The Hudson

The Hudson
A Guidebook to the River

Arthur G. Adams

State University of New York Press Albany

Published by
State University of New York Press,
Albany

For information, address State University
of New York Press, State University
Plaza, Albany, N.Y., 12246

Library of Congress Cataloging in
Publication Data

Adams, Arthur G.
The Hudson, a guidebook to the river

Includes index.
1. Hudson River—Description and
travel—Guide-books.
2. Hudson Valley—Description and
travel—Guide-books.
I. Title.
F127.H8A22   917.47'3'044   79-14846
ISBN 0-87395-406-8

*Maps 1-29 are from the 7.5 planimetric series published by the Map Information Unit
of the New York State Department of Transportation. Thanks are given to
Mr. Paul McElligott for helping make these maps available.*

This book is dedicated to the memory of

Wallace Bruce
1844-1914

Poet, orator, statesman, literary scholar and author of Hudson River and Catskill Mountain guidebooks; whose *Hudson By Daylight* initiated the writer into the mysteries and delights of the Hudson Valley and the Catskills, and whose writings established an ideal toward which all future guidebook writers should strive.

In respectful memory and the hope that the present book follows worthily in his footsteps.

Contents

Maps

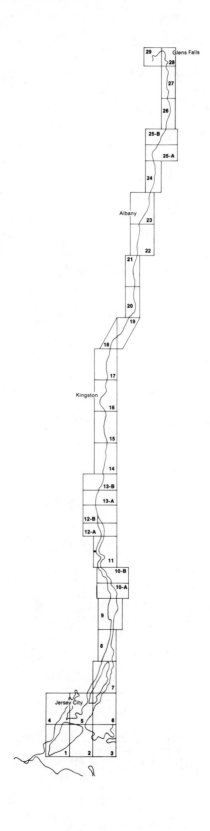

29

Glens Falls

28

27

26

25-B

25-A

24

Albany

23

22

21

20

19

18

17

Kingston

16

15

14

13-B

13-A

12-B

12-A

11

10-B

10-A

9

8

7

Jersey City

4   5   6

1   2   3

Acknowledgments

Numerous people and institutions have been helpful in the research and writing of this book—and they all have my grateful thanks. However, I would like to give particular thanks to the following people and organizations: To Dr. Alfred H. Marks, of the State University of New York, New Paltz, for encouragement and constructive criticism; to Mrs. Frances Reese, of Scenic Hudson Preservation Conference, for encouragement, good advice, and putting me in touch with other people who have been very helpful; to Mr. Charles Keppel for well-informed constructive criticism and evaluation; to Mr. Alfred Van Santvoord Olcott, Jr., for encouragement, valuable information, and the use of unique material from his personal collection and the archives of the original Hudson River Day Line, which his family founded and operated for many years—and simply for his friendship; to the Steamship Historical Society of America, for information from its membership (some of whom have insisted upon remaining anonymous); to Mr. William G. Muller, Marine Artist, for use of his painting of the steamer *Robert Fulton;* to Mr. Leon R. Greenman, of Walking News Press, for advice on map work; to Mr. Richard Hendel for creating the excellent maps and planning the layout of this complex book; to Mr. William D. Eastman, Director of the State University of New York Press, for his patience in seeing this complicated book through the press; and finally to my wife Daryl, children Christopher and Cynthia, and my mother, for their help, patience and encouragement.

Arthur G. Adams

Preface

Over the course of the years there have been numerous books about the Hudson River. Guidebooks were popular in the nineteenth century. In our own times history books and photographic albums have predominated. All these books served a good purpose, and some, such as Benson Lossing's *The Hudson, From the Wilderness to the Sea,* have intrinsic literary value. The guidebooks of Walton Van Loan, Wallace Bruce, and Ernest Ingersoll were popular until just after the turn of the century. However, since their books went out of print before 1940, there has not been a good detailed point-by-point guide available.

It is the purpose of this book to fill this need. There is renewed interest in the Hudson. People are again beginning to travel upon it, as well as along the roads that follow its banks. This book describes the river and shorelines point by point with historical background. Emphasis is upon points as seen from the water. Inland points of interest are also covered in self-guiding road routes along either shore. These road routes take in all major scenic and historical attractions and also follow some intriguing and picturesque by-ways. For good measure, there are descriptions of the views along the railroad routes on either shore.

Arthur G. Adams

How to Use This Guidebook

Measurement System

All distances in this guidebook are measured in land miles using a decimal system of notation carried generally to the tenth of the mile but occasionally to the hundredth of the mile, where features crowd close upon one another. (Examples: 1.00-1 mile; 1.40-1 4/10 mile; 2.45-2 4/10 and 5/100 miles, etc.) The 1/10-mile readings are fairly accurate, but the 1/100 readings are "by convention," meaning that the distances are not to be taken literally, but only to differentiate from other very nearby features, such as several houses next door to one another, or sharp bends in a road only a few feet apart.

Water measurements were obtained from marking large scale United States Coast and Geodetic Survey navigation charts. The distance from the base point is measured along the main steamboat channel, which is not necessarily in midstream. Points on the shore are measured by dropping a line perpendicular to the direction of the steamboat channel at the nearest point. Therefore, if one is traveling upstream, a feature designated for a stated river mileage will be 90° either to right or left, designated always as E (east) or W (west). Distances and directions are often deceiving on bodies of water such as the Tappan Zee or Newburgh or Haverstraw Bay, and often the steamboat channel is not running parallel to the shoreline. Therefore, one should use the simple rule of first looking directly ahead up the channel, and then at right angles right or left to find a place listed at a specific distance.

Road distances were measured (and checked at least twice in different vehicles) by odometer. Measurement is accurate within one tenth of a mile, but the readings in one hundredths are by convention. Frequently distances will vary with the distance being traveled in different directions. This can come about because of differences in distance at interchanges, cloverleafs, or traffic circles, and sometimes by the necessity of using alternate oneway streets or park drives. Weighted averages have been used where appropriate, our purpose being to simplify matters for the user of the guide.

Railroad mileages are those given in operating employees timetables and engineering charts, and these will sometimes vary slightly from published public timetables (which tend to round off distances to the nearest full mile from major terminals) and from actuality. These later variations have usually come about from minor changes in track alignment and are not of any real significance.

Calibration

This guide describes five possible routes for the tourist:

1) directly up the main steamboat channel;
2) Along a selected scenic road route along the east shore;
3) Along a selected scenic road route along the west shore;

4) Along the West Shore Railroad (Delaware & Hudson Railroad further upstream, above Albany);
5) Along the Grand Central Terminal and Hudson Divisions of the former New York Central Railroad from Manhattan to Albany, which is the route used by M.T.A. commuter and Amtrak long-haul trains.

Consequently it has been necessary to correlate distances along the different possible routes. Distance along the river has been used as the standard, and every measurement along the road or rail routes has been assigned an equivalent river mileage, or E.R.M. number. Consequently, when following any given land route, it will be possible to find what is on the opposite shore by looking up what features share the same ERM number.

In assigning distance designations along a river whose vestiges can be traced from the Adirondacks to Bermuda and whose precise source is a point of some dispute, it was necessary to assign some base line for measurement. I have chosen a line running exactly east and west along Forty-second Street in Manhattan as the 0.00 base line. While it might be argued that Sandy Hook, the Narrows, or the Battery would be more suitable, I believe that the following practical reasons are sound. Most tourists of the Hudson River start their tour from this line, as Grand Central Terminal is located on Forty-second Street, the Day Line operates from Pier 81 at the foot of West Forty-first Street, and the Circle Line Sightseeing Yachts operate from Pier 83 at the foot of West Forty-third Street. Both of the latter are reached by the Forty-second Street crosstown bus, which passes Grand Central terminal. The former West Shore Ferry terminal was at Forty-second Street and the passenger rail terminal was almost directly across the river at Weehawken. The railroad measured all distances from Weehawken Terminal.

Many motorists will wish to use the Lincoln Tunnel, which runs between Fortieth Street and Weehawken. The junction of Boulevard East and Forty-eighth Street in Weehawken has been chosen as the 0.00 point for the west side road route, as it is very close to the former Weekawken Railroad and Ferry Terminal, which was reached by Pershing Avenue, an eastern extension of Forty-eighth Street. The streetcars also descended the Palisades at this point, and it is possible to drive from the Lincoln Tunnel Administration Building to this point, along the foot of Kings Bluff, via Baldwin Avenue and up the Palisades on Pershing Avenue, or along an upper route following the Boulevard East.

Concurrently on the east shore, the junction point of West Forty-second Street Manhattan and Twelfth Avenue (West Side Highway) is directly on the scenic route and convenient to the Lincoln Tunnel and midtown Manhattan hotels.

Use of this baseline has necessitated use of negative numbers south of here as far as -910.00 at Bermuda; -16.00 at Rockaway Point, on the east-shore road route, and -117.20 from the Twin Lights at Atlantic Highlands. However, this last figure includes a great deal of backtracking and looping around to gain scenic vantage points. It is only -23.00 in terms of Equivalent River Mileage (E.R.M.). For simplicity point measurements on the scenic lower east and west side road routes are given in positive distances measured from Rockaway Point and from the Twin Lights (but the negative E.R.M. numbers are intercalated).

In several instances alternate routes are indicated, each utilizing the same base points. Because of one-way streets and prohibitions on left turns in many cases, and in order to obtain the most striking vantage points, it is highly recommended that the lower road routes be traversed from south to north — indeed it is almost impossible to do otherwise in Brooklyn and lower Manhattan. To expedite this, an alternative express route has been shown from the Forty-second Street baseline, south to both Rockaway Point and the Twin Lights. These express routes also serve as interesting alternates and can be used in either direction.

Practical Notes

The Henry Hudson Drive, along the base of the Palisades, is closed during much of the winter and early spring because of danger from falling rocks. Hook Mountain and Tallman Mountain Parks are closed in wintertime. Rockland Cemetery and Greenwood Cemetery are private property. One enters as a guest, and the sanctity of the grounds must be respected. Often it is not possible to follow the direct route through the United States Military Academy Grounds at West Point. The Storm King Highway makes an attractive alternate.

Boat travelers should take note that Day Line steamers do not make regular landings above West Point; they normally cruise only so far as Poughkeepsie but do not land there or at Newburgh anymore. Also, during commencement week there are no landings at West Point.

Amtrak trains operate from Grand Central Terminal in Manhattan. Most other Amtrak trains operate from Penn Station, and a subway or taxi transfer is necessary for those coming from New England, the south or the west via the old Pennsylvania Railroad route. The M.T.A. operates local train service between Grand Central and New Haven which makes an easier connection for those connecting with the Hudson River Line. Remember that trains no longer stop in downtown Albany, but at the Albany-Rensselaer station, which is a short taxi ride across the river. There is no scheduled service on the West Shore Railroad. Excursions in the past have operated from the Erie-Lackawanna (Conrail) Terminal at Hoboken and followed the Jersey Junction Line to the former site of Weehawken Terminal. Tourists without an automobile can also avail themselves of Conrail-New Jersey-D.O.T. North Jersey Shore trains from Penn Station Manhattan to Perth Amboy, South Amboy, Mattawan, Middletown, Red Bank, and Long Branch. Several city subway lines operate to Coney Island, and some BMT Division trains operate across the Manhattan Bridge, offering good views. The IND Division trains also operate to Rockaway via Jamaica Bay. Staten Island Rapid Transit trains operate on an above-ground route from St. George Ferry Terminal to Tottenville. There is no longer any ferry service across to Perth Amboy.

1

**From the Ocean's Depths
to New York Bay**

Introduction to the Hudson River

The Hudson River

The Hudson rises from numerous springs in the Adirondack region that feed three of its principal branches. Lake Tear of the Clouds, at an elevation of 4,322 feet on the southwestern slope of Mount Marcy is generally recognized as the river's principal source.

Feldspar Brook is the outlet of Lake Tear of the Clouds. It in turn flows into what is today called the Opalescent River. Formerly this was called either the North Branch or Main Branch of the Hudson. The branch we now simply call the Hudson River was formerly called the West Branch. Its source is Hendrick Spring, northeast of Long Lake, whose waters flow north to the Saint Lawrence River. The waters of Hendrick Spring are first collected in Fountain Lake. The West Branch continues south through Round Pond and Catlin Lake and then turns east and flows through Rich Lake and Harris Lake to a junction with the Opalescent River near Newcomb, which is about fifteen miles from Lake Tear of the Clouds. A third branch, known as the North Fork, has its head at Henderson Lake and joins the Opalescent River at the outlet of Sanford Lake.

From Newcomb, the Hudson flows generally southeast to the community of North River, receiving on the way the waters of the Boreas River. It then continues south to Riparius, below which it combines with Mill Creek, coming from the southwest. It continues south past The Glen to Thurman Station, where it receives the waters of the Schroon River from the northeast. From here the river continues south, bowing slightly to the west, to take up the waters of Stony Creek. At Luzerne it receives the waters of the Sacandaga River from the west. From here south to Corinth, at the head of Jesup's Great Falls, the river is broad and smooth flowing. Below the falls the river starts to curve first east and then northeast, flowing through Lake Moreau and making several loops before arriving at the dam and falls at Glens Falls. It is crossed by the bridge at routes 9 and 32, just below the dam and above the falls.

This is the northern terminus of our detailed descriptions. It is 115 miles from Lake Tear of the Clouds. Outside of the dam, the principal feature here is the Pruyn's Island log pool, just above it. In the years when the upper Hudson was a great logging river, logs were driven down and collected at the great boom here. A great deal of the water is diverted along power canals of the Finch Pruyn Co. on the north side of the falls, and frequently the flow of water over Glens Falls is disappointing, though there is sometimes a spectacular scene during the spring runoff. Before the recent reconstruction of the highway bridge, it was possible to descend a stairway from the midpoint of the bridge to one of the numerous rocky islands in the falls, where the cave that was described by James Fenimore Cooper in *The Last of the Mohicans* is located. All access to this famous cave is now closed off. To this point, the Hudson has flowed primarily through wilderness. From here to its mouth, it will flow through a densely populated region with intensively cultivated lands. It is a "river of history," and was for many years the nation's greatest commercial artery. It is with this lower portion that we shall concern ourselves.

The next seven miles to Fort Edward are full of rapids, most prominently Baker's Falls, just above the town of Hudson Falls. Its banks are crowded with industry, including pulp and paper mills and chemical plants at Fort Edward, where the river turns decisively south. It continues straight south for the next forty-four miles to the Government Lock at Troy, at the head of tidewater. This stretch passes through a broad pastoral valley given over largely to dairy farming in its upper reaches and industry in its nether ones. It is in fact a canalized river, forming a part of the Champlain Canal, and there are several dams and locks along the way. It flows past Fort Miller, Thomson, and Northumberland, where it receives the waters of the Batten Kill from the east. Next is Schuylerville, where it is fed by Fish Creek from the west. Along the right bank, running south from here to Bemis Heights, is the Saratoga Historic Battlefield Park, where a decisive battle of the American Revolution was fought in October of 1777, in which the British, under Gen. John Burgoyne, were forced to surrender to Gen. Horatio Gates.

Near Stillwater, the Hudson receives the waters of the Hoosic River from the east. Then it flows south past Mechanicville and Waterford, where the New York State Barge Canal (successor to the Erie Canal) enters from the west. Between here and the city of Cohoes, the Mohawk River—called the Maquaas Kill in early times—flows into the channel west of Van Schaick and Simmons islands. On the east shore is the Lansingburgh section of Troy. South of Van Schaick Island is Green Island. The Federal Lock is located between Green Island and Troy, on the east bank.

From here to the south, the river is tidewater—salty as far north as New-

burgh and brackish to just above Poughkeepsie, although, in some conditions, fresh water can be drawn from the Hudson at Chelsea, ten miles below. North of there, is quite fresh.

From Troy, the river flows through broad flats, and, until 1930, when extensive dykes were built, it was often quite shallow, with a shifting channel. The Berkshire Mountains are visible to the east, and the Catskills to the southwest.

Below Troy, the river flows almost directly southward, with only a few short and sharp bends near West Point and Bear Mountain in the Highlands. The principal broader stretches, from north to south, are Newburgh Bay, Haverstraw Bay, and the Tappan Zee. From Hudson and Athens, on the west bank, south to the Highlands just below Newburgh, the banks are more precipitous, and the river is paralleled to the east by the Taconic Range and to the west by the Catskill Mountains, and further south by the Shawangunk Mountains and Plattekill Hills. Below Newburgh, at Cornwall, the Hudson breaches the main chain of the Appalachian Mountains in what are called the Hudson Highlands. The range to the east is called the Taconics, and the one to the west the Ramapos. South of the Highlands, the east bank remains relatively high all the way to Manhattan Island. The west bank immediately below the Highlands is made up of a series of low mountains: Buckberg, Little Tor, and High Tor are the principal ones, below which are Hook and Clausland mountains. The Palisades run from just below Sneden's Landing to behind Jersey City, with the highest portion extending from the New York-New Jersey state line to Weehawken. The Highlands served as an important military bulwark during the Revolution, and West Point remains an important military base to this day.

The Hudson River below the George Washington Bridge from Manhattan to Fort Lee is often called the North River, which was a name that was originally given to it to distinguish it from the East

River and the South River (Delaware).
At the foot of Manhattan Island, the river
is joined by the East River and opens
out into Upper New York Bay. To the
southeast is Brooklyn, located on Long
Island. To the west is a low peninsula
terminating at Bergen Point in Bayonne
and separating New York Bay from
Newark Bay, which in turn has collected
the waters of the Passaic and Hackensack river systems. Bayonne is separated
from Staten Island by the Kill Van Kull, a
tidal estuary that connects New York
and Newark bays. Another estuary called
the Arthur Kill separates Staten Island
from the New Jersey mainland and
connects Newark Bay with Raritan Bay.
There are several high hills on Staten
Island: Todt Hill, Grimes Hill and
Latourette, in the Dongan Hills.

The Upper Bay narrows between
Brooklyn and Staten Island and is simply
called the Narrows. It is spanned by the
great Verrazano Narrows Bridge. Below
the Narrows is Lower New York Bay. To
the east is Coney Island, separated from
Brooklyn by Gravesend Bay. To the west
is Raritan Bay, at the mouth of New
Jersey's greatest river, of the same
name. To the south are Sandy Hook Bay
and the Atlantic Highlands of New Jersey. The long sand spit of Sandy Hook
extends almost four miles due north
from Atlantic Highlands and separates
the mouth of the Shrewsbury River and
Sandy Hook Bay from the open sea.
Here the Hudson seems finally to lose
its identity. About 10,000 to 15,000
years ago, however, prior to the last
glacial period, the entire land mass
was higher, and the Hudson extended
another 120 miles further out to sea.
A submerged trough, known as the
Hudson Canyon, has left vestiges halfway to Bermuda, another 330 miles
beyond the continental shelf.

The principal tributaries on the west
bank south of Albany are the Norman's
Kill, Catskill Creek, Esopus Creek,
Rondout Creek, Black Creek, Quassaic
Creek, Moodna Creek, Popolopen Creek,

Miniseongo Creek, and the Sparkill.
The principal tributaries on the east side
are Papscanee Creek, Moordener Kill,
Vlockie Kill, Schodack Creek, Stockport
Creek, Roeliffe Jansen Kill, Landsman
Kill, Indian Creek, Wappinger's Creek,
Fishkill Creek, Indian Brook, Annsville
Creek (Peekskill Creek), Croton River,
Pocantico River, and Neperhan or Saw
Mill River. The Spuyten Duyvil Creek,
which separates Manhattan from the
mainland to the north, is not, properly
speaking, a tributary but rather a tidal
estuary, as is also the East River. The
East River and Spuyten Duyvil Creek are
connected by the Harlem River, which is
another tidal estuary that separates Manhattan from the Bronx on the mainland.

The larger towns and cities past which
the Hudson flows are Glens Falls, Hudson Falls, Fort Edward, Waterford,
Cohoes, Troy, Albany, Rensselaer, Hudson, Catskill, Saugerties, Kingston,
Poughkeepsie, Newburgh, Peekskill,
Haverstraw, Nyack, Yonkers, New York
City, Weehawken, Hoboken, Jersey City,
and Bayonne.

The Hudson is actually a fjord or
drowned river. Taking Forty-second
Street in Manhattan as a base line, we
can consider that the Hudson has a
length of 314 miles from Lake Tear of
the Clouds to the north, and 580 miles
to its last vestige in the Southwestern
Canyon to the south, beyond the continental shelf, which is a total identity of
894 miles. The section of the river that
most people think of is the 200 miles
from Manhattan to Glens Falls. It is
sometimes remarked that the Hudson is
a very big river for its size. Taking this
grand total length into consideration, we
can understand why this is the case.

In 1625, Johannes De Laet, in his
New World, or Description of West-India,
(Amsterdam, n.d.) tells how the early
Dutch explorers and settlers had divided
the Hudson into "reaches." These are
stretches of the river, all of which could
be seen point to point, and on which
sailing conditions were somewhat uni-

Headwaters of the Hudson

New York Harbor and adjacent waters

form. Their names remained in common use all through the age of sail and into the early steamboat days. They had fallen into such disuse, however, that when in 1975 we asked Capt. William O. Benson of Sleightsburg, a noted authority on steamboating who had been active on the river for forty-five years, to clarify a point, he wrote, "During my day on the Hudson the only reaches I ever heard older men speak about was 'Percey's Reach' between Hamburgh and Hudson Lighthouse." This was not very helpful, for Captain Benson is not a young man, and the name Percey's Reach seems rather new and does not belong in the traditional canon—it is frankly apocryphal. The exact definition of the reaches is hard to relate to present-day place names; however, after much study of various authorities, I will venture the following breakdown:

1) The Great Chip Reach: The Palisades were known by the old Dutch settlers as the "Great Chip." This extended from Weehawken to the New Jersey-New York state line for about 18 miles.

2) Tappan Reach: Equivalent to the Tappan Zee. From state line to Verdrietege Hook (that is, Tedious Hook or Hook Mountain).

3) Haverstroo Reach: Equivalent to Haverstraw Bay. From Verdreitege Hook to within view of Pyngyp or Timp Mountain on the west side. The Old Dutch mariners used to change tack when they were within range of Pyngyp Mountain, and the booms of the sloops would sound a "ping" or "pyngp" when they swung over. In modern parlance this would be from Hook Mountain to Stony Point.

4) Seylmakers' Reach, or Sailmakers' Reach: Stony Point to Peekskill.

5) Crescent Reach or Cook's Reach: A crescent-shaped stretch from Peekskill to Manitou through the Kittatinny Mountains or Highlands. The Indian name Kittatinny is no longer applied to the Highlands but is preserved in the name of the southern part of the Shawangunk Mountains in New Jersey. The Indians applied the name to the entire Ramapo and Highland Mountains.

6) Hoge's or High Reach: Manitou to Gee's Point, opposite Constitution Island at West Point.

7) Martyr's Reach: Also called Martelaire's Reach. Between Constitution Island, which the Dutch navigators called Martelaer's Island, and Storm King Mountain, which they called Klinkersberg. It is claimed that a French family named Martelaire lived on Constitution Island about 1720. A variation on this was Martyr's Reach. The word "martyr" as used in this connection signifies "contending" or "struggling," as vessels coming up the river with a fair wind would frequently find themselves, immediately after passing Constitution Island, struggling with the wind right ahead. Possibly it was an allusion to perilous sailing with downdrafts from the mountains and a rocky shoreline. Vorsen or Foxes' Reach were still other names that were applied to Martyr's Reach between Constitution Island and Storm King Mountain.

8) Fisher's Reach: Storm King to Wappinger's Creek: Includes Newburgh Bay.

9) Lange Rack or Long Reach: Wappinger's Creek to Whiskey Point.

10) Vasterack or Vaste Reach: Whiskey Point to Athens. Refers to the great width of Hudson around Inbocht Bay. Rodger's Island was formerly called Vasterack Island.

11) Kleverack or Claverack: Clover Reach—Athens to Fourmile Point. This was also the name of Van Rensselaer's lower manor house near Hudson.

12) Backerack or Baker's Reach: Four-mile Point to Fordham Point.
13) Jan Playsier's Reach: Fordham Point to Hinnenhoeck (Nutten Hook).
14) Hart's or Hunter's Reach: Hinnenhoeck to Kinderhoeck (Nutten Hook to Stuyvesant).

Changes in the channel, islands, and shorelines, as well as of place names, make it extremely difficult to determine accurately the limits of these reaches; yet they remain a pleasant subject for speculation.

The Hudson was known by many names, and the Indians had various ones. To the Iroquois it was the Cohohatatia, or "place to catch shad." To the Lenapes and Mahicans it was the Muhheakunnuk or Mahicannittuck, or "great waters constantly in motion" (referring to the tides), which came to have the secondary meaning, "place where the Mahicans dwell." The Mahicans also called it the Shatamuc, Shattemuc, or Shattemuck. In 1524 Verrazano called it simply the Grande Rivière, or Angoleme. In 1525, Gomez dubbed it the Rio San Antonio, and it was later called the Rio de Gomez, or Guamas. About 1569, it appears on several maps as the Norumbeza. In 1609, Henry Hudson called it the Manhattes, from the tribe at its mouth. In 1611, the Dutch named it the Mauritius River or Mauritz Rivier, or River of the Prince, after Prince Maurice of Nassau. In 1625, Johannes DeLaet called it the Rio de Montaigne or River of the Mountains. The Dutch also used the name the Nassau River, also in honor of the prince, but soon came to call it simply the Groote or Great River. The English called it variously the Manhattan River, Great River, River of the Mountains, North River (Noordt in Dutch), or, most commonly, Hudson's River, which name ultimately remained, shortened to simply Hudson River.

Tides are felt as far north as the Federal Lock at Troy, where the tide rises six inches and at Albany, where it rises two feet. Highest tides occur when the moon is in the southeast or the northwest. A log would take almost a year to float from Troy to the sea. Normally, it would be carried eight miles downstream and seven and a half miles back upriver each day. Some authorities give the figures twelve miles down and seven to nine miles up per day; much depends upon the rate of stream flow. Wallace Bruce has said that a drop of water would take three weeks to get from Albany to New York City.

The salt line or wedge is normally at Newburgh, but in recent years it has ranged as far north as Poughkeepsie in 1966, and as far south as the Battery in New York in 1968. Normally, salt is 30/1000 parts at New York City. The river is most salty from late summer to early spring, when runoff from the mountains commences. It is saltier at lower depths.

There are considerable shoals at Edgewater that are caused by a process called flocculation, wherein salinity causes silt in suspension to precipitate to the extent of 4,000,000 cubic yards per year. To remove this material and keep the channels to sufficient depth for shipping, the United States Army Corps of Engineers maintains large dredges. One of these, the Driftmaster, which is based at Gravesend Bay, removes 24,000 tons each year. The great new dredge Essayons went into operation in 1950. It is 525 feet long and cost $11,500,000. Two huge pumps attached to long tubes can pick up 8000 cubic yards per shipload. The material is then taken six and a half miles southeast of Ambrose Light and dumped through twenty-four trap doors in the bottoms of the hoppers. The river is navigable by large river steamers to Troy, and by ocean-going vessels to the Port of Albany. "The Hudson Tide," a short article from the 1901 edition of Wallace Bruce's *Hudson by Daylight* is of interest:

The tide in the Hudson River is the continuation of the tidewave, which comes up from the ocean through New York Bay, and is carried by its own momentum one hundred and sixty miles, growing, of course, constantly smaller, until it is finally stopped by the dam at Troy. The crest of this wave, or top high water, is ten hours going from New York to Troy. A steamer employing the same time (ten hours) for the journey, and starting at high water in New York, would carry a flood tide and highest water all the way, and have an up-river current of about three miles an hour helping her. On the other hand, the same steamer starting six hours later, or at low tide, would have dead low water and an ebb-tide current of about three miles against her the entire way. The average rise and fall of the tides in New York is five and one-half feet, and in Albany two feet.

The flood tide may carry salt water, under the most favorable circumstances, so that it can be detected at Poughkeepsie, but ordinarily the water is fresh at Newburgh.

To those who have not studied the tides the following paragraphs will also be of interest.

The tides are the semi-diurnal oscillations of the waters of the ocean, caused by the attraction of the moon and sun.

The influence of the moon's attraction is the preponderating one in the tide-rising force, while that of the sun is about two-fifths as much as that of the moon. The tides therefore follow the motion of the moon, and the average interval between the times of high water is the half length of the lunar day, or about twelve hours and twenty-five minutes.

The tide-waves always travel west. When the configuration of the coast line drives it into a corner, as in the Bay of Fundy, or the mouth of the Severn, the tides rise to very great heights—fifty, seventy-five, or even one hundred feet. The lowest regular tides are on the islands in mid-ocean. (Bruce, *Hudson by Daylight*, New York: Bryant Literary Union, 1901, p. 306.)

Geology of the Hudson

In addition to various geological references scattered through these pages, the following facts from the *American Geological Railway Guide*, by James Macfarlane, quoted in Bruce's *Hudson by Daylight*, (pp. 307-09), will be of interest.

The State of New York is to the geologist what the Holy Land is to the Christian, and the works of her Palaeontologist are the Old Testament Scriptures of the science. It is a Laurentian, Cambrian, Silurian and Devonian State, containing all the groups and all the formations of these long ages, beautifully developed in belts running nearly across the State in an east and west direction, lying undisturbed as originally laid down.

The rock of New York Island is gneiss, except a portion of the north end, which is limestone. The south portion is covered with deep alluvial deposits, which in some places are more than 100 feet in depth. The natural outcroppings of the gneiss appeared on the surface about 16th street, on the east side of the city, and run diagonally across to 31st street on 10th avenue. North of this, much of the surface was naked rock. It contains a large proportion of mica, a small proportion of quartz and still less feldspar, but generally an abundance of iron pyrites in very minute crystals, which, on exposure, are decomposed. In consequences of these ingredients it soon disintegrates on exposure, rendering it unfit for the purpose of building. The erection of a great city, for which this island furnishes a noble site, has very greatly changed its natural condition. The geological age of the

New York gneiss is undoubtedly very old, not the Laurentian or oldest, nor the Huronian, but it belongs to the third or White Mountain series, named by Dr. Hunt the Montalban. It is the same range which is the basis rock of nearly all the great cities of the Atlantic coast. It crosses New Jersey where it is turned to clay, until it appears under Trenton, and it extends to Philadelphia, Baltimore, Washington and Richmond, Va., and probably Boston, Massachusetts, is founded on this same formation.

On the opposite side of the river may here be seen for many miles the Palisades, a long, rough mountain ridge close to the water's edge. Its upper half is a perpendicular precipice of bare rock of a columnar structure from 100 to 200 feet in height, the whole height of the mountain being generally from 400 to 600 feet, and the highest point in the range opposite Sing Sing 800 feet above the Hudson, and known as the High Torn [sic]. The width of the mountain is from a half mile to a mile and a half, the western slope being quite gentle. In length it extends from Bergen Point below Jersey City to Haverstraw, and then westward in all 48 miles, the middle portion being merely a low ridge. The lower half of the ridge on the river side is a sloping mound of detritus, of loose stones, which has accumulated at the base of the cliff, being derived from its weathered and wasted surface. This talus and the summit of the mountain are covered with trees, with the bare rocky precipice called the Palisades between, and many fine country residences may be seen on the level summit, from which are beautiful views of the river, the harbor and City of New York. Viewed from the railroad or from a steamboat on the river, this lofty mural precipice with its huge weathered masses of upright columns of bare rock, presenting a long, straight unbroken ridge overlooking the beautiful Hudson River, is certainly extremely picturesque. Thousands of travelers gaze at it daily

without knowing what it is. This entire ridge consists of no other rock than trap traversing the Triassic formation in a huge vertical dike. The red sandstone formation of New Jersey is intersected by numerous dikes of this kind, but this is much the finest. The materials of this mountain have undoubtedly burst through a great rent or fissure in the strata, overflowing while in a melted or plastic condition the red sandstone, not with the violence of a volcano, for the adjoining strata are but little disturbed in position, although often greatly altered by the heat, but forced up very slowly and gradually, and probably under pressure. Subsequent denudation has laid bare the part of the mountain now exposed along the river. The rock is columnar basalt, sometimes called greenstone, and is solid, not stratified like water-formed rocks, but cracked in cooling and of a crystalline structure. Here is a remarkable but not uncommon instance of a great geological blank. On the east side of this river the formations belong to the first or oldest series of Primary or Crystalline rocks, while on the west side they are all Triassic, the intermediate Cambrian, Silurian, Devonian and Carboniferous formation being wanting. This state of things continues all along the Atlantic coast to Georgia, the Cretaceous or Jurassic taking the place of the Triassic farther south.

Montrose to Cornwall. This celebrated passage of the Hudson through the Highlands, is a gorge nearly 20 miles long from 3 miles south of Peekskill to Fishkill, and is worn out of the Laurentian rocks far below mean tide water. The hills on its sides rise in some instances as much as 1800 feet, and in many places the walls are very precipitous. The rock is gneiss, of a kind that is not easily disintegrated or eroded, nor is there any evidence of any convulsive moment. It is clearly a case of erosion, but not by the present river, which has no fall, for tide water extends 100 miles up the river beyond the Highlands. This

Hypothetical Course of the Hudson River in Schooley Time. According to the Theory of Superimposed Subsequent Drainage. (*The Geology of the Hudson River*—A. Van Santvoord Olcott, Jr.)

The Hudson submarine canyon as contoured by A. C. Veatch on the basis of echo sounding by the U. S. Coast and Geodetic Survey. Streams are shown and contours drawn in accordance with Veatch's belief that submarine canyons represent submerged subaërial valleys. Contour interval: on shelf, 5 fathoms (30 feet) to depth of 85 fathoms; on slope 25 fathoms (150 feet). Reproduced from Chart IB, Special Paper No. 7, Geological Society of America.

therefore was probably a work mainly performed in some past period when the continent was at a higher level. Most likely it is a valley of great antiquity.

Opposite Fishkill is Newburgh, which is in the great valley of Lower Silurian or Cambrian limestone and slate. North of that, on the west side of the river, the formations occur in their usual order, their outcrops running northeast and southwest. On the N.Y.C. & H.R.R.R., on the east side, the same valley crosses, and the slates from Fishkill to Rhinebeck are about the same place in the series; but being destitute of fossils and very much faulted, tilted and disturbed, their precise geology is uncertain. See the exposures in the cuts at Poughkeepsie. The high ground to the east is commonly called the Quebec group.

A series of great dislocations with upthrows on the east side traverse eastern North America from Canada to Alabama. One of these great faults has been traced from near the mouth of the St. Lawrence River, keeping mostly under the water up to Quebec just north of the fortress, thence by a gently curving line to Lake Champlain or through Western Vermont across Washington County, N.Y., to near Albany. It crosses the river near Rhinebeck 15 miles north of Poughkeepsie and continues on southward into New Jersey and runs into another series of faults probably of a later date, which extends as far as Alabama. It brings up the rocks of the so called Quebec group on the east side of the fracture to the level of the Hudson River and Trenton.

Catskill Mountains. For many miles on this railroad are beautiful views of the Catskill Mountains, 3,800 feet high, several miles distant on the opposite or west side of the river, and which furnish the name for the Catskill formation. The wide valley between them and the river is composed of Chemung, Hamilton, Lower Helderberg and Hudson River. The geology on the east or railroad side is entirely different.

Albany. The clay beds at Albany are more than 100 feet thick, and between that city and Schenectady they are underlaid by a bed of sand that is in some places more than 50 feet thick. There is an old glacial clay and boulder drift below the gravel at Albany, but Professor Hall says it is not the estuary stratified clay.

The foregoing article can be very briefly summed up in the following simple statements:

(1) The Palisades are composed of metamorphic basalt or diabases. (2) The Highlands are composed primarily of granite and gneiss with various intrusions. (3) From Beacon to Albany the composition is of shales and limestones; or mainly sedimentary rock, with contorted strata resulting from the Taconic revolution in the late Ordovician period.

For the lay reader, the following table should be helpful:

AGE	YEARS AGO	PRINCIPAL ACTION
Pre-Cambrian Period		
Archean	more than 1,000 million	Grenville sediments layed down
Algonkian	1,000 million	" " " "
Paleozoic Period		
Cambro-Ordovician	500 million	Ramapo fault formed
Late Ordovician	400 million	Taconic revolution
Silurian Devonian	300 million	Storm King and Fishkill faults
Permian	200 million	" " " " "
Post-Paleozoic Period		
Triassic	175 million	Lava intrusions: Palisades formed
Cretaceous	100 million	
Tertiary	35 million	General rising of area
Quarternary	1 or 2 million	Ice ages: area depressed. Hudson filled with silt, and sea intrudes

It has been stated that the Hudson is actually a fjord. The only other true fjord on the North American east coast is Somes Sound on Mount Desert Island in Maine.

Pollution

For many years raw sewage and industrial wastes have been poured into the Hudson. In recent years treatment plants have been built and marine life such as crabs are returning to the river. The water is noticeably clearer. However, marine boring worms cannot live in New York Harbor. Possibly the most polluted points on the river are the Albany Pool and the raw sewage outlets in Manhattan. Among the worst are those at Fifty-ninth Street and Ninety-sixth Street. The 172d Street outlet, known as the Medical Center Sewer has coliform bacteria count of 10M/100ML and the Seventy-second Street outlet spouts straight, untreated sewage. Manhattan sewage takes six days to reach the sea and sometimes penetrates upriver to the Tappan Zee. A large new treatment plant is presently under construction on filled land between 137th and 145th Streets. In 1977, 175 million gallons of raw sewage per day were poured into the Hudson at Manhattan.

Other sources of pollution are a pier at 130th Street where garbage scows are loaded (to be emptied just outside the lower bay) and various industrial sources including refined syrups and sugar wastes at Yonkers, paint from the General Motors plant at Tarrytown, oil for the Conrail railroad yard at Harmon; wastes from the paper mills near Glens Falls, and tinning and pickling wastes from the Anaconda Copper plant at Hastings.

Sometimes the river is afflicted by the red tide, which consists of microscopic dinoflagellates called Glenodinium and Prorocentrum. These cause the eyes, nose, ears, and throat to burn. As this penetrates along the shoreline it is a menace to Long Island and Jersey shore resorts. However, the local variety is not the same as the more virulent Florida variety, which is called Gymnodinium Breves.

So-called thermal pollution is not, strictly speaking, pollution. It is simply the raising of the water temperature above normal that is caused by outflow of cooling water from power plants. This causes significant changes in marine life.

-580.00 The Abyssal Plain.

The last significant vestiges of the Hudson Canyon are discernable in the debris at the bottom of the Continental Shelf, more than halfway to Bermuda.

-241.00 Rim of the Continental Shelf—the Hudson Canyon.

Eleven thousand years ago, before the last glacier retreated, the continental shelf was above sea level. Before entering the Atlantic, the Hudson River then ran 120 miles farther southeast than it does at present. The old channel is now smothered with silt and is not discernable northwest of Mud Hole, near Ambrose Light. From Ambrose Light (about 26 miles from shore) to about 131 miles from shore, the Hudson Channel is noticeably deeper than the rest of the ocean floor. From 131 miles to the rim of the continental shelf (and beyond) it is much deeper and is known as the Hudson Canyon. At the rim of the continental shelf the bottom of the canyon is 1½ miles below the surface of the water and five miles wide.

In 1930, the United States Coast and Geodetic Survey made echo soundings and found the canyon to be 9,000 feet deep near the rim of the shelf and 15,000 feet deep 160 miles beyond the shelf, just before it disappeared in the abyssal plain sloping towards Bermuda. This canyon was formed by turbidity currents. Sediments disclose shallow water shells. Dr. William Beebe studied the canyon's life forms in the 1920s and described his findings in *Arcturus Adventure*. He called the canyon the "Hudson Gorge." It was his opinion that "long after the last animal and insect from the heart of Africa and New Guinea has been collected and named, and the north and south poles have been crossed and recrossed with tourist planes, strange fish and other creatures will still be brought to light within a day's motor boat run of New York City" (William Beebe, *Report on the Eleventh Expedition of the Department of Tropical Research of the New York Zoological Society, New York, 1928*).

Among these strange fish are Bathytractes drakei; Haplophryme hudsonius; Dragonfish (Chanliodus sloanei); and Stylophthalmus, which has a bill like a duck, eyes on the tops of long stalks, and a long, threadlike body lined with what look like scores of glowing portholes.

-131.00 Inland End of the Hudson Canyon—Outer End of the Hudson Channel.

The submerged Hudson Channel is here nearly five miles wide and two-thirds of a mile deeper than the ocean floor.

-116.00 The Gully.

A deep hole in the former delta —now submerged.

-26.00 The Inland End of Submerged Hudson Channel.

Here the submerged channel is only twenty feet deeper than the ocean floor.

-26.00 The Dumping Grounds.

In this vicinity are various dumping grounds for garbage and other types of waste, brought out to sea in scows. Among them are: Doorknob Grounds, filled with rubbish from the Manhattan East Side Urban Renewal; Subway Grounds, filled with material excavated in building the Eighth Avenue Subway; New or Seagull Grounds, where organic garbage from New York City is dumped (scavenging gulls hover over this area). Acid Grounds is to the east of the main shipping channel. Here are dumped sulphuric acid and iron sulphate wastes from the National Lead Company plant at Sayreville, New Jersey. Special dumping barges now make two trips a day. Formerly the wastes were dumped directly into the Raritan River. Acids have killed all marine life near the Acid Grounds. Certain of the other grounds attract fish, however.

-25.75 The Ambrose Light Tower
(40° 27' N x 73° 49' W), East of the Channel. This tower marks the outer end of Ambrose Channel, which is the main approach to New York Harbor. Built in 1966, it has two decks and a helicopter pad and is permanently manned. Built in 190 feet of water, it rises 75 feet above the surface. The tower replaces lightships that were previously anchored here. The original red-painted lightship (now on display at the South Street Seaport Museum), built in 1907 at Camden, New Jersey, by the New York Shipbuilding Company, measured 135 by 29 feet, was designated Light No. 87 of the former United States Lighthouse Service. It was manned by civilians. The service was later taken over by the United States Coast Guard, which operates the present light tower. The original lightship was in use here until 1932 and subsequently was stationed at other stations until retirement in recent years. Other similar lightships served the Ambrose Station until erection of the present tower in 1966.

From here to just below Sneden's Landing, eighteen miles north of Forty-second Street, Manhattan, where the New Jersey-New York state line is located, all the land to the west of the channel belongs to New Jersey, except for Swinburne, Hoffman, Staten, Liberty, and Ellis Islands, which belong to the State of New York. All land on the east side belongs to New York. North of Sneden's Landing, which is in New York State, the Hudson flows entirely within New York State. North of Paulus Hook, the middle of the river serves as the state line. The present boundaries were

established in 1719 and were formally ratified in 1772.

New York State

New York State is the thirtieth in size and second in population of all the states in the United States. Its area is 49,576 square miles, its 1977 population, 18,120,000. Its capital is Albany, and its largest city is New York, with a population of 7,646,818. The eleventh state to be admitted to the union, its total road and highway mileage is 107,743, and its total railroad mileage is 5,578.

New Jersey

New Jersey is the forty-sixth state in size and ninth in population. It is the most densely populated state in the Union with 933.7 persons per square mile. Area: 7,836 square miles. Population in 1977: 7,316,000. Capital—Trenton. Largest city: Newark, with a population of 382,288. Third state to be admitted to the Union. Total road and highway mileage: 32,704. Total railroad mileage: 1,838.

On 24 June 1664 the land now known as New Jersey was sold by the Duke of York (later King James II of England) to John, Lord Berkeley and Sir George Carteret. It was named New Caesarea or New Jersey in honor of Sir George Carteret, who had been governor of the Isle of Jersey. The first governor of New Jersey was Philip Carteret. The Proprietors divided the new colony into East Jersey and West Jersey on 1 July 1676. Berkeley sold his undivided share of West Jersey in 1674 to John Fenwick in trust for Edward Byllinge, who was a Quaker. Byllinge assigned his share to William Penn and other Quakers. Carteret's widow sold her share in East Jersey to William Penn and eleven others in 1680. Ultimately there were twenty-four proprietors. From 1688 till

1689 the Jerseys were annexed to the Colony of New England for administrative purposes, but on 17 April 1702, under Queen Anne, New Jersey became a royal province. However, between 1702 and 1738 New Jersey shared the same governor as New York.

Monmouth County New Jersey

The land on the New Jersey shore, adjacent to the lower New York Bay and Raritan Bay and including Sandy Hook, is designated Monmouth County. On 17 April 1665, Governor Richard Nicolls of New York granted a patent to a group of Englishmen who were mainly Baptists and Quakers from Rhode Island and the settlement of Gravesend in New York. This patent embraced all of present Monmouth County and large parts of Ocean and Middlesex Counties. Principal early settlements were between the Shrewsbury and Navesink rivers and at Middletown, on the south shore of Raritan Bay.

Long Island

The land on the east of New York Bay is a large, fish-shaped island, 118 miles long, known as Long Island. It was called Paumanok by the Indians. It varies from twelve to twenty miles in width and extends east-northeast from the mouth of the Hudson River. It is separated from Staten Island by the Narrows, and from Manhattan and the Bronx by the East River. It is separated from the New York mainland and Connecticut by Long Island Sound, to the north. To the south is the Atlantic Ocean. The two "tail fins" are at the east end. The more northerly and shorter one is known as Orient Point, and the longer southern one is Montauk Point. Between these points, from west to east, are Great Peconic Bay, Little

Peconic Bay, Noyack Bay, Gardiners Bay, Napeague Bay, and Block Island Sound. Islands in these bays, from west to east, are Shelter Island, Ram Island, and Gardiners Island.

The north shore is hilly and strewn with boulders. A glacial terminal moraine runs the length of the island. The central section is flat and sandy with pine growth predominent. The southern portion is low and sandy. There are long and narrow barrier reef islands along the southern shore, separated from the main island by the broad, shallow Jamaica Bay, Zacks Bay, Great South Bay, Moriches Bay, and Shinnecock Bay.

The island was first settled by the Dutch in 1636. Present population is about five million. The western end belongs to New York City: the borough of Brooklyn (Kings County) and the Borough of Queens (Queens County). East of Queens is Nassau County, and Suffolk County is at the eastern end of the island. The eastern end of the island is largely devoted to agriculture, resorts, and oyster fishing. Whaling was formerly important; many early settlers came from New England and Nantucket. Much of the eastern end remains rural. Famous resort towns include Southampton, Easthampton, and Amagansett. The central portion is devoted to suburban homes, light industry, aviation plants, and test airfields. Jones Beach is a large south shore resort for day-trippers that is located on a barrier island. Fire Island, to the east, caters to a more Bohemian element. Many wealthy society people have estates along the scenic north shore. The western end is more industrialized and has many row houses and apartment houses in Queens and Brooklyn. LaGuardia and Kennedy International (formerly Idlewild Airport) airports are in Queens County. The island was also known as Nassau Island in early times. It is served by the New York City subway system and lines of the Long Island Rail Road. There are ferry steamers from Port Jefferson to Bridge-

Monmouth Middlesex County Area

Middlesex County — Perth Amboy

Hudson County, New Jersey

port, Connecticut, and from Orient Point to New London, Connecticut. Long Island belongs entirely to New York State.

Lower New York Bay

Lower New York Bay is an arm of the Atlantic Ocean that is enclosed by the shores of northeastern New Jersey, Staten Island, and Long Island. It is separated from the open sea by Sandy Hook Bar, which runs six miles between Sandy Hook and Rockaway Point along the southeastern edge of the bay. The bar is breached by the Ambrose Channel. The western portion is also known as Raritan Bay. Tributaries are, clockwise from Sandy Hook, the Shrewsbury-Navesink rivers, Raritan River, Arthur Kill (separating Staten Island from mainland New Jersey) and the Narrows (separating Staten Island from Long Island), which connect with Upper New York Bay. Van Der Donck's map of New Netherlands calls it Port May, or Godyns Bay. See James Fenimore Cooper's *"Water Witch"* and James Kirke Paulding's *"New Mirror For Travellers"*, for excellent descriptions.

-23.00 The Highlands of the Navesink and Twin Lights

The Neversink Highlands hold a position of honor among the American Hills. They stand near the principal portal of the continent—the first land to greet the curious eyes of the stranger, and to cheer the heart of the returning wanderer. The beauty of these wooded heights, the charming villas that stud their sides, the grace of their undulating lines, give to the traveller prompt assurance that the country he visits is not only blessed with rare natural beauty, but that art and culture have suitably adorned it. The delight with which the wearied ocean-voyager greets the shores that first rise upon the horizon has often been described; but, when these shores have a rare sylvan beauty that opens hour by hour to view as the vessel draws near—when, instead of frowning rocks or barren sands, he beholds noble hills clothed to their brows with green forests, fields and meadows basking with summer beauty in the sun, cottages nestling amid shrubbery, and spires lifting above clustering treetops—the picture possesses a charm which only he who first beholds it can fully realize. It is such a green paradise that the Neversink Hills offer to the gaze of every ocean-wanderer who enters the harbor of New York. These highlands are situated in New Jersey, extending several miles along the coast in a southerly direction. At their feet flows the Shrewsbury River; beyond the river stretches a narrow strip of sand, upon which the surf of the Atlantic ceaselessly beats. This strip or tongue of sand extends northerly into the sea, somewhat beyond the reach of the hills, which, suddenly trending westward, form, in connection with the Hook, what is known as Sandy-Hook Bay. The ship entering from the sea stretches past this point of sand, leaving the hills to the left; but from their receding forms the voyager soon turns to greet the rising shores of Staten Island. . . . The outer bay, or Lower Bay, as it is commonly called, has upon its west side a deep estuary, between the New Jersey and Staten Island shores, known as Raritan Bay. Shrewsbury River, which is probably more an estuary than a river, enters the sea between Raritan Bay and the Hook.

This description, written in 1872 by O. B. Bunce for *Picturesque America*, edited by William Cullen Bryant (New York: D. Appleton, 1872, p.p. 173-4.),still holds true today. The highest of the elevations is Beacon Hill, which is 266 feet above sea level. This is the highest location along the Atlantic coastline south of Mount Desert Island in Maine. There is considerable confusion about the proper name of these hills. Verrazano called them the Montagne di S. Polo. Often they are simply called the Atlantic Highlands. However, the name Atlantic Highlands more properly belongs to the small town at their feet on the south shore of Sandy Hook Bay. The name Navesink is in general use today among cartographers. Most Jerseyites simply refer to "the Highlands" (never meaning the Highlands of the Hudson, which they inclusively call "Bear Mountain"). Even in 1872, there was much confusion, and we shall again quote Mr. Bunce:

In regard to the designation of these hills, there exists a fearful orthographical confusion. The word is sometimes spelled "Navasink," sometimes "Navisink," then again as "Nevisink," and lastly as "Neversink," as in Philip Freneau's poem "Neversink". The correct method can be determined only by a knowledge of its origin, and of this there appears to be some doubt. "Navasink" is supposed to be an Indian word, meaning "fishing-place," and, of course, applied to the river; but others claim that this is simply a common instance of a natural desire to find an aboriginal root for our nomenclature, and that the term is really "Neversink," having been bestowed by the sailors, as expressive of the long time which these hills remain in view to the outward voyager. There is more romance and originality in the Indian term, but, so far, the weight of authority does not appear to be in its favor. (Ibid.)

We disagree with this last affirmation, having in mind the Neversink River in the Catskills, which is and was a fishing place par excellence, and whose name is of undoubted Indian derivation. Other Indian names such as Matawan, meaning "place of the beaver," are found both on the shores of Raritan Bay and along the mid-Hudson.

These Navesink Highlands offer fine views of the Atlantic, Sandy Hook, Long Island, New York Bay, Staten Island, and much of New Jersey, and, in clear weather, of Manhattan, the Verrazano-Narrows Bridge, and the Watchung Mountains of New Jersey. They are still "dotted with villas and cottages" and have many picturesque winding roads and small chapels and crossroad hamlets on the banks of the Navesink and Shrewsbury rivers. The peninsula between these two rivers is occupied mainly by large estates with beautiful landscaping and architecture. The bustling town of Red Bank, formerly an important point for shipping oysters to the New York market, is at the head of navigation on the Navesink River. Formerly served by steamboats from New York, it may be reached by Conrail North Jersey Shore trains from Penn Station and Newark.

The most interesting feature of the Highlands of the Navesink is the historic Twin Lighthouse. This ridge, the highest point found on the shore of the Atlantic, emerged from the sea about 125 million years ago and resisted erosion because it was capped with ironized conglomerate stone. Beacon Hill and the rest of the ridge is an erosional remnant, or cuesta. Because of this advantageous elevation near the entrance to New York Harbor, it was considered as a suitable location for a major lighthouse, and as early as 1764 a beacon was erected here. This was replaced in 1828 by a double lighthouse, which served until construction of the present Twin Lights in 1862. The early lighthouses were lighted by tallow candles. After 1812, the Argand lamp was in general use until about 1852, when the Fresnel lens came into use. The Argand lamp, named for its inventor, the Swiss chemist Aimé Argand (1755-1803), made use of circular wicks that admitted air to the center of the flame and thereby increased the intensity of combustion. These lamps burned either spermaceti oil or gas and were the brightest lights known at the time. The Fresnel lens is named for its inventor, the Frenchman,

Augustin Jean Fresnel (1788-1827). It is a circular compound lens that polarizes light in the horizontal axis and can send beams a great distance. It has generally superseded the use of mirrors in light-houses and for beacon lights. The United States Lighthouse Service (now incorporated into the Coast Guard) was organized in 1852, and this was the immediate impetus for the construction of the great new Twin Lights in 1862. Writing of these lights, in 1872, Mr. Bunce notes

We soon reach Beacon Hill, crowned by a double-towered light-house furnished with "Fresnel" lights of remarkable capacity. The square tower has the most powerful light on the coast, the rays of which reach a distance of thirty-five miles, or as far as the altitude of the tower lifts the horizon. This light gives the mariner the first intimation of his nearness to our shores, just as the green slopes of the hill it surmounts greet him with the first show of land. This magnificent light is of French construction, was exhibited and secured the prize at the great French exposition (Paris 1867), and was purchased by our government at a cost of thirty thousand dollars. The light in the corresponding tower was manufactured in imitation of it, and although upon the same principle, is scarcely so powerful. A visit to this light-house will repay us; the view from the tower is superb, and the mangnificent lenses of the lamp are well worth our curious attention. The obliging light-house keeper will draw the curtain, and show, reflected upon the convex central crystal, an exquisite miniature of all the expanse of land and sea and sky—such a landscape as the most gifted painter would despair of being able to imitate. (Ibid.)

The northwestern tower is octagonal, and the southeastern one is square; each is 50 feet high. They are constructed of red sandstone and linked by a gabled central pavilion, forming a total frontage of 300 feet. The entire structure is crenellated. The towers and facade are of rusticated sandstone, but the back is built of red brick. Since World War II, the lights have been superseded by radar and are not operational. The Twin Lights are now a museum. Visitors may climb the octagonal tower. This museum is maintained by the Navesink Twin Lights Historical Society and is open from Memorial Day to Labor Day. Also on view are the first United States Life Saving Station of 1842 (moved here from another location) and Marconi's radio tower, from which he made the first successful transatlantic radio transmission in 1907.

-21.50 Sandy Hook (W).
Sandy Hook is a long, low, and narrow strip of sandy land, about five miles in length, extending north by northwest from the mouth of the Shrewsbury River east of Beacon Hill. It separates the Atlantic Ocean on the east from Sandy Hook Bay on the west. It is the southern cape of Raritan Bay. While now a peninsula, it has been an island or barrier reef at various times in the fairly recent past. Originally, the Shrewsbury and Navesink Rivers each emptied directly into the Atlantic farther south, near Rumson. In 1778, an inlet was cut through by the sea during a gale, but this was closed again in 1800. Another was cut in 1830, of such size that steamboats passed through, but this was closed by 1866. At present, the shoreline is continuous and unbroken from Shark River Inlet to the tip of Sandy Hook, which is about 13 miles. The Navesink River empties into the Shrewsbury River east of Rumson, and the Shrewsbury flows north to empty into Sandy Hook Bay (part of Raritan Bay) inside Sandy Hook at the foot of the Highlands.

This long and strongly curved hook was built up by currents in Sandy Hook Bay in stages that have resulted in coves on the inland side. A seawall has been built along the ocean side to prevent future erosion. A government bulletin notes that

technically, Sandy Hook is a compound, complex, recurved barrier sand spit. It was formed from a series of currents eroding both the ocean and bay shore-lines. For nearly 10,000 years these currents have continually worked on changing the Sandy Hook Shoreline. The currents create a constantly changing beach area by removing sand from the south end of the hook and transporting it northward. This sand is deposited at the northern tip of Sandy Hook where it widens and elongates the Hook. . . . The waves generally strike the shoreline from the southeast. This produces a deflected runoff of water towards the north. This littoral current transports sand northward and has led to the present spit formation. In geological terms a spit which curves toward the mainland is called a hook. This particular formation has grown over 7,000 feet since 1764, and because of this con-stant growth, the Sandy Hook Channel, just off the northern tip of the Hook, must be dredged periodically in order to keep the channel open to ship traffic. (*Sandy Hook Visitors Information*, National Park Service. Washington: US Government Printing Office, 1978)

Construction of the present seawall from Sea Bright to the Hook was started after a violent storm in 1914. The work was completed in 1921. It utilized in part material excavated in construction of the Holland and Lincoln tunnels. It is continually being strengthened. The cen-tral portion of the hook is composed of sand dunes, and the western border of salt march, tidal pools and coves. Typi-cal vegetation includes cordgrass, sea rocket, salt hay, seaside goldenrod, poi-son ivy, holly trees, foxtail reeds, bay-berry, prickly pear cactus, beach plums, sumac, eastern red cedar trees, wild black cherry, golden heather, Indian fig, tree of heaven, green briar, groundsel, apple trees, shad bush, high bush blue-

berry, privet, and honeysuckle. Because of driving salt spray, there are few large trees.

Principal features on the inside of the hook, from south to north are: Plum Island (now joined to the hook by a narrow isthmus); Spermaceti Cove (partly enclosed by small crescent-shaped Skeleton Hill Island); and shal-low, open Horseshoe Cove. Fort Han-cock and the United States Coast Guard Station are at the northern tip.

Sandy Hook has long been closed to the public, as it was an Army Base. In recent years, portions of the hook have been set aside as a state park, part of the new Gateway National Recreation Area, which is administered by the National Park Service. There are bathing beaches and nature trails. Inquiries may be made to Area Manager, P. O. Box 437, Highlands, New Jersey 07732; or telephone (201) 872-0115. Caution: the beaches become extremely crowded in July and August, and tourists should check traffic conditions in advance.

Sandy Hook Lighthouse
The first Sandy Hook lighthouse began operation on 11 June 1764. It was built by Isaac Conro of New York City with money collected from the merchants of that city. It was 103 feet tall with an oil-burning lantern that was 7 feet high. Originally, the lighthouse was only 500 feet from the end of the hook, but the continual buildup of sand now leaves it 7,000 ft. (one-and-a-half miles) from the tip. In 1950, the light was listed as "45,000 candle-power, third-order elec-tric light, fixed white, in a white stone tower, 85 feet above ground and 88 feet above water, visible for 15 miles." (Ibid.)

Historic Fort Hancock
One of the first important military actions on the hook was on 5 July 1778, when the forces of the British General Sir Henry Clinton, retreating after the Battle of Monmouth Courthouse, embarked from here to New York City in barges.

The following are extracts from the brochure "Sandy Hook's Bicentennial Story," distributed by the Gateway National Recreation Area.

As the threat of a second war with England grew, the Federal Government purchased all the land north of the lighthouse in 1806 to build the preliminary fortifications for New York Harbor defense. . . . a "massive log fort" was constructed half a mile north of the lighthouse. The fort was manned by the Monmouth County Militia during the War of 1812. Plans for a more permanent fortification on Sandy Hook were made in 1847 by Army Captain Robert E. Lee, then Recorder for the Engineer Board. . . . Work began on a massive granite star-shaped fort in 1859 and continued intermittently until construction was suspended in 1869. It was never completed largely because the technical improvements of weapons and explosives during the Civil War made granite forts obsolete. During the 1890s most of the fort walls were partially dismantled for various Army building projects around the Hook. Construction of the first heavily fortified solid-concrete shore batteries were begun in 1890. The Mortar Battery (1890-1892) mounted 16 12 inch breech-loading Seacoast mortars which could fire 700 lb projectiles in high arcs that would descend almost vertically on the lightly armored decks of warships. They were clustered in four pit-like emplacements and manned by almost 200 men. Battery Potter (built 1890-1898) mounted two 12 inch high power guns mounted on a hydraulic lift barbette carriage and had a useful range of eight miles using a 1,000 lb projectile—which was sufficient distance to match or outshoot the guns of contemporary battleships. This remained operational until 1903.

From 1876 until after the First World War, when all operations were moved to Aberdeen, Maryland, the Army used Sandy Hook for its proving grounds.

In 1950, while a missile was being developed that could destroy a high altitude aircraft, the Army established ARAACOM (Army Anti-aircraft Command). A unit of this defense command, consisting of various battalion batteries of the 52nd Artillery Brigade, was assigned the primary mission of defending the New York area in 1952. Initially armed with 90 mm and 120 mm anti-aircraft guns, the Brigade later received the Nike Ajax, the first missile to protect American cities against air attack, in 1954-55. The Nike Ajax had a range of over 30 miles and an altitude of 60,000 ft.

By 1957 most of the remaining gun batteries were inactivated. A year later the Nike Ajax were replaced by the Nike Hercules, which had a range of 96 miles altitude of 100,000 ft. and were designed to use either a conventional or nuclear warhead. Aircraft nearing this area could be detected by the radar tracking post at Fort Hancock. If identified as hostile, the radar post would coordinate the firing of Nike Hercules from the launching area against approaching aircraft. In recent years the continuing technical development of missiles has made the Nike Hercules obsolete. This has led to the removal of these weapons from Sandy Hook and the deactivation of Fort Hancock in 1974.

For many years fortifications at Sandy Hook were simply officially designated the fortifications at Sandy Hook "Fort at Sandy Hook." On October 30, 1895, General Army Order #57 designated the fortification at Sandy Hook as Fort Hancock, thus honoring Major General Winfield Scott Hancock of Civil War fame (1824-1886). Around the turn of the century the officers-row of houses was constructed. By the time of the First World War, Fort Hancock had become a formidable coastal defense site bristling with heavy ordnance. World War Two saw the post expand into an anti-aircraft site and an Eastern staging area for troops being readied for European duty.

The post was also a primary reception center in the New York area at the end of the war for returning European theater veterans.

Historical Incidents.
On New Years Eve day in 1783 *H.M.S. Assistance*, a British warship, sent a detachment of fourteen men to the hook to round up some deserters. Led by twenty-year-old 1st Lt. Hamilton Douglas Halyburton, the group met a tragic fate when a blizzard trapped them on the hook.

A similar incident is recounted by Benson Lossing in his book, *The Hudson —From the Wilderness to the Sea:*

About a mile below the pier, near the lighthouse, on the inner shore of the Hook, once stood an elegant monument, erected to the memory of a son of the Earl of Morton, and thirteen others, who were cast away near there, in a snow storm, during the revolution, and perished. All but one were officers of a British man-of-war, wrecked there. They were discovered, and buried in one grave. The mother of the young nobleman erected the monument, and it remained, respected even by the roughest men of the coast, until 1808, when some vandals from a French vessel-of-war, landed there, and destroyed that beautiful memorial of a mother's love. (Troy, N.Y.: H. L. Nims & Co., 1866, p. 464.)

Sandy Hook seems to have been a place of ill omen. In 1609, one of Henry Hudson's crewmen, John Coleman, was the first white man to be killed in this area by an Indian. He was shot through the throat with an arrow while exploring the Kill van Kull in a small boat. To preserve his body, his fellow crewmembers buried him on Sandy Hook, which long bore the name Coleman's Point.

In 1620, a Dutch immigrant ship bound for New Amsterdam was wrecked on Sandy Hook. The passengers and crew got ashore and decided to walk to Manhattan, because they were afraid of Indians. However, Penelope van Princis, who was only eighteen years old, refused to leave her seriously wounded husband, and she stayed to care for him in the bitter winter cold. They were found by local Raritan Indians, who killed her husband and left Penelope for dead with a fractured skill and serious wounds of the left arm and abdomen. She crawled into a hollow tree and hid for days living on bark and frozen tree gum, until two Indians found her. One expressed the wish to kill her; the other prevailed upon him to take her to a nearby village, where she was nursed back to health. Word of her plight reached New Amsterdam, and she was soon ransomed. Four years later, she married an Englishman, Richard Stout, and moved with him back to New Jersey, to be among the first settlers of Middletown. The Indian who had befriended her visited them often. Once, at considerable risk to himself, he warned them of an intended massacre. Penelope lived to the age of 101 and left 502 direct descendants when she died.

In the early 1870s, the Southern Railroad of New Jersey was built south from Spermaceti Cove to Long Branch. When Spermaceti Cove was found to be too shallow for the connecting steamboats, the terminal was moved to Horseshoe Cove. Eventually these services were absorbed by the New York & Long Branch and Central railroad of New Jersey. The former railroad right-of-way is now part of the Salt Marsh Hiking-Nature Trail. There is an unsubstantiated belief that Captain Kidd buried treasure on Sandy Hook.

-21.50 Rockaway Beach, Long Island(E).
Popular seaside resort and residential area.

-21.25 Sandy Hook Bar.
Sandbar extending from Sandy Hook on the west to Rockaway

31

Point on the east, separating Lower New York Bay from the open Atlantic Ocean. It is breached by the Sandy Hook and Ambrose Channels, which are the major shipping lanes. The natural depth of water is twenty-one feet, but it was deepened to twenty-three feet in 1837.

Since 1694, ships have taken on their harbor pilots here and the pilot boats are stationed here as well. Members of the two separate associations, the United New Jersey Sandy Hook Pilots Benevolent Association and the United New York Sandy Hook Pilots Benevolent Association, used to race each other to get the job as each ship appeared. These days, they have made peace and take alternate turns. They take the ships as far up the Hudson as Yonkers, where members of the Hudson River Pilots Association, based in that city, take over from them.

-21.25 Keansburg, New Jersey, (W). On south shore of Raritan Bay, beyond Sandy Hook.

-20.00 Raritan Bay This is the western extremity of the Lower New York Bay and the outlet of the Raritan River. It is bounded on the north by Staten Island and on the west by Middlesex County, New Jersey, and on the south by Middlesex and Monmouth Counties, New Jersey. The cities and ports of Perth Amboy (population 38,798) and South Amboy (population 9,338) are at the head of the bay, and the city of New Brunswick (population 41,885) is ten miles up the Raritan River. Principal tributaries are the Arthur Kill, to the north; the Raritan River, to the west; and

Matawan, Chingarora, Thornes, Waycake, Pews, Comptons Creeks, and the Shrewsbury River to the south. The southeastern portion of Raritan Bay, inside Sandy Hook, is also known as Sandy Hook Bay.

Raritan River

All thy wat'ry face
 Reflected with a purer grace,
Thy many turnings through the trees,
 Thy bitter journey to the seas,
Thou Queen of Rivers, Raritan!
 John Davis—1806
 "Ode to the Raritan, Queen of Rivers"

The Raritan is the largest river entirely within the state of New Jersey. It is roughly 100 miles from the headwaters of the south branch at Budd Lake in Morris County to Raritan Bay at Perth Amboy. It drains more than 1000 square miles. The first white settlers were Dutch. They moved in prior to 1650. The name Raritan comes from the Indian word Laletan, meaning "forked river." This has also been interpreted as "gentle" or "smooth-running." All are accurate descriptions of the river. The local Indians were called Raritangs or Naraticongs. They grew maize, pumpkins, beans, and fruit. The early settlers found the region good for growing grain and raising cattle

The South Branch starts at Budd Lake in Morris County and flows south past Schooley's Mountain through Bartley, Naughtright, Long Valley, Middle Valley, and High Bridge. It continues past Clinton and Hamden. Here the river turns east and flows past Flemington Junction, Three Bridges, Woodfern, Neshanic, and South Branch. The North Branch starts at Ralston, in Morris County, at the confluence of Burnett and Indian Brooks. It flows southeast past Pleasant Valley and south into Somerset County past Peapack, Gladstone, Far Hills, Pluckemin, and Burnt Mill, where it is joined from the west by the Lamington River. It continues south past North Branch and Milltown to its junction with the South Branch, just west of Raritan. The combined stream, now officially known as the Raritan River, flows east past Raritan, Somerville, and Finderne to Manville and Zarephath, where it is joined from the south by the Millstone River. Continuing east, we pass Bound Brook, Piscataway, Fieldville, and Somerset before coming to New Brunswick on the south shore and Highland Park on the north shore. We are now in Middlesex County. This is now a tidewater area and the river is navigable by ships to New Brunswick. Continuing east we pass Weston's Mills on the south shore and Greensand, Bonhamtown, and Nixon on the north.

Lawrence Brook and South River enter the Raritan just west of Sayreville on the south shore. The river here is quite wide, with extensive salt marshes and abandoned claypits on either side, the remnants of a once extensive brick-making industry. We pass Phoenix on the south and finally enter Raritan Bay at the confluence of the tidal estuary Arthur Kill from the north. Perth Amboy is on the north shore and South Amboy on the south.

At New Brunswick, the Raritan is crossed by high bridges of the Pennsylvania Railroad, Route 1, and the New Jersey Turnpike, and by a lower-level bridge of Route 27 between New Brunswick and Highland Park. Just west of Perth Amboy, it is crossed by the twin high-level Governor Alfred E. Driscoll Bridge of the Garden State Parkway and the Thomas A. Edison Bridge used by Route U.S. 9, immediately to the east. Also at Perth Amboy are the long, low-level, swing, Victory Vehicular Bridge, and that of the New York, & Long Branch Railroad—the outermost bridge on the river, at its confluence with Raritan Bay. Crab Island is located north of Sayreville. Also near Sayreville is the large plant of the National Lead Company. There is a large power generating station

at South Amboy and several railroad car dumpers. South Amboy was the terminal of the pioneer Camden & Amboy Railroad across New Jersey. The Delaware & Raritan Canal parallels the south bank of the Raritan from Zarephath to New Brunswick, where the last lock lowers it to tidewater.

The Arthur Kill

The Arthur Kill is a deepwater tidal estuary separating Staten Island and New Jersey. The state line runs down the middle of its channel. It empties into Newark Bay at the north and Raritan Bay at the south. From south to north the principal tributaries are: Woodbridge Creek, Smith Creek, Rahway River, Pile's Creek, Morse's Creek, Elizabeth River, on the west bank. Fresh Kills, (fed by Richmond Creek from the south), and Old Place Creek are on the Staten Island side. Principal islands, which are both in New York State, are the Island of Meadows, at the mouth of Fresh Kills, and Prall's Island near Tremley Point and the mouth of the Rahway River.

Principal locations from south to north along the New Jersey side are: Perth Amboy, Barber, Sewaren, Woodbridge, Port Reading, Tufts Point, Chrome, Carteret, Tremley Point, Warner's Station, Grasselli, Bayway, and Elizabethport. On the Staten Island side: Tottenville, Richmond Valley, Charleston, Port Mobil, (formerly Port Socony), Smoking Point, Fresh Kills, Island of Meadows, Travis, Bloomfield, Pralls Island, Gulfport, Port Ivory, and Howland Hook. Bridges from south to north are: Outerbridge Crossing, between Perth Amboy and Tottenville; Goethals Bridge, between Elizabeth and Howland Hook; and the lift bridge of the Staten Island Rapid Transit Railroad (freight only), between Elizabeth and Howland Hook. There were formerly ferries between Tottenville and Perth Amboy and Port Ivory and Elizabethport. The Arthur Kill was part of the popular

1. Arthur Kill

inside or north shore route between New Brunswick and the Amboys and Newark, Manhattan, Jersey City, and Hoboken in the early days of steamboating.

The Central Railroad of New Jersey (Conrail) parallels the Arthur Kill on the New Jersey side. This was formerly the Elizabeth & Perth Amboy Railroad. The Sound Shore Branch and Chrome Branch also serve the area. An electrified branch of the Pennsylvania Railroad (Conrail), used by North Jersey Shore Trains, connects the Pennsylvania Mainline at Rahway with Perth Amboy, via Woodbridge. At Perth Amboy, both the Central of New Jersey and Pennsylvania lines connect with the New York & Long Branch, which is also electrified across the Raritan River Drawbridge to South Amboy.

The New Jersey Turnpike and U.S. Routes 1 and 9 parallel the Arthur Kill inland from the Central of New Jersey tracks. Major oil refineries of Gulf Oil Corporation, Socony-Mobil Corporation, and Standard Oil of New Jersey (Esso-Exxon) are located along the estuary and are served directly by deepwater tankers. There are major plants of the Nassau Smelting & Refining Division of Western Electric Company and of Proctor & Gamble, Ivory Soap Division, at Tottenville and Port Ivory on Staten Island. The shores are marshy and largely devoted to heavy petrochemical industry, tank farms, and cemeteries. The area was formerly a resort that was popular with fishermen, crabbers, and marsh hunters. There is considerable heavy-tonnage shipping, and these waters are not recommended for pleasure cruising in small boats. The upper reaches of the Rahway River, near Rahway and Cranford, are very scenic. They are kept as parkland and are popular for canoeing. The Elizabeth River is littered with trash and is given to violent flooding after heavy rains or snow.

The Rahway Reformatory, a major state prison and a prison farm are at Rahway. The Raritan Arsenal is located at Carteret. The west bank is bounded by Middlesex County to the south and Union County to the north. Elizabeth is the county seat of Union County which was settled from New England in 1664. The tall white office tower is the Union County Court House, built in 1905 by the architects Ackerman & Ross.

Outerbridge Crossing

Named in honor of Eugenius H. Outerbridge, first chairman of the Port of New York Authority, the Outerbridge Crossing and the similar Goethals Bridge were the first facilities constructed by the Port Authority. In conjunction with the Verrazano-Narrows Bridge, these bridges provide access from New Jersey to Long Island and serve as part of the metropolitan area's southerly highway bypass system.

Length of Center Span	750 ft.
Total Length of Truss Spans	2,100 ft.
Length of New Jersey Viaduct	4,758 ft.
Length of Staten Island Viaduct	1,920 ft.
Total Length of Elevated Structure	8,778 ft.
Width of Bridge (Main Span)	62 ft.
Width of Roadway (Main Span)	42 ft.
Width of Roadway (Viaducts)	50 ft.
Channel Clearance at Midspan	135 ft.
Opened to Traffic 29 June, 1928	
Traffic Volume (Eastbound) 1975	3,004,000

Goethals Bridge.

Goethals Bridge was built as a memorial to Maj. Gen. George W. Goethals, builder of the Panama Canal and first consulting engineer of the Port Authority.

Length of Center Span	672 ft.
Total Length of Truss Spans	1,152 ft.
Length of New Jersey Viaduct	2,831 ft.
Length of Staten Island Viaduct	3,126 ft.
Total Length of Elevated Structure	7,109 ft.
Width of Bridge (Main Span)	62 ft.
Width of Roadway	42 ft.
Channel Clearance at Midspan	135 ft.
Opened to Traffic 29 June, 1928	
Traffic Volume (Eastbound) 1975	9,868,500

Kill van Kull.

The Kill van Kull is a deepwater tidal estuary connecting Newark Bay and the Arthur Kill with Upper New York Bay. It separates the north shore of Staten Island from Bayonne, in Hudson County, New Jersey. It was while sailing through this estuary in a small boat, making explorations in 1609, that John Coleman, one of Henry Hudson's crew members, was shot through the throat by an Indian. This was the first recorded incident of bloodshed in the New York area. Coleman was buried on Sandy Hook.

Shooters Island (one-third of which is in New Jersey and two-thirds in New York) is at the west end at the mouth of Newark Bay. The Kill van Kull serves as the state line between New Jersey and New York. It is one of the entrances to the busy ports of Newark Bay. From west to east, these are its principal points: on Staten Island there are Mariners Harbor, Arlington, Elm Park, Port Richmond, West New Brighton, Livingston, Sailors Snug Harbor, New Brighton, and St. George. In New Jersey, there are Bergen Point, Port Johnson and Constable Hook. Robbins Reef with its light is at the junction with Upper New York Bay. It is crossed by the Bayonne Bridge between Bayonne and Elm Park. There was formerly a ferry here.

The Bayonne Bridge
The Bayonne Bridge is the longest steel arch bridge in the world. The mid-span clearance of 150 feet permits ocean-going vessels to use this entrance to Port Newark and the Elizabeth-Port Authority Marine Terminal without interference.

Length of Arch Span	1,675 ft.
Length of New Jersey Viaduct	3,010 ft.
Length of Staten Island Viaduct	2,010 ft.
Total Length of Elevated Structure	6,695 ft.
Width of Bridge	85 ft.
Width of Roadway	40 ft.
Channel Clearance at Midspan	150 ft.
Height of Arch above water at Crown	327 ft.
Opened to Traffic 15 November, 1931	
Traffic Volume (Eastbound) in 1975	1,979,400

The south shore of the Kill van Kull is paralleled by the freight-only branch of the Staten Island Rapid Transit line between St. George and Port Ivory. The waterway can best be seen by driving along Richmond Terrace on Staten Island. Sailor's Snug Harbor is worth a visit. The currents of the Kill are swift, and there is considerable ship traffic. It is not recommended for small boats, however.

Staten Island

Staten Island is the large island on the west side of the narrows. Roughly oval in shape, it incorporates an area of fifty-seven square miles with a maximum length of fourteen miles and breadth of eight miles. On the north, it is separated from Bergen Point (Bayonne) New Jersey by the Kill van Kull. On the west, it is separated from the New Jersey mainland by Newark Bay and the Arthur Kill. Raritan Bay is to the south, and Lower New York Bay and the Narrows is to the east. Upper New York Bay is to the northeast.

The western portion of the island is low and swampy. It is drained by Old Place Creek, the Fresh Kills, and Richmond Creek. The remainder of the island consists of indeterminate hills and upland. One principal ridge runs from southwest to northeast along the eastern side of the island. Its principal elevations are Latourette (241 feet), Grimes Hill (370 feet) and Todt Hill (410 feet). Todt Hill is the highest point on the Atlantic Seaboard south of Mount Desert Island in Maine. Principal indentations on the southeastern shore are Princess Bay and Great Kills Harbor. Ward's Point at the confluence of the Arthur Kill and Raritan Bay is the southernmost point in New York State.

The original inhabitants were the Raritan and Hackensack tribes of the Lenni-Lenape Indians. They called the island Eghquaons, which means "place of high sandy banks." At the time of European discovery, the island was heavily wooded. For a more detailed description of early topography, the reader is referred to James Fenimore Cooper's "Water Witch."

In 1609, Henry Hudson named the island Status Eylandt in honor of the States General of the Netherlands, which had financed his voyage. In 1630, the Dutch West India Company granted Staten Island to Michael Pauw, who also held extensive grants at the present site of Jersey City. However, in 1634, title reverted to the Dutch West Indian Company because Pauw had failed in planting any settlements.

Planting settlements was not so easy a matter because of Indian hostility. In 1639, David Pietersen De Vries received a grant and started a colony at the Watering Place, near present-day Tompkinsville. This was named from the fact that there were several good springs where ships replenished their water supplies. This settlement ws wiped out by Indians in 1641.

In 1640, Cornelis Melyn attempted to establish a patroonship and planted a colony that was destroyed in 1643. He made a second attempt at the Watering Place in 1650, but this too was destroyed in 1655. In 1659, Melyn gave up his patroonship.

Peace with the Indians was established by a treaty in 1660, and, in 1661, Governor Peter Stuyvesant gave permission to nineteen Dutchmen and Frenchmen from the Palatinate to settle at Oude Dorp, or Old Town, just inland from present day Fort Wadsworth. The leader of this colony was Pierre Billeau, a Walloon. A small garrison was established for its protection, and there were church services every two months. These were conducted by Dominie Drisius, who preached in English, French, and Dutch. The Dutch generally accepted French settlers so long as they made no attempts at claiming French sovereignty.

The English conquered the island in 1664 and renamed it Richmond, in honor of the Duke of Richmond, second son of Charles II. All settlers were required to take an oath of allegiance. Long Island and Staten Island were incorporated together into the West Riding of Yorkshire. The seat of government was established at Gravesend on Long Island, and court continued to be held there until 1675.

In 1670, Governor Francis Lovelace made a "final purchase" from the local Indians. He required that the young Indians also sign the deed, so that it would not quickly be forgotten. This same year it was estimated that there were about one hundred families, mainly Dutch and French, settled on Staten Island. In 1668, some Waldensians had settled and established a church near Stony Brook; and some Huguenots had settled at Fresh Kill, which is now known as Greenridge.

The original settlers lived in cabins of squared logs, but these were gradually replaced by more substantial stone houses of long and low massive construction. Stone, timber, and shingles were easily procured, and lime was made from oyster shells collected along the shore. The stonework was irregular, and door and window placement was asymetrical. The houses were usually only one room deep and had no hallway. Steep gables were favored, but the houses differed from those elsewhere in the colony in that they lacked the graceful overhanging eaves and, also, the original unit was usually the largest section.

In 1671, the village of New Dorp was settled on the shore, east of the present village of that name. Also that year, the settlement of Oude Dorp spread to the nearby fertile valley, and this new section was laid out as the New Lots of the Old Town, now known as Dongan Hills. In 1682, Thomas Dongan became governor of the province of New York. He would hold this office until 1688. He lived for some time on Staten Island but later returned to Ireland where he became the Earl of Limerick, dying there in 1715 at the age of eighty-one. In 1683, Governor Dongan called the first Provincial Assembly, and Staten Island was organized into Richmond County. The county seat was established at Cuckold's Town, near New Dorp, which was given the more dignified name of Richmond Town.

It was the English custom to give grants of eighty acres, or multiples thereof, to settlers and speculators. In 1684, Governor Dongan granted two large manorial estates on Staten Island, one near Ward's Point to Christopher Billopp, and one, located in the central part of the island, to John Palmer. Dongan himself shortly thereafter acquired the Palmer manorial lands. This immense tract became known simply as The Manour.

After Louis XIV of France revoked the Edict of Nantes in 1685, there was a considerable influx of French Huguenot settlers to Staten Island. Also about this time, a dispute arose between the colonies of New Jersey and New York for possession of the island. The Duke of York, according to an old tradition, offered title to whichever colony boasted a native son who could first circumnavigate the island within twenty-four hours. The honors went to Capt. Christopher Billopp of New York in 1687, and Staten Island has belonged to New York ever since. In 1688, the four townships of Northfield, Southfield, Westfield, and Castletown were established, corresponding to the earlier precincts and Castleton Manour.

In 1775, the New York City Council chartered a ferry route to Manhattan. This was served by small sailing boats known as piraguas. During the American Revolution, the British took control of Staten Island in the summer of 1776 and held it until the autumn of 1783. The state of New York established a quarantine station on the northern extremity of the island in 1799. In 1858, the local natives burned it down in protest of the fact that two years earlier there were over five hundred cases of yellow fever held at the station. The facility was then replaced by a hospital ship anchored in the Upper Bay. However, today there is again a quarantine station located at Rosebank.

The island was devoted to fishing and agriculture until the 1830s. The principal crops were corn, wheat, and rye. Some grapes were grown for wine, and there were extensive cherry and apple orchards and many cider mills. From the 1830s on, the island became popular as a resort and suburban residence for wealthy New Yorkers. Many large villas were erected, enjoying the fine views of the harbor and Narrows. The great landscape architect, Frederick Law Olmstead, creator of Central Park, made his home on Staten Island and developed plans for a greenbelt, which was never created during his lifetime. Today his plans are being implemented, and a scenic hiking trail system has been named the Olmstead Trailway. Among the famous nineteenth-century residents were Francis Parkman, Guiseppe Garibaldi, and Cornelius Vanderbilt. Vanderbilt was a native of Staten Island and started his vast transportation empire with a small ferryboat plying between there and Manhattan. The elaborate Vanderbilt family mausoleum in the Moravian Cemetery near New Dorp is one of the island's most interesting sights.

During the Civil War, Staten Island was a pocket of Southern sympathy, and there were particularly violent draft riots. After ferry and railroad services were consolidated at St. George in 1886, that town rapidly became the principal community and county seat. In 1898, Staten Island was consolidated with New York City as the Borough and County of Richmond. Some heavy industry settled along the western shore, including a smelting plant at Richmond, refineries along the Arthur Kill, and a large soap factory at Port Ivory. However, most development has been residential, Richmond being the most rural of the New York boroughs. The island is served by the Staten Island Rapid Transit Railroad, which provides freight service and passenger service between St. George and Tottenville. In past years, ferry lines have operated to Perth Amboy, Elizabeth, Bayonne, and Brooklyn, as well as to Manhattan. Today only the St. George line to Manhattan survives, the others having been replaced with the Outerbridge Crossing, Goethals Bridge, Bayonne, and the Verrazano-Narrows bridges. This last great bridge across the Narrows was completed in 1965, and the island's population has boomed since then to over 310,000. Interstate Highway 278 connects the Goethals and Verrazano-Narrows bridges and serves as an important southern bypass around New York City, connecting New Jersey with Long Island.

Silver Lake, near Stapleton, is the southern termination of the Catskill aqueduct system. The recreational facilities offered by Staten Island include many beaches along the eastern shore. Midland and South beaches are connected by the Franklin D. Roosevelt Boardwalk, which offers superb views of the Lower Bay. Among the many parks are Wolfe's Pond Park, Great Kills Park, New Springville Park, Latourette Park and golf course, Willowbrook Park, Clove Lakes Park, Silver Lake Park, and Barrett Park with the Staten Island Zoo, which contains one of the largest snake collections in the world. Also of interest are the High Rock Nature Conservation Center, Moravian Cemetery, and the Jacques Marchais Center of Tibetan Art with its oriental garden. Old Richmondtown is a historic restoration with three dozen buildings recreating a seventeenth-century village. There is a historical museum, several old churches and homes, and a lighthouse in the vicinity. This complex is operated by the Staten Island Historical Society.

Staten Island is particularly rich in educational institutions, hospitals, and asylums for the aged and infirm. Among the more notable institutions are Saint Paul's Seminary, Augustinian Academy, Notre Dame College, Willowbrook State School, Saint Francis Seminary, Wagner College, Staten Island Community College, Mount. Loretto Academy, Staten Island Academy, Saint Joseph-by-the-Sea Home, Sailors' Snug Harbor, The Goodhue Home, Staten Island Hospital, United States Public Health Service Hospital at Rosebank, and the United States Quarantine Station. There is a major military base at Fort Wadsworth, overlooking the Narrows, and a United States Coast Guard station at Saint George. Principal historic landmarks include the Billopp Conference House, Voorlezer's House, Saint Andrew's Church, the Moravian Church at New Dorp, and the Stillwell-Perrine House at Dongan Hills.

Newark Bay

Newark Bay is a deepwater bay, five miles long by one and a half miles wide to the west of Bayonne and Upper New York Bay. It is the outlet of the Passaic and Hackensack rivers in New Jersey. It lies entirely in New Jersey, although it debouches into both the Arthur Kill and Kill van Kull, north of Staten Island, at its south end. It is bounded on the east by Bayonne and Jersey City, and on the west by Elizabethport and Newark. Kearny is at the north end, between the mouths of the Passaic and the Hackensack. Bayonne, Jersey City, and Kearny are in Hudson County. Newark is in Essex County, and Elizabethport in Union County.

Elizabeth Port Authority Piers are bounded on the north by the Elizabeth Channel, and Port Newark is bisected by

City Channel, also known as Port of Newark Channel. Both port complexes are on the west shore. Behind the massive port complexes are the Newark Branch of the Central Railroad of New Jersey (Conrail), the New Jersey Turnpike, and Newark International Airport. This is the busiest part of the entire Port of New York and is equipped to handle container ships. Principal features on the eastern shore from south to north are Bergen Point, City Park, Bayonne Park and Lagoon, Roosevelt Stadium, Droyer's Point and the Hackensack River. On the west shore are Elizabethport, Port Elizabeth, Oyster Creek, Elizabeth Channel, Port Newark, City Channel, Passaic Valley Sewage Plant, the Passaic River, and Newark. There is a large lift bridge of the Central Railroad of New Jersey (Conrail) across the mouth of the bay. Further north, between Port Newark and Jersey City, are another railroad bridge of the Pennsylvania Railroad and Lehigh Valley (Conrail) and the Newark Bay Bridge of the New Jersey Turnpike's Holland Tunnel extension, the latter of which offers good views. Newark Bay is busy and dirty, and the water can be rough. It is not recommended for small boats.

The Passaic River

The Passaic is one of the major rivers of New Jersey. It rises near Mendham in Morris County and flows east past Ledell's Pond at Washington Corner, near Jockey Hollow in Morristown National Historical Park (Washington spent a winter here during the Revolution) to Van Doren's Mill, Osborn Pond, Osborn Mill, and the Great Swamp National Wildlife Refuge near White's Bridge in Millington. This is the vast remains of the former large Lake Passaic, which was once contained by the Watchung Mountains.

Here the river has been trending southeastward, but after passing Milling-ton, it makes a sharp bend and starts to flow northeast past Stirling, Gillette, Meyersville, Berkeley Heights, New Providence, Chatham, Florham Park, and Hanover. Much of this area has a New England aspect and is a popular suburban neighborhood. It can be seen best from an Erie-Lackawanna (Conrail) Gladstone Branch train. Flowing north from Hanover, we pass Swinefield Bridge, Hanover Neck, and Rockaway Neck, where the Passaic is joined by the waters of the Rockaway River from the north. Here the Passaic makes a great loop to the west around the Great Piece Meadows, passing Pinebrook Bridge, Horseneck Bridge, and Two Bridges, where it is joined from the north by the Pompton River. The Pompton itself has been formed by the junction of the Ramapo River, which rises west of the Hudson Highlands, and the Pequannock River, which rises in the eastern hills of Sussex County. The Pequannock also receives the waters of the Wanaque River, which is the outlet of Greenwood Lake that lies half in New Jersey and half in New York State, south of Monroe, New York.

By the time the Passaic River reaches Two Bridges, it is now in Passaic County and is flowing east. It passes North Caldwell, Fairfield, and Totowa, to the first falls at Little Falls. Here it turns northeast past West Paterson and Prospect Park to Paterson, where it passes to the north of Garret Mountain. This portion was formerly paralleled by the Morris Canal. At Paterson, it goes over the Great Falls, which, with its abundant water power, gave birth to the industrial city of Paterson. Below the Great Falls, the Passaic makes a great loop to the north, passing Hawthorne and Haledon on the northern bank. Here it turns decisively south, with Bergen County now on the east bank. Paterson is now on the west bank and Fairlawn and Elmwood Park (formerly East Paterson) on the east. Here the river enters Dundee Lake and between Clifton and

41

Garfield falls over the Dundee Dam. This is the head of tidewater navigation. Between Garfield and Wallington, it receives the waters of the Saddle River, which rises near Monsey in Rockland County in New York and flows south through Bergen County. It makes an S loop between Wallington and the city of Passaic on the west bank and continues south with Rutherford, Carlton Hill, Lyndhurst, North Arlington, Arlington, Kearney, East Newark, and Harrison on the east bank; and Nutley, Avondale, Belleville, and Newark on the west bank. It enters the Newark Bay just below Newark.

The Hackensack River

The east branch of the Hackensack River rises in Rockland Lake (also known as Snedeker's Pond) atop the Palisades at Hook Mountain in Rockland County. It meanders west, down off the Palisades, through Swartwout Lake and Conger's Lake, thence south through Valley Cottage and southwest into Lake De Forest. Lake De Forest is an artificial reservoir formed by damming the west branch of the Hackensack River near Clarksville. The west branch rises in a bog south of Little Tor Mountain east of Pomona. It meanders eastward to near New City and then turns directly south and flows into the northern end of Lake De Forest. From Lake De Forest, it flows south past Clarksville and West Nyack into Lake Tappan (another artificial reservoir) at Orangeville. This section, also known as Blue Hills, is on the border between Rockland County, New York, and Bergen County, New Jersey. It is the heart of the old Dutch settlement area. From Lake Tappan it continues south past Rivervale, New Jersey, and Harrington Park into the artificial Oradell Reservoir at Closter. Here it receives the waters of the Dwarskill from the slopes of the Palisades to the east, and of the Pascack River from the west. The Pascack rises near Spring Valley in New York and flows south past Pearl River, New York, and Montvale, Park Ridge, and Woodcliff Lake, New Jersey, before entering the large Woodcliff Lake Reservoir. At Park Ridge, it receives the waters of the small Pearl River from the east. South of Woodcliff Lake the Pascack continues south and east past Hillsdale, Westwood, and Rivervale to Oradell Reservoir. Below the dam at Oradell, the Hackensack continues south past New Milford and River Edge, where tidewater navigation begins. From here south we pass New Bridge, Teaneck, and Bogota on the east side; and Hackensack, South Hackensack, and Little Ferry on the west. At Ridgefield Park (here confusingly known as Little Ferry Station) the Overpeck Creek enters from the east. The Overpeck in turn receives the waters of Wolf Creek. From here south the Hackensack flows through the vast Hackensack Meadows, which are vast areas of marsh grass and cattails that are now being filled in to make land for industry and provide garbage dumping area. In colonial times, this was a swampy cedar forest. From here south, we have Moonachie, Carlstadt, East Rutherford, Kingsland, North Arlington, Arlington, and Kearny on the west; and North Bergen, Secaucus and Jersey City on the east bank. (During the Revolutionary period, Dow's Ferry crossed from the foot of Saint Paul's Avenue in Jersey City, to Kearny.) Here it enters the north end of Newark Bay. Principal tributaries south of Overpeck Creek are Losen Slote, Moonachie Creek, Bashe's Creek, Cedar Creek, Berry's Creek Canal, Berry's Creek, Kingsland Creek, and Saw Mill Creek on the west. On the east are Bellman's Creek, Paunpeck Creek (also known as Cromakill Creek), Mill Creek, Fish Creek, and Penhorn Creek. Droyer's Point is on the east side of the junction with Newark Bay. Laurel Hill, also known as Snake Hill and mentioned by Washington Irving, is on the east bank between Secaucus and Penhorn Creek, near the New Jersey Turnpike and the Pennsylvania Railroad. It is nearly half quarried away.

For all its proximity to densely populated areas, the Hackensack is a difficult river to see. Its northern reaches can be seen from local roads, but the large reservoirs are fenced off. The Pascack branch and the stretch between Hackensack and Oradell can be seen from trains of the Pascack branch of Erie-Lackawanna (Conrail, formerly the New Jersey & New York Railroad). The lower reaches can best be seen from the New Jersey Turnpike and local roads near Secaucus. The stretch from Overpeck Creek to Bogota can be seen from either the West Shore Railroad or the New York, Susquehanna & Western, neither of which presently offers passenger service. The Hackensack is navigable for small pleasure boats north to New Milford. Above there, it is largely controlled by the Hackensack Water Company, and all trespassing is forbidden. The former Dayliner *Chauncey M. Depew* is permanently anchored at Secaucus as the Aratusa Supper Club. She is beautifully restored, and the food is excellent, if rather expensive.

-19.00 Romer Shoal is to the southwest.
There are rich pastures of plankton in the area, and consequently excellent striped bass fishing.

-17.10 Romer Shoal Light to the west.
Bend in channel to the north.

-17.00 Fort Tilden to the east.
Located on Rockaway Beach Point in Queens County, New York. It is an active military installation and the home of the 99th Army Signal Battalion, 411th Army Engineer Brigade, Army 306th Engineer Company, and a United States Coast Guard Station.

-17.00 Ward's Point, Staten Island, and Tottenville Beach to the west.
This is the southernmost point in New York State.

-16.00 Rockaway Point and lighthouse, Queens County, to east.

-16.00 Old Orchard Shoal Light to west. Seguine Point, Staten Island, to west.

-15.60 Great Kills Light to west, offshore. Huguenot Beach, Staten Island, to west.

-15.50 Crooke's Point, Staten Island, to west.

-15.50 Breezy Point, Queens County, to east.

-15.50 West Bank Light, offshore to west.

-15.00 Great Kills Beach, Staten Island, to west.

-15.00 Rockaway Inlet to east.
This is the entrance to Jamaica Bay, spanned by the Marine Parkway Lift Bridge—it separates Rockaway Beach Point and Queens County on the south from Brooklyn and Kings County to the north.

-14.60 Oakwood Beach, Staten Island, to west.

-14.60 Manhattan Beach, Brooklyn, to east.

-14.50 Brighton Beach, Brooklyn, to east.

-14.50 New Dorp Beach, Staten Island, to west.

-14.10 Northern End of Ambrose Channel

-14.10 Coney Island Beach, Brooklyn, to east.

-14.10 Northern end of East Bank Shoals to east.
They extend south to -16.50.

-14.10 Elm Tree Light on Staten Island to west.

-14.10 Miller Field, Staten Island, to west.

-14.10 Swinburne Island, to west, at southern end of West Bank Shoals.
Formerly a quarantine detention station with crematorium and pesthouse.

-14.00 Latourette Hill on Staten Island (241 ft.) to west.

-14.00 Richmond, Staten Island, to west.
This is a site of historic restorations.

-14.00 New Dorp, Staten Island, to west.
An early settlement.

-13.50 Midland Beach, Staten Island, to west.

-13.00 Norton Point and Lighthouse, Coney Island, Brooklyn, to east.

-13.00 Seagate, Coney Island, Brooklyn, to east.
An exclusive residential area.

-13.00 Coney Island to east.

This island, once separated from the mainland, is part of Brooklyn. Famous for bathing beaches, amusement parks and its Boardwalk, in the nineteenth century this was a fashionable resort with large summer hotels served by many steamboats and railroads. Among the railroads were the Manhattan Beach Railroad; Sea Beach Railroad; Long Island Rail Road; Brooklyn, Bath and Coney Island Railroad; Brooklyn, Flatbush and Coney Island Railroad; and Prospect Park and Coney Island Railroad. This gives some measure of the popularity of the beach. Today all these lines are part of the subway system. Steamboats ran to Locust Grove, Norton Point, and the great tubular iron pier that was built out into the ocean. The early trains had open cars with striped red and white awnings and were pulled by steam locomotives known as dummy engines. Because the tracks ran down carriage roads and streets, the engines were disguised as passenger cars in order not to frighten the horses. Principal resorts

were Brighton Beach, Manhattan Beach, and Coney Island Beach. The principal amusement parks were Luna Park, Dreamland Park, and Steeplechase Park. Originally, the island was covered with sand dunes, and wild rabbits were abundant, thence the name Coney Island.

-12.80 Hoffman Island to west.
At midpoint of West Bank Shoal. There was formerly a small coastal defence battery located here, as well as a military prison and a quarantine detention station.

-12.75 West Bank Shoals to west.

-12.50 Grant City, Staten Island, to west.

-12.25 Dongan Hills, Staten Island, to west.

-12.25 Gravesend Bay to east.
Separating Coney Island from the mainland.

-12.25 Gravesend to east.
A section of Brooklyn and an early settlement.

-12.20 Bensonhurst to east.
Residential section of Brooklyn.

-12.20 Bensonhurst Park to east.
Waterfront recreational area.

-12.00 Bath Beach to east.
Residential section of Brooklyn that was formerly a summer resort.

-12.00 South Beach, Staten Island, to west.

-11.50 Arrochar, Staten Island, to west.
A residential community.

-11.50 New Utrecht, Brooklyn, to east.
An early settlement.

-11.25 Dyker Heights, Brooklyn, to east.
Elevation 106 feet.

-11.25 Dyker Beach Park, east.
A large city park. Formerly the eight-story Grand View Hotel was built on piles out over the water here. There were four levels of balconies running

around the building that had a mansard-roofed tower. The view was out over the lower bay and the Narrows.

11.20 Fort Hamilton, Brooklyn, to east.

The name applies to a residential neighborhood and a military installation. The original fort stood upon the heights and was built in 1832. It was enlarged and strengthened during the Civil War and mounted sixty heavy guns, some of them *en barbette*. It remains an active army base with a chaplains' school and Veterans' Administration Hospital.

11.00 The Narrows.

This is a channel separating upper and lower New York Bay. Staten Island to the west, Long Island to the east.

-11.00 The Verrazano-Narrows Bridge.

Connecting Brooklyn and Staten Island. This is the world's longest suspension bridge. Its center span is 4,260 feet, and its side spans are each 1,215 feet. Its total length, including approaches, is 13,700 feet. The bridge is 103 feet wide, with two levels of six traffic lanes each. The towers are 690 feet above mean high water. Clearance at the center is 228 feet above mean high water. The deepest foundation is 170 feet below mean high water. It is supported by four cables of 35⅝ inches in diameter, consisting of sixty-one strands, with 428 wires per strand or 26,108 wires per cable. Each cable is 7,205 feet long, and the total length of wires comes to 143,000 miles. There are 161,000 tons of steel in the structure; and 724,600 cubic yards of concrete in the anchorages, tower piers, roadway, and approaches. The bridge

was opened in November of 1964, and the lower level was completed in 1969. It carries Interstate Route 278. It was used by 35,000,000 vehicles in 1970. It is a toll bridge and is operated by the Triborough Bridge and Tunnel Authority. The bridge was designed by the firm of Ammann & Whitney (Otho Ammann designed the George Washington Bridge), and Milton Brumer was the chief construction engineer.

-10.75 Fort Lafayette, east.

This fort formerly stood on Hendrick's Reef, 200 yards from the Brooklyn shore and was originally called Fort Diamond. Its construction was begun in 1812 but was not completed until the start of the Civil War. It mounted 75 heavy guns and also served as a political state prison during the Civil War.

-10.75 Hendrick's Reef, to east.

Brooklyn

The Borough of Brooklyn in Greater New York City occupies the southwestern tip of Long Island on the east side of the Narrows. It is oval in shape, occupying an area of seventy-one square miles. Its greatest lengths are eleven miles from north to south and ten miles east to west. It is bounded on the north by Newtown Creek and the English Kills. On the north and east, it is bounded by the borough of Queens, Old Mill Creek, Jamaica Bay, Pumpkin Patch Channel, Rulers Bar Hassock, and The Raunt, and, on the south, by Rockaway Inlet and Lower New York Bay. On the west, it is bounded by Gravesend Bay, the Narrows, upper New York Bay, Buttermilk Channel, and the East River.

Principal waterways and bays are Wallabout Bay, Newtown Creek, and the English Kills that are either on or empty

2. The Narrows

3. Coney Island

into the East River; Sheepshead Bay, Gerritsen Creek, Mill Creek, Gerritsen Inlet, Mill Basin, East Mill Basin, Paerdegat Basin, Fresh Creek, Hendrix Creek, and Old Mill Creek, emptying into Jamaica Bay; Gravesend Bay abutting on the Narrows; Gowanus Bay and Canal, Erie Basin, and Red Hook Basin abutting on Upper New York Bay; and Buttermilk Channel, separating Brooklyn Heights and Governor's Island. The East River separates Brooklyn from Manhattan.

The Borough is broken into the following thirty-one recognized sections: Northwestern quadrant: Greenpoint, Williamsburgh, Brooklyn Heights, South Brooklyn, Red Hook, and Park Slope; northeastern quadrant: Bushwick, Bedford-Stuyvesant, East New York, Brownsville, Crown Heights, Prospect Park, and Flatbush; southeastern quadrant: Borough Park, Kensington, Flatlands, Bergen Beach, Canarsie, and Sheepshead Bay; southwestern quadrant: Sunset Park, Bay Ridge, Fort Hamilton, Dyker Heights, New Utrecht, Bath Beach, Bensonhurst, Gravesend, Seagate, Coney Island, Brighton Beach, and Manhattan Beach.

Coney Island, once a true island on the southern shore facing on lower New York Bay, has since become attached to the mainland by means of land fill. Sheepshead Bay and Gravesend Bay are at the east and west end of the former channel that separated the island from the mainland. Norton Point is at its west end in the Seagate district and separates Gravesend Bay from lower New York Bay.

The Borough of Brooklyn is contiguous with Kings County. The southern portion is low ground. The early settlers found it sandy but fertile. The southeastern section had large grassy plains that were devoid of forest. This land, especially around Canarsie, was good for growing maize. The western end of a terminal moraine that ran east and west traversed the southern portion of the

region. This moraine extends far east out onto Long Island and there are numerous erratic boulders in this belt.

In the north-central region is a long ridge of medium height running roughly east and west, known as Crown Heights. Grand Army Plaza and the Brooklyn Museum now crown this ridge. In early times, this was stony and densely forested. It served important defensive purposes in the Battle of Long Island in 1776. Its western terminus, known as Brooklyn Heights, fronts on Buttermilk Channel and the East River. Further south, fronting on Upper New York Bay, are Cowans Heights, which are now inside the limits of Greenwood Cemetery; and 106 feet high Dyker Heights, facing on Gravesend Bay and the Narrows near Fort Hamilton. The northeastern and far northern sections were originally densely wooded. Most of Brooklyn is now well built over.

The aboriginal inhabitants of Brooklyn were the Canarsie Indians, whose Sachem was Sessys. Ownership of parts of the area was disputed by the neighboring Rockaway Indians, whose principal settlements were in present-day Queens.

As early as about 1624, there were scattered Dutch settlements at New Amersfoort near Flatlands, facing on Jamaica Bay. An Indian pathway, which much later developed into Flatbush Avenue, ran from Bergen Island, on Jamaica Bay, to opposite Manhattan, at the later site of Fulton Ferry, which is a distance of 10½ miles. Soon after settlement, Flatlands became a palisaded village. Between 1634 and 1636, scattered settlements were made in the section then called Midwout, which is now part of Flatbush. In 1636, Jacob Van Curler made extensive land purchases from the Indians.

Twenty-two Dutch and Walloon families settled at Gowanus in 1636 and at Wallabout Bay in 1637. Also, between 1638 and 1639, the Dutch West India Company acquired the Indian title from the Canarsie tribe for most of present-day Brooklyn. In 1642, a Cornelius Hooglandt was licensed to operate a flat-bottomed rowboat ferry across the East River from New Amsterdam. The landing on the Long Island side soon became known as "The Ferry." Between 1641 and 1650, numerous Swedes and Normans settled along Newtown Creek in what was then called Woodtown or Bushwick. This is now part of present-day Williamsburgh. Later, Frenchmen settled in this same area.

In 1643, a patent was granted to Lady Deborah Moody, widow of Sir Henry Moody of Garsden in Wiltshire. In 1640, she had moved to Massachusetts for religious reasons. Becasue of their non-conforming views, she and her son, Sir Henry, were excommunicated and sought asylum in the New Netherlands. The settlement at Gravesend was "dedicated to freedom of religion." Forty house plots were set out in a palisaded enclosure, with forty farms located outside the stockaded area. The enclosure contained sixteen acres. In 1644, the settlement was almost wiped out by Indians but managed to hang on. Lady Moody died in 1658, and Sir Henry moved on to Virginia. In 1645 or 1646, the settlement at "The Ferry" on the East River was incorporated as Breuckelen, which is Dutch for "broken Ground." Also in 1646, a settlement was made in "The Clove" at present-day Bedford. A patent was granted for a settlement at Flatbush in 1651, and a Dutch church was established in 1654.

Land near the Narrows and Gravesend Bay was informally settled as early as around 1643, but in 1652 the Nyack Patent was granted to Cornelius Van Werckhoven, schepen of Utrecht in Holland, and a member of the Dutch West India Company. He repurchased this land from the Indians. He died in either 1655 or 1656, before he could establish his patroonship. However, in 1657, Jacques Cortelyou, who had been the tutor of his children and manager of his estates,

purchased this tract and founded the village of New Utrecht. This was a palisaded village consisting of twenty plots and a blockhouse. It was surrounded by twenty fifty-acre farms. In 1675, a disastrous fire almost destroyed the settlement. In 1677, a Dutch church was organized. By 1661, five Dutch towns and one English town had been established in Brooklyn.

New Amsterdam was conquered by the English in 1664. That same year a twenty-year lease of the Brooklyn ferry was given to William Merritt, at the rental of twenty pounds per year. He was to operate flat-bottomed scows powered by oars and sometimes by sail. These boats had no keels. Also the name of Breuckelen was officially changed to Brooklyn. In 1665, a conference was called at Hempstead and the Dukes Laws were promulgated by Governor Richard Nicolls. Long Island and Staten Island were incorporated into the West Riding of Yorkshire, with the seat of government at Gravesend. In 1670, the Rockaway Indians made claim to the Flatbush area, and the town was repurchased and a firm eastern boundary established. Shortly thereafter, in 1671, a new settlement, known then as Oostwoud (East Woods), or the New Lots of Flatbush, was established in the area later known as New Lots or East New York.

The first Colonial Assembly was called in 1683. The ridings were abolished, and counties were established. Brooklyn became Kings County, possibly because it was the most fertile and rich part of the colony. There were further minor reorganizations after the Jacob Leisler Rebellion in 1691. During the American Revolution, Brooklyn was the site of the important and disastrous Battle of Long Island. After 1776, Brooklyn remained in British control. The infamous prison ships were anchored in Wallabout Bay, and those who died in them were buried in shallow graves on the site of the present Navy Yard.

The first steam ferry, owned by Robert Fulton and his brother-in-law, William Cutting, was put into service to Manhattan in 1814. It was double-ended and named the *Nassau*. Fulton Ferry operated until 1924.

In 1816, Brooklyn was formally incorporated as Brooklyn Ferry, and again incorporated as a city in 1834. In 1841, the *Brooklyn Daily Eagle* was formed, of which Walt Whitman served as editor from 1846 to 1847. From here on, Brooklyn grew rapidly. Williamsburgh was absorbed in 1855, making it the third largest city in the United States. The Brooklyn Bridge was under construction from 1869 till 1883. It was designed and constructed by John and Washington Roebling at a cost of $15,500,000. The main span is 1,595 feet. The new bridge and steam ferries gave terrific impetus to Brooklyn's growth. Handsome Greek Revival houses were built on Brooklyn Heights, and Brooklyn fast became a fashionable suburb. Finally, in 1898, with a population of around one million, Brooklyn became a borough of the city of New York. Present population is about three million.

With construction of rapid transit lines and subway tunnels to Manhattan, Brooklyn became a city of fine homes and mansions. It was frequently called the City of Homes or the City of Churches. Among the more prominent churches are the Reformed Protestant Dutch Church at Flatbush, organized in 1654 (the present building was built 1796); Saint Ann's Episcopal Church, established in 1784; and the Plymouth Church where Henry Ward Beecher preached from 1847 onwards. In the twentieth century, agriculture gave way to apartment houses and private home development in southern and eastern Brooklyn, and the great main streets were laid out. It is interesting to note that the early colonial homes in Brooklyn were mainly built of wood and lath, owing to a shortage of building stones. The graceful curved eaves and porticos of Dutch Colonial architecture reached a high point of perfection in Brooklyn. The Lefferts Homestead in Prospect Park is a beautiful example of this. Unfortunately, very few of these homes survive.

Trade and industry also developed in the nineteenth century. The Erie Canal Basin was established in 1825 with extensive warehouses built by Francis Bannerman & Sons. In the early 1860s, the great India Docks and Atlantic Docks, with substantial granite warehouses covering over forty acres, were erected. The great brick Empire Stores were built on the East River in the 1870s. These were the forerunners of the later tremendous Brooklyn Eastern District and Bush Terminals and present-day Port Authority Ocean Terminals. Brooklyn also developed extensive machinery, textile, paper, and chemical goods industries. It is served by the Brooklyn Branch of the Long Island Rail Road, with a major terminal at Flatbush Avenue, numerous elevated and subway lines, and the freight-only branch of Conrail (formerly New York Connecting Railroad), from Bushwick to Bay Ridge, near the Brooklyn Army Terminal. The former New York Naval Shipyard which once handled the Navy's heaviest work, is greatly reduced in size; its facilities on Wallabout Bay are leased to private operators.

The great Verrazano-Narrows Bridge, completed in 1965, replaces the former Sixty-ninth Street Ferry to Staten Island. Brooklyn is joined to Manhattan by the Brooklyn-Battery Tunnel and the Brooklyn, Manhattan, and Williamsburgh suspension bridges across the East River. The latter two carry subway trains as well as motor vehicles. The Kosciusko Bridge across Newtown Creek carries Interstate 278-A, the Brooklyn-Queens Expressway, into Queens. The Marine Parkway Bridge carries Flatbush Avenue across Rockaway Inlet to the Rockaway Peninsula in Queens County. Other principal highways in Brooklyn are the Gowanus Expressway along the Upper

New York Bay, and the Belt Parkway (Route 27-A), also called the Shore Parkway, along the shores of the Narrows and Gravesend and Jamaica Bays. Floyd Bennett Field, the former New York Naval Air Station, is located in the southeasternmost portion of the Borough near Jamaica Bay. Fort Hamilton, built originally in 1831 as a harbor defense at the entrance of the Narrows, now serves as an administrative center and school for military chaplains. The former Manhattan Beach Civil Defense Training Center is now given over to the Kingsborough Community College.

A now extinct, unique Brooklyn institution was Ebbets Field, the former home of the Brooklyn Dodgers baseball team. The team was originally called the trolley dodgers because of the plethora of streetcar lines that once operated in Brooklyn. They are now gone, along with the ball club.

Brooklyn was also once a fashionable resort, with large hotels at Manhattan Beach and Brighton Beach. The great Manhattan Beach Hotel, Hotel Brighton, and Oriental Hotel were colossuses of their day. An iron pier out into the ocean accommodated the landing of excursion steamers or the Iron Steamboat Co. and other lines from such points as Manhattan, Newark and Jersey City, bringing day-trippers to the famous surf bathing beaches of Coney Island. At a later day, these fashionable hotels gave way to the boardwalk, bathhouses, and amusement parks such as famous Luna Park; Dreamland Park; and Steeplechase Park, with its great parachute jump tower and roller coaster rides. Sheepshead Bay was the center for party fishing boats and such large seafood restaurants, as F.W.I.L. Lundy's.

Among Brooklyn's cultural attractions are the Brooklyn Museum of Art; the Brooklyn Academy of Music, with both an opera house and concert hall; and the Brooklyn Public Library. The Brooklyn Botanical Garden is possibly the finest in the United States. There is also a small zoo. Prospect Park is in the center of the city; and the Grand Army Plaza, at its northern end, with its monumental arches and colonnades, is reminiscent of the Arc de Triomphe in Paris. A fine formal Parade Ground is adjacent to the southern end of 526-acre Prospect Park.

Other major parks include Brooklyn Marine Park on Jamaica Bay; Dyker Beach Park near Gravesend; McGolrick Park; McCarren Park; Fort Greene Park; Tompkins Park; Bushwick Park; Lincoln Terrace Park; Sunset Park; Owl's Head Park, overlooking the Narrows; Manhattan Beach Park; the Jamaica Bay Wildlife Refuge Islands; Canarsie Park; Plum Beach; McKinley Park; and Shore Road Park overlooking the Lower Bay. The very extensive and beautiful Greenwood Cemetery on Cowans Heights also served as a park in the nineteenth century.

The principal educational institutions include Brooklyn College of CUNY; Polytechnic Institute of Brooklyn; Pratt Institute; St. John's University; St. Joseph's College for Women; Packer Collegiate Institute; Long Island University, and Kingsborough Community College.

-10.75 Vandeventer's Point on Staten Island, west.

-10.75 Grasmere, Staten Island, to west.
Residential neighborhood.

-10.75 Fort Wadsworth, Staten Island, to west.
Active military base. Part of harbor defenses started ca. 1812. Originally called Fort Richmond, but later renamed in honor of General Peleg Wadsworth, (1749-1829) who served in the Battle of Long Island. The massive waterfront bastions were never completed, such type of construction having been outmoded by heavy artillery. However, the area of the fort bristled with cannon.

4. Elizabeth

5.   Jersey City

6. Brooklyn

-10.65 **von Briesen Park on west.**

-10.50 **United States Quarantine
Station on west.**

-10.00 **Rosebank, Staten Island, on
west.**

- 9.75 **Catskill Aqueduct**
passes beneath water from
Brooklyn to Staten Island in a
bell-and-spigot pipeline.

- 9.75 **Todt Hill, Staten Island, on
west.**
Elevation 410 feet. Highest
point on Atlantic shoreline
South of Mount Desert Island,
Maine.

- 9.70 **Clifton, Staten Island, west.**

- 9.70 **Pouch Terminal docks and
warehouses on west.**

- 9.70 **Shore Road Park, Brooklyn,
on east.**

- 9.65 **Foreign Trade Zone No. 1
on west.**

- 9.60 **Stapleton Port Authority
Trailership Terminal on west.**

- 9.60 **Stapleton, Staten Island, on
west.**
Site of former Doyle's Ferry
Wharf.

- 9.00 **Bayridge Section of
Brooklyn on east.**

- 9.00 **Bennett Point on east.**

- 9.00 **Tompkinsville, Staten
Island, on west.**
Formerly known as the Watering
Place, because in early days
sailing ships filled their water
casks from springs in the neighborhood.

- 8.75 **Owl Head to east.**

- 8.50 **Sixty-ninth Street Brooklyn.**
Former terminal of ferry from
Staten Island.

- 8.50 **Ducksberry Point on west.**

- 8.50 **Emerson Hill on west.**

- 8.50 **St. George, Staten Island,
on west.**
Seat of Richmond Borough and
county government. Commercial center of Staten Island.
Terminal of ferry from Manhattan and of Rapid Transit lines.

- 8.25 **Owl's Head Park, Brooklyn,
east.**

- 8.25 **Kill van Kull, west.**

- 8.20 **66th St., Bay Ridge,
Brooklyn, east.**

- 8.20 **Constable Hook and Point,
Bayonne on west.**
Site of many oil refineries.

Bayonne, New Jersey

Bayonne occupies a low peninsula separating Upper New York and Newark
bays. It is three miles long by less than
one mile average width, widening out at
the south end into Bergen Point on the
west and Constable Hook on the east. It
is bounded on the north by the Greenville section of Jersey City; on the west
by Newark Bay; on the south by the Kill
van Kull, which separates Bayonne from
Staten Island; and on the east by Upper
New York Bay.

It was first settled by Dutch traders in
about 1650. Later, small farms were
established, and some fishermen lived
along the shore, but the area was largely
undeveloped until the nineteenth century. An early road ran from Bergen
(present-day Jersey City) to the ferry
between Bergen Point and Staten Island.
This was part of a major stagecoach
route between New York City and Philadelphia. This early road was later developed into Hudson County Boulevard,
which has since been renamed Kennedy
Boulevard. In the nineteenth century,
the Central Railroad of New Jersey was
built south from Jersey City to the tip of
the peninsula and then crossed Newark
Bay to Elizabethport on a long bridge.
This railroad extended eventually to
Allentown and Wilkes-Barre, Pennsylvania, with important connections to Philadelphia and Harrisburg. Trains of the
Reading Company and Baltimore & Ohio
also operated over the Jersey Central.
Today it serves as a secondary line of
Conrail. The Lehigh Valley and Pennsylvania Railroads also built a jointly

shared bridge across Newark Bay to Port Newark from the north end of Bayonne. This is also part of the Conrail system today.

Irénée Dupont, one of the founders of the Dupont Chemical Company, first settled in Bayonne in 1800, when he arrived from France. His home, called La Tourette, faced the Kill van Kull. In later years it was turned into a resort hotel and greatly enlarged. It operated for many years and was finally razed in 1926. This was the beginning of Bayonne as a society resort. Many wealthy New Yorkers took advantage of the pleasant seaside atmosphere and built large suburban homes overlooking the water. There were numerous golf courses, bridle trails, picnic groves, and tennis courts and clubs. The town even boasted an opera house. Many large mansions and churches from this era remain. In 1840, Hudson County was split off from Bergen County.

In 1875, the first oil refinery was established in Bayonne. Soon the Standard Oil Company of New Jersey came to occupy much of Constable Hook. Deepwater docking for tankers and oil barges, good rail connections, and proximity to the New York and New England markets favored the further development of refineries. However, these had the unpleasant consequences of polluted waters and malodorous vapors that destroyed Bayonne's desireability as a resort or suburban area for the affluent. The wealthier residents moved farther west along the Jersey Central to such towns as Roselle, Cranford, Plainfield, and Somerville. Immigrant labor flowed in to work on the Hook, and inexpensive row houses and tenements were built to accommodate them. Refinery activity was at its zenith during World War II when the Big Inch Pipeline was completed from the southwest with Bayonne as its eastern terminal. At the present time Texaco and Richfield Oil have facilities at Bergen Point; and Asiatic Oil, Tide Water Oil, and Exxon have large

facilities at Constable Hook. Other major industries are Baker Castor Oil, General Cable, National Sulphur, Bergen Port Chemical, and American Radiator. Conrail serves Port Johnson on the Kill van Kull on Constable Hook and has extensive marshalling yards. The United States Army Military Ocean Terminal occupies a long pier on Upper New York Bay; this was formerly occupied by the United States Naval Supply Center.

Generally speaking, residential areas are west of the railroad, and heavy industry is east of it. Bayonne is connected to Staten Island by the Bayonne Bridge across the Kill van Kull, and with Port Newark by the high-level bridge of the New Jersey Turnpike Hudson County Extension across Newark Bay. There are three major parks along Newark Bay. The population of Bayonne in 1977 was 72,743.

-8.18 Upper New York Bay
This was called the Bay of Santa Margarita by Verrazano.

-8.15 Robbins Reef and Light on west.
The bass caught near here taste oily. Seals play on the surrounding rocks.

-8.10 Brooklyn Army Terminal on east.

-8.00 Bayonne on west.

-7.75 Oyster Island on west.
Very tiny.

-7.75 U. S. Army Military Ocean Terminal on west.
(Formerly Pamrapo).

-7.50 Bush Terminal docks and warehouses on east.

-7.50 Bay Ridge Channel on east.

-7.25 Cowan's Heights on east.
Elevation 220 feet. Now in Greenwood Cemetery

-7.00 Port Authority-Port Jersey Industrial Marine Center on west.

-7.00 Bayonne-Jersey City Line on west.

-6.52 Gowanus Cove on east.

Port Authority Marine Terminal.

-6.52 Gowanus Creek leading to Gowanus Canal with its several basins on east.
Gowanus is a corruption of "Cowan's." The canal provides constricted navigation.

-6.50 Port Authority Columbia Street Marine Terminal on east.

-6.50 Caven Point Army Terminal on west.

-6.50 Greenville Section of Jersey City on west.

-6.50 Oyster Bay on west.

-6.50 Erie Basin on east.
Former terminal for Erie Canal barges.

-6.50 Breakwater Terminal on east.
On outer side of Erie Basin.

-6.50 Henry Street Basin on east.
(formerly Brooklyn Basin)

-6.50 Port Authority Erie Basin Grain Terminal on east.

-6.50 Red Hook Channel on east.

-6.25 Red Hook Container Port on east.

-6.00 Black Tom Island on west.
Now a part of the mainland.

-6.00 Gallows Point on west.
Formerly property of National Docks Corporation and Lehigh Valley Railroad; now being redeveloped as Liberty Park.

-6.00 Claremont section of Jersey City to west.

Jersey City

Jersey City occupies a peninsula between the Hudson River and Upper New York Bay on the east and the Hackensack River and Newark Bay on the west. The portions bordering the water are low and were originally swampy. A rocky ridge runs down the center; it is low at the south end and gains height and breadth at the north end. It constitutes the far southern end of the Palisades. At Jersey City the top forms a plateau about a mile wide. Jersey City is bounded on the north by Penhorn Creek, a tributary of the Hackensack, and the municipalities of Secaucus, North Bergen, Union City, and Hoboken. To the south it is bounded by the City of Bayonne, which occupies the southern tip of the peninsula.

The Hudson shoreline is indented, from north to south, by Harsimus Cove, Morris Canal Basin, and the Tidewater Basin. Jersey City measures four miles from north to south and about two and a half miles from east to west, or roughly ten square miles. It is densely built up with homes and industry. Principal industries are meatpacking, ink, chemicals, steel and large plants owned by Continental Can and Colgate-Palmolive Soap Company. It was formerly a major steamship terminal and was Cunard's original terminal in the Port of New York. Harborside Terminal is one of the world's largest warehouse structures. It fronts on the Hudson River. Formerly there were major passenger train and ferry terminals of the Central Railroad of New Jersey, Pennsylvania Railroad, and Erie Railroad along the Hudson. All these lines have been absorbed into Conrail, and the trains have been rerouted to Penn Station in Manhattan and the Lackawanna Terminal in Hoboken. No ferry routes remain. Two subway tunnels of the P.A.T.H. rapid transit system connect with downtown and midtown Manhattan. P.A.T.H. trains also operate to Newark and to Hoboken from four stations in Jersey City: Pavonia, Exchange Place, Grove-Henderson, and Journal Square, site of the modern P.A.T.H. Intermodular Transportation Center that includes a bus terminal and a large parking garage for private automobiles. There remain numerous freight yards, including the Pennsylvania's former Greenville and Harsimus Cove yards, and the Erie's Croxton Yard, in the Hackensack Meadows. Jersey City is also served by the New York, Susquehanna & Western Railroad.

The Holland Tunnel provides vehicular access to downtown Manhattan and connects with the Hudson County Extension of the New Jersey Turnpike. Major highways to the west are the Lincoln Highway (Routes 1 and 9), the Pulaski Skyway (Routes 1 and 9A), and the Jersey City and Newark Turnpike (Route 7). Principal north-south arteries are Kennedy Boulevard, atop the plateau, and Tonnele Avenue (Routes 1 and 9) along the western foot of the ridge. Residential and commercial areas predominate atop the plateau, with industry in the lower areas, although there is considerable residential development there as well. Much area is devoted to outmoded railroad freight yards that are being gradually redeveloped.

Jersey City's population in 1977 was 260,545—the second largest in the state after Newark. Major sections are Greenville, a residential area at the southern end of town; Caven Point, devoted to industry along Upper New York Bay; and Black Tom, which is also on the Upper Bay. Formerly it was largely devoted to railroad yards of the Jersey Central System. During World War I Black Tom was the site of a large and famous ammunition explosion. Bergen, atop the plateau, was the early nucleus of the city and one of the first parts settled; Communipaw, van Vorst, Paulus Hook, Harsimus, and Pavonia range along the Hudson shoreline. Commercial centers are at Exchange Place in Paulus Hook, on the Hudson shoreline, where there are banks, warehouses, and the giant Colgate-Palmolive headquarters and plant; and at Journal Square, north of old Bergen, where there are the P.A.T.H. Transportation Center, many banks and office buildings, and the large and palatial Loew's and Stanley theaters. Roosevelt Stadium is located on Newark Bay at Droyer's Point. The Medical Center, one of the largest hospitals in the New York metropolitan area, is near Bergen and Communipaw.

The largest of the many parks are the still-developing Liberty Park on the Upper Bay and Lincoln Park, on the west side, which runs down to the Hackensack River. Here is located J.E. Fraser's famous statue of Lincoln, executed in 1929. Other major parks include County Park; Columbia Park; Bayside Park; Audubon Park; Grand Park; Lafayette Park; Leonard Gordon Park; and Montgomery Park.

Principal cemeteries include Saint Peter's and Holy Name, on the West Side; and Jersey City Cemetery, New York Bay Cemetery, and Bayview Cemetery, on the east side. These all provide significant open areas with long vistas. Squares are of importance in Jersey City and form the nucleus of residential areas consisting of brownstone and similar row houses, some of which are of considerable distinction. Many are being renovated and restored. Principal squares are Hamilton Park Square; van Vorst Park Square; and Washington Park Square, at the junction of Grand and Washington Streets in the Paulus Hook section.

Saint John's Roman Catholic Church, on Kennedy Boulevard north of Journal Square, is of architectural interest with its massive limestone and granite construction and high campanile. Other landmarks are the former Brunswick Laundry, Jersey Central Terminal and Fairmont Hotel, and Saint Peter's Preparatory School and College.

Jersey City had an exciting past. According to Robert Juet, who chronicled Henry Hudson's voyage of 1609, the crew was met by friendly Lenni-Lenape Indians on 3 September at Gamoenipa (now called Communipaw.) This name means "over the river." This region was occupied by the Hackensack Indians, who belonged to the Lenni-Lenape nation.

In 1610, the first permanent settlement was made at Ahasimus (now called Horsimus or Harsimus). An attempt at settlement had been made at Communipaw in the previous year, but this was probably simply a temporary trading post. Oloffe Van Cortlandt was among the first settlers in the Jersey City area. In either 1616 or 1618, a village was planted at Bergen by the Dutch East India Company. The meaning of the name Bergen has always been an enigma. Some authorities claim that it was named for Bergen in Norway, as there were possibly some Norwegians among the early settlers. Another theory is that it was named for Bergen-op-Zoom in Holland, which is much more likely. A third theory posits that the name is derived from the word *bergen*, denoting a "ridge between two marshlands." As this describes the situation perfectly, it is the most likely origin. In 1621, the Dutch West India Company acquired the lands of the Dutch East India Company, and in 1630 they granted the Pavonia patroonship to Michael Pauw. This grant also included Staten Island. By 1636, Cornelius van Vorst was in command of the Pavonia settlement. It consisted of thatch-roofed houses and was palisaded and well armed. In 1641, Myndert Myndertsen van der Horst was also given a grant in Jersey City.

Trouble soon developed with the Indians, aggravated by the stupid and stubborn attitude of the company's director, William Kieft. Bloody Indian raids in 1643 virtually destroyed the settlements on the New Jersey side of the Hudson. The problems between the Indians and the settlers were resolved in 1658 when Kieft's successor, Peter Stuyvesant, repurchased the lands from them.

By 1660, Bergen had become a palisaded village with a Dutch Reformed Church, which was the first in New Jersey. That same year Jacques Cortelyou was laying out a village at Communipaw, and William Jansen was being granted a charter to operate a horse ferry from there to New Amsterdam. Security was gained by following Governor Stuyvesant's order to concentrate the settlements, although by this time the local Indians were not causing any serious trouble.

Bergen's first municipal government was established in 1661, and the first school was built in 1662. In 1664, the English gained control. In 1675, Bergen was unofficially designated a county, and this was made official in 1683. Development was gradual under the English, who allowed the Dutch ways to continue. In 1762, a line of stages was established from Paulus Hook to New Bridge on the Hackensack River. A race track was established at Paulus Hook in 1771, which was popular with "bloods" from Manhattan. The English began to call Paulus Hook "Powles Hook," and both spellings have been used interchangeably to this day. Originally the Powles Hook area was a small island, separated from the mainland by marshes. During the American Revolution a small redoubt or fort was built there. It was commanded by the patriot general Hugh Mercer. On September 23rd in 1776, it was cannonaded by the British, who gained command that day and were to hold it for the rest of the war, with one notable exception. On August 18th in 1779, Major "Lighthorse" Harry Lee recaptured the fort from the British, but he immediately abandoned it as difficult to hold and of little strategic value. It was mainly a moral victory, similar to Wayne's capture of Stony Point.

After the war, in 1804, Anthony Dey acquired property at Powles Hook, which was soon taken over by a group called Associates of the Jersey Company. The population then was only twenty persons. Major impetus to growth came in 1812 when Robert Fulton established a steam ferry from Powles Hook to Cortland Street in Manhattan. This latter evolved into the important Pennsylvania Railroad ferry route. Fulton lived in Jersey City until his untimely death in 1815. Establishment of the steam ferry assured the future growth and importance of Jersey City. In 1820, a "City of Jersey," or "Jersey City within Bergen County" was incorporated, centering at Powles Hook. A revised charter was granted in 1829, and the town was reincorporated simply as Jersey City in

1838. In 1840 Hudson County, including all that area within present-day Jersey City, was split off from Bergen County. The villages of van Vorst, Hudson City, and Bergen were annexed in 1851 and 1869. In 1873, the village of Greenville was also annexed, and a new charter was granted.

Shortly after 1824, the Morris Canal was completed, with its terminus in Jersey City, south of Powles Hook. The Erie Ferry at Pavonia was established in 1859 and the Jersey Central Ferry in 1902 from Communipaw. The Hudson and Manhattan subway tubes were completed in 1908 to Morton Street in Manhattan and to downtown Manhattan in 1909. The Holland Tunnel was completed in 1927.

Historic Landmarks are:

(1) Dr. Barrow's Mansion, Ionic House, 85 Wayne Street. A restored Greek Revival mansion built in the 1830s. Five Ionic columns support a flat pediment across facade.

(2) Robert Fulton House, 77-79 Grand Street.

(3) Governor Ogden-Conrad Home, 248 Ogden Avenue.

(4) Hampton Court, 1-7 Wayne Street.

(5) Schurmann House, 240 Ogden Avenue.

(6) Saint Mary's Residence, 240 Washington Street.

(7) van Vorst Farmhouse, 531 Palisade Avenue.

(8) van Wagenen-Quinn Home, 298 Academy Street. Formerly called the Apple Tree House. Washington and Lafayette planned strategy here.

(9) Old Bergen Reformed Church, 797-809 Bergen Avenue. Greek revival, 1841.

(10) Grace van Vorst Church, 264 Erie Street. Gothic revival designed by Detlef Lienau, 1853.

(11) City Hall, Mercer and Grove Streets. Limestone and granite eclectic designed by Lewis H. Groome, 1895.

(12) New Jersey Title Guarantee & Trust Co., 83-85 Montgomery Street, 1888, Yellow brick with cast terra-cotta ornaments and Art Deco Portal added in 1931. Now an apartment house.

(13) Hudson County Courthouse, 591 Newark Avenue. Granite-faced classical structure now out of use. Designed by Hugh Roberts; completed in 1910.

(14) Jersey Central Railroad Depot, at the foot of Johnston Avenue. French Chateau styling, 1902-14; undergoing restoration.

Liberty Island
-5.50 Liberty Island and Statue of Liberty to west.

Liberty Island is in New York State and was originally called Bedloe's Island after Isaac Bedloe, who had obtained a patent for it under Governor Francis Nicholson (1688-89). It has an area of 10.38 acres. The island served as New York's first quarantine station, established by Dr. John Bard (1716-99). Between 1811 and 1841, a strong fortification named Fort Wood was erected on the island.

In 1875, the historian Edouard de Laboulaye conceived the idea of a monument commemorating the alliance of France and the United States in achieving American independence and symbolizing the friendship of the two nations. This monument was to be a gift from the people of France. He organized the Franco-American Union and had raised about $250,000 by 1882. The promoters turned to Frederic Auguste Bartholdi (1834-1904), an Alsatian sculptor who had already earned a name for himself for such colossal monuments as *Switzerland Succoring Strasbourg; Vercingetorix,* at Clermont-Ferrand; and the gigantic *Lion of Belfort* at the Citadel in Belfort, which commemorated the heroic defence of that fortress from 1870 to 1871 during the Franco-Prussian War. Bartholdi conceived the idea for the statue as he sailed into New York

Harbor. The statue was to be called *Liberty Enlightening the World.* It was to be the figure of a woman lifting a lighted torch in her right hand. The statue was to be 152 feet tall and made of copper sheets, which would soon oxidize to a green patina in the salt air. It was to be supported by a wrought iron armature.

First Bartholdi made a model nine feet high. Today this model stands near the pont de Grenelle on a small island in the Seine in Paris. Workmen then hand hammered copper sheets 3/32" thick on wooden forms. The supporting armature was designed by Alexandre Gustave Eiffel (1832-1923), who was to build the famous Eiffel Tower in 1889. A circular stairway with 168 steps leads to an observation platform in the diadem, with a straight ladder branching off near the top and ascending through the uplifted right arm and hand, then through the base of the torch, to a circular platform around the flame of the torch. The entire statue weighs 225 tons and was shipped from France in 214 cases in 1885.

Joseph Pulitzer, editor of the *New York World,* organized an American subscription to build a suitable base. He raised $225,000 and engaged the American architect Richard Morris Hunt (1828-1895) to design the base. Hunt had been the first American to study architecture at the École des Beaux-Arts in Paris, and he was later one of the organizers of the American Institute of Architects. He designed a pedestal 154 feet high in neo-Greco style built of concrete faced with granite. This sat atop the eleven-pointed rampart of Fort Wood, dating from 1811. The statue was formally presented to the United States in 1884, shipped in 1885, and assembled in less than 18 months. It was dedicated by President Grover Cleveland on October 28, 1886. It was designated a national monument in 1924 and put under control of the National Park Service in 1937. An elevator rises through the pedestal, but it is necessary to climb the circular stairway to ascend to the observation platform in the head.

This climb is not recommended for anyone who has a weak heart or who suffers from vertigo. The ladder to the torch is closed to the public because the extra weight and vibration in the arm (which is not in plumb with the rest of the statue but shoots up at an angle,) would create dangerous stress in the framework. Only workmen ascend to maintain the powerful lights that illuminate the torch.

There is an American Museum of Immigration in the base, with both permanent and changing exhibits. The statue is open daily year around. Ferries leave from the Battery hourly between 9:00 A.M. and 4:00 P.M., with extra sailings in July and August.

In 1886 the Jewish-American poetess Emma Lazarus (1849-87), who was a native of New York, wrote a sonnet eulogizing the monument.

The New Colossus

Not like the brazen giant of Greek fame,
With Conquering limbs astride from land
to land;
Here at our sea-washed, sunset gates
shall stand
A mighty woman with a torch, whose
flame
Is the imprisoned lightning, and her
name
Mother of Exiles. From her beacon-hand
Glows world-wide welcome; her mild
eyes command
The air-bridged harbor that twin cities
frame.
"Keep, ancient lands, your storied
pomp!" cries she
With silent lips. "Give me your tired,
your poor,
Your huddled masses yearning to
breathe free,
The wretched refuse of your teeming
shore.
Send these, the homeless, tempest-tost
to me
I lift my lamp beside the golden door!"

-5.10 Atlantic Terminal—India Wharf, Brooklyn to east.

-5.00 Baltic Terminal Brooklyn to east.

-5.00 Buttermilk Channel to east.
Between Governor's Island and Brooklyn. So named because in Dutch times the channel was so shallow that the women of the island were able to walk across to Brooklyn at low tide to buy their buttermilk. In 1776, General Israel Putnam stretched a *chevaux de frise* across the channel to impede British vessels from entering the East River and force them to pass beneath the guns on Governor's Island and the Battery.

-5.00 Governor's Island.
Located to the east at the mouth of the East River. Separated from Brooklyn by Buttermilk Channel, the island has an area of 173 acres and maximum elevation of 40 ft. It was originally called Nutten or Nooten Island by the Dutch (this means Nut Island). In 1637, Governor Wouter Van Twiller purchased it from the Indians for a few trinkets, allegedly two axeheads and a few nails. In 1638, its rents were reserved as a perquisite of the governor; thus the name Governor's Island, which became official, however, only in 1784.

Fortifications were first authorized in 1703 but were not undertaken until the time of the Revolution. In 1784, a Dr. Price of Brooklyn built a racetrack on the island. This operated only until 1797, because it was inconvenient to bring the horses across on barges. Fort Jay was commenced in 1794 on a knoll near the center of the island. It was not completed until the early nineteenth century. In 1800, General Ebenezer Stevens took command of the fortifications and expanded them greatly in 1812. The original fort, later to be renamed Fort Columbus, was shaped like a five-pointed star. A second major fortification, now called Castle William, was built

between 1807 and 1811 to the plans of Lt. Col. Jonathan Williams. It was circular, with a diameter of 200 feet and a height of 40 feet. The walls were 8 feet thick. In the nineteenth century it was nicknamed "the cheese box" because of its shape. While originally an important fortification, Castle William was later changed to a disciplinary barracks. Fifteen hundred Confederate prisoners were held in it during the Civil War, and in 1863 draft rioters attempted to storm the castle and free them.

In 1878, Fort Jay became the headquarters of the 2d Corps Area, and shortly after 1900, the federal government reclaimed much eroded land around the perimeter. A small fortification at the southern tip of the island was called South Battery. In 1906, Fort Columbus was described as shaded with old Lombardy poplars. Eventually a nine-hole golf course was laid out around the fort, and this is still in existence. For many years, until 1964, Fort Jay occupied the entire island and was the principal military installation in New York City, where it served as headquarters of the lst Army Command. During the days of army occupancy, there was also a polo field on the island. Today the principal occupant of Governor's Island is the Coast Guard. It is the largest Coast Guard base in the United States, with 6000 people working there on weekdays. It is the headquarters of the 3rd Coast Guard District and home port to several large cutters. There is also a Coast Guard training center. A medical air reserve unit is based on the island, and some of Fort Jay is devoted to government housing. Governor's Island is linked to Manhattan by two ferry boats making the 1500 foot crossing to the foot of Whitehall Street. Access to the island is controlled, but open house is held on weekends during the summer. A large, white brick ventilator tower for the Brooklyn-Battery Tunnel is located just offshore from the northeastern corner of the island.

-5.00 Brooklyn Heights on east.
Residential district of fine homes, many dating from Greek Revival period and the brownstone era. Excellent views from the public terrace.

-4.80 Brooklyn Port Authority Fulton Marine Terminal to east.

-4.80 Ellis Island to west.

Ellis Island, known to the Indians as Gull Island, to the Dutch as Oyster Island, and to the English as Gibbet Island and Ellis Island, has grown from 3.7 acres to 27.5 acres by means of landfill. The English used to hang pirates on the island, which originally belonged to New Jersey. In 1794, it was purchased by the wealthy merchant Samuel Ellis and at that time reverted to the state of New York. At the time of purchase, it was called Bucking Island. Fort Gibson was established in 1808 when the United States Government purchased the island. Fort Gibson served both as a fortress and naval munitions magazine. In 1892, the United States Immigration Service established its major immigration depot here. The monumental buildings on the island date from 1898. The island served this function until 1943. From 1943 to 1954, it served as a detention station for enemy aliens and more recently as a holding station for immigrants with some defects in their credentials. In 1956, Ellis Island was declared surplus property and offered for sale. Various proposals have been put forward for use of the island, but the general consensus is that it should be preserved as a museum or national monument to the immigrants who helped to build America. In 1965, President Lyndon Johnson signed a bill making Ellis Island a part of Liberty National Monument. On 5 November, 1975, a rededication ceremony was held. Over 15,000,000 New Americans had entered the "golden door" and passed through Ellis Island. New York is still the largest immigration port of entry welcoming over 100,000 new citizens each year. However, most of these enter through airports and the new liner piers. Ellis Island is accessible by passenger ferry from the Battery, Liberty Island, and Liberty Park in Jersey City.

-4.70 Fish Point on west.

-4.70 East River on east.

-4.50 Communipaw Bay on west.

-4.00 The Battery to east.
Southern tip of Manhattan Island at confluence of Hudson and East Rivers. Known to earliest settlers asKapsee, the Dutch named it Schreyer's, or Weeper's Point (perhaps from gallows and gibbet erected here around 1650). The name Battery derives from a strong battery of ninety-two cannon lined up along the waterfront in 1693 by the British, in fear of a French attack. Ultimately a stone fort with four bastions was erected. This was called Fort George, and its precincts included the governor's house and most of the government offices. As described by Benson Lossing:

At the beginning of the war for independence, Fort George and its dependencies had three batteries—one of four guns, near the Bowling Green; another (the Grand Battery) of twenty guns, where the flag-staff on the Battery now stands; and a third of two heavy guns at the foot of Whitehall Street, called the White Hall Battery. Here the boldness of the Sons of Liberty was displayed at the opening of the revolution, by the removal of guns from the battery in the face of a connonade from a British ship of war in the harbor. From here was witnessed, by a vast and jubilant crowd, the final departure of the British army, after the peace of 1783, and the unfurling of the banner of the Republic from the flag-staff of Fort George, over which the

British ensign had floated more than six years. The anniversary of that day—"Evacuation Day"—(the 25th of November) is always celebrated in the City of New York by a military parade and feu de joie. . . .

At White Hall, on the eastern border of the Battery, there was a great civic and military display, at the close of April 1789, when Washington, coming to the seat of government to be inaugurated first president of the United States, landed there. He was received by officers and people with shouts of welcome, the strains of martial music, and the roar of cannon. He was then conducted to his residence on Franklin Square, and afterwards to the Old Federal Hall on Wall Street, where Congress held its sessions. . . .

The present Battery or park, looking out upon the bay of New York, was formed early in the present century; and a castle, pierced for heavy guns, was erected near its western extremity. For many years, the Battery was the chief and fashionable promenade for the citizens in summer weather; and State Street, along its town border, was a very desirable place of residence. The castle was dismantled, and became a place of public amusement. For a long time it was known as Castle Garden; but both are now deserted by fashion and the Muses. All of old New York has been converted into one vast business mart, and there are very few respectible residences within a mile of the Battery. At the present time (September, 1861), it exhibits a martial display. Its green sward is covered with tents and barracks for the recruits of the Grand National Army of Volunteers, and its fine old trees give grateful shade to the newly-fledged soldiers preparing for the war for the Union."

Castle Clinton was designed by a certain Colonel Jonathan and erected between 1808 and 1811 a bit off-shore—connected by catwalks with the mainland. It was built in the style of French military architecture. When it was turned into a concert hall and opera house in 1823, a roof was added. The Swedish soprano Jenny Lind made her American debut here on September 11, 1850 under the auspices of P. T. Barnum. The top price ticket sold for $250. and the concert brought in a total of $18,000. Miss Lind contributed her share of the receipts to various New York City charities, thus winning the hearts of her hosts.

In 1851, a great celebration was held here upon the opening of the Erie Railroad from Piermont to Lake Erie. President Millard Filmore embarked upon the steamboat "Erie," along with many other dignitaries, to start a ceremonial journey the entire length of the new line.

Castle Garden served as the principal immigration station from 1855 till 1892, when Ellis Island became the principal depot. It was next remodeled, in 1896, by McKim, Mead & White, as an aquarium, and was used as such until 1941 when the acquarium was moved to Coney Island. It is now restored as a fortress.

Passenger ferries leave from the Battery to Liberty Island, and there are loading gates of steamboats along the seawall.

2
New York City
and
the New Jersey Palisades

The largest metropolis of the United States and the fifth largest city in the world, New York City's 1977 population figures were: New York, 7,646,818; Metropolitan area, 9,634,400.

The following tabulation of comparisons will be of interest:

World's Largest Cities (1977)   Population

1	Shanghai, China	10,820,000
2	Tokyo, Japan	8,738,997
3	Mexico City, Mexico	8,299,209
4	Manilla, Phlippines	7,800,000
5	New York City, New York	7,646,818

The area of New York City, including water surfaces, is 365 square miles. The city comprises five boroughs, each co-extensive with a county:

Manhattan, New York County (an island)
Bronx, Bronx County (on the mainland)
Brooklyn, Kings County (on Long Island)
Queens, Queens County (on Long Island)
Richmond, Richmond County (Staten
    Island)

The island of Manhattan is the center of the city. It is separated from the Bronx by the Harlem River and Spuyten Duyvil Creek and from Queens and Brooklyn by the East River. It is separated from Staten Island by Upper New York Bay. Brooklyn and Staten Island are separated by the Narrows, connecting upper and lower New York Bay. New Jersey is to the west of Staten Island and Manhattan. Major islands belonging to the city are: In the East River: Rikers Island, Hart Island, City Island, Randall's Island, Roosevelt Island (formerly Blackwell's and Welfare Island), Ward's Island, and Governor's Island; in New York Bay: Ellis Island, Liberty Island (formerly Bedloes Island), Hoffman Island, Swinburne Island, and West Bank Island; in the Kill van Kull: Shooter's Island. There are also many islands and pols in Jamaica Bay. Coney Island is now connected with the mainland of Brooklyn.

New York City was the provincial capital and became the state capital until 1797. It was the capital of the United States from 1785 to 1790. It was here that George Washington was inaugurated, in 1789. By 1790, New York had outstripped Philadelphia and had become America's largest city with a population of over 33,000. By 1800, the population was up to 60,5l5. The first of the great bridges, the Brooklyn Bridge, was built in 1883, and this paved the way for the formation of the present city. Until 1898, Brooklyn was a separate city. In 1898, New York took one of the most significant steps in its history and adopted a new charter, which transposed it into a metropolis of five boroughs, with a hugely increased population. Blessed with one of the world's finest harbors, with over 500 miles of waterfront, it expanded rapidly upon completion of the Erie Canal in 1825 and subsequently of the New York Central and New York & Erie railroads to the interior and became the nation's principal seaport. Today much of this port activity has moved to the New Jersey shoreline on the mainland.

In 1946, New York was chosen as the permanent headquarters of the United Nations. The nation's financial center, New York is a leading center of manufacture and commerce. Among its principal industries are clothing, textiles, printing, publishing, machine shop and metal products, food, and chemicals. As center of the garment industry, it is an important fashion center. The headquarters of many large industrial firms are located here, as well as the stock and commodity exchanges and a Federal Reserve Bank. The World Trade Center facilitates international trade.

While the traditional Broadway theater was for a short while somewhat in eclipse because of high production costs, it is making a comeback and New York remains an important theatrical center with many off-Broadway and off-off Broadway theaters. New York is also a major art and music center with many famous museums, three major opera companies and a half-dozen major orchestras. Columbia University, New York University and C.U.N.Y. are among the city's many institutions of higher learning.

The first subway was built in 1904, and New York now has the nation's largest rapid transit system. Principal railroad depots are Grand Central Terminal, Pennsylvania Station, 125th Street Station (Amtrak and Conrail), Flatbush Avenue, Hunt's Point, and Jamaica (Long Island Rail Road) and Hudson Terminal, located at the World Trade Center (P.A.T.H. transit to New Jersey). The Hoboken, N.J., terminal of Conrail also serves as a major gate of entry. Principal bus terminals are at Forty-first Street (Port Authority) and at the George Washington Bridge. The three major airports serving the city are John F. Kennedy International Airport (formerly Idlewild), LaGuardia Airport, and Newark International Airport in New Jersey. Ocean steamships and cruise liners leave for all parts of the world from the Hudson River Passenger Terminal. Excursion boats of the Hudson River Day Line and Circle line leave from the foot of Forty-second Street. The Staten Island Ferry and Statue of Liberty Ferry depart from the Battery.

The problems that have beset all large American cities are especially acute in New York. Because of high costs, labor difficulties and taxes, much industry has left the city. This is also the case with many industrial office headquarters, resulting in unemployment, with its related welfare costs and high taxes. Although the city continues to exert its attraction on the affluent, many middle-class people have fled to the suburbs.

For many years, the New York metropolitan area's transit and commuter railroad systems have been breaking down, making working in the City less attractive to commuters. The private corporations providing these services have been hard hit by government subsidized truck and air competition and ill able to support the losses of running a large commuter operation, and even less able to keep it modern and attractive to riders. Only with recent infusions of state and federal funds has it become possible to begin to rehabilitate and modernize these services. In the meantime, many large firms, such as Western Union, Pepsico, and I.B.M., have moved to the suburbs.

Other problems are related to the obsolescence of the old-fashioned finger piers in Manhattan which required transshipment from truck or rail to ship by means of expensive lighterage operations and carfloats. Gradually much of this activity has been moved to the "Jersey Side." Also, with the grave financial problems, and attendant breakdown, of reliable and competitive freight services of the railroads serving the Port of New York, much traffic has been lost to other ports such as Halifax, Baltimore, Boston, Norfolk, and Philadelphia. There is also an unusually high level of theft and damage at the New York docks, which makes it an unattractive gateway for high-value merchandise. Another factor is the jet plane, which has largely replaced transatlantic ocean liners . Vacationers no longer visit Manhattan before boarding ship. At most, the traveller has a few hours' layover at Kennedy Airport. This has hurt the city's hotel and entertainment industries.

With all this loss of revenue and jobs, the city's tax base has been eroded, and the city has gone into debt and had to curtail basic services such as police, fire, and sanitation. All of this leads to a dirty city where crime is less well contained than previously.

New York City still has the seeds of greatness. It is still the Mecca for active, intelligent, and creative people from all over the world. It has tremendous reservoirs of talent and ability. It has a fine and extensive infrastructure of public utilities and transport facilities. It has a remarkable bank of buildings that can be renovated and recycled. It can once again become the greatest city in the world.

The Port of New York and The Port Authority

With 500 miles of deepwater shoreline along protected waters, not more than ten miles from the open sea, and located at the mouth of a great navigable river, it is natural that New York grew into the world's largest seaport. Completion of the Erie Canal in 1825, and the New York Central and Erie Railroads shortly thereafter, caused New York to become the principal seaport for the eastern United States. The Port of New York includes facilities located in both New York and New Jersey, along the Hudson and East Rivers, New York Bay, Newark Bay, and adjoining estuaries. Port statistics are compiled by the Port Authority of New York and New Jersey. The following statistics will give an overview of present day (1975) port activity:

1975 Oceanborne Foreign Trade

	Long tons	Dollars
Exports	6,402,000	$11,751,983,000.
Imports	46,599,127	$14,697,272,000.
Total	53,001,127	$26,449,255,000.

1975 Exports in Long Tons

Machinery	718,000	Tallow	115,000
Chemicals	611,000	Non-ferrous metals	134,000
Steel products	229,000	Fruit and vegetables	92,000
Vehicles	279,000	Paper products	189,000
Textiles	253,000	Drugs and cosmetics	81,000
Grain	416,000		

1975 Imports in Long Tons

Sugar	771,000	Lumber	184,000
Steel products	376,000	Liquors and wines	449,000
Bananas	567,000	Meat	343,000
Coffee	427,000	Vehicles and parts	299,000
Newsprint	142,000	Chemicals	345,000
Petroleum	37,155,000		

1975 World Distribution of Oceanborne Exports

North America	1,754 Long Tons
Middle America	514,347 " "
South America	441,185 " "
Europe	2,490,443 " "

Middle East	494,498	"	"
Africa	250,647	"	"
Far East	1,244,980	"	"
Australasia	122,701	"	"

1975 Waterborne Coastwide Trade in Long Tons

Shipments	2,950,000
Receipts	4,600,000
Total	7,550,000

1975 World Distribution of Oceanborne Imports

North America	322,078	Long Tons	
Middle America	1,514,715	"	"
South America	653,053	"	" Excludes Petroleum
Europe	3,051,446	"	"
Middle East	64,847	"	" Excludes Petroleum
Africa	318,671	"	"
Far East	1,662,898	"	"
Australasia	554,854	"	"

Petroleum imports acccount for over 95% of New York's bulk cargo.

1975 Overseas Passenger Vessels

	Passengers
Arriving	222,576
Departing	219,718
Total	442,294

1964 Total: 1,039,838 Passenger arrivals and departures

1975 Foreign air passengers, arrivals and departures: 10,667,802

1975 Marine Terminal Summary

All terminals:	
ship arrivals	3,583
general cargo (long tons)	11,581,036

New Jersey terminals:	
ship arrivals	2,198
general cargo (long tons)	10,094,932

New York terminals:	
ship arrivals	1,385
general cargo (long tons)	1,486,104

Cumulative Port Authority investment in marine terminals: $516,163,000.

In the clipper ship days, the favored docking spaces were at the foot of South Street in the East River, in lower Manhattan. Auxiliary docking was in Brooklyn. With the coming of the steamboat, ships tended to dock in lower Manhattan along the North or Hudson River. Even ships coming in from Long Island Sound via the East River usually docked at North River piers. With the development of oceangoing steamships, the piers along the Hudson in midtown Manhattan became popular, as did those in Jersey City and Hoboken. This remains true for large passenger liners. Through the years, traffic has shifted to terminals on the New Jersey shores because of more modern facilities, easier access to railroads and highways, and elimination of lighterage and shoreside vehicular congestion. Principal marine terminals now operated by the Port Authority are:

Brooklyn—Port Authority Marine
  Terminal
Erie Basin—Port Authority Marine
  Terminal
New York City Passenger Ship
  Terminal
Columbia Street Marine Terminal
  (Brooklyn)
Port Newark
Elizabeth—Port Authority Marine
  Terminal
Hoboken—Port Authority Marine
  Terminal

In addition, the United States Army has its extensive military ocean terminal in Bayonne, on Upper New York Bay, and also at Caven Point in Jersey City, as well as the Brooklyn Army Terminal at Sixty-third Street and Upper New York Bay. The privately operated Bush and Brooklyn Eastern District Terminals are in Brooklyn, on Upper New York Bay and the East River, respectively, and the private Pouch Terminal at Clifton on Staten Island, just above the Narrows. Sea-Train Lines and Sea-Land Lines have extensive container ship terminals at Weehawken and Edgewater, New Jersey. The refineries tend to be concentrated on Constable Hook in Bayonne and along the New Jersey shore of the Arthur Kill.

The Port Authority of New York and New Jersey is a self-supporting corporate agency of the two states. Functioning without burden to the taxpayer, it was created as the Port of New York Authority in 1921 by treaty between the two states, to plan, develop, and operate terminal, transportation, and other facilities of commerce and to improve and protect the commerce of the bi-state port. In 1972, the Authority's name was changed to identify more accurately its status as a bi-state agency of New York and New Jersey. Port Authority commissioners, six from each state, are appointed by the governors of New Jersey and New York. They serve without pay for overlapping terms of six years. The Port Authority is responsible for the operation of six interstate tunnels and bridges, a regional system of four airports and two heliports, seven marine terminals, two bus terminals, and two union motor truck terminals. In 1962, the Port Authority Trans-Hudson Corporation (P.A.T.H.), a subsidiary of the Port Authority, assumed responsibility for operation and rehabilitation of the former Hudson Tubes, a vital rapid transit system which links Newark, Jersey City, and Hoboken with lower and mid-Manhattan. The first element of the Journal Square Transportation Center was opened in December 1973.

The World Trade Center, under construction since 1966, opened its doors to its first tenants in 1970. The Trade Center, principal headquarters for international trade activities in the New York/New Jersey area, also houses the Port Authority administrative staff. These facilities represent an investment of over $3.4 billion. The Port Authority and its rail subsidiary, P.A.T.H., employ a career staff of over 8,000 people in the development and operation of the following facilities:

Rail & Bus Commuter Facilities
    Port Authority Bus Terminal (Midtown)
    George Washington Bridge Bus Station
    Port Authority Trans-Hudson System
      (P.A.T.H.)
    Journal Square Transportation Center

Air Terminals
    John F. Kennedy International Airport
    LaGuardia Airport
    Newark International Airport
    Teterboro (N.J.) Airport (for private
      aviation)
    Port Authority-Downtown Heliport
    Port Authority-West Thirtieth St.
      Heliport

Marine Terminals
    As listed above

Tunnels and Bridges
    Bayonne Bridge
    George Washington Bridge
    Goethal's Bridge
    Holland Tunnel
    Lincoln Tunnel
    Outerbridge Crossing

Miscellaneous Facilities
    World Trade Center
    Development offices in Chicago,
      Cleveland, Washington, New York,
      London, Tokyo, and Zurich

Manhattan

Manhattan Island is 12½ miles long and 2½ miles wide at its widest point. It is bounded on the west by the Hudson or North River, on the north by Spuyten Duyvil Creek, on the east by the Harlem River (called Muscoota by the Indians), Hell Gate, and the East River, on the south by the East River and Upper New York Bay. The far northern portion of the Harlem River and eastern reaches of Spuyten Duyvil Creek are also known as either the New York Ship Canal or the Harlem River Ship Canal, as its present

navigable condition is the result of dredging a shallow backwater.

The point at the far southern tip of the island, known today as the Battery, was known to the earliest settlers as Kapsee. It was originally a semi-detached rocky point, the intervening space being filled-in land. The Dutch also called it Schreyer's Hook, or Weeper's Point in English. On the Hudson side, Greenwich Point was at present day Gansevoort Street and Jeffrey's Hook under the approach of the George Washington Bridge. On the East River, Horn's Hook is just below Hell Gate at 89th Street, and Corlear's Hook is just south of the Williamsburg Bridge. Turtle Bay was located on the East River at the present United Nations site. Much of the present shoreline is filled land, both along the East River (south of Corlear's Hook) and along the Hudson River (north as far as Gansevoort Street, the former Greenwich Point.) This process is continuing today between the Battery and Canal Street. This last-named street is named for an actual former canal. Cooper described it in his novel, *The Water Witch*, (New York; G. P. Putnam's Sons, pp. 21-2) which is set before the Revolution.

A deep, narrow creek penetrated the island at this point, for the distance of a quarter of a mile. Each of its banks had a row of buildings, as the houses line a canal in the cities of Holland. As the natural course of the inlet was necessarily respected, the street had taken a curvature not unlike that of a new moon. The houses were ultra-Dutch, being low, angular, fastidiously neat, and all erected with gables to the street. Each had its ugly and inconvenient entrance, termed a stoop, its vane or weathercock, its dormer-windows, and its graduated battlement-walls. Near the apex of one of the latter, a little iron crane projected into the street. A small boat, of the same metal, swung from its end,—a sign that the building to which it was appended was the ferry-house.

An inherent love of artificial and confined navigation had probably induced
the burghers to select this spot as the
place whence so many craft departed
from the town; since it is certain that the
two rivers could have furnished diverse
points more favorable for such an object,
inasmuch as they possess the advantage of wide and unobstructed channels.

Fifty blacks were already in the street,
dipping their brooms into the creek, and
flourishing water over the sidewalks,
and on the fronts of the low edifices.
This light, but daily duty was relieved
by clamorous collisions of wit, and by
shouts of merriment, in which the whole
street would join, as with one joyous and
reckless movement of the spirit. The
language of this light-hearted and noisy
race was Dutch, already corrupted by
English idioms, and occasionally by English words. . . .

As the movement of the ferry-boat
was necessarily slow, the alderman and
his companion were enabled to step into
it before the fasts were thrown aboard.
The periagua, as the craft was called,
partook of a European and an American
character. It possessed the length, narrowness, and clean bow of the canoe,
from which its name was derived, and
the flat bottom and lee-boards of a boat
constructed for the shallow waters of
the Low Countries. Twenty years ago
vessels of this description abounded in
our rivers, and even now their two long
and unsupported masts, and high narrow-
headed sails, are daily seen bending like
reeds to the breeze, and dancing lightly
over the billows of the bay. . . .

Though, in some respects, of singular
aquatic habits, the original colonists of
New York were far less adventurous, as
mariners, than their present descendants. A passage across the bay did not
often occur in the tranquil lives of the
burgers; and it is still within memory of
man, that a voyage between the two
principal towns of the State was an
event to excite the solicitude of friends,
and the anxiety of the traveller. The

perils of the Tappan Zee, as one of the
wider reaches of the Hudson is still
termed, were often dealt with by the
good wives of the colony, in their relations of marvels; and she who had
oftenest encountered them unharmed,
was deemed a sort of marine Amazon.

This canal has been filled in for many
years. However, the filled in land made
poor footing for the elevated West Side
highway, and the former location is
spanned by a large and easily distinguished arch bridge.

The island is blessed with few natural
watercourses. Minetta Brook flowed
from the center of the island to the
Hudson near Fortieth Street, but today
it is merely a covered sewer. Another
stream flowed from the vicinity of Fifth
Avenue and Fifty-ninth Street to the
East River. A small natural pond, named
Collect Pond, was near Foley Square. It
has been filled in. The present ponds,
lakes and reservoir in Central Park are
artificial. Manhattan Island is quite rocky,
but formerly contained some rather fertile farmland. The southern portion is
fairly level, but the central portion is
covered with indeterminate hills. Among
these are Murray Hill, Lenox Hill, Mount
Morris, and Harlem Heights. Further
north are Morningside Heights, Mount
Washington (highest point in Manhattan),
Washington Heights, Morris Heights, and
Inwood Hill, at the northernmost tip of
the island. There are several low traverse valleys. The most prominent are at
Harlem, where the fertile Harlem Plains
bordered the East River, and at Dyckman
Street between Fort Tryon and Inwood
Hill. Cooper's novel, *Satanstoe*, (New
York: G. P. Putnam's Sons, pp. 81-2) gives
a good description of the topography
immediately prior to the Revolution:

The roads on the island of Manhattan
were very pretty and picturesque, winding among rocks and through valleys,
being lined with groves and copses in a
way to render all the drives rural and

79

retired. Here and there, one came to a country-house, the residence of some person of importance, which by its comfort and snugness, gave all the indications of wealth and of a prudent taste.

Early villages on the island were Kingsbridge, on the Harlem River near the bridge that still bears that name; Carmansville atop Mount Washington; Manhattanville, on the Hudson near present day 130th Street; Elm Park, near 110th Street, and Broadway; Bloomingdale, near Columbus Circle; Harlem, on the Harlem River near 125th Street; Yorkville, near the Harlem River and Eighty-ninth Street; Murray Hill, near Park Avenue and Fortieth Street; Greenwich Village, at its present location; and New Amsterdam, at the foot of the island. Broadway follows the former Bloomingdale-Manhattanville and Manhattanville-Kingsbridge roads.

New Jersey is to the west, across the Hudson River. Riverdale and Marble Hill are to the north, across the Spuyten Duyvil Creek. The Bronx, Randalls Island and Wards Island are to the east, across the Harlem River. The Astoria and Long Island City sections of Queens are to the east, across the East River, as are the Greenpoint and Williamsburg sections of Brooklyn. Downtown Brooklyn, Brooklyn Heights and Governors Island and Upper New York Bay are to the south.

Manhattan is the principal borough of New York City, with a population of approximately two million and an area of twenty-two square miles. It is the governmental, financial, cultural, and commercial center of the city. The borough of Manhattan is coextensive with New York County, which is not, as generally thought, confined to Manhattan Island. Both the borough of Manhattan and county of New York include a small enclave on the mainland, north of Spuyten Duyvel Creek, known as Marble Hill. This is completely surrounded by the Bronx.

Formerly, Manhattan Island was connected to the mainland and adjacent islands by an extensive network of ferry routes. Today only those to Staten Island and Governor's Island from the Battery remain in service, along with passenger launch service to Liberty and Ellis Islands. The first bridge to the mainland was a royal monopoly. It was called the Kingsbridge, and crossed the Harlem River near Marble Hill. Today there are twenty bridges connecting Manhattan with New Jersey and the other islands and boroughs: one water aqueduct, one footbridge, two railroad bridges, and sixteen vehicular bridges, two of which also carry subway trains. There are also four vehicular, two railroad, and thirteen subway-rapid transit tunnels, not to mention aqueduct, power, and telephone wire tunnels. The principal railroad depots are Pennsylvania Station, Grand Central Terminal and Conrail-125th Street Station. Principal bus depots are the Port Authority Bus Terminal in midtown and the George Washington Bridge Bus Terminal. The Port Authority operates a heliport at Thirtieth Street on the Hudson River. Steamship piers are located along the East River between Corlear's Hook and the Battery, and along the Hudson River from the Battery to Fifty-ninth Street.

Principal remaining open areas on Manhattan are the following parks: Central, Riverside, Fort Washington, Fort Tryon, Inwood Hill, Highbridge, Colonial, Hudson, St. Nicholas, Morningside, Mt. Morris, Thomas Jefferson, Hamilton Fish, W.H. Seward, Gabriel's, Carl Schurz, Franklin, DeWitt Clinton, City Hall, Corlear's Hook, Bryant, Bowling Green, and Battery. There are also several squares (Tompkins, Union, Stuyvesant, Madison, Manhattan, Washington, and Gramercy) and such green spaces as Baker Field, the United Nations Plaza, Trinity and St. Paul's churchyards, and Trinity Cemetery. Fine panoramic views are obtained from many office buildings and bridges.

Manhattan has an interesting history. The name is a corruption of the Mohican word "Menohanet," meaning "people of the islands." Three groups of the Manhattan Indians lived on Manhattan Island. The Werpoes, with their Sachem Meijeterma, lived near present-day Foley Square and the former Collect Pond on the lower portion of the island. Rechewac was the sachem of the Rechewanis, who occupied the middle east side of the island. Their name means "little sand stream." The Inwood section of upper Manhattan was the home of the Weckquaesgeeks. The original Indian purchase of the island was made by Peter Minuit in 1626 for $24 worth of hardware, kettles, and rum. In 1715, the freeholders of New Harlem, by special tax, raised a fund with which Col. Stephen Van Cortlandt made a final settlement with the Manhattan Indians. The last bears and wolves had been driven from the island in 1686.

The first permanent settlement on the island was made under the auspices of the Dutch West India Company in 1625. The plan of the city was drawn by Cryn Fredericksz. The first street laid out was Pearl Street. The first church was built in 1633 at what is now 39 Pearl Street. Fort Amsterdam was built in 1635. This consisted of the Director's House, a barracks, a guard house, and a block house, all surrounded by palisades. In 1638, the first sale of property was made to a private owner, the Dutch West India Co. having held title to all land until this time. A strong palisades or wall was erected along the present course of Wall Street in 1653, this was the upper limit of New Amsterdam. Above this were the commons. During the remainder of the seventeenth and early eighteenth centuries, the other villages mentioned above were founded and individual farmsteads were settled throughout the island.

Under British rule after 1664, New Amsterdam became New York and Fort Amsterdam became Fort James. In 1693, under threat of French invasion, a battery of ninety-two cannons were lined up along the Kapsee, thus giving the Battery its name. The first Trinity Church was erected in 1696. The present structure dates from 1830 and is the third on the site. The oldest building in the city is Fraunces Tavern, which was built in 1719 as a townhouse for Stephen DeLancey. It was converted to a tavern in 1762. The present St. Paul's Chapel was built between 1764 and 1766, and the spire erected in 1794. George Washington worshiped there while living in New York as President. Manhattan was in British control from 1776 until the end of the Revolutionary war. It was the capital of the United States from 1789 until 1790. George Washington was inaugurated as the first president of the United States in 1789 at Federal Hall, on the site of the present Sub-Treasury Building at Broad and Wall Streets.

We cannot continue the story of the growth of Manhattan into the great metropolis it is today. However, it should be observed that this greatness was achieved because of its unrivaled harbor, the access to the interior provided by the Hudson River and later by the Erie Canal and the railroads that paralleled them.

In his three novels, *Satanstoe, The Water-Witch*, and *Afloat and Ashore*, James Fenimore Cooper gives some interesting descriptions of early New York. *Satanstoe* takes place in 1757, *The Water-Witch* in around 1708, and *Afloat and Ashore* after the Revolution (ca. 1814).

I dare say there were fifty young ladies promenading the churchwalk when I reached it, and nearly as many young men in attendance on them; no small portion of the last being scarlet-coats, though the mohairs had their representatives there too. A few blue-jackets were among us also, there being two or three king's cruisers in port. As no one presumed to promenade the Mall who was not of a certain stamp of respectability, the company were all gayly dressed; and I will confess that I was much struck with the air of the place, the first time I showed myself among the gay idlers. The impression made on me that morning was so vivid that I will endeavor to describe the scene as it now presents itself to my mind.

In the first place there was the noble street, quite eighty feet in width in its narrowest part, and gradually expanding as you looked towards the bay, until it opened into an area of more than twice that width, at the place called the Bowling Green. Then came the fort, crowning a sharp eminence,* and over-looking everything in that quarter of the town. In the rear of the fort, or in its front, taking a water view, lay the batteries that had been built on the rocks, which were black and picturesque, and over the batteries they supported, was obtained a view of the noble bay, dotted here and there with some speck of a sail, or possibly with some vessel an-chored on its placid bosom. Of the two rows of elegant houses, most of them brick, and, with very few exceptions, principally of two stories in height, it is scarcely necessary to speak, as there are few who have not heard of, and formed some notion of Broadway; a street that all agree is one day to be the pride of the Western world.

In the other direction, I will admit that the view was not so remarkable, the houses being principally of wood, and of a somewhat ignoble appearance. Never-theless, the army were said to frequent those habitations quite as much as they did any other in the place. After reaching the Common, or present Park, where the great Boston road led off into the coun-try, the view was just the reverse of that which was seen in the opposite quarter. Here all was inland and rural. It is true the new Bridewell had been erected in that quarter, and there was also a new jail, both facing the Common; and the king's troops had barracks in their rear; but high, abrupt, conical hills, with low marshy lands, orchards and meadows,

*The Kapsee

gave to all that portion of the island a peculiarly novel and somewhat pictur-esque character. Many of the hills in that quarter, and indeed all over the widest part of the island, are now surmounted by country-houses, as some were then, including Petersfield, the ancient abode of the Stuyvesants, or that farm which, by being called after the old Dutch governor's retreat, has given the name of Bowery, or Bouerie, to the road that led to it; as well as the Bowery House, as it was called, the country abode of the then lieutenant-governor, James De Lancey; Mount Bayard, a place belong-ing to that respectable family; Mount Pitt, another that was the property of Mrs. Jones, the wife of Mr. Justice Jones, a daughter of James De Lancey, and various other mounts, houses, hills and places, that are familiar to the gentry and people of New York.

But the reader can imagine for himself the effect produced by such a street as Broadway, reaching very nearly half a mile in length, terminating at one end in an elevated, commanding fort, with its background of batteries, rocks, and bay, and at the other with the Common, on which troops were now constantly parad-ing, the Bridewell and jail, and the novel scene I have just mentioned. Nor is Trinity itself to be forgotten. This edifice, one of the noblest, if not the most noble of its kind in all the colonies, with its Gothic architecture, statues in carved stone, and flanking walls, was a close accessory of the view, giving the whole grandeur and a moral.

As has been said, I found the Mall crowded with young persons of fashion and respectability. This Mall was near a hundred yards in length; and it follows that there must have been a goodly show of youth and beauty. The fine weather had commenced; spring had fairly opened; Pinkster blossoms (the wild honeysuckle) had been seen in abundance throughout the week; and every thing and person appeared gay and happy. (Satanstoe, pp. 98-101)

Here he soon stopped before the door of a house which, in that provincial town, had altogether the air of a patrician dwelling.

Two false gables, each of which was surmounted by an iron weathercock, intersected the roof of this building, and the high and narrow stoop was built of the red freestone of the country. The material of the edifice itself was, as usual, the small, hard brick of Holland, painted a delicate cream color.

A single blow of the massive glittering knocker brought a servant to the door. (*The Water-Witch,* p 15.)

New York, in that day, and on the Hudson side of the town, commenced a short distance above Duane Street. Between Greenwich, as the little hamlet around the State prison was called, and the town proper, was an interval of a mile and a half of open fields, dotted here and there with country-houses. Much of this space was in broken hills, and a few piles of lumber lay along the shores. St. John's Church had no existence, and most of the ground in its vicinity was in a low swamp. As we glided along the wharves, we caught sight of the first market I had ever seen—such proofs of an advanced civilization not having yet made their way into the villages of the interior. It was called "The Bear," from the circumstance that the first meat ever exposed for sale in it was of that animal; but the appellation has disappeared before the intellectual refinement of these later times—the name of the soldier and statesman, Washington, having fairly supplanted that of the bear! Whether this great moral improvement was brought about by the Philosophical Society, or the Historical Society, or "The Merchants," or the Aldermen of New York, I have never ascertained. If the latter, one cannot but admire their disinterestedness and modesty in conferring this notable honor on the Father of his Country, inasmuch as all can see that there never has been a period when their own board has not possessed distinguished members, every way qualified to act as godfathers to the most illustrious markets of the republic. But Manhattan, in the way of taste, has never had justice done it. So profound is its admiration for all the higher qualities, that Franklin and Fulton have each a market to himself, in addition to this bestowed on Washington. Doubtless there would have been Newton Market, and Socrates Market, and Solomon Market, but for the patriotism of the town, which has forbidden it from going out of the hemisphere in quest of names to illustrate. Bacon Market would doubtless have been equivocal—too much so to be tolerated under any circumstances. . . .*

We passed the Albany basin, a large receptacle for North River craft, that is now in the bosom of the town and built on, and recognized in it the masthead of the Wallingford. . . .We rounded the Battery, then a circular strip of grass, with an earthen and wooden breastwork running along the margin of the water, leaving a narrow promenade on the exterior. This brought us to Whitehall, since so celebrated for its oarsmen, where we put in for a haven. (*Afloat and Ashore,* pp. 38-39.)

-3.80 Pier A Manhattan to east.

Presently serving as a fireboat station for the Fire Department Marine Division, this interesting old pier was built between 1884 and 1886, making it the oldest in the city. It is also the only surviving specimen of block and bridge construction. It has a seventy-foot-high lookout tower with a clock built by Seth Thomas which strikes ship's bells. It was originally entirely clad in galvanized sheet iron and decorated with classical zinc ornaments. Originally housing the city's Department of Docks, it has since housed the city's Marine and

Aviation, and Ports and Terminals Departments, the harbor police, and the fire department as well as serving as landing place for excursion steamers. In 1964, the entire exterior of the pier was covered with aluminum sheet metal. It is an official New York City landmark and is listed in the National Register of Historic Places. It is presently undergoing restoration.

-3.80 New York Custom House visible to east.

-3.75 Battery Place to east.
Communipaw to west.

-3.74 Former Central Railroad of New Jersey ferry terminal to west.
At the foot of Johnston Avenue. Built in 1889, it is presently undergoing restoration as part of the Liberty Park complex. It is to serve as a visitor's center.

-3.74 New landfill to old pier line on east.

-3.73 Tidewater Basin and Morris Canal Basin to west.

-3.71 Paulus Hook (Powles Hook) to west.
In Jersey City, this is the site of early fortifications.

-3.71 Colgate-Palmolive plant and ten-story office building on west.
The plant was established in 1847. Atop it is the world's largest conventional clock with a face fifty feet in diameter and a minute hand twenty-six feet long. It was erected in 1924.

-3.70 Exchange Place, Jersey City, to west.
Former site of Cunard Line piers and Jersey City Depot of Pennsylvania Railroad and ferries. It was the eastern depot for various other railroads, and was the western terminus of Robert Fulton's first steam ferry line.

-3.70 Cortlandt Street on east.
Robert Fulton's first successful trip in the *Clermont* started from this site on September 4, 1807. Later it served as Manhattan terminal for Fulton's steam ferry to Paulus Hook, and for Pennsylvania Railroad and West Shore Railroad ferries until March 24, 1959, when the *S.S. Stony Point* made her last sailing.

-3.70 P.A.T.H. downtown twin tubes.
Twin rapid transit single track tunnels connecting the World Trade Center in Manhattan with Journal Square and Exchange Place in Jersey City. Each tube is over a mile long. They were originally built by the Hudson & Manhattan Railroad, which was organized in 1901, and were completed on July 17, 1909.

-3.70 The World Trade Center and the Twin Towers.
This facility of the Port Authority of New York and New Jersey occupies a sixteen-acre site in Manhattan bounded by Liberty Street on the south, Church Street on the east, Vesey Street on the north, and West Street on the west. The project includes two 1,350 foot, 110-story tower buildings, two nine-story buildings, a new eight-story U.S. Customs building, and a five-acre landscaped plaza. It also serves as the downtown terminal for the P.A.T.H. rapid transit system. It stands on the site of the former Hudson Terminal Buildings and Washington Market. There are nine million square feet of office space in this complex. Each floor in the twin towers is approximately one acre in size and is column-free to assure flexibility in layout. There is below-grade parking for almost 2,000 cars. An enclosed observation deck is located on the 107th floor, and an open promenade is on the 110th floor (roof) of the South Tower of the World Trade Center. The maximum observation point elevation is

I,377 feet. Observation decks are open from 9:30 A.M. until 9:30 P.M. every day of the year. There is a charge.

More than 1.2 million cubic yards of earth and rock were excavated to make way for the Trade Center. This material was placed in the Hudson River to create 23.5 acres of new land deeded to the City of New York, and which will ultimately become part of the Battery Park City Project. Construction of the Trade Center utilized more than 200,000 tons of steel and 425,000 cubic yards of concrete. At peak construction periods, 3,500 workers were on jobsite. There are 43,600 windows with over 600,000 square feet of glass in the twin towers. Automatic window washing machines on stainless steel tracks clean the exterior. There are 102 passenger elevators in the project. More than 6,500 sensors throughout the Center register temperatures, pressures, power consumption, and other variables and feed data into a computer which provides instantaneous information for any necessary remedial action.

The architects were Minoru Yamasaki and Associates of Troy, Michigan, and Emery Roth and Sons of New York. Engineering was: Structural—Skilling, Helle, Christiansen and Robertson of New York and Seattle; Electrical— Joseph R. Loring and Assoc. of New York; Mechanical—Jaros, Baum and Bolles of New York; Functional Planning —World Trade Center Planning and Construction Division of Port of New York Authority; Foundations—Engineering Department, Port of New York Authority. General Contractor was Tishman Realty and Construction Co. of New York.

-3.69 Harborside Warehouse west:
The world's largest warehouse complex.

-2.50 Canal Street to east.

-2.50 The Holland Tunnel.
This is another facility of the Port Authority, and was the first Hudson River vehicular tunnel. It connects Canal Street in Manhattan with Twelfth and Fourteenth Streets in Jersey City. The tunnel was opened November 13, 1927, when President Calvin Coolidge, in Washington, D.C., pushed an electric button which caused two huge American flags to part at each entrance to the tunnel. The $70-million-dollar tunnel was named for its chief construction engineer, Clifford M. Holland, who died of exhaustion in 1924 just two days before sandhogs digging from each side met in one of the tunnel's two tubes. His bust and a memorial plaque are at the Manhattan entrance. This was the first major tunnel to pose a ventilation problem. It was solved by construction of four ventilation buildings, two on each side of the Hudson River, housing immense fans which can provide a change of air every ninety seconds. This was, then, the first tunnel with forced ventilation.

The length of the tunnel (portal to portal) is 8,588 feet in the north (westbound) tube and 8,371 feet in the south (eastbound) tube. Each roadway is 20 feet wide with an operating headroom of 12'6" and an external diameter of roughly 30 feet. Maximum depth from Mean High Water to Roadway is 93 ft. 5 in. By June 30, 1977, over 713,462,300 cars had passed through—over 22,000,000 in 1976 alone. There is a toll, which is collected eastbound only on the New Jersey side.

-2.30 P.A.T.H. Uptown Tubes.
These first railroad tunnels under the Hudson River completed on March 11, 1094, were opened on February 25, 1908 from Hoboken to Morton St., Manhattan (extended uptown to West Thirty-third Street in 1910). Originally constructed by the Hudson & Manhattan, owing to an engineering miscalculation, the two shafts did not quite meet in the middle of the river, and it was necessary to connect them with an S curve halfway under the

river. To this day, operating speeds are therefore restricted. Each tube is single track. The builder was W. G. McAdoo and chief engineer was Charles M. Jacobs.

-2.38 Morton St. to east.

-2.28 Harsimus or Horsimus Cove to west.:

Largely filled in. Formerly site of many railroad float bridges.

-2.20 Hoboken to west.

Hoboken is a city comprising exactly one mile square between the Hudson River and the foot of the Palisades. Population in 1976 was 45,380. The name is derived from the Indian word "Hackingh" or "the place of tobacco pipes," and it is recorded that the Indians did indeed make such pipes from the red clay hereabouts. The region was originally quite picturesque. As late as 1840, the landscape painter Asher B. Durand wrote in his *Journal*," . . . for real and unalloyed enjoyment of scenery, the rocks, trees and green meadows of Hoboken will have a charm that all Switzerland cannot boast." While this is obvious hyperbole, many other early writers testify to the rural charms of the area.

As early as 1642, the Dutch had established a settlement and a brewery. The first farmers settled in about 1630, and Governor Stuyvesant procured a deed from the Indians in 1658. An unfortunate event occurred in 1643. According to Benson J. Lossing, the story was as follows:

The low promontory below Castle Point was the site of the large Indian village of Hobock. There the pleasant little city of Hoboken now stands (1866), and few of its quiet denizens are aware of the dreadful tragedy performed in that vicinity more than two hundred years ago. The story may be related in few words. A fierce feud had existed for some time between the New Jersey Indians and the Dutch of Manhattan. Several of the latter had been murdered by the former, and the Hollanders had resolved on vengeance. At length the fierce Mohawks, bent on procuring tribute from the weaker tribes westward of the Hudson, came sweeping down like a gale from the north, driving great numbers of fugitives upon the Hackensacks at Hobock. Now was the opportunity for the Dutch. A strong body of them, with some Mohawks, crossed the Hudson at midnight, in February, 1643, fell upon the unsuspecting Indians, and before morning murdered almost one hundred men, women and children. Many were driven from the cliffs of Castle Point, and perished in the freezing flood. At sunrise the murderers returned to New Amsterdam, with prisoners and the heads of several Indians. (Lossing, *The Hudson*, pp. 450-51.)

In 1711, the land in the vicinity passed into the hands of Samuel Bayard, a wealthy New York merchant. In 1771, title passed to William Bayard, a loyalist in the Revolution. The land was confiscated and valued at $90,000. The site was purchased in 1784 by John Stevens, who established his home at Castle Point in 1787.

Originally much of Hoboken was an island surrounded by swamps, but this had been gradually filled in through the years. In 1804, John Stevens laid out a town and a pleasure garden to the north, known as the Elysian Fields, which operated until about 1839, and was a popular resort for New Yorkers. Ferry services were established at an early date. In 1825, John Stevens built 630 feet of circular track on his estate and operated a "steam wagon" thereon—the first steam railroad in America. John Jacob Astor built a home here in 1828, which was a gathering place for authors, including Fitz-Greene Halleck, Washington Irving, Gulian Verplanck, and William Cullen Bryant. John Stevens died in 1838, but in 1850 his son Edwin Stevens hired Alexander Jackson Davis to build him a castle, which soon gave its name to the promontory on which it stood. This building served as the adminstration building of the Stevens Institute of Technology until 1959, when it was torn down to make room for the present high-rise building. Only the gatehouse remains. It is built of irregularly cut greenish stone and has crenellated towers and stepped gables.

In 1855, Hoboken was incorporated as a city. It attracted many German immigrants and seamen, and as late as the 1920s and 1930s, it was a common excursion to visit the German beer cellars at "Hoboken, where German is spoken." The south end of town was soon preempted by the Morris and Essex Railroad (later Delaware, Lackawanna and Western; Erie-Lackawanna; and Conrail) freight and passenger yards and terminals. Rows of brownstone houses (many now undergoing restoration) stood near the river, and light industry and boiler and machine works were located further inland and on the site of the former Elysian Fields. There were also shipyards at the north end, and the Hoboken-Port Authority Marine Terminal is located between Stevens Institute and Lackawanna Terminal.

-2.00 Lackawanna Terminal (west).
A large passenger terminal and ferry depot, this is the last remaining example of this monumental type structure. Built by the Delaware, Lackawanna and Western Railroad in 1907, this green copper-sheathed structure once boasted an impressive campanile tower, which has been replaced by a utilitarian microwave tower. The architect was Kenneth Murchison and the structural engineer was Lincoln Bush. It incorporates many important developments in marine and railroad terminal design, including upper deck ferry loading ramps

and the so-called, "Bush train sheds." While no longer served by ferries, it remains an important and very busy railroad station, and its unique neo-classic architecture is worthy of renovation and preservation. In 1979, the state of NJ D.O.T. undertook a $3,700,000 restoration program.

-1.80 Hoboken-Port Authority Marine Terminal (west).
This facility was financed and developed by the Port Authority under a fifty-year, three-party lease, effective in 1952, among the U.S. Maritime Administration, the city of Hoboken and the Port Authority. There are three modern cargo piers with 5,952 linear feet of wharfage. In 1975, it handled 121,096 long tons. The movie *On The Waterfront*, with Marlon Brando, was filmed here.

-1.50 14th Street Manhattan to east.
Consolidated Edison Building: 37 stories, 475 ft with a clock in the tower.

-1.50 Castle Point (west), also known as Stevens Point.
Former site of the home of Edwin Stevens, which was designed by Alexander Jackson Davis in Gothic Revival style and stood from 1850 to 1959. Now a high-rise building occupies its site, the property of Stevens Institute of Technology. Formerly the marine shops of the Pennsylvania Railroad stood at the foot of the promontory. During the years of activity of the Elysian Fields recreation grounds (1804-1839), the Sibyl's Cave, under Castle Point, a cool, rocky cavern containing a spring, was a popular resort point.

-1.50 Former site of Greenwich Point on east.

-1.20-1.70 Old Chelsea Piers on east:
Thirteenth to Twenty-third Streets

-1.10 Twenty-third Street Manhattan to east.

Site of former large ferry terminals of Jersey Central, Lackawanna, Erie, Pennsylvania railroads. Formerly a copper-sheathed campanile tower. Visible on Twenty-third Street are the massive London Tower Apartments, the Starret-Lehigh Warehouse, and the Metropolitan Life Insurance Building (48 stories, 658 feet, with clock in tower). Built in Italian Rennaissance Eclectic style in 1908-09, it was designed by N. LeBrun and Sons.

-1.00 Elysian Fields (west):

Former pleasure grounds operating from 1804-1839. The site is now covered by industrial buildings, shipyards, and marine terminals, and an approach to the Lincoln Tunnel.

-1.00 Port Authority-West Thirtieth Street Heliport (east),

At foot of West-Thirtieth Street and Hudson River. Leased from the city of New York, it accommodates general and corporate helicopter operations. It opened in 1956. Facilities include a paved area 400 feet by 70 feet with two concrete landing pads, each 80 feet square. Projecting 40 feet out over the water on steel "H" piles. The Terminal building is at the northern end.

-1.00 New York Life Building (east)

massive tower with golden spire (34 stores, 617 feet tall).

-0.75 Weehawken Cove to west.

Outlet of Sluice and Weehawken Creeks.

-0.50 Sea Train Terminal (container-port) to west.

Dea's Point to west.

-0.50 Entrance approach ramps for Lincoln Tunnel to west.

-0.50 Empire State Building to east.

(102 stories, 1,265 feet to tip of tower). Completed 1931, this was for a long period the world's tallest building. Shreve, Lamb and Harmon were the architects. It has sixty three passenger and four freight elevators.

-0.50 33rd Street Manhattan to east.

-0.50 Pennsylvania Railroad Tunnel.

Twin single-track railroad tunnels completed in September and October of 1906. They are built of cast-iron rings 2½ feet long and with 23 ft diameter, each composed of eleven segments and a key, and of a total weight of 11½ tons, embedded in loosely compacted riverbed silt. They are lined with concrete, leaving 18 feet clear internal diameter. A concrete walk, 6 feet in width, extends along each side of the tube at the height of the car windows, in which are imbedded the conduits for the water pipes, the power-cables and the signal-wires. As there is but six inches clearance above the car-roof, ventilation is assured merely by the trains forcing the air ahead of them and fresh air following. The tubes are 6000 feet long, with the western portal in the Hackensack meadows west of the Palisades. Penn Station is at the eastern end.

-0.25 Fortieth Street Manhattan to east.

Outlet Minetta Brook to east. Covered over.

-0.25 Lincoln Tunnel. Ventilator towers to east and west.

-0.25 Lincoln Tunnel.

A facility of the Port Authority of New York and New Jersey, it is the world's only three-tube vehicular tunnel. The width of the roadway in each tunnel is 21 feet 6 inches, with an operating headroom of 13 feet. External diameter of each tunnel is 31 feet and maximum depth from mean high water to roadway is 97 feet.

	North Tube	Center Tube	South Tube
Date opened	1945	1937	1957
Length	7,482 ft.	8,216 ft.	8,006 ft.

Traffic volume 1975—33,499,200.

Direct ramps connecting the Lincoln Tunnel with the Port Authority Bus Terminal facilitate the handling of commuter buses by removing them from Manhattan streets, and provide direct access for automobiles to the three-level roof parking.

0.10 Former Delaware and Hudson Canal Co. Depot to west:
site now occupied by banana docks.

0.10 Kings Bluff, Weehawken.
This bluff was named for James Gore King, whose estate, Highwood, occupied the site. The duel between Aaron Burr and Alexander Hamilton on July 11, 1804, in which Hamilton was killed, took place on the grounds of this estate, which were a recognized dueling ground. There were at least fifteen recorded duels at this place. On Septmeber 2, 1799, Burr fought another duel with John B. Church, in which neither was hurt. On November 23, 1801, Hamilton's son Philip was killed in a duel with a certain Mr. Eaker. The same set of dueling pistols was used in all three duels. Other notable duels fought here were between DeWitt Clinton and John Swartwout on August 1st 1802 in which Swartwout was wounded; and between Oliver Hazard Perry and John Heath on October 19, 1818, in which neither was wounded. The actual duel plot was blasted away during the construction of the Jersey Junction Railroad.

0.00 Fortieth Street Manhattan: Pier 81,
Hudson River Day Line terminal.

0.00 Forty-second Street Manhattan:
Grand Central Terminal.

0.00 Forty-third Street Manhattan:
Pier 83, Circle Line sightseeing yachts.

0.00 Former site of West Shore Railroad Terminal and Bonn's elevator.

0.00 Weehawken (west):
A township, incorporated in 1859. A residential community atop the Palisades with extensive railroad yards of the Conrail system, it is the former eastern terminus of the New York, Ontario & Western and West Shore Railroads. There is a double track railroad tunnel one mile long through the Palisades. Weehawken developed rapidly in the late nineteenth and early twentieth century by the building of streetcar lines. Many German and Swiss immigrants settled here. The name comes from the Indian word for a "palisaded place" or one surrounded by "rows of trees." This was a popular picnic ground for New Yorkers in the early nineteenth century. Fitz-Green Halleck wrote in his poem, "Fanny,"

Weehawken! In thy mountain scenery set,
All we adore of Nature and her wild
And frolic hour of infancy is met.

From *"Fanny"* by Fitz-Green Halleck, George Dearborn, NYC 1819.

The dome, visible atop the cliffs, back from the edge, belongs to the church of St. Michael's Monastery in Union City.

0.30 Site of former New York Central RR Pier 7 grain elevator to west.

0.30 Passenger ship terminal.
Operated by the Port Authority since 1974, its construction involved the rebuilding of three obsolete piers dating from 1933 between Forty-eighth and Fifty-second Streets to provide six ship berths with the most modern passenger facilities. The second level of the terminal is heated or air conditioned year round and is used for passengers and baggage. The ground level is used as a service area for delivery of equipment and ships' stores. Flat roofs provide parking for 1,000 vehicles. The terminal cost was in excess of two million dollars and employs 171 people with an annual payroll of $2,145,000. It handled 433,050 passengers in 1975.

0.60 Old steamship "finger piers" on east.

1.00 Site of New York Central RR car float slips on east.

1.00 Slough's Meadow
At the foot of the palisades is now covered by Conrail freight yards.

1.50 Guttenberg on west:
A town with a heavy German population. There was formerly a brewery here. The town has very short frontage on the Hudson River. It runs far west with a residential section atop the palisades.

The Palisades.
This striking series of cliffs along the western shore is composed of columnar basalt and is named for their similarity in appearance to a wooden palisaded fortification. Their geology is described in detail under the Geological Heading on page 15. The actual geological formation is actually more extensive, running from Bayonne, New Jersey to the vicinity of Pomona, New York, York, about forty-eight miles, than the section commonly designated the Palisades. Generally speaking, they are said to start at Kings Bluff on the south end and continue north to Tallman Mountain, just south of Sparkill Creek near Piermont, New York. The highest point is Indian Head, opposite Hastings-On-Hudson, with an elevation of 522 feet. The top of the Palisades is generally level for about a mile back from the cliffs, and slopes from there down to the valley of the Hackensack River. Originally densely wooded throughout, the southern end is now devoted to dense residential development, while the northern end remains in forest devoted to recreation and conservation. The northern cliffs are park land and are under the protection of the Palisades Interstate Park Commission formed in 1900 to preserve this unique area against quarrying and other unsightly encroachments. In past years, wealthy New Yorkers purchased extensive wood lots atop the Palisades to supply themselves with heating wood. The logs were pitched down from atop the cliffs to docks below. Many of these pitching places are known as "gutters," and the names of these former docks are still used by hikers as landmarks. Until the formation of the Palisades Interstate Park, there were small farms at the base of the cliffs and on terraces above the river. Pears were one of the staple crops, and many of the "Undercliff" dwellers also pursued shad fishing and stone quarrying and logging. Today the entire area is devoted to recreation. The Henry Hudson Drive runs beneath the cliffs and the Palisades Interstate Parkway and Route 9W run along the top. From Fort Lee south to Weehawken, many large high-rise apartment houses have been built in recent years. They offer their tenants spectacular views. However, while attractive enough in themselves, their erection is changing the character of the area and is tending to dwarf the Palisades themselves.

1.85 79th Street Yacht Basin on east.

1.85 Riverside Drive.

This famous street runs from Seventy-second Street north to Dyckman Street. Its embankments, terraces, and pergolas were designed by the noted landscape architect Frederick Law Olmstead (ca.1909) in the classic eclectic style. It is fronted by gracious townhouses and apartment buildings and is separated from the river by Riverside Park. In the 1930s, the Hudson Division of the New York Central Railroad south of 123rd Street was covered over by landscaped terraces and the Henry Hudson Parkway constructed from the north end of the West Side Elevated Highway at Seventy-second Street to the Henry Hudson Bridge at the north end of Manhattan. This parkway runs closer to the river edge than does Riverside Drive and is a limited access highway. It is presently in poor repair and there are tentative plans to rebuild it as part of the proposed Westway which will also replace the defunct West Side Elevated Highway further south.

1.85 Boulevard East.

This street runs along the top of the Palisades from King's Bluff to Hudson Heights at the Hudson-Bergen County Line. Many luxurious highrise apartments are being constructed along it.

1.85 Conrail (former West Shore Railroad/New York Central) freight yeards are along the foot of the Palisades.

Site of former marine shops of the New York Central Railroad and coal piers of the New York, Ontario & Western and New York, Susquehanna & Western Railroads. During the 1940s and 1950s, many shanty dwellers lived aboard decaying barges aground on the shallow flats.

2.45 Block House Point on West: site of a Revolutionary War blockhouse. Benson Lossing tells its history succinctly in *The Hudson* as follows:

In the summer of 1780, a few weeks before the discovery of Arnold's treason, that block-house was occupied by a British picket, for the protection of some woodcutters, and the neighboring New Jersey loyalists. On Bergen Neck, below, was a large number of cattle and horses, belonging to the Americans, within reach of the foragers who might go out from the British post at Paulus's Hook, now Jersey City. Washington's head-quarters were then inland, near Ramapo. He sent General Wayne, with some Pennsylvanian and Maryland troops, horse and foot, to storm the block-house and to drive the cattle within the American lines. Wayne sent the cavalry, under Major Henry Lee, to perform the latter duty, whilst he and three Pennsylvanian regiments marched against the block-house with four pieces of cannon. They made a spirited attack, but their cannon were too light to be effective, and, after a skirmish, the Americans were repulsed with a loss of sixty men, killed and wounded. After burning some wood-boats near, and capturing those who had them in charge, Wayne returned to camp with a large number of cattle driven by the dragoons.

This event was the theme of a satirical poem, in three cantos, in the ballad style, written by Major Andre, and published in Rivington's Royal Gazette *in the city of New York.* (Lossing, *The Hudson*, pp 439-41.)

2.45 Soldiers and Sailors Monument to east, at corner of Eighty-ninth Street and Riverside Drive: Designed by Charles W. and Arthur A. Stoughton in the Beaux Arts

Eclectic style. Constructed between 1900 and 1902, it is dedicated to soldiers who lost their lives in the Civil War. It is in the form of a Greek temple with a peristyle of twelve Corinthian columns. Sculptural work is by Paul Duboy.

3.00 Shadyside on west.
Named for former Shady Side Hotel. Formerly known as Bull's Ferry. Presently an industrial area.

3.30 Former Ford Motor Company assembly plant on west.
Now a deepwater terminal and warehouse. This is the south end of the village of Edgewater. A tunnel of the New York, Susquehanna & Western RR penetrates the Palisades here to the Hackensack Meadows.

3.30 Former site of Stryker's Bay on east.
Now filled in by construction of Riverside Park and Henry Hudson Parkway.

4.30 Sunnyside on west.
A section of the village of Edgewater. Possibly named in contradistinction to Shadyside?

4.30 Riverside Church and Interchurch Center on east
at corner of 122nd Street and Riverside Drive. This is one of the largest churches in New York. Built 1930 in neo-Gothic style with a twenty-four-story, four hundred foot tower housing the seventy-four-bell Laura Spellman Rockefeller Carillon. The nineteen-story Interchurch Center is faced with Alabama limestone and houses church and church-related organizations of the Orthodox and Protestant religions. Columbia University is located behind the church and center.

4.40 Grant's Tomb on east.
Tomb of General and President Ulysses Simpson Grant (1822-1885), located at the corner of 123rd Street and Riverside Drive. It houses President Grant and his wife Julia Dent Grant. There are also reliquary rooms displaying Civil War flags and other mementoes. The tomb is officially called the General Grant National Monument. Built between 1892-1897, it was designed in competition. The winning architect, John H. Duncan, chose to build in the classic eclectic style. The square base in the Doric mode is surmounted by circular peristyle in the Ionic mode with a stepped conical dome. The structure is reminiscent of the tomb of King Mausolos at Halicarnassos. The interior is similar to Napoleon's tomb in the chapel of the Hotel des Invalides in Paris, but is much smaller. It is built of white granite and cost $600,000.

4.40 Former Lackawanna ferryboat S.S. Binghamton
is anchored along the shoreline at Edgewater to the west. Converted to a floating restaurant and supper club, it operates under the tradename *Binghamton's.* It is the only remaining typical large steam ferryboat on the Hudson.

4.75 Formerly swimming baths
were moored in the Hudson here on the East side. They were partially submerged barges with lattice bottoms to permit ingress of the river water. It is ironic that this is presently the most highly polluted place in the river with untreated sewage entering here.

4.75 Site of former Recreation Pier at end of 130th Street.
This was also used by the Hudson River Day Line and Night Line and various excursion boats, and by the Iron Steamboat Company.

4.75 Riverside Drive Viaduct on East:
between 129th and 135th Streets, (length 1,688 feet), it carries a

60-foot-wide roadway and two sidewalks 10 feet wide. It is built of steel girders and masonry at the southerly end. Opened for traffic in 1903.

4.75 Visible behind the Riverside Drive Viaduct is the high 125th Street viaduct of the Broadway Line of the I.R.T. Division of the New York subway system. This is a large steel arch viaduct. The 125th Street station is atop the viaduct.

4.80 Site of former 125th Street Ferry to Edgewater on east.
It is a peculiarity that West 125th Street and West 130th Street come together at an angle at the riverfront. Thus 130th Street pier and 125th Street ferry were next to each other, with the 130th Street pier to the south.

4.80 Edgewater, N. J., to the East:
village at foot of the Palisades. Largely residential at the northern end, it has retained a rural atmosphere (population 4,987). The southern end is devoted to industry, and there were formerly large plants of the Jack Frost Sugar Company and Alcoa located here. Served by New York, Susquehanna & Western Railroad, it is the former terminus of the 125th Street Ferry and numerous electric interurban lines serving northern New Jersey. At one time shad fishing was a major local industry. The old Ox Hill Road was one of the pioneer roads up the Palisades.

4.80 Cliffside Park, N.J., residential community atop the Palisades.
The section along the cliffs is known as Grantwood, after the tomb across the river. The very large apartment houses are known as the Winston Towers and stand on the site of the former large Palisades Amusement Park. This was one of

America's largest amusement parks and featured a giant salt-water pool with machinery to simulate ocean waves, three giant roller-coasters, (the Scenic Railway; the Sky Rocket; and the Bob-Sled), which was located dramatically atop the Palisades cliffs, and a large ferris wheel, also located at the edge of the cliffs.

The development of both the residential area and the amusement park was fostered by the ferry and various trolley lines crossing here.

4.80 Harlem section of Manhattan, to the east.
Originally a valley of rich farms in colonial days, it later became the location of luxurious country estates and later an area of stylish townhouses and apartment flats. As the wealthy white population moved further uptown and across to New Jersey, the area became popular with blacks, and is now the largest single black community in the United States. As the blacks are becoming more affluent and moving farther afield, Hispanic people are gradually moving into Harlem, particularly along the East Side and Riverside Drive north of 125th Street.

4.90 Manhattanville section of Manhattan to east.

4.95 Site of the Grange, home of Alexander Hamilton, to east.

5.00 Undercliff section of Edgewater to west.
Largely residential but once an art colony.

5.00 Large new sewage treatment plant
under construction along the river on the east. Site was once occupied by yards and docks of the Iron Steamboat Company and various coal companies.

7.00 Carmansville section of Manhattan.

Named for colonial era builder, developer, and merchant Richard F. Carman who owned extensive tracts in the area and developed village of Carmansville. Well-known inhabitants of this section were Roger Morris, Madame Jumel, the widow of Aaron Burr, and John James Audubon. The section is sometimes known as Audubon Heights or Audubon Park.

7.10 Columbia-Presbyterian Medical Center on east:

large complex of buildings devoted to the care of the sick, medical research, and teaching. Completed in 1928 and designed by James Gamble Rogers, it is the site of the famed Harkness Pavilion. The medical center is to the north of the site of the early New York Institution for the Deaf and Dumb, founded in 1817.

7.10 Former landing on the west known variously through the years as Tillie Tudlem, Tilly Toodlum, Pleasant Valley, Burdett's Ferry, and Fort Lee Park.

At the bottom of a clove giving easy access to the top of the Palisades, it was once the site of resort hotels and was a popular steamboat landing. Some wine grapes were grown here in the nineteenth century.

7.15 Site of former Powder Dock, or DuPont Dock, on west.

7.20 Site of Hazard's Dock on west.

7.30 Fort Washington on east,

atop Washington Heights, the highest point in Manhattan (elevation 268 feet). The name now applies to the entire neighborhood of apartment houses. Originally named for a Revolutionary War fortification. this location is described by Benson Lossing in *The Hudson:*

. . . we reach the station-house of the Hudson River Railway, which stands at the southern entrance to a deep rock excavtion through a point of Mount Washington, known for a hundred years or more as Jeffrey's Hook. This point has an interesting revolutionary history in connection with Mount Washington. At the beginning of the war, the great value, in a strategic point of view, of Manhattan Island, and of the river itself —in its entire length to Fort Edward—as a dividing line between New England and the remainder of the colonies, was fully appreciated by the contending parties. The Americans adopted measures early to secure these, by erecting fortifications. Mount Washington (so named at that time) was the most elevated land upon the island, and formidable military works of earth and stone were soon erected upon its crown and upon the heights in the vicinity from Manhattanville to Kingsbridge. The principal work was Fort Washington. The citadel was on the crown of Mount Washington, overlooking the country in every direction, and comprising within the scope of vision the Hudson from the Highlands to the harbour of New York. The citadel, with the outworks, covered several acres between One Hundred and Eighty-first and One Hundred and Eighty-sixth Streets.

On the point of the chief promontory of Mount Washington jutting into the Hudson, known as Jeffery's Hook, a strong redoubt was constructed, as a cover to chevaux-de-frise and other obstructions placed in the river between that point and Fort Lee, to prevent the British ships going up the Hudson. The remains of this redoubt, in the form of grassy mounds covered with small cedars, are prominent upon the point. . . . The ruins of Fort Washington, in similar form, were also very conspicuous until within a few years, and a flag staff marked the place of the citadel. But the ruthless hand of pride, forgetful of the past, and of all patriotic allegiance to the most cherished traditions of American citizens, has levelled the mounds, and removed the flag-staff; and that spot, consecrated to the memory of valorous deeds and courageous suffering, must now be sought for in the kitchen-garden or ornamental grounds of some wealthy citizen, whose choice celery or bed of verbenas has greater charms than the green sward of hillock beneath which reposes the dust of a soldier of the old war for independence!

"Soldiers buried here?" inquires the startled resident. Yes; your villa, your garden, your beautiful lawn, are all spread out over the dust of soldiers, for all over these heights the blood of Americans, Englishmen, and Germans flowed freely in the autumn of 1776, when the fort was taken by the British after one of the hardest struggles of the war. More than two thousand Americans were captured, and soon filled the loathsome prisons and prison-ships of New York.

Fort Washington mounted twenty heavy cannon and several smaller pieces and mortars. Its chief strength consisted in its position. The fort was commanded by Colonel Magaw of Pennsylvania, assisted by Lambert Cadwalader of that same state. The total American force was 2000 men, including those driven in from Ft. Tryon and Cock Hill Fort.

The British and German combined forces was about 5000 men; the British under Sir William Howe and the Hessians and Waldeckers under Baron Wilhelm von Knyphausen. The decisive action was on the morning of November 16, 1776, at which time Generals Greene and Washington were at Fort Lee, watching the battle from across the river. Knyphausen led 500 Hessians and Waldeckers from the north, having first taken Cock Hill and Fort Tryon. A Division of 800 English and Hessians under Lords Percy and Cornwallis, and Colonel Stirling and Brigadier Matthews attacked from the south and east. Despite hard fighting Magaw had to surrender by 1:30 P.M. when the Union Jack was raised over the fort—which was shortly thereafter renamed Fort Knyphausen.

7.30 Jeffery's Hook on east.

Site of revolutionary fortification and of Jeffry Point Lighthouse. The lighthouse is no longer operational. It is located directly beneath the George Washington Bridge. When it was proposed to dismantle the red lighthouse public feeling led to its permanent preservation. Hildegarde Swift wrote a children's story entitled "The Little Red Lighthouse and the Great Gray Bridge," which sold 2 million copies. Both the spelling Jeffery's Hook and Jeffry Point are used officially by different government agencies.

7.30 Fort Lee to west.

(present population 30,631). Largely devoted to highrise apartment houses and highway interchanges funneling into the George Washington Bridge, it was a center of the movie industry until the mid-1930s. It was originally called Pickletown. Its elevation is 260 feet.

Fort Lee takes its present name from a fortification erected in July 1776, by Gen. Hugh Mercer, and named for General Charles Lee, who aided in the defense of New York City. Maj. Gen. Israel Putnam suggested that the Hudson be obstructed by placing sunken ships in the channel. These, in conjunction with Forts Lee and Washington, would prevent British ships from sailing upriver. On November 16, 1776 General Washington watched the assault and surrender of Fort Washington from Fort Lee. When he received word that Lord Cornwallis had landed 6000 British troops 5 miles north of Fort Lee, he immediately ordered retreat to Hackensack and ultimately across New Jersey before Cornwallis cut him off. Much artillery and supplies were left behind and food was left cooking in the pots, so hasty was the retreat.

Prior to this, the troops had spread out over an area known as Nolan's Ground and set up hut villages inland from the fort. Also on August 16th 1776, the British warships *Phoenix* and *Rose* were attacked by American fireships and galleys just off Fort Lee. The Fort has recently been restored by the Palisades Interstate Park Commission as Fort Lee Historic Park. The fortifications have been reconstructed, and there is a visitor center, museum, and scenic overlooks.

7.30 George Washington Bridge.
This bridge was built and is operated by the Port Authority of New York and New Jersey. It was designed by Othmar H. Ammann. Ground was broken in October 1927. It was opened for traffic on October 25, 1931. An additional two lanes were added to the upper deck in 1946. Construction of the six-lane lower level started in September 1958. The lower level was completed at 10:45 A.M. on June 16, 1960 when the seventy-sixth and final section, weighing 62 tons and measuring 108 feet wide and 60 feet long was raised from a barge below the center of the bridge and fitted into the gap between the previously erected sections. The writer, quite unexpectedly, personally witnessed this final operation from the deck of the sidewheel steamer *Alexander Hamilton.* No doubt the construction crews purposely awaited the passing of the daily "up boat" to complete this historic operation. No previous public notice had been given.

The George Washington Bridge spans the Hudson River between West 178th Street Manhattan and Fort Lee, passing directly over Jeffery's Hook and lighthouse. It forms part of Interstate Highway I-95. Upon its completion, it became the world's only fourteen-lane suspension bridge. Total bridge investment by 1975 came to $215,800,000. In 1975, it carried over 76,000,000 vehicles.

Bridge Statistics:
Length of River Span—3,500 ft.
Length of main span between anchorages—4,760 ft.
Width of bridge—119 ft.
Width of roadway—90 ft.
Height of towers above water—604 ft.
Channel clearance of bridge at midspan under lower level—212 ft.
Bridge is supported by four main cables —two on each side.
There are sidewalks on either side of the upper level.

Provision was made in the tops of the towers for restaurants and observation platforms to be reached by elevators from the sidewalks, but these were never completed.

7.30 George Washington Bridge Bus Station to east.
Operated by the Port Authority, it replaces various former bus sidewalk loading areas. It was designed by Dr. Pier Luigi Nervi and was opened on January 17, 1963. It can accommodate 200 buses and 10,000 passengers in a peak hour and has direct passageways to the IND subway station. The terminal measures 400 feet by 185 feet on three levels and cost $15,400,000. On a typical weekday, it handles 28,000 passengers on 1,200 buses. In 1975, it handled ten million passengers on 440,000 bus movements.

7.40 Taylorville section of Fort Lee to west atop Palisades.

7.50 Coytesville Section of Fort Lee to west atop Palisades.

7.50 Carpenter's Beach to west

7.60 Ross Dock to west
Has parking facilities and recreation fields.

7.60 Floraville to west
On western slope of Palisades.

8.00 The Miraculous—Glen to west

8.00 Linwood section of Fort Lee to West atop Palisades.

8.00 St. Michael's Villa and St. Peter's College atop Palisades to west

8.10 Allison Point to west

8.20 Fort Tryon to east

Located atop ridge in Fort Tryon Park north of intersection of Fort Washington Avenue and West 193rd Street. This Revolutionary War redoubt mounted two guns. Commanded by Colonel Rawlings, a small American force yielded to greatly superior Hessian forces under Baron Knyphausen on the morning of November 16, 1776. It was subsequently occupied by the British until end of the war and was greatly strengthened by them.

8.30 The Cloisters to east

Atop ridge in Fort Tryon Park, the site was formerly occupied by a small castle built by A. C. Richards in 1864 and known as Wood Cliff. The property belonged to C.K.G. Billings until 1926. The Cloisters, which is now a branch of the Metropolitan Museum of Art, was presented to the city by John D. Rockefeller, Jr. It is a museum of medieval art incorporating whole sections of abandoned European monasteries, which have been brought here and reassembled.

8.70 Tubby Hook to east:

site of former Dyckman Street Ferry to Englewood Cliffs.

8.75 Inwood Hill Park on east:

a high wooded land incorporating a climax forest—on Manhattan Island! This is the site of a former Indian village called Shorakapkok, or "as far as the Sitting-Down Place."

9.70 Englewood and Englewood Cliffs to west

(population 24,985): mainly a residential community with most of the homes located on the gentle western slopes of the Palisades, and in the Northern Valley. The business center is in the western part of town. There are numerous corporate headquarters office buildings along Route 9W atop the Palisades. Prior to the Revolution, Englewood was known as English Neighborhood, to distinguish it from the predominently Dutch surrounding area. During the Revolution, a Liberty Pole was erected here, and for a while the town was called Liberty Pole. With the coming of the Northern Valley Railroad of New Jersey, the name Englewood was adopted. The southwestern part of town was called Nordhoff, and the northwestern part was called Highwood.

9.70 Englewood Creek to west:

a small stream with waterfalls down the Palisades.

9.70 Site of Palisades Mountain House

(elevation 375 ft.). This was a large brick and stone, four story hotel built atop the Palisades. It had porticos on three sides and towers and a Mansard roof in the best Victorian style, and commanded a fine view up and down the river. It was located south of Palisades Avenue, on the edge of the cliffs. It was built by a syndicate headed by Andrew D. Bogert, and also including William B. Dana, William Walter Phelps, George S. Coe, Garret A. Lydecker, Jacob S. Wetmore, and Sen. Cornelius Lydecker. The hotel opened on June 7th 1860. The operating lessee was Dave Hammond, who also managed the stylish Murray Hill and

Plaza Hotels in Manhattan. He installed William Perry as acting manager at the Mountain House. The hotel attracted a high class clientele, and to make access easier, the hotel, through a subsidiary company, built a road down the cliff (the present Palisades Avenue, then called Palisades Turnpike) and a steamboat dock. It also built a well-constructed footpath down the cliffs. The hotel burned down in 1884 and was not rebuilt. The property was sold to William Outis Allison, who built a mansion on the site which stood until 1903. The location was known as Allison Point. St. Joseph's Orphanage acquired the property in 1907, and it now belongs to St. Peter's College.

9.70 Englewood Yacht Club to West

Former landing of the Dyckman Street Ferry. Small excursion steamers used to land at the two-story pier here until the 1940s. The area is now surrounded by Palisades Interstate Park.

9.70 Site of Cock Hill Fort to east

On the northernmost tip of Manhattan Island, this was a small Revolutionary redoubt mounting two guns, captured by the Hessians under Baron Knyphausen on November 16, 1776.

9.70 Spuyten Duyvil Creek to east:

Separates Manhattan Island from the mainland and connects the Hudson and Harlem Rivers (also called Harlem River Ship Canal). The name was also spelled Spitondivell, or "Spitting Devil," possibly from the strong currents. Another derivation is "in spite of the Devil," and derives from Washington Irving's story about Peter Stuyvesant's trumpeter, Anthony Corlear, as told in his *Knickerbocker History of New York:*

It was a dark and stormy night when the good Anthony arrived at the famous creek (sagely denominated Haerlem river) which separates the island of Manna-hata from the main land. The wind was high, the elements were in an uproar, and no Charon could be found to ferry the adventurous sounder of brass across the water. For a short time he vapoured like an impatient ghost upon the brink, and then, bethinking himself of the urgency of his erreno, took a hearty embrace of his stone bottle, swore most valorously that he would swim across, en spijt den Duyvel (in spite of the devil!) and daringly plunged into the stream.—Luckless Antony! scarce had he buffetted half way over, when he was observed to struggle most violently as if battling with the spirit of the waters—instinctively he put his trumpet to his mouth and giving a vehement blast—sunk forever to the bottom!

The potent clangour of his trumpet, like the ivory horn of the renowned Paladin Orlando, when expiring in the glorious field of Roncesvalles, rung far and wide through the country, alarming the neighbors round, who hurried in amazement to the spot—Here an old Dutch burgher, famed for his veracity, and who had been a witness of the fact, related to them the melancholy affair; with the fearful addition (to which I am slow of giving belief) that he saw the duyvel, in the shape of a huge Mossbonker with an invisible fiery tail, and vomiting boiling water, seize the sturdy Antony by the leg, and drag him beneath the waves. Certain it is, the place, with the adjoining promontory, which projects into the Hudson, has been called Spijt den duyvel, or Spiking devil, ever since. (Washington Irving, *Knickerbocker History of New York*, New York: G. P. Putnam's Sons, 1880, pp. 497-98.)

On June 12, 1693, William and Mary granted to Frederick Philipse authority to build a bridge at "a certain neck or island of land called Papparinnomo and to collect tolls" This was the origin of the present Kingsbridge. This place was also called "The Wading Place." It was the southern end of the East Side Kings Highway, which ran from King's Bridge to the ferry at Crawlier, over against Albany.

During the French and Indian Wars, Lord Loudon had broadened an old Indian trail. Under later Royal authority, it was widened to "The Queens Road, to be forever the Highway, of the breadth of four rods, English measurement, at the least." In 1703, the New York Provincial Assembly authorized improvements of the Kings Highway from Kings Bridge to Albany. The road was much used by cattle drovers in early days. This crossing was at the junction of Spuyten Duyvil Creek and the Harlem River.

9.70 Baker Field,
the football stadium of Columbia University, is visible to the east at the far tip of Manhattan Island.

9.70 Railroad Bridge to east:
an opening swing bridge of the Hudson River Railroad (Conrail) across the mouth of Spuyten Duyvil Creek to the east, usually kept open because there is far more boat than train traffic on this particular line, which is used for freight only and runs down along the west side of Manhattan. Passenger trains, bound for Grand Central Terminal, swing east here and follow the north bank of Spuyten Duyvil Creek, as do most freight trains.

9.70 Henry Hudson Bridge to east
(across Spuyten Duyvil Creek). Operated by the Triborough Bridge and Tunnel Authority, this is a fixed arch bridge designed by Robinson and Steinman and Madigan-Hyland. Chief construction Engineer was Emil Praeger. Construction started June 1935. Opened to traffic December 12, 1936. Length of arch span 800 feet. Length each side span 300

feet. Total length of structure, including approaches, 2,000 feet. There are three traffic lanes on the upper level and four on the lower. Clearance above the mean high water at midspan 142.5 feet. Total cost was $4,949,000. It carries the Henry Hudson Parkway. Its total traffic in 1972 was 15,480,762 vehicles.

9.75 Bloomer's Dock to west
9.80 High Tom Rock to west
(elevation 360 feet).

9.85 Berrian's Neck to east:
at junction of Spuyten Duyvil Creek and Hudson River, near the present Spuyten Duyvil railroad station. This was the site of a small Revolutionary War fortification.

9.85 The Bronx to east

This is both a borough of New York City and a county of New York State. It stretches along the Hudson from here to River Mile 12.30, and embraces the neighborhoods of Riverdale and Mount Saint Vincent along the riverfront.
with a population of about 1,500,000. It is bounded on the north by Westchester County, on the east by Long Island Sound, and on the South by the East River and Bronx Kills. The western boundaries are the Harlem River, Spuyten Duyvil Creek, and the Hudson River. Three major watercourses run from north to south within the Bronx: Tippetts Brook or Creek, rising east of Yonkers and flowing into the Spuyten Duyvil Creek near its junction with the Harlem River. This was known to the Indians as Moshula, and its banks were a favorite camping grounds of a warlike Mohegan tribe. The Bronx River flows south to the East River from Kensico Reservoir, north of White Plains. The Hutchinson River rises in the town of Eastchester and flows into the East River near its junction with Long Island Sound.

The first recorded settler was Jonas Bronck, a Dane, who received his grant from the Dutch West India Company in 1641. The name Bronx is a corruption of his name. This family also settled upriver near Coxsackie. The next major settlement was a patent given to Adriaen van der Donck in 1646. Donck's Colony sold 7,708 acres of this patent to Frederick Philipse and two associates in 1672. Frederick Philipse was the first lord of the neighboring manor of Philipsborough. In 1686, he bought out his two associates, and the Philipse Manor then extended from Manhattan to the Croton River and east to the Bronx River, which flows for approximately 20 miles. He established his manor houses at Yonkers and on the Pocantico at North Tarrytown. His adopted daughter, Eva, and son-in-law, Jacobus Van Cortlandt, were the first Van Cortlandts to own property in the Bronx. The present manor house, located in Van Cortlandt Park, was erected in 1748 by their son Frederick Van Cortlandt. Other English manorial grants were: Fordham in 1671; Pelham in 1687; and Morrisania, granted in 1697 to Lewis Morris (1671-1746), first lord of the manor. These were all considerably east and south of the Hudson River.

Originally the Bronx was part of New York and Westchester Counties. Eventually, the entire area became part of New York County, which had been originally erected in 1683. The present Bronx County was taken from New York County in 1914. Principal elevated areas are Tetard's Hill, along the Hudson; University Heights, along the Harlem River; and Fordham Heights, between the Harlem and the Bronx Rivers.

The Bronx has three large parks: Van Cortlandt Park in the north, which em-braces the Van Cortlandt manor and the cottage where Edgar Allan Poe lived from 1846 to 1849 and where he wrote his famous poem "The Raven"; Pelham Bay Park and Bronx Park with its large and famous zoological and botanical gardens. Yankee Stadium is located along the Harlem River. Major educational establishments include Fordham University; New York University, (with its Hall of Fame on University Heights); Lehman College of CUNY; Manhattan College; and the New York State Maritime College at Fort Schuyler. Railroad service is provided by the former Hudson River, Harlem and Putnam Divisions of the defunct New York Central and the New York, New Haven and Hartford, now all part of Conrail. It was also served by the abandoned New York, Westchester & Boston Electric Railroad which had its southern terminus here. This line never got out of Westchester County, much less to Boston. Numerous subway and elevated lines serve the borough.

The Bronx is mainly a residential community. Large tenement and apartment buildings are prevalent in the south and central sections and private homes in the east, northern, and western sections. There are many fine private mansions in Riverdale, and this section was the home of former mayor Fiorello LaGuardia and Arturo Toscanini, the conductor.

There are important produce and lumber markets here, and clothing, textiles, food products, chemicals, machinery, bank notes, and musical instruments are manufactured.

3

The Hudson Below the Highlands

9.90 Tetard's Hill to east
Here in 1608, Henry Hudson skirmished with Indians.

9.90 Site of former Fort Independence
on Tetard's Hill near present Henry Hudson Monument. A smaller Continental Army fortification abandoned on November 2, 1776, before the Battle of Fort Washington.

9.90 Henry Hudson Monument:
statue atop tall column to east

9.90 University Heights in the Bronx can be seen by looking east up Spuyten Duyvil Creek.

10.30 Undercliff to west:
site of former settlement. Sometimes called "Under The Mountain."

10.75 Powder Dock to west

10.75 Clinton Point atop Palisades to west

11.00 Riverdale to east
Wealthy residential section of the Bronx.

12.20 Mount Saint Vincent College to east
This interesting location is well described by Benson Lossing in his *The Hudson* of 1866:

A mile and a half below Yonkers, on the bank of the Hudson, is Font Hill, formerly the residence of Edwin Forrest (1806-1872), the eminent American tragedian. The mansion is built of blue granite, in the English castellated form, a style not wholly in keeping with the scenery around it. It would have been peculiarly appropriate and imposing among the rugged hills of the Highlands thirty or forty miles above. The building has six towers, from which very extensive views of the Hudson and the surrounding country may be obtained. The flag, or stair tower, is seventy-one feet in height.

To this delightful residence Mr. Forrest brought his bride, Miss Catherine Sinclair, daughter of the celebrated Scotch vocalist, in 1838, and for six years they enjoyed domestic and professional life in an eminent degree. Unfortunately for his future peace, Mr. Forrest was induced to visit England in 1844. He was accompanied by his wife. There he soon became involved in a bitter dispute with the dramatic critic of the London Examiner, *and Macready the actor. This quarrel led to the most serious results. Out of it were developed the mob and the bloodshed of what is known, in the social history of the City of New York, as the "Astor Place Riot," (1849) and with it commenced Mr. Forrest's domestic troubles, which ended, as all the world knows, in the permanent separation of himself and wife." (Ed. Note: She brought a Divorce Suit against him in England in 1852.) "Font Hill, where he had enjoyed so much happiness, lost its charms, and he sold it to the Roman Catholic Sisters of Charity, of the Convent and Academy of Mount St. Vincent. This institution was founded in 1847, and the academy was in 105th Street, between the Fifth and Sixth Avenues, New York. It is devoted to the instruction of young ladies. The community, numbering about two hundred Sisters at the time of my visit (1865), was scattered. Some were at Font Hill, and others were at different places in the city and neighborhood. The whole were under the general direction of Mother Superior Mary Angela Hughes. At Font Hill they erected an extensive and elegant pile of buildings, of which they took possession, and wherein they opened a* school, on the 1st of September, 1859. It was much enlarged in 1865. They had, in 1860, about one hundred and fifty pupils, all boarders, to whom was offered the opportunity of acquiring a thorough education. The chaplain of the institution occupies the "castle."

Today Mount St. Vincent is a full-fledged coed Catholic college. There is a local railroad station here.

12.20 Near this point the steamer *Henry Clay* burned and ran aground with great loss of life on Wednesday, July 28, 1852. The story is shortly told by John H. Morrison in his *History of American Steam Navigation*. The *Henry Clay* had left Albany that morning and was racing the *Armenia* downstream:

When a short distance below Yonkers, caught fire and was burned to the water's edge. The vessel was run ashore about two miles below Yonkers dock, in the vicinity of Forrest's Castle, or Riverdale. It was one of those accidents on the water which seem to electrify the community and cause them to ask, if there is any safety from such appalling disasters.

Morrison describes the steamboat race with the *Armenia* and a slight collision between them near Rhinebeck. He continues:

The effect of the collision was to cause the "Armenia" to drop astern, and the Henry Clay *then took and maintained the lead, increasing the distance between them up to the time of the breaking out of the fire at 3:15 P.M. It is supposed that just previous to the fire, the blower*

having been put in operation for increasing the draft of the furnaces, and that the furnace doors not being securely fastened, the strong blast from the blower had forced open the furnace doors and drove the flames from the furnace against the wood-work in the vicinity of the boiler, that was in the hold of the vessel, which took fire immediately and burned with alarming rapidity. The vessel was run ashore head on, but the larger number of passengers being aft of the engine and boiler were obliged to take to the water, which was here very deep almost to the shore, though a number remained on board the vessel until actually forced by the fire to take to the water. It is believed that over one hundred lives were lost by this lamentable occurrence; should not be called an accident. (John H. Morrison, *History of American Steam Navigation*. New York: W.F. Sametz, 1903, p. 108.)

This seems to be an unlucky place on the river. On Saturday, August 28, 1965 the writer was aboard the southbound paddle steamer "Alexander Hamilton," when it hit some large debris which jammed the paddle wheels and broke the paddle shaft bearings. The "Hamilton" was blown up on the same place where the "Henry Clay" had burned. Fortunately no great damage was done and we were towed home eventually by the tug "Carol Moran." The damage was repaired overnight and the "Hamilton" made its scheduled run the next day.

12.20 Lambier Dock to the west
12.30 Tenafly to the west

This New Jersey residential community was first settled by the

Dutch in 1640. It was incorporated in 1894. The first real impetus to growth came with construction of the Northern Valley Railroad which started its residential growth, which continues today. Present population is 14,827. This is double what it was just after World War II. The village proper is at the west foot of the Palisades in the Northern Valley. The west slope of the Palisades was devoted to luxurious homes and estates at the lower levels and forest on the upper slopes and plateau on top. To this day, only Clinton Avenue connects the village in the valley with Route 9W near Clinton Point. Most recent growth has been development of the middle western slopes.

12.30 Greenbrook Falls to west
Greenbrook arises in the Kelder's Pond in Greenbrook Sanctuary atop the Palisades.

12.30 New York City/Westchester County line to east

12.30 Westchester County.
From here to 42.60, the Putnam County line, Westchester County occupies the east shore of the river. Westchester County is bordered on the west by the Hudson River, on the north by Putnam County, on the east by Fairfield County, Connecticut, and on the south by Fairfield County, Connecticut, Long Island Sound, and the Bronx.

The county covers an area of 435 square miles. It is largely residential in character, but has several large cities in the southern part and is rural in the northern and eastern parts. It is home to many Manhattan commuters who travel the rail lines of the former New York Central Hudson and Harlem Divisions and the main line of the former New York, New Haven and Hartford, which runs along the Long Island Sound shoreline on its way to New Haven and Boston. The former New York & Putnam line of the New York Central formerly ran from the Bronx to Brewster, but has been abandoned north of Elmsford and handles only freight on the southern portion. All remaining lines are now part of the Conrail System.

The County of Westchester was established in 1683 and named for Chester in England. The present County Seat is White Plains. Yonkers is the largest city.

The Indians called the tract stretching from Spuyten Duyvil Creek to Hastings-On-Hudson and between the Hudson and Bronx Rivers, Kekesick.

An early Dutch settlement was along the Hudson shoreline. New Englanders soon moved in along the eastern borders of the county, and French Huguenots settled around New Rochelle on Long Island Sound. Under the English several manor grants were established: 1693-Philipsburg; 1697-Van Cortlandt (stretching along the Hudson from Croton River to Anthony's Nose); 1701-Scarsdale; and the small Ryck's Patent enclave near Peekskill.

In his 1821 novel, *The Spy*, James Fenimore Cooper describes Westchester County in the following terms:

The country which lies between the waters of the Hudson and Long Island Sound, is, for the first forty miles from their Junction, a succession of hills and dales. The land bordering on the latter then becomes less abrupt, and gradually assumes a milder appearance, until it finally melts into the lovely plains and meadows of the Connecticut. But as you approach the Hudson the rugged aspect increases, until you at length meet with the formidable barrier of the Highlands. Here the neutral ground ceased. . . .

The county of Westchester, after the British had obtained possession of the Island of New York, became common ground, in which both parties continued to act for the remainder of the war of the Revolution. A large proportion of its inhabitants, either restrained by their attachments, or influenced by their fears, affected a neutrality they did not feel. The lower towns were, of course, more particularly under the dominion of the crown, while the upper, finding a security from the vicinity of the continental troops, were bold in asserting their revolutionary opinions, and their right to govern themselves. Great numbers, however, wore masks, which even to this day have not been thrown aside; and many an individual has gone down to the tomb, stigmatized as a foe to the rights of his countrymen, while, in secret, he has been the useful agent of the leaders of the Revolution; and, on the other hand, could the hidden repositories of divers flaming patriots have been opened to the light of day, royal protections would have been discovered concealed under piles of British gold. . . .

The royal army held the two points of land that commanded the Southern entrance of the river into the mountains [Stony Point and Verplanck's Point]; but all the remaining passes were guarded by the Americans.

We have already stated that the pickets of the continental army were sometimes pushed low into the country, and that the hamlet of the White Plains was occasionally maintained by parties of its troops. At other times, the advanced guards were withdrawn to the northern extremity of the county, and, as has been shown, the intermediate country was abandoned to the ravages of the miscreants who plundered between both armies, serving neither. . . . [These later were known as "Cowboys" and "Skinners."] (James Fenimore Cooper, The Spy. New York: G. P. Putnam's Sons, undated, pages 2 and 306.)

12.50 Chimney Rock to west
12.50 Hawthorne section of
Yonkers to east:
a residential area of private detached homes. Fay Park is in the vicinity.
13.00 Ludlow section of Yonkers to east:
mixed residential and light commercial. A local railroad station is located here.
13.00 Huyler's Landing to West
An old house built here in 1840 was an important transfer point

for goods and passengers between the city and the interior of New Jersey.
13.50 Walker Hollow to west:
A low point on the Palisades.
14.00 Yonkers

(population 204,297). Residential and industrial city located at junction of Hudson River and the Saw Mill River (formerly known as Neperah or Neperhan River), whose water power gave impetus to industrial growth. Locust Hill and Rose Hill front along the Hudson and are backed by Nodine Hill and Valentine Hill, upon whose slopes a skirmish was fought after the Battle of White Plains.

An Indian village by the name of Nappeckamack was located here. West of the Saw Mill River is a large rock called Meech-keek-assin, or A-mac-ka-sin. The Indians paid reverence to this stone as an evidence of the permanency and immutability of their deity. The name Nappeckamack signified "the rapid water settlement," taken from the cascades of the Neperahan River.

In 1639, the Dutch West India Company purchased a tract of 24,000 acres hereabouts called the Kekeskick Tract from the Indians. In 1646, a patent was confirmed to Adriaen Cornelissen Van der Donck. He was a learned man, the first lawyer and historian in New Netherlands. He was given the nickname "jonker" or "yonkeer," meaning "the young lord," from which the present name of Yonkers is derived. Van der Donck named his colony "Colen Donck," meaning "Donck's Colony." Van der Donck died in 1655, and Colen Donck was broken up after arrival of the British in 1664. Frederick Philipse and two associates purchased 7,708 acres, running along the Hudson from Spuyten Duyvil Creek to his other property near the Pocantico River at Castle Philipse. By 1686, he had bought out his two associates. On April 1st 1688, he purchased the Pocantico tract from the Indians, and by 1693, when he was created lord of the manor of Philipsburgh, his land extended from Spuyten Duyvil Creek to the Croton River and east to the Bronx River and covered 90,000 acres or about 200 square miles.

The history of this notable Hudson Valley family is worthy of note. Frederick Philipse I (1626-1702) was born and baptised in Bolswaert, Friesland, Netherlands, the son of a slater. He came to New Amsterdam with his family in 1647, and by 1653 was serving as carpenter and architect for Peter Stuyvesant. He commenced trading and purchasing land. In 1662, he married a rich widow, Margaret Hardenbroeck, relict of Peter Rudolphus de Vries. He then commenced trading on a worldwide scale in furs, whale oil, tobacco, sugar, cocoa, sassafras, logwood, grain, breadstuffs, animals, lumber, cloth, spices, ivory, slaves, wampum, rum, brandies, wine, tinware, molasses, flour, and manufactured goods. He established profitable mills upon his estates, and by 1674 he was the wealthiest man in New Amsterdam. He was named alderman by Governor Andros and also served as a member of the governor's council from 1675 to 1698.

On June 12, 1693 William and Mary granted him a royal charter for the erection of the manor of Philipsborough. In return for the status of lord of the manor, he owed the crown an annual fealty of fourteen pounds, twelve shillings. He held absolute title to the land except for any findings of gold or silver, which remained vested in the crown. He had the rights of Court Baron and Court Leet, having jurisdiction over all civil and criminal matters except treason.

By about 1680, he had three mills. The upper mill was on the Pocantico, the lower mill at Yonkers, and a third on the upper Nepperhan River. There were 40 families or about 200 individuals at the upper mill alone.

Frederick Philipse I had four children —Philip, Adolph, Annetje, and Rombout. In 1692, one year after the death of his first wife, he remarried Catharine Van Cortlandt Derval, daughter of Oloff Stevense Van Cortlandt. After his death in 1702, the upper mills were inherited by Adolph (1665-1750). He held the posts of member of the King's Council, judge of the Supreme Court, represen-

tative and speaker of the assembly and Westchester County Highway Commissioner. In 1720, he enlarged the upper manor. Among his occupations was the bolting of wheat and baking of ship biscuits. His tenants held only verbal leases.

Frederick Philipse II (1695-1751) inherited the lower mills at Yonkers upon his grandfather's death in 1702 and the balance of the family property upon Adolph's death in 1750. In that year he also acquired the so-called Highland Patent, incorporating most of present-day Putnam County. He married Joanna Brockholls, daughter of Lt. Gov. Anthony Brockholls. He served as justice of the Supreme Court from 1731 to 1751. His elder daughter Susannah married Col. Beverly Robinson and lived on the Highland Patent. His younger daughter Mary was a great beauty, and it was rumored that George Washington considered proposing to her. She eventually married Roger Morris, one of Washington's associates on Braddock's staff. Frederick Philipse II greatly enlarged and beautified the original Manor House of 1681 at Yonkers. He added a stone section to the west and in 1745 built a brick north wing. These additions created a stately Georgian country seat. He planted boxwood hedges, flower gardens, trees, and ornamental shrubs and created a deer park. His establishment numbered thirty white and twenty negro servants.

His son Frederick Philipse III, the last lord of the manor, also lived at Yonkers, leasing the upper mills to William Pugsley for £200 per year. He married Elizabeth Rutgers, a widow. Frederick III was a royalist and in 1776 was arrested and banished to Connecticut. He was attainted of treason in 1779 and his property confiscated and sold. In 1783, he sailed for England, where he died at Chester on April 30, 1785. That same year the Yonkers manor house, along with 300 acres, was sold to Cornelius P. Low. In 1865, the manor belonged to W.W. Woodworth and in 1868 was acquired by the village of Yonkers to serve as village hall. In 1872, major interior changes were made to create a large Gothic council chamber. Recently

8. Yonkers

it has been acquired and restored by the New York State Division for Historic Preservation, and it is now open as a museum.

The upper manor was purchased at auction by Gerard G. Beekman, Jr. in 1784. Upon the death of his widow in 1822, the upper manor was broken up. The manor house and the immediately adjacent property passed through the hands of many owners until 1937. At that time, the property was being fore-closed by a bank and in danger of being sold to developers. John D. Rockefeller Jr. intervened to save the historic site and established the Sleepy Hollow Res-torations, which has now returned the manor mill to its earliest condition and operates it as a museum. The rest of the estate was sold in odd parcels to 287 different individuals in 1784.

Returning to the history of Yonkers proper, we note that 16,000 British troops camped here in 1780. By 1781, American soldiers were encamped on Locust Hill. A battle took place just off Yonkers between American gunboats and the British frigates *Rose* and *Phoe-nix*. The Hudson River Railroad reached Yonkers in 1849 and the town grew rapidly as a suburb popular with wealthy New York City merchants. Business also came, and in 1854 Elisha G. Otis estab-lished his elevator works, which still remain a principal Yonkers industry. In 1857, David Saunders opened a large machine shop, and in 1865 Alexander Smith and Halcyon Skinner revolution-ized carpet manufacturing with introduc-tion of the first Axminster power loom. The carpet mills grew to enormous size along the Neperhan River. Today they are no longer used for carpet manufac-turing, but are rented out as loft space. Other manufactured products include clothing, books, patent medicines, re-fined syrups and sugars, and insulated wire and cable produced by the Habir-shaw Cable & Wire Division of the Phelps Dodge Corporation.

Yonkers was incorporated as a village in 1855 and chartered as a city in 1872.

The first American golf game was played here on the St. Andrew's golf course on November 1, 1888. As recently as 1940, Yonkers was served by fourteen pas-senger railroad stations. Today service is provided only on the former Hudson River Railroad line of Conrail, by the Metropolitan Transportation Authority and Amtrak. Once an important river port, the municipal pier is now too frail and dilapidated for docking large river-boats. The former ferry to Alpine has been discontinued.

14.10 Yonkers Municipal Pier on east

14.20 Outlet of Nepperhan, or Saw Mill River, to east
Now covered over as a storm sewer. A mill was built here in 1646.

14.30 Former Alpine Ferry terminal on east

14.30 Philipse Manor on east

14.40 Otis Elevator Company plant on east

14.40 Alpine, New Jersey, on west
Rural residential town atop Pali-sades. Former ferry to Yonkers.

14.40 Alpine Grove to west,
also formerly known as Occi-dental Grove or Riverview Land-ing (at base of Palisdes): a former popular destination for excursion boats.

14.45 Alpine boat basin to west

14.45 Cornwallis' "headquarters" to west
An old colonial tavern at the foot of the Palisades and the road up the cliffs through Alpine Gorge that was used in Revolutionary days. It is supposed that the British spent a night here pre-paratory to scaling the cliffs to take Fort Lee. Here Lord Grey disembarked in October 1778, and crossed to the Hackensack Valley, surprising and massacring Colonel Baylor's patriots, despite their surrender and calls for mercy. Major General "No Flint"

Grey killed thirty continental soldiers under Col. George Baylor at River Vale, New Jersey, after they had surrendered. This location was known as Closter Dock, taking its name from the early Closter Patent and the village of that name at the west foot of the Palisades. Patroon Frederick Closter had a sloop ferry.

14.50 Glenwood section of Yonkers on east

14.50 Former New York Central Railroad electric power plant on east

14.50 Cape Fly-Away on west
High crag of the Palisades.

14.60 Trevor Park to east

14.60 Boar's Hill to east

14.70 Armstrong F.M. radio tower to west
(See west side road 15.50.)

14.70 Excelsior dock on west:
site of Excelsior Grove, another former popular steamboat excursion park.

15.00 Grey Crag to west
Largest separated section of cliff on Palisades. Measures about 300 feet long by ten to twenty feet wide. Reached by a foot-bridge from top of Palisades. In winter and spring, 300 feet high ice columns appear where the water plunges over the cliffs.

15.50 Twombly Landing to west:
named for a former owner who gave property to Palisades Interstate Park. Because of layers of oyster shells found here, this is believed to have been the site of Indian camps.

15.80 Bombay Hook to west
(elevation 500 feet). Also called Boompes Hook, a corruption of the Dutch "Boomje" meaning "little tree," the highest, most isolated and conspicuous pillar of rock in the Palisades, literally curving 70 feet high between two large slides. Also formerly called Point Comfort. A face of

a "man in the rock" can allegedly be seen near the base of the north face.

16.00 Untermyer Park to east
Named for Samuel Untermyer (1899-1940) who developed gardens and landscaped grounds around his former home. The site of former home of New York governor and United States presidential candidate Samuel J. Tilden, it was originally built for hat manufacturer John Waring. The house is now razed, its grounds being maintained by the city of Yonkers.

16.10 Greystone section of Yonkers to east
Seton Academy and Thompson Institute are located here. The remains of the Old Croton Aqueduct may be seen.

16.40 Ruckman Point to west
(Elevation 520 feet).

17.00 Forest Dock to west
Yonkers/Greenburgh town line to east.

17.75 Hastings-On-Hudson to east
(elevation 140 feet; population 9,479). A residential community named for the English birthplace of William Saunders, a local manufacturer, it was incorporated in 1879. This was the home of Horace Greeley (1811-1872) and Glasgow, the estate of Admiral David Farragut (1801-1870), the commander of the Union fleet in the battle of Mobile Bay. Here Dr. John W. Draper (1811-1882), president of the New York University Medical School, in 1841, took the first outdoor photograph of the human face in direct sunlight. Chemicals, copper, and paving blocks are manufactured here, and there is a large plant of the Anaconda Wire & Cable Company. The famous Mount Hope Cemetery is in the east end of the town.

During the Revolution a party of Hessians was surprised and cut to pieces by troops under Col. Sheldon at the battle of Edgar's Lane. Here also 6000 British troops under Cornwallis crossed to attack Fort Lee. In 1777, a division of American soldiers under General Lincoln encamped here. This also was the first spot appointed as the meeting-place of André and Arnold. Circumstances prevented the meeting, and it was postponed. Here, in the mansion of Van Brugh Livingston, Gen. Nathaniel Green met the chief of three commissioners from Gen. Henry Clinton, in conference concerning Maj. André. (The meeting led to no positive results.). Washington had his headquarters here towards the close of the revolution, and here, in November 1783, Washington met with George Clinton, "Civil Governor of the State of New York," and Sir Guy Carleton, the British commander, to confer on the subject of prisoners, the loyalists, and the evacuation of the city of New York by the British forces.

17.75 Indian Head to the west: highest point on Palisades (elevation 522 feet.).

17.90 Giant's Stairway to west: Natural stone stairway up cliffs used as a hiking route. The borough of Rockleigh, New Jersey lies on the west slope Palisades.

17.90 Point Lookout to west

18.00 Station Rock to west: New Jersey/New York state line. Here, atop the cliffs, is a 6 foot memorial shaft erected in 1882.

18.30 High Gutter Point and Skunk Hollow to west

18.65 Lamont Geological Observatory of Columbia University on west

The former estate of C.F. Park, it is now a seismological station.

18.90 Rockland County.

Running along the west bank of the Hudson from mile 18.00 to mile 42.60 Popolopen Creek. This was formerly a part of Orange County, known as "Orange County under the Mountains." Owing to administrative difficulties from the Orange County seat at Goshen, and the fact that its economy was more like that of Bergen County in New Jersey, it was erected as a separate county in 1798. The present New Jersey/New York boundary was determined in 1687. The first recorded settlements were in 1683 near Tappan. This land was purchased from the Indians in 1681 and 1682 and the Indian Deed was acknowledged by Governor Carteret of New Jersey on July I in 1682. On March 24, 1686, Governor Dongon of New York granted a patent to 16 Dutch farmers including Lambert Adriaense Smidt, Adriaen Lambertse Smidt, and Hendrick Gerritse Blauvelt, who owned the land in common until divisions were made in 1704 and 1721. This was known as the Tappan Patent. A Dutch Church was organized in 1694 and the first house of worship built in 1716. The Tappan Patent stretched from the Hudson to the Hackensack. Another tract near Snedens Landing was granted on February 20, 1685 to George Lockhart. This was again confirmed as a patent on June 27, 1687. Another major early grant was the Kakiat Patent, granted on June 25, 1696 to Daniel Honan and Michael Hawdon, speculators. This stretched west from the Hackensack to the vicinity of present day Tallman's, and north to the foot of the Ramapo Mountains. It was settled from people from Hempstead, Long Island, and they established their seat at New Hempstead—now New City, the present county seat. Other early settlements were at Jan Claus's land, near Greenbush, which is near present-day Blauvelt and Orangetown. The Tappan settlement included what is presently Old Tappan, New Jersey. Present-day Rockland county is abuted on the east by the Hudson River, on the southwest by Bergen and Passaic counties in New Jersey, and on the northwest by Orange county in New York. It is roughly an equilateral triangle. Principal watercourses are the Hackensack River, and its tributaries including Pascack Brook; Saddle River; Mahwah River and Ramapo River, which all ultimately empty into Newark Bay. Minnisceongo Creek, Cedar Pond Brook and Sparkill Creek empty into the Hudson River. Principal natural lakes are Rockland Lake and Swartwout and Congers Lakes, at the headwaters of the East Branch of the Hackensack River, and Hessian Lake near Bear Mountain. Most of the other large "lakes" are actually artificial reservoirs or recreational lakes of a manmade type. They include Lake De Forest and Lake Tappan on the Hackensack River (Built by the Hackensack Water Company), and Owl Swamp, Lake Welch, Cranberry Lake, Pine Meadow Lake, and Lake Sebago in Harriman Interstate Park. There is an escarpment along the Hudson—a sort of northern continuation of the Palisades. The Ramapo Mountains cover the northwestern part of the county. The central portion is a high plateau and rolling hills drained by the Hackensack, Saddle, and Ramapo rivers. Principal parks are Tallman Mountain State Park, Blauvelt Interstate Park, Nyack Beach State Park, Rockland Lake State Park, Hook Mountain State Park, High Tor State Park, Bear Mountain State Park and Harriman Interstate Park, all under the Palisades Interstate Park Commission. There are also the Kakiat and Pomona County Parks and Tackamack Town Park near Blauvelt and the Stony Point Battleground Reservation. Almost one-third of the county is devoted to parkland and reservations, thus preserving the original natural beauty of the area.

The County is divided into four large towns: Orangetown, Clarkstown, Stony Point, and Ramapo. Principal towns and villages are: Tappan, Nyack, Haverstraw, Pearl River, Spring Valley, New City, Sloatsburg and Suffern. The county is largely residential with some farming and small scale industry. Principal rail lines are the West Shore line of Conrail (formerly New York Central) running north and south between Tappan and Bear Mountain through the Hackensack and Hudson valleys; The old Erie Mainline from Piermont to Suffern (now largely abandoned between Blauvelt and Nanuet); the Erie Mainline (former Erie-Lackawanna now Conrail) along the Ramapo Valley between Suffern and Sloatsburg; the former New Jersey & New York line from Pearl River to Nanuet (formerly with branches to New City and Thiells and West Haverstraw), now the Pascack Line of Conrail; and the former Northern Railroad of New Jersey from the New Jersey State Line to Nyack (now abandoned from Sparkill to Nyack) also part of the Conrail system. Passenger service is only available on the former Erie mainline in the Ramapo Valley. Principal highways are the New York Thruway from South Nyack to Sloatsburg; the Palisades Interstate Parkway from Palisades to Bear Mountain; Route 9W from Palisades to Bear Mountain, along the Hudson River; and Route 17 from Suffern to Sloatsburg.

18.90 Sneden Landing to west
In the village of Palisades, New York, it was formerly known as Paramus and was the western terminal of Dobbs Ferry. On June 27, 1687 a patent of 3410 acres was granted to George Lockhart. In 1698, William Merritt, who held the mortgage, assumed title and was known to be occupying the site in 1701. On May 14, 1705, it was sold to John Corbett, an English sea captain, who died in 1717. Among the earliest settlers were members of the Sneden family,

who were descended from Jan Snedick who emigrated from Holland to New Amsterdam in 1657. Robert Sneden is known to have owned property here in 1752, and probably as early as 1745. His wife Mary, or Molly, Sneden (1709-1810) ran the ferry to Dobbs Ferry. She lived to the ripe age of 101 years and 18 days and is buried at Palisades Cemetery. She and all her children except John were Tories. This location came to be known as Sneden's Landing as early as 1759. The orthography is confusing. Principal variants are: Sneeding, Sneydon, Snyden, Suyden, Sueden, and Snyding. At various times, the locality was called Rockland and Paramus.

David Cole, in his 1884 *History of Rockland County* gives the following information:

To protect the landing place at Sneden's the Americans erected a work, which was visited by a British spy on June 27th, 1781, and thus described: "It is a redoubt about a mile and half from the landing, on a very rough rocky height, picketted in all around with tops of trees and branches; no way to get in without climbing over; about four rods within this circle is a round breastwork running quite round the height, eight feet high, with a gate to pass in on the west side. Within that circle, about three rods, is another breastwork running round the top of the height, about the same height as the other, on which is wooden embrasures built, in which they have one piece of cannon on a travelling carriage. On the south side of the inward work a gate opens into the first breastwork. The rise of the height is so much as to cause the top of the first breastwork to be no higher than the bottom of the second. At this time it was commanded by a Lieutenant, two Sergeants, two Captains, and twenty-five men in the works.

At one time during the war Garret O'Blenis and a half-dozen comrades were watching a British vessel, which had anchored off Sneden's Landing—

now Palisades. At last their watch was rewarded by seeing a barge filled with men start for the shore. Concealing themselves behind the rocks, the Americans permitted the barge to approach within a few yards of the landing, and then fired into her. After the first surprise the enemy endeavored to force a landing, assisted by the guns of the ship. For a few moments the conflict was severe, but, unaware of the numerical strength of the shore party, the foe at length withdrew. The only man seriously wounded among the patriots was Garret O'Blenis, who had a ball pass through his right arm and completely through his body, smashing two ribs and perforating the right lung in its course. His wound was regarded as mortal, but, after several months' illness, he entirely recovered. (David Cole, *History of Rockland County*, N.Y.: J.B. Beers & Co., 1884.)

19.00 Dobbs Ferry
(population 10,353). Residential suburb in the Greenburg Hills on East shore. The original Indian name was Weec-ques-guck, or Wecquaskeck, meaning "place of the bark kettle." It was originally part of the Philipse Patent, but when the manor was confiscated and sold in 1785, the property here was acquired by Philip Livingston and two associates. By 1796, Livingston had sole possession. One of the earliest settlers was Jan Dobbs, a Swede from the Delaware, who established a ferry in 1698. In 1781, Washington established headquarters here and met with the count de Rochambeau to plan the Yorktown campaign, which ended the Revolution. Towards the end of the Revolution, the British fleet lay in these waters and in May of 1783 Sir Guy Carleton met here with Washington at the Van Brugh Livingston House to discuss plans for Bri-

tish evacuation of New York. A sloop of war then fired a seventeen gun salute, the first salute by Great Britain to the United States of America.

The oldest portion of the Van Brugh Livingston House was erected in 1690 by Frederick Philipse, 1st lord of the manor. In 1806, Philip Livingston made a large addition in the Federal Style. Another interesting building is the Zion Episcopal Church at Cedar and Main Streets, erected in 1834. Washington Irving was a Vestryman here from 1837 to 1843. It is built of stone. In 1854 the tower was heightened and mullions and buttresses added. Estherwood, now owned by the Masters School, is a large mansion, built around 1890 by James Jennings McComb, a wealthy New York merchant, in the French Rennaisance style, with turrets, carved balconies, and a glass conservatory. In the Victorian period, there was a popular summer hotel known as the *Glen Tower.*

19.50 Crumkill Creek to west

19.50 Salt Marsh to west

19.50 Tallman Mountain and Park to west
Also spelled Taulman.

19.50 Wickers Creek to east:
Derived from Indian Wysquaqua.

20.10 Ardsley-On-Hudson on east
A residential area formerly called Abbotsford after Sir Walter Scott's ersatz castle, where the great poet and novelist attempted to live like a laird despite his bankruptcy and to fulfill his dream of bourgeois romanticism. This image appealed to wealthy merchants of the late nineteenth century and many of them built imposing homes here in the Baronial style. Among

these imposing homes are Graytowers, or Belzover Castle, and Cottenet House. Cyrus West Field (1819-1892), who completed laying of the Atlantic cable after twelve years of effort, built a large mansion here in about 1860. This baronial approach is reflected in the Ardsley Club, built in monastic style, and the railroad station, which was built to harmonize with Stanford White's Casino, with its Tudor timbering. The casino was demolished in the 1930s to make way for an apartment complex. Nevis, the home of James Alexander Hamilton (1788-1878), third son of Alexander Hamilton, was named after his father's birthplace in the British West Indies. It was originally a simple Greek revival building with doric columns, but was extensively remodeled by Stanford White in 1889. It has an Early Republican garden. Mrs. T. Coleman DuPont gave the estate to Columbia University in 1934 for establishment of a horticultural and landscape architecture center. There are over 2,640 trees of 56 varieties and 1,928 ornamental shrubs on the property making it one of the largest arboretums in the United States. It now houses the Columbia University Nevis Laboratoreis for Physics Research.

20.80 Sparkill Creek on west
The name is a redundancy, as "kill" means "creek." It was formerly called Tappan Slote, as was the village at its mouth. It rises in Sparkill Brook in Rockleigh and Cooper Pond in Northvale, both in New Jersey. Thence it flows northeast into the Hudson through a gap between Tallman and Nebo Mountains. This is the only sea-level gap in the Palisades range between Bay-

onne and Bear Mountain. Some geologists believe that Sparkill Creek and the Hackensack River once formed a secondary channel of the Hudson, flowing west of the Palisades. As the general level of the land rose, the waters of the Hudson receded, leaving only the present small creek, with no connection with the Hackensack. In 1841, the Erie Railroad took advantage of this natural gap to gain the Hudson without tunneling or going over the mountain. Ice was once cut from the creek just west of the Route 9W viaduct, where remains of dams and forms can still be seen.

20.80 Irvington-on-Hudson on east

(population 5,878). Area about 2000 acres. This land was originally part of the Philips manor. In later years it belonged to Justus Dearman and was called Dearman's Station. In 1850, streets were laid out and parcels sold at auction, and, in 1854, the name Irvington was adopted in honor of its most famous resident, Washington Irving. Ironically, Irving's home, Sunnyside, was pulled into the incorporation of adjacent Tarrytown in 1870, prior to the incorporation of the village of Irvington in 1872. In the mid-nineteenth century the entire Irvington-Ardsley area was known as Abbotsford.

Early settlers included Wolfert Ecker, (sometimes spelled Acker), Barent Dutcher, Captain John Buckout (who lived to the age of 103), and Captain Jan Harmse. The Harmes-Conklin-Odell Tavern on Broadway was built in 1690. During the Revolution this was neutral ground. British troops under Gen. Sir John Vaughan (famous for burning Kingston) camped near the Odell Tavern in 1776. The British burned the Wolfert Ecker home, which then belonged to Jacob Van Tassel. It was a favorite hangout of the patriots and a real thorn in the side of the British. This house was later made famous by Washington Irving under the name Wolfert's Roost. He later purchased the house in 1835 and

rebuilt it into the famous Sunnyside. This house is now within the Tarrytown corporate limits.

The Abbotsford area attracted wealthy and romantic people who proceeded to act out their architectural dreams. Francois Cottenet built a two and one-half story French Victorian chateau named Nuits in 1892. It was built with stone from a quarry at Nuits on the Cote d'Or in France. Strawberry Hill, a stone mansion in Norman Victorian Gothic style on North Broadway was built in 1849. This was named after the home of English novelist Horace Walpole. Another extravaganza was the Octagon House built in 1860 on West Clinton Avenue by wealthy meat packer Philip Armour. This was built according to the ideas of Orson Fowler who, around 1849, wrote articles extolling this type of design. In more recent years it has belonged to the late well-known Hudson River historian Carl Carmer. He believed the house was haunted. It features a great octagonal dome and cupola. Louis Comfort Tiffany lived in Irvington and, about 1870, built some cottages for his employees that are still standing. They are two story stone with Mansard roofs. He also designed the stained-glass windows in the Presbyterian Church on Broadway.

The various developments were all called parks. They included: Spiro Park, Ardsley Park, Joffrey Park, Matthiessen Park, and Barney Park. Very exclusive cooperative apartments, known as the Half-Moon Apartments were built in Ardsley in the 1930s. An interesting building on Broadway is Villa Lewaro. It was built in 1917, at the cost of $350,000, by Sarah J. Walker, a black woman who had amassed a fortune from the sale of a patent hair straightener. It was designed in Anglo-Palladian style by Vertner Tandy, the first black admitted to the American Institute of Architects. It was also built despite the strong opposition of the wealthy white neighbors. However, Madame Walker soon won their admiration and respect, as she was a real lady. The unusual name was coined by her friend Enrico Caruso, from the name of her daughter, A'Lelia Walker Robinson. Today it is the Anna E. Poth Home for Convalescent and Aged Members of the Companions of the Forest in America. Among the other prominent residents of the area were Cyrus W. Field, layer of the Atlantic Cable; Chauncey M. Depew, president of the New York Central Railroad, United States senator, and celebrated wit and after-dinner speaker; Amzi Lorenzo Barber, the asphalt magnate; and Albert Bierstadt, the noted landscape painter. Other interesting local structures include: Abercombie House (1850), carpenter Gothic; Buckout-Jewell House (pre-Revolutionary); Eliphalet Wood House (1869), Victorian with tower; Irvington Presbyterian Church (1869), Romanesque by James Renwick; and St. Barnabas Episcopal Church (1853), stone Gothic. The Brisbane-Walker Building, three-story stone, Beaux Arts, was designed early in the century by Stanford White for the Cosmopolitan Magazine. It can be seen from the river. Just below it, near the railroad, at the foot of Main Street, is the red brick factory of Lord & Burnham, one of the first manufacturers of greenhouses and glass, boilers, heaters, and other horticultural equipment.

21.20 Erie Pier to west

A mile-long pier built in 1841 as a railroad and steamboat terminal by the Erie Railroad. The pier is no longer used by the railroad. Lamont Observatory keeps its oceanographic ship moored here. There is a small lighthouse.

21.25 Piermont to west

In early days, this village was known as Tappan Slote or Tappan Landing and sometimes as Bogerttown. Prior to the Revolution, a grist mill was built here, and a store was operated by Abraham Mabie, who kept it until the close of that war. About 1783, the store was acquired by Major Abraham Taulman, who managed it until his death in

1835. This was the first port of entry in Rockland County and an important point of access to the interior. During this period, the name of Tappan fell into disuse, and the place came to be called either Taulman's Landing, or simply The Landing. Besides the Taulmans, other prominent early families included the Haddocks and Myers, and an industrious negro named John Moore who built a saw mill. In 1815, William Ferdon built a woolen mill which spun yarn and manufactured blankets. The growth of Piermont depended almost entirely upon the opening of the Erie Railroad in 1841. It served as eastern terminus, and there were locomotive and car works here. Eventually two round houses, a machine, car and paint shop, foundry, and planing mills were built.

The railroad facilities eventually covered four acres. This was the period of Piermont's greatest prosperity. In 1860, its population reached 2,426. The village of Piermont ws organized in 1850. The name Piermont was coined in 1839 by Eleazor Lord, the first president of the Erie. It combined the name of the long pier with the mountainous nature of the surrounding country. At this time, Sparkill came into use for the creek instead of Tappan Slote. In 1852, the directors of the Erie obtained permission to relocate their terminal at Pavonia, and Piermont fell into an irremediable decline. The principal industry here today is the paper plant of Clevepac Corporation, near the former Erie terminus. There are many quaint old corners and charming vistas. The Arie Smith, or Onderdonck, House near the upper landing was often fired upon by British ships during the Revolution. Paradise Lane has several mid-nineteenth century homes with good potential for restoration. Castlewood, the 1850 home of Eleazor Lord, and the 1840 Verdon-Blauvelt house are also notable.

21.25 Tappan.

This is inland from Piermont. This village is chiefly notable as the place of the imprisonment, trial, and execution of Major John André. George Washington made his headquarters in the Johannes DeWindt House (1700), which is now maintained as the Masonic Washington Shrine. Major André was incarcerated in the Mabie House Tavern, built in 1755 and now known as the '76 House, (still a restaurant). Washington was in Tappan from August 8 to August 23 in 1780. André's trial or court martial ran from September 28 to October 2, 1780, on which date he was executed.

21.45 Tappan Zee.

We are now in the Tappan Zee, which is 12 miles long by 2 to 2.4 miles wide. The bottom is composed of shells, mud, and glacial rubble, and bedrock is 500 feet farther down. There are oyster seedbeds here. The name Tappan Zee is derived as follows: Tappan is the Indian word for "cold springs" and Zee is Dutch for "sea," a term they freely gave to any large body of water. Some Mohegan Indians dwelt on the eastern shore, but the western was inhabited by the Tappan and Saulrikan subtribes of the Unami Lenni Lenapes. The name was sometimes corrupted to Topan.

In his *History of Rockland County*, David Cole tells of military activity in this area:

As early as September 8th, 1776, Washington ordered the removal of his sick to the neighborhood of Tappan. Later, when General Scott encamped in

Haverstraw to protect the stores which were there, he ordered ten tons of lead moved from Tappan to Major Smith's at Upper Nyack—the property now [1884] *owned by Joseph Hilton. When Colonel Tyler had ceased to harry the Tories in Orangetown for a moment, and had withdrawn to Ramapo, Abraham Post, of Tappan, was ordered to remove eleven chests of armorer's tools, with bellows, anvils, &c, to the store of Abraham Mabie at the Slote. In 1780, General Greene had his headquarters in the stone house near the old road, which led from Sneden's Landing to Orangeburg, and which is now occupied by E. N. Taft and owned by Wm. Peet. . . .*

The River shore from Taulman's Point at Piermont, north, was much exposed to the depredations of foraging forces from the enemy's ships, and the chief duty of Colonel Hay and the Minute Men was to guard this long and exposed line. On the first appearance of the British vessels, on July 12th, 1776, the enemy made two attempts to land at Nyack, but were repulsed through the watchfulness of Colonel Hay's men, who, by reason of their small number—only 400—and the distance to be patroled, were on duty night and day. On July 16th the fleet sailed up as far as Haverstraw and anchored off Kiers' landing, but here, too, their attempts to land were prevented. So deficient was the guard in the necessary munitions of war that Hays appealed for powder and ball to supply his men. Fortunately General George Clinton was able to reinforce him at the time, and shortly after he was sent twenty pounds of powder. For nine days the vessels remained off Haverstraw, but only once succeeded in obtaining provisions from the west shore. On that occasion they burned the house of a man named Halstead and took his pigs.

At last, on July 25th, the vessels sailed slowly down the river, anchoring for a time off Teller's, now Croton Point, to obtain some provisions from the

Westchester shore. But their presence had roused the spirit of battle in the patriots, and on August 3rd, 1776, the American galleys, Lady Washington, Spitfire, Whiting, and Crown, under Benjamin Tupper, attacked their vessels, Phenix, Captain Parker and Rose, Captain Wallace, off Tarrytown and fought them for two hours. (Ibid.)

This is perhaps a good time to tell the old Dutch Storm Ship legend as told by Washington Irving. This mysterious ship was often supposed to have been sighted in the Tappan Zee:

The Storm Ship legend harks back to the early days before the English came to bedevil the Dutch calm on the river. Then a mysterious ship, flying the Netherlands color is said to have been seen entering the river with sails bellied by winds nowhere else apparent, riding forward against a strong ebb tide. The astonished burghers signaled a command to her to stop and show her papers; but the ship sailed on. Then a gun at the Battery sent a ball thundering toward her. But her hull did not stop the ball, nor did the ball check her course. On she sped past the Palisades, straight up the Tappan Sea, around the frowning heights of Verdrietege Hook, until she disappeared from sight and for ever. She was never seen to pass down-river and out to sea. But that is not the last of her here, as many Tappan fisherman has attested, for she is the Storm Ship, says Bacon, that makes mysterious journeys, never heeding shoal or headland, tacking when the wind is fair and running free in the teeth of a gale, with never a concession to any weather that mortals give heed to. Into the moonlight she comes suddenly from some unknown quarter and as suddenly, while the eye is fixed upon her, vanishes completely as a bubble that floats for a moment where a wave has broken, and then, in a twinkling, is dissipated. (Tales from Irving, New York: Bryant Literary Union, 1902, p. 30.)

There is another legend of a certain Rambout Van Dam of the Bronx who, after carousing all one Sunday morning at a party in the Rockland Hills, near Piermont, swore to row all the way back to Spuyten Duyvil, and was drowned by the devil for his blasphemy. Clearly this, and the legend of Anthony Van Corlear at Spuyten Duyvil, all hark back to the old Dutch legend of the Flying Dutchman—Vanderdecken—whose story is used as the basis of Richard Wagner's opera *Der Fliegende Hollander.* It is interesting to see how the Dutch colonists fleshed out the old legend to suit their new surroundings.

21.45 Sunnyside on east:

The home of Washington Irving from 1835 until his death in 1859. It was built by Wolfert Ecker sometime in the 17th century and was owned by Jacob Van Tassel during the Revolution. Irving loved the old house, which he called Wolfert's Roost, and remodeled it extensively between 1835 and 1837. He turned the old farmhouse into a romantic dwelling "made up of gable ends . . . full of angles and corners as an old cocked hat."

It combines features of English, Spanish, Dutch, and Hudson River Gothic architecture into a happy and very personal blend, reflecting the personality of its owner. Irving never married, but he lived here with his brother Ebenezer and his nieces. He entertained greatly and Oliver Wendell Holmes, William Makepeace Thackary, and Louis Napoleon were among his guests. He took meticulous interest and care of the grounds. The study, in particular, reflects the great author's personality. The house has been restored by Sleepy Hollow Restorations and is maintained as a museum. I recommend it very highly. Formerly some New York Central local trains used to stop at Sunnyside.

21.50 Mount. Nebo to west
(elevation 672 ft.).

21.50 Rockland Cemetery on upper slopes of Mount. Nebo.
(For further details see article on west side road route, mile 21.30.)

22.00 Grand-View-On-Hudson to west:
residential community, formerly served by the Northern Railroad of New Jersey, Nyack Branch.

22.00 Clausland Mountain to west:
550 foot elevation. The name is a corruption of "Jan Claus's land—an early name for Greenbush, to the west of the mountain.

22.25 Requa Landing to east

22.25 Lyndhurst to east

Lyndhurst is one of the finest and most important private estates extant along the Hudson River. Along with Sunnyside, Philipsburg Manor, Van Cortlandt Manor, Boscobel, and the Vanderbilt Mansion at Hyde Park, it serves as excellent documentation of both a period and style of architecture and decoration. Lyndhurst has been restored by the National Trust for Historic Preservation in a style reconciling the contributions of the three families who lived in it—the Pauldings, the Merritts, and the Goulds.

Lyndhurst is a Gothic Revival residence in the Pointed style. It was designed in 1838 by Alexander Jackson Davis (1803-1892), who was the greatest exponent of the Gothic Revival style in America, for Gen. William Paulding. Paulding was a former New York congressman and ex-mayor of New York City. He lived at Lyndhurst with his son Philip Rhinelander Paulding.

In 1864, Lyndhurst was purchased by a New York City merchant named George Merritt. He retained Alexander Jackson Davis to further enlarge the house. During the 1865 enlargement, the house lost its symmetrical layout and became asymmetrical, which was more typical of the Greek Revival style. At this time, a tower was built on the west and a porte cochère on the east, with a new large wing to the north which almost doubled the size of the house. The house was built of Sing Sing marble. The interior details such as the ribbed and vaulted ceilings, the stained glass windows, parquetry floors, door and window trip, mantels, and even the furniture, were all designed by Davis and presented a unified conception. The great taste-maker of that time, Andrew Jackson Downing, wrote of Lyndhurst: "The eye is struck by the picturesque outline of towers, turrets, gables, and pinnacles; and with the pleasing variety afforded by the windows decorated with mullions and tracery."

In 1880, Lyndhurst was purchased by the railroad financier Jay Gould. He and his daughters, Helen and Anna, respected the integrity of Davis's design and embellished the property with objects d'art and established a library. In 1964, Anna, Duchess of Talleyrand-Périgord, left Lyndhurst to the National Trust to be operated and maintained in memory of her parents as a non-profit museum.

The mansion is not the only attraction at Lyndhurst. In 1870, George Merritt had a gigantic greenhouse built for him by Lord and Burnham of neighboring Irvington. It was modeled after Roulault's Conservatory in the Jardin des Plantes (1833) in Paris. The cupola was reminiscent of John Nash's Royal Pavilion of 1818 at Brighton, and Samuel Sloan's Longwood at Natches, Mississippi, sometimes known as "Nutt's Folly," of 1861. The greenhouse was 380 feet long. The central section was 95 feet wide and 80 feet long, and the wings on the east and west measured 148 feet each and were 36 feet wide. A 100-foot high tower rose from the dome of the central section and was topped by a glass cupola 25 feet in diameter. Facilities included reception rooms, sleeping quarters, billiard room, bowling alley, gymnasium, carpenter shop, and seed rooms. In the cellar were coal rooms, boiler rooms, water tanks, store rooms for materials and potting tools, and a mushroom cellar.

The tower was surmounted by a bulbous, Saracenic, onion dome-shaped cage, used as an aviary. Shortly after Jay Gould purchased the property in 1880 this Arabian Nights creation burned. Gould had Lord and Burnham reconstruct the greenhouse, but without the Moorish tower. Gould specialized in the growing of orchids. The greenhouse is presently dilapidated, but restoration work is under way.

23.10 Tappan Hill to east
(elevation 400 feet).
23.20 Tappan Zee Bridge.

This bridge carries the mainline of the New York State Thruway between Tarrytown and South Nyack. It is one of the largest bridges in the United States; total length is 15,764 feet, or almost 3 miles. The main structure is a Cantilever through truss span of 1,212 feet (2 cantilevers @ 340 ft and 532 ft suspended span), with anchor spans of 602 ft. The remainder of the west end consists of conventional steel stringer design and the east end of deck truss design. There are 153,900 cubic yards of concrete, 14,610 tons of reinforcing steel and 59,250 tons of structural steel (including railing). A total of 132,050 square yards or 27¼ acres of pavement comprises the roadway. This required 714,285 cubic feet or 26,455 cubic yards of concrete. Some 42,702 cubic yards were used in the eight foundation cassions alone. In the bridge foundations, a total of 1,602,200 feet (303 miles) of timber piles were used, as well as 330,500 feet (62.5 miles) of steel "H" piles and 33,400 feet (6.3 miles) of 30-inch steel pipe piles filled with concrete.

The bridge's roadway comprises six lanes, three in each direction separated by a 10-foot center mall, which can be used for emergency parking except around the curve on the westerly end where 3,233 feet of median barrier has been installed.

Overall width of the structure is ninety feet between railings, with each roadway thirty-seven feet wide. An emergency walk three feet wide runs along each side of the bridge. The height of the bridge pavement above the river at the center of the main span is 157.3 feet; the clearance from the river to the bottom of the steel is a minimum of 138 feet in the channel, and the height of the two main towers above the river is 293 feet. In 1975, a total of 25,000,000 vehicles crossed the bridge. Peak capacity is estimated at 27,000,000 per year. The structure cost $80,800,000. The first test borings were sunk in June 1951, and actual construction begun in March of 1952. The bridge opened in on December 15, 1955.

Designers were Madigan-Hyland consulting engineers. Major contractors were: American Bridge Division-U.S. Steel Corporation, Merritt, Chapman and Scott, Garafano and Eyclid, and Construction Aggregates Corp.

One of the unique features of the bridge is the use of eight concrete caissons supported on steel piles driven to rock, which serve as buoyant underwater foundations to support approximately seventy per cent of the structure's dead weight. The largest of these caissons is half the size of a city block and weighs 15,000 tons. The two caissons supporting the main piers measure 190 x 100 x 40 feet. The concrete caissons were poured in molds at Grassy Point, above Haverstraw, and floated downriver into place.

While the bridge is an engineering masterpiece, the writer cannot help but feel that it is unfortunately situated and destroys one of the finest water vistas in the world.

23.20 Carroll Castle to east.
Prominent on small hill south of Hackley Hill, this castle with

crenellated towers now serves as offices for the Axe-Houghton investment group. Built in 1900.

23.25 Hackley Hill to east
(elevation 450 feet).

23.50 The Bight to west:
an old name for a small cove.

23.60 Cornelison Point on west.

23.60 South Nyack on west.
The earliest settlers were John Claesen Kuyper and Theunis Roelofse Van Houten, who settled here in 1686. The Michael Cornelison House dating from 1770 was often fired upon by British ships, and was briefly occupied by the enemy early in the war. The area is now entirely residential in character.

24.00 Tarrytown on east

(population 11,115). There was formerly a ferry here to Nyack. This area was originally part of the Philips Manor. In later times, the Beekmans were the large landowners in the vicinity. Incorporated in 1870, the town's famous residents have included Commodore Oliver Hazard Perry (1785-1819), the hero of the battle of Lake Erie in the War of 1812; his brother Commodore Matthew Calbraith Perry (1794-1853), who opened up Japan to United States trade in 1853 and was an early advocate of naval steamships; and General John C. Fremont (1813-1890), the "pioneer pathfinder of the West."

There are two theories of how Tarrytown got its name. The more prosaic, and more likely, theory is that it derives from the Dutch word "tarwe," which means "wheat," which was grown here. Washington Irving would have us believe that it got its name because the local farmers, when they went to market here, would tarry at the local taverns. Who knows! Maybe Irving was correct.

Marymount College (for Catholic women) is located here as was the famous Miss Mason's Castle School for Girls, which operated from 1891 to 1933

in a crenelated castle built as a private home in 1856 and razed in 1944. Of particular architectural and historic interest is Christ Church on Broadway at Elizabeth Street. It is a small brick church built in 1838. Washington Irving worshiped here from 1843 till his death in 1859. He was a warden, and his funeral was held here. The Warner Library on North Broadway was built in 1928 in the Beaux Arts style. It has a frieze, decorated cornice, formal portico, and arched windows set in recessed panels. The massive cast bronze bas-relief doors were taken from a Renaissance Italian baptistry.

On September 23, 1780, a most significant event in American history took place on North Broadway when John Paulding, David Williams, and Isaac Van Wart captured Major André. Wallace Bruce, in his *Guide To The Hudson* tells the following story:

The following quaint ballad-verses on the young hero give a realistic touch to one of the most providential occurrences in our history:

> *He with a scouting party*
> *Went down to Tarrytown,*
> *Where he met a British officer,*
> *A man of high renown,*
> *Who says unto these gentlemen,*
> *"You're of the British cheer,*
> *I trust that you can tell me*
> *If there's any danger near?"*

> *Then up stept this young hero,*
> *John Paulding was his name,*
> *"Sir, tell us where you're going*
> *And also whence you came?"*
> *"I bear the British flag, sir;*
> *I've a pass to go this way,*
> *I'm on an expedition,*
> *And have no time to stay.*

Young Paulding, however, thought that he had plenty of time to linger until he examined his boots, wherein he found the papers (plans of the fortifications at West Point), and, when offered ten guineas by André, if he would allow him to pursue his journey, replied: "If it were ten thousand guineas you could not stir one step."

Young André was very much of an aristocrat and, while stationed down in New York, had written a long satiric doggerel poem entitled "The Cow Chase," concerning an episode near Bulls Ferry, New Jersey, and mocking the American patriots, and their leader, General Anthony Wayne. It closed with the following verse:

*And now I've closed my epic strain,
I tremble as I show it,
Lest this same warrio-drover, Wayne,
Should ever catch the poet.*

The "Cow Chase" was given wide circulation. When André was captured by the Americans, some anonymous wag wrote the following verse, which was widely sung:

*When the epic strain was sung
The poet by his neck was hung—
And to his cost he finds too late
The dung-born tribe decides his fate.*

(Bruce, *Hudson by Daylight,*
pp. 88-96)

24.10 Chevrolet Motors assembly plant to east.
A Maxwell plant until 1916, this is now one of the largest assembly plants in the east.

24.20 André Brook to east.

24.25 Tarrytown Lighthouse to east.
Its ironclad tower was completed in 1883.

24.30 Kingsland or Beekman's Point to east.

24.50 Nyack to west

(population 6,659). This residential village was incorporated in 1833. Claes Jansen Kuyper von Purmarent obtained a New Jersey patent for two tracts in this area in 1671. It was later settled by his son Cornelius Cuyper. The first recorded settler was Harman Tallman in 1675. His father, Douwe Harmanszen Tallman, joined him sometime betwen 1678 and 1686. Another early settler was Michael Cornelison. The Salisbury House on Piermont Avenue dates from 1770.

During the Revolution, Nyack saw some interesting skirmishing. The following extract is from David Cole's *History of Rockland County.*

Nyack, then but a hamlet of perhaps a dozen houses, became, before the end of the war, an object of the enemy's bitter aversion. This was partly due to those patriotic actions of its inhabitants, which ended in the repulsion more than once of their forces when they attempted to land for fresh provisions or water; partly because it was a rendezvous for the whale boat fleet, which patroled the river, and partly because of the residence at this place of Henry Palmer who had rendered himself obnoxious to the British.

Captain Palmer had owned a vessel and been employed in the carrying trade for one of the largest firms in New York, before the Revolution. When the news of the Battle of Bunker Hill reached that city, he was offered great financial advantages to serve the cause of the King but refused absolutely. Shortly after he conveyed two cargoes of arms and ammunition, which had been seized by the Sons of Liberty, from New York to the camp of the Continental Army. New York soon became uncomfortable for this patriot, and he removed with his family to a house, which formerly stood in Upper Nyack, on the east side of Broadway, opposite the old mountain road, by Garret E. Green's residence.

Owing to these causes, the British vessels, whenever they passed up the river, greeted the residents of the Nyack valley with a shotted salute from their guns. For their protection, those residents erected an earth work on the land east of the Methodist Church and just north of Depew Avenue, which covered the first dock in the village; while the section known as Upper Nyack, was defended by a swivel mounted on Major John L. Smith's place, and a company of Minute Men, under his and his brother— Captain Auri Smith's command.

As soon as hostilities had begun in this Colony the Shore Guard was placed on duty; this following order governing those stationed at Nyack.

Haverstraw, October 16th, 1776. General orders for the commanding officers at the place called the Hook.

Guards to mount daily at 4 or 5 o'clock in the afternoon, with sentries fixed as the commanding officer sees expedient. No soldier to fire a gun unless a sentry after hailing a craft or person three times, or at the enemy, or on an alarm. On every alarm, twenty hands to be sent to the commanding officer with intelligence. No person to pass without a permit from some commanding officer, or the committee from whence he came. No craft to be taken without liberty from the officer of the party of the place where said craft is. No liquor to be sold after 7 o'clock at night unless to a traveller, and none to be sold to any person in liquor. No sentry to leave his post until relieved. The commanding officer at the Hook to consult with the Major of the Riflemen, at New York, about the countersign. These orders to be read morning and evening to the guards until further orders.

A. Hawkins Hay,
Commanding Officer.

In October 1776, the enemy attempted to land at Nyack, but were repulsed by the Shore Guard, not however till their cannon balls had marked Sarvent's house. In December of the same year, they effected a foot-hold and, besides looting a house, took off some cattle. In the summer of the following year—1777 —two boats attempted to land at the present Piermont, at the point now known as the upper dock, at daybreak. After a sharp conflict with the Shore Guard they were repulsed with three killed. Several of the Shore Guard were wounded, but none fatally. (Cole, *History of Rockland County*.)

During the 19th century, Nyack was a resort. Popular hotels of that era were the Mansion House, Pavilion, Clarendon, Smithsonian, Tappan Zee House, and Prospect House, formerly called the Palmer House. Many of these hotels doubled as young ladies' finishing schools during the winter.

Through the years, principal industries have included the manufacture of organs, sewing machines, and leather goods. There was a ferry to Tarrytown until 1941. Nyack was formerly the terminus of the Northern Railroad of New Jersey.

24.50 Pocantico River to the east.

Also formerly called Gory Creek. The present name is derived from the Indian "pocanteco" or "weehkanteco," meaning "deep woods." It rises in the Pocantico Hills near the large private estate of the Rockefeller family named Kykuit, which means "lookout point." It then flows southwest through Sleepy Hollow and empties into the Hudson through a small cove, now largely silted up into marshland, just below the mill dam erected by Frederick Philipse I.

This area was part of the Philipse Manor, and the upper mill was built here in about 1680 by Frederick Philipse I. He erected a dam and a mill which ground corn and wheat. Sloops anchored just below the dam, and the location also became an important trading post. Shortly after settlement, there were two hundred settlers, making up about forty families. The manor house was also built to serve as a fortress. It was built of rough-hewn blocks of native stone and fieldstone, mortared with river-bank clay. It was whitewashed. It had leaded glass casement windows with heavy wooden shutters. The dam served to create a millpond to create water power and also allowed the cove to silt up to create marshland for the growing of salt hay, then an important commodity. Frederick Philipse I also built a church in 1697 or 1699. Adolph Philipse inherited the upper mills in 1702, and they passed to Frederick Philipse II in 1750. His son Frederick Philipse III was a Royalist and his property was confiscated and sold at auction. The upper mill property was purchased in 1784 by Gerard G. Beekman Jr. After the death of his widow in 1822 the property passed through many hands until it was purchased by John D. Rockefeller Jr., in 1937, and the present restoration work was subsequently commenced by the Sleepy Hollow Restorations."

It has been completely re-.stored and operates as a museum. A visit is highly recommended, as it gives one an excellent idea of early life along the river.

24.75 Philipse Manor to east:
The name refers to a railroad station and a 20th-century residential neighborhood. This is officially known as North Tarrytown. The large and beautiful Sleepy Hollow Cemetery is located here, with the graves of such notables as Washington Irving, Carl Schurz, Robert G. Ingersoll, Andrew Carnegie, and Whitelaw Reid.

25.25 Upper Nyack to west.
This was also known in Revolutionary times as Sarvent's Land-ing. There is a "smuggler's tunnel" running from the river bank to Broadway, built about 1750. However, it is possible that this was actually built for use by the Shore Guard during the Revolution.

Toward the close of July, 1777, the British sent a galley ashore to destroy a sloop which was moored to a dock at Abram Sarvent's place in Upper Nyack. To oppose this endeavor, Henry Palmer, Abram Sarvent, Cornelius Cuyper, Peter Freeland and Major Smith hastily collected, and concealed themselves in a quarry near the dock. Waiting till the enemy was within safe range, the patriots opened fire. The galley was at once put about and pulled out of gun shot for a time. A second attempt to force a landing, though assisted by the ship's guns, ended in failure. A third attempt was made, but the loss of the British was too great for further hope of success. The galley was then pulled up opposite Henry Palmer's house, and fire opened against that building from the bow carronade. So accurate was the aim of the gunners, that every shot struck the house or tore up the earth in the door yard. Mrs. Palmer, fearing each moment that a ball would pass through the building, took her infant in her arms and, creeping alongside the house, till out of range, at length crossed the mountain and found a safe asylum at the house of a friend. In her flight, a ball struck the bank so close to the fugitive as to spatter dirt over herself and child.

The morning after the fight at Sarvent's Landing, the bodies of nine British sailors floated ashore and were buried by the Americans.

9. Nyack/White Plains

On another occasion Captain Palmer with a few comrades fired into a British vessel which was becalmed and floating with the tide. Thirty-six of the enemy were killed or wounded in this slaughter while of Palmer's force but one man was injured. He was wounded by a splinter from the rock behind which he was concealed.

Dreadful warfare did the patriots wage against the enemy's ships with the swivel, which was mounted east of Broadway, in Upper Nyack, opposite the residences of Joseph Hilton and S. C. Eaton, on property now [1884] belonging to Wilson Defendorf. At best this famous gun would barely carry a ball a half mile, and as the ships kept in the channel, some two and a half miles away, no very great injury was done by this long range shooting. Once however, during the war, two boats attempted to land at this shore for water and the Shore Guard opened so hot a fire with muskets and swivel, that one boat's crew surrendered at once while the other, braving the fire, pulled for the ships. The captured crew was sent to Tappan. (Cole, History of Rockland County.)

The Old Stone Church on Broadway, oldest in Rockland County, dates from February 1813. It is built of red sandstone. Founders were William Palmer, Nicholas Williamson, and John Green. Originally Methodist Episcopal, it is now Interdenominational. Upper Nyack is a residential community with many large fine homes. Nyack Beach State Park is located at the end of Broadway in the north end of town.

26.50 Verdrietege Hook to west.
Triassic red sandstone cliffs 730 feet high. There was formerly quarrying here prior to creation of the Palisades Interstate Park, which has subsequently acquired much of the area and developed it for recreation. The name derives from the Dutch and means "tedious hook," probably because it took so long for sailing craft to pass it. As there is no single clearly defined point, it was also called Point-No-Point. Still another early name applied to the point was Calico Hook. Much of the property in this area once belonged to Isaac I. Blauvelt.

26.50 Ball Mountain
(650 foot elevation): slightly to the west of the southern end of Verdrietege Hook.

27.00 Hook Mountain to west:
the northern part of Verdrietege Hook, also sometimes called Diedrick Hook.

27.50 Scarborough to east.
A railroad station and a fine residential area within the corporate limits of the town of Briarcliff Manor.

27.60 Kemeyst Cove to east.
28.10 Sparta to east:
section within the town of Ossining, with many fair to well-preserved buildings from the early to mid-nineteenth century.

28.50 Sing Sing State Prison to east.
The location of New York State's famous electric chair, it presently contains 2,719 prison cells.

On the southern borders of the village of Sing Sing (Ossining) is a rough group of small hills, called collectively Mount Pleasant. They are formed of dolo-

mitic, or white coarse-grained marble, of excellent quality and almost inexhaustible quantity, cropping out from a thin soil in many places. At the foot of Mount Pleasant, on the shore of the river, is a large prison for men, with a number of work-shops and other buildings, be-longing to the State of New York. A little way up the slope is the prison for women, a very neat and substantial building, with a fine colonnade on the river front. These prisons were built by convicts about thirty years ago, when there were two establishments of the kind in the State, one in the city of New York, and the other at Auburn, in the interior. A new system of prison discipline had been adopted. Instead of the old sys-tem of indolent, solitary con-finement, the workhouse feature was combined with incarceration in separate cells at night. They were made to work diligently all day, but in perfect silence, no recognition by word, look, or gesture, being allowed among them. The adoption of this sys-tem, in 1823, rendered the prison accommodation insuffi-cient, and a new establishment was authorized in 1824. Mount Pleasant, near Sing Sing, was purchased, and in May, 1826, Captain Lynds, a farm agent of the Auburn prison, proceeded with one hundred felons from that establishment to erect the new penitentiary. They quarried and wrought diligently among the marble rocks at Mount Pleas-ant, and the prison for men was completed in 1829, when the convicts in the old State prison in the city of New York were removed to it.

It had eight hundred cells, but these were found to be too few, and in 1831 another story was added to the building, and with it two hundred more cells, making one thousand in all, the present number. More are needed, for the number of convicts in the men's prison, at the beginning of 1861, was a little more than thirteen hundred. In the prison for women there were only one hundred cells, while the number of convicts was one hundred and fifty at that time.

The ground occupied by the prisons is about ten feet above highwater mark. The main build-ing, in which are the cells, is four hundred and eighty feet in length, forty-four feet in width, and five stories in height. Be-tween the outside walls and the cells there is a space of about twelve feet, open from floor to roof. A part of it is occupied by a series of galleries, there being a row of one hundred cells to each story on both fronts, and backing each other. Between the prison and the river are the several workshops, in which var-ious trades are carried on. In front of the prison for women is the guard-house, where arms and instructions are given out to thirty-one guardsmen every morning. Between the guard-house and the prison the Hud-son River Railway passes, partly through two tunnels and a deep trench. Upon the highest points of Mount Pleasant are guard-houses, which overlook the quarries and other places of industrial operations.

In the prison for men, and in the workshops, everything is car-ried on with the most perfect order; every kind of labour, the *meals, the religious exercises in the chapel, are all conducted according to the most rigid rules. The discipline is consequently quite perfect.* Reformation, *not merely* punishment, *is the great aim, and the history of the prison attests to the success of the effort. Severe punishments are becoming more and more rare, and the terrible Shower Bath, which has been so justly condemned by the humane, is now seldom used, and then in the presence of the prison physician. Only when all other means for forcing obedience have failed, is this horrid punishment inflicted. It is admitted, I believe, that the Mount Pleasant or Sing Sing prison is one of the best conducted penitentiaries in the world.* (Lossing, *The Hudson,* pp. 298-300.)—1866.

28.65 Rockland Lake Landing to west:

previously called Hunters Landing, Slaughter's Landing and Slauter's Landing. Originally this served the back country much as Huyler's and Sneden's Landings. In 1711, John Slaughter purchased a tract of land in the Clove, at the present Rockland Lake, and built a landing which bore his name until changed by Barmore, Felter & Co. in 1835.

In 1850, Francis Powley built a marine railway here to use for the construction and repair of vessels engaged here in the ice and quarry business. In 1872, John Mansfield established a stone-crusher which he later sold to M.M. Miranda. Around 1884, an average of from 75 to 90 vessels loads of crushed stone were shipped annually, and employment was given to from 25 to 65 men according to the demand. In 1873, James W. Smith fitted up a pleasure ground known as Sylvan Grove. The Knickerbocker Ice Company built a gravity railroad from Rockland Lake atop the cliffs to the landing in 1858. In the 1860s, this was the principal ice depot on the Hudson.

28.65 Rockland Lake to west:

atop Hook Mountain (elevation 300 feet). This is an irregular ellipse, half a mile in length and three quarters of a mile at its greatest width and covers about 500 acres. It is supplied by springs in its own bosom, and clear mountain brooks. It is the headwater of the Hackensack River, which was originally known as the Demarest Kill, after a family of early settlers. The Indian name was Quaspeck Pond; but the name Quaspeck and also Snedecker's Pond were used interchangeably until the formal adoption of the name Rockland Lake in 1835. A post office of the later name was opened in 1842.

In 1694 the Pond or Quaspeck Patent was granted to Jarvis Marshall and William Welch, "speculators." The southern end of the pond was settled by Germans about 1711, although a certain John Hutchins had settled here as early as 1700. John Slauter settled on the west side in 1711 and Tunis Snedeker at the northern end in 1731. In 1775, John Ryder settled at the northeastern corner and Hermanus Hoffman at the southeastern one.

The water is of singular purity and has long been recognized as producing good ice. In 1835 John J. Felter, John G. Perry, and Edward Felter cut a sloopload of ice from the lake and sold it at an almost clear profit in New York. In 1836, they formed the firm of Barmore, Felter & Co., with a capital of $2,000. They purchased Slaughter's Landing and soon built a gravity railroad to lower the ice to boats in the river. Business grew rapidly, and the firm soon evolved into the Knickerbocker Ice Company, which was still doing business in New York City in 1978. During the heyday of natural cut ice, this was the largest of many such firms doing business along the river, and they also had other tributary lakes and ice depots along the Hudson.

28.75 Rockland Lighthouse to west:

built to guide traffic to Rockland Lake Landing.

28.75 Ossining to east

(population 21,659): a large residential town and the site of Sing Sing Prison. The main portion of the village has an elevation of 100 ft. The name comes from the Indian 'Sink-Sink—also variously given as "Sin-Sing," "Sing-Sin," or "Sint-Sinck"— meaning "a stony place." Indeed, there are many stones here— mainly dolomitic marble. This is an excellent building material and formerly much was shipped from here. Also a great deal was burned to make builders lime. Other old spellings were: Cinque Singte, Cinque-single, Sinck Sinck, and Sin-sing. The name also applied to the brook which flows into the Hudson here. Silver was mined in the late eighteenth and early nineteenth centuries and copper was mined for a short time after 1820.

On August 24, 1685, Frederick Philipse purchased all the land along the Hudson River between the Pocantico and Croton Rivers from eight Indians—Weskenane, Keanarhan, Mamannane, Crawman, Wennicktanon, Weremenhore, Wappus and Aquaines—of the Sint-Sinck tribe. After the American Revolution, the Philipse lands were confiscated by the commissioners of forfeiture and sold off in much smaller freeholds, frequently to the former tenants of the patroon. At this period the locality was known as Hunter's Landing. The earliest settlement in the neighborhood was at Sparta, in the southern part of the present town, where there was a convenient natural dock. The southern portion of Ossining was known as Mount Pleasant.

The village of Sing Sing was incorporated in 1813. The Sing Sing prison was established in 1826. During the nineteenth century diverse manufacturing developed. The best known was the patent medicine works of Dr. Benjamin Brandreth, "the pill factory." Many Italian immigrants settled here to work in the marble quarries. In about 1900, many people were boycotting prison-made goods and mistook privately manufactured products made in the village of Sing Sing for prison-made merchandise. Naturally this hurt the local tradesmen. To end this confusion the name of the town was officially changed to Ossining in 1901, and the name Sing Sing applies only to the prison today. Ossining is the home of the Maryknoll Catholic Missions, which operates a large seminary and home for retired missioners. It is notable for its unique pagoda topped tower. The Maryknoll Fathers were particularly active in the Orient and today operate on a worldwide basis

Verplanck
Point
Verplanck
Tomkins Cove
Montrose
Quarry
Trailer Park
Cem
Junk Yard
Ten Eyck's Beach
Peekskill
Sea Plane Base
Greens
Cove
Park
Route of Colonial King's Ferry
STONY
POINT
STONY POINT
STATE PARK
Lighthouse
Stony Point
COUNTY
PARK
Water
Tanks
Montrose
Point
HEIGHTS
Hillside
Cem
Stony Point
Bay
Georges
Island
FRANKLIN D ROOSEVELT
VA HOSPITAL
Sewage
Disposal
Belfry
Cedar
Pond
Stony Point
Library
Immaculate Conception Sch
WESTCHESTER CO
ROCKLAND CO
Oscawana
Island
COUNTY PARK
Trailer
Park
Trailer
Park
Grassy
Point
Sewage
Disposal
WT
Bronk
CONVEYOR
St Gregory Barbarigo
Sch
WT
Sewage
Disposal
WT
Sewage Disposal
BM
13
State Rehabilitation
Hospital
North Garnerville
Sch
Cem
Junk
Yard
Samsondale
BAGAN
Junk
Yard
WT
Powerplant
Creek
West Haverstraw
Sewage
Disposal
Bowline
Point
Garnerville
Miniscongo
HUDSON
Union Free
Sch
HAVERSTRAW
BM 198
GURNEE AVE
St Peters
Sch
HAVERSTRAW
HAVERST
Little Tor
SOUTH
Cemetery
Water
Tank
Sewage
Disposal
BAY
HIGH
TOR
STATE
PARK
Parking
Swimming
Pool
MOUNTA

with particular activity in South America. Their Bishop Walsh was known for his long imprisonment by the Chinese Communist Government.

28.80 Sing Sing Brook to east:
also known as Sint-sinck Brook and Kil Brook. (Note the use of only one "l" in Kil.)

29.50 North Park to east:
a residential area.

29.50 Crawbuckie Point to east:
former base of fishing operations.

29.50 Teller's Point to east.
This is the dividing point between the Tappan Zee to the south and Haverstraw Bay to the north. Strictly speaking, Teller's Point is the southward-pointing tip of the larger Croton Point. It separates Croton Bay from the main channel of the Hudson. The present name comes from William Teller who purchased the point from the Indians for a barrel of rum and twelve blankets. It was also formerly called Sarah's Point in honor of his wife. The Indian name for the location was "Senasqua." In later years, the property passed into the ownership of R.T. Underhill, M.D., and his brother. Dr. Underhill had an Italian villa here and also operated a vineyard and winery. There were eighty acres devoted to the growing of Isabella and Catawba grapes, and, around the turn of the century, about 10,000 gallons were bottled annually. The old natives and the Indians both believed the point to be haunted by dead Indians, and "the Sachems of Tellers Point," were household words in the neighborhood. It is believed that there was once a great Indian battle here.

The British ship "Vulture" lay offshore here and was driven downstream by a cannonading. This was a proximate cause of Major Andre's capture at Tarrytown.

29.50 Croton Bay to east:
an outlet of the Croton River, separated from the main channel of the Hudson by Teller's Point. Crawbuckie Point is at its eastern end. Henry Hudson anchored here in the *Half Moon* on the evening of October 1, 1609. This was once a great resort of canvasback ducks and other water fowl. Governor Thomas Dongan came here to hunt them in 1683. The bay was formerly quite deep and harbored great quantities of shad. However, the great Croton Reservoir Dam was swept away by a flood in 1841 and great quantities of earth were carried down which have silted up the bay to an average depth of only five feet. What is shown on modern charts as a tidal flat near the New York Central drawbridge across the Croton River used to be known as Dover Kill Island.

30.25 Croton River to east.
This stream is almost 100 miles long, rising in the Pawling Mountains of Dutchess and Putnam Counties, and among the lakes of northern Westchester County. Another principal source is Lake Mahopac in Putnam County. This lake has an elevation of 800 feet, and was originally called Ma-cook-pake, which was Indian for "large inland lake." The last great convention of the Southern Tribes of the Hudson was held on an island in this lake. The Croton River flows generally southwesterly through a series of man-made reservoirs belonging to New York City. Principal tributaries are the Cross River and Mohansic River, sometimes called the Muscoot. The great

Cornell or Croton Dam is about three miles upstream.

The Indian name for the river was the Kitchawan, or Kitch-a-wong, signifying "large and swift current." The Dutch renamed it Croton in honor of an Indian Sachem of that name. There is another theory that Croton is the corruption of another Indian name, Kenotin, signifying "wind or tempest."

The river drains an area of about 350 square miles. This, and its relative proximity to New York, made it an attractive place to build reservoirs. A dam was built in 1837, and construction commenced on a stone aqueduct to the city. The original dam was swept away by a flood in 1841, but it was immediately rebuilt to a higher level. Between 1884 and 1890, the system was again enlarged to the capacity of 100,000,000 gallons per day. Total the 38 mile long old aqueduct, opened for use 1842, is out of use, but the reservoirs continue to contribute their waters to the Catskill and Delaware Aqueduct systems. John Bloomfield Jervis was the principal engineer. In early days, there was a very high covered bridge across the Croton Gorge at the head of navigation. Also, in the middle of the last century it was the location of an important iron foundry.

30.25 Crotonville to east:
a small village on the south side of the mouth of the Croton River.

30.25 Van Cortlandt Manor to east:
the seat of the Van Cortlandt family on the north bank of the Croton River, (more fully described under east side road route mile 37.80.), built in 1683.

30.50 Croton Point to east.
Separating Croton Bay from main channel of the Hudson River, it projects southwesterly into the stream, its extremity, known as Teller's Point, pointing due south. Its average elevation is only twenty feet. The 504-acre Westchester County Croton Point Park is located here. (See Teller's Point.) Benson Lossing describes the area as follows:

A little west of the cemetery, at the neck of land which connects Croton Point with the main, stood the old fort or castle of "Kitch-a-wan," said to have been one of the most ancient Indian fortresses south of the Highlands. It was built by the Sachem Croton, when he assembled his parties for hunting or war. In a beautiful nook, a little east of the site of the fort, on the borders of Haunted Hollow, is the "Kitch-a-wan" burying-ground. Around this locality hovers the memory of many a weird story of the early times, when the superstitious people believed that they often saw, in the groves and glens there, the forms of the departed red men. They called them the Walking Sachems of Teller's Point.

(Lossing, *The Hudson*, p. 315.)

In the nineteenth century, grapes, apples, and melons were grown here.

30.90 Enoch's Neck to east:
northern extremity of Croton Point.

31.00 Potato Rock to east:
small rocky island off Croton Point.

31.00 Collaberg Landing to east.

31.00 Harmon on east:
large yards and station on former New York Central Railroad. Here, electric locomotives are taken off long-distance trains and are replaced by diesel power (steam

in the old days). Consequently, there are large locomotive shops here. The station has been re-named Croton-Harmon.

31.00 Harmon Park on east:
a residential development built by aviation pioneer Clifford B. Harmon, part of Croton-On-Hudson.

31.50 Long Clove to west.
The word comes from the Dutch "kloof," for cleft, gap, or ravine. We will encounter this name frequently along the Hudson. Route 9W comes through this Clove from the Hackensack to the Hudson Valley. It is at the north end of Hook Mountain. The West Shore Railroad also comes through a tunnel just to the south of Long Clove and runs northward along a ledge above the river.

31.50 Snedeker's Landing or Waldberg Landing on west.

The land in this area originally belonged to Marshall and Welch's Pond's Patent of 1694. Tunis Snedeker settled in the neighborhood in 1707. In 1835, Abram B. Snedeker built a hotel here. In 1840, Abraham B. Conger purchased land in the area and eventually built a residence he named Waldberg. The name gradually spread to the entire neighborhood, and prior to 1860, had been adopted by the residents of the school district as the name of the locality. New Lake, somewhat inland, was renamed Congers Lake. The lack of sufficient depth of water at Haverstraw village led to the construction of a ship yard and marine railway here in 1845 for the repair of vessels engaged in the brick business. It operated successfully until 1851 when it was superseded by other yards.

Snedeker's Landing derives historical interest as the landing place of the spy Major André on September 21st, 1780. This is probably the best place to tell the story of the André incident, as we have been travelling through the scenes of its action since Dobbs Ferry and will continue to do so until we pass West Point.

Benedict Arnold was disaffected with his rank and command in the continental army and "sulking in his tent" like Achilles when he was given command of West Point.

The entire story is well told by Benson Lossing, in his *The Hudson:*

Arnold twice received honorable wounds during the war—one at Quebec, the other almost two years later at Saratoga; both were in the leg. The one last received, while gallantly fighting the troops of Burgoyne, was not yet healed when, in the spring of 1778, the British army under Sir Henry Clinton, evacuated Philadelphia, and the Americans, under Washington, came from their huts at Valley Forge to take their places. Arnold, not being able to do active duty in the field, was appointed military governor of Philadelphia. Fond of display, he there entered upon a course of extravagant living that was instrumental in his ruin. He made his headquarters at the fine old mansion built by William Penn, kept a coach and four, gave splendid dinner parties, and charmed the gayer portions of Philadelphia society with his princely display. His station and the splendour of his equipage captivated the daughter of Edward Shippen, a leading loyalist, and afterwards chief justice of Pennsylvania; she was then only eighteen years of age. Her beauty and accomplishments won the heart of the widower of forty. They were married. Staunch Whigs shook their heads in doubt concerning the alliance of an American general with a leading Tory family.

Arnold's extravagance soon brought numerous creditors to his door. Rather than retrench his expenses he procured money by a system of fraud and prostitution of his official power: the city being under martial law, his will was supreme. The people became incensed, and official inquiries into his conduct were instituted, first by the local state council, and then by the Continental Congress. The latter body referred the whole matter to Washington. The accused was tried by court-martial, and he was found guilty of two of four charges. The court passed the mildest sentence possible—a mere reprimand by the commander-in-chief. This duty Washington performed in the most delicate manner. 'Our profession,' he said, 'is the chastest of all; even the shadow of a fault tarnishes the lustre of our finest achievements. The least inadvertence may rob us of the public favor, so hard to be acquired. I reprimand you for having forgotten that, in proportion as you had rendered yourself formidable to our enemies, you should have been guarded and temperate in your deportment towards your fellow citizens. Exhibit anew those noble qualities which have placed you on the list of our most valued commanders. I will myself furnish you, as far as it may be in my power, with opportunities of regaining the esteem of your country.'

What punishment could have been lighter? yet Arnold was greatly irritated. A year had elapsed since his accusation, and he expected full acquittal. But for nine months the rank weeds of treason had been growing luxuriantly in his heart. He saw no way to extricate himself from debt, and retain his position in the army. For nine months he had been in secret correspondence with British officers in New York. His pride was now wounded, his vindictive spirit was aroused, and he resolved to sell his country for gold and military rank. He opened a correspondence in a disguised hand, and in commercial phrase, with Major John André, the young and highly accomplished adjutant-general of the British army.

How far Mrs. Arnold (who had been quite intimate with Major André in Philadelphia, and had kept up an epistolary correspondence with him after the British army had left that city) was implicated in these treasonable communications we shall never know. Justice compels us to say that there is no evidence of her having any knowledge of the transaction until the explosion of the plot at Beverly.

Arnold's deportment now suddenly changed. For a long time he had been sullen and indifferent; now his patriotism glowed with all the apparent ardour of his earlier career. Hitherto he had pleaded the bad state of his wounds as an excuse for inaction; now they healed rapidly. He appeared anxious to join his old companions in arms; and to General Schuyler, and other influential men, then in Congress, he expressed an ardent desire to be in the camp or in the field. They believed him to be sincere, and rejoiced. They wrote cheering letters to Washington on the subject; and, pursuant to Arnold's intimation, they suggested the propriety of appointing him to the command of West Point, the most important post in the country. Arnold visited Washington's camp at the same time, and, in a modest way, expressed a desire to have a command like that of West Point, as his wounds would not permit him to perform very active service on horseback.

The change surprised Washington, yet he was unsuspicious of wrong. He gave Arnold the command of "West Point and its dependencies," and furnished him with written instructions on the 3rd August, 1780. Then it was that Arnold made his headquarters at Beverly, and worked vigorously for the consummation of his treasonable designs. There he was joined by his wife and infant son. He at once communicated, in his disguised writing and commercial phraseology, under the signature of "Gustavus," his plan to Sir Henry Clinton, through Major Andre, whome he addressed as "John Anderson." That plan we have already alluded to. Sir Henry was delighted with it, and eagerly sought to carry it out. He was not yet fully aware of the real character behind "Gustavus," although for several months he had suspected it to be General Arnold. Unwilling to proceed further upon uncertainties, he proposed sending an officer to some point near the American lines, who should have a personal interview with his correspondent. "Gustavus" consented, stipulating, however, that the messenger from Clinton should be Major André, his adjutant-general.

Arnold and André agreed to meet at Dobbs Ferry, twenty-two miles above New York, upon what was then known as neutral ground. The British waterguard prevented the approach of Arnold. Sir Henry, anxious to complete the arrangement, and to execute the plan, sent the "Vulture" sloop of war up the river as far as Tarry Town, with Colonel Robinson, the owner of Beverly, who managed to communicate with Arnold. A meeting of Arnold and Andre was arranged. On the morning of the 20th of September, the latter officer left New York, proceeded by land to Dobb's Ferry, and from thence to the "Vulture," where it was expected the traitor would meet him that night. The wily general avoided the great danger. He repaired to the house of Joshua Hett Smith [near West Haverstraw], a brother to the Tory chief justice of New York, and employed him to go to the "Vulture" at night, and bring a gentlemen to the western shore of the Hudson. There was delay, and Smith did not make the voyage until the night of the 21st, after the moon had gone behind the high hills in the west. With muffled oars he paddled noiselessly out of Haverstraw Creek [Minisceongo Creek], and, at little past midnight, reached the "Vulture." It was a serene night, not a ripple was upon the bosom of the river. Not a word was spoken. The boat came alongside, with a concerted signal, and received Sir Henry's representative. Andre was dressed in his scarlet uniform, but all was concealed by a long blue surtout, buttoned to the chin. He was conveyed to an estuary at the foot of Long Clove

Mountain, a little below the Village of Haverstraw. [Waldberg Landing].

Smith, led the officer to a thicket near the shore, and then, in a low whisper, introduced "John Anderson" to "Gustavus," who acknowledged himself to be Major-General Arnold, of the Continental Army. There, in the deep shadows of night, concealed from human cognizance, with no witnesses but the stars above them, they discussed the dark plans of treason, and plotted the utter ruin of the Republican cause. The first faint harbingers of day began to appear in the east, and yet the conference was earnest and unfinished. Smith came and urged the necessity of haste to prevent discovery. Much was yet to be done. Arnold had expected a protracted interview, and had brought two horses with him. While the morning twilight was yet dim, they mounted and started for Smith's house. They had not proceeded far when the voice of a sentinel challenged them, and André found himself entering the American lines. He paused, for within them he would be a spy. Arnold assured him by promises of safety; and before sunrise they were at Smith's house, on what has since been known as Treason Hill. At that moment the sound of a cannon came booming over Haverstraw Bay from the eastern shore; and within twenty minutes the "Vulture" was seen dropping down the river, to avoid the shots of an American gun on Teller's Point. To the amazement of André, she disappeared. Deep inquietude stirred his spirit. He was within the American lines, without flag or pass. If detected, he would be called a spy—a name which he despised as much as that of traitor..

At noon the whole plan was arranged. Arnold placed in André's possession several papers—fatal papers!—explanatory of the condition of West Point and its dependencies. Zealous for the interests of his king and country, André contrary to the explicit orders of Sir Henry Clinton, received them. He placed them in his stockings, under his feet, at *the suggestion of Arnold, received a pass from the traitor in the event of his being compelled to return to New York by land, and waited with great impatience for the approaching night, when he should be taking a boat to the "Vulture."*

(Lossing, *The Hudson,* 289-93.)

To conclude the story, André, in disguise, crossed the King's Ferry to Verplanck's Point and went by land to the old bridge across the Croton River where he was suspected. He was making his way by land back to New York when he was apprehended at Tarrytown. Arnold returned to the Beverly House, across from West Point, and was eating breakfast when word reached him of Andre's capture. He immediately left the table and ran to the river where he was rowed downstream to the *Vulture.* Soon after this, he joined the British army and was sent on a marauding expedition up the James River in Virginia. He ended his days in England, an abhorred outcast.

31.75 Nordica Hill on the east:
Nordica Hill, named for opera singer Lillian Nordica (1859-1914), whose real name was Lillian Norton and who resided at Croton. She sang at the Metropolitan and was famous for Wagnerian roles.

32.00 Croton-On-Hudson on east
(population 7,523): a residential community, first settled c.1609. Many Irish and Italian laborers working on the Croton Dam settled here. Incorporated in 1898, it has a separate local railroad station. There was an artist's colony here after World War I, and an early "progressive" school, the Hessian Hills School, was opened in about 1932.

32.00 Haverstraw Bay.
This bay is 6 miles long, from Croton to Stony Point, and 3 miles wide. The Indian name was Kumachenack. The area on the east side was formerly called "Mother's Lap." High Tor and Hook Mountains are on the west side, and the Spitzenberg Mountains, Blue Mountain, Prickly Pear, Torment, Hessian, Airy, and Nordica Hills on the east side.

32.40 Short Clove on the west.

33.00 Mount Airy on the east.

33.00 High Tor to the west
(elevation 827 feet). A part of the Verdreitig Mountains, its geology is similar to that of Hook Mountain. There was formerly an airplane beacon atop the mountain. It is traversed by the Long Path hiking trail. Long a major landmark to navigators on the Hudson, it served as a beacon site during the Revolution. In the 1930s, the New York Trap Rock Company started quarrying out the back of the mountain. The noted playwright, Maxwell Anderson, wrote a play entitled *High Tor* in 1937, which helped stimulate sentiment for preservation of the mountain. This verse play had a pessimistic ending, but the mountain had a happier ending. The Hudson River Conservation Society raised $12,000 and purchased the mountain from the heirs of Elmer Van Orden. In 1943, the property was acquired by the Palisades Interstate Park Commission. They removed the airplane beacon, which had been subject to repeated vandalism. Little Tor (elevation 710 feet, is to the north on the same ridge and is also reached by the Long Path. Everett Crosby's High Tor Vineyards are on the back slopes. Henry Varnum's painting of High Tor entitled *Grey Day* is in the Metropolitan Museum of Art.

33.10 Hessian Hill to the east
(elevation 550 feet). Senasqua Beach to east.

33.20 Torment Hill to the east
(elevation 600 feet).

33.25 Haverstraw to west
(population 8,198). The name comes from the Dutch "haver-stroo" or "oat straw," which grew abundantly in the swamps (the Dutch word is "hauver") along the Hudson and Minisceongo Creek. In 1671, two tracts were granted under New Jersey patents to Hendrick Van Bommel, and another to Balthazar De Hart and Nicholas DePew. Florus Willemse Crom and Minne Johannes settled here in 1681 and Reyn Van Ditmarsen in 1683. The Haverstraw Precinct was set off in 1719. In 1825, followers of Robert Owen established the Franklin Community here, the first American Communist experiment. The town was incorporated in 1854.

In the 1820s, red sandstone was quarried here in great quantities. Ten to twelve vessels a day would leave the docks beneath Hook Mountain.

In the early 1800s, James Wood discovered the modern method of burning brick. As there was abundant good clay and straw (both necessary ingredients) in the vicinity, brick-making soon became an important industry. At first the bricks were mass produced in moulds compressed by a device known as Hall's Improved Machine. However, in the 1850s, a local man, Richard A. Ver Valen, developed a better machine which was soon adopted and which gave great impetus to the brick industry. Coal dust and sand were mixed with the clay to impart durability to the bricks. This gave the industry a great advantage in the neighborhood, as there was also suitable sand in good quantity. Cheap water transportation to New York also aided in growth of this major industry. In 1883, there were forty-two brick yards in operation between Long Clove and Jones Point, employing 2,400 men and with a production of 302,647,000 bricks. In 1884, there were forty-three yards between Long Clove and Tomkins Cove. At the height of production there were forty brickyards in Haverstraw alone, producing 326,000,000 bricks per annum. While bricks were also produced at other points upriver, Haverstraw was the capital of this industry. With the advent of poured concrete construction and the playing out of the clay beds the industry gradually faded away to nothing. Old clay pits, usually filled with water, can be seen in the grassy meadows between Haverstraw and Grassy Point along the Minisceongo Creek. There were major strikes in 1853 and 1877, and it was necessary to call in the militia. Both were caused by the manufacturers' cutting wages.

Today Haverstraw has light manufacturing and a large Hispanic population. Many row-type townhouses have been built in the outskirts in recent years.

33.50 Bowline Point to west:
slightly north of Haverstraw and between the Hudson and Minisceongo Creek. There is a recreation park here with a large lagoon. This is also the site of a large power plant owned jointly by the Orange & Rockland Utilities and Consolidated Edison Company of New York.

33.50 Prickly Pear Hill to east.
(elevation 536 feet). Washington encamped here in 1782 and used the peak as an observatory. The name comes from a species of cactus which grows abundantly here.

34.40 Oscawana to east:
a small hamlet and local railroad station. End of third-rail electrification on railroad.

34.65 Oscawana Island to east.
It has rocky ledges, now connected to the mainland by railroad causeways and siltation.

34.50 Little Tor to west.
(elevation 710 feet). See article on High Tor.

34.65 Samsondale to west:
a residential section of Haverstraw inland from Bowline Point.

34.65 Garnersville to west:
inland from Samsondale, on Minisceongo Creek. This was a nineteenth-century "company town" centered around the Rockland Print Works (textile printing and dyeing) owned by the Garner Family. Red brick Gothic style mill buildings were surrounded by rows of company houses for the workers and detached small villas for the managers. Brush Court, the Garner family mansion was located in the west end of town. The textile operations moved south in the 1930s and the mills are sublet to a variety of light manufacturing firms. This is a good example of a Victorian factory community and is still largely intact.

34.70 Furnace Brook to east.

35.00 Grassy Point to west.
This low point was originally very beautiful, being covered with a dense oak and chestnut forest and bordered by marshes and salt meadows. It is separated from the mainland by the serpentine MiniSceongo Creek and Cedar Pond Brook. The mouth of this creek was crossed by what was called the Penny Bridge.

John Allison, who died in 1754, purchased the area from a certain Albert Minnie "and others." Allison left the tract to his son Joseph Allison, who in turn left it to his three sons, John, Joseph, and William. On April 9, in 1798, they sold this land to Jacob Sabriska, who shortly thereafter resold it to William Denning, Jr. On July 4th 1798, Mr. Denning sold it to his father, William Denning Sr., a wealthy lawyer, for use as a summer estate. Mr. Denning Sr. erected a handsome summer home which he used until his death.

After several years Denning sold ten acres at the south end to William Smith, a, a nephew of Joshua Hett Smith. Smith beautified the grounds and built a large two-story house which he called Rosa Villa.

After the death of Mr. Denning (who was a brother-in-law of Joshua Hett Smith), the property passed through the hands of Philip Verplanck, Isaac L. Pratt, and Dr. Lawrence Proudfoot. Later the property passed into the ownership of David Munn, Thomas Murphy, Abraham B. Conger, and others. It was eventually subdivided.

Dr. Lawrence Proudfoot built the first steamboat landing here in 1830. It was a popular landing because it offered adequate depth of water near the regular steamboat channel and was long an important way-landing, serving a considerable back country. Dr. Proudfoot also built a hotel and ran a bar room. In 1845, O.C. Gerow opened a general store, and James Creney opened a hotel in 1848. John I. Wiles opened a wheelwright shop and foundry in 1845, which was carried on for many years under the name of F.J. Wiles & Co. It specialized in manufacturing machinery for the quarry and brickmaking industry. During this period, there was also a shipyard and a marine railway.

A post office was established in 1834, which went under the name of North Haverstraw until 1836. In the late nineteenth and early twentieth centuries, the brick industry dominated and the forests were all cut down. Dun-colored sand hills, ugly clay pits, brick kilns, brick sheds, and tumbledown shanties covered the point, which was always under a pall of smoke and dust. Today there is a modern plant of the U.S. Gypsum Company. Several popular yacht clubs are located on the point, and, with the returning cleanliness of the waters, crabbing is again a popular pastime in the vicinity. It is an excellent place to recapture the old-time river flavor. According to an old legend, Captain Kidd buried treasure here.

35.00 Treason Hill to west.
This is the hill upon which formerly stood the home of Joshua Hett Smith, which was visited by Major André on September 22, 1780. The house no longer exists. It stood on the present site of the New York State Rehabilitation Hospital on Route 9W. (See article on André under mile 31.50, Snedeker's Landing.)

35.00 West Haverstraw to west.
(population 8,558): a residential community, formerly the northern terminus of the New Jersey & New York Railroad and of most West Shore Railroad commuter trains.

35.00 Crugers to east.
A small hamlet and local railroad station named for John Peach Cruger, who was married to Elizabeth, granddaughter of States Morris Dyckman, owner of Boscobel on adjacent property. This place was also formerly called Cruger's Park.

35.25 Franklin D. Roosevelt Veterans' Administration Hospital on east.
Formerly and more simply known as Montrose Veterans' Hospital. The hospital stands on the former estate of Boscobel, which belonged to States Morris Dyckman (1755-1806). The name means "beautiful woods" in Italian, and this name was most likely quite descriptive of the area in earlier times. In order to make room for new construction in the 1950s, the mansion was taken apart and moved and reassembled near Cold Spring. It has been completely restored with beautiful grounds and gardens and is now operated as a museum.

35.35 Minisceongo Creek to west.
Also formerly known as Nappie's Kill, this creek rises in two major branches. The northern one rises in Palisades Interstate Park and is formed by the waters of Horse Chock Brook and Beaver Pond Brook. The artificial Lake Welch was formed by damming its waters. This branch flows southeastward to a junction with the southern branch near Letchworth village. The southern branch rises near Mount Ivy and flows northeastward to the junction. From Letchworth village, the stream flows east past Thiells and Garnersville to Samsondale, where it flows over Miner's or Minne's Falls to tidewater. It then turns northward behind Bowline and Grassy points and flows in a

serpentine and meandering manner through marshlands to an outlet at Stony Point Bay. Near its outlet, it receives the waters of Cedar Pond Brook. The old Penny Bridge crossed it near the outlet.

35.35 Cedar Pond Brook to west.
Formerly known as Florus' Falls Creek and Flora's Falls Creek and also simply Cedar Brook, it rises in Lake Tiorati in Palisades Interstate Park and flows generally southeasterly as Tiorati Brook. Just west of Stony Point it is joined from the northwest by the waters of Timp Brook. It then flows east through a picturesque ravine near Stony Point village. This is now a park and is crossed by a viaduct on Route 9 W. It then goes over some small falls to tidewater and meanders eastward through salt marshes to Minisceongo Creek, near its outlet into Stony Point Bay.

35.40 George's Island to east:
now attached to mainland by marshes. A public beach and park slightly to the north take their name from George's Island.

35.75 Montrose Point to east,
also known as Parson's Point. The Wagenals' House, a two-story clapboard with temple facade, ca. 1840, is on the south side of the point. The Montrose railroad station is located inland.

35.75 Stony Point Bay to west,
formerly known as Brewster's Cove. Between Grassy Point on the south and Stony Point on the north, it receives the waters of Minisceongo Creek.

35.75 Stony Point to west.
(village with population of 8,270). It was originally part of Haverstraw and was called North Haverstraw. In 1847, it was given a separate post office, and the name was changed to Flora Falls (a corruption of Florus' Falls). In 1865, Stony Point township split off from Haverstraw, and in 1870 the name of the village was changed to Stony Point. The original owner of the land hereabout was Florus Crom, and the falls derived their name from him. There was a large iron works along Cedar Pond Brook in the mid-nineteenth century. A Methodist Society was formed in 1834. In 1844, William Knight opened a chemical works near Cedar Pond for the manufacture of pyroligneous acid, used at the Garnersville Print Works. Today the town is largely residential.

36.20 Stony Point to west.

This is a high rocky headland jutting straight out into the river (elevation 150 feet). The river here is scarcely more than half a mile wide. Low, sandy Verplanck's Point is opposite to the northeast. Located at the southern gateway to the Highlands and commanding a narrow river pass, Stony Point was of considerable strategic military value during the Revolution. The Kings Ferry, which was a vital communications link, was located immediately to the north.

The Americans built a fort here early in the Revolution. They built another, called Fort Lafayette, on Verplanck's Point, just across the river. On June 1, 1779, both were captured from the Americans by British forces, which had been conveyed up the Hudson by Admiral Collier. Verplanck's Point, which was protected by only seventy men, was taken by Gen. Sir John Vaughan. Stony Point, which was garrisoned by only about forty men under Capt. Armstrong, was occupied by troops under the personal command of Sir Henry Clinton. The small American garrison did not attempt a defense, but retreated upon approach of the British, and the fort changed hands without bloodshed. The next morning, the British trained the cannons and guns of Stony Point upon

Fort Lafayette on Verplanck's Point. Gen. Vaughan attacked Fort Lafayette from the rear simultaneously with the bombardment from Stony Point. The Americans surrendered themselves as prisoners of war.

The first months of 1779 found the British Commander, Sir Henry Clinton, located at New York City. George Washington and the Continental Army were encamped at Middlebrook, New Jersey, in the Raritan Valley, on the foothills of the Watchung Mountains. Clinton was playing a cat and mouse game, attempting to draw Washington into a full scale battle that would be decisive. When he could not gain this end, he had decided upon the campaign against the Highland fortifications. He decided to devote 6000 troops to this venture, with a minimum goal of gaining control of the important King's Ferry, thus lengthening the American supply lines.

To strengthen the Highlands, Washington marched his troops from Middlebrook to Smith's Clove in the Western Highlands. He posted troops at New Windsor and strengthened the garrisons of the various Highland fortifications. Lacking sufficient strength to penetrate farther up the Hudson, Clinton garrisoned Stony Point and Verplanck's Point with 1,000 troops and ordered raids on Connecticut coastal towns in another attempt to lure Washington into open field. Stony Point was garrisoned by men of the 17th Regiment of Foot; grenadier's companies of the 71st Regiment; and some artillery—all under the command of Lt. Col. Henry Johnson of the 7th Regiment. Washington burned to regain control of Stony Point, but felt that it was too strongly defended to be worth the attempt.

. . . General Anthony Wayne, known as "Mad Anthony," on account of his impetuosity and daring in the service, was then in command of the Americans in the neighborhood. Burning with a desire to retake the forts, he applied to Washing-ton for permission to make the attempt. It would be perilous in the extreme. The position of the fort was almost impregnable. Situated upon a high rocky peninsula, an island at high water, and always inaccessible dryshod, except across a narrow causeway, it was strongly defended by outworks and a double row of abattis. Upon three sides of the rock were the waters of the Hudson, and on the fourth was a morass, deep and dangerous. The cautious Washington considered; when the impetuous Wayne, scorning all obstacles, said, "General, I'll storm hell if you will only plan it!"

Permission to attack Stony Point was given (July 10, 1779), preparations were secretly made, and near midnight, on the 15th of July, Wayne led a strong force of determined men towards the fortress.

(Lossing, *The Hudson*, pp. 282-83.)

At about 8 o'clock in the evening, on July 15th, a force of one thousand picked men were formed into two columns near Springsteel's farm, back of Buckberg Mountain. One detachment, under the command of Colonel Richard Butler, had come from an encampment at Queensboro, in back of Bear Mountain, on the upper reaches of Popolopen Creek. That same morning, all the Massachusetts Light Infantry were marched to the headquarters of General Wayne at Sandy Beach, fourteen miles from Stony Point. It was a scorchingly hot day. At noon they started their eight hour march over narrow trails over Dunderberg Mountain. Advance word had been sent to kill all the dogs in the vicinity so that their barking would not betray the troop movements.

Some advance espionage had been undertaken by a negro slave named Pompey, whose master was an ardent patriot. He had gotten into the habit of visiting Stony Point to sell fresh strawberries and cherries to the troops stationed there, and was able to obtain the countersign, "The fort's our own," of which good use was made in tricking the outlying sentries.

Shortly before midnight, when ebb tide was expected, Pompey led the troops towards Stony Point. Several outlying pickets were quickly dispatched and the troops soon arrived at the causeway.

Here the army split into three main parts. The southern group were under the overall command of Gen. Wayne, and Lt. Col. De Fleury. The northern group were commanded by Col. Butler and Maj. Stewart. A small group under Maj. Murfee was to keep up a diversionary fire and attack the main landward approach. The two main bodies, under Wayne and Butler, were to skirt the southern and northern sides of the point and then turn to join in the middle of the fortifications. Each of the main columns was led by twenty picked men, under Lieutenants Gibbon and Knox, who cut through obstructions.

Because he believed that success demanded surprise and swift, close combat, Wayne ordered his men to carry unloaded muskets with fixed bayonets. No guns were to be loaded under penalty of death. Each soldier and officer put a piece of white paper in his hat to distinguish himself from the foe.

The attack began shortly after midnight. General Wayne forded the marsh on the south, covered at that time with two feet of water. The other column, under Colonel Butler and Major Murfee, crossed the causeway. They then split, with Colonel Butler going along the north side, and the men in the center, under Major Murfee, opening a diversionary fire.

. . . They advanced undiscovered until within pistol-shot of the picket guard on the heights. The garrison were suddenly aroused from sleep, and the deep silence of the night was broken by the roll of the drum, the loud cry "To arms! to arms!" the rattle of musketry from the ramparts and behind the abattis, and the roar of cannon charged with deadly grape-shot. In the face of this terrible storm the Americans made their way, by force of bayonet, to the center of the works. Wayne was struck upon the head by a musket ball that brought him upon his knees. "March on!" he cried. "Carry me into the fort, for I will die at the head of my column!" The wound was not very severe, and in an hour he had sufficiently recovered to write the following note to Washington:

> "Stony Point, 16th July, 1779
> 2 o'clock, A.M.

"Dear General,—The fort and garrison, with Colonel Johnston, are ours. Our officers and men behaved like men who are determined to be free.

> "Yours most respectfully,
> "Anthony Wayne."

(Lossing, *The Hudson*, pp. 283-284.)

It is recorded that General Wayne was carried over the rampart by his two aides, Fishbow and Archer, after being wounded. Only fifteen minutes of bloody, savage, fighting brought the British to surrender. Only fifteen Americans were killed and eighty-three wounded. Estimates of the number of British killed vary from twenty to sixty-three, with no count of wounded. It is believed that about sixty escaped. We took 543 prisoners.

The next morning the cannons were again turned upon Fort Lafayette, which was then commanded by Lt. Col. Webster. However, Sir Henry Clinton sent relief, and the Americans did not succeed in recapturing Fort Lafayette. Lacking the men to hold Stony Point, Wayne evacuated it three days later on the night of July 18th, after destruction of the fortifications and removal of ordnance and stores to the value of $180,000. These were loaded on a

galley and started for West Point. However, off Jones Point, the galley was
fired upon and sunk by the British ship
Vulture.

The main importance of this victory
was to raise American morale. It also
removed about 600 British troops from
action. Most of the prisoners were
inturned near Easton, Pennsylvania,
whence they were escorted by Count
Casimir Pulaski and his cavalry troop
that was posted at Minisink, now known
as Port Jervis. Congress ordered a gold
medal struck in honor of the event and
presented to General Wayne. Silver
copies of this medal were given to two
of the subordinate officers engaged in
the enterprise. Cash was distributed to
the troops.

Clinton immediately reoccupied Stony
Point on July 20th and built stronger
fortifications. However, he lacked the
troops to penetrate further into the
Highlands and withdrew from Stony
Point and Fort Lafayette in October of
1779. He then turned his attention to
the war in the south.

A battlefield museum was opened in
1936, and the area is now maintained by
the Palisades Interstate Park Commission.

The other major feature of Stony Point
is the lighthouse. It was built of fieldstone in 1826 upon the site of the old
central powder magazine. It was thirty
feet high with a fixed white light, at an
elevation of 179 feet above the water. It
operated for one hundred years, when it
was replaced with a small modern
electric light on the rocks nearer the
water. There was also a mechanical fog
signal housed in a pyramidal wooden
housing. Old engravings show what
appears to be a weight suspended by a
rope running over a pulley, similar to the
apparatus of some grandfather's clocks.
Possibly this activated a bell or worked a
bellows and trumpet.

36.25 Green's Cove to the east.
It receives the waters of
Meahagh Creek. Montrose Point

is to the south; Verplanck's Point
is to the north.

36.50 Lake Meahagh to the east.
This Indian name stands for a
creek which formerly meandered
through marshes east of Verplanck's point. It was dammed
for the purposes of cutting ice
and was renamed Knickerbocker
Pond, for the ice company which
operated there.

36.50 Collaberg Mountain to east,
also called Coleberg Mountain.

36.75 King's Ferry:
former colonial ferry between
Verplanck's Point and Stony
Point.

36.75 Verplanck Point on east.
Formerly Verplanck's Point, this
is a broad and low sandy peninsula between the Hudson River
on the west and south and
Meahagh Creek, or Knickerbocker Lake, now known as
Lake Meahagh on the east. It
rises to elevations of 100 feet at
its northern end. The Indians
called it Meahagh Point. It was
purchased from the Indians in
1683 by Stephanus Van Cortlandt. It next passed to his son
Johannes, whose daughter Gertrude married Philip Verplanck,
who gave it the present name.

It was the eastern terminus of
the important King's Ferry. Early
in the Revolution, the Americans
built a fort near the southern
extremity, overlooking the Hudson, which they called Fort Lafayette. The details of this fort's
history have been told in the
preceding article on Stony Point,
with whose history it is inextri-
cably joined.

After the withdrawal of the
British from Fort Lafayette in
October 1779, the Americans
again took possession and put
James Livingston in command.
On September 20 and 21, 1782
Gen. Washington was encamped

here and reviewed the American troops and Rochambeau's French troops, and held a large military banquet.

This was also the place where Henry Hudson first came to anchor after leaving the mouth of the river. He attracted many Indians, one of whom was shot and killed when he attempted to steal a pillow and several other articles from a cabin. Another Indian was drowned after his hand had been cut off by a sword during an attempt to climb into one of the ship's boats.

During a period of intense land speculation in 1836, a large village was mapped out and several fine mansions erected. Previously the area had been given over to the growth of corn and potatoes. Toward about the middle of the nineteenth century, the Cambrian limestone began to attract quarry operations. Brick making was also carried on for many years. Many fishermen of Italian descent live here now.

36.80 Quarries to west:
see article on Tomkin's Cove.

36.80 Ten Eyck's Beach to west.
Named for an old ferryman named Tenyck who operated the ferry from 1784 until the mid-1860s and who lived here, at the eastern terminus of the King's Ferry.

37.00 Mountain panorama to west
(from west to east):
Pingyp Mountain (elevation 1023 feet), Buckberg Mountain (elevation 793 feet), the Timp (elevation 846 feet), Bald Mountain (elevation 1100 feet), and Dunderberg Mountain (elevation 1086 feet). (Pingyp also spelled Pyngyp, and Buckberg was also known as Boulderberg.)

Pyngyp is from the Latin "piniger" or "pine bearing."

Another possible explanation of the name Pingyp comes from an old Dutch nautical term, "pijngjip," which is an onomatopoeic word describing the sound made as the boom of a fore and aft rigged vessel, such as a schooner or sloop, comes around on a tack. This is a cracking sound. Possibly the old Hudson mariners, who used the neighboring mountains to steer by, used this mountain as a point for changing course.

The name Timp comes from the Dutch "timpje," meaning a small cake or bun.

37.00 Mountain panorama to east
(from west to east):
Manitou Mountain (elevation 700 feet), Gallows Hill (elevation 400 feet), Jacob's Hill (elevation 600 feet), Fort Hill (elevation 320 feet), the city of Peekskill, Blue Mountain (elevation 640 feet), and Spitzenberg Mountain (elevation 560 feet). Both Blue Mountain and Spitzenberg are in what is called the Spitzenberg Mountains. Both lie within the limits of the Westchester County Park Commission's Blue Mountain Reservation. This is a forest preserve. The mountains are glacier-smoothed hogbacks. There are open bluestone ledges on the south side of Spitzenberg which offer a breathtaking view over Haverstraw Bay. The rock is norite, a blend of hornblende and mica. It is gray colored with a pink tinge. There are also emory deposits.

37.35 Bulsontown to west.
Inland beyond Buckberg Mountain.

37.35 Tomkin's Cove to west.
This locality is noted for its limestone quarrying industry. As early as 1789, John Crom built a small lime kiln, but nothing much else developed during the next

half century. In 1838, Daniel Tomkins discovered the limestone in this area only by searching carefully from Hoboken to the present Tomkin's Cove. During and after his search, he made several trips on foot between Haverstraw and Newark. The limestone beds which he discovered occupy a superficial area of nearly 600 acres, extending to the rear of Stony and Grassy Points, where they disappear beneath the red sandstone formation. They're traversed by white veins of carbonate of lime. Some of it is black and variegted, which makes pleasing ornamental "marbles," but most of it is blue.

"In the spring of 1838, having purchased twenty acres of land the year before for $100 an acre, Daniel Tomkins embarked at Newark, New Jersey, on board a sloop named Contrivance, *with sixteen men, one woman, one horse, one cow, and a small quantity of lumber, and set sail for his new home. Upon arriving at the now thriving hamlet of Tomkin's Cove, the men and woman were landed by small boat, while the animals were lowered into the water and allowed to find their own way to shore. A shanty for shelter was at once erected, and on the following day the work of quarrying out the limestone was begun.*

This branch of business proved a success from the outset, and has steadily continued to increase in importance. Beside the manufacture of lime, the company owning the cliff has added to its business by crushing limestone for macadamizing purposes.

When first begun, the business at Tomkins Cove was carried on under the name of Tomkins, Hadden & Co. At a later period, the firm was changed to Calvin Tomkins & Co., and the members were Calvin and Daniel Tomkins and Walter Searing. In 1859, the Tomkins Cove Lime Company was formed, and since that time the business has been conducted in its name."

(Cole, *History of Rockland County*)

The principal cliff workings were nearly 200 feet high and stretched along the river for one-half mile. Several wharves were erected for the easy transfer to sloops and barges. The lime was slaked before shipment to prevent combustion. By 1865, the works were producing a million bushels per year and employed 100 men. Thousands of tons of stone annually were shipped to kilns in New Jersey. Each year, 20,000-25,000 tons of "gravel" were shipped to New York City, where they were used to macadamise roads in Central Park and private driveways.

Calvin Tomkins & Co. opened a store near the landing in 1842. In 1850, a shipyard was started and a marine railway built. The post office was established March 15, 1860.

Calvin Tomkins was born in 1793 near Orange, New Jersey. He served in the War of 1812 and came to this area in 1834, after having established several successful businesses in Newark, New Jersey. His brother Daniel joined him in 1838, as described above. Eventually their business included brick yards, plaster manufacturing facilities, and large real estate holdings, and extended as far away as New Brunswick, Canada. In 1858, Calvin Tomkins built a large private mansion for himself using poured concrete as the prime building material. It is believed that this was New York State's first poured concrete building. It is Gothic in style and is embellished by curved and carved bargeboards, diamond panes, and rich moldings. There is a central hot-air heating system employing sheetmetal-lined ducts embedded in the concrete walls. The interior is richly decorated. After Mr. Tomkin's death in 1892 at the age of 99, the property came into the hands of Charles S. Wood. Today it is operated at the Boulderberg Manor Restaurant.

37.35 Ramapo Fault and Escarpment on east and west.
Buckberg and Dunderberg Mountains represent the eastern end of the Ramapo Mountains, which extend southwest to the area of Oakland, New Jersey. The name was also spelled Ramapaugh, Remopuck, Remepog, Ramopog, and Ramapaw—which in Indian dialect means either "rugged· country of the waterfalls," or "place of sloping rock." The fault line along its southern foot was created in the Cambro-Ordovician period. This has been supposed to be a relatively inactive fault line. However, in recent years, earthquakes in the vicinity of Mahwah and Oakland, New Jersey, have raised serious questions. The chief concern is that the Indian Point Nuclear Power Plant sits almost directly on top of the fault line.

37.37 Lovett plant of Orange and Rockland Utilities, Inc. on west.

Originally designed to use coal brought in by seventy-five car unit trains, it now burns low-sulphur oil, brought in by barge, to meet air environmental standards. Boilers and furnaces are designed so that they can operate on either fuel.

37.40 Overhead power cables across river.

37.40 Boulderberg Manor on west: see Tomkin's Cove article for details.

38.00 Former Reserve Fleet Anchorage on west.
Between 1946 and 1971, one hundred eighty-nine ships were anchored here. Most of them were Liberty Ship type freighters built for World War II, but a few fighting ships and passenger liners, including the big *George Washington,* were also stored here, anchored side to side in long rows perpendicular to the shoreline. Up until 1963, the ships were used to store surplus grain. Each ship could store 6000 tons, or 225,000 bushels. Ninety-four men under a fleet superintendent kept watch over the "mothball fleet." Ships were reactivated for the Korean conflict, the Suez Crisis, and the Vietnam War. Ships were also stored here after World War I.

38.25 Rose Town on west.

38.25 Indian Point on east.
Site of Indian Point Park, operated by the Hudson River Day Line. This park offered facilities for picnicking, dining in a cafeteria, swimming, strolling through the woods, or simply relaxing. The Day Line claimed that this property had been a meeting place for Indians. It covered 320 acres and included a farm for the raising of vegetables for use on the steamers. It opened for business in 1923. There were two piers here, and

they were sometimes used for winter storage of ships. The Day Line steamers continued to call here until 1956. The property was then sold to Consolidated Edison Company for construction of a nuclear power plant.

The $90,000,000 nuclear reactor steam-electric generating station was scheduled for completion in 1960, but did not get into operation until 1963. The plant is now (1978) being doubled in capacity. Tours of the facility are available. Conservationists voiced concern about the warm water being returned to the river, and, in 1963, there was an incident where large numbers of striped bass fingerlings were drawn into the water intakes and killed. Many are concerned about the proximity of the Ramapo Fault.

38.50 Buchanan to east:
a small residential community inland from Indian Point.

38.50 Caldwell's Landing to west.
Formerly called Gibraltar. This was part of the Cheesecocks Patents. Joshua Colwil settled here before 1800. He was descended from John Cholwell, one of the original patentees. On March 19th, 1800, he was granted by legislative act the right, in conjunction with Joseph Travis, of Peekskill, to run a ferry across the river from his landing to that of Travis, in the south end of Peekskill. In the early 19th century there was a popular hotel located here. In his *New Mirror For Travellers* of 1828, James Kirke Paulding says of the Donderbarrack:

. . . at whose foot dwells in all the feudal majesty (only a great deal better) of a Rhoderick Dhu, the famous highland chieftain,

Caldwell, lord of Donderbarrack, and all the little hills that grow out of his ample sides like warts on a giant's nose. To this mighty chieftain, all the steam boats do homage, by ringing of bells, stopping their machinery, and sending their boats ashore to carry him the customary tribute, to wit, store of visiters, whom it is his delight to entertain at his hospitable castle. This stately pile is of great antiquity; its history being lost in the dark ages of the last century, when the indian prowled about these hills, and shot his deer, ere the rolling wave of the white man swept him away forever.

(Paulding, *New Mirror For Travelers,* 115-16.)

During the War of 1812, the Navy wished to establish a shipyard here, which would be less exposed to enemy attack than the one at Brooklyn. However, Colwil, or Caldwell, was a Federalist, and considered the war iniquitous. He placed so disproportionate a valuation upon his property that the government at once abandoned the project.

A post office was opened here in 1885. Shortly thereafter Charles H. Jones, a resident of Long Island, who owned some property in the vicinity, prevailed upon the postal and railroad authorities to give his name to the locale.

38.50 Jones Point to the west.

39.00 Lent's Cove to the east:
the outlet of Dickey Brook. Indian Point is to the south and Charles Point to the north. British troops landed here for a raid on Peekskill in 1777.

39.00 Dickey Brook to the east:
rises on northern slopes of Blue Mountain and flows southwest,

through Lounsbury Pond, to just north of Buchanan, thence northwest into Lent's Cove.

39.25 Charles Point to the east: separates Lent's Cove on the south from the outlet of Mac-Gregory Brook on the north. It is the site of the Fleischmann Yeast plant of Standard Brands, the largest of its type in the world. It is self-contained with 130 buildings and its own electric and steam plants.

39.40 MacGregory Brook to east: rises in eastern section of Peekskill, near Beecher Park, and flows west to Lake Penelope, thence southwest to Peekskill Bay.

39.45 Travis Point to east. This is a small point near southern end of Peekskill Bay, at foot of Mount St. Francis, the former eastern terminal of the ferry to Caldwell's Landing operated by Joshua Colwil and Joseph Travis.

39.50 Peekskill Bay to east. At outlet of Peek's Kill, or Annsville Creek. Roa Hook is to the north and Flatrock, Fort Hill, and the city of Peekskill are to the east. Travis and Charles Points are to the south. It is very shallow, varying from 3 to 5 feet in depth, save for a channel 7 feet deep leading to the wharves. Some shoals have only one foot of water. Boatmen beware!

39.50 Peekskill to east. A city with population of 19,283, Peekskill is primarily residential, located at northern extremity of convenient rail commuting to New York City. There is some manufacturing of yeast, gin, food products, and jewelry, as well as several foundries.

The Indians called this area Appamaghpogh, and the immediate vicinity of Peekskill Sackhoes. It belonged to the Kitchawong Tribe. In 1665, this area was granted as the Ryck's Patent and for many years formed an enclave in the surrounding Van Cortlandt Patent. A Dutch trader by the name of Jan Peek founded a trading colony here in 1697, on the banks of the creek which bears his name. He had sailed up this creek in the belief that it was the main channel of the Hudson. He was disabused when his ship hung up on a sandbar.

Neighboring Van Cortlandtville, two miles up the creek from the Hudson, was the seat of the Upper Manor of Van Cortlandt. In 1767, Catherine Van Cortlandt, daughter of the 1st lord of the manor, who was married to Andrew Johnson, founded St. Peter's Episcopal Church. It has recently been restored. In its churchyard are buried fifty-four Revolutionary soldiers and John Paulding, one of André's captors. This graveyard was established in 1752. Nearby is the family graveyard of the Van Cortlandt family.

Cornelia, daughter of Pierre Van Cortlandt, who was married to Gerard G. Beekman, lived at the Upper Manor. Her house served as George Washington's headquarters in 1776, 1777, and 1778. This area was used as a supply depot by the Americans and came to be called Continental Village. The depot and village were burned by the British on October 9, 1777. Across the creek, to the north, is Gallows Hill. Here, in August 1777, a British spy by the name of Nathan Palmer was hanged by General Israel Putnam. In response to a letter of inquiry from

the British Command concerning Palmer's fate, Putnam answered: "Nathan Palmer was taken as a spy, tried as a spy, and will be hanged as a spy. P.S.—He is hanged."

Peekskill was incorporated as a village in 1816 and as a city in 1940. The Peekskill Military Academy, which is over one hundred years old, was the first academy in the country after West Point to incorporate the military feature into its training. St. Mary's School For Girls occupies a conspicuous site atop Fort Hill.

Notable natives have been John Paulding, one of André's captors, Peter Cooper, early industrialist and philanthropist, Henry Ward Beecher, a famous preacher, and Chauncey M. Depew, president of the New York Central Railroad, senator, orator, and wit.

39.60 Fort Hill to east.
This hill lies within Peekskill's city limits. St. Mary's School for Girls occupies its summit.

39.60 Flatrock to east:
at the foot of Fort Hill, near the railroad.

39.75 Annsville Creek to east.
Formerly called Peek's Kill and Peekskill Creek, its Indian name was Sackboes Creek. Its present name comes from the small community of Annsville, about one mile upstream on the north bank. It is tidal for about a mile upstream, where it is formed by three branches, all flowing generally from the northeast. The northernmost branch is simply called Annsville Creek and rises in Philipstown in the Manitou Mountains. The middle branch is called Sprout Book in its lower reaches and Canopus Creek, and rises between the Taconic and Manitou Mountains, after which it flows southwest through Canopus Hollow. The southernmost branch, called Peekskill Hollow Brook, rises in Lake Peekskill, and flows southwest along the base of the Manitou Mountains.

This creek was named after early settler Jan Peek who mistook it for the main channel of the Hudson, until he ran aground on a sandbar. He established a trading post on its banks in 1697.

Its mouth is spanned by a railroad bridge and causeway 1,496 feet long called Cortlandt Bridge. Another Indian name was Magrigaries.

4
The Highlands of the Hudson

40.00 Dunderberg Mountain to west:

elevation 865 feet. This name is Dutch for "Thunder Mountain," as it was believed to brew storms. Another old Dutch name for it was Donderbarrack. According to Washington Irving, in his story "The Storm Ship,"

The captains of the river craft talk of a little bulbous-bottomed Dutch goblin, in trunk hose and sugar-loafed hat, with a speaking-trumpet in his hand, which, they say, keeps the Donder Berg. They declare that they have heard him, in stormy weather, in the midst of the turmoil, giving orders in Low Dutch, for the piping up of a fresh gust of wind, or the rattling off of another thunderclap. That sometimes he has been seen surrounded by a crew of little imps, in broad breeches and short doublets, tumbling head over heels in the rack and mist, and playing a thousand gambols in the air, or buzzing like a swarm of flies about Anthony's Nose; and that, at such times, the hurry-scurry of the storm was always greatest. One time a sloop, in passing by the Donder Berg, was over-taken by a thunder-gust that came scouring round the mountain, and seemed to burst just over the vessel. Though tight and well ballasted, she laboured dreadfully, and the water came over the gunwale. All the crew were amazed, when it was discovered that there was a little sugar-loaf hat on the mast-head, known at once to be the hat of the Heer of the Donder Berg. Nobody, however, dared to climb to the mast-head, and get rid of this terrible hat. The sloop continued labouring and rocking, as if she would have rolled her mast overboard, and seemed in continual danger, either of upsetting, or of running on shore. In this way she drove quite through the Highlands, until she had passed Pollopel's Island, where, it is said, the jurisdiction of the Donder Berg potentate ceases. No sooner had she passed this bourne, than the little hat sprung up into the air like a top, whirled up all the clouds into a vortex, and hurried them back to the summit of the Donder Berg, while the sloop righted herself, and sailed on as quietly as if in a mill-pond. Nothing saved her from utter wreck but the fortunate circumstance of having a horse-shoe nailed against the mast—a wise precaution against evil spirits, since adopted by all the Dutch captains that navigate this haunted river.

There is another story told of this foul-weather urchin, by Skipper Daniel Ouslesticker, of Fish Kill, who was never known to tell a lie. He declared that, in a severe squall, he saw him seated astride of his bowsprit, riding the sloop ashore, full butt against Anthony's Nose, and that he was exorcised by Dominie Van Geisen, of Esopus, who happened to be on board, and who sang the hymn of St. Nicholas, whereupon the goblin threw himself up in the air like a ball, and went off in a whirlwind, carrying away with him the nightcap of the Dominie's wife, which was discovered the next Sunday morning hanging on the weather-cock of Esopus church steeple, at least forty miles off. Several events of this kind having taken place, the regular skippers of the river for a long time did not venture to pass the Donder Berg without lowering their peaks, out of homage to the Heer of the Mountains; and it was observed that all such as paid this tribute of respect were suffered to pass unmolested.

(Washington Irving, "The Storm Ship")

Another interesting feature of this mountain is the uncompleted Dunder-berg Spiral Railroad. It had been planned to hold the great Columbian Exposition on Verplanck's Point in 1893. However, this plan fell through owing to a financial panic and ensuing depression. However, in 1889, a corporation had been formed by T.L. and H.J. Mumford of Mauch

Chunk, Pennsylvania, to build a palatial hotel atop Dunderberg and a series of inclined planes and a gravity railroad on the southern and eastern faces of the mountain. There was such a system in operation at Mauch Chunk for many years and it was a great popular tourist attraction. There was nothing chimerical about this project. The hotel on the summit was to be reached by two inclined planes, such as now operate on Mt. Beacon, totaling one mile in length. The cars were to return to the level of the river over a nine-mile course of loops and dips offering pleasant views of the surrounding countryside. They were to descend by gravity alone. Grading was begun in 1890. However, funds ran out in 1891, and the railway was never completed. Some of the grading, including a short tunnel, can still be seen by hikers on the mountain. The old highway skirted the foot of the mountain, near the present West Shore Railroad. The new Route 9W crosses a shoulder of the Dunderberg, offering fine views, particularly after the leaves are off the trees. The popular Dunderberg-Suffern hiking trail starts here.

Anthony Wayne's troops crossed the mountain on an old trail, somewhat inland from the river, prior to the attack on Stony Point, on July 15, 1779. Also, on the afternoon of October 6, 1777, British troops were led across this same trail, under cover of mist and fog, by a loyalist resident in the vicinity, on their way to attack Forts Clinton and Montgomery. A diversionary attack was made upon Fort Independence on Roa Hook, across the river.

40.20 Kidd's Point on west.

This point takes its name from a curious and rather involved incident. Captain William Kidd was born near Greenock, Scotland in about the middle of the seventeenth century. He later resided in New York City, near the corner of William and Cedar Streets, and here he was married. He made the acquaintance of Robert Livingston, the wealthy merchant, and it is believed that Livingston backed some of Kidd's later ventures. In April, 1696, he sailed from England in command of the *Adventure Galley,* with full armament and eighty men. He captured a French ship, and, on arrival at New York, put up articles for volunteers; remained in New York three or four months, increasing his crew to one hundred and fifty-five men—mostly from above the Highlands. He sailed then to Madras, Bonavista, and St. Jago, Madagascar. He then went to Calicut and then back to Madagascar. After this he took the Moorish ship *Quedah Merchant.* Kidd kept forty shares of the spoils, and divided the rest with his crew. He then burned the *Adventure Galley,* went on board the *Quedah Merchant,* and steered for the West Indies. Here he left the *Merchant,* with part of his crew, under one Bolton as commander. He manned a sloop and took his spoils to Boston, via Long Island Sound. It is claimed that he set goods on shore at different places. In the meantime, in August 1698, the East Indian Company informed the Lords' Justice that Kidd had committed several acts of piracy, including the taking of the *Quedah Merchant.* When Kidd landed at Boston, he was arrested by the Earl of Bellomont, and sent to England for trial in 1699. He was found guilty and executed at the Water Gate of the Tower of London in 1701. It is generally believed in the Hudson Highlands that the crew of the *Quedah Merchant,* which Kidd left at Hispaniola, sailed for their homes in the Highlands and further upriver, passing New York in the night, en route to Livingston Manor. They encountered a gale in the Highlands, and thinking they were pursued, ran her near the shore near Kidd's Point and scuttled her, the crew taking to the woods with such treasure as they could carry. It was believed that much treasure went down with the *Quedah Merchant.*

A modern tale of skullduggery is appended to this, as told by Benson Lossing, in his *The Hudson* of 1866:

. . . several years ago . . . the steam engine of an immense pumping apparatus was in operation at Donder Berg Point. Concerning that engine and its co-workers, there is a curious tale of mingled fraud, superstition, credulity, and "gullibility," that vies with many a plot born in the romancer's brain. It cannot be told here. The simple outlines are, that some years ago an iron cannon was, by accident, brought up from the river depths at this point. Some speculator, as the story goes, at once conceived a scheme of fraud, for the success of which he relied on the average ignorance and credulity of mankind. It was boldly proclaimed, in the face of recorded history, that Captain Kidd's piratical vessel was sunken in a storm at this spot with untold treasures on board, and that one of its cannons had been raised. Further, that the deck of his vessel had been penetrated by a very long augur, hard substances encountered by it, and pieces of silver brought up in its thread—the evidence of coffers of specie below. This augur with its bits of silver was exhibited, and the story believed. A stock company was formed. Shares were readily taken. The speculator was chief manager. A coffer dam was made over the supposed resting place of the treasure-ship. A steam engine and huge pumps, driven by it, were set in motion. Day after day, and month after month, the work went on. One credulous New York merchant invested 20,000 dollars in the scheme. The speculator took large commissions. Hope failed, the work stopped, and nothing now remains to tell the tale but the ruins of the coffer dam and the remains of the pumps, which may be seen on a level with the surface of the river, at high water.

(Lossing, *The Hudson*, 242-3.)

Wallace Bruce adds the additional information that it was claimed that the ship could be seen on clear days, with her masts still standing, many fathoms below the surface; and that the Treasurer of the firm disappeared with $30,000.

Kidd's Point is also called Caldwell's Point, Jones Point and Donder Berg Point.

40.30 Roa Hook on east.
Also called Royer's Point, it is located at the northern side of the mouth of Annsville Creek.

40.30 Site of Fort Independence on east:
on the high bluff at the western end of Roa Hook.

40.30 The Highlands:

ahead and on either side north to Newburgh Bay. These mountains were well described by Charles Callison, Executive Vice President of the National Audubon Society, while testifying against construction of a pumped storage facility at Storm King Mountain. He said:

. . . the Highlands are the most beautiful stretch of river scenery in the United States. [Its beauty is directly related] to the dominant geological feature of the eastern United States, the Appalachian Mountains. [It is] one of the very few places where the main chain of the Appalachians is broken by a river. . . . the French Broad, at the base of the Great Smokies, cuts through the main chain. And the Susquehanna, starting in central New York's Otsego Lake, journeys southwest and then turns southeast to go through several of the Appalachian ridges of Pennsylvania. The Delaware, Connecticut, and James Rivers also cut through one or more of the main chains of the mountains, often with striking beauty. Yet nowhere, in my opinion, is the impact as great as it is through the Highlands. In the Smokies, of course, the French Broad cuts a

*deeper valley and is flanked by higher
mountains. But there the river is shallow
and narrow, a small stream practically
hidden by the scale of the mountains. At
the Delaware Water Gap there are also
high hills. Yet in the Highlands—and
only in the Highlands—the river cuts the
Appalachian at sea level. And with a
relative breadth it creates river scenery
of an unequaled scale, bounded on both
banks by the precipitous hills. Here we
have not simply a river, but an estuary
. . . with the tides of the Atlantic literally
cutting through the mountains. Here
alone we have ocean-going vessels
passing through a great mountain chain
and traveling ninety miles on to the
heartland. And here, too, and again here
alone—we have Storm King Mountain—
a headland unique in its height and
sheer rise from the river.*

> (Federal Power Commission
> Hearing Testimony, November,
> 1966 *"Storm King Pumped
> Storage,"* U.S. Govt. Printing
> Office.)

At a much earlier date, James Fenimore
Cooper observed in his novel, *The Spy*
that:

*To be seen in their perfection, the
Highlands must be passed immediately
after the fall of the leaf. The scene is
then the finest, for neither the scanty
foliage which the summer lends the
trees, nor the snows of winter, are
present to conceal the minutest objects
from the eye. Chilling solitude is the
characteristic of the scenery; nor is the
mind at liberty, as in March, to look
forward to a renewed vegetation that is
soon to check, without improving, the
view.*

The Indians called these mountains
the Kittatinny Mountains, a name since
abrogated by the southern extension of
the Shawangunks in New Jersey. Technically speaking, the mountains on the
western side are the Ramapo Moun-

tains, and those on the eastern side are
the Manitou Mountains, a southern
extension of the Taconic-Berkshire
Chain.

The Appalachian Trail, affectionately
known to hikers as the "A.T." crosses the
Hudson River here on the Bear Moun-
tain Bridge. This trail, conceived by
Benton Mackaye in 1921, runs from Mt.
Katahdin in Maine, to Mt. Oglethorpe, in
Georgia, along the crest of the Older
Appalachians. The first section was
completed in 1923, and the entire trail
in 1937.

Old guidebook writers placed the
Southern Gateway to the Highlands at
Dunderberg, and the Northern Gateway
at Storm King. This area was of great
strategic importance during the Revolution, as the narrowness and bends of the
Hudson made sailing ships vulnerable to
gun batteries on shore. Principal fortifications in the area included Stony Point,
Fort Lafayette, Fort Independence, Fort
Clinton, Fort Montgomery, West Point,
Fort Putnam, and Fort Constitution—not
to mention numerous small gun emplacements and the various Chevaux-de-frise
and chains. Washington made his headquarters and chief supply depots here
and just above at Newburgh, New
Windsor, and Fishkill, and inland at
Smith's Clove and Continental Village.
The Highlands made possible keeping
intact the lines of communications and
supply between New England and the
rest of the colonies, and kept the British
from the breadbasket of the central
Hudson region.

40.30 The Race.

This is the stretch of river from
here to Bear Mountain, also
known formerly as the Horse
Race, and the Devil's Horse
Race, from the swiftness of the
current here, the fastest on the
river. This is one of the narrowest
parts of the river below Albany,
with depths up to 165 feet. The
river is only ⅜ mile wide.

40.30 Camp Smith on east.
Above Roa Hook. This is the summer training grounds of the New York State National Guard. Infantry and artillery are trained here. The camp is named in honor of former Governor Alfred E. Smith, but is much older. Mine Mountain, at the northern end of the reservation has abandoned iron mines.

40.50 Dickiebusch Brook on east:
rises in Dickiebusch Lake in Camp Smith Reservation and empties into Peekskill Bay at Roa Hook.

40.75 Fish Island on east.
This is the smallest named island in the Hudson. Close to the eastern shore, it is little more than a rock awash in rough high water.

41.00 Flat Point on east.
This bluff on Manitou Mountain was formerly tunneled by the New York Central Railroad. In the 1950s, it was "daylighted," i.e., its top was blasted off to make it an open cut, to improve clearance for automobile rack cars.

41.00 Deep Hole on east:
143 feet deep, just off Flat Point.

41.00 Round Island on west.
The high, rocky southeastern tip of Iona Island, it is round in shape.

41.00 Snake Hole Creek on west:
between Iona Island and Dunderberg Mountain.

41.00 Salisbury Meadow on west:
between mainland and Iona Island. Drained to the south by Snake Hole Creek and to the north by Doodletown Brook, it was formerly called Salisbury Island. It is wet marshland, but has dry hummocks at low tide. There is a causeway from Route 9W on the mainland to Iona Island that affords good close

views. The area is important in the incubation of marine life and the nesting of water fowl, and it is presently a wildlife refuge.

41.00 Ring Meadow on west.
This name refers to that portion of Salisbury Meadow on the southern end of Iona Island, east of Snake Hole Creek.

41.00 Manitou Mountain on east.
With an elevation of 720 feet, Manitou Mountain lies within the Camp Smith Military Reservation.

41.50 Iona Island on west.
Formerly known as Beveridge's Island and Weyant's Island, it is about 300 acres in size, 200 of which are marsh meadow. Only about 40 acres are suitable for cultivation. There are rocky outcroppings, and the maximum elevation, near the northern end, is 60 feet. It is separated from the mainland by Snake Hole Creek on the south and by Doodletown Brook and Doodletown Bight on the west and north. The West Shore Railroad cuts across the island, via a causeway and small bridge on the south and a long low trestle on the north. It is connected to Route 9W on the mainland by a low causeway across Salisbury Meadow. There was formerly a railroad station here. The sea breeze stops here, but its mild effect is visible upon vegetation. The spring season is two weeks in advance of that at Newburgh, only fourteen miles northward. In the mid-nineteenth century, C. W. Grant, M.D., a noted horticulturist and arborist, had extensive vineyards and orchards here. Twenty acres was devoted to the vine, and there were between 2,000 and 3,000 bearing pear trees and small fruit of every kind. According to Benson

Lossing, he had eleven propagation houses, and produced more grapes and other fruit plants than all other establishments in the United States combined.

Later in the century it served as a summer resort and in the 1870s was a popular destination for excursion steamers from New York. The island served as a U.S. Naval Arsenal from 1900 until after World War II. It was rumored to be strongly defended on the waterside by artillery. The government also stored rubber here. There was a circular iron shot tower with a conical top, painted with red and white checks which gave a picturesque effect, but has since been removed. The island is now under the jurisdiction of the Palisades Interstate Park Commission.

There was once a great railroad disaster here when an express train piled into the rear of a stopped passenger train made up of wooden coaches. One of the trains involved belonged to the NYO & W.

41.60 Broccy Creek and Reservoir to east.

Rising in Broccy Creek Reservoir at an elevation of 537 feet in a col between Anthony's Nose and Mine Mountain in the Camp Smith Reservation, it flows southwest to the Hudson. The name was corrupted from the Dutch Brocken Kill, or Broken Creek; an intermediately used name was Brockey Kill.

41.60 West Mountain to west.

Elevation 1257 feet. It is located at head of Doodletown Hollow and is traversed by the Timp-Torne and Suffern-Bear Mountain hiking trails. There is a shelter here.

41.60 Doodletown to west.

This is the name of a hollow and village between Dunderberg on the south, West Mountain on the west, and Bear Mountain on the north. It is on the mainland behind Iona Island. The name most likely comes from the Dutch "Dooddel" or "Dead Valley." The name may have come from its dark and shadowy appearance, or dead trees in the vicinity. Many people think the name is derived from Yankee Doodle, but the name seems to have applied at an earlier date than that of the tune's original popularity. This land was part of the Richard Bradly Patent of 1743. The French Huguenot June family settled here in 1776. In the nineteenth century, the area was settled mainly by woodmen engaged in cutting and hauling wood to the landing northwest of Iona Island, for the boats and brickyards. When Mr. Beveridge bought Iona Island, he erected a church edifice here in 1851. This was called the Mountville Church. It was also used as a schoolhouse. In later years, around 1945, Doodletown had a population of about 100 persons, mostly working in the Palisades Interstate Park or on Iona Island at the arsenal. Today it is a ghost town. It is here that forces under Sir Henry Clinton, on their way to attack Fort Clinton, met their first American resistance. The American militia was composed of farmer lads, few of them over twenty-five years old.

41.60 Timp Brook to west.

It rises in a col between the Timp and Bald Mountain and flows northeast into Doodletown Brook at Doodletown.

41.60 Doodletown Brook to west.

Rising in a col between West Mountain and Bear Mountain, it flows east through Doodletown Hollow to Doodletown Bight near Salisbury Meadow.

41.75 Doodletown Bight to west.

An outlet of Doodletown Brook, between Iona Island and Bear Mountain, it is a shallow bay. It is crossed at its mouth by a low and long trestle of the West Shore Railroad. It is also known as Doodletown Cove.

42.00 Chevaux-de-Frise across river.

The name "chevaux-de-frise"—is the French term for any sort of portable wire or metal entanglements. As part of the fortifications of the Highlands, it was proposed that the Americans stretch chains across the Hudson to prevent British warships from sailing upriver. The first one was proposed by General G.M. Scott of the New York Militia, to be stretched from Fort Lee to Fort Washington. He proposed using heavy wooden beams shod with iron and bolted together in the form of tetrahedons, the ends of the beams extending beyond the joints into horns. They would be fourteen feet beneath the surface of the water and impale any wooden vessel running upon them. Robert Erskine, operator of the Ringwood iron mines and furnaces, and Washington's chief surveyor, undertook to manufacture such a chain. However, Forts Washington and Lee were lost to the British before anything could be done.

In 1776, Erskine undertook to manufacture a similar chain to be stretched across the Hudson between Bear Mountain and Anthony's Nose. This one was actually installed and consisted of heavy iron chain supported on wooden floats and protected on the downriver side by wooden booms. When the British captured forts Clinton and Montgomery in 1777, they dismantled this chain and took it overseas where they used it for many years to protect the harbor at Gibralter. It had cost the Americans $250,000.

A second similar chain was installed between West Point and Constitution Island in 1779. These were manufactured in the Ramapo Mountains at the Sterling and Ringwood iron works and installed under direction of Captain Thomas Machin. A similar chain was proposed between Plum Point and Pollepel's Island.

42.10 Site of ice storage sheds on west.

The Knickerbocker Ice Company used to cut ice from Highland Lake (Hessian Lake) and send it down long chutes to be stored in great sheds located on the shore of Doodletown Bight. It shipped 30,000 tons annually.

42.40 Bear Mountain to west.

With an elevation of 1,284 feet, it was formerly called Bear Hill, or earlier, Bread Tray Mountain. It is supposed that bears were common in the vicinity. However, it is possibly a corruption of "bare" mountain, referring to its rather bald summit. It is the focal point of the Bear Mountain State Park section of Palisades Interstate Park. There is a large lodge here, administrative offices, a ski run, ski jump, toboggan run, athletic fields, recreational lake, picnic grounds, swimming pool, museums, nature trails, and zoo. There are two steamboat piers and an inactive railroad station. It is a regular port of call for the Hudson River Day Line and a popular destination for other charter excursion boats. Bear Mountain Inn is open year round and has complete facilities. It used to be a popular training camp for athletic teams. The Pell and Harriman families formerly had residences near here, and Fort Clinton, the ruins of which can still be seen, were near the Bear Mountain Bridge. The Appalachian Trail crosses over Bear Mountain. The Perkins Memorial Drive goes to the summit where there is an observation tower. These are a memorial to George W. Perkins, who was president of the Palisades Interstate Park Commission until his death in 1920. The park took its present form under his direction. Originally, in 1908, the state of New York had acquired the Bear Mountain area as a new site of Sing Sing Prison, and prisoners were actually moved here and work started on clearing the land.

There was a great public outcry against this misuse of the area, and when Mrs. Mary A. Harriman gave her gift of 10,000 acres in the vicinity, she stipulated that the prison project be abandoned. The Bear Mountain Inn was opened in 1922.

42.40 Site of Fort Clinton on the west.

Located on the bluff just to south of toll booths of the Bear Mountain Bridge, this was the site of exciting activity during the Revolution, as told by Benson Lossing in his *The Hudson*.

. . . Fort Montgomery was on the northern side of (Popolopen) the creek, and Fort Clinton on the southern side. They were constructed at the beginning of the war for independence, and became the theatre of a desperate and bloody contest in the autumn of 1777. They were strong fortresses, though feebly manned. From Fort Montgomery to Anthony's Nose a heavy boom and massive iron chain were stretched over the river, to obstruct British ships that might attempt a passage toward West Point. The two forts were respectively commanded by two brothers, Generals George and James Clinton, the former at that time governor of the newly organized State of New York.

Burgoyne, then surrounded by the Americans at Saratoga, was, as we have observed . . . in daily expectation of a diversion in his favour, on the Lower Hudson, by Sir Henry Clinton—in command of the British troops at New York. Early in October, the latter fitted out an expedition for the Highlands, and accompanied it in person. He deceived General Putnam, then in command at Peek's Kill, by feints on that side of the river, at the same time he sent detachments over the Donder Berg, under cover of a fog. They were piloted by a resident Tory or loyalist, and in the afternoon of the 6th of October, and in two divisions, fell upon the forts. The commanders of the forts had no suspicions of the proximity of the enemy until their picket guards were assailed. These, and a detachment sent out in that direction, had a severe skirmish with the invaders on the borders of Lake Sinnipink, a beautiful sheet of water lying at the foot of the lofty Bear Mountain, on the same general level as the foundations of the fort (Clinton). Many of the dead were cast into that lake, near its outlet, and their blood so incarnadined its waters, that it has ever since been vulgarly called "Bloody Pond."

The garrisons at the two forts, meanwhile, prepared to resist the attack with desperation. They were completely invested at four o'clock in the afternoon, when a general contest commenced, in which British vessels in the river participated. It continued until twilight. The Americans then gave way, and a general flight ensued. The two commanders were among those who escaped to the mountains. The Americans lost in killed, wounded, and prisoners, about three hundred. The British loss was about one hundred and forty.

The contest ended with a sublime spectacle. Above the boom and chain the Americans had two frigates, two galleys, and an armed sloop. On the fall of the forts, the crews of these vessels spread their sails, and, slipping their cables, attempted to escape up the river. But the wind was adverse, and they were compelled to abandon them. They set them on fire when they left, to prevent their falling into the hands of an enemy. "The flames suddenly broke forth," wrote Stedman, a British officer and author, "and, as every sail was set, the vessels soon became magnificent pyramids of fire. The reflection on the steep face of the opposite mountain (Anthony's Nose), and the long train of ruddy light which shone upon the water for a prodigious distance, had a wonderful effect; while the ear was awfully filled with the continued echoes from the rocky shores, as the flames gradually reached the loaded cannons. The whole was sublimely terminated by the explosions, which left all again in darkness.

Early on the following morning, the obstructions in the river, which had cost the Americans a quarter of a million of dollars, Continental money, were destroyed by the British fleet. Fort Constitution, opposite West Point, was abandoned. A free passage of the Hudson being opened, Vaughan and Wallace sailed up the river on their destructive errand to Kingston and Clermont.

(Lossing: *The Hudson*, 262-4.)

Two of the ships the Americans lost were the frigate *Montgomery*, with twenty-four guns, and the frigate *Congress*, with twenty-eight guns. Sir Henry Clinton abandoned the forts after hearing of General Burgoyne's surrender at Saratoga.

Sir Henry Clinton's total force was about 4000 men. He left 2000 of them encamped below Peekskill and making feints on Peekskill and Fort Independence. Another 2000 men, under his personal command, crossed to the west bank at Kings Ferry and marched north,

across Dunderberg Mountain to Doodletown on October 6. They split into two groups. One division of 900 men went around the back of Bear Mountain to attack Fort Montgomery. They were met by American reinforcements of 400 men, but still managed to take the fort. The troops consisted largely of Hessians.

The other group of 1,100 men attacked Fort Clinton, after an active skirmish on the shores of Lake Sinnipink. The garrisons of the forts were composed mostly of untrained militia. They fought nobly and well, but could not stand up to the much larger force of disciplined troops. Many escaped, but a considerable number were slain or made prisoners. Governor George Clinton fled across the river from Fort Montgomery in a boat, and at midnight was with General Putnam at Continental Village. There is a persistent legend that he slid down the steep slopes from the fort to the shore on the seat of his pants. General James Clinton forced his way to the rear of Fort Clinton, where he received a bayonet wound in his thigh. However, he reached his home in New Windsor in safety.

42.40 Hessian Lake on west.

Its elevation is 155 feet. Originally called Lake Sinnipink, it is called Hessian Lake or Bloody Pond after the battle of Fort Clinton. The bodies of Hessian troops were thrown into the lake and incarnadined the waters. In the nineteenth century, it was called Highland Lake. During this period, the Knickerbocker Ice Company cut 30,000 tons of ice here annually. Today it is a principal feature of Bear Mountain Park. There is a paved path around the lake, and its banks are popular for picnicking. There are rowboats for hire. The Bear Mountain Inn is at the south end and the new Lodge at the north end.

42.40 Anthony's Nose on east:

elevation 900 feet. There was an Indian settlement called Wiccapee here. The tip of the mountain is pierced by a tunnel of the New York Central Railroad over 200 feet in length.

The most interesting feature of this promontory is its name. Estevan Gomez called it "St. Anthony's Nose" on his charts, possibly in honor of St. Anthony the Great of Egypt, founder of monastic life. (Born 251 A.D. at Coma in Heraclea, a town in upper Egypt.)

Washington Irving, in his *Knickerbocker History of New York*, has a more picturesque story to tell:

And now I am going to tell a fact, which I doubt much my readers will hesitate to believe, but if they do they are welcome not to believe a word in this whole history—for nothing which it contains is more true. It must be known then that the nose of Anthony the trumpeter was of a very lusty size, strutting boldly from his countenance like a mountain of Golconda, being sumptuously bedecked with rubies and other precious stones—the true regalia of a king of good fellows, which jolly Bacchus grants to all who bouse it heartily at the flagon. Now thus it happened, that bright and early in the morning, the good Anthony, having washed his burly visage, was leaning over the quarter railing of the galley, contemplating it in the glassy wave below. Just at this moment the illustrious sun, breaking in all his splendour from behind a high bluff of the Highlands, did dart one of his most potent beams full upon the refulgent nose of the sounder of brass—the reflection of which shot straightway down hissing hot into the water, and killed a mighty sturgeon that was sporting beside the vessel. This huge monster, being with infinite labour hoisted on board, furnished a luxurious repast to all the crew, being accounted of excellent flavour excepting about the wound, *where it smacked a little of brimstone— and this, on my veracity, was the first time that ever sturgeon was eaten in these parts by Christian people. When this astonishing miracle became known to Peter Stuyvesant, and that he tasted of the unknown fish, he, as may well be supposed, marvelled exceedingly; and as a monument thereof, he gave the name of Anthony's Nose to a stout promontory in the neighbourhood, and it has continued to be called Anthony's Nose ever since that time.*

The above refers to Anthony Van Corlaer, a real historical personage, who was allegedly drowned attempting to swim across Spuyten Duyvil Creek.

In his *New Mirror For Travellers* of 1828, James Kirke Paulding offers a few choice remarks:

Turning the base of Donderbarrack, the nose of all noses, Anthony's Nose, gradually displays itself to the enraptured eye, which must be steadily fixed on these our glowing pages. Such a nose is not seen every day. Not the famous hero of Slawkemburgius, whose proboscis emulated the steeple of Strasburg, ever had such a nose to his face. Taliacotius himself never made such a nose in his life. It is worth while to go ten miles to hear it blow—you would mistake it for a trumpet. The most curious thing about it is, that it looks no more like a nose than my foot. But now we think of it, there is still something more curious connected with this nose. There is not a soul born within five miles of it, but has a nose of most jolly dimensions—not quite as large as the mountain, but pretty well. Nay, what is still more remarkable, more than one person has recovered his nose, by regularly blowing the place where it ought to be, with a white pocket handkerchief, three times a day, at the foot of the mountain, in honour of St. Anthony. In memory of these miraculous restorations, it is the custom for the passengers

*in steam boats, to salute it in passing
with a universal blow of the nose: after
which, they shake their kerchiefs at it,
and put them carefully in their pockets.
No young lady ever climbs to the top of
this stately nose, without affixing her
white cambric handkerchief to a stick,
placing it upright in the ground, and
leaving it waving there, in hopes that all
her posterity may be blessed with goodly
noses.* (p.117.)

42.50 Bear Mountain Bridge overhead.

When built in 1924, this was the
world's longest suspension span.
As early as 1889, a railroad
bridge was projected for this
"natural" bridgepoint. The present bridge was privately built at
a cost of $5,000,000. It was
designed by Howard Baird of
New York City. Construction took
place between April 1923 and
November 1924. The central
span is 1632 feet long, and total
length 2,258 feet. It is 185 feet
above the water. It was acquired
by the state of New York in 1940
for $2,300,000. Routes U.S. 6
and U.S. 202 and the Appalachian Trail all make use of it. It is
a toll bridge.

42.60 Orange County on west.

From Popolopen Creek to Cedarcliff, the
west bank is occupied by Orange County.
It is bounded on the south by Rockland
County and Passaic and Sussex Counties in New Jersey and by the State of
Pennsylvania, and on the west by Sullivan and Ulster Counties in New York,
and on the north by Ulster County. It
covers an area of 829 square miles and
embraces nineteen townships and five
incorporated cities and villages.

It is one of the original counties of
New York State, having been erected in
1683 by Governor Thomas Dongan. It
was named in honor of King William III
of England, who also was Stadtholder of
Holland and Prince of Orange. Rockland
County was taken from it in 1798, but
some area was gained from Ulster
County that same year. The county has
two half-county seats, Goshen and Newburgh, but most official offices are at
Goshen, the original shire town.

The original inhabitants were the Mun-
cee Tribe of the Delaware Indians. They
had all left the area by 1740. Orange
County did not suffer from being preempted by gigantic patents. The largest
was the Evans Patent, but it was revoked
in 1699 by the lord of Bellomont, governor of New York, and the area was
reissued in the form of eighty-two
smaller patents between 1709 and 1775.
Generally these were limited to 2000
acres. However, several partners could
group together to qualify for a larger
patent. Among the larger ones were the
Chesekook, Wawayanda, and Minisink
patents. The so-called "German Patent"
was promised to German Palatinate settlers by Queen Anne of England in
1708, but not confirmed until 1719,
when they had already settled on the
land.

The county is composed of the follow-
ing townships: Newburgh, New Windsor,
Deer Park, Mount Hope, Greenville,
Wawayanda, Minisink, Goshen, Wallkill,
Crawford, Warwick, Chester, Monroe,
Tuxedo, Woodbury, Highlands, Blooming
Grove, Hamptonburg, and Montgomery
and the incorporated cities and villages
of Newburgh, Cornwall, Walden, Port
Jervis, and Middletown.

Principal water courses are the Hudson on the east and the Delaware River
on the southwest. It is also traversed
from south to north by the Wallkill River,
which rises in New Jersey and flows into
Ulster County, and its tributary Shawangunk Kill, which rises on the eastern
slopes of the Shawangunk Mountains
within Orange County. The Neversink
River rises in the Catskills and flows
south to the Delaware at Port Jervis. Its
tributary the Basha Kill flows south along
the western foot of the Shawangunk

Mountains. Moodna Creek is the principal outlet to the Hudson, along with Popolopen Creek. The former D & H Canal followed the western foot of the Shawangunk Mountains from Port Jervis to Ulster County. There is excellent fertile black dirt truck farming land along the Wallkill in southwestern Orange County, east of the Shawangunks.

Principal lakes include: Greenwood Lake (half in New Jersey), Lake Washington, Orange Lake, Chadwick Lake, Lake Tiorati, Lake Mombasha, Wickham Lake, Ramsdell Lake, also known as Beaver Dam Lake, and the smaller— Silver Stream Reservoir, Popolopen, Stillwell, Silver Mine, Stahe, Island Pond, Cahasset, Massawippa, Long Pond, Round Pond, Tomahawk, Turkey Hill Pond, Skanatati, Skemonto, Tuxedo, Sterling, Sterling Forest, Walton, Round, Cromwell, Orange & Rockland Lake, Glenmere, Forest, Cranberry, Silver, Highland, Monhagen, Hessian, Shawangunk, Cahoonzie, and Big Pond Lakes.

Principal mountain ranges are the Shawangunks, running from southwest to northeast, along the western portion of the county; the Catskills in the far western tip; the Plattekills, along the Hudson and the Highlands of the Hudson, actually the northern end of the Ramapo Mountains; as well as the isolated Schuenemunk Mountain near the Highlands.

Principal highways are Route 9W, along the Hudson; the New York Thruway, following Smith's Clove and paralleling the Hudson west of the Highlands and Plattekills; Interstate I-84 from the Newburgh Bridge to Port Jervis; and Route 17, the Quickway, from Harriman northwest to the Sullivan County border.

Principal railroads are the West Shore along the Hudson and the Erie, following the Ramapo River and Smith's Clove, heading west to Middletown and Port Jervis, thence up along the Delaware with branches to Newburgh, Montgomery, and Pine Bush; the Middletown

and New Jersey (part of the old Oswego Midland route) from Slate Hill to Middletown; the former Lehigh & Hudson from Maybrook south to New Jersey; and the former New Haven line from the Poughkeepsie Bridge to Maybrook. The now-abandoned Lehigh & New England ran from Maybrook to the New Jersey border near Pine Island, and the abandoned New York, Ontario & Western ran from the Hudson at Cornwall, westward to Middletown and thence over the Shawangunk Mountains into Sullivan County, with branches to Port Jervis and Kingston and Monticello.

Two noted early settlers were Sarah Wells and William Bull, whom she married. They were of Irish extraction. Later, the Frenchman Hector St. John de Crevecoeur purchased a farm near Goshen. He wrote the famous *Letters From An American Farmer,* describing agricultural life in the early nineteenth century. Famous native sons include Cadwallader Colden of Coldenham who lived in the county between 1727 and 1760 and served several terms as colonial governor of New York. William H. Seward, who later became Vice President of the United States and purchased Alaska ("Seward's Folly") was born in Florida, near Goshen. Benjamin B. Odell, a shipping magnate of Newburgh, was governor of New York from 1900 to 1904; and W. Averell Harriman, of Harriman, was governor of New York from 1955 to 1958.

42.60 Popolopen Creek to west.

Also formerly known as Popolopen's Kill, Pooploop's Kill and Fort Montgomery Creek or simply Montgomery Creek, it rises about six miles to the west in Popolopen and Stillwell Lakes in the Forest of Dean area behind the West Point Military Reservation. There was a dam at the head of navigation and the small lake behind it was known as Roe Pond. The area near Roe Pond is very rugged and picturesque, and was given the name "Hell Hole" by the West Point cadets who practiced summer manoeuvres there. Popolopen Torne rises 941 feet above it to the north. The creek is crossed near its outlet by the high viaduct of Route 9W and the low trestle of the West Shore Railroad.

In the past this area was known for its iron mining operations. Between 1746, when the first mining operations began in the Forest of Dean region, and 1934, when the last mine shut down, roughly 2,000,000 tons of high grade ore was taken from these hills. The ore is a pinkish calcite with crystalized magnetite, producing between sixty and sixty-one percent iron, with a low sulphur content which was excellent for non-Bessemer production. Benson Lossing visited in area in 1865, the same year that commercial operations got under way on a large scale. He noted a mill dam, flume, and water wheel at the head of navigation, about one mile from the Hudson. The wheel was used to provide pumping and hoisting power for the Forest of Dean Iron Ore Company, who started operations that year. They ran the mine until 1894, when it was abandoned. In 1905, with modern electric equipment, the Hudson Iron Company found it profitable to reopen the mines. The business was taken over between 1914 and 1934 by the Fort Montgomery Iron Corporation. They used 2½-ton skips at the mine, where they had a tipple and crushing plant. From thence, the ore was taken three miles over a narrow gauge steam railroad, along the creek to the head of the falls. Here the ore

was dumped into large buckets on a suspended wire ropeway to be conveyed for 1¼ miles to either barges anchored in the creek, or cars of the West Shore Railroad.

42.65 Site of Fort Montgomery to west.

(See article on Fort Clinton.) The West Shore Railroad goes through a short tunnel here below the site of the fort.

42.65 Putnam County to the east.

From here to Fishkill, just below Beacon, we have Putnam County on our right. It is one of the smallest in New York State, having only 235 square miles. It is bounded on the south by Westchester County and on the east by Connecticut and the north by Dutchess County, from which it was taken in 1812. It was named in honor of Revolutionary War General Israel Putnam. The county seat is Carmel, well inland to the east. The county is quite mountainous, and largely devoted to country estates, parks, and small agriculture. The mountains are the southwestern end of the Taconics. Principal water courses are the Croton River, draining the eastern precincts and Fishkill Creek draining northwest into the Hudson in Dutchess County. The Canopus Creek flows southwest into Annsville Creek and the Hudson. Principal towns are Brewster, Cold Spring, and Garrison. Major roads all run from north to south except Interstate I-84, which runs from the Newburgh Bridge to the Connecticut border via Brewster. Route 9N follows the Hudson; Route 9 parallels it further inland (the old New York and Albany Post Road); the Taconic State Parkway bisects the county from north to south. The New York

Central Railroad follows the Hudson, and the Harlem Division runs from south to north through the Croton River Valley. The former, now abandoned New York and Putnam ran from Westchester County to Brewster via Lake Mahopac. The former New Haven (now Conrail) has a line running from Poughkeepsie to Danbury, Connecticut, via Brewster. The most famous native son was Daniel Drew, who came from Carmel. It is a question whether he was famous or notorious. The countryside is very picturesque and the natives have a liking for dirt roads (well maintained and oiled) and actively work to preserve a rural atmosphere.

42.65 Popolopen Torne to west.
(elevation 941 feet).

42.75 Fort Montgomery village to west.

42.75 Brook's Lake to west,
behind village of Fort Montgomery.

43.40 Garrison Pond on west.
In village of Fort Montgomery, along Route 9W.

43.40 Manitou on east.
Formerly called Highland, it is a station on the railroad.

43.70 Mystery Point on east.

44.40 Canada Hill on east.
(elevation 820 feet).

44.40 South Mountain Pass on east.
Between Canada Hill and Anthony's Nose, it leads to Canopus Hollow and was used by the old highway before construction of the highway along the ledges of Anthony's Nose.

44.40 Copper Mine Brook to east.
It rises in South Mountain Pass.

44.60 Curry Pond to east.

43.40 to 44.60 on west:
estates of John S. Gilbert, William Pell, and Arthur Pell.

Active at turn of the century, they are now broken up.

44.80 Con Hook on west.
Formerly spelled Cohn's Hook, and pronounced Connosook, it is a low rocky headland jutting directly out into the channel with a 125 foot depth. The water immediately north and south is only one half foot deep, sheerly dropping off to 108 feet and 72 feet depths. A menace to navigation, it has a flashing beacon with a 2½-second signal. Henry Hudson anchored here on his way up river on September 14, 1609. The estate of J. Pierpont Morgan was located above the Hook.

45.00 Crown Ridge to west.
(elevation 1000 feet).

45.00 Cragston Lakes to west.
Atop the first bluffs, this is the site of the former estate of Alfred Pell.

45.00 Pell's Pond to west.
(up on ridges).

45.00 Crystal Lake to west.
(up on ridges).

45.00 White Rock to east.
(elevation 885 feet).

45.50 Bare Rock Mountain to west.
Also called Mt. Eyrie, its elevation is 1,210 feet

45.50 Former Estates
of Charles Tracy, Captain Roe, "Benny' Havens, and John Bigelow.

45.50 Sugarloaf Hill to east.
(elevation 730 feet). Wallace Bruce says:

. . . so named as it resembles, to one coming up the river, the old-fashioned conical-shaped sugarloaf, which was formerly suspended by a string over the centre of the hospitable Dutch tables, and swung around to be occasionally nibbled at, which in good old Knickerbocker days,

*was thought to be the best and
only orthodox way of sweetening
tea.*

(Bruce, *Hudson by
Daylight*, p. 118.)

The Dutch was "Suycker Broodt."

45.50 Third Order Villa to east:
Former estate of S.J. Livingston.

45.65 Glenclyfe Siding to east:
former home of Hamilton Fish.

45.70 Beverly Dock to east.
Benedict Arnold escaped from
here to the British ship *Vulture*
on the morning of September
24, 1780, after he learned of the
capture of Major André. Benson
Lossing tells us that:

*. . . His six oarsmen on that
occasion, unconscious of the
nature of the general's errand in
such hot haste down the river,
had their musceles strengthened
by a promised reward of two
gallons of rum; and the barge
glided with the speed of the
wind. They were awkened to a
sense of their position only when
they were detained on board the
"Vulture" as prisoners, and saw
their chief greeted as a friend by
the enemies of their country.
They were speedily set at liberty, in New York, by Sir Henry
Clinton, who scorned Arnold for
his meanness and treachery.*

(Lossing, *The Hudson*,
p.240)

**45.70 Beverly Robinson House site
to east.**
Located above Beverly Dock, it
was burned in 1892. It was built
in 1758 and belonged to the
Tory Beverly Robinson. Benedict
Arnold made it his headquarters
while in command of West Point
and escaped from here on the
morning of September 24, 1780.

The scene is described in a
lively manner by Wallace Bruce:

*. . . Alexander Hamilton and
General Lafayette sat gayly chat-
ting with Mrs. Arnold and her
husband (over breakfast) when
the letter from Jamison was received. Arnold glanced at the
contents, rose and excused himself from the table, beckoning to
his wife to follow him, bade her
good-bye, told her he was a
ruined man and a traitor, kissed
his little boy in the cradle, rode
to Beverly Dock, and ordered
his men to pull off and go down
the river. The "Vulture," an English man-of-war, was near Teller's
Point, and received a traitor,
whose miserable treachery
branded him with eternal infamy
in both continents.*

(Bruce, *Hudson by
Daylight*, p.114.)

46.20 Highland Brook to west.
46.20 Buttermilk Falls to west.
On Highland Brook, this site is
well described by Benson Lossing:

*. . . a small stream comes rushing
down the rocks in cascades and
foaming rapids, falling more than
a hundred feet in the course of
as many yards. The chief fall,
where the stream plunges into
the river, is over a sloping granite
rock. It spreads out into a broad
sheet of milk-white foam, which
suggested its name to the Dutch
skippers, and they called it
"Boter Melck Val"—Buttermilk
Fall. The stream affords water-
power for flour-mills at the brink
of the river. The fall is so great,
that by a series of overshot
water-wheels, arranged at different altitudes, a small quan-*

tity of water does marvellous execution. Large vessels come alongside the elevator on the river front, and there discharge cargoes of wheat and take in cargoes of flour.

Rude paths and bridges are so constructed that visitors may view the great fall and the cascades above from many points. The latter have a grand and wild aspect when the stream is brimful, after heavy rains and the melting of snows.

On the rough plain above is the village of Buttermilk Fall.
(Lossing, *The Hudson*, p.255.)

The mill that Lossing was referring to in 1865 was the grist mill of David Parry, built about 1838. It stood just south of the fall of the cascades into the Hudson. The water is ninety feet deep right off shore here. When the West Shore railroad was built, it was necessary to demolish the mill and hang bridges parallel to the cliffs out over the water to carry the railroad. Parry also operated a resort hotel above his mill, to the south of the falls. Buttermilk Falls are on private property and not open to the public. They can only be seen from the water or a West Shore train.

46.25 Highland Falls Village to west.
Formerly called Buttermilk Falls, it is basically a service village for the adjacent United States Military Academy at West Point. It offers small stores, motels, and housing for base personnel. Ladycliff College is located here. It was formerly a resort town. The historical landscape painters Emanuel Leutze (1816-1868) and Robert W. Weir (1803-1889) both resided here.

46.40 Ladycliff College to west.
Atop the cliffs north of Buttermilk Falls is this Catholic college, formerly Ladycliff Academy for Girls. It occupies the site of earlier Cozzens's Hotel and Cranston's Hotel. Cozzens originally operated a resort on the West Point grounds. In 1849, he built a much larger one south of the military reservation, somewhat north of the present Ladycliff College. In about 1860, it burned down, and he built a larger one on the high rocky bluff overlooking Buttermilk Falls. It was later operated under the name Cranston's, and was acquired by a Catholic order in 1900 for use as an academy.

The hotel was situated 180 feet above the river and accommodated between 250 and 500 guests. It was visited by the Prince of Wales in 1865. There were cottages attached and extensive pleasure-grounds with walks, rustic bridges, etc.

46.40 Monastery of Mary Immaculate to east.
This monastery is run by the Capuchin Franciscan fathers as a friary and convent. The southern end was built ca. 1890; it is 4-story red brick with copper-crowned cupola. The northern end was built in 1932; it is red brick, two-story.

46.40 Castle Rock to east.
A spire-topped castle atop 630 foot hill, it is three-story stone with tower and was built 1881 for William H. Osborn.

46.70 Cozzens's or Cranston's Landing to west.
(The Highland Falls railroad depot.)

46.75 U.S. Hotel Thayer to west.
On West Point grounds, this hotel is owned and operated by the United States government. It is open to the general public.

Built in 1924, renovated 1978, it was named in honor of Sylvanus Thayer, an early West Point superintendent.

46.75 Arden Point to east.

It was named for the former estate of T.B. Arden, "Ardenia."

46.80 Arden Brook to east.

It was formerly called Kedron Brook. In the mid-nineteenth century, there was a mill near the upper end of the ravine.

46.80 Fort Hill to east.

Also known as Redoubt Hill, from Revolutionary War fortifications, its elevation is 810 feet.

47.35 West Point (United States Military Academy) to west.

West Point has been called the Gibralter of America because of its strategic situation. In sailing days, ships had to change course here, because of the sharp bends in the river, and virtually came to a halt. In the narrow waters, they became easy targets for guns on shore. Early in the Revolution, fortifications were built both on West Point and Constitution Island on the opposite shore. Constitution Fort, on Constitution Island, was completed in September 1775. In 1778, a chain was stretched across the river from West Point to Constitution Island. Fort Clinton, originally called Fort Arnold, was completed at West Point in the spring of the same year. In 1779, Fort Putnam was built atop Mount Independence, behind Fort Clinton. It was on a virtually impregnable crag and provided covering protection to Fort Clinton. There were several smaller batteries. Battery Knox faced the river near Fort Clinton. Redoubt Wyllis and Redoubt Meigs both faced to the south and were located on lower ground southeast of Fort Putnam. In early Army orders this group of fortifications was designated as "the citadel and its dependencies." After the failure of Arnold's plan to hand it over to the British in 1780, West Point was never again threatened, and the American flag has flown over it since 1778. It was first occupied by the United States Army on January 20, 1778, making it the nation's oldest continually occupied military post.

In October 1776, Congress appointed a committee to prepare plans for a military school. Shortly after the Revolution (1783), Washington suggested West Point as a possible site for a military academy. In 1793, in his annual message, Washington again recommended West Point as a location. In 1794, Congress organized a corps of artillerists to be stationed at West Point, with thirty-two cadets attached. In 1798, the number was increased to fifty-six cadets. On March 16, 1802, Congress formally authorized the founding of a military academy at West Point, and it opened on July 4th of that year with ten cadets. Under Major Sylvanus Thayer, who served as Superintendent from 1817 to 1833, West Point became a military school of the first order; the basic system established by Thayer is continued today.

The cadets live a strict military life in an atmosphere of learning. All cadets receive considerable basic military instruction, particularly in the last two years. The curriculum includes much mathematics, physics, and engineering and leads to a B.S. degree. The graduates are then required to serve with the Army for a number of years. Graduation from West Point is held in great esteem in the Army and is often the key to high advancement in the ranks. Many other graduates, and even drop outs, have gone on to great success in civilian life as well. Among the most famous graduates are Robert E. Lee, Ulysses S. Grant, Andrew Jackson, Philip Henry Sheridan, Douglas MacArthur, George Patton, and Dwight D. Eisenhower. Edgar Allan Poe and James A McNeill Whistler became famous, although they did not complete their terms. For many years West Point was the nation's premier school of civil engineering.

In the nineteenth century, West Point was a popular summer resort, because of the attractions of the beautiful scenery and interesting historic associations. It is still a popular place for pleasure excursions, and visitors are always welcome and treated with courtesy and respect. The regular outdoor band concerts, and July 4th pyrotechnic displays are very popular with the natives of the surrounding towns. Athletic events draw large crowds—particularly football games at Michie Stadium, where many people arrive by bus and steamer. Reviews on the parade grounds are perhaps the most popular event, and the military museum and organ recitals in the chapel also draw large ttendance. It is a regular stop of the Day Line steamers, and there is ample time between boats to see the most important and interesting sights.

Principal points of interest are as listed here. I shall give full descriptions only of those points not seen from the river. These later will be fully described at the appropriate river mileage, although some of them are considerably inland.

1) Hotel Thayer—described at ERM 46.75.

2) Cavalry and Artillery Drill Field— now known as South Athletic Field —across from Hotel Thayer.

3) Michie Stadium—open only during games. This football field with seating capacity of 26,000 was named in honor of Dennis Mahan Michie, class of 1892, captain of the first West Point football team, killed in action at San Juan, Cuba in 1898.

4) Redoubt Meigs—near junction of Wilson and Kinsley Hill Roads.

5) Redoubt Wyllis—immediately north of Redoubt Meigs.

6) Lusk Reservoir—opposite Michie Stadium on Mills Road.

7) Fort Putnam—on Mount Independence, north of Michie Stadium. Approached by a steep foot trail from Mill's Road, it was originally built in 1778 and partially restored in 1907-10. Its elevation is 451 feet above the river.

8) Cadet Chapel—the dominant structure on the reservation. Its elevation is 300 feet above the river. It is located on DeRussy Road.

9) Catholic Chapel of the Most Holy Trinity—on Washington Road near Mill Road. Modeled on an English Carthusian abbey church, it was consecrated in 1900.

10) Old Cadet Chapel—In the cemetery on Washington Road. Built in 1837 on the site of Jefferson Hall and moved to its present site in 1911, it is in Renaissance Revival style with a Roman Doric portico. Inside is an oil painting by Robert W. Weir entitled *Peace and War.* Black marble shields on the walls are inscribed in gold with the name, rank, and dates of birth and death of every Revolutionary War general. One bearing only a date of birth and rank, omits the name of Benedict Arnold.

11) Thayer Hall—near lower landing. (See article ERM 47.50.)

12) Grant Hall—opposite Administration Building on Thayer Road. Adjacent to the South Cadet Barracks, it is the cadet reception hall, built in Tudor Gothic style.

13) Administration Builting—Thayer Road. Built in 1904. Designed by Cram, Goodhue & Ferguson— mainly work of Cram. Dark gray granite trimmed with limestone in Gothic style with a 160-foot tower-keep on its southwest corner. Built of solid masonry, it has battlements, buttresses, and cross-mullioned and traceried windows. The entrance is ornamented with heraldic seals of the Government and the Washington coat of arms, and is guarded by a raised portcullis. It contains the Ordnance Museum.

14) Central Cadet Barracks (1851)— behind Grant Hall.

15) Washington Hall—Jefferson Road. Built in 1925-9. Designed by Gehron & Ross architects. This is the

cadet mess hall. In Gothic style, its large stained glass window depicts outstanding events in the life of Washington.

16) Superintendent's Quarters—Jefferson Road (ca. 1820). This building was once occupied by Robert E. Lee.

17) Battle Monument—Trophy Point (off Washington Road). The monument was erected to the memory of the 2,230 officers and privates of the regular Army killed in action in the Civil War. A Roman Doric column, five feet in diameter and forty-six feet high stands upon a five-step circular stairway,broken by eight plain pedestals around the perimeter, each of which supports a sphere flanked by two cannons. The column supports a winged statue of Fame, by Frederick Mac-Monnies. The rest of the monument was designed by Stanford White.

18) Kosciusko Monument—Cullum Road, on site of old Fort Clinton. Designed by John H. Latrobe, class of 1822, it was erected by the corps of cadets in 1828. (See article ERM 47.76 for details about Kosciusko.)

19) Site of Fort Clinton (Fort Arnold). Cullum Road and Clinton Place. See article ERM 47.75.)

20) Officers' Club (mess)—Cullum Road. (See ERM 47.70.)

21) Bachelors' Building—Cullum Road. (See REM 47.72.)

22) Cullum Memorial Hall—Cullum Road. (See ERM 47.71.)

23) Flirtation Walk—A gravel and rock foot trail which leaves Cullum Road just north of the Bachelors' Building and winds three quarters of a mile down the cliff to the river, past the lighthouse at Gee's Point, the beach where the western end of the great chain was anchored, the site of the chain battery, and the remains of the earthworks of Fort Clinton, and ends at Battle Monument. Just before passing the lighthouse the path is overhung by "Kissing Rock," so called because, according to tradition, if a cadet passes underneath with his best girl and fails to kiss her, the rock will crush them both.

24) Kosciusko's Garden—near south end of Flirtation Walk. According to Benson J. Lossing:

. . . a pleasant terrace in the steep bank of the river, which is called Kosciusko's Garden. At the back of the terrace the rock rises perpendicularly, and from its outer edge descends as perpendicularly to the river. This is said to have been Kosciusko's favourite place of resort for reading and meditation, while he was at West Point. He found a living spring bubbling from the rocks, in the middle of the terrace, and there he constructed a pretty little fountain. Its ruins were discovered in 1802 and repaired. The water now (1865) rises into a marble basin. Seats have been provided for visitors, ornamental shrubs have been planted, and the whole place wears an aspect of mingled romance and beauty. A deep circular indentation in the rock back of the fountain was made, tradition affirms, by a cannon-ball sent from a British ship, while the Polish soldier was occupying his accustomed loitering place, reading Vauban, and regaled by the perfume of roses.
(Lossing, *The Hudson,* pp. 233-234.)

25) Battery Knox—formerly immediately above Kosciusko's Garden.

26) Site of West Point Hotel—was located on Trophy Point. It is also known as Roe's Hotel.

27) Stony Lonesome—desolate area west of Michie Stadium

28) Benny Haven's—name of a bartender in village of Highland Falls who sold refreshment to the cadets in violation of the regulations. Affectionately mentioned in many old songs and jokes.

47.35 West Point South Dock and Depot to west.

This is not the original West Point landing. According to Benson Lossing, "The road from the plain to the landing at West Point was cut from the steep rocky bank of the river, at a heavy expense to the government. The wharf is spacious, and there a sentinel was continually posted (1865), with a slate and pencil, to record the names of all persons who arrive and depart. This was for the use of the Superintendent, by which means he is informed daily of the arrival of any persons to whom he might wish to extend personal or professional courtesies." The road to the landing is named Williams Road. When fresh recruits used to arrive at West Point by train, they were made to run up this hill as their first reception at the Point. The scene will be familiar to those who saw the motion picture *The Long Gray Line.* Note the Gothic railroad station. This is a regular landing of the Day Line. The schedule between here and New York City is the world's oldest scheduled passenger steamer route, having been established by Fulton's *Clermont.*

47.35 Fort Defiance Hill to east. (elevation 900 feet.)

47.35 Garrison to east:

A residential village with local railroad station and passenger ferry to West Point (formerly vehicle ferry). Originally called Garrison's after a local family, it is in the town of Phillipstown, which was organized ca.1858.

Garrison was used as the site for filming some of the scenes of *Hello Dolly!* because of its supposed resemblance to Yonkers in the 1890s. There are many nineteenth-century buildings left in the village. Many Continental Army troops were stationed here during the Revolution.

47.50 Thayer Hall to west.

Formerly the Riding Hall, it was designed by Cram, Goodhue & Ferguson and built in 1911. It rises from the river shore to the level of the east edge of the plain. Formerly an arena covering more than 16,000 square feet was provided for cavalry practice. There were stalls for 100 horses. The area has since been broken up and used for classroom space. It is of granite Gothic construction; a power house is located in the lower portion and the roof is used for parking.

47.50 Mount Independence to west. (elevation 451 feet.)

47.50 Fort Putnam to west:

atop Mount Independence. Built under the direction of Colonel Rufus Putnam in 1778-1779, by men of his Massachusetts regiment, it was partially restored 1907-10.

47.65 Site of Phillipse Manor to east.

The seat of the Phillipse family's Highland Patent, this included most of present day Putnam County.

47.70 Phillipse Brook to east.

47.70 Gordon School to east.

The former home of M.P. Moore, it is in Stone Gothic, (1847), designed by Richard Upjohn.

47.70 Duck Island to west.

Formerly amidst ½ foot deep shallows, now filled in to create athletic fields at the foot of the bluffs.

47.70 Officers' Mess to west.
Atop the bluffs on Cullum Road, it is also known as the Officers' Club. One of three neoclassic buildings in a row designed by McKim, Mead & White and built between 1898 and 1903, this is the most southerly of the three. It is built of granite and is two stories high. The Bachelor Officers' Mess is one of the oldest in the service.

47.71 Cullum Memorial Hall to west.
The middle of the neoclassic group on Cullum Road, it is granite, two stories, with hipped roof. The main facade is adorned with four three-quarter engaged Ionic columns. The river front has undergone extensive modifications in recent years.

47.72 Bachelors' Building to west.
This is the most northerly of the neoclassic group.

47.73 Site of Battery Knox to west:
Atop bluffs.

47.75 Site of Fort Clinton to west
(originally Fort Arnold): atop bluffs. Built in the spring of 1778 under the direction of Thaddeus Kosciusko, then colonel in Continental Army and chief of the Engineers' Corps, it was 600 yards around within the walls with embankments 21 feet thick at the base and 14 feet high. It was 180 feet above the river and could accommodate 600 persons. It has been partially restored.

47.76 Kosciusko's Garden to west:
partway up bluffs. (See item 24 under West Point article, ERM 47.35, for details.)

47.76 Kosciusko's Monument to west:
atop bluffs on site of Fort Clinton. Designed by John H. Latrobe, class of 1822, it was erected by the corps of cadets in 1828. I quote from Lossing with reference to Thaddeus Kosciusko:

Kosciusko was much beloved by the Revolutionary Army, and his memory is held in reverence by the American people. He was only twenty years of age when he joined that army. He had been educated at the Military School of Warsaw. He had not completed his studies, when he eloped with a beautiful girl of high rank. They were overtaken by the maiden's father, who made a violent attempt to seize his daughter. The young Pole was compelled either to slay the father or abandon the daughter, He chose the latter, and obtaining the permission of his sovereign, he went to France, and there became a student in drawing and military science. In Paris he was introduced to Dr. Franklin, and fired with a desire to aid a people fighting for independence, he sailed for America, bearing letters from that minister. He applied to Washington for employment. "What do you seek here?" asked the leader of the armies of the revolted colonies. "I come to fight as a volunteer for American independence," the young Pole replied. "What can you do?" Washington asked. "Try me," was Kosciusko's prompt reply. Pleased with the young man, Washington took him into his military family. The Congress soon afterwards appointed him engineer, with the rank of colonel. He returned to Poland at the close of the Revolution, and was made a major-general under Poniatowski. He was at the head of the military movements of the Revolution in Poland, in 1794, and was made a prisoner, and carried to St. Petersburg . . . . After the Empress Catherine died, the Emperor Paul liberated him, offered him command in the Russian service, and presented

him with his own sword. He declined it, saying, "I no longer need a sword, since I have no longer a country to defend." He revisited the United States in 1797, when the Congress granted him land in consideration of his services. He afterwards lived in Switzerland, and there he died in 1817. A public funeral was made for him at Warsaw. Twelve years afterwards, the cadets of West Point, actuated by love for the man and reverence for his deeds, erected a beautiful marble monument to his memory, within the ruins of Old Fort Clinton, at a cost of about $5,000.

(Lossing, *The Hudson,* p. 229-232)

47.76 There are eddies
in the channel here, caused by the bend in the river and water entering from Indian Brook.

48.20 Flirtation Walk to west.
(See item 23 under West Point article, ERM 47.35, for details.)

48.20 Sheridan Monument to west:
on Gees Point. Philip Henry Sheridan (1831-1888) was a Union general in the Civil War. He was a member of the class of 1853 at West Point. He distinguished himself at Perryville and in the Chattanooga Campaign and Wilderness Campaign. He beat Lee at Five Forks and cut him off at Appomattox Courthouse. On Sherman's retirement in 1883, he was made commanding general of the United States Army.

48.20 Gees Point on west.
Also Gee's Point. Possibly a corruption of "Geese" Point. There is a lighthouse here. There is 88 feet of water just off the point and the river bends sharply to the west. There is also a fog bell here.

48.25 Warner Ridge to east.

48.25 Saint Basil's Academy to east.
Now a Greek Orthodox seminary., Present building is Tudor style, ca.1920. At about the turn of the century, this property belonged to M.M. Gouverneur and later to Jacob Ruppert, the brewer.

48.35 Dick's Castle to east.
I quote the flyer published by Mr. Anton Chmela, the present owner:

On top of a high hill in the midst of the city of Granada, Spain, rises a complex of buildings referred to as the "Alhambra." Parts of the structure date back to the ninth century. The palace has no architectural unity but consists of a series of halls and courtyards built at need. The walls and ceilings were adorned with geometric designs, and the ornamental stone lions guarding many of the fountains are heresies of Christian influence that came during the fifteenth century.

Dick's Castle is not a replica of the Alhambra, but the flavor of Moorish architecture and Christian motifs has been preserved in a structure that was caught in the renaissance of new building ideas in the United States between 1900 and 1930. The late Mrs. Evans R. Dick was impressed with the Alhambra and decided to build a residence here in Garrison that would have been the "showplace of the Hudson Valley." Her dream was short-lived, when in 1911 after six years of construction, her husband's financial means were destroyed by a stock market slump initially indicated by the earlier 1907 crash. The Dick fam-

ily had spent close to $3,000,000 when building was halted, and had their vision been completed some $7,000,000 would have been spent.

Although work had stopped, Mrs. Dick refused to sell the castle for any price. Years passed and no one looked after the building. Vandals broke in and destroyed the inner courtyard. Ornamental figurines were torn from the walls. In 1944 the castle was finally purchased from the Dick family by an Austrian engineer.

Work is presently under way to finish one wing of the castle. Plans call for a museum which will house a collection of items, mostly models, that will illustrate the history of American industry. The courtyard will be restored preserving the Moorish style that first prompted Mrs. Dick to begin a venture which the present owners hope to finish.

(Brochure privately printed by Anton Chmela ca. 1975.)

The writer has visited with Mr. Chmela and observed further work in progress. There are many exquisite details and the years have mellowed even the dilapidation. It is a very romantic place. The castle is located on a hill with an elevation of about 400 feet. The views from the upper floors are outstanding.

Upon Mrs. Chmela's death in 1979, the property was sold to the Dia Art Foundation, who plan to use the castle as a museum, exhibiting the works of Hudson Valley artists. Dia plans to complete the castle as rapidly as possible and it will remain open to the public.

48.40 Cat Hill to east:
Elevation 800 feet.

48.40 Indian Brook to east.
Rises in Catfish Pond south of Moneyhole Mountain, east of Cat Hill. It first flows northwest for about one mile where it turns southwest after receiving the waters of Loch Lyall, via Loch Lyall Brook. This bend is near the Albany Post Road (Route 9). It then flows southwest for two miles through very picturesque ravines and over waterfalls. After passing under a high viaduct on Route 9D, it flows into a shallow bay opposite Gees Point. This bay is virtually shut off from the Hudson by the causeway of the New York Central Railroad. This bay also collects the waters from several small brooks flowing from Dale's Pond, Lath's Pond, and Cat Pond, and through the meadows separating Constitution Island from the mainland. The north bank of Indian Brook is followed by a very scenic and picturesque narrow dirt road between route 9D and Route 9. The falls on this stream are very picturesque and were a popular place of resort in the nineteenth century. They were dubbed "Fanny Kemble's Bath" after a noted incident in 1832 or 1833 when this famous and attractive young actress got soaked and almost killed herself climbing them.

48.50 World's End
mid-channel between Gees Point and Constitution Island. This is the deepest place in the Hudson River—202 feet.

48.50 Site of chain across river 1778-1779.
This chain was installed under the direction of Captain Thomas Machin. It was manufactured at forges in the Ramapo mountains. The links were made of iron bars, 2½ inches square. Their average length was a little over two feet and their weight about 140 pounds each. According to Lossing:

The chain was stretched across the river at the narrowest place, just above Gee's Point (the extreme rocky end of West Point) and Constitution Island. It was laid across a boom of heavy logs, that floated near together. These were sixteen feet long, and pointed at each end, so as to offer little resistance to the tidal currents. The chain was fastened to these logs by staples, and at each shore by huge blocks of wood and stone. This chain and boom seemed to afford an efficient barrier to the passage of vessels; but their strength was never tested, as the keel of an enemy ship never ploughed the Hudson after the fleet of Vaughan passed up and down in the autumn of 1777, and performed its destructive mission.

(Lossing, *The Hudson*, p.227-28.)

The chain was installed in April of 1778. It was protected by a "chain battery" at West Point. Part of the chain is on display at Trophy Point.

48.50 Constitution Island to east.

A rocky island with a maximum elevation about 100 feet, it is bounded on the north by Foundry Cove, on the west and south by the main channel of the Hudson, and on the east by marshes traversed by small brooks flowing from Dale's Pond, Lath's Pond, and Cat Pond. Its eastern side is traversed from south to north by the New York Central Railroad, which attains it by means of long causeways across the mouth of Indian Brook and Foundry Cove. It belongs to the United States Military Academy and is not open to the public except on special tours operating from the ferry landings at West Point and Garrison. Advance reservations are required.

It is claimed that a French family by the name of Martelaire lived here about 1720. In any event, it was acquired by the Philipse family from the first subdivision of the Highland Patent in 1754 until 1836, when it was purchased by Henry Warner. The stretch of the Hudson here is called the Martelaer's Rack, or Martyr's Reach. It is possible that this derived from the early settler Martelaire. However, Lossing has another possible explanation: "It was called by the Dutch navigators Martelaer's Island, and the reach in the river between it and the Storm King, Martelaer's Rack, or Martyr's Reach. The word martyr was used in this connection to signify "contending" and "struggling," as vessels coming up the river with a fair wind would frequently find themselves, immediately after passing the point of the island into this reach, struggling with the wind right ahead." As the name seems to have been in use from very early times, the story of the Frenchman Martelaire seems just a bit too pat to ring true.

The island was fortified early in the Revolution at the suggestion of Bernard Romans. It was first garrisoned on September 21, 1775, and the fort was called "Constitutional Fort," in honor of the British Constitution. It soon became simply Fort Constitution. A block house or powder house was built near the high western tip of the island, and its ruins can still be seen. It was the eastern terminus of the great chain from West Point. Washington's bodyguards were mustered out here in December of 1783.

After the Revolution, it generally became known as Constitution Island, although the Warner Family used the old name of Martelaer's Rock well into the twentieth century.

Henry Warner, who purchased the island in 1836, was a New York City lawyer. He had financial reverses shortly after purchasing the island and retired here to a simple house he called "Wood Crag." This house was built of stone and clapboard, with parts dating back to before the Revolution. A large addition was put on about 1845. His household consisted of his sister, and his two daughters, Susan (1819-1885) and Anna (1827-1915). They lived a simple life here. The girls were very religious and never married. They conducted Bible classes and befriended homesick cadets. Aside from a rare trip to Boston or New York, they never left the island. However, they did attain a wide fame.

In 1850, G.P. Putnam published a novel by Susan Warner entitled *The Wide Wide World,* which turned out to be a tremendous best-seller, selling hundreds of thousands of copies. It went through thirty editions. The book was quite sentimental, but struck the popular note. A second novel entitled *Queechy* sold almost as well, and its name was even given to a lake in Columbia County near the foothills of the Berkshires. Susan used the pen name of Elizabeth Wetherell. Anna Warner also tried her hand at writing with some substantial success. She wrote under the name Anna Lothrop and specialized in children's books. In 1876, the two collaborated on a novel entitled *Wych Hazel.*

The sisters always wanted the island to go to the military academy and refused large offers for it. However, Congress would never appropriate the small price they asked—and needed for their maintenance. In 1908, Anna and Mrs. Russell Sage gave the island to the government. The gift was accepted at the direction of President Theodore Roosevelt. The terms of the gift provided for Anna Warner to live there until her death (1915) and for the maintenance of the island and house "as is" forever. These wishes have been followed out substantially ever since. At the time of writing the boat leaves from West Point South Dock and the Garrison Marina on Tuesday and Wednesday afternoons, June through September. Phone 914-446-8676 (Mon.-Fri. 10-11:30 A.M.) for reservations.

48.50 Targes Rock to east:
also called Powder House Point and Magazine Point.

48.60 Valley Point to west:
referring to Washington Valley.

48.60 Trophy Point and Battle Monument to west.
This was the site of Roe's West Point Hotel in the nineteenth century. There are unexcelled views northward from here. Besides the Battle Monument (see item #17 in West Point article, ERM 47.35) there are various other old cannon and mortars on display.

48.60 West Point North Dock to west. or south.
This was the original West Point landing where Fulton's steamboat docked.

48.60 West Point Post Exchange to west or south:
a large modern brick building.

48.60 Mount Independence and Fort Putnam to south.
(Refer back to ERM 47.50.)

48.60 Cadet Chapel to south.
At 300 feet above the river, this is the dominant structure on the reservation. Designed by Cram, Goodhue & Ferguson, it was completed in 1910. It is built of granite in neo-Gothic style and cruciform in plan. There is a high buttressed tower at the crossing of the nave and transepts. The aisle walls of the nave are solid masonry, but the clerestory walls are all glass except for stepped stone buttresses. The interior decoration is lavish and allegorical in nature. The magnificent pipe organ has 12,500 pipes. The service is interdenominational, but similar to that of the Episcopal church.

48.65 Boscobel Restoration to east.
This was originally at River Mile 35.25. (Please refer back.) Res-

toration of eighteenth century home of States Morris Dyckman (1755-1806), with fine collections of English china, silver, and books and period furnishings. The house is in the style of Robert Adam. The gardens are extensive and very beautiful. The house is open daily except Tuesdays, Thanksgiving, Christmas, and January and February. It is located on Route 9D.

48.90 Crow's Nest Brook to west: rises in a bog at l,200 foot level of Crow's Nest Mountain.

48.90 Murray's Ravine to west.

It is near the shore of the Hudson. Crow's Nest Brook flows through it.

48.90 Washington Valley to west.

This is a long broad valley along the southern foot of Crow's Nest Mountain, Hill of Pines, Mose Gees Mountain, and Mount Rascal, at the northern end of the United States Military Reservation. It is traversed by Routes 293 and 218. The West Point golf course is at its eastern end. As with so many other places, it takes its name from the fact that Washington used to stay in a house here when visiting West Point, winter of 1779. Moore House, now demolished.

49.00 Foundry Cove to east.

It was named for former West Point Foundry which operated here between 1817 and 1884. During the War of 1812, President James Madison ordered the creation of four foundries in different parts of the country. Cold Spring was chosen as one, as it could be protected by West Point. James Kirke Paulding, the writer, was serving as secretary of the board of naval commissioners at the time and gave the direction of the foundry to Gouverneur Kemble (1786-1875). The foundry was a pioneer in much technology and built America's first iron ship, the revenue cutter *Spencer.* Its greatest fame came from the "Parrott gun," much used in the Civil War, and invented by Robert P. Parrott, who was one of the directors of the firm. There were very close ties between the firm and the administration of West Point. For many years it operated a fleet of seven sloops plying between Cold Spring and New York City. The *Victorine,* was supposedly the fastest on the river. The foundry ultimately closed down because it could not compete with more modern plants. Some of the iron used was mined behind Mt. Taurus. The Putnam County Historical Society maintains a museum. The only remaining building is the foundry office, dating from 1865.

Foundry Cove is the outlet of Foundry Brook, which rises east of Schofield and Breakneck Ridges in Cold Spring Reservoir and Jacox Pond and flows southwest to just south of Cold Spring.

The Foundry Cove is bounded on the south by Constitution Island, on the east by a marsh and on the north by bluffs on the south side of Cold Spring. Formerly there was a wharf used by the foundry on the north side, but only a few stones remain. The Cove is crossed by a causeway of the New York Central Railroad with a low short bridge in the center. It is mostly shoal water only two to four feet deep, with the exception of a few holes.

To the east of it is the Boscobel Restoration. Just to the north of Boscobel is the mid-nineteenth century Victorian mansion of the painter Thomas Prichard Rossiter (1818-1871), who lived here from 1859 until his death. The mansion of Gouverneur Kemble is also nearby on the north side of the Cove, as is the Roman Catholic Chapel of Our Lady of Cold Spring, brick, in style of Etruscan temple, ca. 1834, on a bluff looking out over the water.

49.00 Town of Philipstown to east.
Name derives from early patent and includes such villages as Cold Spring, Garrison, and Manitou. At Philipsburg, where the Continental Army was encamped, almost every soldier was innoculated with the kine-pox, to shield him from the ravages of smallpox. This was before Jenner, and considered a dangerous manouevre. Jenner's first cow-pox vaccination was in 1796.

49.30 Falls Brook to west.

49.40 Rose's Brook to west.

49.50 Crow's Nest Mountain to west.
(elevation 1,396 feet). Also frequently shortened to "Cro' Nest." This name is also given to a huge hollow among the summits of these hills, which suggests the idea of an enormous crow's nest. It has inspired several local poets:

Where Hudson's waves o'er
  silvery sands
  Winds through the hills afar,
And Cro' Nest like a monarch
  stands,
  Crowned with a single star.
  George Pope Morris,
  (Poems of George Pope
  Morris, p. 233)

This the middle watch of a
  summer night,
  The earth is dark, but the
  heavens are bright,
The moon looks down on old
  Cro' Nest—

She mellows the shade on his
  shaggy breast,
And seems his huge grey form
  to throw
  In a silver cone on the wave
  below.
    from "The Culprit Fay" by
    Joseph Rodman Drake

Crow's Nest is bounded on the south by Washington Valley, on the west by Mount Misery and Whitehorse Mountain, and on the north by Storm King Valley and Storm King Mountain. The southern peak has an elevation of 1403 feet, although in early days the northern peak, with 1,396 feet elevation was considered the true Crow's Nest. It is traversed by both Old and New Storm King Highways. The southern portion is within the United States Military Reservation. The northern portion belongs to the Palisades Interstate Park Commission, and some of the western part belongs to Harvard's Black Rock Forest Preserve. In the early days West Point trainees and trial artillerists at the West Point Foundry used the southern and eastern escarpments for target practice. One major reason why the Military Academy makes its part of the mountain out of bounds to the public is that there are believed to be substantial numbers of unexploded shells on the mountainside.

49.50 Site of former Foundry Dock to east:
north of Foundry Cove.

49.50 Our Lady of Cold Spring R. C. Church to east.
This church is in the form of an Etruscan temple, ca.1834.

49.50 Cold Spring Village to east.
This attractive residential village takes its name from a large cold spring which, it is said, boats plying the Hudson used to fill their water butts. In the nineteenth century the West Point Foundry gave impetus to the

town's growth, and many small-scaled eighteenth and nineteenth-century structures survive in a good state of preservation. Gouverneur Kemble and the painter Thomas Prichard Rossiter lived here, and the locality was a popular resort of such literary lights as Fitzgreen Halleck, Washington Irving, and Joseph Rodman Drake, who was inspired to write his lyrical quasi-epic while taking a moonlight walk along the shore here.

The waterfront remains a lovely and lively place with its tree shaded nineteenth-century bandstand and stone mooring walls. The Hudson View Inn at the landing is charming and has been continuously dispensing hospitality since 1837. It is a fine place to watch the boats passing by of an afternoon, or to visit on a full moonlit evening when the Hudson looks like burnished silver.

49.55 Undercliff to east.
On southern slopes of Mount Taurus. This was the home of the noted publisher and poet, George Pope Morris (1802-1864). Built by John C. Hamilton, son of Alexander Hamilton.

49.55 Old Storm King Highway to west.
Between West Point and Cornwall carved from the cliffs of Crows Nest and Storm King Mountains, it affords magnificent views. It is narrow and winding.

49.55 New Storm King Highway to west.
Going across the tops of Crow's Nest and Storm King further inland, it affords quite a different set of fine views. Used by Route 9W, completed ca.1940, it is a modern all-weather highway.

50.00 Kidd's Plug Cliff to west.
This must have been destroyed either by quarrying or construction of the Old Storm King Highway—or possibly by artillery practice. I give Benson Lossing's description in 1865:

High up on the smooth face of the rock, is a mass slightly projecting, estimated to be twelve feet in diameter, and by form and position suggesting, even to the dullest imagination, the idea of an enormous plug stopping an orifice. The fancy of some one has given it the name of Captain Kidd's Plug, in deference to the common belief that that noted pirate buried immense sums of money and other treasures somewhere in the Highlands. Within a few years ignorant and credulous persons, misled by pretended seers in the clairvoyant condition, have dug in search of those treasures in several places near West Point; and some, it is said, have been ignorant and credulous enough to believe that the almost mythical buccaneer had, by some supernatural power, mounted these rocks to the point where the projection is seen, discovered there an excavation, deposited vast treasures within it, and secured them by inserting the enormous stone plug seen from the waters below. It is plainly visible from vessels passing near the western shore. Kidd's Plug Cliff is a part of the group of hills which form Cro' Nest. . . .

(Lossing, *The Hudson,* p. 217-18.)

50.50 Little Stony Point to east
(elevation 13 feet). Until recently, this was the site of a stone crusher, tipple, and barge loading dock of the Hudson River Stone Corporation who had a quarry on the lower southwestern slopes of Mt. Taurus.

50.50 Quarry to east

(See article above.) This was the last of the notorious stone quarries operating in the Hudson Highlands. The Hudson River Stone Corporation started blasting here in 1931.

50.55 Mount Taurus or Bull Hill to east.

(elevation 1420 feet). According to Wallace Bruce,

The mountain opposite Cro' Nest is Bull Hill, or more classically, Mt. Taurus. It is said that there was formerly a wild bull in these mountains, which had failed to win the respect and confidence of the inhabitants, so the mountaineers organized a hunt and drove him over the hill, whose name stands a monument to his exit.

(Bruce, *Hudson by Daylight,* p. 130.)

Table Rock, at the 1000-foot level, is a popular lookout point on the hiking trail over the mountain. As described in the preceding two articles, this mountain was subject to quarrying until quite recent times. In 1970 the Taconic State Park Commission acquired Mount Taurus and included it, along with neighboring Breakneck Ridge and Sugar Loaf, in the Hudson Highlands State Park. Catskill Aqueduct passes under in mile long tunnel.

Benson Lossing tells us that: "It is the old 'Bull Hill' which in Irving's exquisite story of 'Dolph Heyliger,' 'bellowed back in the storm' whose thunders had 'crashed on the Donder Berg, and rolled up the long defile of the Highlands, each headland making a new echo.' "

51.00 The Clove to west.

Also known as Storm King Valley, Mother Cronk's Cove, and Donderbarrak (Thunder-chamber) and Valley of Hope,

This clove is situated between Crows Nest Mountain to the south and Storm King Mountain to the west and north. Formerly there was a considerable cove in the Hudson River, but this has been largely cut off and turned into a shallow backwater by the causeway of the West Shore Railroad, which has caused much of it to silt up. The Old Storm King Highway follows around the clove at the 200 foot level and the new one at the 1000 foot level. Storm King Brook rises between Whitehorse Mountain and Crow's Nest and flows generally northeasterly through the clove. Stillman's Spring is near the 200 foot level. The area is heavily timbered.

There was a pre-Revolutionary settlement at the foot of the clove. It is recorded that a family named Cronk had a small farmstead on the mountaintop back of the clove, and this may account for the old name "Mother Cronk's Cove." Lossing tells us that a New York City resident named Lambertson had a solitary summer retreat here in 1865. Somewhat later part of this land belonged to Dr. Matthew Beattle of Cornwall, who sold it to Dr. Earnest C. Stillman of Cornwall. He, in turn, gave much of his land further inland to Harvard University for forestry research. The Clove now belongs to the Palisades Interstate Park Commission.

In 1824, the sloop *Neptune* capsized here drowning thirty-five persons. The name "Donderbarrak" or "Thunder Chamber" comes from the old Dutch belief that the storm-goblins stored their thunder here. The name "Valley of Hope," has a rather interesting history. During the Revolution West Point was thought of as the Gibralter of America. When the question came up of a National Capital, much thought was given to its security from enemy attack. Consequently, serious consideration was given to this valley as our national capital, because of its mountain ramparts and easy access by the Hudson. Speculators soon bought up the property in this Valley of Hope. The hopes fell flat when Washington was created in the District of Columbia. It is quite difficult to picture what would have happened if the Capital had been located here. As the nation grew, probably the expansion would have been around Cornwall and Newburgh.

51.25 Breakneck Brook to east: between Mount Taurus and Breakneck Ridge.

51.25 Storm King Station to east: now defunct. Nathaniel Parker Willis convinced the New York Central Railroad to give this name to the small way-station once located here.

51.50 Breakneck Mountain to east. This is actually the western end of a long ridge running southwest to northeast. Its highest elevation is 1,213 feet. Breakneck Brook and Mount Taurus are to the south, Sugarloaf Mountain to the north. A popular hiking trail runs along the ridge.

According to the old legend, the bull that was chased over Mount Taurus was finally chased onto the top of this ridge and fell off a cliff, breaking his neck.

This ridge was subjected to extensive quarrying of the dark granite at a relative early date, and still bears ugly scars. Lossing tells us that:

Several years ago (1846) a powder blast, made by the quarriers high up on the southern declivity of the mountain, destroyed an object interesting to voyagers upon the river. From abreast the Storm King, a huge mass of rock was seen projected against the eastern sky in the perfect form of a human face, the branches of a tree forming an excellent representation of thick curly beard upon the chin. It was called the TURK'S HEAD. . . . Its demolition caused many expressions of regret, for it was regarded as a great curiosity, and an interesting feature in the Highland scenery on the river.

(Lossing, *The Hudson*, p. 209.)

The name Turk's Face Mountain was used into the twentieth century. However, in 1901, Wallace Bruce tells us that it was called St. Anthony's Face. There seems to have been some confusion with Anthony's Nose. The mountain is now part of Hudson Highlands State Park. The pressure tunnel of the Catskill Aqueduct comes up at the northwestern foot of the mountain, near the shore, and then passes beneath Breakneck in a 1000-foot-long tunnel. The tip of the ridge is pierced by tunnels of the New York Central and Route 9D. There is hikers' access parking at the north end of the tunnel, where the trail starts up the ridge. There are tremendous cliffs in the old quarry section on the southwest face.

51.50 Breakneck Point on east.

51.50 Wey-Gat.

This is Dutch for "Wind Gate," the name for that part of the river between Storm King Mountain and Breakneck Mountain. In the nineteenth century, this place was called the Northern Gate of the Highlands.

51.50 Storm King Mountain to west.

(elevation 1340 feet). This is the northeastern buttress of the Hudson Highlands, with Butter Hill to the southwest and Storm King Clove and Whitehorse Mountain to the south. The Old Storm King Highway traverses the cliffs above the Hudson on a narrow ledge at the 200-foot level, offering magnificent views. The New Storm King Highway climbs the back of the mountain to the 900-foot level, offering more limited views.

The earliest name given to this mountain by Europeans was Klinkersberg, (so-called by Henry Hudson, from its glistening and broken rock.) Lossing tells us that:

The Storm King, seen from the middle of the river abreast its eastern centre, is almost semicircular in form, and gave to the minds of the utilitarian Dutch skippers who navigated the Hudson early, the idea of a huge lump of butter, and they named it "Boter Berg" or "Butter Hill." It had borne that name until recently (1865), when Mr. Willis successfully appealed to the good taste of the public by giving it the more appropriate and poetic title of Storm King.

(Lossing, *The Hudson*, p. 208.)

The western extension of the ridge is still called Butter Hill. There was a named train on the West Shore called the "Storm King." It was a mid-afternoon express from Albany to Weehawken.

. . . when the Storm King smites his thunderous gong,
Thy hills reply from many a bellowing wave;
And when with smiles the sun o'erlooks thine brow,
He sees no stream more beautiful than thou.

Anon.

51.55 Catskill Aqueduct.

The aqueduct passes beneath the river here in an inverted siphon 1100 feet below the river, in solid rock. The tunnel is horseshoe shaped, being 17 feet high and 17½ feet wide—large enough for a railroad train to pass through. The water flows at a rate of 4 m.p.h. and passes 500,000,000 gallons per day. Granite towers can be seen on either side of the river atop the tunnel shafts. On the east side the water continues through another 1000 foot tunnel beneath Breakneck Mountain and another, a mile long, beneath Mt. Taurus. The aqueduct tunnel is 1400 feet below the high water mark. It was completed in 1919.

51.55 Dutchess County to east.

For the next 47 miles to just above Tivoli, the eastern shore belongs to Dutchess County. Dutchess is one of the original ten counties erected in 1683 and is named in honor of the wife of the Duke of Albany and York, later James II. It has an area of 8I6 square miles and extends inland from the Hudson sixteen miles to the Taconic Mountains. It is bounded on the west by the Hudson

River; on the north by Columbia County; on the east by Salisbury, Litchfield, and Fairfield Counties in Connecticut; and on the south by Putnam County, New York, which was taken from Dutchess in 1812. It is comprised of twenty townships and the incorporated cities of Beacon and Poughkeepsie. The townships are: Red Hook, Milan, Pine Plains, Northeast, Rhinebeck, Clinton, Stanford, Amenia, Washington, Pleasant Valley, Hyde Park, Poughkeepsie, La Grange, Unionvale, Dover, Pawling, Beekman, East Fishkill, Wappinger, and Fishkill. Principal towns and cities are: Poughkeepsie, Beacon, Pawling, Millbrook, Millerton, Tivoli, Red Hook, Rhinebeck, and Hyde Park.

Principal mountain ranges are the Taconics along the Connecticut border and the Fishkill Range, including North and South Beacon Mountains in the northern Hudson Highlands. There are several north and south running ridges of hills parallel to the Hudson and the Taconics. Principal watercourses are the Roeleff Jansen's Kill, Wappinger's Creek, and Fishkill Creek, flowing west to the Hudson. Principal lakes are: Whaley Lake, Quaker Lake, Lake Walton, Sylvan Lake, Tamarack Lake, Hunn's Lake, Swift Pond, Indian Lake, Strauss Marsh, Round Lake, Upton Lake, Long Pond, Silver Lake, Spring Lake, Halycon Lake, Miller Pond, Thompson Pond, and Stissing Pond. Principal parks are: Taconic State Park, Rudd Pond Area, and Margaret Lewis Norrie State Park. The Taconic State Parkway, a toll-free scenic highway, runs the length of the county from north to south about five miles inland from the Hudson. Principal railroads are the main line of the New York Central, along the Hudson River; the former New Haven lines from Poughkeepsie Bridge to Pawling and Brewster and from Fishkill Junction to Hopewell Junction, and the Harlem Division of the former New York Central along the base of the Taconics from Brewster and Pawling north to Dover Plains, Amenia,

Millerton, and Copake Falls (the northern section largely defunct), all presently in the Conrail System. Both MTA and Amtrak operate over the Hudson River Line. The county is largely rural with many truck and dairy farms and large private estates. Poughkeepsie is the County Seat.

The area was originally populated by the Wappinger Indians. On February 8, 1682, a license was granted to Francis Rombout, Jacobus Kipp, and Gulian Ver Planck to purchase land from the Indians. On August 8, 1683, they purchased a tract of 85,000 acres from Nimham, chief of the Wappingers. They in fact cheated the Indians. First they bargained to purchase for a given price "all the land they could see," and then conducted the Indians to the top of South Beacon Mountain, the highest elevation between theCatskills and the Seacoast and indicated a tract of land sixteen miles back from the Hudson to the Taconics. The Indians honored this bargain for many years, but in 1740 Chief Daniel of the Wappingers sought to have it set aside in a celebrated law trial—to no avail. This large patent was known as the Rombout Patent. Gulian Ver Planck died before the patent was issued, but his place was taken by Stephanus Van Cortlandt. Jacobus Kipp married Ver Planck's widow, thereby succeeding to the share of his defunct partner. Letters of patent were granted by King James II to Rombout, Van Cortlandt, and Kipp. In 1698, Lt. Colonel Henry Beekman had a large patent centering on Rhinecliff. The Schuyler Patent of 1688 included tracts north and south of Poughkeepsie and Cruger's Island. To a large extent Dutchess County remained under the manorial system until the mid-nineteenth century. Much of the eastern portion of the county was settled by Quakers and Yankees from New England. Only limited industrial development came with the steamboats and railroads. For many years drovers would herd their cattle to the steamboats at Poughkeepsie for

shipment to New York City, and consequently the main roads developed running from east to west. In the later
nineteenth and early twentieth centuries, Dutchess was favored by the
wealthy for country estates and some of
the finest face on the Hudson River.
There was a limited iron and steel
industry at Poughkeepsie in the mid-
nineteenth century. Commercial impetus
was given by construction of the Poughkeepsie Railroad Bridge in 1886. The
principal industry in Dutchess County
today is International Business Machines
(IBM), with principal plants at Poughkeepsie and Fishkill.

52.30 Cornwall-on-Hudson to west.
A former resort area, now a
residential village at the northern
foot of Storm King Mountain,
south of Moodna Creek, much of
the town is on a plateau or
terrace affording fine views over
Newburgh Bay and many attractive homesites. It was the home
of such well-known nineteenth
century literary figures as Lyman
Abbott, E.P. Roe, and Nathaniel
Parker Willis, whose estate Idlewild became well known through
his magazine writings and his
book *Outdoors At Idlewild.* Idlewild was designed by Calvert
Vaux, then practicing at Newburgh. After Willis's death in
1869, the property passed to the
novelist Edward Payson Roe.
The New York, Ontario &
Western Railway branched off
westward from the West Shore at
Cornwall. In 1892, the N.Y.O. & W.
built a large pier here for the
transfer of coal to barges. The
former village of Canterbury is
now the principal shopping section of Cornwall.

52.80 Site of New York, Ontario &
 Western pier to west.
52.80 Sugarloaf Mountain to east.
(elevation 900 feet.)

52.80 Pollepel Island to east.
Also variously called Pollepel's
Island, Pollepel Eiland, Polly
Pell's Island, Pot Ladle Island,
and at an earlier time Cheese
Island. An Indian tribe called it
Menahtis, meaning a small island. The Polypus is the name of
a prickly pear of the cactus
family which once grew abundantly on the island. The Dutch
Poptlepel or Polopel means
spoon or potladle.
The island is mostly rock and
covers 6¾ acres with a maximum elevation of 115 feet. It is
1,010 feet from the eastern
shore of the Hudson, but the
breakwaters forming the small
harbor come to within 650 feet
from shore. There are flats of
shallow water both north and
south of the island, but a channel
deep enough for steam tugboats
between it and the mainland.
A chevaux-di-frise was constructed between the island and
Plum Point on the western shore
in 1776.
The Indians believed the island was haunted and would not
stay on it at night—which made
it somewhat of a refuge for
those fleeing from them. The
early Dutch mariners believed
the island marked the northern
limit of the domain of the gob-
lins of Dunderberg. New sailors
to the Hudson were inoculated
against the Heer of Dunderberg
by being ducked in the river as
their boats passed the island
when entering the highlands. In
1866, Benson Lossing tells of a
lone fisherman who lived on the
island with his insane wife. Later
another fisherman named Ward, a
relative of Henry Ward Beecher,
lived on the island. At one time
Matthew Vassar wanted to ac-
quire the island as a site for a

monument to Henry Hudson, but he failed to arouse interest or backing. Since the Revolution, the island belonged to William Van Wyck from 1788 until his devisees sold it to Walter C. Anthony in 1888. That same year it was deeded to Mary G. Taft, who sold it to Francis Bannerman on December 5, 1900.

Francis Bannerman VI was born in Dundee, Scotland, in 1851 and came to America when he was three years old. His family settled in Brooklyn, and his father established a business selling articles acquired at Navy auctions. His son followed in his footsteps and entered the business in a large way after the Civil War. Francis Bannerman was descended from one of the few MacDonalds to survive the massacre at Glencoe in 1692. He was a Scottish patriot, a founder of the Caledonian Hospital in Brooklyn, a member of the St. Andrew's Society, and a strict Presbyterian. After his purchase of Pollepel Island in 1900, Francis Bannerman commenced construction of a Scottish castle for a summer retreat and an arsenal for his business. He built the present structure with its crennelations, turrets, moats, battlements, etc., with the intent to be both romantic and functional at the same time. It was still incomplete at the time of his death in November of 1918.

The Bannerman family continued to use the island arsenal. The main place of business was at Broadway in New York City, but it was moved to Blue Point, Long Island, in 1959. The island was used for storage of ammunition, arms, and explosives. It was the center of a worldwide business.

For many years the great castle of Bannerman's Island Arsenal attracted the attention of travellers on the river steamers and the New York Central Railroad and Route 9D. In 1967, the Bannermans sold the island to the people of the state of New York. They removed all the old military merchandise, giving much of it to the Smithsonian Institution for their museum. The Taconic State Park Commission took possession on July 1, 1968. For a short while they offered public tours of the island. On the night of August 8, 1969, a great fire destroyed all the buildings. Only romantic ruins remain.

53.20 Moodna Creek to west.
It was originally known as Murderer's Creek because of legends of Indian treachery in the immediate neighborhood. The name was changed at the behest of N. P. Willis, whose estate Idlewild abutted the stream. It rises in Tomahawk Lake near Blooming Grove and flows northeast to near Washingtonville, where it is joined from the northwest by the waters of the Otter Kill. It then flows east, by the northern end of Schunnemunk Mountain, to Salisbury Mills and Mountainville, where it turns north past Firthcliffe and then turns east after receiving the waters of Silver Stream from the northwest. It flows into the Hudson through tidal marshes south of Plum Point. It gives its name to a great high viaduct of the Erie Railroad near Salisbury Mills, and flows through some of the most idyllic scenery in the eastern United States. Its pollution by several paper mills became a cause célèbre, but the stream is now relatively pure.

53.30 Sloop Hill to the west.

53.30 Plum Point to west.
Also variously called Plumb Point and Nicoll's Point, it was settled in the 1680s by an individual named Patrick Mac-Gregorie. During the Revolution, it was fortified with a battery of fourteen guns. The Gregorian Colonial mansion was the home of Alfred P. Sloan.

54.00 Wade's Brook to east.

54.10 Gordon's Brook to east:
flowing from Melzingah Reservoir

54.50 New Windsor to west.
(population 18,932). A residential suburb of Newburgh, this little town is best known as a cantonment site for the Revolutionary Army—particularly after the cessation of active hostilities. Washington made his headquarters at the Ellison House here between June 22 and July 21, 1779, and between December 1, 1779, and June 25, 1780. Generals Knox, Greene, and Gates and Colonels Biddle and Wadsworth also had headquarters nearby. In neighboring Vail's Gate, Generals St. Clair and Gates used the Edmonston House as headquarters, and General Lafayette used the Brewster House. The New York Military Academy, a preparatory school for West Point, and one of the oldest in New York State is located here. Its brick and concrete Gothic buildings cover a 350-acre campus. The New Windsor Cantonment was one of three winter camps occupied by the Continental Army for eight months in 1782-83. It is also called Temple Hill from the Temple, a large meeting hall wherein Washington refused a crown. The Masonic Order maintains a shrine here.

54.90 Dutchess Junction to east.
A defunct railroad junction between main line of New York Central and branch of New York, New Haven and Hartford, it has been superseded by Fishkill Junction.

55.00 Fishkill Bay and Creek to east.
The Bay has extremely shallow shoal water; depths range from one-half to four feet. It is separated from main body of Newburgh Bay on the north by Denning Point. Fishkill Creek rises behind Beacon Ridge and flows generally southwest to the Hudson. Name from the Dutch Vischer's Kil, or Fisherman's Creek (Indian name: Mawanassigh).

55.00 Denning Point to east.
Eastern terminus of Revolutionary period ferry to Newburgh and New Windsor and eastern terminus for Erie Railroad rail car ferry, this was also known as Fishkill Hook. There were burial grounds of the Wiccapee and Shenandoah Indians here.

56.00 Mount Beacon to east.
Highest point(s) in the Fishkill Mountain Range, it actually has two summits: North Beacon (elevation 1531 feet and South Beacon (1635 feet). These are the highest points between the Catskills and the seacoast. It was formerly called Grand Sachem Mountain, in the Wequehache, or Endless Hills. Its present name comes from beacon fires used as signals during the Revolution. The gigantic fires were built up of rectangular pyramids thirty feet high built of logs filled with brush wood. James Fenimore Cooper set some of the most exciting action of his novel,

The Spy, on the slopes of this range.

The summit of North Beacon can be reached easily by the Mount Beacon Incline Railway (Box 327 Beacon, N.Y. Tel: 914-831-8070). This unique cable railway is the steepest of its length in the world with an average gradient of 64%. The track, which is also built on a curve, is 2364 feet long. In the middle is a double track section known as the Brown Patent Turn-Out, where the two cars pass each other. The railway was designed by the Otis Elevator Corporation, who also built the machinery. The roadbed was built by the Mohawk Construction Company, and the cars were built by the Ramapo Iron Works at Hillburn, N. Y. Total lift is 1,200 feet. The two cars each seat fifty-four passengers and travel at a rate of 500 feet per minute—one car ascending while the other descends. Motive power comes from powerful electric motors turning a drum at the top around which is wound the cable. The cars have a 10,000 lb. load capacity. The 1⅜-inch-thick steel cable has a capacity of sixty-two tons. The system was designed with a twelve times safety factor. Safer than most modern office building elevators, the Otis Double Grip Safety Device, activated by a centrifugal governor, can hold 50,000 lbs. There are also hand brakes on the cars and on the cable drum. In normal operation, the cars are controlled by Otis Electric Limit Stops, as in most modern elevators. The system was opened on May 30, 1902, and has operated since without accident. It was long operated by the Mount Beacon-on-Hudson Association.

There are some summer homes and a dance hall and casino at the top. The line also carries some freight and has served as a ski lift. The regular season is from May through October. At various times there has been talk of building a hotel or motel atop the incline. The view is spectacular. This is a must for the serious sightseer.

56.00 Quassaic Creek to west.
It rises south of Plattekill and flows generally south by southeast past Savilton, Cronomer Valley, and Glenwood Park; thence behind Newburgh. Here it turns east and flows into the Hudson south of Newburgh. Principal tributaries are Bushfield Creek (Orange Lake) and Gidneytown Creek.

56.00 Newburgh to west.

(population 26,219). An industrial and residential city located along the river edge and on a plateau 300 feet above the river, it was first settled in 1709 by German Palatinates, who established the Palatine Parish by Quassaic under the Lutheran Minister Joshua Kocherthal. The town was named after Neuberg-on-Rhine. However, the Palatinates were almost penniless and, by 1762, most had moved west into Pennsylvania to find richer farmlands. They were superseded by Scots and Englishmen who modified the name of the town to Newburgh, in honor of Newburgh-on-Tay in Scotland. George Washington had his headquarters here towards the end of the Revolution, from March 31, 1782, until late August 1783. He established his headquarters in the house of the Huguenot Jonathan Hasbrouck. This is now preserved as an historic site and museum. While at Newburgh, Washington received the infamous Newburgh letter. It was anonymous but threatened revolt by the army if their pay was not immediately forthcoming. Washington shamed the would-be rebels into being patient by remarking that his eyesight had grown dim in the service of his country. Here he also received the Nicola letter offering him the crown. This too he scorned. It was at Newburgh that the Continental army was finally disbanded upon signing of the Treaty of Paris in 1783.

After the Revolution, Newburgh developed as a trading center for the rich agricultural area further inland. Produce was shipped from here to New York City. By 1798, Major Isaac Belknap, and three other entrepreneurs had established four lines of sloops trading between Newburgh and New York City. Construction of the Newburgh & Cochecton Turnpike quickened the growth of this "gateway city" on the new road to western expansion. Ultimately the road was to go on to Canandaigua, but construction of the Erie Canal in 1825 diverted the path of western trade to Albany. The Erie Railroad opened a branch from Chester on its main line in 1850, reaching the Hudson via the Valley of the Moodna and the Quassaic Creek Ravine. It was planned to establish a railroad car ferry to Fishkill, where connections further east were to be maintained by the Dutchess & Columbia Railroad and the New York & New England. This plan was aborted by construction of the railroad bridge at Poughkeepsie in 1886.

Newburgh was incorporated as a City in 1865. During the early nineteenth century, Newburgh was a whaling port and home of China and ivory traders—a true seaport. In the mid-nineteenth century the famous landscape architect Andrew Jackson Downing lived and worked here, as well as his younger associates Calvert Vaux, Frederick Law Olmstead, and Frederick C. Withers. The school of Hudson River Bracketed Architecture was indigenous to Newburgh. By 1842, industry had grown to such an extent that there were three flouring mills, three plaster mills, an extensive brewery, a rotary pump manufactory

mills, three plaster mills, an extensive brewery, a rotary pump manufactory and factories manufacturing floor cloths, soap, candles, morocco leather, buckskin, ploughs, combs, tobacco products, chairs, carriages, guns, whips, and sashes and blinds. There were also two iron foundries, two tanneries, four lumber yards, six coal yards, two ropewalks, two freestone and marble yards, a steam engine factory and general machine shop, a steam boiler factory, two ship yards, a marine railway, an extensive brick yard, and three printing offices.

In later years Newburgh produced major quantities of flannels, overalls, paper boxes, iron products, hats, wire products, furniture, building supplies, paints, soap, electric motors, reed chairs, flour, feed, wallpaper, and lawn mowers. The West Shore Railroad was put through town in 1883. There was a ferry service to Fishkill-Beacon from 1743 until 1963. In the late nineteenth and early twentieth century, the Orange Traction Company operated local streetcars and the electric interurban Newburgh & Wallkill Valley Railway to Orange Lake and Walden. Newburgh was a major steamboat landing, and the Marvell Shipyard here built many of the most famous Hudson River steamers, including the *Hendrick Hudson* and *Robert Fulton*, not to mention innumerable steam ferryboats.

Downing Park was designed as a memorial to Andrew Jackson Downing by Vaux & Olmstead, and its beautiful grounds offer fine prospects of the surrounding countryside. Newburgh is the seat of Mount Saint Mary College. Of particular interest architecturally are the Orange County Courthouse (1841) by Thornton M. Niver; St. George Episcopal Church (1819), Greek Revival; and the Dutch Reformed Church (1830), Greek Revival, by Alexander Jackson Davis.

Newburgh is a city in decline. Regressive tax policies have driven industry away. The steamboat industry died after

World War I, and Newburgh lost its importance as a point of transshipment. Discontinuation of the ferry in 1963 and its replacement by a new bridge north of town diverted more trade from the area, as did the cessation of West Shore passenger trains and elimination as a landing by the Hudson River Day Line because of decay of the dock. The construction of a new dock in 1973 was futile, as it is too delicate to withstand the impact of a large ship against the bulkheads. There has been chronic unemployment with a staggering welfare load. When an aggressive city manager attempted to limit welfare, he got into serious trouble. The major stores have moved out to the suburbs as has industry and the middle class population. Crime is rampant and many people in Orange County who used to shop in Newburgh are afraid to go there. Most of the County Administration has moved to Goshen and Middletown. An ill-advised urban-renewal policy has demolished much of the precious architectural heritage, which might have made Newburgh into a nineteenth-century Williamsburg. While some restoration work and renewal programs are going forward, the future of this once attractive city is still very much undecided.

56.10 Hasbrouck House and Washington Monument Belvidere to west.

The Hasbrouck House was built in 1724 and was enlarged in 1750-53 when it was purchased by Jonathan Hasbrouck. It is in the Dutch Colonial style with a low roof, but has similarities to the typical Huguenot stone house. It had reached its present form in 1770. George Washington and his wife lived here from April 4, 1782, until August 18, 1783. It was here that Washington wrote his famous "crown letter" rejecting a monarchy, and here that, on June 7, 1783, he parted with his guard. His army lay in camp five miles westward at New Windsor. Knox and Lafayette were frequent visitors. In 1850, the State of New York purchased the house from the Hasbrouck family. This was the first historic preservation effort by any state or federal agency.

The grounds include a large lawn, well and well-sweep, flagpole, museum building (erected in 1910), and the grave of Usual Knapp, a member of Washington's life guard.

The Washington Monument Belvidere was completed in 1888. I quote from the report of the committee to erect the monument:

. . . the committee, after much reflection, had come to the conclusion that the most appropriate monument to carry out the spirit of the joint resolution would be a structure of rude but imposing nature, built of the native stone. Such a structure would typify the rugged simplicity of the times and personages it was intended to commemorate.

In addition to this, the site of the proposed monument afforded an opportunity for distant display, which could not well be ignored. The grounds are on a bluff overlooking the river, and in full view of travelers on the cars and passing steam-boats. The monument therefore should be of sufficient proportions to attract the eye of the millions who annually pass up and down the river.

Another fact to which the attention of the committee was called was that these Headquarters are visited every year by thousands of excursionists from the city of New York and tourists from all parts of the world. A very natural, and probably the first, impulse of strangers visiting a monument is to ascend it, and for this reason the committee was of opinion that if the structure to be erected could be surmounted by an accessible outlook it would be a very desirable feature.

. . . the committee commissioned Mr. Maurice J. Power, of New York, who has had a wide experience and great success in monumental structures, to pre-

pare a design. Mr. Power called to his aid Mr. John H. Duncan, of New York, artist and architect.

The design prepared by Mr. Duncan and adopted by the committee represents a Tower of Victory, built of native stone, of a rectangular form. The dimensions or ground lines are 37 by 32 feet, with a total height of 53 feet. Four large archways open into the atrium, one on each side. In the center of the atrium, upon a polished pedestal of red granite, will stand a life-size bronze statue of Washington, modeled by the sculptor O'Donovan. (Note: This statue was not a success and has been removed to the museum.)

From the ground floor two commodious circular stair-cases (one for ascent and the other for descent) lead to a belvedere, or open outlook, capable of holding over three hundred persons.

The view from the belvedere will prove a very attractive feature to the thousands of strangers who visit these Headquarters every year. (Note: It is presently closed to the public.) It embraces a broad expanse of river and mountain scenery, with outlying valleys. North and South Beacon, upon whose towering tops the signal fires were lit during the Revolution, are directly in front, whilst to the right will be seen the Northern Gate to the Highlands and West Point in the distance.

("The Centennial Celebration and Washington Monument at Newburgh, N.Y.," Report of the Joint Select Committee Washington, Government Printing Office, 1889.)

56.10 Site of former Marvell Shipyard to west,
along riverfront below the Hasbrouck House park.

56.25 Site of former Newburgh-Beacon ferry terminal.

56.25 Site of former steamer landing.

56.30 West Shore Railroad passenger terminal:
classic red brick ca.1900.

56.30 Fishkill and Beacon to the east

(Beacon population 13,255). A residential city with light manufacturing, the present city of Beacon was incorporated in 1913 and incorporated the former villages of Fishkill Landing and Matteawan. The name Matteawan is Indian, and its derivation is somewhat confused. It means either "a country of good fur" or "a confluence of streams," which would in effect denote good beaver and other fur-bearing animal country. (The name is not uncommon elsewhere, and usually the location fits this description.) The area was originally populated by the Pachami branch of the Wappinger Indians, although Wiccapee and Shenandoah tribes had burial grounds on nearby Denning Point.

The present village of Fishkill is two miles inland and incorporates the former villages of Glenham and Wolcottville. It derives its name from the Dutch name for the local creek—Vischer's Kil, or Fisherman's Creek.

The entire neighborhood was part of the Rombout Patent of 1682. (See article on Dutchess County for more details—ERM 51.55.) Other partners in the patent were Gulian Verplanck, Jacobus Kipp, and Stephanus Van Cortlandt. Catharyna, daughter of Francis Rombout was born in New York City in 1687. At the age of sixteen, she married Roger Brett, a lieutenant in the English navy. They settled here in 1714 and built the house at 50 Van Nydeck Avenue, Beacon, which is still standing and is now a museum. After her husband's death, Madam Brett, as she was locally called, became an active businesswoman. Her mill was the principal local industry. Unlike most other landowners, it was her practice to sell her lands rather than lease them. This led to commercial development. She died in 1764 and is buried in the old Reformed Church at Fishkill.

Gulian Verplanck also built a large home about 1700, known as Mount Gulian. During the Revolution it was used as headquarters by Gen. Baron von Steuben, and here, on May 13, 1783, General Knox and other Continental Army officers founded the Society of the Cincinnati.

During the Revolution, Fishkill became a major supply depot and hospital area. It was first used as such after the Battle of White Plains. Many American Revolutionary soldiers are buried in the area. Part of Washington's army was encamped here from March of 1782 until August 1783. The Van Wyck House, which served as headquarters for Gen. Israel Putnam, served as the model for the Wharton House in Cooper's *The Spy,* of which many of the most exciting actions take place in this neighborhood. The Brinckerhoff House served as Washington's headquarters. The ferry, which had been established in 1743, served as a vital communications link inside the American lines.

After the Revolution, there was considerable commercial development. Between 1812 and 1816, the Long Wharf and ferry slips were built and an inn was established at the wharf. After 1814, John Jacob Astor, Peter Schenck, and Philip Hone, attracted by waterfalls on the Fishkill, built a cotton mill and foundry. Bricks, cotton goods, silk, machinery, wagons, and hats were also made here. About 1872, Alexander T. Stewart established his Beacon Piece and Dye Works, which was originally called the Groveville Mills. It produced carpets. The workers' homes are well preserved and provide a good example of a nineteenth century industrial community.

The Fishkill-Beacon area also attracted wealthy estate owners. Tioranda was built in 1859 by Richard Morris Hunt for George Joseph Howland, a shipping magnate. It is Gothic-Victorian with contrasting black and white glazed bricks. It is now known as Craig House and is used as a sanitarium.

Also part of the Craig Sanitarium is Wodenethe, the former estate of Henry Winthrop Sargent, to whom Andrew Jackson Downing dedicated his *Architecture of Country Houses,* in 1850. The house was built in 1825 and was extensively remodeled by Calvert Vaux in 1853. It is painted yellow with white trim and is three-story with a hipped roof.

Mount Gulian, the Verplanck family home, burned in 1931. This was the home of Gulian Crommelin Verplanck (1786-1870). He was admitted to the bar in 1807 and took part in politics, writing against the Clinton faction. His verse satires are collected in *The Bucktail Bards* (1819). Verplanck served in the New York legislature and in the U.S. House of Representatives. From 1821 to 1824, he was a professor at the General Theological Seminary, and wrote *Essays on the Nature and Uses of the Various Evidences of Revealed Religion* (1824). He was associated with William Cullen Bryant and R.C. Sands in writing the annual *Talisman.* However, Verplanck is best remembered for his three-volume edition of Shakespeare's plays in 1847, and he remains among the greatest of Shakespeare scholars.

The 900-acre estate of his former neighbor John J. Scanlon has been taken over by the state of New York for the Matawan Correctional Facility, formerly referred to as Matteawan State Hospital for the Criminally Insane.

The principal local industry is IBM. There is also a major Veteran's Administration Hospital.

56.30 Newburgh Bay.
Eight miles long, extending from Cornwall on the south to Chelsea at the north, its widest section (1.6 miles) is opposite the mouth of Moodna Creek north of Cornwall. The eastern shore is largely

shoal water, the principal channel being nearer the western shore.

57.00 Sherman's Dock on west.

57.20 Newburgh-Beacon Bridge.
A unit of the New York State Bridge Authority, it opened to traffic November 2, 1963. This is a combination deck truss and continuous deck bridge, designed by Modjeski & Masters. Principal contractors were Frederick Share Corporation, Dravo Corporation and Bethlehem Steel Corporation. Overall length is 7855 feet. Length of main span is 1000 feet. The bridge has a two-lane roadway. Vessel clearance is 135 feet and the highest point of steel above water is 252 feet. The highest point of roadway slab above water is 192 feet. There are 24 spans, 23 piers, and 2 abutments. The deepest foundation goes 165 feet below the surface of the water. Actual construction was started in March 1961. Total cost was $70,000,000. It carries Interstate 84. A toll is charged. A twin structure is planned for completion in 1980.

57.30 Matawan Correctional Facility to east.
Formerly referred to as the Matteawan State Hospital for the Criminally Insane.

58.00 Balmville to west.
Named for the "Balm of Gilead tree," also known as the Bonville oak tree, the oldest living thing in Orange County. This tree was a seedling in 1699. It is 90 inches in diameter with a circumference of 25 feet, 5 inches. A "protected" tree, it is surrounded by a fence.

5
The Central Hudson

58.00 Brockway to east.
This is the site of a former brick yard.

58.50 Purdy Ridge to east.
(elevation 342 feet).

58.50 Cronomer Hill to west.
(elevation 728 feet).

59.50 Castle Point—U.S. Veterans Hospital to east.
(elevation 170 feet). Opened in 1924 for care of tubercular war veterans, it can accommodate 400 patients. It is a series of light red brick buildings with a tall water tower.

59.75 Mud Hole to west.
A shallow cove now cut off from the river by the West Shore railroad tracks, so named because it seemed to the railroad builders that this took so much fill that it was a bottomless hole.

60.00 Middle Hope to west.
This village is inland on Route 9W.

60.25 Low Point to east.

60.25 Van Wyck Ridge to east.
(elevtion 393 feet).

60.25 Chelsea to east.
This was formerly called Carthage Landing. There is an active yacht club here which is home to a considerable fleet of small sailboats. The Delaware Aqueduct Tunnel is here and an intake station.

61.00 Roseton to west.
Here was the home of Sen. John Bailey Rose, owner of the Rose Brick Co. The house is now the Beau Rivage Restaurant and overlooks the river. It is two-story Greek Revival clapboard with Ionic columns, ca. 1810. Roseton is a station on the West Shore Railroad.

61.25 Clay Pitts to west.
Jova brickyard.

62.00 Danskammer Point to west.
A low, flat rocky point jutting out into water 36 feet deep, it was long a menace to navigation. Formerly there was a projecting point. This was broken off when it was run into by the large steamer *Cornell* one misty morning in 1890. The present lighthouse was built on the fragments which fell into the water. It takes its name from the Dutch "teufel's danskammer," or "devil's dance-hall." This name was given it by Lt. Cowenhoven in 1663, who saw Indians doing ceremonial dances by firelight here. This was a usual meeting place for Indians to hold their ceremonial dances, and Henry Hudson witnessed such a ceremony on his first visit. It is recorded that one of the dances was called the "kintikaeye."

Benson Lossing tells us that

On this rock the Indians performed their peculiar semi-religious rites, called 'pow-wows,' before going upon hunting and fishing expeditions, or the war-path. They painted themselves grotesquely, built a large fire upon this rock, and danced around it with songs and yells, making strange contortions of face and limbs, under the direction of their conjurors or 'medicine' men.' They would tumble, leap, run and yell, when, as they said, the Devil, or Evil Spirit, would appear in the shape of a beast of prey, or a harmless animal; the former apparition betokened evil to their proposed undertaking, and the latter prophesied of good. For at least a century after the Europeans discovered the river, these hideous rites were performed upon this spot, and the Dutch skippers who navigated the Hudson, called the rock Den Duyvel's Dans Kamer. Here it was that Peter Stuyvesant's crew were "most horribly frightened by roystering devils," according to the veracious Knickerbocker.

(Lossing, *The Hudson*, p.196.)

More recently the point has been the location of large power plants of Central Hudson Electric Company and large oil barges are anchored immediately alongshore in deep water.

62.75 Hughsonville to east.
This village is inland on Route 9D. The landing was formerly known as Farmer's Landing.

62.75 Soap Hill to west.
Its prominent cliffs rise to an elevation of 320 feet.

63.00 Wappinger's Creek and Falls to east.
This is also the name of a town about a mile up the creek. Wappinger's Creek takes its rise in several lakes in Clinton and Stanford townships east of Staatsburg and Hyde Park. The stream first takes its proper name just south of Willow Brook Village, at the confluence of Hunn's Lake Creek and Willow Brook. It then flows southwest past Hibernia to Salt Point, where it is joined from the north by the waters of Little Wappinger's Creek. It continues southwest past Pleasant Valley,Rochdale, and Manchester Bridge to the neighborhood of New Hackensack, and forming the boundary between Poughkeepsie and La Grange townships. North of the village of Wappinger's Falls, it forms Wappinger's Lake. Here it goes over a seventy-five-foot fall to tidewater. Near its outlet to the Hudson, it is crossed by a highway swing bridge and a bascule bridge on the New York Central Railroad. The village (population 5,607), is on a plateau with an elevation of 116 feet. Local industries included a bleachery and an overall factory. The name comes from the local powerful tribe of Wappinger Indians.

63.20 Diamond Reef in midstream.
This rocky reef with only five feet depth surrounded by water sixty-two feet deep to west and sixty-eight feet deep to east is also known as New Hamburg Reef. It is known for excellent striped bass fishing.

63.20 Cedarcliff to west.
It was formerly known as Hampton and Hampton Ferry. It is a local station on the West Shore Railroad.

63.30 New Hamburg to east.
This is a local station for Wappinger's Falls on New York Central Railroad.

63.50 Hampton Point to west.
Also known as Peck's Dock, it is noted for fine white cedar trees. Dolomite (magnesium limestone) is quarried on both sides of the river for concrete and road building. The quarries here belong to the New York Trap Rock Division of Lone Star Industries.

63.75 Site of former Indian fishing encampment to west.

64.00 Vineyards to west.

64.20 Site of area's earliest settlement (ca. 1695) to west.
This later became an important textile manufacturing center.

Three quarters of a mile west of here is Mill House built in 1714 by a man known as "Gomez the Jew" or Mr. Gomez. He had built a mill nearby in 1711. The house has the distinction of being the oldest standing dwelling house in North America built by a member of the Jewish faith. Gomez was quite prosperous and the Maune Kill was also known as Jew's Creek from his mills. In 1772, he sold his house to Wolfert Acker, who expanded the house. The third owner was Henry Armstrong, a novelist. He wrote a Civil War novel called *Rutledge* while living here.

64.50 Maune Kill to west.

Formerly known as Jew's Creek from the mills of "Gomez the Jew" in the eighteenth century, it rises on the eastern slopes of the Marlboro or Plattekill Mountains and flows over falls in the village of Marlboro.

64.50 Marlboro to west.

It is also spelled Marlborough. This is the name of both a village and a town in Ulster County. It is a station on the West Shore Railroad and a formerly active steamboat landing. There was once a profusion of arbor vitae trees in the area. This was a fruit-growing center. Until the 1930s, this landing used to dispatch a boatload of raspberries daily to New York City in season. It is alleged that the aroma would spread over the river for miles. Here was the home of Col. Lewis DuBois, of 5th Regiment of the Continental Line (1728-1802). His home (ca.1763) is believed to be the first clapboard house built in Ulster County. Washington visited here. The hotel was built in 1858. McCourt House (brick) dates back to ca. 1830. There are wineries in this area.

64.50 Ulster County to west.

From here to West Camp (Wanton Island, ERM 100.50) the west bank is occupied by Ulster County. Ulster was one of the ten original counties established in 1683 and was named in honor of the Duke of York's earldom in Ireland. It has a present area of 1,143 square miles but has lost some area in the south to Orange. It presently consists of twenty townships: Hardenburgh, Denning, Shandaken,

Woodstock, Olive, Hurley, Marbletown, Rochester, Wawarsing, Shawangunk, Gardiner, New Paltz, Plattekill, Marlborough, Lloyd, Esopus, Rosendale, Kingston, Ulster, and Saugerties. The city of Kingston is the county seat. Other principal towns are Saugerties, New Paltz, Rosendale, and Ellenville.

Principal watercourses are: Esopus Creek, rising near Slide Mountain in the Catskills and flowing east to the Hudson at Saugerties. Rondout Creek, rising in the high Catskills and also flowing east to the Hudson at Kingston. The Wallkill River rises in Lake Mohawk in northern New Jersey and flows northeast through Orange County to Ulster County at Wallkill. It continues northeast past New Paltz to a junction with Rondout Creek just east of Rosendale.

Principal lakes are Rondout Reservoir and the large Ashokan Reservoir, both belonging to the city of New York. There are three principal groups of mountains. The Catskills occupy the western half of the county. The Shawangunk Mountains are in the southwestern part of the county and the Plattekill Mountains parallel the Hudson River.

The county was settled very early. Henry Hudson made his voyage of discovery in 1609. By 1614, there was an active trading post at Kingston, before the landing of the pilgrim fathers at Plymouth Rock. Early settlement was by the Dutch, with a strong infusion of French Huguenots in the Hurley and New Paltz areas.

In 1708, during the governorship of Lord Cornbury (1702-1708), Queen Anne granted a patent of approximately two million acres to Major Johannis Hardenbergh, Esq., formerly "High Sheriffe of Ulster Countie," and six other grantees. This patent covered most of present day Ulster, Delaware, Sullivan, and Greene Counties. As most of this area was mountainous and unfit for farming, the major had difficulty finding settlers. Among the first were German Palatine refugees from the Rhineland. (The Palatinates, victims of the French in the religious wars in Europe, had sought help from England. Queen Anne, sympathetic to their plight and, among other things, aware of the Hardenbergh patent in the Catskills and the need for settlers, agreed to help them.) They first were settled along the Hudson River (1710-1711) and unsuccessfully attempted the manufacture of tar and pitch. After much suffering, they took up farming. Others moved south and settled at Newburgh.

Vagueness about the boundaries of the patent caused decades of litigation, particularly pertaining to the western one which was variously construed as being the Bear Kill at one extreme and the West Branch of the Delaware at the other. In 1749, Ebenezer Wooster surveyed the property and divided it into large sections called Great Lots, averaging between 10,000 and 30,000 acres. By the time matters were settled, most of the original grantees for whom Major Hardenbergh was fronting were long dead. For many years the heirs of the original grantees cherished their "titles" and speculated with them, but few enjoyed any substantial benefit.

In 1672, a smaller patent entitled the Fox Hall Patent had been granted to Capt. Thomas Chambers. This was located above Esopus. It soon lapsed because of lack of heirs. Much of the land around Kingston belonged to the Kingston Commons. The mountainous nature of the territory and confusion over titles and boundaries inhibited settlement of much of Ulster County. The remaining area, unlike that on the east bank of the Hudson, was settled by small freeholders.

Most of eastern Ulster County is devoted to farming—largely orchards and vineyards. The balance is devoted to watershed purposes, forest preserves, parklands, and the resort industry. Principal early industries were tanning and bluestone quarrying. Building of the Wallkill Valley, Ulster & Delaware and West Shore Railroads did much to foster

the resort industry. Tourism remains the county's principal industry. There is an IBM Plant at Kingston and other light industry at Kingston, Woodstock, and Ellenville. Kingston serves mainly as an administrative and shopping center.

64.50 Howland to east.

64.70 Casper Creek to east.
It flows southwest into Hudson from southeastern section of Poughkeepsie. It was formerly called Casperkill or Jan Casper's Kill; Indian names were Thanakonok and Pietawickquasseick.

64.70 Young estate to west.
This was a point of deep-channel shipping of fruit in the late nineteenth and early twentieth centuries.

64.90 Quarry and crusher to east:
Lone Star industries.

64.90 Channing Ville to east.
This is about one mile inland.

64.90 Lake Pontusco to east.
Also known as Cobalt Lake, it is located on Casper Creek.

64.90 Pegg's Point to west.

65.00 Clinton Point to east.

65.00 Stoneco Post Office to east.
Here is located the New York Trap Rock dolomite quarry.

65.10 Sand pit to west:
behind Peggs Point.

65.50 Quarry to east.

65.50 Old landing to west.
The *Trojan* was burned here in a local labor war in 1940. This was a winter lay-up berth for river steamboats.

66.00 Barnegat to east.
Helen Wilkinson Reynolds tells us, in her *Dutch Houses In The Hudson Valley Before 1776:*

From the oysterbeds along the Atlantic coast shell-lime was . . . obtained to add to the filling for the walls (of houses) and, later, limestone-ridges in the Hudson Valley were exploited, as for example at Barnegat (the "fire-hole") in the town of Poughkeepsie, a place which earned its name in the eighteenth century from the flames flaring out of the many kilns in which limestone was calcined there.

The property where the present quarries are located was once the site of DeWitt Clinton's country home.

66.00 Gallaudet Home for Aged and Infirm Deaf-Mutes to east.
This home is located on a 100-acre estate established in 1872 by Dr. Thomas G. Gallaudet (1822-1902) son of Thomas H. Gallaudet (1787-1852) who initiated systematic education of the deaf in America. It is inland from the quarry region.

66.50 Camelot to east:
a local railroad station.

66.50 Cliffs to west.
These cliffs are named Lange Rack on the Coast and Geodetic Service navigation chart #283. The name Lange Rack properly applies to the Long Reach of the Hudson hereabouts, rather than to any land features.

67.00 Van Keurens to east.

67.00 Elderhoj art colony to west.
This is a stuccoed building in Moorish style, early twentieth century.

67.10 Captain Sherbourn Sears House to west.
This two-story clapboard, mid-eighteenth century house was modernized in mid-nineteenth century. This was formerly the property of "Father Devine," alias Joe Baker, born in Savannah, Georgia, in the 1890s. This flamboyant personality set himself up as a prophet. He came to New York in 1915 with twelve disciples and set up a commune in Brooklyn. Later he moved to Harlem. His adherents claimed he was God Himself. His followers went by the names of children and angels and dedicated all their property and earnings to the commune. He owned many businesses—a number of them in Ulster County.

67.25 Rudco to east.

67.25 Spring Brook to east.
Benson Lossing tells an interesting story about this location:

About four miles below Poughkeepsie is an ancient stone farmhouse and a mill, at the mouth of Spring Brook, at the eastern terminus of the Milton Ferry. Here, during the old war for independence, lived Theophilus Anthony, a blacksmith, farmer, miller, and staunch Whig, who used his forge for most rebellious purposes. He assisted in making a great chain that was stretched across the Hudson in the Highlands at Fort Montgomery, to prevent the British ships of war ascending the river and carrying invading troops into the heart of the country. For this offence, when the chain and accompanying boom were forced, and vessels of Vaughan carried the firebrand to Esopus or Kingston, the rebel blacksmith's mill was laid in ashes, and he was confined in the loathsome "Jersey" prison-ship at New York, where he had ample time for reflection and penitence for three weary years. Alas! the latter never came. He was a sinner against ministers, too hardened for repentance, and he remained a rebel until the close of his life. Another mill soon arose from the ashes of the old one, and there his grandsons, the Messrs. Gill were grinding wheat when we were there for the descendants of both

*Whigs and Tories, and never
inquired into the politics of the
passengers upon their boat at the
Milton Ferry. (1860)*

(Lossing, *The Hudson*,
p. 193.)

67.50 Milton to west.
Formerly known as Milton Ferry,
this town was once the center of
a Quaker intellectual colony. It
once shipped large quantities of
strawberries, raspberries, currants, and grapes. It was the
home of novelist Mary Hallock
Foote. Several active wineries
are located here. This is a major
orchard area.

67.60 IBM plant to east.
Its water towers are visible.

67.65 Sand's Dock to west.
This is the site of the Ward family
shipyard.

68.00 Long Point to east.

68.80 Locust Grove to east.
This is the former home of
Samuel F.B. Morse (1791-1872),
inventor of the telegraph. It is a
two-story Italian villa with wings,
begun in 1830 and renovated in
1852, on a 100-acre estate.

69.10 Southwood Estate to east.
This is a two-story brick house
with tower and Mansard roof (ca.
1865). Sunfish Cove is to east.

69.15 Mine Point to east.
Distinguished by a tomb, it is in
the grounds of the Poughkeepsie
Rural Cemetery. It is also known
as Lookout Point.

69.20 Blue Point to west.
This is the site of the Hudson
Valley Winery. These waters were
allegedly the favorite anchorage
of the Storm Ship. (See article
on Tappan Zee—mile 21.45.) It
was formerly called Juffrouw's
Hoeck (Madam's Point).

70.10 Fox Point to east.

**70.10 Vassar Brothers' Hospital to
east.**
This institution in a group of
red-brick buildings was founded
by two nephews of Matthew
Vassar.

70.40 Oakes to west.

70.45 Lewisburg to west.

70.50 Mid-Hudson Bridge.
This is a unit of the New York
State Bridge Authority. This
beautiful suspension bridge was
opened to traffic on August 25,
1930. The bridge has an overall
length of 3000 feet, with a main
span of 1500 feet. It carries two
vehicle lanes and two pedestrian
sidewalks. Vessel clearance is
135 feet. The east pier was
carried down to a record depth of
135 feet below water to reach
solid rock. Principal building contractors were: American Bridge
Company, Blakeslee-Rollins Corporation, David Schoentag, Inc.,
and Scott Brothers Construction
Company. Total cost was
$5,890,000.

The bridge was designed by
Ralph Modjeski (1861-1940),
partner in the firm of Modjeski &
Moran, engineers. This noted
bridge designer was born in
Cracow, Poland, and came to the
United States in 1876, after
studying engineering in Paris.
He was perhaps the leading
bridge designer of his day. Other
principal spans of his are the
Huey P. Long Bridge at New
Orleans; the Iowa-Illinois Memorial Bridge at Davenport, Iowa;
the Ben Franklin Bridge over the
Delaware at Phildelphia; and
large structures for the Southern
Pacific Railroad over the Columbia and Willamette Rivers. In
later life he resided at Saugerties. His partner was Daniel E.
Moran.

His mother was the famous tragic actress Helena Modjeska (1844-1909). After a successful European career, she came to the United States in 1877. She was best known for her Shakespearean roles.

70.50 Poughkeepsie to east.

(population 32,029). The "Queen City" of the Hudson. The city is partly upon a hill-side, sloping to the river, but chiefly upon an elevated plain, back of which is College Hill, whose summit is 500 feet above the town. The plain has a 200-foot elevation.

There are several theories as to the derivation of the name Poughkeepsie. One is that it comes from the Indian "Pooghkepesingh", meaning "where the water breaks through or falls over," possibly referring to the rapids on the Fall Kill. Another theory is that it means "reed-covered lodge by the little water place," The most likely is the theory propounded by Benson J. Lossing (a native of this vicinity) in his book *The Hudson:*

The name is a modification of the Mohegan word, Apo-keep-sinck, signifying "safe and pleasant harbour." Between two rocky bluffs was a sheltered bay (now filled with wharves—Ed. Note-1860—near foot of Main Street), into the upper part of which leaped, in rapids and cascades, the Winnakee, called Fall Kill by the Dutch. The northerly bluff was called by the Dutch "Slange Klippe," or Adder Cliff, because of the venomous serpents which were abundant there in the olden time. The southern bluff bears the name of Call Rock, it having been a place from which the settlers called to the captains of sloops or single-masted vessels, when passage in them was desired. With this bay, or "safe Harbour," is associated an Indian legend, of which the following is the substance:—Once some Delaware warriors came to this spot

with Pequod captives. Among the latter was a young chief, who was offered life and honour if he would renounce his nation, receive the mark of the turtle upon his breast, and become a Delaware brave. He rejected the degrding proposition with disdain, and was bound to a tree for sacrifice, when a shriek from a thicket startled the executioners. A young girl leaped before them, and implored his life. She was a captive Pequod, with the turtle on her bosom, and the young chief was her affianced. The Delawares debated, when suddenly the war-whoop of some fierce Hurons made them snatch their arms for defense. The maiden severed the thongs that bound her lover, but in the deadly conflict that ensued, they were separated, and a Huron chief carried off the captive as a trophy. Her affianced conceived a bold design for her rescue, and proceeded immediately to execute it. In the character of a wizard he entered the Huron camp. The maiden was sick, and her captor employed the wizard to prolong her life, until he should satisfy his revenge upon Uncas, her uncle, the great chief of the Mohegans. They eluded the vigilance of the Huron, fled at nightfall, with swift feet, towards the Hudson, and in the darkness, shot out upon its bosom, in a light canoe, followed by blood-thirsty pursuers. The strong arm of the young Pequod paddled his beloved one safely to a deep rocky nook near the mouth of the Winnakee, concealed her there, and with a few friendly Delawares whom he had secured by a shout, he fought, conquered, and drove off the Huron warriors. The sheltered nook where the maiden lay was a "safe harbour" for her, and the brave Pequod and his friends joyfully confirmed its title to Apo-keep-sinck.

(Lossing, *The Hudson,* pp. 187-8.)

A very nice tale if you can swallow it! More possibly, it simply referred to a safe

canoe anchorage. Another derivation of Call Rock is from the Dutch "Kaal" Rock, signifying barren or bald.

Lossing gives a list of various spellings as found in records and maps: Pakeepsie, Pacapsey, Pakepsey, Paughkepsie, Pecapesy, Pecapsy, Pecapshe, Pochkeepsinck, Poeghkeepsing, Poeghkeeksingk, Poeghkeepsink, Pochkeepsey, Pochkeepsen, Pochkeepsy, Pochkepsen, Pochkyphsingh, Pockeepsy, Pockepseick, Pockepseng, Pokepsing, Poghkeepsie, Poghkeepsinck, Poghkeepsing, Poghkepse, Poghkepsen, Poghkeepsink, Poghkeepson, Poghkeepse, Pokeepsigh, Pokeepsingh, Pokeepsink, Pokeepsy, Pokepsinck, Pokkepsen, Poughkeepsey, Poukeepsie, Poukeepsy, Pikipsi, Picipsi, Pokepsie, Pokeepsie, Poughkeepsie, Total—42.

The area was originally populated by the Wappinger or Wappingi Indians. In 1683, Chief Massany gave a deed to two Hollanders and the first settlement was made in 1687. Baltus Van Kleek built a substantial home near the mouth of the Fall Kill in 1705. This stood until 1835. This house was pierced with loopholes for musketry, near the roof, that being a necessary precaution against Indian attacks. The New York legislature met here during two sessions in 1777 and 1778 when New York was held by the British and after Kingston had been burned by Vaughan.

In 1788, the township of Poughkeepsie was incorporated. That same year, in June, a State Convention met here to consider the Federal Constitution. Among the members were Alexander Hamilton, George Clinton, John Jay, and Chancellor Livingston. They voted to accept it by one vote. This, and passage by Virginia of ratification, put the Federal Constitution into effect, on July 26, 1788.

The village of Poughkeepsie was formed in 1799, and incorporated as a city in 1854. It is the county seat of Dutchess County.

Joel Benton, a local writer, tells us that Poughkeepsie:

. . . soon became the center of a large trade running in long lines east and west from the river. Dutchess county had at this time but a sparse population. There was a post-road from New York to Albany; but the building of the Dutchess Turnpike from Poughkeepsie to Sharon, Connecticut, connecting with one from that place to Litchfield, which took place in 1808, was a capital event in its history. This made a considerable strip of western Connecticut tributary to Poughkeepsie's trade.

Over the turnpike went four-horse Concord stages, with berailed top and slanting boot in the rear for trunks and other baggage. Each one had the tin horn of the driver; and it was difficult to tell upon which the driver most prided himself—the power to fill that thrilling instrument, or his deft handling of the ponderous whip and multiplied reins. Travelers to Hartford and Boston went over this route; and an east and west through and way mail was a part of the burden. A sort of overland express and freight line, styled the Market Wagon, ran in and out of the town from several directions. One or more of these conveyances started from as far east as the Housatonic River, and they frequently crowded passengers in amongst their motley wares.

Speaking of the stage-driver's horn recalls the fact that when the steamboat arrived—which was so solitary an institution that for some time it was distinctly called "The Steamboat"—the tin horn did duty also for it. When it was seen in the distance, either Albanyward or in the New York direction, a boy went through the village blowing it to arouse those who wished to embark on it. It is said the expectant passengers had ample time, after the horn was sounded, to make their toilets, run down to the river (or walk down) and take passage on it.

Poughkeepsie honored in May 1824, the arrival of Lafayette, and dined him, besides exchanging speeches with him, both at the Forbus House, on Market

Street, very nearly where the Nelson House now stands, and at the Pough-keepsie Hotel. It was one of Poughkeep-sie's great days when he came. Daniel Webster has spoken in her Court House; and Henry Clay, in 1844, when a presidential candidate, stopped for a reception.

In 1844, the New York State Fair was held here somewhere east of what is now Hooker Avenue. It was an occasion thought important enough then to be pictured and reported in the London Illustrated News. Two years after the telegraph wires were put up in this city, before they had yet reached the City of New York. Considering the fact that Prof. S.F.B. Morse, the telegraph inventor, had his residence here, this incident was not wholly inappropriate.

> ("Vignettes of Poughkeepsie," in The Four Track Series, published by the New York Central System, No. 36, Jan. 1902, p.20.)

Thus go Mr. Benton's reminiscences. The New York Central railroad came through in 1849. The large railroad bridge across the Hudson was built in 1886, thus making Poughkeepsie an important railroad center.

In Picturesque America, edited by William Cullen Bryant, E. L. Burlingham gives the following description of Poughkeepsie:

The "rural city," as one of our writers has called it, lies very pleasantly upon its group of gentle hills, and overlooks a bright and sunny portion of the river-view. By day, one may quarrel a little with the smoke of its busy founderies, but by night these become the most strangely beautiful and striking feature in many miles of the Hudson's scenery. They light the river like weird beacons, and the sound of their great furnaces comes across the water in the stillness, as the panting of giants that toil when the weaker forces of the world are all asleep. (p. 3.)

Other nineteenth-century industries included Adriance, Platt & Co., who manufactured the famous Buckeye Mowers and Reapers; the Phoenix Horsehoe Company; the Knitting-Goods Establishment; and various shoe, shirt, silk thread, and hardware factories.

More modern industries have produced ball bearings, cream separators, dairy equipment and office machinery, cough-drops, candy, and computors. Important local firms are the DeLaval Co., International Business Machines, and Smith Brothers Cough Drops. This last named firm was established in 1850 by William Wallace Smith and Andrew Smith, of the flowing beards, who used their photographs printed upon each box of cough drops. They were commonly known throughout the land as "Trade" and "Mark." The present factory was built in 1914, and the cough drops are still popular both as candy and as an effective medicinal. The Smith Brothers also long operated a good restaurant on Market Street. The writer can remember accompanying his father on business trips when a small boy and eating there. It had old fashioned wooden paneling and paddle fans. We would arrive from Newburgh on the Dayline steamer (these were the days of gas rationing during World War II) and take a bus up Main Street from the Landing and put up overnight at the old Nelson House. Poughkeepsie was a busy place at that time, and the proximity of President Franklin D. Roosevelt's home at Hyde Park nearby and the wartime projects of IBM gave the town considerable importance.

For many years, from 1895 until 1950, the Intercollegiate Rowing Association regatta was held on the Hudson here. It was finally removed to Marietta on the Ohio River. Excursion trains full of fans would be parked on the high bridge for viewing. The winning crews would paint their initials on the rocks along the western shoreline. Some faint ones can still be made out.

Poughkeepsie is an educational center. The Dutchess Community College, Marist College, and Vassar College are all located here. Also, for many years, Poughkeepsie was the seat of the famous Eastman College, a popular business and commercial school. Matthew Vassar (1792-1868) was born in England and came to America with his father in 1796. The family operated successful breweries in Poughkeepsie. In 1861, he founded the Vassar Female College, "where women can learn what is useful, practical and sensible." He gave more than $800,000 to the school. Today the school is coeducational.

In recent years Poughkeepsie has seen considerable economic decline. The city became a "two-industry town," i.e., De Laval and IBM, with both the advantages and disadvantages of such a limited economic base. River shipping has declined to zero and its importance as a railroad junction was diminished first by the creation of Penn Central and Conrail, and then by the "temporary" closing of the railroad bridge and the trade route it upheld after a fire several years ago. The bridge has not been repaired, although several industrial associations and the Interstate Commerce Commission are agitating to make Conrail repair and reopen it. Much of the river-slope part of town has been torn down to make way for urban renewal. New parks have been built along the waterfront and a fine automobile expressway takes through traffic off the local streets. There have been new public housing projects, a new civic center and mall and auditorium and other major physical improvements. The dilapidated steamboat landing has been removed and the waterfront generally cleaned up.

However, with the lack of activity, this is like the mortician's "prettying up" the corpse. For lack of a proper landing place, the day boats no longer put in at Poughkeepsie. There is still a crying need for additional diversified industry.

There is too much unemployment in the area.

There are many interesting eighteenth and nineteenth century homes and commercial buildings. Among the most interesting are the following:

1) A group of Greek Revival Houses on Mill Street (ca. 1840-50)
2) Commercial buildings on Main Street (mid nineteenth century)
3) Vassar Brothers' Institute, two-story brick Georgian (ca. 1765)
4) Victorian and Greek Revival townhouses on Mill Street
5) Home of George Clinton, two-story brick Victorian (ca. 1765)
6) Glebe House, brick Georgian, (ca. 1767)
7) Old Ladies' Home, Greek Revival (1836)
8) Soldiers' Fountain, South Avenue and Montgomery Street (1870): Civil War memorial, cast iron, at entrance to Eastman Park
9) Eastman House, three-story brick, Italianate Victorian (ca. 1870)
10) Frear House, one-story stone 18th century)
11) Springside: summer home of Matthew Vassar, board and batten, (ca. 1850). House and grounds designed by Andrew Jackson Downing. This is considered the best remaining example of Downing's residential landscape architecture.

Old churches include:
1) Church of St. Peter (R.C.), Italianate Victorian (1853)
2) Episcopal Church of the Holy Comforter, stone Gothic Revival (1860), designed by Richard Upjohn
3) Second Baptist Church, clapboard Greek Revival, (ca.1840)

Poughkeepsie is the northern terminus of the MTA Hudson Line suburban rail service and an express stop for Amtrak. It was once the northern terminus of Hudson River Day Line excursion service. Since dilapidation of the dock, the boats still cruise to Poughkeepsie daily during the season, but do not land.

70.50 Call Rock to east.
It is at the eastern foot of the Mid-Hudson Bridge. See Poughkeepsie article for derivation of name.

70.51 Former steamboat landing to east, at the foot of Main Street.

70.52 Fall Kill to east.
Formerly Winnakee Brook, it rises in northeastern section of Poughkeepsie township and flows southwest to Hudson through northern portion of the city.

70.52 College Hill to east.
(elevation 365 feet). It was formerly property of Sen. Morgan and William Smith, who gave it to the city as a park.

70.52 Adder or Snake Cliff to east.
Formerly the Dutch "Slange Klippe," it was named for the former profusion of snakes.

70.52 Railroad Cantilever Bridge.
This bridge was begun in 1873, but work was stopped for several years. Work was resumed in 1886 and finished in less than three years' time by the Union Bridge Company. Length is 12,608 feet, with main span of 2,260 feet. The main span of 2,260 feet. The track is 212 feet above the water. Vessel clearance of center span is 165 feet. Breadth of river at this point is 3,094 feet. Cost of bridge: $3,500,000. It is for railroad only. It is presently out of commission and is part of the Conrail System. Repair of fire damage and reactivation are problematical.

71.50 Marist College to east

71.50 Water intake and Purification plant to east:
City of Poughkeepsie.

71.50 Illinois Mountain to west.
(elevation 1129 feet).

71.50 Twaalfskill Creek to west.
It rises west of Blue Point and flows northeast to the Hudson through a picturesque ravine.

71.50 Highland to west.
It was formerly called New Paltz or Elting's Landing. The main part of the village is uphill and out of sight. Settled by Huguenots in about 1677, it is the former western terminus of the ferry to Poughkeepsie. It was bombarded by the British in 1777. Interesting buildings are Ferryman Inn or Yelverton House, eighteenth-century saltbox; Mid-Hudson Hotel (1850) with stepped gables; and Davis Place (ca. 1830).

72.00 Site of Woodcliff Amusement Park to east.

72.75 Hudson River State Hospital to east.
This mental hospital, founded in 1871 on property purchased from James Roosevelt, has a brick Victorian Gothic main building designed by Vaux & Withers. Its grounds have grown from 208 to 1,730 acres. Now there are 83 buildings.

72.75 Lange Rack Cliffs to west.
This is the former start of a four-mile course of Intercollegiate crew races. Some faded painted trophies may still be seen on the rocks.

73.20 Roosevelt to east.
This is a former local New York Central station.

73.20 Dog Head Cove Point to west:
site of early nineteenth-century Coe House.

73.80 Culinary Institute of America to east.
Red brick Gothic buildings with white trim dating from 1903, with a five-story main building on a seventy-acre campus, this was

formerly St. Andrews-on-the Hudson, a Jesuit Seminary and Monastery. Since 1972, it has been the home of America's premier school for commercial chefs and food service personnel. The school was founded in 1946 in New Haven, Connecticut. Offering exclusive training for cooks in the broadest sense, the Institute is the only facility of its kind awarding a degree for purely vocational training in the culinary arts. The degree is awarded upon completion of four trimesters of courses and a trimester of externship. This private, non-profit, educational facility has a curriculum that is known and respected throughout the world.

The school operates the Escoffier Restaurant and Rabelais Grill, as well as a coffee shop and diner. All are open to the general public, but the gourmet Escoffier Restaurant requires reservations (telephone 914-452-9600).

74.00 Maritje Kill to east.
It rises south of East Park and flows southwest to the Hudson.

74.25 Crum Elbow Point to west.
Also called Krumm Elbow. There are several possible derivations, both from the Dutch. The more popular one is from "Krom Elleboge" or "crooked elbow." However, the original Dutch name for the location was Kromme Hoek, or "rounded point." Father Divine once owned a 500-acre estate here which was called Negro Heaven. It was operated as a communal farming project. There was a large pavilion and boathouse.

74.75 Crum Elbow, home of Franklin Delano Roosevelt to east.
The following is taken from the brochure of the National Park Service:

Franklin D. Roosevelt, 32nd President of the United States was born in this home on January 30, 1882. He was the only child of James and Sara Roosevelt.

Franklin Roosevelt spent much of his life here. Here Franklin— the toddler, the little boy, the young man—was shaped and grew to maturity. Here he brought his bride, Eleanor, in 1905, and here they raised their five children. From here he began his political career that stretched from the New York State Senate to the White House. Roosevelt was a State senator, 1911-13, Assistant Secretary of the Navy under Woodrow Wilson, 1913-20, and unsuccessful vice-presidential candidate in 1920. Then, in 1921, he contracted infantile paralysis. During his struggle to conquer the disease he spent much time here. He refused to become an invalid and reentered politics. He was elected Governor of New York in 1928 and 1930 and President of the United States in 1932. As Governor and President, he came here as often as he could for respite from the turmoil of public life. On April 15, 1945, three days after his death in Warm Springs, Georgia, President Roosevelt was buried in the family rose garden. Seventeen years later, on November 10, 1962, Mrs. Roosevelt was buried beside the President.

The central portion of the building, the oldest section, dates to the early 1800s. When James Roosevelt bought the house, then called "Spring Wood," in 1867, it had a clapboard exterior.

The main house has undergone many renovations and additions with the passage of years. In 1916 it assumed its present form.

The central part, its clapboards removed, was covered with stucco and fronted by a porch with a sweeping balustrade and a small colonnaded portico. On each end, the Roosevelts added a two-story wing.

The house was designated a National Historic Site on January 15th 1944. A gift from President Roosevelt, the site then consisted of 33 acres containing the home, outbuildings, and the grave site. The site was formally dedicated on April 12, 1946, the first anniversary of the President's death, and now contains 188 acres.

The Franklin D. Roosevelt Library and Museum, which are NOT part of the National Historic Site, are located nearby. They contain the President's books, papers, ship models, gifts, and personal belongs. (National Park Service, GPO 1974-585-454/7.)

75.25 Crum Elbow Point Light to east.

75.50 Rogers Point to east.

75.50 Mt. Hymettus to west.
(elevation 900 feet. John Burroughs gave it this name because of his luck in finding many bees, beehives, and wild honey on its slopes. Mount Hymettus in Greece is famous for its fields of flowers, many bees, and honey.

76.00 Plattekill Hills to west.

76.40 Santa Maria Novitiate to west.
Two-story brick Italianate Victorian building, mid-19th century.

76.40 Hyde Park to east.
Originally called Stoutenburgh after Jacobus Stoutenburgh who lived here in 1741. However, as early as 1705, Peter Fauconier, private secretary of Edward Hyde, Viscount Cornbury, royal governor of New York, obtained a patent for land in this vicinity.

Subsequently the name was changed from Stoutenburgh to the more aristrocratic Hyde Park. Of particular architectual interest in the town are the railroad station, with bracketed overhang, and the Eymard Seminary. This building, originally a private mansion named Crumwald, dates from 1889 and is Romanesque in style with towers and dormers. Saint Peter Julian Eymard was the founder of the congregations of the Fathers of the Blessed Sacrament and of the Servants of the Blessed Sacrament. He was born at La Mure d'Isére, France in 1811 and early evinced a great sensitivity to the Real Presence in the Blessed Sacrament. He devoted his entire life founding an order devoted to perpetual adoration of the Blessed Sacrament. He died in 1868.

76.40 East Park to east:
inland from Hyde Park.

76.60 Crum Elbow Creek to east.
It rises near East Park and flows generally west to the Hudson, through several small ponds near the Vanderbilt Mansion.

76.60 Frothingham Dock to west.
This is the western terminus of a former horse-powered ferry to Hyde Park.

77.00 Vanderbilt Mansion National Historic Site to east.

The following article is taken from the brochures of the National Park Service which administers the site:

The history of the 211 acre grounds goes back much further than that of the mansion. The grounds had been maintained as a country seat by prominent individuals since colonial days. The fine old trees and spreading lawns had been carefully developed for generations.

Hyde Park, as the estate was first

called, is said to have been named by Peter Fauconnier, the private secretary of Edward Hyde, Viscount Cornbury, later third Earl of Clarendon and Governor of New York from 1702 to 1708. Fauconnier held office in the colony as collector and receiver general and also owned extensive tracts of land, including a part of the patent of Hyde Park. This patent was granted in the reign of Queen Anne on April 18, 1705. The town of Hyde Park, established in 1821, took its name from the estate.

Dr. John Bard, noted physician and pioneer in hygiene, acquired the entire Hyde Park patent during the two decades following the death of Fauconnier in 1746. Dr. Bard lived principally in New York City until about 1772, when he moved to Hyde Park. He built a house just north of the present St. James Church and began to develop the virgin land of the estate. After the Revolution, Dr. John Bard returned to private practice in New York. There he assisted his son, Dr. Samuel Bard, as attending physician to George Washington, then in his first term as President of the United States. Dr. John Bard retired to Hyde Park again in 1798, and there, a year later, he died.

Dr. Samuel Bard received the property by transfer shortly before his father's death. Educated at King's College, (now Columbia University) and at Edinburgh, he, like his father, was an eminent physician.

The younger Dr. Bard built a new mansion at Hyde Park. This was a large house on the high elevation rising about 300 feet above the Hudson River and commanding a superb view of this beautiful stream, of the Shawangunk Range to the west, and of the Catskill Mountains to the north. Continuing to improve the grounds, Dr. Bard also undertook experiments in horticulature and farming. He imported small fruits from England, larger ones from France, melons from Italy, and vines from Madeira. Dr. Bard and his wife lived at Hyde Park until 1821, when they died within a day of each other.

Their only surviving son, William Bard, inherited Hyde Park, which had been reduced by land sales to 540 acres, but lived there only until about 1828. In that year he sold the estate to Dr. David Hosack of New York City. Dr. Hosack, who had been a professor of natural history at Columbia College, was a former partner of Dr. Samuel Bard, and received the latter's medical practice when he retired.

Dr. Hosack, who was deeply interested in plants, flowers, and trees, revived horticultural experimentation and gardening at Hyde Park. He engaged Andre Parmentier, a Belgian landscape gardener, to lay out roads, walks, and scenic vistas. This work was probably done between 1828 and 1830. The rare and exotic specimens which grace the lawns and park appear to date principally from that time.

In 1840, 5 years after the death of Dr. Hosack, John Jacob Astor bought the mansion tract from the heirs. Mr. Astor almost immediately made a gift of the estate to his daughter, Dorothea Astor Langdon, and her children. Walter Langdon, Jr., a son, became the sole owner of the estate in 1852. He continued to live at Hyde Park until his death in 1894. During this period the greenhouses and flower gardens were enlarged and the farmland east of the Albany Post Road was reunited with the property by purchase in 1872.

The Langdons had no children, so Hyde Park was offered for sale in 1895. It was purchased by Frederick William Vanderbilt, the grandson of Commodore Cornelius Vanderbilt who had founded the family fortune.

Mr. Vanderbilt had the Langdon House torn down. On its site he erected the present structure, which was completed in 1898 at a cost of $660,000 without furnishings. Care was used in choosing the furnishings; Continental motifs, especially Italian and French, predominate. Mr. Vanderbilt greatly improved the grounds and built new farm buildings, carriage houses, and entranceways.

The Vanderbilts occupied the mansion during the spring and autumn. Entertaining at the large mid-Hudson Valley estates during the early 1900's was usually limited to weekends. Mr. Vanderbilt died in 1938, having willed the estate to Mrs. Vanderbilt's niece, Mrs. Margaret Van Alen, now Mrs. Louis Bruguiere.

Vanderbilt Mansion was designated a national historic site on December 18, 1940, following Mrs. Van Alen's gift of the estate to the United States for that purpose. The site consists of 212 acres of beautiful grounds overlooking the Hudson River, together with the mansion house and related buildings. Vanderbilt Mansion is a symbol of an era. It is a magnificent example of the great estates built by wealthy financial and industrial leaders between 1880 and 1900.

The Stately mansion of Indiana limestone is the focal point of the Vanderbilt estate. Designed by McKim, Mead and White, this 3-story American "royal palace," built at a cost of $660,000, is one of the finest examples of Italian Renaissance architecture in the United States and a fitting symbol of the Gilded Age.

When Frederick Vanderbilt (1857-1938) purchased the estate from Walter Langdon, Jr., in 1895, he was influenced by its proximity to New York City and its scenic charm. Also, his neighbors would be the Rodgerses, the Roosevelts, the Millses, and, farther upriver, the Astors —all families of prominence and wealth. But more importantly, Vanderbilt found the land ideal for pursuing his interests in purebred livestock and horticulture. The grounds of the estate were enlarged in 1905 when Vanderbilt purchased the Sexton estate adjoining his property on the north.

In 1895 the Vanderbilts had the Pavilion constructed and lived there while the mansion was built. (McKim, Mead and White in Classic Greek style.) The Langdon House was torn down in 1896 and that October Vanderbilt began construction of his 54-room mansion. It was finished in December 1898. During the next few months furnishings were in-

stalled and in May 1899 the first of many gala parties was given. The Vanderbilts look forward to returning each spring and fall to their Hudson River estate. Their summers were spent elsewhere, but in winter they came here on weekends and at Christmas, living in the Pavilion, for the mansion was closed. During these visits they took particular delight in sleighing.

The mansion was lavishly furnished in continental motifs, mostly Italian and French. Noted decorators Georges A. Glaenzer and Ogden Codman designed the decor of some of the rooms, while McKim, Mead and White did the others. Cost was no hinderance to the Vanderbilts.

Like other wealthy families along the Hudson, the Vanderbilts entertained lavishly. Gala balls were held in the 30 by 50 foot drawing room, and refreshments were served in the spacious oval reception hall with its large fireplace imported from a European palace. Guests included nobility and leaders in business, politics and the arts such as the Duke of Marlborough, who was Vanderbilt's niece's husband, and Franklin D. Roosevelt.

The Vanderbilts played an important role in the economy of the community, hiring local residents when possible, to work in the mansion, on the grounds, the farm, coachhouse, and Italian gardens. When the Vanderbilts were at Hyde Park, 17 household helpers were needed at the mansion alone. They also took an active interest in the welfare of nearby villages.

Much of these activities ceased after Louise Vanderbilt's death in 1926. Frederick, though a power in the business world, was a quiet and reserved man who cared little for social life, preferring walks on the mansion grounds, yachting and overseeing the care of his gardens and purebred livestock. When he died in 1938, the mansion and grounds were left to Louise Vanderbilt's niece, Margaret Van Alen (the late Mrs. Louis Bruguière), since the Vanderbilts had no children.

(Vanderbilt Mansion-National Historic Site United States Department of the Interior-Form 1962 0-625246)

It is open daily from 9 a.m. to 5 p.m. except New Year's Day and Christmas. This is a must for the serious tourist.

77.20 West Park to west.

This was the home of the author and naturalist John Burroughs (1837-1921). He was born in Roxbury, New York, the son of a farmer. He later taught school in Olive Bridge and worked as a Treasury Clerk in Washington and as a journalist. In 1874, he designed and built his home, Riverby, in West Park, and gave himself over to horticulture and pomology, and most importantly to the writing of the many nature essays for which he is best known. Much of this writing was done in his "bark study" overlooking the Hudson, where he was visited by Walt Whitman, John Muir, and Theodore Roosevelt. He also had a retreat on the southern slopes of Shaupeneak Mountain called Slabsides, and maintained a summer home near Clump Mountain west of Roxbury in the Catskills, which he called Woodchuck Lodge. Primarily an essayist, he was also a poet and an avid explorer, and the first to make a recorded visit to the summit of Slide Mountain, highest of the Catskills. He is buried near Roxbury.

His son Julian Burroughs also lived at West Park, and his home was called "The Nest." He was an architect and designed the elaborate stables for the estate of Colonel Oliver Hazard Payne, for whom he also served as estate manager between 1914 and 1918.

The Payne estate is now the Marist Brothers novitiate. The main mansion was built in 1910 from designs by Carrere & Hastings, of New York, best known for the Main Branch of the New York Public Library on Fifth Avenue. The mansion is a chateau in the French style with 36 rooms. It makes extensive use of marble and California tile. Mr. Payne was an oil magnate and an associate of John D. Rockefeller.

The Church of the Ascension (Episcopal) on Route 9W was built in 1842. It has two ogee windows and is of unusual charm. The West Shore Railroad leaves the riverbank and cuts inland for the rest of the way to Albany just south of West Park.

77.75 Bard's Rock and Creek to east.
It rises west of Hogback Hill and flows southwest to the Hudson.

78.30 Bolle's Island to east.
This is now joined to the mainland.

78.50 Hogback Hill to east.
(elevation 364 feet).

78.75 Blunt's Island to east.
It is now joined to the mainland.

78.75 Site of Placentia to east.
This was the country seat of James Kirke Paulding (1779-1860), one of the Knickerbocker school. He was a popular novelist and best known for his *The Dutchman's Fireside.* He also wrote the interesting *New Mirror For Travellers & Guide To The Springs* in 1828, one of the earliest Hudson River guidebooks. He was also active in politics and served as Secretary of the Navy under Martin Van Buren. He lived at Placentia in elegant retirement for many years, enjoying his books, his pictures, and his friends, among whom was Washington Irving. After his death, the estate was sold to Robert T. Lord and was renamed Gros Bois.

79.00 Esopus Island.
It is just east of midstream and has channels on either side.

79.25 Black Creek to west.
It rises on the western slopes of

Illinois Mountain and flows north into Chodikee Lake (Grote Binnewater) (also known as Black Pond). Then it continues over several waterfalls and through some narrow gorges before turning northeast by north to enter the Hudson below the town Esopus. Its waters are dark with tannin from cedar and hemlock trees—thus its name.

79.50 Esopus to west.
Formerly known as Van Pelt's, this town was founded in 1811. On the riverfront is located Rosemont, the former home of Alton B. Parker, New York State jurist and 1904 Democratic Presidential candidate. The house dates from before the Revolution and is two-story clapboard.

79.50 Brown's Dock to west.

79.75 Indian Rock to west.
This is the site of the Walter P. Seaman House (1870), a two-story clapboard building.

79.75 Norrie Point to east.
This is a state park with a public yacht basin and marina. It is part of Margaret Lewis Norrie State Park.

79.75 Shaupeneak Mountain to west.
(elevation 910 feet).

79.90 Indian Kill to east.
Formerly Ficket's Creek, it rises in Staatsburg Reservoir and flows southwest to the Hudson north of Norrie Point.

79.90 Mt. St. Alphonsus Seminary to west.
Of the Roman Catholic Redemptorist order, its massive gray stone building was erected in 1900. It is 4½-story Romanesque.

80.25 Pelham Dock to west.
It is also known as Pell's Dock. Here was the 1,200-acre model orchard and fruit farm of Robert L. Pell, Esq. He had over 25,000 trees in his orchards and was one of the largest fruit shippers in the world. He shipped apples to Queen Victoria, as well as large quantities of table grapes, currants, and small fruits. His estate was known as Cliffwood.

81.20 Staatsburg to east.
It is inland and is not seen from the river. It was first settled by Dr. Samuel Staats and Dirck Van der Burgh. In the 1850s, large ice storage sheds were erected here, and the Staatsburg Ice Tool Works was established in 1858.

St. Margaret's Episcopal Church was built in 1891, designed by Richard Upjohn. It is Gothic style and has two three-panel stained glass windows of the 13th century taken from Chartres Cathedral. They were the gift of Ogden Mills, Sr., as a memorial to his wife, Ruth Livingston Mills.

81.50 Cave Point to west.
Inland and not visible from the river is the village of Ulster Park.

81.60 Mills Mansion State Historic Site to east.
Located in Mills Memorial State Park, this is operated by the Taconic State Park Commission. The following is taken from the official descriptive brochure:

The Mills Mansion, with grounds, architecture and furnishings still intact, is an elegant relic of the turn of the 20th century. Its story, however, extends back a century earlier in the state's history. In 1792 General Morgan Lewis, New York's third governor, purchased the land and built a home on the present mansion site. Governor Lewis was married to Gertrude Livingston, the sister of Chancellor Robert P. Livingston of Clermont, and the house has had close associations with the Liv-

ingston family ever since.

When the original mansion burned in 1832, Morgan Lewis and his wife immediatley had it rebuilt in the popular Greek Revival style of their day. At the end of the 19th century, the home was in the Possession of Ruth Livingston Mills, great-granddaughter of the original builder, and wife of Darius Ogden Mills (1884-1937) a wealthy financier and philanthropist. At this time the old Greek Revival building was heavily remodeled in accordance with designs prepared by the prestigious architectural firm of McKim, Mead and White. Two large wings were added to the existing central core and the exterior was embellished with balustrades, pilasters and swags. The interior, decorated in the style of Louis XV and Louis XVI, remains rich with marble fireplaces, oak paneling and gilded ceiling and wall decorations installed at that time.

The Mills family usually came to Staatsburg in the autumn when, with their neighbors and house guests, they could sail on the river, ride horses kept in their large stable, or play golf at a course installed behind the house. The household staff numbered about 25 and many more were employed in the gardens, greenhouses, and extensive farming enterprises.

In 1937, Mrs. Henry Carnegie Phipps, in memory of her parents Ruth and Ogden Mills, gave the house and its grounds to New York State. The exterior is encased in white marble in the French Renaissance style. It has 65 rooms and cost $500,000. It is now open as a museum.

(Undated, anonymous, information leaflet issued by Taconic State Park and Recreation Commission — no form number)

81.70 Lewis Pier to east.

81.75 Dinsmore or the Locusts to east.
This is the estate of William B. Dinsmore, who, with Alvin Adams, founded the Adams Express Co. in 1840.

81.80 Dinsmore Point to east.
There is currently a serious error in this matter. The current Coast & Geodetic Survey Navigation Chart #283 incorrectly labels Esopus Meadows Point, on the west shore, as Dinsmore Point. Consequently the name has been transferred in popular usage.

82.30 Esopus Meadows Lighthouse
near mid-river to left of shipping channel. Esopus Meadows are a shallow area of the Hudson on the west side, with weedy shoals and water only a single foot or so deep. It is treacherous, and even very small craft can easily be wrecked. The main channel here is curved close to the Eastern shore. There are sharp reefs. It is protected by Esopus Meadows Light (1872) at the south end. The lighthouse is of Victorian design on an artificial island. It is one-story clapboard with tower.

82.30 Esopus Meadows Point to west.
This point is incorrectly labeled Dinsmore Point on the U.S.C.and G. Navigation Chart #283.

82.75 Vanderburgh Cove to east.
Cut off from river by New York Central Railroad causeway, it is an outlet of Fallsburg Creek and Landsman Creek.

82.75 Fallsburg Creek to east.
It rises south of Rhinebeck and flows southwest to Vanderburgh Cove. The former Beekman's Mills' dock is near its mouth. It is also known as Dow's Dock.

82.80 George Holliday Mansion to east.

82.90 Landsman Kill to east.
Also known as Landsman Creek and Vanderburgh Creek, it rises southwest of Rhinebeck and flows south to Vanderburgh Cove. It was named for Casper Landsman, first miller on stream.

83.00 Mirror Lake to west.
Out of sight, inland on a plateau, it is also known as Binnewater Pond.

83.10 Prospect Hill to west (elevation 360 feet).

83.10 Jones Point to east.

83.10 Linwood to east.
Ancestral home of the late Col. Jacob Ruppert. He was a wealthy brewer, real estate owner, and onetime owner of the New York Yankees baseball team. It has been more recently owned by his nephew, J. Ruppert Schalk.

83.20 Ruins of Rhinecliff to east.
This is a brick Victorian mansion (1852), described in novels and in the autobiography of Edith Wharton whose aunt lived here.

83.20 Jones Island to east.
This is a tiny islet just off Jones Point.

83.30 Hemlock Point to west.

83.30 Wildercliff to east.
Built by a famous Methodist preacher, Rev. Freeborn Garrettson (1752-1827) in about 1799. It had many distinguished guests including Bishop Asbury and other dignitaries of the Methodist Church. He married Catherine Livingston (1752-1849). Their daughter, Mary Garrettson (1794-1879), lived here until her death. The house later passed to E.R. Jones and A. Frinck. It is a two-story clapboard with gambrel roof. The wings are later additions.

83.50 Wilderstein to east.
This is a victorian mansion with minaret-like towers and similar details, built by John Warren Ritch for Thomas Suckley in 1852. Additions were made in 1888 by Arnout Cannon. Landscaping is by Calvert Vaux. It is still occupied by members of the Suckley family.

83.80 Swan Plot to east.
This is a long shallow reef of one-and two- foot depth, parallel to the eastern shore. There is a channel of between a twenty-one-and a twenty-six-foot depth between it and the shore, but it is open to deep water only at the southern end. There are only seventeen feet at the northern end.

83.80 Ellerslie Dock to east.
The railroad passes through a tunnel here.

84.40 Big Rock Point to west.

84.50 Hussey's Mountain to west.
(elevtion 1005 feet). It is also called Huzzy Hill.

84.50 Ellerslie to east.
This is the Hilltop estate and palatial summer home of former Vice Presidnet Levi P. Morton. The 600-acre estate was owned earlier by the Hon. William Kelly. It is now Farley Military Academy.

85.00 Sturgeon Point to east.

85.25 Port Ewen to west.
This village was built entirely by the Pennsylvania Coal Company and was named in honor of its president, John Ewen. It was laid out in 1851 and had a population of about 1,400, most of whom worked on, or built, the company's coal barges. The Gurney Brickyard and a large ice storage yard were also located here. The shrine of Our Lady of the Hudson is located here.

86.00 Sleightsburg to west.
This is an old river town, popular with retired rivermen. Capt. William O. Benson, well-known his-

torian and writer on the Hudson River and steamboats, resides here. This is the former southern terminus of the cable ferry across Rondout Creek.

86.25 Rhinecliff to east.

Station and landing for Rhinebeck, about a half mile inland. It is not seen from the river. The name derives from the name of the Rhine River and "beck," which means cliffs. William Beekman came from the Rhine in Germany in 1647 and purchased the area around Rhinebeck from the Indians. He gave homes to several poor families who came with him. The area closer to the river was originally called Kipsbergen. The families of the Kips purchased lands extending four miles along the river. The original deed, signed by three Esopus Indians, is dated July 28, 1686. A confirming Royal Patent is dated June 21, 1688. On May 26, 1702, the land of the patent was divided among five partners. Kipsbergen was absorbed into Rhinebeck Precinct on December 16, 1737. The Rhinebeck area is noted for the violet-growing industry and the Beekman Arms Hotel, established in 1700 and claimed to be the oldest continuously operating hotel in the United States. The Long Dock used to be the terminus of the Rondout Ferry. It was also formerly known as Hoffman's Landing. It is presently an Amtrak stop. This was also formerly the western terminus of the Hartford & Connecticut Western Railroad, later the Rhinebeck Branch of the Philadelphia & Reading.

86.25 Rondout Creek to west.

It rises in two branches on the western and southern slopes of Slide Mountain in the Catskills and flows generally southeast through Peekamoose Lake, Rondout Reservoir, and Honk Lake to the vicinity of Napanoch. It then turns northeast along the northwestern foot of the Shawangunk Mountains, past Kerhonkson, Port Jackson, St. Josen, Accord, Alligerville, Kyserike, and High Falls. Here it breaches the Shawangunk Mountains and continues past Rosendale, Creeklocks, Bloomington, and Eddyville, where it falls to tidewater—the head of navigation from the Hudson. The portion between Napanoch and Eddyville was paralleled by the defunct Delaware & Hudson Canal. Just above Creeklocks, it receives the waters of the Wallkill River, which rises in northern New Jersey.

Below Eddyville, it broadens out with tidal marshes and with Gumaer Island in the middle. Barges come up this far to be loaded with aggregate. There were lime kilns along the shore here and bluestone yards at Wilbur, the next town downstream. Here the creek is crossed by the 1200-foot long, 150-foot high truss bridge of the West Shore Railroad, built in 1883. Further towards the Hudson are the old canal villages of Connelly and Sleightsburg on the south bank, and Rondout on the north bank. These formerly were connected by a cable ferry, since replaced by the Route 9W suspension bridge. Immediately west of the road bridge is the famous Island Dock where, in past years, immense piles of coal were unloaded from canal boats prior to reshipment in river and coastal barges and schooners. On the north bank is the Strand section of Rondout, which was the former commercial center of the central Hudson valley. Here was located the ferry terminal of the Rhinecliff Ferry and the home port of the Cornell tug and barge fleet, the *Mary Powell, Baldwin,* and *Romer.*. Still further towards the Hudson, on the north bank, are former limestone quarries, later used as mushroom growing caves, and the Ponckhockie Cliffs and neighborhood of Ponckhockie. There were formerly many ship and boatyards in the vicinity. Jetties extend out into the Hudson River on either side, with mud flats to the north and south. There is a navigation light at the tip of the south jetty, and a two-story brick light house tower, built in 1915, at the tip of the north jetty. Just north of this, across some mud flats is Kingston Point.

86.30 Kingston Point to west.
Formerly called Columbus Point, it used to be an important river landing and transfer point to the trains of the Ulster & Delaware Railroad. For many years, the Hudson River Day Line maintained a pleasure park here. Now there are oil depots and a public park.

86.30 Delaware & Hudson Canal to west.
This canal extended from Honesdale, Pennsylvania, to Rondout. It was built to carry coal.

86.30 Ponckhockie to west.
Inland from Kingston Point, this is a neighborhood of Kingston. Its name is also spelled Ponk Hockie, signifying "burial grounds" in Indian language. The name also applies to Manlius limestone cliffs on the north shore of Rondout Creek, known as the Vlightberg. An old cement mine here was called the Glory Hole.

86.30 Rondout to west.
Originally a seprate city at the junction of Rondout Creek (formerly called the Wallkill River at this place) with the Hudson River, it was originally called Bolton. Rondout was merged into the city of Kingston in 1878, along with neighboring Ponckhockie and Wilbur. This was a major steamboat center, being the home port to the famous *Mary Powell,* and the paddlewheel towboats *Norwich* and *Austin,* which used to pull long tows of coal barges from the outlet of the Delaware & Hudson Canal here to New York City. There were ferries to Rhinecliff, Sleightsburg, and Connelly. The waterfront area was called the Strand. Ulster & Delaware passenger trains used to originate both at Kingston Point and Rondout, before climbing the steep hill to the Union Station in upper Kingston. Urban renewal is fast clearing away the typical old "river town" type commercial buildings, although there are still quite a few fine older churches and homes on the slopes above the town.

86.30 Kingston to west.

(population 25,544). This is the seat of Ulster County. The Indian name for the area where the city now stands was At-kar-karton, the great plot or meadow on which they raised beans and corn. It was the location of a settlement of the Esopus Indians, largely an agricultural tribe. According to Wallace Bruce, "all of the country-side in this vicinity was known as Esopus, supposed to be derived, according to Ruttenber, from the Indian word "seepus," a river. A "sopus Indian," was a Lowlander, and the name is intimately connected with a long stretch of territory from Esopus village, near West Park, to the mouth of the Esopus at Saugerties.

Although traders had operated from

the Rondout area as early as 1614, the first permanent settlers came to the area about 1652. The area near the waterfront was first simply called Redoubt, but was later corrupted to Rundoubt and finally Rondout. The later settlers built on a high piece of ground overlooking the fertile Esopus Flats meadowlands, to the northwest. This area had been used previously by the Indians to grow maize and was prime farmland. Although the settlers purchased the land from the Indians, their gradual encroachment caused resentment and, in 1659, the First Esopus War broke out and caused the settlers to request a garrison to defend them. At this time the settlers were rather thinly spread out on individual farms. In 1658, Governor Peter Stuyvesant directed that a stockaded town be erected at Wiltwyck ("Wild place"), as the settlement was then known. This area was bounded by the present North Front, Green and Main Streets, and Clinton Avenue. According to Wallace Bruce:

The east, north and west fronts ran along elevations overlooking the lowlands and having a varying altitude of from twenty to thirty feet. The enclosure comprehended about twenty-five acres of land. There were salients, or horn works at each end of the four angles, with a circular projection at the middle of the westerly side, where the elevations were less than upon the northerly and easterly sides. The church standing upon the ground . . . was enclosed with a separate stockade, to be used as the last resort in case of disaster, and, projecting from this separate fortification, a strong blockhouse commanded and enfiladed the approaches to the southerly side, which was a plain.

Bruce, *Hudson by Daylight*, p. 182.)

The fortifications included a guard house, barracks, and blockhouse. The stockade consisted of a wooden palisade made of spike-topped logs. There were tunnels running from the basements of the buildings inside the stockade to the low-lying meadows roundabout.

The Dutch Reformed Church was organized in 1659. The first was built of logs, and has been succeeded by five later buildings. The present fine Gothic structure, designed by Minard Lefever, was built in 1852. According to Dr. Van Slyke, one of the pastors.
This church claims a distinction which does not belong even to the Collegiate Dutch Churches of Manhattan Island, and, by a peculiar history, stands identified more closely with Holland than any other of the early churches of this country. When every other church of our communion had for a long time been associated with an American Synod, this church retained its relations to the Classis of Amsterdam, and, after a period of independency and isolation, it finally allied itself with its American sisterhood as late as the year 1808.

(Bruce, *Hudson by Daylight*, p. 199.)

It is still considered the Mother Church of the Dutch Reformed Church in America. Dominie Blom was the first preacher.

A formal charter was granted to Wiltwyck in 1658, and work on the stockade was completed in 1661.

On June 7, 1663, a band of Indians attacked Wiltwyck and neighboring Hurley and massacred many inhabitants. This was the outbreak of the Second Esopus War. In November, a punitive expedition was mounted which finally broke the power of the Indians.

In 1665, the colony came under English rule. English troops garrisoned here under the command of a Capt. Brodhead behaved obnoxiously. When the citizens remonstrated they were accused of causing what was called the Esopus Mutiny. Governor Nicolls intervened, and the "mutiny" devolved into legal squabbles and was finally forgotten.

Dutch rule was restored between 1673 and 1674. Under the English there was peaceful development. The name of the settlement was changed to Kingston in 1679. During the French and Indian Wars (1754-1760), Kingston served as a base for frontier military operations. During this period the name Esopus was frequently used instead of Kingston. This became more the case after the outbreak of the Revolution in 1775.

During the Revolution, Kingston served as capital of the state of New York, and was the first meeting place of the New York State senate in 1777. After the defeat of Gen. Burgoyne at Saratoga, Gen. John Vaughan sailed up the Hudson on a punitive expedition. On October 13, 1777 he burned Esopus, sparing only one house. The inhabitants fled to Hurley, where a small force of Americans hanged a messenger who was caught carrying dispatches from Gen. Clinton to Burgoyne. The constitution was formally announced at Kingston on April 22, 1777. The first court was held here on September 9 and the first legislature on September 10. Adjourning on October 7, they convened again August 18, 1779, and again in 1780 from April 22 to July 2, also for two months beginning January 27, 1783.

Consequently, it can be seen that Kingston was a hotbed of patriot activity. Wallace Bruce states that: "The burning of Kingston seemed unnecessarily cruel, and it is said that Vaughan was wide of the truth when, to justify the same, he claimed that he had been fired upon from dwellings in the village." In any event, this was the last military action in the area. The stone-walled buildings were quickly rebuilt, and development continued after the war. Many of the settlers were Huguenots, who intermarried with the Dutch and English. The present courthouse was built in 1818 on the site of a previous one, in which the New York State Constitution was adopted in 1777. George Clinton, who was born in 1739, was inaugurated as the first governor of the state of New York at Kingston in 1777. The ceremony took place outside the court house. Clinton was surrounded by the Council of Safety and a square formed by two companies of soldiers. He was proclaimed governor by Egbert Dumond, the sheriff of the county, reading his proclamation from the top of a barrel, and closing it with the words, "God save the people," for the first time taking the place of "God save the king." In 1812, Governor Clinton was buried in the yard of the Dutch Reformed Church, across the street.

Fulton's first successful steamboat of 1807 began the development of neighboring Rondout as an important river port. Completion of the Delaware & Hudson Canal in 1828 added to the importance of the port. Kingston developed as a transport and finance center for the tanning, ice, brick, and bluestone industries, as well as into a farm produce marketing center.

The coming of the railroads increased Kingston's importance as a transport center. The Wallkill Valley Railroad was completed to a junction with the Erie Railroad at Montgomery in 1872. In 1875, the New York, Kingston & Syracuse (later the Rondout & Oswego and the Ulster & Delaware) was completed from Kingston Point to Stamford, in the western Catskills. It was later extended to a junction with the Delaware & Hudson Railroad at Oneonta. In 1883, the West Shore Railroad from Weehawken to Albany was completed through Kingston. The Ellenville & Kingston branch of the New York, Ontario & Western reached Kingston in 1902. For many years Kingston boasted a union terminal served by four steam railroads and an electric traction line.

The turn of the present century was the high point of Kingston's prosperity. Kingston was merged with neighboring Rondout and Wilbur in 1878. There was ferry service from Rondout across Rondout Creek to Sleightsburg and Connelly and across the Hudson to

Rhinecliff, where there were connections with the Hudson River Railroad (New York Central) and Hartford & Connecticut Western. Steamers of all lines stopped at Kingston Point until 1953. An electric streetcar line ran along Broadway connecting uptown Kingston with the ferry to Rhinecliff at Rondout. The union terminal, city hall, Y.M.C.A., library and hospital were all located along Broadway. Many fine mansions were built on the heights overlooking Rondout. During this era, the Cornell and Coykendall families were prominent in business and public improvements.

Then the decline began. In 1904, the Delaware & Hudson Canal was abandoned, being superseded by railroads bypassing Kingston. This ended the great coal transfer activity at island dock and eliminated the need for the many towboats and barges. People began driving to the Catskills rather than traveling by boat and train. Ulster & Delaware passenger service, long only a pathetic remainder, ended in 1954. In 1957, the New York, Ontario & Western was totally abandoned, its passenger service having been discontinued many years earlier. In 1958, the last West Shore passenger train left town. The Rondout Creek ferry was discontinued after completion of the Route 9W suspension bridge in the 1930s. The Rhinecliff ferry stopped upon completion of the Kingston-Rhinecliff bridge. Construction of the New York Thruway outside of town diverted still more activity from Kingston. Only the coming of the light-aggregate industry and IBM brought any new activity to the area. Although still the principal trading town on the west bank of the Central Hudson Valley, Kingston is a relatively quiet place today. However, it is becoming more and more recognized as a place of historic interest because of its many well-preserved old buildings and interesting 19th century residential, ecclesiastical, and commercial architecture. There is presently talk of building an authentic "Steam Town" here, with steam train excursions on the scenic

Ulster & Delaware and possibly bringing the sidewheel steamer *Alexander Hamilton* to a permanent berth in Rondout Creek. This would make Kingston the tourist center of a county in which tourism is the principal industry. Certainly this would be a fitting memorial to a city that saw its greatest glory as a steamboat and railroad center.

88.00 Astor Cove to east.
This cove is cut off from river by a railroad causeway. The former Hartford & Connecticut Western Railroad cut inland here. The William Astor estate was near here, as was the Beekman Manor House.

88.25 Clifton Point to east.
Formerly Rutsen's Landing, here was located Ferncliff, the country residence of Vincent Astor, son of John Jacob Astor.

88.25 East Kingston to west.
88.00 to 91.00 The Flats.
This is an extensive and continuous shallow area just west of mid-stream. There are navigation channels on either side. Depths average two and three feet.

88.75 Mt. Rutsen to east.
(elevation 350 feet).

89.45 Whiskey Point to west.
89.60 Mills Point to east.
This is also known as Mill Dock.

89.60 Flatbush to west.
90.00 Kingston-Rhinecliff Bridge.
A unit of the New York State Bridge Authority, it carries New York State Route 199. Opened to traffic February 2, 1957, it was designed by D.B. Steinman. Principal contractors were Harris Structural Steel and Merritt, Chapman & Scott. The bridge is of the continuous deck design and has an overall length of 7,793 feet. The main span is 5,200 feet with a vessel clearance of 152 feet. There are two vehicle lanes. A toll is charged eastbound.

91.00 Heath to the west.
Also Lake Katrine.

91.25 Astor Point to east.

91.30 Picnic Point to east.

91.30 Rokeby to east.
This is not visible from river. It is the former estate of William B. Astor, a two-story stuccoed stone, Federal style, ca. 1815, with later mansard roof, tower, and other renovations. Benson Lossing gives us some interesting history:

. . . Rokeby, the seat of William B. Astor, Esq., who is distinguished as the wealthiest man in the United States. (1866) It was formerly the residence of his father-in-law, General John Armstrong, an officer in the war for independence, and a member of General Gates's military family. Armstrong was the author of the celebrated addresses which were privately circulated among the officers of the Continental Army lying at Newburgh, on the Hudson, at the close of the war, and calculated to stir up a mutiny, and even a rebellion against the civil power. The feeble Congress had been unable for a long time to provide for the pay of the soldiers about to be disbanded and sent home in poverty and rags. There was apathy in Congress and among the people on the subject; and these addresses were intended to stir up the latter and their representatives to the performance of their duty in making some provision for their faithful servants, rather than to excite the army to take affairs into their own hand, as was charged. Through the wisdom and firmness of Washington, the event was so overruled as to give honor to the army and benefit the country. Washington afterwards acquitted Major Armstrong of all evil intentions, and considered his injudicious movement (instigated, it is supposed, by Gates) as a patriotic act.

Armstrong afterwards married a sister of Chancellor Livingston, and was chosen successively to a seat in the United States senate, an ambassador to France, a brigadier-general in the army, and secretary-of-war. He held the latter office while England and the United States were at war, in 1812-14. He was the author of a "Life of General Montgomery," "Life of General Wayne," and "Historical Notices of the War of 1812." Rokeby, where this eminent man lived and died, is delightfully situated, in the midst of an undulating park, farther from the river than the other villas, but commanding some interesting glimpses of it, with more distant landscapes and mountain scenery. Among the latter may be seen the range of the Shawangunk, in the far southwest. Here Mr. Astor's family reside about eight months of the year.

(Lossing, *The Hudson*, pp. 175-77.)

91.50 Goose Island to east:
formerly Daisy Island.

91.50 Ulster Landing to west.
Here is located Wrongside, a two-story brick and clapboard mansion dating from about 1825. Its name was given to the estate by the Livingstons, who felt their relative who built it should have done so on the east bank of the river.

91.55 Tyler Point to west.

91.75 Barrytown to east.
Formerly known as Lower Red Hook Landing, after the town of Red Hook which is located several miles inland. This is a local railroad station. Wallace Bruce

tells us that: "It is said when General Jackson was President, and this village wanted a post office, that he would not allow it under the name of Barrytown, from personal dislike to General Barry, and suggested another name; but the people were loyal to their old friend, and went without a post office until a new administration." The present writer thinks this story is apocryphal, as he can find no references to a "General Barry." However, William T. Barry was Postmaster General during Jackson's administration. It is easy to see how the facts might have been mixed up. Actually Barry was a good friend of Jackson's. Did the residents get their post office only on condition of naming it after Mr. Barry? The location is notable for possessing a pair of Octagonal houses designed by Alexander Jackson Davis, about 1860. Edgewater, a two-story Federal mansion with a Doric portico dates from about 1820.

92.30 Trap Cliff to east.

92.35 Hog's Back.
Slightly to east of mid-channel, this is a reef with as little as four feet of water, marked by a flashing white light, with channels on either side.

92.35 Glenerie to west:
inland on Esopus Creek.

92.35 Washburn Brothers Brick Yards to west.

92.60 Annandale-on-Hudson to east.
This is neighborhood of distinguished homes. Bard College is located here. It was founded by Dr. John Bard in 1860 as St. Stephen's College for Sons of Episcopal Clergymen. Since 1928, it has been a unit of Columbia University. It is located on the 2000-acre Ward Manor estate, the former home of Robert B. Ward, the prominent baker. The Ward mansion is two-story stuccoed Tudor, dating from 1918. There is an interesting gatehouse dating from 1915, which is a two-story castellated structure with a tower.

The Chapel of Holy Innocents was designed in 1860 by Charles Babcock, an associate of Richard Upjohn. It is built on the site of an earlier church built in 1857, which burned in 1858. The interior has been redecorated by Ralph Adams Cram.

Blithewood is an estate established in 1795 by Gen. John Armstrong (1758-1843) whose history has been given under the heading of Rokeby (ERM 91.30). He married Alida, the sister of Chancellor Livingston. In 1810, he sold Blithewood and moved to Rokeby. Blithewood was then purchased by John Cox Stevens (1785-1857), another brother-in-law of Chancellor Livingston. He was a yachtsman and a founder of the New York Yacht Club and a backer of *America,* leading to the creation of the America's Cup. In 1835, Robert Donaldson acquired Blithewood. During his tenure, the grounds were landscaped by Andrew Jackson Downing who also designed the gatehouse. It is recorded that Dr. John Bard lived here after 1853. The present late Georgian style mansion was erected by Andrew C. Zabriskie in 1899.

92.75 Skillpot Island to east.
This island is in South Bay, inside the railroad causeway. Skillpot was an old Dutch term for a large turtle. This is a very small island.

92.75 Montgomery Place to east.

This is one of the most interesting estates along the Hudson because of its sad history. This is best told by Benson Lossing:

Adjoining Annandale is Montgomery Place, the residence of the family of the late Edward Livingston, brother of the Chancellor, who is distinguished in the annals of his country as a leading United States senator, the author of the penal code of the State of Louisiana, and ambassador to France. The elegant mansion was built by the widow of General Richard Montgomery, a companion-in-arms of Wolfe when he fell at Quebec, and who perished under the walls of that city at the head of a storming party of Republicans on the 31st of December, 1775. Montgomery was one of the noblest and bravest men of his age. When he gave his young wife Janet a parting kiss at the house of General Schuyler, at Saratoga, and hastened to join that officer at Ticonderoga, in the campaign that proved fatal to him, he said, "You shall never blush for your Montgomery." Gallantly did he vindicate that pledge. And when his virtues were extolled by Barre, Burke, and others in the British parliament, Lord North exclaimed, "Curse on his virtues: he has undone his country."

The wife of Montgomery was a sister of Chancellor Livingston. With ample pecuniary means and a good taste at command, she built this mansion and there spent fifty years of widowhood, childless, but cheerful. The mansion and its 400 acres passed into the possession of her brother Edward, and there, as we have observed, members of his family now (1866) reside. Of all the fine estates along this portion of the Hudson, this is said to be the most perfect in its beauty and arrangements. Waterfalls, picturesque bridges, romantic glens, groves, a magnificent park, one of the most beautiful of the ornamental gardens in this country, and views of the river and mountains, unsurpassed, render Montgomery Place a retreat to be coveted, even by the most favoured of fortune.

Lossing, The Hudson, pp. 173-74.)

The following sequel is told in Stone's *History of New York City:*

In 1818 the Legislature of New York— DeWitt Clinton, Governor—ordered the remains of General Montgomery to be removed from Canada to New York. This was in accordance with the wishes of the Continental Congress, which in 1776, had voted the beautiful cenotaph to his memory that now stands in the wall of St. Paul's Church, fronting Broadway. When the funeral cortege reached Whitehall, N.Y., the fleet stationed there received them with appropriate honors; and on the 4th of July they arrived in Albany. After lying in state in that city over Sunday, the remains were taken to New York, and on Wednesday deposited, with military honors, in their final resting place, at St. Paul's. Governor Clinton had informed Mrs. Montgomery of the hour when the steamer "Richmond," conveying the body, would pass her home. At her own request, she stood alone on the portico. It was forty years since she had parted from her Richard, to whom she had been wedded but two years when he fell on the heights of Quebec; yet she had remained faithful to the memory of her "soldier," as she always called him. The steamboat halted before the mansion; the band played the "Dead March," and a salute was fired; and the ashes of the venerated hero, and the departed husband, passed on. The attendants of the Spartan widow now appeared, but, overcome by the tender emotions of the moment, she had swooned and fallen to the floor.

(Bruce, *The Hudson by Daylight,* p. 193.)

In her *Biographies of Francis Lewis and Morgan Lewis,* Julia Delafield gives the following interesting description of Janet Montgomery:

Mrs. Montgomery's eyes had the peculiarity of being always half shut. The lid was probably too long. In a miniature that the General had taken to send to Ireland, she is represented looking down, reading a letter. It gives the idea of a handsome woman. Her complexion, even in her old age, did honor to her Scotch descent. She had a noble head, well placed on her shoulders, and like her sisters, Mrs. Garretson and Mrs. Lewis, she was above the middle height, and extremely graceful. Sprightly sense, sweetness of temper, and overflowing good humor attracted round the sisters men of the highest position as well as talent.

(Julia Delafield, *Biography of Francis Lewis & Morgan Lewis*, N.Y.: Scribners, 1877.)

Mrs. Montgomery originally called Montgomery Place the Chateau de Montgomery. Edward Livingston lived from 1764 to 1836. He had the grounds landscaped by Andrew Jackson Downing and the house enlarged by Alexander Jackson Davis. The building is a two-story Federal mansion. The remodeling was done in 1840 and again in the 1860s. In 1900, the property belonged to Carleton Hunt and his sisters. In 1940, it was the property of General John Ross Delafield, the great-grandson of Edward Livingston.

92.75 South Bay to east.
This bay is now cut off from river by a railroad causeway. It is very shallow, only one and two feet deep. Blithewood and Montgomery Place face onto South Bay.

92.80 Sawkill Creek to east.
This creek empties into South Bay.

92.80 Whale's Back to east.
(elevation 300 feet).

92.85 Turkey Point to west.

93.75 Cruger Island to east.
Also called Cruger's Island, it is now joined to the mainland. Wallace Bruce tells us that:

There is an old Indian legend that no person ever died on this island, which a resident recently (1900) said still held true. It is remarkable, moreover, in possessing many antique carved stones from a city of Central America built into the walls of a temple modeled after the building from which the graven stones were brought. The "ruin" at the south end of the island is barely seen from the steamer, hidden as it is by the foliage, but it is distinctly noted from the windows of the New York Central in the winter season. Col. (John Church) Cruger has spared no expense in the adornment of his grounds, and a beautiful drive is afforded the visitor. The bogus ruins were built about 1840 to simulate the Romantic atmosphere of Thomas Cole's paintings. The island was later given by William B. Ward to the New York Association for Improving the Condition of the Poor for use as a summer camp and health resort.

94.25 Saddle Bags.
West of the main vessel channel in the river, these are treacherous reefs in roughly the shape of a pair of saddle bags. Depths are between five and thirteen feet.

94.50 Beckwith Hill to east.
(elevation 400 feet).

94.50 Glasco to west.
Located at the eastern terminus of the Glasco Turnpike from Woodstock, at the base of the Catskill Mountains, it takes its name from a large sign originally painted on a wharf warehouse which a glass company formerly used to trans-ship its products. The glass was made between 1809 and 1855 at Shady, near Woodstock, and brought here over the Glasco Turnpike for

transfer to boats. The area was originally settled by Palatinates.

94.50 North Bay to east.

Formerly called De Koven's Cove or Bay, it is cut off from the river by a railroad causeway, and is now almost completely silted up. Benson Lossing gives us the following interesting information, which is at the root of the popular but incorrect story that Fulton built the *Clermont* at North Bay. It was actually built at New York City and Hoboken:

Mr. Livingston's chief honour as a man of science, and promoter of useful interests, is derived from his aid and encouragement in efforts which resulted in the entire success of steam navigation. As early as 1797, he was engaged with an Englishman named Nesbit in experiments. They built a steamboat on the Hudson River, at a place now known as De Koven's Cove, or Bay, about half a mile below Tivoli, or Upper Red Hook Landing. Brunel, the engineer of the Thames Tunnel, and father of the originator and constructor of the "Great Eastern" steamship, was the engineer. The enterprise was not successful. Livingston entered upon other experiments, when he was interrupted by his appointment as United States minister to the court of France. In Paris he became acquainted with Robert Fulton's experiments there.

(Lossing, *The Hudson*, p. 169.)

Upon returning to America, Fulton did spend some time at *Clermont* nearby, perfecting his designs for the North River Steamboat. Thus it is easy to see how the confusion has arisen.

94.80 Stony Creek to east.

It flows into northern end of North Bay.

94.80 Magdalen Island to east.

Also spelled Madalin and Madaline, it was formerly Goat Island. A great depth of 47 feet of water is immediately offshore. It would be possible to draw a steamboat up alongside and tie it to a tree.

95.30 Sycamore Point to east.

95.80 Catskill Mountains to west.

95.80 Tivoli to east.

Formerly known as Upper Red Hook Landing. Between 1798 and 1802, a Frenchman by the name of Peter de Labigarre built a home here which he called the Chateau de Tivoli. He hired an itinerant draftsman named Charles Balthazar Julien Fevret de Saint-Memin, who was an expatriot officer of the Guard of King Louis XVI. He was also a portrait painter. In any event, he drew up impractical plans of a town with 60-feet-wide streets in a gridiron pattern. Of these streets, only Flora and Diana remain today. The speculation was a failure, and the lots did not sell. Monsieur DeLabigarre died in 1807 and Chancellor Livingston bought them all at a foreclosure sale.

The Callendar House, two-story frame in the Federal style with wings and quoins (ca. 1790) was formerly the property of Johnston Livingston. Sunning Hill and The Pynes, a two-story clapboard mansion date from about 1790. St. Paul's Protestant Episcopal Church on Wood Road dates from 1868. It was designed by Robert E. Livingston, grandson of the chancellor. It is Victorian Gothic in style and was modified in 1922 by the addition of eight burial vaults to receive the remains of the Livingstons.

96.00 Rose Hill to east.

This is a 2-story brick Italianate Victorian villa, ca. 1870. Wallace Bruce gives us this information:

The residence of J. Watts De-Peyster stands on a commanding bluff north of the railway station and it was beside his open fireside many years ago that he told the writer how his house was saved from Vaughan's trip up the river to burn the Livingston Manor House. Rose Hill, the home of his ancestors, was mistaken for "Clermont," but a well-stocked cellar mollified the British Captain. "Rose Hill," was named after the old Watts Mansion in Edinburgh, which has recently (1900) been removed to make room for a railway.

Rose Hill projects so far out into the river that it is beyond the islands two miles below, which, at one time, were about in the center of the wide expanse of water between the main shores. To give a better idea, however, of the projection, steamboats which pass down to the front have to sheer in so far in making their landing at Tivoli, a quarter of a mile below, that they disappear from sight of those looking southward and watching them from the piazza of the mansion. Rose Hill itself has grown like one of the old English family houses, with the increase of the family, until, in strange but picturesque outline—the prevailing style being Italian, somewhat in the shape of a cross—it is now 114 feet long by 87 feet deep. The tower in the rear, devoted to library purposes, rises to the height of about sixty feet. This library, first and last, has contained between twenty and thirty thousand volumes. Such indefi-nite language is used, because the owner has donated over half this number to the New York Historical Society, the New York Society Library, and a number of other similar organizations in different parts of the United States. As a working library, replete with dictionaries and cyclopaedias, in many tongues and on almost every subject, it is a marvel. It is likewise very valuable for its collections on military and several other special topics. From it was selected and given to the New York Historical Society, one of the finest possible collections on the History of Holland, from the earliest period down to the present time. In spite of all these donations it is still a curiosity shop; not only for the bibliophile, but for a curio-seeker.

(Bruce, *Hudson by Daylight*, p.199.)

96.25 Long Pier to west.

This is a former steamboat landing south of the mouth of Esopus Creek. It was also formerly known as Saugerties Landing.

96.50 Esopus Creek to west.

Rising on the slopes of Panther and Slide Mountains in three branches, the combined steam begins near the settlement of Slide Mountain Post Office. The principal source is Winnisook Lake. Blossom Falls are on the middle branch. From Slide Mountain, the stream flows in a big curve first west, and then north, through the Big Indian Valley to the village of Big Indian. Here it turns southeast to Phoenicia, Mount Pleasant, and Boiceville and finally enters Ashokan Reservoir. Below the dam at Olive Bridge, it continues southeast to Lomontville, where it makes a bend to the northeast and flows through broad fertile flats between the Catskill foothills and the northern tip of the Shawangunks. It passes the early Dutch settlements of Marbletown, Hurley, and Kingston. It continues north through marshes, past the village of Lake Katrine, to a junction with Plattekill Creek above Glenerie Falls. It turns sharply right under the West Shore Railroad and goes over Glenerie Falls. It then turns sharply north at the foot of the falls and flows through a gorge which is straight, rugged, and very narrow, to the vicinity of Saugerties. Here it is dammed just below the Route 9W bridge and forms a fair size lake. In the nineteenth century, the falls were used for water power for the paper mills. Below the dam the creek flows through another deep gorge and makes a sharp turn to the east, where it becomes still tide water. The shores are lined with marinas and boatyards for the final short stretch to the Hudson, which it enters between tidal flats and jetties on either side. There is a Coast Guard station and lighthouse on the Washburn's Point jetty on the north side.

96.50 Washburn's Point to west.
This lighthouse is two-story brick with a tower. It was built 1869.

96.50 Saugerties to west

The name derives from "Da Zaagertijis," which is Dutch for "saw mills." These were built on Esopus Creek prior to 1663. The remains of a similar one, presently in progress of restoration, can be seen on the neighboring Sawyer's Kill near Seamon Memorial Park, north of the village. Settled by the Dutch, it was developed by the Livingstons. It once had extensive lumbering, white lead, and

paper industries and shipped much bluestone. Principal among the paper companies were the Sheffield Paper Company, the Barkley Fibre Company (pulp wood), the Martin Company (cardboard), and the Cantine Coated Paper Company.

Saugerties in around 1800 is well described by Cooper in his novel *Afloat and Ashore*. The following describes the Mynderse House and grounds almost perfectly, with its main house built in 1690 and "new" wings of 1743:

My father died on the farm on which he was born, and which descended to him from his great-grandfather, an English emigrant that had purchased it of the Dutch colonists who had originally cleared it from the woods. The place was called Clawbonny, which some said was good Dutch, others bad Dutch; and now and then a person ventured a conjecture that it might be Indian. Bonny it was in one sense at least, for a lovlier farm is not on the whole of the wide surface of the Empire State. What does not always happen in this wicked world, it was as good as it was handsome. It consisted of three hundred and seventy-two acres of first-rate land, either arable or rich river bottom in meadows, and of more than a hundred of rocky mountain side, that was very tolerably covered with wood. The first of our family who owned the place had built a substantial one-story stone house, that bears the date of 1707 on one of its gables; and to which each of his successors had added a little, until the whole structure got to resemble a cluster of cottages thrown together without the least attention to order or regularity. There were a porch, a front door, and a lawn, however; the latter containing half a dozen acres of a soil as black as ones hat, and nourishing eight or ten elms that were scattered about as if their seeds had been sown broadcast. In addition to the trees and a suitable garniture of shrubbery, this lawn was coated with a sward that, in the proper

seasons, rivalled all I have read or imagined of the emerald and shorn slopes of the Swiss valleys.

Clawbonny, while it had all the appearance of being the residence of an affluent agriculturist, had none of the pretension of these later times. The house had an air of substantial comfort without, an appearance that its interior in no manner contradicted. The ceilings were low, it is true, nor were the rooms particularly large; but the latter were warm in winter, cool in summer, and tidy, neat, and respectable all the year round. Both the parlors had carpets as had the passages and all the better bedrooms; and there were an old-fashioned chintz settee, well stuffed and cushioned, and curtains in the "big parlor," as we called the best apartment—the pretending name of drawing—room not having reached our valley as far back as the year 1796 or that in which my recollections of the place, as it then existed are the most vivid and distinct.

We had orchards, meadows, and ploughed fields all around us; while the barns, granaries, stiles, and other buildings of the farm were of solid stone, like the dwelling, and all in capital condition.

There was a mill, just where the stream that runs through our valley tumbles down to a level below that on which the farm lies, and empties itself into a small tributary of the Hudson. This mill was on our property, and was a source of great convenience and of some profit to my father. There he ground all the grain that was consumed for domestic purposes for several miles around; and the tolls enabled him to fatten his porkers and beeves, in a way to give both a sort of established character. In a word, the mill was the concentrating point for all the products of the farm, there being a little landing on the margin of the creek that put up from the Hudson, whence a sloop sailed weekly for town. My father passed half his time about the mill and landing, superintending his workmen, and particularly giving directions about the fitting of the sloop, which was his property also, and about the gear of the mill.

There had been a generation of sloops which bore the name of Wallingford, as well as generations of men, at Clawbonny; and this every river-man knew. In point of fact, we counted four generations of men and six of sloops. Now, none of these vessels was worthy of being mentioned, but this which my father had caused to be built; but she had a reputation that extended to everybody on the river.

I had a dozen slaves, also; negroes who, as a race, had been in the family almost as long as Clawbonny. About half of these blacks were singularly laborious and useful, namely, four males and three of the females; but several of the remainder were enjoying otium, and not altogether without dignitate, as heirlooms to be fed, clothed, and lodged, for the good or evil they had done. There were some small-fry in our kitchens, too, that used to roll about on the grass, and munch fruit in the summer, ad libitum, and stand so close in the chimney-corners in cold weather, that I have often fancied they must have been, as a legal wit of New York once pronounced certain eastern coal mines to be, incombustible. These negroes all went by the patronymic of Clawbonny, there being among them Hector Clawbonny, Venus Clawbonny, Caesar Clawbonny, Rose Clawbonny, and Julietta, commonly called Julee, Clawbonny—who was black as a crow—and Romeo Clawbonny; who were the Pharaoh, Potiphar, Samson and Nebuchadnezzar, all Clawbonnys in the last resort. Neb, as the namesake of the herbivorous King of Babylon was called, was about my own age, and had been a sort of humble playfellow from infancy; and even now, when it was thought proper to set him about the more serious toil which was to make his humble career, I often interfered to call him away to be my companion with the rod, the fowling-piece, or in the boat, of which we had one that frequently descended the *creek and navigated the Hudson for miles at a time, under my command. The lad, by such means, and through an off-hand friendliness of manner that I rather think was characteristic of my habits at that day, got to love me as a brother or comrade. It is not easy to describe the affection of an attached slave, which has blended with it the pride of a partisan, the solicitude of a parent, and the blindness of a lover. I do think Neb had more gratification in believing himself particularly belonging to Master Miles, than I ever had in any quality or thing I could call my own. Neb, moreover, liked a vagrant life, and greatly encouraged Rupert and myself in idleness, and a desultory manner of misspending hours that could never be recalled. The first time I ever played truant was under the patronage of Neb, who decoyed me away from my books to go nutting on the mountain, stoutly maintaining that chestnuts were just as good as the spelling-book, or any primer that could be bought in York.*

We were all four of us seated on a rude bench that my mother had caused to be placed under the shade of an enormous oak that stood on the most picturesque spot, perhaps, on the whole farm, and which commanded a distant view of one of the lovliest reaches of the Hudson. Our side of the river, in general, does not possess as fine views as the eastern, for the reason that all our own broken, and in some instances magnificent, background of mountains, fills up the landscape for our neighbors, while we are obliged to receive the picture as it is set in a humbler frame; but there are exquisite bits to be found on the western bank, and this was one of the very best of them. The water was as placid as molten silver, and the sails of every vessel in sight were hanging in listless idleness from their several spars, representing commerce asleep.

(James Fenimore Cooper, *Ashore and Afloat* pp. 2, 3, 5, 23.)

At the southern end of town, on Route 9W, there are several sharp bends in the road and bluestone walls are layed up along the roadside. Several old houses and churches in this neighborhood are reminescent of the following extract from Cooper's *Miles Wallingford*.(p.137.)

*St. Michael's churchyard is beautifully ornamented with flourishing cedars. These trees had been cultivated with care, and formed an appropriate ornament for the place. A fine cluster of them shaded the graves of my family, and a rustic seat had been placed beneath their branches, by order of my mother, who had been in the habit of passing hours of meditation at the grave of her husband.*This scene describes the grave of Grace Wallingford, "The Lily of Clawbonny," a character quite obviously patterned after Cooper's own beloved sister who had died young. The scene might equally well fit the Church of the Ascension in West Park.

The old commercial neighborhood, Cantine paper mill, and falls of the Esopus, as well as Barclay Heights with its mansions, are worth a visit. Seamon's Park has extensive floral displays and an annual autumn Chrysanthemum Festival. The Wede Marine Museum is located here.

96.75 Sawyer's Kill to west.
This creek flows south from the Great Vly Swamp southwest of the Kalkberg to the Hudson. It was named for the saw mills along its banks.

96.75 Columbia County to east.
From here to mile 126.60, opposite Barren Island, the eastern bank is occupied by Columbia County. It occupies an area of 643 square miles and is largely devoted to agriculture and dairy operations. It was taken from Albany County in 1786 and named in honor of Christopher Columbus. Hudson is the county

seat. Chatham and Hillsdale are the only other two towns of any size. It is bounded on the west by the Hudson River, on the north by Rensselaer County, on the east by Massachusetts and on the south by Dutchess County. The Taconic range of the Berkshire Mountains run along the eastern border. The county is drained to the east by the Green River, which flows into the Housatonic, and to the west, or Hudson, by the Roeliffe Jansen Kill (also known as Livingston Creek and Ancram Creek) and by Claverack Creek and Stockport Creek (also known as Major Abraham's Creek or Kinderhook Creek). The Hudson River Railroad runs along the Hudson and is now part of the Conrail Mainline. The former Boston & Albany Railroad runs from the Massachusetts State Line to Castleton, cutting through the townships of Chatham and Kinderhook in Columbia County. The Harlem Division of the former New York Central (now defunct) runs from Copake Falls in Dutchess County to Chatham. Formerly a line of the Rutland Railroad came down to Chatham from Renssalaer County. The New England Branch of the New York Thruway parallels the Boston & Albany, and the Taconic State Parkway, coming up from Dutchess County, terminates at the Thruway, just north of Chatham. Principal lakes are Queechy Lake, Copke Lake, and Knickerbocker Lake. Formerly there was a considerable iron industry centered near Hudson and Ancram.

97.50 Rock Island to west.

Near the shore, it is small and surrounded by shallow water of one- and two-foot depth.

97.90 Clermont Wharf to east.

97.90 Clermont to east.

Formerly the estate of the Livingston family, it is now maintained as Clermont Mansion State Historic Site by the Taconic State Park & Recreation Commission.

The history of the mansion and estate with the Livingston family and the entire history of this part of New York State are a single story, best told by giving the history of the family.

The Livingstons are of Scottish ancestry, of the family of the Earls of Linlithgow. Robert Livingston (1654-1728) was descended from Mary Livingston, one of the "four Marys" who attended Mary Queen of Scots during her childhood and education in France. He was born at Roxburghshire, Scotland, and lived in Holland until coming back to the British Isles at the age of nine. After the death of his father, he came to America in 1673 and settled in the Albany area. He married Alida Van Rensselaer, a widow, and a daughter of the Schuyler family. He soon became wealthy through his active trading ventures and influential family connections. He is said to have been a friend of Captain Kidd, and a powerful promoter of his enterprises. Between 1684 and 1715, he made many purchases from the Indians of land on the eastern bank of the Hudson. These lands ran along the Hudson for twelve miles and back eastward, fanning out to a breadth of thirty miles. He later purchased tracts on the western shore, which were part of the Hardenburgh Patent. A patent was granted for the eastern lands by Gov. Thomas Dongan in 1686 under the name, "the Lordship and Manor of Livingston." This was confirmed by King George I. In 1710, Gov. Robert Hunter had helped Livingston consolidate his various holdings which then came to a total of 162,248 acres. He paid to the King's treasury "an annual rent of twenty-eight shillings, lawful money of New York," or about $3.50. Benson Lossing tells us that: "This magnificent estate was constituted a manor, with political privileges. The freeholders upon it were allowed a representative in the colonial legislature, chosen by themselves, and in 1716 the lord of the manor, by virtue of that privilege, took his seat as a legislator. He had already built a manor-house, on a grassy point upon the banks of the Hudson, at the mouth of Roeliffe Jansen's Kill." (Lossing, *The Hudson,* pp. 166-167.) This Manor House was called *Linlithgow* after the city in Scotland. It was later taken down by his great-grandson. He was Secretary of Indian Affairs from 1695 to 1728 and served as representative to the New York Provincial Assembly (1709-II and 1715-25) becoming its speaker in 1718. He had two sons:

1) Philip Livingston (1686-1749) established the senior branch of the family. He married Catharine Van Brugh and had three sons. This senior branch retained possession of the manor at Linlithgow. His sons were:
   a) Peter Van Brugh Livingston (1710-1792) In 1775, he was elected president of the First Provincial Congress.
   b) Philip Livingston (1716-1778) A signer of the Declaration of Independence and an active member of the Continental Congress.
   c) William Livingston (1723-1790). He moved to New Jersey in 1772. He was a member of the First and Second Continental Congress, and was elected the First Governor of New Jersey in 1777.

2) Robert L. Livingston (1688-1775) established the junior branch of the family. Although his father had given his older brother, Philip, the major part of his estate, coming to 247,000 acres and the manor house at Linlithgow, he provided for young Robert by giving him an estate of 13,000 acres south of the Roeliffe Jansen Kill, which was known as the Lower Manor. Young Robert built a fine mansion which he called Clermont, as was also called the small village further inland. He had five daughters (all of whom made advantageous or distinguished marriages) and one son, Robert R. Livingston (1718-1775).

Robert R. Livingston, Sr. (1718-1775) was often called "the Judge", as he served as judge of the Admiralty Court from 1759 to 1763 and as judge of the Supreme Court of the colony from 1763 to 1775. He was an active patriot and a member of the Stamp Act Congress and writer of the letter of protest sent by that congress to the king. He also established powder mills which supplied Washington's army. He was the chairman of the New York Committee of Correspondence. His son was also an active patriot and had a distinguished public life.

Robert R. Livingston, Jr. (1746-1813) became famous as "Chancellor Livingston," as he served in that capacity from 1777 to 1801. Next to governor, this was the most powerful post in the new state of New York. He was a strong advocate of the rights of the colonies and, as a member of the Second Continental Congress, was one of the five elected to draft the Declaration of Independence. The Revolution reached his home of Clermont in October of 1777 when a British landing party sailed up the Hudson, burned Kingston, and proceeded on to burn Clermont. The family and servants escaped after burying or hiding their valuables. After the war, as Chancellor, he administered the oath of office when Washington became the first president of the United States in 1789. In 1781, Livingston became First Minister of Foreign Affairs, and later served as Minister to France under Jefferson, when he negotiated with Napoleon for the Louisiana Purchase. While in France, he met Robert Fulton and became his partner in the successful development of the steamboat. The *North River Steamboat* of *Clermont* stopped at the Chancellor's dock on her maiden voyage up the

Hudson in 1807. In 1794, the Chancellor finished a new home just south of Clermont, which he called Arryl House. This burned in 1908, but the ruins are still visible. It was an elegant, French-inspired building and became the show-place of the Hudson.

Judge Livingston's younger son, Edward Livingston (1764-1836) served as the first Secretary of State of the United States and had a long and distinguished career.

Old Clermont continued to be a home to the Livingston family through the years until 1962, when the property was given to New York State as an historic site. The center part of the house was built shortly after the British burned the original house in 1777, and part of the walls from the earlier building were incorporated into it. The north wing was added in 1802 as an office where the tenants could pay their rent. The south wing was added in 1830 to give the family more room. It was again enlarged in 1893. The steep, chateauesque roof was added in 1874.

The house and grounds are now open to the public as an example of historic preservation in process.

97.90 Cross Hill to east.
(elevation 322 feet).

97.91 Roundtop to east.
(elevation 341 feet).

97.92 Little Roundtop to east.
(elevation 300 feet).

98.00 Green Flats.
These are slightly to east of mid-stream. The main vessel channel is to the west. Depths are between one-half and seventeen feet. It is also known as Lower Flats-Middleground.

98.25 Canoe Hill to west.

98.25 Bristol to west.
Bristol Beach is an undeveloped county park of seventy-three acres with a sandy beach in a protected cove. The water is clean. From the twenty-two-acre beach area you can wade out

600 feet before reaching the main channel.

98.50 Malden-on-Hudson to west.
Site of Staples House (ca. 1837) and a Methodist Church in the bracketed style dating from 1867, it was the home town of John Bigelow (1817-1911), noted editor, author, and diplomat. From 1848 to 1861, he shared with William Cullen Bryant in the ownership and editing of the *New York Evening Post.* His antislavery and free-trade editorials were especially vigorous. In 1861, he was appointed consul general at Paris and served as United States minister to France from 1865 to 1866. He is credited for preventing French recognition of the confederacy.

99.00 Bigelow Blue Stone Company dock and quarry to west.

99.25 The Maelstrom.
Slightly to east of the western vessel channel, between Green Flats and Upper Flats. is a narrow but rather deeper channel (eleven- to sixteen-foot depths) between the shallow flats of one-half and one-foot depths, and connects the main channel, on the west of the flats, with the secondary deepwater channel to the east of the flats. During the change of tide, the waters rush through here in eddies and whirlpools. *The American College Dictionary* defines maelstrom as follows: 1) a famous whirlpool off the NW coast of Norway, 2) any great or violent whirlpool, 3) a resistless confusion of affairs, or influence.

99.60 Eve's Point to west.

99.61 Evesport to west.

100.00 Upper Flats (Livingston Flats).
These are to the east of mid-

stream. The vessel channel is to the west. The flats are covered with grass and are only one-half to one foot deep.

100.00 Livingston Channel to east.
East of upper flats, this is a secondary channel along the eastern shore, petering out at the northern end. Access is only from southern end. Depths are between twenty-one and forty-one feet.

100.25 West Camp Landing to west.
100.30 West Camp to west.
Queen Anne of England sent Palatinate refugees here in 1710 in an unsuccessful attempt to manufacture turpentine.

100.50 Wanton Island to west.
100.50 Greene County to west.
From here to Barren Island, at mile 126.60, the western shore is occupied by Greene County. It has an area of 653 square miles. Catskill is the county seat. It was taken from Albany and Ulster Counties in 1800 and named in honor of Revolutionary War general Nathaniel Greene, of Rhode Island, who had been given lands in the towns of Windham, Ashland, Jewett, and parts of Lexington and Hunter, to the eastern base of the mountains. He established a cloth factory at Red Falls. Presently the county consists of the townships of: Halcott, Prattsville, Ashland, Lexington, Jewett, Durham, Hunter, Catskill, Cairo, Athens, Greenville, Coxsackie, and New Baltimore. The eastern portion of the county consists of low ridges, interspersed with fertile valleys parallel to the Hudson. The western part of the county is comprised of the Catskill Mountains and a high plateau, drained to the northwest by Schoharie Creek, and the East,

West, and Batavia Kill. The eastern escarpment of the Catskills and lowlands are drained by Kaaterskill Creek, Lake Creek, Basic Creek, Potic Creek, and Catskill Creek—all emptying into the Hudson via Catskill Creek. The county is bordered by the Hudson River on the east, Albany and Schoharie counties on the north, Delaware County on the west, and Ulster County on the south.

Principal bodies are North, South, and Black Lakes. The West Shore Railroad runs parallel to the Hudson, as does Route 9W and the New York Thruway. Principal east-west routes are State Routes 81, 145, 23, and 23A. Principal towns are Catskill, Athens, Coxsackie, Cairo, Palenville, Greenville, Tannersville, Windham, Hunter, and Prattsville. Much land is devoted to state parks and forest preserves. Recreation is the principal industry, and this was the classic area of the Catskill Mountains. There is considerable quarrying for Portland cement along the Hudson.

100.50 Cheviot to east.
This is a characteristic nineteenth-century farm and river village.

100.90 Cementon to west.
Formerly Smith's Landing, it was named for the many cement plants in the neighborhood.

101.25 East Camp to east.
I quote from Benson Lossing: "In the year 1710 Governor Hunter, by order of Queen Anne, bought of Mr. Livingston 6,000 acres of his manor, for the sum of a little more than £200, for the use of Protestant Germans then in England, who had been driven from their homes in the Lower Palatinate of

the Rhine, then the dominions of a cousin of the British Queen. About 1,800 of them settled upon the manor lands, and at a place on the opposite shore of the river, the respective localities being known as East and West Camp." (Lossing, *The Hudson,* p. 167.) They were expected to produce tar, turpentine, and other naval stores. However, they were inexperienced, and the local trees were not suited to produce such products. Robert Livingston contracted to furnish bread and beer for 6¢ per day for adults and 4¢ for children. He also sold them flour and meat and gave them cash advances. Everybody lost by the transaction and the colonies were disbanded in 1712. Many of the Palatinates settled elsewhere in the Hudson Valley and Catskills.

101.50 Germantown to east.
It has a local railroad station. (See above for history.)

102.45 Silver Point to west.
There were formerly ice houses here.

102.50 Duck Cove to west.
Here there is grassy shoal water.

102.65 Marsh Island to west.
There are trees on the island.

102.65 Alsen to west.
Inland on Route 9W and West Shore RR, it has large cement works.

102.90 Long pier to west.
Here are elaborate facilities for loading cement barges. There are six hoppers.

103.00 North Germantown to east.

103.25 Dewitt Point to west.

103.25 Tree-covered shoals to west.
These immediately offshore at DeWitt Point.

103.40 Post Creek to west.

103.50 Inbocht Bay to west.
Also called Embought Bay, it has grassy water of one-half-foot depth. It is fed by Mineral Spring Brook and Post Creek.

104.00 Mineral Spring Brook to west.
It flows south from swale between Kykuit Hill and the Kalkberg Cliffs into north shore of Inbocht Bay.

104.00 Greene Point to west.
At the north end of Inbocht Bay, this is the site of Van Arden House, a two-story clapboard mansion, mid-nineteenth century.

104.00 Nine Mile Tree to east.
This is an oldtime navigational sighting point.

105.00 Burgett Creek to west.
This creek drains marshes south of Catskill and east of Kykuit Hill.

105.25 Roeliffe Jansen's Kill to east.
The Indians called it Saupenak, and it formed the boundary between the Mohegans to the north and the Wappingers to the south. The present name is derived from Killaen Van Rensselaer's estate overseer around 1630. It was also known as Livingston Creek and Ancram Creek. It rises near Hillsdale in eastern Columbia County and flows south into Dutchess County, whence it turns and takes a northwesterly course to the Hudson.

105.25 Linlithgo to east.
Robert Livingston built his first manor house on a grassy knoll on the north bank of Roeliffe Jansen's Kill near its outlet into the Hudson about 1699. This building burned about 1800 and was immediately replaced by one slightly to the east. This

too burned in 1918. These manor houses were always occupied by the senior branch of the Livingston family, according to primogeniture. The first eight generations of the Livingstons were buried in vaults of the Livingston Memorial Chapel (Dutch Reformed), which was built in 1722 and rebuilt in 1870.

The name Linlithgo is a corruption of Linlithgow. The Livingstons were descended from the earls of Linlithgow in Scotland. Linlithgow is the county town of West Lothian (formerly Linlithgow), and near the south shore of Loch Linlithgow and west of Edinburgh. The burgh was a residence of Scottish kings; Linlithgow Palace, on an elevated promontory above the loch, was the birthplace of James V and Mary Queen of Scots. The parish church of St. Michael was founded by King David I of Scotland. Linlithgow was the scene of the murder of James Stuart, first earl of Murray.

A bit farther inland from the Hudson are the remains of the works of the Hudson River Ore & Iron Company, which were worked in conjunction with the Iron Mountain Mines between 1875 and 1898. The Burden Iron Works were also in the vicinity.

105.45 Linlithgo Station to east.
This was formerly Livingston Station.

105.50 Washburn Dock to east.
This is a ruined long pier with trees growing on it.

105.50 Mount Tom to east.
(elevation 519 feet).

106.00 Foxes' Creek to east.
Rising near Mt. Tom, its course was followed by a railroad spur leading to the Burden Iron Works.

106.20 Burden Dock to east.
A former trans-shipment point for iron and iron goods, it is now a ruin.

106.35 Oak Hill Landing to east.

106.35 Oak Hill to east.
(elevation 265 feet).

106.40 Blue Hill to east.
(elevation 660 feet).

106.50 The Kalkberg to west.
This is derived from the Dutch for "chalk rock." The name has also been corrupted to "Callabarrachs," "Collar Back," and "Calderberghs." It is a long limestone ridge of abut 250 feet elevation parallel to the Hudson running from Cementon on the south to Quarry Hill, west of Catskill at the north. Van Luven Lake sits atop the ridge at 213 feet. In the nineteenth century it was a popular scenic drive from Catskill, as good views were obtained of both the Catskill Mountains and the Berkshires, as well as of the Hudson River. Subsequent quarrying for the cement plants has despoiled large areas and placed much of it off limits. It represents the easternmost reach of the Catskills.

106.50 Ramshorn Creek to west.
This is a short crooked creek through the marshes east of Kykuit Hill.

106.50 The Fly to west.
Corruption of the Dutch Da Vly, this means "the swamps or marshes."

106.50 Kykuit Hill to west.
This is roughly translated from the Dutch as "beacon hill." The early settlers used it as such to warn of the approach of Indians. John Overbagh settled here in 1722.

107.20 Greendale to east.

A local railroad station and former terminus of steam ferry to Catskill, it was also formerly known as Oak Hill Station and Catskill Station. Oak Hill, a two-story brick mansion with mansard roof and veranda, was built in 1763 by John Livingston (1750-1822). It is in the Federal style and was extensively remodeled in the mid-19th century.

107.25 Catskill Creek to west.

Catskill Creek rises near Franklinton in Schoharie County and flows southeast past Livingstonville, Preston Hollow, Cooksburg, Oak Hill, East Durham, Freehold, South Cairo, and Leeds, to a confluence with the Kaaterskill Creek at Cauterskill. It is the dividing line between the Helderberg Mountains to the north and the Catskill Mountains to the south. It was followed by the early unsuccessful Canajoharie & Catskill Railroad, which was never extended west of Cooksburg, and by the Susquehanna and the Schoharie Turnpikes. At Leeds, it is crossed by the historic old stone bridge. Above Cauterskill it flows through the picturesque Austin's Glen, which is crossed by a bridge on the New York Thruway just south of Exit 21. Formerly the narrow gauge Catskill Mountain Railroad followed it through the Glen. East of Cauterskill, it is crossed by the high trestle of the West Shore Railroad (1883) and what is now a footbridge, but was formerly used by the Catskill Mountain Railroad, at a lower level. It flows through the village of Catskill where it is crossed by the vehicular Uncle Sam bascule bridge. Below this is the old port where the Catskill Evening Line boats used to tie up. After flowing past the promontory of Hopp's Nose on the south bank, it flows into the Hudson south of Catskill Point. Hopp's Nose, also known as Hop-O-Nose, is a rock formation projecting into the stream and is said to have caused many steamboat accidents. It was named for the prominent nose of a local redman named Hopp. Claes Uylenspiegel, a fur trader, had a cabin here prior to 1650.

Principal tributaries are: Basic and Potic Creeks on the north and the Shingle Kill and Kaaterskill Creek on the south.

Kaaterskill Creek

This is probably the most famous waterway in the Catskills. It rises in a marsh west of the village of Haines Falls, near which it flows over a 160-foot cataract at the head of Kaaterskill Clove. In mid-clove it is joined from the north by the waters of Lake Creek, which rises in North and South Lakes and then flows over the scenic Kaaterskill Falls and Bastion Falls. After going over many rapids and waterfalls, it leaves the clove at Palenville. A bit further east it goes over Kaaterskill High Falls and then dips down into Ulster County. It then turns decisively north through deep picturesque valleys to Cauterskill, where it flows into Catskill Creek.

107.25 Catskill to west.

With a population of 5,317, Catskill is the seat of Greene County. It is one of the alleged home towns of the legendary Rip Van Winkle. It is the actual home town of Samuel Wilson, who, as a sutler in the War of 1812, became known as "Uncle Sam." Wilson resided in a house on West

Main Street from 1817 to 1824. In that same house, Martin Van Buren (later eighth president of the United States, and a native of Kinderhook across the Hudson) had married Hannah Hoes in 1807.

The first recorded visit of a white man to Catskill was by Henry Hudson in 1609, when he found "a very loving people." He traded with the local Mahican Indians, who had recently been ignominiously defeated by the neighboring warlike Mohawks in a battle on Rodgers Island, just above the mouth of Catskill Creek. After this, the Mohawks claimed hegemony over the Mahicans, who shortly thereafter dispersed.

The first recorded settlement is that of Claes Uylenspiegel, a fur trader who had a cabin at Hop-O-Nose before 1650. Also prior to 1650, Hans Vos, after whom is named the Vosenkill, established a mill on that stream. Jan Jansen van Bremen also built on the present site of the Van Veighten House beneath Jefferson Heights, at the ford across Catskill Creek on the King's Highway. In the late seventeenth century, Marte Gerritse Van Bergen settled in the neighborhood of Leeds, which was the original Old Kaaterskill. In 1677, Capt. Sylvester Salisbury, an officer of the British troops that took over New Netherlands from the Dutch, acquired many thousands of acres along Catskill Creek. In 1705, Francis Salisbury erected a handsome two-story mansion at Leeds.

With the development of river commerce, the center of activity shifted down the hill from Jefferson Heights to Het Strand, or the landing, on the present site of Catskill village. The town was incorporated in 1806. Impetus for this was given by completion of the Susquehanna Turnpike (ca. 1800) to Wattle's Ferry (Unadilla) on the Susquehanna River. An eastern segment extended from Salisbury, Connecticut, to Greendale, across the Hudson from Catskill. This made Catskill the natural ferry place for westward migration from New England. It was also a good place for shipping the produce of the interior downriver to New York City. In 1838, the steamboat *Frank* began plying regularly between Catskill and the City. The ferry also soon came under steam. The *Frank* was soon followed by the *Utica, Washington, Thomas Powell, New Champion, Andrew Harder, Kaaterskill, Catskill, William C. Redfield, Thomas McManus,* and *Onteora.*

As if all this road and river activity was not enough to assure prosperity, the Canajohrie & Catskill Railroad was built and operated between Catskill and Cooksburg from 1840 to 1842, when it was closed down after an accident. The tanning industry in the mountains made Catskill a busy deepwater port for the receipt of raw hides for tanning and the shipment of tanned hides. As the tanning business declined, the Catskill Mountain House (1824), high atop South Mountain on the great wall of Manitou, with its tremendous view over the Hudson River Valley, began to attract many travelers. Prior to 1824, Erastus Beach of Catskill had been operating stage coach lines up and down the Hudson Valley and into the interior. His relative, Charles L. Beach, soon assumed control of these operations and also acquired the Catskill Mountain House. He then turned it into the "Yankee palace in the clouds." He also improved the old mountain turnpike starting at Catskill.

The work of the landscape painter Thomas Cole (1801-1848), who settled in Catskill shortly after his first visit in 1825, and Washington Irving's tale of *Rip Van Winkle,* and William Cullen Bryant's poem "Kaaterskill Falls," focused interest on the Northern Catskills. It was halfway between the metropolis and the pleasure meccas of Saratoga Springs and Ballston Spa. Catskill became the natural gateway to the Catskills, and Catskill Point, where through steamers stopped, was developed. This was an important landing for both Night and Day Line boats until the final Day Line sailing in 1953. The

Catskill Evening Line, eventually controlled by Beach interests, sailed right up Catskill Creek into the village. Completion of the Hudson River Railroad on the east shore of the Hudson in 1851 made Greendale, sometimes called Catskill Ferry, an important location.

To complete this transport nexus, in 1882, Beach interests completed the narrow gauge Catskill Mountain Railroad from Catskill Point to Pallenville, with a branch to Cairo. Eventually connections were built to the top of the Mountain via the Otis Elevating Railway and the Catskill & Tannersville Railway, another narrow-gauge line built by the Beaches. There were three stations in Catskill: the Point, the Village, and a station near the West Shore Railroad depot, which was up above on a hill, south of the trestle over Catskill Creek. The Catskill Mountain Railroad operated until 1918. The West Shore had come through town in 1883. Changing vacation patterns and the automobile killed the resorts and the steamboats and little railroads that served them. Later the New York Thruway also bypassed Catskill.

Around the turn of the century, the shale brick industry was extensive and also provided paving materials for New York City. As early as 1808, there was an iron foundry. Today liqueurs and cement products are manufactured. At the turn of the century, Catskill boasted its own fine resort, the Prospect Park Hotel, on a terrace north of the village and overlooking the river. Its broad verandahs commanded a fine view of the Hudson and the distant Berkshires.

107.25 Catskill Point to west.
This is a former important steamboat landing and terminus of ferry to Greendale and of the Catskill Mountain Railroad.

107.30 Prospect Park Hotel site to west.
Now occupied by St. Anthony's friary, this hotel opened in the 1860s. It is described by Wallace Bruce as follows: *Just out of the villge proper, on a beautiful outlook, stands the charming Prospect Park Hotel, unrivaled in its beauty of location. It has a most delightful piazza, four hundred feet long, sixteen feet wide, supported by Corinthian pillars twenty-five feet high, with many private balconies, and charming views from every room. The main building is two hundred and fifty feet front, with wing one hundred and fifty feet by forty, situated in a large and beautiful park. This handsome park adjoins the best residence portion of the village, thus affording miles of elegant shady walks and drives near at hand. The views and scenery from the "Prospect," are unsurpassed. . . .*

108.00 Church Hill and Olana Castle to east.
(elevation 500 feet). The home of landscape painter Frederick Edwin Church (1826-1900), this unique house in the Persianesque style was designed by the world-renowned painter of the Hudson River School as a three-dimensional presentation of his ideal of beauty. He consulted with architect Calvert Vaux on "practical matters."

Perched atop a hill with extensive views of the Hudson River and Catskill Mountains, Olana is extravegantly beautiful, alive with color, drama and detailing of the Eastern art that entranced Church. The name Olana means "our castle on high." It is now a state historic site and open to the public. The castle has thirty-five rooms and was completed in 1872.

108.50 Rogers Island to east of main vessel channel.
Formerly known as Vastrack

264

Island, this is a large, low-lying island, separated from the eastern shore by a shallow channel obstructed by a submerged dike, called Hallenbeck Creek. Wallace Bruce tells us that on Rogers Island

. . . the last battle was fought between the Mahicans and Mohawks' and it is narrated that " as the old king of the Mahicans was dying, after the conflict, he commanded his regalia to be taken off and his son put into the kingship while his eyes were yet clear to behold him. Over forty years had he worn it, from the time he received it in London from Queen Anne. He asked his son to kneel at his couch, and, putting his withered hand across his brow, placed the feathery crown upon his head, and gave him the silver-mounted tomahawk—symbols of power to rule and power to execute. Then, looking up to the heavens, he said, as if in despair for his race, 'The hills are our pillows, and the broad plains to the west our hunting-grounds; our brothers are called into the bright wigwam of the Everlasting, and our bones lie upon the fields of many battles; but the wisdom of the dead is given to the living." This battle was in 1625.

(Bruce, *Hudson By Daylight* p.220.)

108.60 Rip Van Winkle Bridge.
This is a unit of the New York State Bridge Authority. A cantilever bridge costing $2,500,000 and opened on July 2, 1935, it was built by the Frederick Share Corporation. There are two vehicle lanes; vessel clearance is 145 feet. The bridge is

5,041 feet long with a main span of 800 feet. A toll is charged eastbound.

108.75 Hamburg to west.
This is a fishermen's settlement.

109.25 Corlaer Kill to west.

109.25 Moreno Point at north end of Rogers Island.

110.00 Brandow Point to west.

110.00 Mount Merino to east.
(elevation 540 feet). This is one of the first places to which Merino Sheep were brought in this country.

110.90 Overhead power cables
(clearance 145 feet).

111.25 Hudson Light.
On an island to the west of the navigation channel, it is a brick Victorian structure with gambrel roof and tower (1874).

111.25 South Bay to east.
Now largely filled in, this was the site of the Hudson Iron Works in the mid-nineteenth century. Its chief business was the conversion of the crude ore into "pigs" ready for the manufacturer's use. Two kinds of ore were used: hematite from West Stockbridge and magnetic from the forest of Dean Mines, in the Hudson highlands. In 1860, it produced about 16,000 tons of pig iron.

111.25 New York State Reformatory for Women to east.

111.25 Hallenbeck Hill to west
(elevation 304 feet).

111.25 Swallow Rocks.
These rocks are at southern end of Middle Ground Flats, between the main navigation channel on the east and the secondary western channel. The western channel was formerly used for navigation. This was formerly called Doper's Island and Noah's Brig. There are interesting stories associated with the place.

In 1845, the steamer *Swallow,* while racing with two other boats, *Express* and *Rochester,* from Albany to New York, rammed these rocks, broke up, and caught fire. Fifty of the three hundred passengers were killed. Currier and Ives circulated a lurid lithograph of the disaster. Later Ira Buchman hauled the wreckage seven miles inland and built himself a two-story home known as the Swallow House.

The other story may be apochryphal and concerns a certain Captain Noah. According to the story, on one foggy twilight Captain Noah, with a fleet of rafts, sighted "a dark object riding the waters." It looked like a brig under sail. "Brig Ahoy!" he shouted. No answer. "Brig Ahoy! Answer, or I'll run you down!" No reply. Captain Noah kept to his course. Suddenly there was a crash and wood crunched on rock. Captain Noah had mistaken two trees on the island for masts with sails set.

111.25 Athens to west.

Originally called Loonenburg or Lunenburg, it was first settled in 1686; but there is evidence that prehistoric Indians mined flint stones at Flint Hill 12,000 years ago, at a site now belonging to the New York Archeological Association. The old Indian village of Potick was located a short distance back from the River. The Looneburg Patent of 17,500 acres, running from Coxsackie to Catskill Creek and embracing the Athens area, was purchased by Adrian Van Loon, a Walloon whose family had come to America in 1581, shortly after Jacques Cartier had first ex-

plored the St. Lawrence in 1534. They had migrated down through the Adirondacks into the Hudson Valley about 1598. Jan Van Loan built a house in Athens in 1708, although a previous owner of the patent had acquired an Indian deed from a certain Caniskeek on April 30, 1665.

The Zion Lutheran Church was organized in 1703, and its first pastor, the Rev. Justus Falkner, was the first Lutheran minister ordained in America.

Isaac Northrup is credited with moving for incorporation of the village in 1805. Athens soon became a port for merchant sailing ships and whalers and supported a considerable shipbuilding industry. The natives favored classic style architecture. This all reflects the "Yankee culture" of the many settlers from New England. A steam ferry to Hudson was established prior to 1836, and in 1867 Athens became the southern terminus of the Saratoga & Hudson River Railroad, known as "the white elephant line," because it never made a profit. Its route along Murderer's Creek northwest of town became the Athens Branch of the West Shore Railroad in 1883. It is now abandoned. Other parts of the Saratoga & Hudson River survive as bits of the West Shore Main Line, Penn Central, South Bethlehem branch, and the Delaware & Hudson. The Van Loan & Magee Co. built steamboats. Steamboats connecting Athens with New York City were the *John Taylor,* and *Erastus Corning* of the John H. Starin Line. Starin later became prominent in Long Island Sound and coastal shipping. The Starin boats to Athens carried cattle as well as passengers. In 1873, the Athens steamboat terminal suffered a disasterous fire, and the business declined from then on.

The Schoharie Turnpike was completed to Cooksburg in 1802, starting from Athens. However, the Susquehanna Turnpike starting from Catskill, and the short lived (1840-1842) Canajoharie & Catskill Railroad offered strong competition to the Athens route.

Development of faster steamboats which did not stop at Athens, completion of the West Shore Railroad (1883), Hudson River Railroad (1851), Delaware & Hudson Railroad (1868), and the Rip Van Winkle Bridge (1935) all served to divert traffic from this once important transportation center. Ice harvesting and brickmaking were the last major industries in the area.

During its heyday, Athens had cultural pretensions, with fine architecture and an opera house which can still be seen on Second Street (now known as the Brooks building). Located west of town are the once-popular picnic resorts of Black, Green, and Hollister Lakes. There are many well-preserved fine old buildings in the town. The Haight-Gantley-Van Loan Mansion (1812), with its Oval Ballroom, built by Gen. Samuel Haight, is particularly elegant.

112.00 to 113.75 Middle Ground Flats.
This is a low flat island in midstream. The main shipping channel is to the east.

112.00 Hudson to the east.
With a population of 8,940, Hudson is the seat of Columbia County. It is the western terminus of Hudson & Chatham Branch of the Boston & Albany Railroad, also known as the Claverack Branch of the New York Central. It is an Amtrak passenger stop today. Formerly a ferry to Athens and to Catskill left from here.

Jan Frans Van Hoesen purchased land here from the Indians in 1662. However, the story of its permanent settlement is best told by Benson Lossing:

About thirty miles below Albany, lying upon a bold, rocky promontory that juts out from the eastern shore at an elevation of fifty feet, with a beautiful bay on each side, is the City of Hudson, the capital of Columbia County, a port of entry, and one of the most delightfully situated towns on the river. It was founded in 1784 by thirty proprietors, chiefly Quakers from New England. Never in the history of the rapid growth of cities in America has there been a more remarkable example than that of Hudson. Within three years from the time when the farm on which it stands was purchased, and only a solitary storehouse stood upon the bank of the river at the foot of the bluff, one hundred and fifty dwellings, with wharves, storehouses, workshops, barns, etc., were erected, and a population of over fifteen hundred souls had settled there, and become possessed of a city charter.

(Lossing, *The Hudson*, p. 146.)

Most of the settlers came from Nantucket and Provi-

19.   Hudson South

dence. One of the reasons for the rapid growth was that they brought prefabricated buildings with them. This was a remarkable innovation at the time. The original settlement was called Claverack Landing. Even at this early date, the city had a mill, a shipyard, two tanneries, and a covered ropewalk. In 1790, twenty-five schooners, including both whalers and traders, showed Hudson as their registered home port. A city charter was granted in 1785—the third in the state.

Parade Hill, or Promenade Hill, a public park atop the riverfront bluffs was granted to the Common Council in 1795 by the "proprietors." It commands extensive views of the Helderbergs and the Catskills. Today machinery, woolen knit goods, ginger ale, shirts, matches, dresses, and flypaper are manufactured, and there are large cement plants at the southeastern end of town.

112.00 Prospect Hill to east.
(elevation 375 feet).

112.00 Greenport Center to east.
It is inland from the Hudson.

112.50 North Bay to east.
This bay is cut off from river by a railroad causeway.

113.00 Murderer's Creek to west.
This creek rises south of Coxsackie and flows southeast into the western channel of the Hudson north of Athens.

113.80 Priming Hook to east.

113.80 Hasbrouck Hill to east.
(elevation 205 feet).

114.25 Stottville to east.

114.30 West Flats to west.
Shoal water.

115.45 Fourmile Point to west.
Here is located an early nineteenth-century stone lighthouse with clapboard wings.

115.45 Vosburgh Swamp to west.
Inland from Fourmile Point.

115.75 Stockport Creek to east.
Formed by the junction of Kinderhook Creek from the north and Claverack Creek from the south, it was formerly called Major Abraham's Creek. Abram Staats built a one-story stone house in 1664 on the north bank of the creek near its junction with the Hudson, replacing one of 1654 that had been burned by Indians.

115.80 Stockport Station to east.
Henry Hudson landed here in September 17, 1609.

116.20 to 116.80 Stockport Middle Ground.
There are channels to either side and a main vessel channel to the west.

116.45 Columbiaville to east.
It cannot be seen from river.

116.75 Judson Point to east.

117.00 Gay's Point to east.

117.35 Fitch's Wharf to west.

117.35 Unnamed man-made island to east of main channel.

118.00 Lampman Hill to west.
(elevation 270 feet). This hill is the property of Leonard Bronck Lampman.

118.00 Fordham Point to east.

118.20 Little Nutten Hook to east.

118.50 Coxsackie lower landing to west.

118.75 Coxsackie to west.
Pronounced "Cook-sackie," its name is from the Indian Kaak-aki. Authorities are divided on the meaning of the term. Some say it means "place where geese gather," others "place of owls," and others "cut banks." Still another theory is that it is a corruption of the Dutch "Koeksrackie," meaning "Cook's Little Reach."

Coxsackie was settled in 1661 by Pieter Bronck of Albany, who built a house somewhat inland near Route 9W in 1663, which is now used as a museum by the Green County Historical Society.

On May 17, 1775, 225 men gathered in the house of Leendert Bronck, who was a member of the Committee of Correspondence and Safety, to sign what has been called the Coxsackie Declaration, prior to the signing of the national Declaration of Independence, stating that "Americans would not consent to be ruled, save by themselves," and "never to become slaves," and to oppose the "arbitrary and oppressive Acts of the British Parliament." It was signed in the wake of the news of the battles of Lexington and Concord as committee couriers sped along the King's Highway in front of the Bronck homestead.

In about 1824, the Robert Owen-inspired Forestville commonwealth, a communal socio-religious community, was established here. The town of Coxsackie was incorporated in 1867. Today there are granite works, and valves are manufactured. There was formerly a ferry to Newton Hook.

118.80 Nutten Hook to east.
This was formerly known as Newton Hook or Newton Hook Station. It once had a ferry to Coxsackie. The large Stack Icehouse is located here.

119.00 Coxsackie Upper Landing to west.

119.50 to 120.20 Coxsackie Island to west of main vessel channel.
There is a secondary channel to the west of the island with depths of 10 to 22 feet. It was formerly known as Hauver Platte and Budd's Island.

120.50 Rattlesnake Island to west.
The main channel lies to the east of the island. There is a lighthouse at the northern end. It used to be called Coxsackie lighthouse, and the island was Lighthouse Island. For many years, this lighthouse was staffed by two spinsters and the informal name of Old Maids' Light was used among the rivermen.

121.00 Kinderhook Point to east.
Name means "children's point."

121.45 Stuyvesant to east.
This is a local railroad station. Henry Hudson landed here. This was the original location of the village of Kinderhook. However, the settlement was soon moved inland because of the mosquitoes and malaria.

121.50 Coxsackie Creek to west.
It rises in West Coxsackie and flows northeast to the Hudson River. It is fed from the northwest just before entering the Hudson by Sickles Creek, originally called Clove Kill.

121.50 Robinson Hill to west.
(elevation 558 feet).

122.00 Kinderhook Village to east.
It is inland and cannot be seen from the river. It is on Kinderhook Creek. The original settlement was on the Hudson at the site of the present Stuyvesant. In the churchyard of the Dutch Reformed Church, north of the village, is the grave of Edmond Charles "Citizen" Genet (1763-1834), who married the daughter of Gov. George Clinton and became an American citizen. He was the French minister to the United States in 1793, and his activities caused some embarrassment to George Washington.

Kinderhook was the birth and burial place of Martin Van Buren (1782-1862), eighth president of the United States. His home, Lindenwald, was built in about

1810. He lived here after his presidency until his death. The house, called the "house of history," is open as a museum. It contains some items which belonged to Van Buren as well as period furniture and historical portraits.

The Van Ness House was built by Peter Van Ness who served in the colonial wars and commanded a regiment at Saratoga. He was a member of the state convention which adopted the federal Constitution.

The Luycas Van Alen House is a Dutch-style brick house dating from 1736. It also is open as a museum. Kinderhook is rich in well-preserved old houses, as is neighboring Valatie.

121.50 to 122.75 Bronck Island to west.
This island is now joined to the mainland.

123.20 Mill Creek to east.
There was an early settlement at its mouth.

124.00 to 126.50 Houghtaling Island to the east of main vessel channel.
It is now joined to the mainland at its northern end by lower and upper Schodack islands. A shallow (minimum seven foot depth) channel to the east of the island leads to Schodack landing.

124.30 Matthew Point to west.
125.50 New Baltimore to west.
This is the home of former sloop and barge building industries. In 1800, Paul Sherman was building schooners here. Later, local boatyards built canal boats and repaired smaller vessels. Many Quakers settled here in the early nineteenth century. Neat white houses and a New England atmosphere make this a popular retirement place for sea and river captains. There are many eighteenth-century and Victorian houses in the area. Most of the village is on a plateau 100 feet above the Hudson. The 1939 movie *Little Old New York* was filmed here.

126.50 Hannacroix Creek to west.
Also spelled Hannacrois Creek, it rises in the southern Helderbergs and flows through a ravine three miles long and eighty feet deep and over Dickinson Falls southeast to Alcove Reservoir (city of Albany), thence east and northeast to the Hudson River.

126.50 Former channel between lower Schodack and Houghtaling Islands to east.

126.60 Barren Island to west.
Formerly Bear Island, it is now joined to the mainland. A sewage plant is located here. The name is a corruption of the Dutch "Bearn Island." This is the site of the famous "Rensellaerstein" described by Washington Irving in his *Knickerbocker History of New York*.

126.60 Albany County to west.
From here north to the Mohawk River, we have Albany County on the western bank. It has an area of 531 square miles and is bounded on the east by the Hudson River, on the south by Greene County, on the west by Schoharie County and on the north by Schenectady County and Saratoga County. The central and southwestern part of the county is taken up by the Helderberg Mountains. Principal drainage is by Catskill and Hannacroix Creeks and the Mohawk River into the Hudson. The largest bodies of water are Alcove and Basic Reservoirs. Principal rail lines are the West

Shore from Ravena to Rotterdam Junction; the New York Central Mainline from Albany to Schenectady and the Delaware & Hudson from Duanesburg to Albany and thence north to Cohoes. The New York Thruway parallels the West Shore Railroad. Albany was one of the original ten counties formed in 1683, and named in honor of one of the titles of the Duke of Albany and York, later King James II. It is comprised of the towns of Rensselaerville, Westerloo, Coeymans, Bethlehem, New Scotland, Berne, Knox, Guilderland, Green Island, and Colonie and the city of Albany. Principal towns are Albany, the county seat, and capital of the state of New York, Menands, Watervliet, and Cohoes.

126.60 Rensselaer County to east.
This county runs along the eastern bank from here to mile 164.30, opposite Stillwater in Saratoga County. It is bounded on the south by Columbia County, on the west by the Hudson River, on the north by Washington County, and on the east by the states of Vermont and Massachusetts. Troy is the county seat. It has an area of 665 square miles and was taken from Albany County in 1791. It was named in honor of the early patroons.

It is an area of undulating hills. The principal watercourse is the Hoosic River, flowing northwest into the Hudson near Schaghticoke. Principal bodies of water are Tomhannock Reservoir, Babcock Lake, Long Pond, Dyken Pond, Wager Pond, Snyder's Lake, Crooked Lake, and Burden Lake.

The New York Central Railroad runs along the Hudson north to Rensselaer, where the main line crosses to Albany. A branch continues north to Troy. The Boston & Albany has a line from Chatham to Albany, and the Boston & Maine formerly had a line from Troy to Eagle Bridge. The main line of the Boston & Maine cuts across northern Rensselaer County, following the Hoosic River, from Mechanicville to Williamstown, Massachusetts. There is passenger service only on the New York Central mainline. Rensselaer-Albany is an Amtrak station with service to New York, Boston, Montreal, Buffalo, Detroit, and Chicago. The main highways are Route 7 from Troy to Bennington, Vermont, and Route 2 from Troy to Williamstown, Massachusetts.

Principal towns are Troy, Rensselaer, and Hoosick Falls.

126.50 to 128.75 Lower Schodack Island to east of main navigation channel.
Shallow secondary channel east of island. Now joined to Houghtaling Island at the south and Upper Schodack island at the north. The name Schodack means "place of fire," referring to the permanent council fire which the Mohican Indians maintained here.

127.50 Coeymans to west.
Pronounced: Queeman's, it was settled in 1673 by Barent Pieterse Coeymans. It is a typical sleepy old Dutch river town and is well described by James Fenimore Cooper, under the name of Willow Cove, in his novel *Miles Wallingford.* This was once a major ice-cutting center. The Sutton & Suderley brick plant is still active.

127.50 Mull Island to east.
It is now incorporated into Lower Schodack Island.

127.55 Coeymans Creek to west.
It rises near South Bethlehem and flows southeast to Hudson at Coeymans.

127.55 Ravena to west.
Inland to west of Coeymans, on Route 9W, Thruway and West Shore Railroad.

127.55 Schodack Landing to east.
Located on mainland, east of Lower Schodack Island, at head of navigability of the eastern channel, it was formerly a local railroad station.

128.00 Roah Hook to west.

128.00 Little Schodack Island to east.
This is a very small island in the eastern channel, here known as Hell Gate.

128.50 Mull Plaat to east.
Now incorporated into northwestern shoreline of Lower Schodack Island, its name refers to "mill plot."

129.00 Former site of Hell Gate to east.
Now filled in, this was a narrow channel between Upper and Lower Schodack Islands.

129.00 to 130.50 Upper Schodack Island to east.
The main navigational channel is west of the island. On the east side is shallow, tidal, Schodack Creek, the outlet of Muitzes Kill. Upper Schodack Island is now connected with the mainland at the northern end and Lower Schodack Island at the southern end.

129.00 Schodack Creek (outlet of Muitzes Kill) to east.
It is located east of Upper Schodack Island.

129.80 Alfred H. Smith Memorial Bridge.
This steel and concrete railroad bridge was named after a former president of the New York Central Railroad. It was built for freight trains running between the former Hudson River Railroad and the Boston & Albany Railroad and the large classification yard at Selkirk, two miles west of here, where connection is made with the West Shore line. The bridge is a mile long, including approaches. It is a through truss bridge, with two major river spans. The eastern one is 600 feet long and the western one 400 feet. The bridge crosses not only the main channel of the Hudson, but also Shad Island and the Binnen Kill. Clearance is 135 feet. It cost $20,000,000.

129.90 Castleton-on-Hudson Bridge.
This bridge carries the Berkshire section of the New York State Thruway to a connection with the Massachusetts Turnpike. The mile-long Castleton bridge is 5,330 feet long. Its deck provides for two separated traffic lanes in each direction with a thirteen-foot-wide raised steel center mall. The bridge consists of relatively short continuous-plate girder approach spans on each side of the main and anchor spans. The main spans are of cantilever-truss design. The bridge pavement is 144 feet above the river, and there is 135 feet clearance between the river and the bottom of steel. The two main towers are 256 feet above the river. The substructure is composed of two abutments and forty-two reinforced concrete bents. These are comprised of two tall vertical columns stiffened with an intermediate strut and capped with a heavy concrete beam. The supporting columns range from five feet in

diameter to fourteen feet for those supporting the main span.

A fog horn with a one-mile range blasts northward whenever the visibility is less than 2,000 feet. Ships approaching from the south are warned by a similar system on the neighboring railroad bridge, 400 feet to the south.

The substructure was built by Arthur A. Johnson Corporation and P. Kiewit Sons Co. of New York. Structural steel superstructure was built by Harris Structural Steel Co. of New York. Total cost of the bridge was $17,000,000. The bridge was designed by Madigan Hyland Consulting Engineers, and opened to traffic on May 26, 1959.

129.80 Shad Island to west.

129.80 Binnen Kill to west.
It separates Shad Island from the mainland.

130.50 Baker Creek to west.
It separates Shad Island on the west from Schermerhorn Island on the east.

130.50 to 131.30 Schermerhorn Island to west.
It is virtually joined to the mainland.

131.25 Vlockie Kill to east.

131.25 Selkirk to west.
Inland, this is the site of a major railroad junction and freight classification yard.

131.50 Castleton-on-Hudson to east.
This is an oldtime small river town. Named after the castle-like appearance of the steep bank upon which it is built. It was settled ca.1630 and incorporated 1827. Paper boxes are manufactured here.

131.50 Poplar Island to west.
It is now joined to the mainland.

132.35 Vloman Kill to west.

132.35 Cow Island to east.
It is now joined to the mainland.

132.50 Moordener Kill to east.
In English, its name means Murderer's Creek. There is a legend of a girl tied to a horse by Indians and dragged through the valley.

132.50 Brookview to east.

132.50 Papscanee Creek to east.
Also known as Dead Creek, it separates Campbell, Pixtaway, and Papscanee Islands from the mainland.

132.60 to 134.00 Campbell Island to east.
It is separated from the mainland by Papscanee Creek and from Pixtaway Island by a small stream.

132.70 Cedar Hill to west.

132.70 Stony Point to east.
This point is on the mainland.

133.00 Schodack to east.
This is the former principal settlement of the Mahican Indians.

133.20 Vandenburgh Hill to east.
(elevation 268 feet.)

133.20 Parda Hook to west.
It is said a horse once drowned here in a horse race on the ice. "Pard" is an old name for a spotted horse.

133.50 Pixtaway Island to east.
Between Campbell Island on the west and Papscanee Creek on the east, it is joined to Papscanee Island at its northern end.

133.75 Vierda Kill to east.
It flows into Papscanee Creek.

133.80 Bear Island to west.
This island is now joined to mainland.

134.00 to 137.00 Papscanee Island to east.
The main channel passes to the west. It was formerly called Staat Island.

134.10 Frothingham Lake to west.
It lies inland.

134.35 Staat Point to east.
On Papscanee Island.

134.50 Wemple to west.

135.00 Van Wies Point to west.

135.25 Lighthouse to west.

135.25 Frothingham to west.

135.50 East Greenbush to east.

135.60 Cooper Kill to east.
On Papscanee Island, it drains southwest into the main channel of the Hudson.

136.30 Island Creek to west.
Separating Beacon, Cabbage, and Westerloo Islands from the mainland, it receives waters of the Norman's Kill at its northern end.

136.35 Beacon Island to west.
This island is in the mouth of Island Creek.

136.40 Bethlehem Center to west.

136.50 Glenmont to west.

136.50 Grandview Hill to east.
This was called "Schoti-ack," place of the ever-burning council fire of the Mahicans. Its elevation is 420 feet.

136.50 Cabbage Island to west.
This was formerly called Parr's Island.

136.50 Overslaugh Bar.
We quote at length from Wallace Bruce, writing for publication in 1901:

> The Castleton Bar or "overslaugh," as it was known by the river pilots, impeded for years navigation in low water. A. Van Santvoord, Esq., President of the Hudson River Day Line, and other prominent citizens along the Hudson, brought the subject before the State Legislature, and work was commenced in 1863. In 1868 the United States Government, very properly (as their jurisdiction extends over tide-water), assumed the work of completing the dykes, and they now

> ing the river channel. Mr. Charles G. Weir, U. S. Engineer, in charge of the Hudson river improvements, in a recent report, says that the work of removing shoals and other obstructions that are a menace to navigation is progressing satisfactorily, and that dredges are at work deepening the channel from Coxsackie to the State dam at Troy, in accordance with the act of Congress of September 19, 1890, which calls for a channel 12 feet deep and 400 feet wide from Coxsackie to the foot of Broadway, Troy, and thence 12 feet deep and 300 feet wide to the State dam.

> The plan provides for a system of longitudinal dykes to confine the current sufficiently to allow the ebb and flow of the tidal-current to keep the channel clear. These dykes are to be gradually brought nearer together from New Baltimore toward Troy, so as to assist the entrance of the flood-current and increase its height.

> The engineers report that the greater part of the material carried in suspension in the Hudson river above Albany is believed to come from the Mohawk river, and its tributary the Schoharie river, while the sands and gravel that form the heavy and obstinate bars near Albany and chiefly between Albany and Troy, come from the upper Hudson.

> The discharge of the Hudson between Troy and Albany at its

lowest stage may be taken at about 3,000 cubic feet per second. The river supply, therefore, during that stage is inadequate in the upper part of the river for navigation, independent of tidal flow.

The greatest number of bars is between Albany and Troy, where the channel is narrow, and at least six obstructing bars, composed of fine and coarse gravel and coarse and fine sand, are in existence. In many places between Albany and Troy the navigable depth is reduced to 7½ feet by the presence of these bars.

From Albany to New Baltimore the depths are variable, the prevailing depth being 10 feet and over, with pools of greater depth separated by long cross-over bars, over which the greatest depth does not exceed 9 or 10 feet.

(Bruce, *Hudson By Daylight* p. 233.)

Even after completion of the above described work, the river between Albany and Hudson was cluttered with small islands, and until 1930 only twelve feet deep at low tide. This presented a serious problem to navigation. The channel was later dredged to a depth of twenty-seven feet, enabling large sea-going vessels to proceed to Albany, independent of the tides. Albany was thus made a seaport. In 1954, Congress authorized further deepening of the channel to thirty-two feet.

By the 1960s, the channel had been improved to thirty-four-foot depth and four hundred foot width.

137.00 Teller Hill to east.
(elevation 407 feet).

137.25 Teller Crossing to east.

137.30 Turning Basin to east.
It has a 25-foot depth.

137.75 Norman's Kill to west.
It rises near East Berne in the Helderbergs and flows east through the Normanskill Ravine, or the Vale of Ta-Wa-sentha ("place of many dead" or of "waterfalls,") to Island Creek, west of Westerlo Island. It was named for an early Albany settler who erected a mill near the mouth of the stream. The Delaware and Hudson follows the Norman's Kill through the ravine. The Vale of Ta-Wa-sentha is one of the supposed dwellings of the legendary Hiawatha.

137.75 Greenbush Banks or Heights to east.
(elevation 300 feet).

137.75 Westerlo Island to west.
Site of the Port of Albany with heavy shipping and rail facilities, it incorporates the former Marsh Island.

137.75 Dow's Point to east.
This is the former estate of V.P. Douw.

137.75 Hazelwood to west.

137.75 Kenwood to west.

138.00 Bogart Island to west.
Now incorporated into Westerlo Island.

138.00 Clinton Heights to east.

138.50 Port of Albany to west.
Port for oceangoing vessels.

138.75 Niagara Mohawk Power Company Kenwood Generating Station to west.
This is a large steam-generating station with tall smokestacks.

138.75 Westerloes to west.

138.75 Cuyler Dike to east.

139.00. Island Creek to west.
This is the northern part of a former creek, now canalized. It no longer connects with the southern portions inside

Cabbage and Westerlo Island, as Westerlo Island is now joined to the mainland.

139.00 Greenbush Heights to east.

139.40 Site of former Parker Dunn Memorial Bridge.
Operational from 1933 to 1974, when it was removed, it was named in honor of Parker F. Dunn (1890-1918) a hero of World War I. It had the heaviest known lift span and served as the principal highway crossing at Albany.

139.50 Mill Creek to east.
It is now largely covered over.

139.50 to 140.00 Van Rensselaer Island to east.
It is now part of the mainland and has been partially dredged away.

139.50 Albany to west.

With a population of 115,781, this is the capital of the state of New York and the seat of Albany County.

Albany was visited by Henry Hudson on September 19, 1609. The first settlement was in 1614 when Fort Nassau was built on Castle Island to protect fur traders. It was under the command of Hendrick Christiaensen. This fort was destroyed by a flood in 1617.

In 1623, the Dutch West India Company sent thirty Walloon families to settle in the Albany area. They built another fort, called Fort Aurania (Fort Orange in English), on Castle Island in 1624.

The first large grant of land was made in 1629, to Killaen Van Rensselaer, a pearl and diamond merchant of the Netherlands. This tract centered on Fort Orange and was on both sides of the Hudson River. It covered an area twenty-four by forty-eight miles. Killaen Van Rensselaer was the uncle of Wouter Van Twiller, a director of the Dutch West India Company, and later the third governor of New Netherlands. Van Rensselaer himself did not venture to the New World, but sent his relative Roelf Janssen as overseer. The tenants had to buy all

supplies from the commissary and have their grain ground at the patroon's mill. By 1637, the patent covered 700 square miles. On April 8, 1680, Van Rensselaer had purchased from King Aepgin of the Mahicans "all that tract of country on the west side of the Hudson, extending from Beeren Island up to Smack's Island, and in breadth two day's journey. In 1642, the Van Rensselaers built Fort Crailo at Greenbush. This area was then known as Crawlier. Later this house served as the upper manor. The lower manor, called Claverack, or "clover pasture," was built in 1685 and was active until 1783. A western manor was located at the north end of present-day Albany. In later years it was taken down and moved to Williamstown, Massachusetts. In 1664 or 1670, Richard Van Rensselaer built another house called De Vlackte, or "the flats," opposite Breaker Island south of Watervliet. This house was later sold to Philip Pietersen Schuyler.

By the time of the governorship of Peter Stuyvesant (1647-1664), Killaen Van Rensselaer thought himself so powerful that he instructed his henchman Nicholas Koorn to build a fort, Rensellaerstein, on Barren Island and demand tribute tolls from passing vessels by *wapen recht.*The power of the Van Rensselaers was becoming intolerable to the company, and director general (governor) Peter Stuyvesant ordered the laying out of the town of Beverwyck adjacent to Fort Orange. This was to be considered company property and was placed under the jurisdiction of three magistrates, completely independent of the manor of Rensselaerwyck, which surrounded it for miles on all sides. This was the nucleus of the present city of Albany.

Later, in 1685, Killaen's grandson was confirmed in his rights to the manor of Rensselaerwyck by the English. This was the only one of the major Dutch patroonships to survive under later English domination, and indeed lasted on past the American Revolution. Two hundred years later, in 1838, there were still between 60,000 and 100,000 tenants on farms owned by the sixth lord of the manor, Stephen Van Rensselaer III, known as the "good patroon." He had acceded to the title at the ripe old age of five years.

After the English conquest in 1664, the name of the town was changed from Fort Orange to Albany, in honor of the Scottish title of the Duke of Albany and York, later King James II. In 1686, it was chartered as a city by Gov. Thomas Dongan—the second city to be chartered in the present United States.

During the French and Indian War, a congress was held at Albany, which was attended by such dignitaries as Benjamin Franklin. Members drew up the so-called "Albany plan of union." This served as an important example for later developments before and during the Revolution.

After the Revolution, commercial development began in earnest. Capt. Stewart Dean of Albany sailed his sloop *Experiment* around the world to Canton, China, via Cape Horn between 1785 and 1787. In 1785, a stagecoach line to New York was chartered. The New York State Legislature established itself here in 1797, renting a house for Gov. John Jay —thus making Albany the State Capital.

The greatest impetus came with the development of the steamboat in 1807. The Champlain Canal was completed in 1822 and the great Erie Canal in 1825. The large Cruttendon's Hotel was opened about 1827. The Mohawk and Hudson Railroad was completed in 1831, and the the Hudson River Railroad in 1851. Among later important commercial developments were the improvement of the New York State Barge Canal in 1918 and opening of the thirteen million-dollar port of Albany in 1932, with facilities covering 217 acres, including a large grain elevator, and accommodating seagoing ships of twenty-seven foot draft.

Any review of the history of Albany must make mention of its greatest native son. General Philip Schuyler (1733-1804) was fourth in descent from an ancestor who had come to Beverwyck from Holland in 1650. He was born at Albany and served in the French and Indian Wars. He married Catherine Van Rensselaer, thus uniting with the family of the Patroon. He served in the Provincial Assembly and the Continental Congress in 1775 and 1779. Between 1775 and 1777 he served as Major General of the Northern Department under Washington. He later served as the first United States Senator from New York. After the Battle of Saratoga, he was host to the captive Gen. John Burgoyne at his mansion in Albany. His daughter, Elizabeth Schuyler, married Alexander Hamilton in December 1780. He owned an extensive estate at Schuylerville further up the Hudson near Saratoga.

Important buildings in Albany not described elsewhere are:
1) New York State Office Building. Located west of the capitol, it has thirty-three stories. It was built of limestone and granite in 1930 at cost of $6,500,000
2) Roman Catholic Cathedral of the Immaculate Conception, Madison and Eagle Streets. In Gothic style with spires similar to those at Cologne, it was built in 1852.
3) New York State Bank Building. On the northeast corner of State and Pearl Streets, it is a seventeen-story red brick built in 1927, designed by H.I. Cobb. It incorporates Adam style elements of the original building of 1803 by Philip Hooker.
4) New York State Court of Appeals Building. On Eagle Street between Pine and Columbia, it is in Greek Revival Style. It has a portico with six Ionic columns of white Sing-Sing marble, built between 1835 and 1842. Henry Rector was the architect.
5) Albany County Courthouse. On Eagle Street between Pine and Columbia it is a granite and limestone Ionic-Neoclassic building, 1916.
6) Gen. Philip Schuyler Monument. Located in front of City Hall, this

monument is by J. Massey Rhind.
7) Statue of General Philip Sheridan
(1831-1888). This Civil War general
lead cavalry under Grant. He was
born in Albany. The statue is by
John Quincy Adams Ward. It was
completed by Daniel Chester
French.

6

From the Capital Area to the Adirondacks

139.50 Albany

The tide here is 4½ feet.

139.50 Rensselaer to east.

With a population 10,136, Rensselaer was formed in 1897 by the union of the villages of East Albany, Greenbush, and Bath-on-the-Hudson, also known as Rensselaerwyck. This was the early seat of the Van Rensselaer family.

Fort Crailo, actually a fortified manor house, is located on Riverside Street, south of Columbia. It is open as a free museum. It was built in 1704 as the home of Hendrick Van Rensselaer, whose grandfather was patroon of a huge estate encompassing most of what is now Rensselaer and Albany counties. The rear wing was built in 1762. During the French and Indian War, the house served as temporary headquarters to Gen. James Abercromby (1706-1781) on his way to Ticonderoga. During his visit in 1758, it is alleged that a Dr. Richard Shuckburgh, who was attached to Abercromby's staff, was struck by the very bedraggled appearance of the colonial milita while sitting on the edge of a well. In an idle moment he penned the poem "Yankee Doodle." Thus Fort Crailo came to be called the "Yankee Doodle home."

During the Revolution, twelve of the Crailo Van Rensselaers served the patriot cause, and early in the war, colonial troops assembled on Fort Crailo's grounds.

Beverwyck on Washington Avenue opposite Eighth Street, now St. Anthony's Seminary, was built between 1840 and 1843. It was the manor house of William Paterson Van Rensselaer, younger son of Stephen Van Rensselaer. It is a two and one-half story structure built of stone with Greek Revival details including an Ionic portico. Frederic Diaper was its architect. It has been a Franciscan seminary since 1912.

Dyes, chemicals, felts, and woolens are manufactured here. It is a major junction for railroad passenger service, with lines running to New York, Boston, Montreal, and the west. It is the location of Amtrak's Albany station.

139.65 Quackendary Kill to east.

It is now largely covered over.

139.65 New Highway Bridge.

This bridge connects with Interstate 787.

139.80 Railroad Bridge.

This bridge formerly led to Union Station, Albany, and was used by all passenger trains. It is presently out of service.

140.50 Railroad Bridge.

This bridge was formerly for freight only. It is presently used by all freight and passenger trains.

140.75 Tivoli Lakes to west,

on Patroon Creek.

140.75 Bath-on-the Hudson to east.

This has been part of Rensselaer since 1897.

140.75 Defreestville to east.

Beyond Bath, it is located on Quackendary Kill.

140.80 Patroon Creek to west.

This creek is followed by the line of the New York Central Railroad.

140.80 to 142.00 Lower Patroon Island to west.

The main vessel channel lies to the east.

141.50 Interstate 90 bridge.

141.50 North Albany to west.

141.80 Filtration Plant to west.

141.80 Unnamed inlet to east.
This inlet is separated from the main channel by Bath Dike.

142.25 to 142.80 Patroon Island to west.
The vessel channel lies to the east.

142.65 Overhead power cables
(Authorized clearance 155 feet).

142.80 to 144.80 Little River to west.
Separating Breaker Island from the Mainland, it has depths of from three to ten feet. It is open to small craft from the Hudson only at its northern end.

142.80 to 144.80 Breaker Island to west.
Formerly Cuyler's Island, it was the site of the Park Island race course in 1894.

143.00 Menands to west.

143.00 Loudonville to west
(beyond Menands). This village, with a population of 9,299, named in honor of Lord Loudoun, commander in chief of the British forces in North America in 1757, during the French and Indian Wars. He became governor of Virginia in 1758.

143.50 Moordenaer's Kill to west.
This creek flows into Little River.

143.80 Overhead power cable.
(authorized clearance 138 feet).

143.90 Kromme Kill to west.
This creek flows into Little River.

143.90 Hillhouse Island to west.
This island is now incorporated into Breaker Island.

143.90 Mix's Island to west.
It is now incorporated into Breaker Island.

144.25 Highway Lift Bridge
(Route 378): horizontal clearance 301 feet, vertical clearance: 62 feet closed, 139 feet open.

144.25 South Troy to east.

144.50 Wynant's Kill to east.

144.50 Albia to east.
(atop ridge).

144.50 Burden's Point to east.

144.50 Immaculate Conception Monastery to east.

144.80 Port Schuyler to west.

144.80 Burden's Iron works to east.

145.30 Watervliet to west.
(population 12,404).

145.30 Watervliet Arsenal to west.
This arsenal was established in 1813 during the War of 1812. Its historic structures include: Quarters No. 1: two-story, stone officer's home built 1845; Building No. 24: a three-story trimmed stone enlisted men's barracks with two-story columned porch, built in 1843; Building No. 38: the "cast-iron building," built in 1839 from decorative cast-iron components cast in New York City; and Building No. 110; the Big Gun Shop, a gigantic brick factory building, built in 1889, enlarged in 1918 and 1942.

145.30 Smart's Pond to east.

145.60 Poesten Kill to east.

146.00 Ida Lake to east.

146.00 Mount Ida to east.
(elevation 360 feet). This mount consists of Cambrian rock and glacial clay. It is in the center of Troy Municipal Prospect Park.

146.25 West Troy to west.
This is now part of Watervliet.

146.25 Troy to east.

With a population of 62,918, this city runs seven miles along the river to the east. The Indian name for the vicinity was Pa-an-pa-ack, which means "field of standing corn." It is included in the tract granted to Killaen Van Rensselaer by the Dutch West India Company in 1629. Gradually the area grew up as a market center for Dutch and Palatinate farmers along the Mohawk Valley, as this was the head of tidewater navigation on the Hudson River. As late as 1785, most of the area in the present city was owned by three farmers, all descendants of Derick Vanderheyden. The land immediately to the north belonged to the Lansing family. This area is now called Lansingburgh, but was called New City before the Revolution. The section near downtown Troy was called Ashley's Ferry or Ferry Hook, after Capt. Stephen Ashley who ran a tavern here. The name Troy was adopted in 1789. In 1796, a post office was established. In the 1790s, bricks and paper were manufactured along the Poestenkill. Troy was incorporated as a village in 1798. It had been surveyed as a town in 1786.

The nineteenth century was Troy's golden age of commercial development. The Troy-Schenectady Toll Road was opened in 1802. The first steamboats arrived shortly after 1807. The Champlain Canal came in 1822 and the Erie Canal in 1825. In 1822, Henry Burden established his iron works to manufacture iron plate, bells, and stoveplates. In 1825, Mrs. Hannah Lord Montague invented the "detachable" collar and gave birth to an important local industry. Construction started on the Schenectady & Troy Railroad in 1838 and was completed in 1842. With the coming of the railroad, Charles Veasie and Orasmus Eaton opened railroad coach works here. In 1835, the first bridge across the Hudson was opened to Green Island by the Rensselaer & Saratoga Railroad. Ebenezer Brown attempted commercial production of detachable collars in 1829. In 1834, Lyman Bennett opened the first successful collar factory. In 1845, he added cuffs to his line. Business boomed with the introduction of the sewing machine in 1852. Today the Cluett-Peabody plant on River Street is the largest producer of men's shirts in the world. This nine-story plant produces the famous Arrow shirt and houses an interesting collar museum.

By 1852, fancy clothes, horseshoes, iron products, coal tar, ammonium sulphate, phenol, and benzol were important products. The iron plates for the Monitor were manufactured at Troy. Horatio Winslow's Troy Iron Works were the first in the United States to use the Bessemer Process. Troy was the iron and steel center of the country until Andrew Carnegie opened his mills near Pittsburgh in 1873. The Troy Furnace of Republic Steel is still in operation.

Neighboring Lansingburgh, which was joined to Troy in 1901, was the home of Poor & Co. which manufactured rail joints. Other industries still active today include the manufacture of coke, engineering and surveying instruments, women's wear, and valves and fire hydrants (Ludlow Co.) Immigration of French Canadians about 1860 led to the development of knitting mills.

Troy was an early center of liberal social action and unionism. It was also a center of abolitionist activity. During the fugitive slave trial of Charles Nalle on April 27, 1860, Harriet Tubman led a riot which enabled Nalle to escape.

During the War of 1812, Troy added to Hudson folklore. Samuel Wilson (1766-1854), a former brickmaker and slaughterhouse operator had military contracts. He was what was then called a sutler. Later Wilson lived in Catskill. During his Troy sojourn, it was his business to pack and consign meat to a certain Elbert Anderson who was in charge of a cantonment at Greenbush. He would brand the meat with the initials "EA-US," standing for Elbert Anderson-United States. The "U.S." soon came to refer to "Uncle Sam" Wilson.

Troy was an educational center from early times. In 1814, Emma Willard founded the Troy Female Seminary. This was later called the Emma Willard School. In 1916, Mrs. Russell Sage founded Russell Sage College for

women, in honor of her late husband (1816-1906), a merchant and congressman. He is buried in Oakwood Cemetery.

The Rensselaer Polytechnic Institute, an engineering college, was founded in 1824 by Stephen Van Rensselaer "for the purpose of instructing persons in the application of science to the common purposes of life." Amos Eaton (1776-1842) was appointed senior professor. The original buildings were of Georgian design and built of brick and limestone. Today R.P.I. is one of the nation's top engineering schools with a worldwide reputation.

St. Joseph's Seminary, next to R.P.I., was founded in 1856. Its fine buildings are built of brick in the Romanesque Revival Style. There is a Gothic chapel built in 1933.

The Hudson Valley Community College is also located at Troy.

Major parks include Prospect Park, Frear Park, and Beman Park, as well as Sage Park and areas along the Wynantskill and Poestenkill and Lake Ida.

Other buildings of interest include:

1) The First Baptist Church, on Third Street, between Congress and State. This is a red brick structure with six Ionic columns and a pediment of white wood. It has a tower and tall spire, and dates from 1846.

2) St. Paul's Episcopal Church at the northeast corner of State and Third Streets, is the oldest church in the city. In English-Gothic style, it dates from 1827. It is built of limestone with wood trim.

3) The Emma Willard School is of English Collegiate-Gothic style (with Tudor and early English details). Built of Schoharie limestone, 1821. It has an octogonal tower with gargoyles and open tracery.

4) The Betsy Hart House, 59 Second Street, was built in 1827 for railroad magnate Richard P. Hart. Its style is Georgian Colonial. It was built of marble and has 13 rooms. The house is now owned by the Rensselaer County Historical Society and is now operated as a museum.

On May 10, 1862, a great fire destroyed most of Troy. At noon that day, a fire broke out on the Rensselaer & Saratoga Railroad bridge to Green Island, and the burning sparks were driven by a strong northwest wind into the heart of the city. It was thought that the fire was started by a spark from a locomotive igniting the wooden bridge. People were burned to death in the streets, and 507 buildings were destroyed by 6 P.M. when the fire died down.

In its heyday, Troy was served by freight and passenger trains of the Boston & Maine, Delaware & Hudson, and New York Central Railroads. The overnight Montreal Limited between New York and Montreal used to operate via Troy and the Green Island bridge. Today only the tracks of the former New York Central (now Conrail) still reach Troy. There is no passenger service.

At the head of ship navigation, Troy was an important steamboat port. Several lines of large steamers terminated here. There was also a local steamer to Albany.

146.30 Route 7-Nineteenth Street swing bridge
(horizontal clearance 181 feet; vertical clearance 32 feet).

146.40 South branch or sprout of Mohawk River enters from the west.

146.40-149.00 Green Island to west.
Formerly called Tibbett's Island, this was the site of important railroad locomotive and car shops.

146.50 Starbuck Island to west of vessel channel.
The channel between Starbuck and Green Island has only one- and two-foot depths.

146.50 Mount Olympus to east.
(elevation 535 feet).

146.75 Site of Green Island Bridge.

A former railroad, and later road bridge, this pioneer wooden railroad bridge of the Rensselaer & Saratoga Railroad, was the first bridge across the Hudson River. It opened on October 6th 1835 and burned on May 10th 1862. The most recent bridge was a lift bridge with horizontal clearance of 160 feet and closed vertical clearance of 24 feet and open clearance of 129 feet. It was built by the Delaware & Hudson Railroad in 1884 and was rebuilt in 1925. It was of lattice truss and through plate girder design, and had an overall length of 625 feet. Rail operations ceased in 1963, and the bridge was conveyed to the counties of Albany and Rensselaer for use as an automobile bridge. The bridge collapsed in March 1977.

147.20 Adams Island in mid-stream (channels either side). It was formerly called Big Stony Island.

147.50 Stony Island to west: west of navigation channel, offshore of Green Island.

147.75 Troy government lock and dam. This is the head of tide water navigation. The lock is near the eastern shore.

148.25 Jan Gowsen Island to west. This small island is offshore of Green Island.

149.00 Main sprout or branch of Mohawk River to west.

149.00-150.00 Van Schaick's Island to west. Formerly Cohoes Island, this was the site of the Northern Inland Navigation Co. canal, an unsuccessful project sponsored by Philip Schuyler in 1795. The Van Schaick House was built in 1777: two-story brick with gambrel roof. There was a military encampment on the island during the Revolution. In 1799, Col. Goose Van Schaick went into the "central wilderness" to destroy villages of the Onondaga.

149.80 Cohoes to west.

The name means "canoe falling," with possible reference to the falls of the Mohawk located here. Another interpretation is "the island at the falls." The author's preference is that it refers to the Indian word for salmon or shad, which were caught in the falls and rapids here.

In *Picturesque America* edited by William Cullen Bryant in 1872, R.E. Garczynski writes:

At Cohoes there is a great fall; about a mile above the falls, the river, broad and deep as it is, has been hemmed in by a dam, and a great portion of its waters drawn off by a water-power company. The little town of Cohoes is entirely manufacturing. It is the Lowell of New York. Here are the great Harmony Cotton-Mills; and here, also, are some twenty-five woolen-mills, besides paper-factories and other industries.

The falls of Cohoes are quite close to the Harmony Mills; and a capital view can be obtained of them, either from the bank in rear of one of the mills, or from an island in the river, at some distance below. Very much depends upon the season of the year as regards the impression which the falls make upon the mind of a traveller. In the dry season there is but little water, and hence the upper part of the falls appears like a series of grand rapids. In the early summer there is one tremendous descent of water, falling over seventy feet. The banks on either side are high and shaly, crowned generally with dark pines at the summit, and showing, below, a diagonal stratification, as if they had been upheaved.

(Picturesque America, edited by William Cullen Bryant, p.465.)

Another interesting description of the falls of the Mohawk is given by Benson Lossing in his book *The Hudson* of 1866: *The scenery about the mouth of the Mohawk, particularly in the vicinity of Cohoes Falls, is exceedingly picturesque, and at some points really grand. A highway bridge, nine-hundred feet in length, and a railway viaduct still longer, cross the river over the rapids a short distance below the falls. From the former, a fine distant view of the cataract and the rapids below may be obtained; but the best places to observe them in all their beauty and grandeur, are at the Cataract House, in the village of Cohoes, which stands upon the summit verge of a precipice one hundred and seventy feet in height. Down a steep slope of that precipice, for about fifty feet, the proprietor has constructed a flight of steps, and upon the top of a broad terrace at their foot he has planted a flower garden, for the enjoyment of visitors. Around its edge, from which may be obtained a view of the entire cataract, is a railing with seats, and there the visitor may contemplate at ease the wild scene on every hand. On his left, as he gazes up the river, rush large streams of water from the top of the precipice above him, in almost perpendicular currents, from the waste-sluices of a canal, which, commencing at a dam almost two miles above the falls, conveys water to numerous mill-wheels in the village. By this means immense hydraulic power is obtained and distributed.*

The water-power at Cohoes is under the control of a stock company, who rented it to the proprietors of mills and factories. The entire fall of water controlled by the company is one hundred and twenty feet; and the minimum supply of water is one thousand cubic feet each second. The estimated value of the various articles manufactured here is nearly three millions of dollars per annum.

Below the fall, the water rushes over a rocky bed, in foaming rapids between high banks, to the plain, where the islands divide it into channels, and through these it flows gently into the Hudson.

(Lossing, *The Hudson,* pp. 109-111.)

Cohoes was settled by the Dutch and incorporated in 1869. Knitted goods, paper products, and shoddy are manufactured here. Its population is 18,653. Here are located the great brick mill buildings of the Harmony Mill and Star Woolen Mill with their mansard roofs and towers dating from between 1837 and 1845. There are also many old workers' tenement houses, some dating from the 1870s. This is a typical late nineteenth-century industrial city.

Cohoes is served by the Delaware & Hudson Railroad and Amtrak.

149.80 Mohawk River to west.

Originally called the Maaquas River, after the Indians dwelling along it. It rises near Rome, in central New York State, and flows 140 miles eastward into the Hudson at Cohoes. For most of this distance, it is canalized as part of the New York State Barge Canal. Earlier the Erie Canal had paralleled it, as did the later railroads and highways. From Rome, it flows east past Utica, Herkimer, Little Falls, Canajoharie, Fonda, Fultonville, Auriesville, Tribes Hill, Fort Hunter, Amsterdam, Schenectady, and Crescent to the power dam above Cohoes Falls. In the early nineteenth-century, this was the site of a pleasure resort with terraces and gardens. With the building of the Harmony Mill in 1837, the water was diverted, and large mill buildings and row houses were erected for the workers. The area remains industrialized today, and only a trickle of water flows over the falls. After going over more rapids, it flows into the Hudson's West Channel near Simmons and Van Schaick Islands. It receives the waters of the large Schoharie Creek, which rises in the Catskills, at Fort Hunter, near Tribes' Hill.

149.50 Lansingburg to east.
Formerly New City, before the Revolution, it was incorporated into Troy in 1901.

149.90 Simmons Island to west.
In mouth of Mohawk River. Van Schaick Island to its east and Peobles Island to its north.

149.90 Route 470 highway bridge.

150.40 Peoble's Island to west.
In the mouth of the Mohawk River, this was formerly Van Hover's Island.

150.40 Second Island to west:
in the north sprout of the Mohawk River, between Peoble's Island and the mainland.

150.45 Goat Island to west:
in the north sprout of the Mohawk River, between Peoble's Island and the mainland.

150.60 Bock Island to west:
in the north sprout of the Mohawk River, between Peoble's Island and the mainland.

150.60 Buttermilk Falls to west:
in the channel of the Mohawk River between Peoble's Island and Van Schaick Island.

151.00 Revolutionary War breastworks to west:
on the northern end of Peoble's Island.

151.00 North sprout or channel of Mohawk River to west.

146.75 to 151.00
The Green Island Branch of the Delaware & Hudson Railroad, formerly the Rensselaer &

Saratoga Railroad, ran north from the Green Island bridge at Troy to Waterford along the Hudson, on Green, Van Schaick, and Peoble's Islands. This route was used by the Montreal Limited, which ran by Troy and bypassed Albany and Cohoes, on the main line. The great Gilbert Car Works were located on Green Island. Eaton, Gilbert & Co.

151.00 Entrance of New York State Barge Canal and locks to west.
(Erie Canal).

151.40 Waterford to west.
This is a former important point on the Erie Canal.

151.50 Saratoga County
The western bank from here to Glens Falls is occupied by Saratoga County. Its county seat is Saratoga Springs, its area, 814 square miles. It was taken from Albany County in 1791.

151.40 Route U.S. 4 bridge

152.00 Pleasantdale to east.

153.75 Campbell Island.

155.00 Half Moon to west.

157.00 McDonald Creek to west.

159.00 Lock No. 2.

159.35 Quack Island.

161.00 Mechanicville to west.
With a population of 6,247, it was settled before 1700, incorporated as a village in 1859, and made a city in 1915. There are railroad shops here and bricks, paper and knit goods are manufactured. This is the home of Elmer Ephraim Ellsworth (1837-1861), a Civil War hero. There is an important junction of the Boston & Maine, and Delaware & Hudson Railroads here.

161.00 Anthony Kill to east.

161.25 Highway Bridge.

161.25 Hemstreet Park to east.

161.25 Schaghticoke to east:
beyond Hemstreet Park, on the
Hoosic River.

161.75 Lock No. 3

162.00 Stillwater Junction to west.
The Boston & Maine, and Saratoga & Schuylerville Railroads
used to meet here. The Saratoga & Schuylerville is now
abandoned.

162.40 Riverside to west.

**162.50 Boston & Maine Railroad
bridge.**
Built by the Boston, Hoosac
Tunnel & Western Railway Co.
in 1879, it is on the present
mainline between Boston and
Rotterdam Junction, N.Y.

163.00 Green Island.

163.50 Hoosic River to east.
Originally called the Walloom-
sac, and also spelled Hoosac
and Hoosick, it is the Indian
name for "place of stones." It
rises in Cheshire Reservoir in
the Berkshire Mountains of
Massachusetts, south of Adams.
Then it flows north past Adams
and North Adams, thence west
to Williamstown, where it is
joined from the south by the
Green River. It then turns north-
west and enters Vermont near
Pownal. After passing North
Pownal, Vermont, it enters
New York and flows past North
Petersburg, Hoosick, Hoosick
Falls, and North Hoosick to
Eagle Bridge. Here it turns
directly west and flows past
Buskirk, Johnsonville, Valley
Falls, and Schaghticoke before
entering the Hudson.

164.00 Lock No. 4:
in east channel.

164.30 Stillwater to west.

164.30 Schuyler Creek to west.

164.30 Route 67 bridge.

165.30 Mill Hollow Brook to east.

168.00 Bemis Heights to west.

**168.00 Site of rope ferry, opera-
tional in 1860.**

**168.20-171.20 Saratoga National
Historical Park to west.**
On October 17, 1777, General
Horatio Gates, with a varied
collection of troops calling
themselves an American army,
defeated an invading British
force under Gen. John ("Gentleman Johnny") Burgoyne and
prevented British control of the
strategic Hudson Valley. This
was the turning point of the
American fortunes, and directly
led to French intervention on
the American side.

It was the grand strategy of
the English to gain control of
the Hudson Valley between
Canada and New York City and
thus split New England from
the other colonies. To prevent
this, Washington determined to
hold the Highlands of the Hudson and the upper Hudson
Valley at all costs. In the great
British campaign of 1777, the
chief strategy was for Gen.
John Burgoyne to march down
from Canada via Lake Champlain and hook up with Sir
William Howe and Sir Henry
Clinton, who were to move up
from New York and, with Barry
St. Leger, who was to march
from the west via Oswego and
the Mohawk Valley. Burgoyne
was halted at the Battle of
Saratoga and St. Leger at the
Battle of Oriskany. For reasons
that are not yet determined,
Howe and Clinton failed to
move north from New York
according to schedule. Thus
the campaign was abortive, and
the American victories were a
turning point in the long war.
The British never did succeed
in splitting the colonies, although they made a foray as
far north as Clermont on the
Hudson in 1777 and burned
Kingston.

Generals Philip Schuyler, Benedict Arnold, and Gates led the American side. The Hessian Baron Reidesel and Generals Phillips and Simon Fraser served under Burgoyne.

There is a visitors' center and nine miles of drives with site markers. A free folder maps the battlefield route. Demonstrations are offered afternoons in July and August.

168.50 Mill Creek to west.

169.30 Kidney Creek to east.

171.20 McAuley Brook to east.

171.20 Site of Powers-Briggs rope ferry.

172.45 Site of Sarles rope ferry (operational from the early 19th century to about 1930).

172.80 Wilbur's Basin to west.
This is an old Champlain canal basin.

175.80 Coveville to west.
This was formerly called Do-ve-gat and Van Vechten's Cove.

176.50-178.00 Site of American fortifications of 1777 on hill to east.

178.25 Site of Fort Clinton to west.
This is a French and Indian War fortification.

178.25 Victory Mills to west.

178.50 Fish Kill or Fish Creek to west.

178.50 General Phillip Schuyler House to west.
On the south side of Fish Creek, this is a restored two-story clapboard structure dating back to 1777. The original house was burned at the time of the Battle of Saratoga.

In 1745, there stood a brick mansion on this site, owned and occupied by a kinsman of Philip Schuyler. This house was attacked by a band of Frenchmen and Indians, and the owner was shot and his body consumed by flames. This property

was then bequeathed to his nephew Philip, who built a country mansion on the site. In 1777, Gen. Burgoyne ordered the house burned—an act which he later came to regret upon making the personal acquaintance of Gen. Schuyler, who treated him very well when his prisoner. Schuyler built the present house as replacement soon thereafter, and used it as his country seat until his death in 1804.

178.80 Greenwich to east.
Note—From mile 164.30 on, the eastern and northern bank is occupied by Washington County. It has an area of 837 square miles. Hudson Falls is the county seat. It was taken from Tryon County in 1784 and was named in honor of George Washington. Tryon County had been established in 1772 and named for Gov. William Tryon of New York. It was taken from Albany County and included all settlements west and southwest of Schenectady as well as the present Washington County. Tryon County no longer exists, all its area having been assigned to other counties.

178.80 Schuylerville to west.
The village occupies the site of Gen. Burgoyne's intrenched camp at the time he surrendered. The Bullard Paper Mills were operating here in about 1870. Formerly, a bridge of the Greenwich & Johnsonville Railroad (now defunct) crossed the Hudson from here to Thomson. It was washed out and was never replaced.

178.80 Route 29 bridge.

179.00 Site of Fort Hardy to west.
This dates back to the French & Indian Wars.

179.00 Fort Saratoga to east.

180.00 Lock No. 5 to west.
180.00 Batten Kill to east.
The Di-On-On-Deh-O-Wa or
"great falls" of the Batten Kill
are a short way upstream. The
Batten Kill rises near Ludlow,
Vermont, and flows south past
Danby, Mount Tabor, Manchester, and Arlington. Here it turns
west and flows past West Arlington and into New York State. It
continues west past Shushan,
East Greenwich, Battenville,
Greenwich, and Middle Falls to
the Hudson.
180.10 Site of Hessian camp of
1777 on east.
180.50 Site of crossing of British
forces in 1777.
180.75 Stark's Knob to west:
site of key battery that blocked
British in 1777.
181.00 Dam.
181.30 Northumberland to west.
181.30 Thomson to east.
181.40 Route U.S. 4 bridge.
182.00 Bacon Hill to west.
184.25 Saratoga Dam.
184.25 Lock No. 6 to east.
185.00 Fort Miller to east.
This is a small community.
There was a small fort on the
west shore of the Hudson in the
French and Indian War. There
are no remains.
186.00 Payne's Island.
186.45 Dams.
186.50 Normal Pool.
187.00 Gansevoort to west.
(inland on Route 32).
187.25 Moses Kill to east.
188.00 Galusha's Island.
188.50 South Argyle to east.
189.90 Bell's Island.
190.25 Fort Edward Center to east.
Here are located the Gansevoort Mill House of 1781 and
the Fort Edward Center
Friends' Meeting House (clapboard, early nineteenth century).

190.25 Munro's Island.
192.20 Lock No. 7 of Champlain
Canal.
This canal leaves the Hudson
here and follows Bond Creek to
the northeast and Whitehall, at
the southern tip of Lake Champlain.
192.20 Bond Creek to east.
192.25-193.00 Roger's Island.
Armies were encamped here
during the French and Indian
War. This island was associated
with Maj. Robert Rogers.
192.50 Site of Fort Edward to east.
One of the largest garrisons in
North America during the
French and Indian Wars. It has
left no significant remains. Built
by Phineas Lyman in 1755, it was
briefly occupied by Burgoyne in
1777.
192.50 Fort Edward to east.
It was incorporated in 1849.
Paper milling is the principal
industry. There is a Delaware
& Hudson (Amtrak) passenger
station here.
193.00 McCrae House to east.

This is a clapboard, late eighteenth
century structure. There is a famous
legend associated with this locality. I
shall quote at length from Benson
Lossing's *The Hudson:*

*Fort Edward was strengthened by the
republicans, and properly garrisoned,
when the revolution broke out in 1775.
When General Burgoyne, with his invading army of British regulars, hired
Germans, French, Canadians and Indians, appeared at the foot of Lake
Champlain, General Philip Schuyler was
the commander in Chief of the republican army in the Northern Department.
His headquarters were at Fort Anne, and
General St. Clair commanded the important post of Ticonderoga. In July, Burgoyne came sweeping down the lake
triumphantly. St. Clair fled from Ticon-*

deroga, and his army was scattered and sorely smitten in the retreat. When the British advanced to Skenesborough, at the head of the lake, Schuyler retreated to Fort Edward, felling trees across the old military road, demolishing the causeways over the great Kingsbury marshes, and destroying the bridges, to obstruct the invader's progress. With great labour and perseverance Burgoyne moved forward, and on the 29th of July he encamped upon the high bank of the Hudson, at the great bend where the village of Sandy Hill now stands.

At this time a tragedy occurred near Fort Edward, which produced a great sensation throughout the country, and has been a theme for history, poetry, romance, and song. It was the death of Jenny M'Crea, the daughter of a Scotch Presbyterian clergyman, who is described as lovely in disposition, graceful in manners, and so intelligent and winning in all her ways, that she was a favourite of all who knew her. She was visiting a Tory friend at Fort Edward, at this time, and was betrothed to a young man of the neighborhood, who was a subaltern in Burgoyne's army. On the approach of the invaders her brother, who lived near, fled, with his family, down the river, and desired Jenny to accompany them. She preferred to stay under the protection of her Tory friend, who was a widow, and a cousin of General Fraser, of Burgoyne's army.

Burgoyne had found it difficult to restrain the cruelty of his Indians. To secure their co-operation he had offered them a bounty for prisoners and scalps, at the same time forbidding them to kill any person not in arms for the sake of scalps. The offer of bounties stimulated the savages to seek captives other than those in the field, and they went out in small parties for the purpose. One of these prowled around Fort Edward early on the morning after Burgoyne arrived at Sandy Hill, and, entering the house where Jenny was staying, carried away the young lady and her friend. A negro

boy alarmed the garrison, and a detachment was sent after the Indians, who were fleeing with their prisoners toward the camp. They had caught two horses, and on one of them Jenny was already placed by them, when the detachment assailed them with a volley of musketry. The savages were unharmed, but one of the bullets mortally wounded their fair captive. She fell and expired, as tradition relates, near a pine-tree, which remained as a memorial of the tragedy until a few years ago. Having lost their prisoner, they secured her scalp, and with her black tresses wet with her warm blood, they hastened to the camp. The friend of Jenny had just arrived, and the locks of the maiden, which were of great length and beauty, were recognized by her. She charged the Indians with her murder, which they denied, and told the story substantially as it is here related.

This appears, from the corroborating circumstances, to be the simple truth of a story which, as it went from lip to lip, became magnified into a tale of darkest horror, and produced a wide-spread indignation. General Gates, who had just superseded General Schuyler in the command of the northern army, took advantage of the excitement which it produced, to increase the hatred of the British in the hearts of the people, and he charged Burgoyne with crimes utterly foreign to the gentleman's nature. In a published letter, he accused him of hiring savages to "scalp Europeans and the descendants of Europeans;" spoke of Jenny as having been "dressed to meet her promised husband, but met her murderers," employed by Burgoyne; asserted that she with several women and children, had been taken "from the house into the woods, and there scalped and mangled in a most shocking manner;" and alleged that he had "paid the price of blood!" This letter, so untruthful and ungenerous, was condemned by Gates's friends in the army. But it had the desired effect; and the sad story of Jenny's death was used with power *against the ministry by the opposition in the British parliament.*

The lover of Jenny left the army, and settled in Canada, where he lived to be an old man. He was naturally gay and garrulous, but after that event he was ever sad and taciturn. He never married, and avoided society. When the anniversary of the tragedy approached, he would shut himself in his room, and refuse to see his most intimate acquaintances; and at all times his friends avoided speaking of the American revolution in his presence. The body of Jenny was buried on her brother's land; it was re-interred at Fort Edward in 1826, with imposing ceremonies; and again in 1852, her remains found a new resting-place in a beautiful cemetary, half-way between Fort Edward and Sandy Hill. Her grave is near the entrance; and upon a plain white marble stone, six feet in height, standing at its head, is the following inscription:

> *Here rest the remains of Jane M'Crea, aged 17; made captive and murdered by a band of Indians, while on a visit to a relative in the neighbourhood,* A.D. *1777. To commemorate one of the most thrilling incidents in the annals of the American revolution, to do justice to the fame of the gallant British officer to whom she was affianced, and as a simple tribute to the memory of the departed, this stone is erected by her niece, Sarah Hanna Payne,* A.D. *1852.*

(Lossing, *The Hudson*, pp. 76-79.)

192.80 Delaware & Hudson Railroad bridge.
The first railroad bridges here were built in 1876 and 1880. The present bridge was built in 1924 and reconstructed in 1941. It was engineered by the D.&H. engineering department and was built by AmBridge Company. It carries the main line to Canada.

192.90 Route 197 bridge.
194.00 Gravel pits to east.
194.00 Moreau township to west.

195.30 Power plant to west.
195.50 Baker's Falls.
The river here is abut 400 feet in width. The entire descent of the water, in the course of a mile, is between 70 and 80 feet.

195.60 Sewage disposal plant to east.
195.60 Road bridge.
196.00 Hudson Falls to east.
With a population of 7,917, this is the seat of Washington County. Originally called Sandy Hill, it was settled in 1761 and incorporated in 1810. Papermaking is the principal industry. It is on the Glens Falls (formerly Lake George) branch of Delaware & Hudson Railroad. There is a very attractive town square here.

196.00 Fenimore to west.
196.50 Big Bend.
Here the river bends to the west.

197.00 Gravel pits to north.
197.50 Quarries to north and south.
198.00 Sewage disposal plant to north.
198.50 Quarry to north.
198.50 Paper mills to north.
199.00 Cooper's Cave:
In island in midstream in rapids.

199.10 Glens Falls
(dam and power canals on sides). Again we will quote from Benson Lossing's *The Hudson:*

Glen's Falls consist of a series of rapids and cascades, along a descent of about eighty feet, the water flowing over ragged masses of black marble, which here form the bed and banks of the river. Hawk-eye, in Cooper's "Last of the Mohicans," has given an admirable description of these falls, as they appeared before the works of man changed their features. He is standing in a cavern, or irregular arched way, in the rock below the bridge, in the time of the old French

313

POTTER ROAD 473
473
FIREBREAK
Gravel Pit
Halfway
466
Cem
Keenan Intake ROAD
Res 479
471 PEGGY ANN
PEGGY BM 753
ANN
Creek
ROAD
TUTHILL RD
ADIRONDACKS
Junk Yard
SHERMAN
58 467
WEST
Clendon
AVE
404
ROAD 895
LUZERNE BM 473
Mt Hermon 428
Cem
ROAD
162
Brook
ANN
Trailer
Park
Junk Yard
Gravel Pit
Junk Yard
Gle
220
MOUNTAIN GLEASON ROAD
433
BM
398 389 ROAD 28
SHERMAN
CORINTH
LUZERNE
Ski Area
ROAD
ISLAND
Ski Lift SKI LIFT
MTS
HUDSON
58 28
Sherman Island
Powerplant
BM 393
28
ROAD
479
LAKE LUZERNE
WARREN CO
SARATOGA CO
ROAD
CORINTH 381
32 28
32 Hartman
Cem
Gravel Pit
408 POTTER
Cem
359 BUTLER
402
OLD BEAR
PALMERTOWN
REDMOND
Palmertown
Mtn
ROAD
RANGE

war, with Uncas and Major Heywood, and Cora and Alice Munro, the daughters of the commandant at Fort William Henry, on Lake George, when Montcalm with his motley horde of French and Indians was approaching. "Ay," he said, "there are the falls on two sides of us, and the river above and below. If you had daylight, it would be worth the trouble to step up on the height of this rock, and look at the perversity of the water. It falls by no rule at all: sometimes it leaps, sometimes it tumbles; there is skips — here it shoots; hereabouts, it pitches into deep hollows, that rumble and quake the 'arth, and thereaway it ripples and sings like a brook, fashioning whirlpools and gullies in the old stone, as if 'twere no harder than trodden clay. The whole design of the river seems disconcerted. First, it runs smoothly, as if meaning to go down the descent as things were ordered; then it angles about and faces the shores; nor are there places wanting where it looks backward, as if unwilling to leave the wilderness to mingle with the salt!*

The falls had few of these features when we visited them (1866). The volume of water was so small that the stream was almost hidden in the deep channels in the rock worn by the current during the lapse of centuries.

> (Lossing, *The Hudson*, pp. 67-68.)

Lossing's final comment is still true in 1978. Most of the water is diverted to side canals. Only after a heavy rainfall, or during the spring runoff of melting snows in the Adirondacks, can a fine flow of water be seen. When the writer was a boy, it used to be possible to descend to the rocks in the falls by means of a staircase from the Route 9 bridge. This is now closed off, and it is quite difficult to see the falls today.

199.10 Route 9 bridge.
199.10 South Glens Falls to south.
199.10 Glens Falls to north.

With a population of 17,222, this place was called Chepontuo by the Indians, meaning "a difficult place to get around." The area was part of the 23,000-acre Queensbury Patent. It was first settled in 1763. In 1780, it was destroyed by the British. In 1788, Col. John Glen of Schenectady acquired and built mills here. It was incorporated as a village in 1839 and as a city in 1908. The manufacture of shirts and cellulose was started in 1879. Principal industries are pulp and paper mills and the manufacture of clothing. Glens Falls is the birthplace of Charles Evans Hughes (1862-1948), lawyer, jurist, statesman, and Chief Justice of the United States Supreme Court.

200.00 Pruyn's Island.
200.00 Log Pool.

In past years a great boom was strung across the river here to collect the logs sent downriver during the drives and prevent their going over the falls and being splintered.

314.00 Lake Tear of the Clouds

(elevation 4,322 feet). On the slopes of Mount Marcy, elevation 5,344 feet. This is the highest source of the Hudson.

7

Excursion Information

Lower West Side Road Route

Southbound Express Route to Atlantic Highlands Twin Lights

0.00 Start at east end of Lincoln Tun-
('0.10 nel, 7th Avenue and West
E.R.M.') Thirty-ninth Street, Manhattan. Enter Lincoln Tunnel
westbound.
Take Interstate 495 to the
New Jersey Turnpike,

-4.00 Interstate 95. Enter Turnpike at
Secaucus.

-6.00 Snake Hill on right. Mentioned
by Washington Irving in his
*Knickerbocker History of
New York,* it is now almost
totally destroyed by quarry
operations.

-6.75 Cross Hackensack River. Cross
New York & Greenwood Lake
Railroad (now Conrail).
You have been running parallel
to the former Pennsylvania Railroad main line on the left. This
is now Amtrak's Northeast Corridor Route.

-8.50 Cross the Morris & Essex Division of the former DL&W RR,
now Conrail, former P.R.R.
lines, now Amtrak, and former
Hudson & Manhattan Rail-
road, now P.A.T.H.

-8.55 Cross Passaic River. Newark is
to the right.

-9.00 Pass beneath the Pulaski Skyway, named after Polish
patriot Casimir Pulaski (1784-
1779), who fought in the
American Revolution. A
nobleman by birth, he came
to America with a letter of
introduction to George Washington from Benjamin Franklin. He fought in the battles
of Brandywine and German-
town. In 1778, he resigned
his cavalry command rather
than serve under Anthony
Wayne. He formed his own

cavalry unit, the Pulaski
Legion, and was mortally
wounded while leading a cav-
alry charge in the attack on
Savannah, Georgia. The
Pulaski Skyway carries U.S.
Routes 1A and 9A and pro-
vides panoramic views.

-11.25 Exit for Newark International
Airport, a facility of the Port
Authority of New York and
New Jersey. Operated under
a lease from the city of
Newark dating from 1948, it
was first opened on October
1, 1928 and then consisted of
only 68 acres. Today it has
2,300 acres. There are three
major runways and more than
twelve miles of seventy-five-
foot wide taxiways. Newark is
regularly served by sixteen
scheduled airlines with
flights to all parts of the
world. The beautiful, new
passenger terminals A and B
were completed in 1972-
1973. The airport is fully
equipped with the most
modern navigational equipment. In 1975, the airport
handled 166,000 plane movements, 6,266,000 commer-
cial passengers, 112,000 tons
of air cargo, and 35,000 tons
of air mail in 1975.

-11.25 Exit for bridge across Newark
Bay to Bayonne and Holland
Tunnel.

-12.25 Port Newark on left. Parallel
railroad on left is former line
of Central Railroad of New
Jersey, now Conrail.

-13.25 Elizabeth Port Authority
Marine Terminal on left.
Port Newark was opened by

the city of Newark in 1915 and came under Port Authority operation in 1948. There is berthing space with 23,387 lineal feet of wharfage and 848 acres of shoreside staging area. The port handled 1,873,955 long tons in 1975. There are thirteen miles of roadway and thirty-eight miles of railroad tracks and three major containership terminals.

Facilities include public cold storage warehouses, a frozen meat inspection building, a wine terminal, a fumigation building, seventy miscellaneous service buildings, a public truck scales, a Waterfront Commission Employment Center, a Seamen's Church Institute Recreation Center, and two commercial bank buildings. Major containership facilities belong to the Maersk Red Star Line and Universal Terminal and Stevedoring Corp.

The Elizabeth-Port Authority Marine Terminal is the major containerport of the United States. Twenty-two container cranes serve the same number of container ship berths—16,934 linear feet of wharfage. Port Authority operation began in 1958. In 1975, 8,099,841 long tons of cargo were handled. Major steamship lines operating from the port are Sea-Land Service, Inc.; Puerto Rico Maritime Shipping Authority; Atlantic Container Line, Ltd. Smaller lines are served by the stevedoring facilities of International Operating Co., Pittston Stevedoring Corp. and Maher Terminals, Inc.

-15.25 Elizabethport Cross former main line of Central Railroad of New Jersey, now Conrail.

-15.50 Elizabeth to right. The tall building is the Union County Courthouse.

-16.50 Cross Elizabeth River.

-16.75 Pass beneath western approach to Goethal's Bridge. See article on Arthur Kill. Staten Island to left.

-17.25 Cross Morse's Creek.

-19.75 Cross Rahway River.

-20.25 Raritan Arsenal on right. Carteret on left.

-22.50 Port Reading on left.

-23.75 Sewaren on left.

-23.80 Cross Woodbridge Creek. Woodbridge on right.

-24.00 Cross former Pennsylvania Railroad Perth Amboy Branch, now Conrail, used by North Jersey Shore trains.

-25.00 Exit 11: Leave New Jersey Turnpike. Enter Garden State Parkway, southbound.

-27.00 Perth Amboy to left.

-28.00 (-20.00 E.R.M.) Cross Raritan River on Alfred E. Driscoll Memorial Bridge, named for a former New Jersey governor.

-29.00 Pay toll.

-36.50 Exit 117, Matawan; *exit from* Parkway. Enter Route 36 east.

-49.50 Highlands: *turn right* up Light House road to

-49.70 Twin Lights (-23.00 E.R.M.). See article on River Route.

Lower West Side Road Route

0.00 (-23.00 E.R.M.) Historic Twin Lights. Start downhill on Light House Road.

0.20 *Turn right* on Highland Avenue.

0.30 Cross Portland Road

0.40 *Turn left* under bridge. Navesink River on right.

0.41 *Turn left* again up onto Route 36 West.

0.45 Gertrude Ederle Park on right.

0.50 *Turn right* on Route 36 West, Memorial Drive.

1.60 *Turn right* on Scenic Road.

1.80 *Bend right* on Scenic Road.

2.10 View to right. Eastpointe Apartments to left.

2.60 Viewpoint on right. Bachert's Hofbrauhaus on left.

3.20 *Bear right.*

3.50 View of Raritan Bay on right.

3.60 Atlantic Highlands town line.

4.30 *Turn right* on First Avenue.

5.10 *Turn around:* foot of First Avenue and Sutton Walk. Site of former combined steamboat and railroad pier and terminal.

5.15 *Turn left* on Ocean Boulevard.

6.00 Cross bridge.

6.10 *Turn left* on Lower Road.

6.15 *Bear left* on Hilton Road.

6.30 *Bear left* on Bayside Road.

6.70 Road turns to red dirt (a good road).

8.20 Pavement resumes.

9.50 *Bear left.*

9.60 *Turn right* on Shore Drive. (large willow tree and gazebo; Marie Manor Apartments on right.)

9.80 *Turn left* on Water Witch Avenue.

9.90 *Turn right* on Bay Avenue, Route 8.

10.70 Go under bridge.

10.80 *Turn Right up hill on Highland Avenue.*

10.90 *Turn sharp right* onto Route 36 East and bridge.

11.00 Cross Navesink River. Seawall and Atlantic Ocean straight ahead.

11.20 *Turn right* around cloverleaf to Sandy Hook.

11.60 Gateway National Recreation Area, Sandy Hook.

11.90 Fishing Area No. 1, dunes.

13.30 Ocean bathing area No. 1.

13.50 Spermaceti Cove Visitor Center on right.

13.60 Ocean bathing area No. 2.

13.70 *Turn around.* End of open public road. Entrance to Fort Hancock.

13.70 (-21.00 E.R.M.) See Sandy Hook article.

16.40 Cross Navesink River. Continue on Route 36 West, Memorial Drive.

20.10 *Turn right* on First Avenue, Atlantic Highlands.

20.30 *Turn left* on West Highland Avenue.

20.50 Cross brook.

21.30 *Turn right* on Leonard Avenue.

21.70 *Turn left* on Beach Avenue.

21.90 Leonardo Beach. *Turn around.* State Marina.

22.10 Conover Beach Beacon.

22.10 *Turn right* on Leonard Avenue.

22.60 *Turn right* on Route 36 West.

22.70 Pass beneath U.S. Government Railroad, which connects the U.S. Naval Ammunition Depot at Earle with the Navy long pier at Leonardo on Sandy Hook Bay.

22.80 Entrance Naval ammunition depot.

23.60 *Turn right* on East Road.

24.10 *Turn right* on Main Street. Belford.

24.50 Cross Compton Creek.

24.65 *Turn left* on Port Monmouth Road (Also called Seabrook Ave.).

25.00 Cross former tracks leading to railroad pier.
25.00 *Bear right* at fork.
25.30 *Seabrook* Homestead on right, at foot of Wilson Avenue. Now houses Shoal Harbor Marine Museum with displays of the fishing and shipping trades. Maintained by the Middletown Township Historical Society, this house was built ca. 1664-1668 by Thomas Whitlock, who moved here from Long Island. From 1696 until 1910, it was the homestead of the Seabrook Family. In the late 18th century, it also served as a stagecoach tavern. As this was the only house on the dunes at the time of the Revolution, the British believed that the owners were spying on their ships. Actually, the spy was Col. John Stilwell, who was stationed on a high hill above the beach. The house was also known as the "Spy House."
25.30 *Turn left* on Wilson Avenue.
25.90 *Turn right* on Main Street.
26.30 *Turn right* on Bray Avenue.
26.80 Cross Pew's Creek.
27.40 *Turn left* on Port Monmouth Road.
27.60 *Turn right* on Ocean Avenue.
27.80 *Ideal Beach.*
27.80 *Turn left* on Seabreeze Avenue.
28.00 *Bear right* on Shore Boulevard.
28.00 Keansburg.
28.60 (-21.00 E.R.M.)

28.60 Cross Main Street. *Enter* Center Avenue.
29.00 Point Comfort-Keansburg (-21.00 E.R.M.): former steamboat pier.
29.00 *Turn left* on Carr Avenue.
29.80 *Turn right* on Church Street.
30.00 Cross Waackaack Creek (Waycake Creek). Continue straight.
30.00 Road becomes 10th Street.
30.30 *Turn left* on Laurel Avenue.
30.60 *Turn right* on Route 36 West.
31.70 Cross Thorne's Creek.
31.72 Natco Lake on right.
31.75 Union Beach.
31.75 *Turn right* on Shore Road.
32.00 *Turn left* on Jersey Avenue.
32.10 *Turn right* on Union Avenue.
32.40 Cross Flat Creek.
32.70 View of Raritan Bay, Staten Island, Verrazano Bridge.
32.70 Road becomes Front Street.
33.10 Coneskonk Point.
33.10 *Turn left* on Dock Street.
33.50 *Turn right* on Florence Avenue.
33.90 Cross brook.
34.10 *Turn right* on Broadway.
34.40 Cross Chingarora Creek.
34.50 *Bear right* on First Street.
35.10 Keyport.
35.10 *Turn right* on Broad Street.
35.20 View of Raritan Bay and Matawan Creek.
35.20 *Turn left* on American Legion Drive.
35.50 *Turn right* on Front Street.
35.60 Cross Luppatatcong Creek.
35.90 Cross Matawan Creek.
36.40 Cliffwood Beach.

Option 1   Cliffwood Beach sidetrip.

36.40 *Bear right* on Shore Concourse.
36.50 *Turn right* on Cliffwood Avenue.
37.00 *Bear right* on Shore Concourse South.
37.40 *Turn left* on Beachwood Way.
37.50 *Turn right* on North Concourse.
37.55 Cliffwood Beach: views.

37.55 *Turn left* on Woodcrest Drive.
37.60 *Turn left* on Seawood Drive.
37.75 *Turn right* on North Concourse.
38.00 *Bear left.*
38.05 *Bear right* on Cliffwood Avenue.
38.60 *Turn right* on Route 35 West.

Option 2   Get onto Route 35 West.

You are now at mile 38.60.

38.60 *Head west* on Route 35.

39.10 Cross Whale Creek, Madison township line.

39.10 Leave Monmouth County. Enter Middlesex County.

39.30 Pirate Ship building.

39.30 Florence Harbor section of Cliffwood Beach.

39.30 *Turn right* on Ocean Boulevard.

39.60 *Bear left* on Raritan Boulevard (concrete road): view.

39.90 Back at Pirate Ship building.

39.90 *Turn right* on Route 35 West.

40.50 Cross Marquis Creek.

40.50 Laurence Harbor line.

41.40 Cross Cheesecake Creek: extensive view to right.

41.65 Cross New York & Long Branch Railroad, Conrail system.

42.00 Morgan.

42.40 *Bear Right* on South Pine Avenue.

43.50 *Turn right* on Catherine Street.

43.60 Cross Raritan Valley Railroad (independent short line), running from South Amboy to New Brunswick.

43.70 *Turn left* on South Stevens Avenue.

44.10 South Amboy.

44.10 *Turn right* on Main Street.

44.30 Public Service Electric & Gas Co. power plant on right.

44.40 Pass under Camden & Amboy Railroad (formerly Pennsylvania Railroad; now Conrail system): New Jersey's first railroad—1831.

45.30 Traffic circle.

45.30 *Bear right* on Route 35.

45.90 Begin Victory Bridge across Raritan River.

46.20 Thomas A. Edison Bridge (Routes U.S. 9) and Alfred E. Driscoll Bridge (Garden State Parkway) to left.

46.20 New York & Long Branch Railroad Bridge to right.

46.50 End of Victory Bridge.

46.70 *Turn right* on Main Street.

46.70 Perth Amboy. Settled in 1683 and incorporated in 1718, it was the capital of East Jersey from 1686 until the union of East and West Jersey, and thereafter, for a time, alternate capital with Burlington. Great growth came after 1876, when it became the tidewater terminal of the Lehigh Valley Railroad, and much coal was shipped from here. It is still the seat of the General Proprietors of the Eastern Division of New Jersey. This organization still holds shares and meets regularly to distribute any new lands discovered in its portion of New Jersey. The population is 38,798. Principal industries are the smelting and refining of metals. Formerly there was an extensive brick, tile, pottery, and terra-cotta industry here.

47.50 Cross over the New York & Long Branch Railroad (Conrail system).

47.50 Perth Amboy passenger depot.

47.70 *Turn right* on Hobart Street.

47.80 *Turn left* on Market Street.

48.00 Traffic circle.

48.00 *Turn right* on High Street.

48.40 *Turn left* on Sadowski Parkway.

48.40 Waterfront Pavilion: view of Raritan Bay and River and railroad hopper car dumpers in South Amboy across the river.

48.60 Street becomes Water Street.

48.60 Arthur Kill on right.

48.90 *Turn right* on Gordon Street.

48.95 *Turn left* on Front Street.

49.00 Former ferry to Tottenville, Staten Island.

49.00 *Turn left* on Smith Street.

49.40 *Turn right on State Street.*

49.45 *Turn left* on Fayette Street.

49.50 *Bear right* on New Brunswick Avenue.

49.80 Cross New York & Long Branch Railroad.

50.00 Pass beneath Lehigh Valley Railroad (Conrail system).

50.00 *Turn right* on Amboy Avenue.

50.90 *Turn right* onto Grove Street.

50.95 Enter Outerbridge Crossing across the Arthur Kill to Staten Island.

50.95 Route 440 East.

51.20 Begin bridge.

52.00 Cross Arthur Kill: extensive views of Raritan Bay area.

52.90 End of bridge (pay toll $1.50). Staten Island, New York.

52.00 Tottenville. The southernmost town on Staten Island and in New York State, this is the southern terminus of the Staten Island RapidTransit line to Saint George. Former ferry to Perth Amboy. Settled ca. 1680 as manor of Tottenville, granted to Christopher Billop by Gov. Thomas Dongan. The property immediately adjacent to the Outerbridge Crossing was settled ca. 1712 by members of the Dissosway (Dusachoy, Dusochany, Dusway, etc.) family. They were descendants of the Huguenot Marc du Sauchoy who came to the New Netherlands shortly before 1655.

53.00 *Turn right* on Page Avenue exit.

53.30 *Turn right* on Richmond Valley Road.

53.50 *Turn left* on Arthur Kill Avenue.

53.60 Cross creek.

53.60 Nassau Smelting and Refining Co. plant on left. This division of Western Electric Co. melts down old telephone equipment and cables to retrieve copper and brass for reuse.

53.80 Cross Staten Island Rapid Transit railroad.

53.80 *Bear right.*

54.40 *Turn left* on Main Street—Tottenville.

54.50 *Turn right* on Craig Avenue.

54.80 Cross Amboy Road. Continue on Craig Avenue.

55.20 *Turn right* on Hylan Boulevard. Named for John Francis Hylan (1868-1936), a political leader and mayor of New York City 1918-1925. He was born in Greene County, New York, and attended New York Law School. He was an opponent of Tammany Hall and was known as "Red Mike" Hylan. Hylan Boulevard is the main thoroughfare along the eastern shore of Staten Island.

55.25 Ward's Point to left.

55.25 **(-20.00 E.R.M.)** View of Perth Amboy, New Jersey, and the junction of Arthur Kill and the Raritan River at the head of Raritan Bay.

55.25 Billopp Conference House on right. A National Historic Landmark, in Conference House Park, this was the early home of Christopher Billopp. Here Benjamin Franklin, John Adams, and Edward Rutledge met with Lord Howe and Sir Henry Strachey on September 11, 1776, in an unsuccessful conference to settle with the British.

55.30 *Turn around.* Ward's Point to left. This is the southernmost point in the state of New York.

56.30 Tottenville Pool on right. Continue on Hylan Boulevard.

57.10 Mount Loretto on left. These are the burned-out ruins of Mission of the Immaculate Virgin-Mount Loretto, a home for children founded by Father Drumgoole.

57.50 Princess Bay on right.

58.20 Cross Wolfe's Brook.

58.50 Seguine Point to right.

58.90 (-18.00 E.R.M.) Wolfe's Pond Park on right.
59.60 Arbutus Lake on right. Huguenot Beach on right.
59.65 St. Joseph-by-the-Sea on right.
60.15 Seaside.
60.25 Sea Breeze House on right.
61.40 (-15.50 E.R.M.)
61.40 Great Kill's Bay and Crooke's Point to right.
62.70 Great Kill's Park on right.
63.10 Great Kill's Recreation Area.
63.60 *Turn right* on Guyon Avenue.
64.00 Oakwood Beach (-14.60 E.R.M.)
64.00 *Turn left* on Mill Road.
64.90 *Turn left* on New Dorp Lane.
64.90 Former Miller Field Air Force Base on right, now a park (-14.50 E.R.M.).
65.10 Cross Hylan Boulevard.
65.60 Cross over Staten Island Rapid Transit.
65.60 New Dorp depot.
65.80 *Turn left* on Richmond Road.
65.90 *Bear right* on Richmond Road.
66.20 *Bear left* on Richmond Road.
66.90 Richmondtown Historic area. A 100-acre site established in 1952, the restoration of the former County Center by the Staten Island Historical Society, and the city of New York, this area features demonstrations of weaving, spinning, dyeing, printing, pottery, and carpentry in July and August. There is also a museum.
67.10 *Turn left* into Richmondtown Restoration.
67.30 *Turn right* on Clarke Avenue.
67.40 Parking lot and Staten Island Historical Museum on right.
67.50 *Turn right* on Arthur Kill Road.
67.60 Voorlezer's House on left.
67.60 *Turn right* on Richmond Road.
68.70 *Turn left* on Rockland Avenue.
68.90 High Rock Nature Conservation Center on right.
69.20 *Turn Right* on Manor Road.
69.20 (-14.00 E.R.M.)

69.20 LaTourette Park on left.
69.30 Sea View Hospital on left.
70.50 Junction with Brielle Road on left.
70.70 *Turn right* on Ocean Terrace.
71.00 *Turn right* on Todt Hill Road.
71.70 *Turn left* on Four Corners Road.
72.00 *Bear left.*
72.30 Turn left on Richmond Road.
72.40 Perine House on right, 1476 Richmond Road, Dongan Hills. The house consists of two connecting buildings. The rear stone house is believed to have been erected ca. 1680 by Thomas Stillwell, an important man on Staten Island: constable, sheriff, magistrate, captain of the militia, and member of the colonial assembly. The stone house nearer the road is believed to have been erected ca. 1713 by Nathaniel Britton, Stillwell's son-in-law. Two wooden additions date from 1749 and 1758. In 1746, Britton's widow sold the house to Walter Dongan, nephew of Sir Thomas Dongan. In 1749, his son sold the house to Joseph Holmes, innkeeper. Holmes kept an inn here until his death in 1759. Ultimately the house passed to his daughter Ann Holmes, wife of Edward Perine. The house remained in the Perine family for over one hundred years. Hamilton Britton Perine sold the house to Donald C. Craig in 1913, and in 1915 it was purchased by the Staten Island Antiquarian Society, now the Staten Island Institute of Arts and Sciences. During the Revolution, British soldiers were quartered here.
72.50 *Turn right* on Delaware Avenue.
73.10 Go under Staten Island Rapid Transit.

73.30 *Turn right* on Hylan Boulevard; get into left lane.

73.40 *Turn left* on Cromwell Avenue.

73.60 *Turn right* on Mason Avenue.

73.70 *Turn left on Seaview Avenue.*

74.70 *Turn left* on Seaside Boulevard.

74.70 Franklin Delano Roosevelt Boardwalk on right.

74.90 (-12.80 E.R.M.)

74.90 Hoffman Island on right.

75.20 Parking area on right.

76.20 *Bend left* on Lily Pond Avenue.

76.40 *Turn right* on McLean Avenue.

76.50 *Turn left* on Tompkins Avenue.

76.60 *Turn left* on Major Avenue.

76.70 *Turn right on Lily Pond Avenue.*

76.70 St. Joseph's Hill Academy on left.

77.30 Vandeventer's Point

77.30 U.S. Army Fort Wadsworth on right. The oldest continually-manned fortification on American continent, its museum exhibits depict the history of the U.S. Army. (Free, open Sunday, Monday, Thursday, Friday from 1-4 P.M., Saturday 10-9.)

77.30 *Turn left* on Bay Street.

77.35 Von Briesen Park on right: view of Verrazano Bridge (-11.00 E.R.M.)

77.95 Pass Hylan Boulevard on left.

78.00 **(-10.00)** Rosebank Section.

78.30 Pouch terminal on right (-9.70 E.R.M.).

78.50 Go under Staten Island Rapid Transit.

78.60 U.S. Public Health Service Hospital on left.

78.60 **(-9.65)** Foreign trade zone No. 1 on right.

79.00 Tappen Park on left.

79.20 Stapleton Section, formerly Doyle's Ferry (-9.60 E.R.M.).

79.20 Port Authority Trailer Ship Terminal on right.

79.70 Tompkinsville section.

79.70 *Bear right* on Bay Street.

80.00 St. George.

80.00 U.S. Coast Guard on right.

80.00 Ducksberry Point (-8.50).

80.00 Manhattan Ferry and Staten Island Rapid Transit Terminals on right.

80.00 *Bear left* on Richmond Terrace.

80.10 Richmond Borough Hall on left. This structure has four stories with a clock tower. In the style of a French town hall, it was built in 1906 by Carrere and Hastings, architects.

80.60 Staten Island Museum on left (corner of Wall Street). Art, photography, American Indian and local archeology, science, and natural history exhibits are here. Tuesday-Saturday 10-5, Sunday 2-5.)

80.60 **(-8.25 E.R.M.)**

80.60 Robbins Reef and Constable Hook, Bayonne, on right.

80.60 Kill Van Kull right.

80.90 Pavillion Restaurant on left, in Greek Revival style.

81.60 Sailor's Snug Harbor on left: A group of Greek Revival buildings, in Ionic style, 1831-1833, by Martin E. Thompson, architect. Founded by Captain Robert R. Randall in 1833, it contains over fifty buildings. The marine paintings in the lobbies are interesting, as is a statue of Capt. Randall by August Saint-Gaudens, unveiled in 1884. This home for retired seamen is supported largely by revenues from extensive land holdings in Manhattan.

81.90 Cross Clove Brook (in a corrugated pipe culvert).

83.30 Cross Clove Road.

83.40 *Bear right* on Richmond Terrace.

83.50 Pass beneath Staten Island Rapid Transit.

83.50 Port Richmond.

84.00 Former ferry to Bayonne on right.

84.00 *Turn left* on Nicholas Avenue.
84.15 Pass beneath Staten Island Rapid Transit.
84.60 *Turn right* on Hooker Avenue.
84.70 *Turn right* on Trantor Place.
84.70 Elm Park.
84.70 Entrance to Bayonne Bridge.
85.00 Pass toll booths.
85.10 Begin Bayonne Bridge. (See article in river section.)
85.75 Cross Kill Van Kull.
86.40 End Bayonne Bridge.
86.50 *Turn right* on Kennedy Boulevard (Bayonne).
86.52 Pass under Central Railroad of New Jersey (Conrail).
86.60 *Turn right* on North Street.
86.70 *Turn right* on Roadway.
86.70 Burned out former C.N.J. depot on left.
86.72 Pass under Central Railroad of New Jersey.
86.80 *Turn right* on West Seventh Street.
86.90 *Turn left* on Avenue C.
87.40 Site of former ferry terminal to Staten Island straight ahead.
87.40 View of Bayonne Bridge to right.
87.40 Bergen Point.
87.40 Site of former amusement area along waterfront on right.
87.40 *Turn left* on First Street.
87.40 Kill Van Kull on right.
87.60 Site of former LaTourette on right.
87.60 *Turn left* on Broadway.
87.80 Pass East Third Street. A fine example of a typical nineteenth-century Bayonne home is on right. Note the fence.
88.20 Pass under Central Railroad of New Jersey (Conrail).
88.20 *Turn right* on West Eighth Street.
88.30 Road becomes Avenue "E".
89.00 *Turn right* on East Twenty-first Street (becomes Hook Road).
89.05 Pass under Central Railroad of New Jersey.
89.50 Refinery area.

89.80 *Bend left,* merge into Twenty-second Street.
89.90 Exxon refinery.
89.90 *Turn right* on Route 169.
90.40 End of Route 169.
90.40 *Turn right* on Hook Road.
90.70 *Turn left:* Port Johnson.
90.80 *Turn around* (-8.20 E.R.M.).
90.80 Constable Hook: view of Kill Van Kull, St. George, Staten Island, Atlantic Cement Co. silos on right.
90.80 *Turn around.*
90.90 *Turn right* on Hook Road.
91.20 *Turn left.* Cross railroad track. Start Route 169.
91.70 Pass Twenty-second Street on left. Continue straight on Route 169.
92.20 Ciba-Geigy Chemical Co. on right.
92.90 (-7.75 E.R.M.)
92.90 Military ocean terminal on right.
94.30 Pass under New Jersey Turnpike Extension and cross over Central Railroad of New Jersey (Conrail).
94.50 Cross Broadway to left. Garfield Avenue to right.
94.70 *Turn left* on Avenue C.
94.80 Pass under Lehigh Valley Railroad (Conrail).
94.85 Pass under New Jersey Turnpike Extension.
95.20 St. Vincent's Church on right. It is in Romanesque style.
95.30 *Turn right* on 44th Street.
95.50 *Turn left* on Kennedy Boulevard.
95.70 *Turn right* into Bayonne Park, belvidere.
95.80 *Turn right* on Park Road.
96.10 *Circle left* around Monopteros.
96.50 Continue straight.
96.60 *Turn right* on Park Road.
96.80 *Turn right* again on Park Road.
97.00 Lagoon on right. View of Newark Bay and Turnpike Bridge.
97.10 *Turn left* on Park Road.
97.10 Port Newark across bay on right. Parking available.
97.20 *Bend left* on Park Road.

97.30 *Turn right.*

97.40 Exit from Bayonne Park.

97.40 *Turn left* on Kennedy Boulevard. For many years this road was known as Hudson County Boulevard, and follows the route of an old road from colonial days which went from Jersey City to Philadelphia via Staten Island.

97.50 World War I monument and statue of "Doughboy" on right.

97.50 *Turn right* on West 40th Street.

97.60 Fountains and small park.

97.70 *Turn left* on Avenue C.

98.20 *Turn right* on 51st Street.

98.40 *Turn left* on Broadway.

98.60 Bayonne-Jersey City line.

98.60 Broadway becomes Garfield Avenue.

98.60 Pass beneath Turnpike Extension.

98.80 Pass beneath Lehigh Valley and Pennsylvania Railroads (Conrail), electrified line.

99.40 Bayview Cemetery on left. New York Bay Cemetery on right.

99.60 (-6.50 E.R.M.)

99.60 Entrance to Caven Point Terminal on right.

100.00 Dingson Ryan Memorial Park (formerly Bayside Park) on right.

100.30 *Turn right* on Bayview Avenue.

100.50 Statue of Liberty visible ahead.

100.70 *Turn right* on Burma Road.

100.90 *Bend left on Burma Road.*

101.00 *Turn right* on Statue of Liberty Road.

101.60 Statue of Liberty Park. This area, formerly known as Black Tom, was an important railhead and terminal. It was owned by National Docks Co. and served by Lehigh Valley and Pennsylvania Railroads. It was the site of a tremendous ammunition explosion during World War I. In August of 1916, German saboteurs blew up a munitions plant here. Six months previously, they had destroyed the Kingsland (New Jersey) Arsenal. The United States government brought suit, and the German government was finally ordered to pay $50,000,000 damages in 1940.

101.60 (-4.50 E.R.M.)

101.60 *Turn around.*

102.20 *Turn left* on Burma Road.

102.60 *Turn right* on Garfield Avenue.

103.30 *Turn right* on Garfield Avenue.

103.70 *Turn right* on Caven Point Road.

103.80 *Turn left* on Pacific Avenue.

104.40 Pass Communipaw Avenue. Gothic church is on left.

104.70 *Turn right* on Johnston Avenue.

105.00 (-4.80 E.R.M.)

105.00 Ellis Island on right.

105.50 Former Central Railroad of New Jersey, Baltimore & Ohio and Reading Co. coach and pullman yards on right.

106.00 Former Central Railroad of New Jersey passenger and ferry terminal on right. It is undergoing restoration for use as a visitors' center.

106.00 (-3.74 E.R.M.)

106.00 Morris Canal Basin on left. View of lower Manhattan ahead.

106.00 *Turn around.*

107.30 *Turn right* on Pacific Avenue.

107.60 *Turn right* on Grand Avenue.

108.30 St. Peter's Preparatory School on left.

108.40 Site of fortification on Powle's Hook.

108.40 *Turn right* on Washington Street: "Liberty Tree Corner."

108.60 *Turn left* on Essex Street.

108.80 *Turn left* on Hudson Street. (Note: Inasmuch as these streets run through the Colgate-Palmolive plant complex, they are closed on weekends and holidays; detour via Washington Street to Montgomery Street)

108.80 Site of early Vulcan Iron Works on right.

108.90 Colgate-Palmolive plant both sides.

109.00 (-3.70 E.R.M.)

109.00 Former terminal site of Fulton's pioneer ferry on right.

109.00 Site of former Pennsylvania Railroad passenger and ferry terminal straight ahead and on right.

109.00 *Turn left* on Exchange Place, Montgomery Street.

109.20 United States Post Office on left. Pass Washington Street.

109.25 New Jersey Title Guarantee and Trust Co. Building (Nos. 83-85) on left. This yellow brick structure with cast terra-cotta ornaments and Art Deco portal was built in 1888. Its portal dates from 1931. It has been converted to an apartment house.

109.50 Jersey City city hall ahead. Of limestone and granite, in Eclectic style it was designed by Lewis H. Broome and built in 1835. In the days of Frank Hague, this building became laughingly known for the fact that, prior to election time, there was always a major fire in the basement hall of records.

109.50 *Turn right* on Henderson Street.

109.60 *Bend right* on Henderson Street.

109.70 *Bend left* on Henderson Street: Harborside terminal on right.

110.20 *Turn right* on Pavonia Avenue.

110.60 Site of former Erie Railroad passenger and ferry terminal on left. This was the site of the former Long Dock Co. property. The Pennsylvania Railroad (Conrail) Harsimus Cove freight yards are on right. The present P.A.T.H. Pavonia Station entrance is on left, with a good view of lower Manhattan ahead.

110.60 (-2.50 E.R.M.)

110.60 Holland Tunnel ventilator tower to left, at end of Pier 9, formerly used by American President Lines as both origin and terminus of its Around-the-World freight and passenger service. The tickets for the longest cruise available in the world used to read simply: "Jersey City to Jersey City."

110.60 *Turn around.*

111.00 *Turn left* on Henderson Street.

111.10 *Turn right* on 8th Street.

111.40 *Turn right* on Hamilton Place West. This is a neighborhood of Victorian row homes, many undergoing private restoration under comprehensive renewal program.

111.40 Hamilton Park on right.

111.50 *Turn right* on 9th Street.

111.80 *Turn left* on Henderson Street.

111.90 Pass beneath Erie Railroad (Conrail).

112.00 Cross Holland Tunnel Plaza. The tunnel entrance is on right.

112.00 (-2.50 E.R.M.)

112.30 Pass beneath Delaware, Lackawanna & Western Railroad. (Erie-Lackawanna; Conrail)

112.40 *Turn right* on Observer Highway.

112.80 Former Erie-Lackawanna Railroad offices on right. Former Railway Express Co. terminal.

112.80 Hoboken.

112.80 *Turn left* on Hudson Street.

112.90 *Turn right* on Hudson Place. A former elevated railway and trolley terminal is on right, now used as a bus terminal.

112.95 Lackawanna Terminal.

112.95 (-2.00 E.R.M.)

112.95 Conrail's suburban passenger terminal is on right. The former ferry terminal and offices are straight ahead. There is a P.A.T.H. station here. The statue is of Samuel Sloan, former president of Delaware, Lackawanna & Western Railroad. This is also the site of the original Hoboken Ferry.

112.95 *Turn left* on River Street.

113.15 (-1.80 E.R.M.)

113.15 Hoboken-Port Authority Marine Terminal on right.

113.20 Hudson Square Park on left.

113.30 *Bend right* on Fourth Street and cross Hoboken Shore Railroad.

113.25 *Bend left* on River Road. (Note: At the time of writing, this formerly rough dirt road, running beneath Castle Point, is being improved.)

113.60 Castle Point (-1.50 E.R.M.)

113.60 Stevens Institute of Technology on left. Former Pennsylvania Railroad marine shops stood on right. Hoboken Shore Railroad tracks formerly paralleled this road. Now inactive, they may be abandoned. The former *S.S. Stevens,*an oceangoing passenger liner, was used as a dormitory and anchored on the right until August 26, 1975.

113.70 Site of Sibyl's Cave on left.

114.00 (-1.00 E.R.M.) Elysian Park on left.

114.10 *Turn right* on Hudson Street.

114.30 Bethlehem Steel shipyard on right.

114.40 Site of former Lackawanna 14th Street. Ferry Terminal on right.

114.40 *Turn left* on 14th Street.

114.60 *Turn right* on Park Avenue.

114.80 Cross bridge over Jersey Junction Railroad (Conrail).

115.00 Weehawken.

115.00 (-0.50 E.R.M.) Port Seatrain on right, a major containerport.

115.60 *Bear right* on Boulevard East.

115.60 Entrance to Lincoln Tunnel on left.

115.80 Pass Baldwin Avenue on right. (Note: This is the turnoff for a rather rough alternate route along the foot of the cliffs to the foot of Pershing Avenue at the site of the former West Shore Railroad and Ferry Terminal. This alternate route is paralleled on the left by tracks of the Jersey Junction Railroad (Conrail) and passes on the right large banana docks, which occupy the former site of the Delaware & Hudson Canal Co. dockyard. The famous Weehawken dueling grounds occupied a small bench or plateau part way up the cliffs on the left, which was blasted away at time of construction of the railroad. The Electric Ferry operated from the foot of Baldwin Avenue. The bluff here is known as King's Bluff. A double-track trolley line paralleled Pershing Avenue to the top of the cliffs. The portal to the tunnel of the Guttenberg Steam Railroad division of the North Hudson Railroad can be seen high up on the cliffs under the present roadway.)

115.80 Lincoln Tunnel Administration Building on right.

115.80 (-0.25 E.R.M.)

116.40 King's Bluff area.

116.40 *Turn right* on King Street.

116.50 *Turn left* on Hamilton Place.

116.55 *Turn left* on Hamilton Avenue.

116.55 Statue of Alexander Hamilton on right. This is immediately above the former Weehawken dueling grounds.

116.55 (-0.15 E.R.M.)

116.70 *Continue Straight* onto Boulevard East.

116.80 Hamilton Plaza Park on right.

117.20 Cross 48th Street Weehawken to left. Pershing Avenue to right. This leads to site of former West Shore Railroad and Ferry Terminal to 42nd Street and Cortlandt Street, Manhattan.

West Side Road Route

0.00 Start West Side Road route (0.50 E.R.M.).
Corner of Boulevard East, Pershing Avenue and 48th Street, Weehawken, New Jersey. Head north on Boulevard East.

0.10 Small Park on right.

0.30 West New York City line.

0.50 Donnelly Park on right.

Alternate Route (shore line).

0.60 At this point, Boulevard East crosses what is called 60th Street to the left and Hillside Road to the right.

0.60 *Turn right* on Hillside Road. Descend Palisades. Slough's Meadows, now covered with Conrail freight yards, are seen at the foot of the cliffs to the right. There are good views of Manhattan and passenger liner piers and far down Hudson River. Large new apartment buildings are on the bluff to the left.

0.80 Road bends left at the site of former New York Central Railroad Marine shops, and West New York Ferry on right.

0.90 River View Park atop cliff to left.

1.00 Former N.Y.O. & W. Railway coal docks on right.

1.10 Guttenberg city line, becomes River Road (1.50 E.R.M.).

1.11 Ferry Road to left. Site of former Guttenberg Ferry on right.

117.20 End of Lower West Side road route.
Starting point of West Side road route.

1.35 North Bergen city line.
Note: From mile 1.00 to mile 5.80, River Road is paralleled on the right by tracks of the New York, Susquehanna & Western Railway.

2.00 Bull's Ferry. Blockhouse Point on right. (2.45 E.R.M.). This is the site of a former ferry. Bull's Ferry Road comes down cliff on left.

2.00 Rejoin main route; continue straight on River Road.

Main route (atop Palisades).

0.60 Cross Sixtieth Street-Hillside Road and continue straight on Boulevard East.

0.80 Auf Der Heide Park on right. (formerly River View Park).

1.10 Guttenberg city line. (1.50 E.R.M.)

1.35 North Bergen city line.

2.30 *Turn left* into North Hudson Park.

2.60 *Bear left* on Park Road.

2.90 *Bear left* on Park Road.

3.20 *Turn left* on Seventy-nineth Street. Leave North Hudson Park.

3.40 *Turn left* on Boulevard East.

3.45 *Turn sharp right* on Bull's Ferry Road.

3.50 Go down steep hill.

3.80 Bull's ferry, Blockhouse Point straight ahead (2.45 E.R.M.).

3.80 *Turn left* on River Road (alternate rejoins main route here).

3.81 Edgewater town line. Leave Hudson County, enter Bergen County.

3.90 Lever Brothers' factory on right.

4.10 Shadyside area of Edgewater (3.00 E.R.M.).

4.20 *Bear right* on River Road: Route 505.

4.40 Former Ford assembly plant on right, now Tri-Terminal (3.30 E.R.M.).

4.70 Cross bridge over New York, Susquehanna & Western Railway. The entrance of the railroad tunnel under the palisades is visible to left.

5.00 Hills Bros. coffee plant on right.

5.20 Sunnyside area of Edgewater (4.30 E.R.M.).

5.40 Former Alcoa (Aluminum Company of America) plant on left.

5.40 Binghamton's Restaurant on right. The restaurant is the former Delaware, Lackawanna & Western Hoboken ferryboat *S.S. Binghamton* (4.40 E.R.M.).

5.80 Site of the former Jack Frost sugar refinery on right.

5.80 Site of the former U.S. Postal Service mailbag repair facility on right.

5.80 End of N.Y.S. & W. Railway tracks on right.

6.00 Edgewater (4.80 E.R.M.).

6.00 Cross Edgewater Plaza. The former 125th Street ferry terminal is on the right. The trolley terminal was located here with carbarns on left.

6.10 *Bear right* at junction with Route 5. Continue on River Road.

7.10 Undercliff section of Edgewater. (5.00 E.R.M.).

7.50 Tillie Tudlem (section of Edgewater also known variously through the years as Tilly Toodlum, Pleasant Valley, Burdett's Ferry, and Fort Lee Park. A former steamboat landing and resort.) (7.10 E.R.M.).

7.50 Junction with Henry Hudson Drive on right.

Alternate No. 1 — Undercliff.

(This route can be used in either direction but is closed in winter.)

7.50 Corner of Henry Hudson Drive and Hudson Terrace (Main Street), Fort Lee town line.

7.50 *Turn right* on Henry Hudson Drive. Enter Palisades Interstate Park.

7.80 DuPont Dock or Powder Dock on right. (7.15 E.R.M.).

8.00 Hazard's Dock on right (7.20 E.R.M.).

8.10 Pass beneath George Washington Bridge (7.30 E.R.M.).

8.30 Carpenter's Beach on right (7.50 E.R.M.).

8.40 Turnoff for Ross Dock recreation area on right. Boat ramps are here.

9.50 Allison Park atop cliffs to left.

9.60 The Miraculous Gully to left (7.90 E.R.M.).

9.70 Allison Point to left (8.10 E.R.M.).

9.80 Site of former Dyckman Street ferry terminal on right.

9.80 Englewood Cliffs landing (9.70 E.R.M.).

9.80 Englewood Yacht Club on right.

9.80 Entrance to parking and picnic area to right (pay area).

9.80 *Bear left,* uphill.

10.20 Bloomer's Dock to right (9.75 E.R.M.).

10.20 Junction of Palisades Avenue, which continues to top of the cliffs and Palisades Interstate Parkway and Route 9W, and Henry Hudson Drive. Sometimes the Drive is open to this point in winter.

10.20 *Bear right* on Henry Hudson Drive.

10.50 High Tom on left. (9.80 E.R.M.).

10.50 Frank's Rock on shoreline— lowest point on drive.

10.80 Undercliff (under the mountains). A former active settlement of farmers, pear arbor- ists, quarrymen, woodcutters, and fishermen, it was heavily populated in the Dutch era. Remains of a cemetery may be seen in the area west of the drive. (10.30 E.R.M.).

11.20 Powder Dock on right. Clinton Point on left. (10.75 E.R.M.)

12.30 Lambier Dock on right. (12.20 E.R.M.)

12.60 Cross bridge over Greenbrook.

13.00 Huyler Landing on right. (13.00 E.R.M.)

13.75 *Traffic circle. Bear left* up to cliffs. (13.50 E.R.M.)

Optional sidetrip.

13.75 *Bear right* down cliffs.

14.05 *Alpine grove*—former Yonkers Ferry terminal. It now has boat docks, picnic facilities, pay parking area. (14.00 E.R.M.)

14.05 *Turn around.*

14.35 *Turn sharp right* up hill at circle —rejoin main route.

14.20 Riverview landing to right at foot of cliffs. (14.40 E.R.M.)

14.40 Cape Fly Away to right. (14.50 E.R.M.)

14.50 Palisades Interstate Park Commission Headquarters on right. This is in a fine mansion formerly belonging to the Oltman family.

14.55 *Bear left* and pass under Palisades Interstate Parkway.

14.60 *Turn right* on Route 9W North. Junction with alternate 2— Overcliff Route.

Alternate No. 2 — Overcliff.

(Works best northbound. Open all year.)

7.50 Tillie Tudlem—Junction of River Road, Henry Hudson Drive, and Hudson Terrace (sometimes also called Main Street here).

7.50 *Continue left* uphill on Hudson Terrace (7.10 E.R.M.).

7.50 Fort Lee town line.

7.70 Restoration of Fort Lee on right (E.R.M. 7.30).

7.80 Pass beneath approach to George Washington Bridge (E.R.M. 7.30).

8.00 Linwood section of Fort Lee. Large apartments on left. (E.R.M. 8.00)

8.60 Victorian cottages on left. Remains of stone walls belonging to earlier estates are visible between Hudson Terrace and the Palisades Interstate Parkway on the right.

8.90 Prentice Hall Publishing Co. on left.

9.30 *Turn right* beneath parkway.

9.40 *Turn right* on Allison Park Road.

9.60 *Turn left.* Enter Allison Park. (E.R.M. 7.80) This is a very special portion of the Palisades Interstate Park System. It was originally privately endowed and administered by the trustees under the will of William Outis Allison (1849-1924), a lifelong resident of the immediate area. The park is entirely fenced and opens at 9 A.M. for the daylight hours only. The park is much more formal than most sections of the Interstate Park System and features "formal-rustic" landscaping, manicured lawns, tar paths, and a spectacular clifftop walk with extensive views embracing Manhattan, the Hudson, Spuyten Duyvil Creek, George Washington and Henry Hudson Bridges, and the Cloisters. There are extensive plantings of pine, rhododendron, and mountain laurel. Many wooden and stone benches (one a unique natural stone bench) are located around the grounds. Facilities include paved parking area, a granite Dutch Colonial style rest room building, drinking water fountains, and caretaker's lodge.

9.60 *Circle left* on Park Road.

9.70 Exit Allison Park.

9.70 *Turn right* on Allison Park Road.

9.90 *Continue straight.*

10.00 *Enter grounds* of St. Michael's Villa and St. Peter's College. When entering grounds, note faces carved in dead tree trunk straight ahead. Bear left on two-way drive and circle around to exit. The four-story, turreted, orange brick main building was formerly St. Joseph's Orphanage. There are attractive statues of the Blessed Virgin, St. Joseph and the child Jesus in the center of the turn-around drive. The grounds feature attractive hydrangea plantings, and are at the top of the gully known as the Miraculous (long before any religious orders occupied the site—origin of name is unknown.) (E.R.M. 8.20) Circle around and exit villa grounds.

10.40 *Turn right* back under parkway.

10.50 *Turn right* on Hudson Terrace.

10.80 *Turn right* on Palisades Avenue (Englewood Cliffs) (8.70 E.R.M.).

10.81 Pass beneath parkway.

10.82 *Turn left* on to Palisades Interstate Parkway Northbound.

10.85 Site of Palisade Mountain House on right. (E.R.M. 9.70).

11.80 Rockefeller Lookout (available northbound only). Elevation 400 feet. Paved parking area. 20 minute limit. This point offers extensive views embracing Manhattan, Henry Hudson Bridge, Spuyten Duyvil Creek, Bronx V.A. Hospital, Baker Field, Long Island Sound, and Westchester County.

There is a memorial dedication plaque to John D. Rockefeller, Jr., who dedicated much land to the Palisades Interstate Park Commission and who envisioned the Palisades' Interstate Parkway.

Coin-operated binoculars are available. There are low stone walls along the cliff tops—caution is urged. There are several dangerous open cliff tops but no fences.

13.50 *Pass over* entrance road to Greenbrook Sanctuary from Route 9W. The Greenbrook

Sanctuary incorporates a wild and rugged area with a 6.5 acre pond (source of Greenbrook) known as the Kelders, Dutch for "the cellars." The sanctuary is open only to members of the Palisades Nature Association, P.O. Box 155, Alpine, New Jersey 07620.

14.60 Alpine Lookout (available northbound only.)

This viewpoint with 430 feet elevation, opposite Riverdale and Yonkers, features Chimney Rock. There are many sheer drops but also a substantial fence along the clifftop. Paved parking area with 20-minute limit.

15.50 Armstrong F.M. Radio Transmission Tower visible ahead to left. This was built in 1938 by F.M. radio pioneer Maj. Edwin Armstrong, who taught at Columbia University. It is 485 feet high with triple arms and broadcast over a range of 100 miles. It was the first F.M. radio station, but has since been discontinued.

15.80 Cross small bridge.

16.20 *Exit right* onto Old Closter Dock Road. (This is the Alpine approach road to Route 9W North.)

16.40 *Circle right* under parkway.

16.50 *Turn right* onto Route 9W North. Junction with Alternate 1, Undercliff Route.

Future mileages are based upon the alternate No. 1

14.60 *Head North* on Route 9W.

15.10 Former Ringling family (circus) estate on right.

16.30 *Turn right* on side road to State Line Lookout. This is located at Exit 3 of the Palisades Interstate Parkway.

16.45 State Line Lookout. Elevation 522 feet (E.R.M. 17.70.) Paved parking. Light refreshments available in season. *Turn around.*

16.60 Enter Palisades Interstate Parkway *Northbound.*

17.40 Exit from parkway at exit 4, onto Route 9W North.

17.70 Entrance to Columbia University Lamont Geological Observatory on right. This is a seismological recording station and teaching facility. It is located on the former estates of Dr. John Torrey, noted botanist and incorporates his former red sandstone mansion and gardens, as well as those of the neighboring estate Niederhurst, ca. 1860, a Victorian Italianate mansion. The property is not open to the public.

17.75 New Jersey/New York State line (E.R.M. 18.00).

17.90 Skunk Hollow on right.

18.30 Long Path on right. Blue blazes.

18.50 Palisades (E.R.M. 18.90).

18.50 Pass Washington Spring Road. A 1.5 mile roundtrip to the right to Sneden's Landing (Old Paramus) is suggested for those interested in old houses. The native stone house in Pennsylvania Dutch style atop the cliffs is a modern reproduction built in 1937.

19.50 Rockland Country Club and golf course on left.

19.80 Tallman Mountain Park on right, a unit of the Palisades Interstate Park System. A loop drive around the park is recommended as a short sidetrip. There are two picnic areas. The northern one offers superior views of the Tappan Zee, Piermont Village, Erie Pier, Tappan Zee Bridge,

Crumkill Creek Meadows, and Sparkill Creek. Recreational facilities include picnic areas, swimming pool, athletic fields, tennis, handball, badminton, basketball, football, softball, children's play area. Rest rooms are available. No pets are allowed. The park closes at 9 P.M.

20.00 Pass junction Route 340 on left. Continue straight on Route 9W.

20.10 Palisades/Piermont town line.

20.20 Start Sparkill Creek Viaduct. (E.R.M. 20.80).

20.50 End Sparkill Creek Viaduct.

20.60 *Turn left* at Second traffic light —Hickey Street.

20.70 *Turn right* on King's Highway.

20.80 Large Dutch Colonial home with Ionic columns on verandah on right.

21.10 *Turn right* and enter Rockland Cemetery, established 1847. Drive to grave of Gen. John C. Fremont (1813-1890) "Pathfinder of the West," atop Mt. Nebo. There are good views. Just keep following cemetery roads to top of mountain. Circle back to the entrance. This is a 2.1-mile round trip.

23.20 *Turn right* back onto King's Highway.

23.50 Closed-off back entrance driveway to Dominican convent and St. Agnes Home and School for Children on left.

23.70 Back entrance to St. Thomas Aquinas College on left.

24.20 Olde Stonehouse Inn on right (ca. 1728).

24.30 *Turn right* on Route 303.

24.50 *Turn right* on Greenbush Road.

24.51 Bell-Ann Factory on right.

24.55 Dutch house on right.

24.60 Volkswagen Building on right on former Rockland County Fairgrounds.

25.20 *Turn right* up ravine on Clausland Mountain Road.

25.50 Town of Orangetown Park on left.

26.40 *Turn right* on Tweed Boulevard.

26.70 Expansive view of Tappan Zee on left. Top of Clausland Mountain (E.R.M. 22.00).

27.50 *Turn right* into town of Orangetown Park.

27.85 Parking. Views both east and west. *Turn around.*

28.20 *Turn right* on Tweed Boulevard.

29.20 Driveway to Castlewood on right. This is a private home; do not enter. This former home of Eleazar Lord, first president of the Erie Railroad, is a three-story fieldstone structure, ca. 1850, extensively remodeled by McKim, Mead & White.

29.30 *Turn right* on Route 9W.

29.40 Pass Castle Road on right.

29.90 *Turn right* at second light— Route 340.

29.90 Sparkill.

30.00 *Turn left* off Route 340 onto Piermont Avenue at Erie Railroad crossing.

30.05 *Turn right* on Valentine Avenue.

30.15 Christ Episcopal Church on right: a nineteenth-century, stone crenellated Gothic structure.

30.30 St. Charles A.M.E. Zion Church on right: Stone, built in 1865, rebuilt in 1893.

30.30 Park, lily-pond—former ice pond, and route 9W trestle on left.

30.40 *Turn left* on Ferdon Avenue.

30.50 Pond and dam and former Tappan Landing on Sparkill Creek on left.

30.50 Pass under Route 9W trestle.

30.70 Sparkill/Piermont town line.

30.90 Verdun-Blauvelt house on right: a two-story Greek Revival with Ionic temple facade and fluted columns (ca. 1840) on the southwest corner of Rockland Road.

30.90 Crescent Ribbon Factory on left: red brick with Gothic ornamentation; originally a silk mill.

31.10 First Reformed Church on right, established in 1839.

31.20 Tallman Park drive on right. Closed to all but official vehicles.

31.20 Old chain drawbridge across Sparkill Creek on left: one-way in the opposite direction.

31.20 *Bear right* and cross Sparkill Creek on new bridge.

31.20 View of Carroll Castle across the river in Tarrytown on right.

31.25 *Turn right* at light on Paradise Avenue.

31.30 *Turn around*—area of mid-nineteenth-century houses undergoing restoration.

31.35 *Turn right* at light onto Piermont Avenue.

31.45 Cross former Erie Railroad mainline (now an industrial spur).

31.50 Piermont Village (E.R.M. 21.25).

31.50 Clevepac Corp. paper carton plant on right.

31.50 Former Erie Railroad pier on right (E.R.M. 21.20).

32.00 Area of old houses (E.R.M. 21.25).

    a) Onderdonk Dutch House on left: 756 Piermont Avenue.

    b) Garrison Colonial House on left: 800 Piermont Avenue.

    c) House with gingerbread vergeboards and fluted Corinthian columns on left: 830 Piermont Avenue.

    d) Victorian House with mansard roof on left: 840 Piermont Avenue.

    e) Bracketed House on left: 850 Piermont Avenue.

    f) Colonial house with Victorian modifications on right: 867 Piermont Avenue.

    g) Victorian House with mansard roof on left: 870 Piermont Avenue.

    h) House with trellised porch in Hudson River Gothic Style on right. Facing St. John's R.C. Church

32.30 Piermont/Grand-View-on-Hudson town line. Cross brook. Name of road changes to River Road. Area of more old homes.

    a) Hudson River Gothic cottage on left, 251 River Road.

    b) Federal period mansion on left, 245 River Road.

    c) Colonial cottage on right, 242 River Road.

    d) Bracketed mansion on left, 225 River Road.

    e) Bracketed cottage on left, 221 River Road.

    f) Victorian mansard roof villa on left, 217 River Road.

    g) Several Hudson River Gothic bracketed villas on both sides.

33.30 Double cottage in bracketed style, batten board construction on right (ca. 1820), 108 and 110 River Road.

33.50 Bracketed house on left, 81 River Road.

33.60 Grand View Springs and pool on left, 55 River Road.

33.70 Canaday Eagle Spring Water Co. on left. 35 River Road.

33.80 Stone hermitage style Hudson River Gothic cottage on right (with red sandstone stepped gables). It was formerly the Wayside Sunday School, 1860. 24 River Road.

33.90 Pass under Tappan Zee Bridge (E.R.M. 23.20).

34.00 Grand-View-on-Hudson/Nyack town line.

34.10 Salisbury Manor Apartments and Cornelison Point on right (E.R.M. 23.60).

34.70 *Turn left* at light on Clinton Avenue.

34.80 *Turn right* at light on Broadway.

35.00 St. Paul's Methodist Church on left: romanesque, limestone with dark sandstone trim.

35.10 Christian Science Church on right: Hudson River Gothic board and batten.

35.10 *Turn right* on Cedar Hill Avenue.

35.20 *Turn left* on Piermont Avenue.

35.25 *Bear right.*

35.25 Hudson House on left: 50 Piermont Avenue. Former DePew House, 1836, Hudson River Gothic with late Victorian additions, square cupola.

35.35 St. John's Deliverance Tabernacle on right: 35 Piermont Avenue. Doric style Greek Revival.

35.40 *Turn right* on Burd Street.

35.60 Nyack Lower Landing, former ferry to Tarrytown (E.R.M. 24.50).

35.60 *Turn around* and head back up Burd Street.

35.70 St. George Hotel on right: two-story Victorian coaching inn, 1864, now called "Off Broadway."

35.80 *Turn right* on South Broadway.

35.80 First Reformed Church on left: red brick Gothic with clock in tower.

36.00 Federal mansion on right: 63 South Broadway.

36.10 First Baptist Church on left: brick with Gothic elements, built in 1857, rebuilt in 1881.

36.20 Large Victorian House behind high brick wall, ca. 1846: 235 S. Broadway.

36.30 Upper Nyack town line (E.R.M. 25.25).

36.50 Empire Fire Company No. 1 on left.

36.70 Old Stone Church on right. Built in 1813, it is the oldest church in Rockland County.

36.85 River Plum on right: stuccoed Hudson River Gothic.

36.90 Cross brook.

37.10 Fellowship Reconciliation Center on right: Federal-style mansion with Ionic elements, red brick: 523 Broadway. It was formerly called Shadow Cliff.

37.40 View of Hook Mountain Cliffs ahead.

37.40 River House on right: 531 Broadway, a French Provincial chateau.

37.80 Old Carriage House and view of Hudson River on right.

37.80 Entrance to Nyack State Park.

37.80 *Turn around.*

37.90 *Turn right* on Larchdale Street.

38.00 *Turn left* on Midland Avenue.

38.00 Mary Dell Convent and Outdoor Chapel on right.

37.70 *Turn right* on Old Mountain Road.

38.90 Spook Hollow.

39.10 *Turn right* on Route 9W.

39.60 Turnout located on right for footpath atop Hook Mountain. It is inconspicuous and is located just south of a driveway.

40.10 Nyack/Rockland Lake town line.

40.50 *Turn right.*

40.50 Rockland Lake State Park (acquired by Palisades Park Commission in 1958): swimming, golf course, picnic areas (E.R.M. 28.65).

40.70 Follow road along east side of Rockland Lake.

41.90 Rockland Lake Village.

41.90 Road to Trough Hol and Rockland Lake Landing on right. This is a dead end; official vehicles only. It is a very steep hill; bicycles must be walked.

41.90 *Bend left.*

42.15 Gethsemane Cemetery on right.

42.40 *Turn right.*

42.50 *Turn right* on Route 9W.

42.60 Swarthout Lake on left.

44.10 Junction with Route 303 from left.

44.30 View of Upper Hackensack Valley on left.

44.30 West Portal of West Shore Railroad tunnel, below on left.

44.50 New York Trap Rock Co. High Tor Quarry seen ahead.

44.60 Junction Route 304 on left.

44.70 Enter Long Clove (E.R.M. 31.50).

44.70 Haverstraw town line.

44.90 André Monument on right.

44.90 East portal of West Shore Railroad tunnel on right below.

45.10 Lookout pulloff on right. Extensive view of Haverstraw Bay and Highlands.

45.50 Pass over traprock conveyor.

45.55 Short Clove on left, traffic light (E.R.M. 32.40).

45.60 *Turn right* on Short Clove Road and cross railroad.

45.60 High Tor on left (E.R.M. 33.00).

45.70 Former brick yards on right.

46.10 Old wooden tenements on left. You are now on Maple Avenue.

46.10 *Turn right* on Fairmont Street.

46.11 *Turn right* on West Street. (This seems almost like just one turn.)

46.20 Marina on right.

46.30 *Turn left* on Canal Street.

46.40 *Turn left* on First Street (also called Front Street) "Captains' Row."

46.40 B.P.O.E. Building on right: Victorian ca. 1860.

46.40 Area of interesting old houses on left:
  a) 52 First Street at corner of Van Houten Street: Van Houton House, 1790.
  b) 44 First Street: Major Welch House, two-story brick Victorian with mansard roof and brackets, mid-nineteenth century.
  c) 42 First Street: two-story Hudson River Bracketed, mid-nineteenth century.
  d) 34 First Street: Captain Woolsey House, three-story brick with Ionic portico, ca. 1845.
  e) 20 First Street: Hudson River Gothic cottage.
  f) 10 First Street: Ionic Greek Revival, ca. 1840.

46.45 Emeline Dock on right.

46.50 River View Boat Club and old ferry slip on right.

46.50 Cross Main Street, Haverstraw (E.R.M. 33.25).

46.51 Hudson River Gothic mansion (ca. 1840 on right: 7 First Street.

46.55 Cornell Steamboat Co. dock on right.

46.60 *Turn left* on Broad Street.

46.70 *Turn right* on Rockland Street.

46.80 *Turn left* on Division Street: area of row houses.

46.80 View of Bowline Point and lagoon to right.

46.90 *Turn right* on Broadway.

46.90 View of High Tor to left.

47.10 *Continue straight* at light. Entrance to Bowline Point power plant and Park on right. Suggested two-mile side trip to end and back.

47.10 St. Peter's R.C. Church on left.

47.40 *Bend right* on Samsondale Avenue.

47.60 Cross Minisceongo Creek.

47.65 *Turn right* on Tanneyann's Lane.

47.90 *Turn right* on Railroad Avenue.

48.00 *Turn left* on Grassy Point Road. Power plant on right.

48.50 Cross Minisceongo Creek.

48.60 A cove of the Hudson is on the right. Minisceongo Creek is on the left.

49.40 Grassy Point: former steamboat landing is on the right.

49.40 *Turn left.*

49.60 Old Roman Catholic Church on left: 1889.

49.70 U.S. Gypsum plant on left.

49.70 Minisceongo Yacht Club on right.

49.90 Cross Minisceongo Creek, Penny Bridge.

49.90 View of High Tor to left: Stony Point Bay, Stony Point, and Verplanck Point to right.

49.95 *Turn right* on Beach Road.

50.40 *Turn left* under railroad.

50.60 *Turn right* on Farley Drive.

50.90 *Turn right* on Jackson Drive.

51.00 *Bear left* on Jackson Drive. This becomes Lincoln Oval. Continue around.

51.20 *Turn right* on Georgetown Drive (downhill).

51.30 *Turn right* on Park Road.

51.40 Enter Stony Point Battlefield Park. Memorial Arch and bridge over the railroad.

51.75 *Turn around* parking area. (E.R.M. 36.20).

52.10 Leave Battlefield Park.

52.20 *Turn right* on Park Road North, up ravine.

52.40 *Turn right* on Route 9W.

52.50 Tomkin's Cove town line.

52.80 *Stay straight* on Route 9W. Buckberg Mountain Road on left.

53.00 *Turn right* on Elm Street.

53.30 *Turn left* on Elm Street.

53.40 *Turn left* on Spring Street.

53.40 View of Orange & Rockland Lovett power plant on right (E.R.M. 37.37).

53.50 *Turn left* on Church Street (gravel road) uphill.

53.60 *Turn right* on Route 9W.

53.60 Old schoolhouse, now library, on left.

53.70 Boulderberg Manor Restaurant, former Calvin Tomkins House, on right.

54.00 Entrance drive to Boulderberg Manor on right.

54.20 Pass under power transmission line (E.R.M. 37.40). View of Indian Point.

54.40 Indian Point Atomic Power Plant across river (E.R.M. 38.25).

54.45 Old graveyard on right.

55.40 Hudson River Reserve Fleet Monument on right (E.R.M. 38.00 for article).

55.70 *Turn right* on Old Ayers Road (marked dead end).

56.20 *Turn Right, then left* along railroad.

56.30 Jones Point. View of Peekskill. (E.R.M. 38.50.)

56.30 *Turn around.* It is possible to walk along the tracks to Kidd's Point.

56.50 *Turn left.*

56.60 Site of former Jones Point depot. (E.R.M. 38.45.)

56.65 Cross cement street at diagonal.

56.70 Tabernacle Church on right.

56.90 *Turn right* on Route 9W.

56.95 Hiker's parking on left.

57.30 Dunderberg Mountain. Scenic pulloff on right. (E.R.M. 40.00.) View of Peekskill on right.

57.90 Vista—Bear Mountain on left with tower. Anthony's Nose, Iona Island, and The Race.

59.20 Old road to Doodletown on left (E.R.M. 41.60).

59.50 *Turn right* onto causeway across Salisbury Meadow to Iona Island. Bird Sanctuary.

60.00 *Turn around*—site of former Iona Island depot. (E.R.M. 41.50.)

60.50 *Turn right* on Route 9W.

60.60 Entrance to Bear Mountain Park on left. Site of former Knickerbocker Ice Co. storage depot on right. Doodletown Bight on right. (E.R.M. 42.10.)

60.60 Bear Mountain Bridge seen ahead. Anthony's Nose to right.

61.30 Road down to steamboat landing on right.

61.50 Entrance to Bear Mountain Inn on left. (E.R.M. 42.40.)

61.60 Swimming pool down to right.

61.80 Hessian Lake on left. (42.40 E.R.M.)

61.85 Site of Fort Clinton on right. (E.R.M. 42.40.)

61.85 Rockland/Orange County Line (See article E.R.M. 42.60.)

61.95 Bear Mountain Circle. Continue around going north on Route 9W. This is the junction of Palisades Interstate Parkway, Route 9W, Route 202, and Route 6. Bear Mountain Bridge to right. (E.R.M. 42.50.)

62.00 *Continue north* on Route 9W.

62.20 Start of Popolopen Creek viaduct. (E.R.M. 42.60.)

62.40 End of Popolopen Creek viaduct.

62.45 Site of Fort Montgomery on right. Reached by narrow footpath. (E.R.M. 42.65.)

62.45 *Turn left* on Old Route 9W.

62.80 *Turn left* on Mine Torne Road.

63.00 Pass trail entrance to Hell Hole on left.

63.05 Trail to Brooks Lake on right.

63.10 *Turn around.* Trail to Popolopen Torne on right. Hell Hole on left. Entrance to U.S. Military Academy straight ahead.

63.10 Site of former Queensboro furnace down on left.

64.50 *Cross* old Route 9W. Continue straight on Mine Dock Road.

64.50 *Bear right* downhill.

64.60 *Bear right.*

64.70 Pass beneath Route 9W viaduct.

64.80 *Turn around.* Fort Montgomery depot. Sandy Beach. General Wayne left here for Stony Point on July 15, 1779. It offers a view of Anthony's Nose. (E.R.M. 42.75.)

65.90 Pass beneath viaduct again.

66.00 *Bear left.*

66.10 *Turn right* on Old Route 9W.

65.50 *Turn left* on present Route 9W.

66.70 Garrison Pond on right. Randall House on left (ca. 1770) (E.R.M. 43.40).

67.30 *Turn right* on Route 218.

67.80 Sugarloaf visible across river.

67.90 Union Cemetery on right.

67.90 Highland Falls town line.

68.30 Margaret Corbin monument, reading "Molly, Margaret Corbin, Heroine of Fort Washington, passed her last days on the former Morgan Estate near by." (E.R.M. 44.80.)

68.40 Cragston Residential Park on right. Former entrance gate to Morgan Estate on left, also stone walls. (E.R.M. 45.00.)

68.60 Junction with cutoff to Route 9W on left. Continue straight.

69.10 Ondora Residential Park on right.

70.10 *Turn right* on Havens Road, off Main Street.

70.30 *Bear sharp left.*

70.40 *Bear sharp right.*

70.50 *Turn around.* View across river to Beverly Dock. (E.R.M. 45.70.)

70.50 *Bear right* uphill.

70.70 *Turn right* on Main Street.

70.80 *Bear right.* Leave Route 218.

70.90 Cross Highland Brook at top of Buttermilk Falls. (E.R.M. 46.20.) This is at the corner of Webb Lane, on private property.

71.05 Ladycliff College on right. Site of former Cozzens and Cranston's Hotels.

71.10 *Turn right* on Station Hill.

71.40 Spring on overhanging rock on left.

71.45 *Turn around.* Site of former Cranston's Station-Highland Falls Depot, now a private residence. (E.R.M. 46.70.)

71.80 *Turn right* on Main Street.

71.90 *Enter Gates* of United States Military Academy, West Point.

71.95 Hotel Thayer on right, built in 1924. (E.R.M. 46.75.)

72.20 *Bear right.*

72.30 Go under building. Viewpoint parking on right.

72.40 Thayer Hall on right. (E.R.M. 47.50.)

72.50 Museum entrance on right.

72.50 Parking on roof of former Riding Academy on right.

72.55 Officer's Mess.

72.60 Cullum Hall on right: Ionic Neo-classic with hipped roof, designed by Stanford White of McKim, Mead & White in 1896.

72.70 *Bear right and right again* on Clinton Place.

72.90 Ruins of Fort Clinton on left, built in 1779, formerly Fort Arnold.

72.90 Kosciuszko monument on left. (E.R.M. 47.75-76.)

72.95 Monument on right. Parade Grounds on left.

73.05 Trophy Point on right. Site of former West Point Hotel. (E.R.M. 48.60.) The Battle Monument was designed by Stanford White.

73.15 Chapel visible on hill to left. (See article E.R.M. 48.60.)

73.25 *Go straight* Post Exchange and good view to right.

73.35 Old officers' houses on left.

73.40 Catholic Chapel of the Most Holy Trinity on left.

73.40 Road becomes Washington Road.

73.70 Old Cadet chapel and burial ground on right. This Greek Revival building was built in 1836 of native stone and has been moved several times. It is now used for funerals. The cemetery dates from 1816 and contains the graves of Generals Winfield Scott, Custer, and Goethals.

73.70 Margaret Corbin grave and marker on right.

73.80 *Bear straight right* at fork.

74.00 *Bear left* on Washington Road.

74.30 New Hospital and Cro' Nest Mountain on right.

74.60 Leave U.S. Military Academy, West Point. Washington Gate.

74.65 Washington Valley (E.R.M. 48.90.)

74.65 *Turn right* on Route 218.

75.60 Pass Lee Gate on right.

75.70 Begin Old Storm King Highway. Built by Gen. George Washington Goethals (1858-1928).

75.80 Cross Falls Brook.

76.30 Cross Rose's Brook.

76.40 Cliff on left. Cro-Nest Mountain. Ahead, across the river, are Breakneck Mountain and Mount Taurus (Bull Hill). View ahead of Storm King Mountain on west bank.

76.80 Parking on right. The valley here is called Mother Cronk's Cove. View ahead of Newburgh Bay and Pollepel's Island. (E.R.M. 51.00)

77.00 Stillman's Spring on left.

77.05 Cross Storm King Brook.

77.20 Parking on right. View of Breakneck Mountain across river.

77.30 Cross stream, No. 1.

77.31 Cross stream, No. 2.

77.50 Cliffs of Storm King Mountain on left. View ahead of Breakneck Mountain and Mount Taurus.

77.80 Point of Storm King Mountain. Road is 200 feet above river. Parking on right. View north of Cornwall, Newburgh Bay, city of Newburgh, Pollepel's Island, Beacon Range, across river, and Shawangunk and Catskill mountains to the northwest. (E.R.M. 51.50.)

78.10 Cross stream, No. 3.

78.20 Parking on right.

78.30 Cross stream, No. 4.

78.40 Cross stream, No. 5

78.40 End of Old Storm King Highway.

78.40 Cornwall village line. Road now called Bayview Avenue.

78.80 Camp Olmstead on left. Note Victorian gatehouses.
79.10 *Turn right* on Hudson Terrace. (E.R.M. 52.30.)
79.15 Cross brook.
79.20 *Turn sharp right* on River Street.
79.20 Spring and park on right.
79.30 Cross West Shore Railroad.
79.31 Cornwall Landing (E.R.M. 52.80). Cornwall Yacht Club on right. Site of former N.Y.O.&W. Railway docks and coal trestle. View across river to South Beacon and Break-neck Mountain. It is near here that Consolidated Edison Co. proposes construction of a pumped storage inlet.
79.31 *Turn left.*
79.40 Cross West Shore Railroad again.
79.80 *Go straight* on Shore Road.
80.10 *Turn right* on River Avenue, Cornwall Depot.
80.11 Cross former New York, Ontario & Western Railway tracks.
80.40 Overgrown drive up hill to left went to Idlewild, home of Nathaniel Parker Willis. His water gardens were located to the right near outlet of Moodna Creek.
80.50 Cross Idlewild Brook.
80.70 New Windsor town line.
80.70 Moodna Creek on right. (E.R.M. 53.20.)
80.90 *Bear right.*
81.00 *Turn right* at stop light, on Route 9W.
81.10 Cross Moodna Creek.
81.40 Pass road to Plum Point on right. Colonie Funeral Home on left. Former Leonard D. Nicoll House, 2½-story Ionic Greek Revival, 1843.
81.70 *Turn right* on Old Route 9W.
82.00 Pass drive to Oakland Academy on right.
82.00 St. Thomas Episcopal Church on left. Stone with crenel-lated bell tower, mid-nineteenth-century.

82.10 Junction with Quassaick Ave-nue on left. (Southbound turn here to get on Route 9W southbound.) The road now becomes River Road.
82.15 Thomas Ellison House site on right, with historical Marker. Used as headquarters by Washington at various times between 1779-1781, it was demolished in mid-nineteenth century.
82.20 Enter Historic New Windsor area: many early nineteenth-century buildings.
82.30 Texaco petroleum depot on right.
82.40 Citgo petroleum depot on right (Cities Service Oil Co.)
82.45 Amoco depot on right (Ameri-can Oil Co.-Standard Oil of New York).
82.47 Affron Tank Terminal on right.
82.47 Lightron Corp. on right: manu-factures fluorescent lighting fixtures.
82.70 Exxon Corp. petroleum depot on right.
82.80 Sunoco petroleum depot on right (Sun Oil Co.).
83.10 Mobil Oil Corp petroleum depot on right.
83.30 Cross Quassaic Creek (E.R.M. 56.00.)
83.30 Newburgh city line. Mount Beacon is across the river. The West Shore Rail-road tunnel under the Erie Railroad branch from Grey-court Junction is on right. This is the site of the former Marvel shipyard, on right, now Steel Style Corp.
83.40 Pass under Erie Railroad.
83.60 *Turn left* on Renwick Street.
83.90 *Turn right* on Liberty Street.
84.05 Pass Lafayette Street.
84.10 Hasbrouck House on right (E.R.M. 56.10).
84.15 *Turn right* on Washington Street.

343

84.20 Belvidere on right. Mount Beacon across river.

84.20 *Turn left* on Washington Place.

84.40 *Turn left* on Broadway (E.R.M. 56.20).

84.50 *Turn right* on Grand Street.

84.55 St. Patrick's R.C. Church on left: greystone, ca. 1855, by Rembrandt Lockwood.

84.60 Ebenezer Baptist Church on right (down First Street): red brick, Hudson River Gothic with clock tower and belfry.

84.65 Associated Reform Church on left: clapboard, Federal style, ca. 1790.

84.65 Newburgh Library on right: three-story brick Victorian, ca. 1865.

84.70 St. George's Episcopal Church on left: stone, 1819.

84.75 Newburgh City Club on right: (restored) two-story brick, ca.1845. Designed by Andrew Jackson Downing and Calvert Vaux, later remodeled by Henry Hobson Richardson.

84.75 Newburgh Court House on left: brick Greek Revival with Ionic entablature, ca. 1830.

84.77 New Library on right: former site of Palatine Hotel.

84.77 Spire of First Methodist Church up Third Street to left: Gothic Revival, mid-nineteenth-century, designed by Rembrandt Lockwood.

84.78 Dutch Reformed Church on right: Greek Revival, ca. 1830, by Alexander Jackson Davis.

84.80 Westminster Presbyterian Church on left: brick, ca. 1890.

85.00 Calvary Presbyterian Church on left: ca. 1890, fieldstone Gothic with red tile, patterned roof and stone spire, heavy cast iron fence, and cemetery. It is now a Seventh Day Adventist Church.

85.10 *Turn left* on Clinton Street.

85.20 *Turn right* on Liberty Street.

85.30 St. Mary's Villa on left.

85.60 *Turn left* on Carobene Court.

85.80 *Turn left* on Elmwood Place.

85.85 *Turn left* on Powell Avenue.

85.95 Van Deuser Farm on left: three-story clapboard, bracketed, ca. 1870. It is now a gatehouse.

86.00 Mount St. Mary's College on left: grounds an example of late nineteenth-century Victorian landscape architecture.

86.40 Chapman Steamer No. 1 firehouse on right.

86.50 Street now called DuBois Street.

86.50 Downing Park on right. Designed by Frederick Law Olmstead in honor of Andrew Jackson Downing in 1892.

86.60 *Turn right* on Third Street.

86.61 *Turn right* on City Terrace.

86.85 *Bear left and then right.* Dante statute and formal gardens.

86.90 Hilltop. Views of River. *Turn around* at loop.

87.10 *Bear right.*

87.15 *Bear right* onto Carpenter Avenue.

87.40 *Turn right* off Carpenter Avenue onto Gidney Avenue.

87.80 *Turn right* on Liberty Street.

87.85 *Turn left* on South Street.

88.10 *Turn left* on Montgomery Street.

88.20 Crawford House on left: three-story clapboard, Ionic columns, ca. 1830. Built for David Crawford in Federal style.
Home and museum of the Historical Society of Newburgh Bay and the Highlands, 189 Montgomery Street.

88.50 *Bear left* on North Street.

88.90 *Turn right* on Balmville Road.

89.00 Johnes Home on left.

89.10 Cross over Interstate 84, Newburgh-Beacon Bridge to right. (E.R.M. 57.20.)

89.30 Powelton Country Club on left: one of oldest golf courses in United States, rebuilt in 1929.

89.40 Chadwick House on right: mid-nineteenth-century.

89.60 Eastman House on right: two-story brick cottage. Downing type with jig-saw ornamentation, mid-nineteenth-century.

89.90 St. Agnes Church on right: red brick and clapboard, Hudson River Gothic (ca. 1870).

89.92 Balmville—Balm of Gilead Tree (also known as Bonville Oak Tree). (E.R.M. 58.00.)

89.93 *Bear straight right* to River Road. Follow signs to Beau Rivage.

90.20 *Bear right.*

90.20 Reese House on left: rusticated Victorian with Andrew Jackson Downing influences, ca. 1859.

90.40 Our Lady of Hope Seminary on right: Oblates of Mary, Tudor Style, ca. 1890.

92.60 Rose House on right, now Beau Rivage Restaurant (E.R.M. 61.00.)

92.70 Roseton.

92.90 Hess Oil Co. Roseton Terminal on right.

93.40 Roseton Generating Plant-Danskammer Point on right. (E.R.M. 62.00.)

93.60 Our Lady of Mercy R.C. Church on left: brick, ca. 1890.

93.60 The power plants in this area are a joint venture of Central Hudson Power, Consolidated Edison Co., and Niagara Mohawk, built 1973. Many transformer yards and transmission lines are in this vicinity.

94.20 Cedar Hill Cemetery is on left.

94.40 *Turn right* on Old Marlboro Turnpike, also called Old Post Road.

95.70 Orchards.

95.80 Quarries near Cedar Cliff are visible on right. (E.R.M. 63.20.)

96.10 Quarry Road on right. New York Trap Rock Div. Lone Star Industries.

96.12 Pond and dam with waterfall on left.

96.40 Bracketed mansion on right.

96.70 Christ Episcopal Church on right.

96.75 *Turn right* onto Route 9W off Old Post Road.

96.80 Marlboro village.

96.80 St. Marys R.C. Church on left.

96.85 Riverside Cemetery on right.

97.20 Cross Maune Kill, falls on left. (E.R.M. 64.50.)

97.21 *Turn right* on Dock Road.

97.25 Foundations of nineteenth-century Marlboro Winery on right.

97.70 Former depot and landing. *Turn around.* (E.R.M. 64.50.)

98.20 *Turn right* on Route 9W.

98.30 Marlboro Central School on left.

98.32 Elementary school on right.

98.33 Young estate on right at end of Young Avenue (E.R.M. 64.70).

98.50 Marlboro town line, Pegg's Point to right. (E.R.M. 64.90.)

100.10 Hepworth Farms on left, reputed to be the first fruit stand in the Hudson Valley.

100.70 Milton town line.

100.71 *Turn right* on South Road.

100.80 Micajiah Lewis homestead on right: 1-story stone, pre-1760, remodeled.

101.10 *Bear right* at fork.

101.20 *Turn right* on Maple Avenue.

101.40 *Turn left* on Watson Avenue (red fire hydrant on left).

101.60 *Turn right* on Dock Road.

101.70 Former Milton Railroad depot and landing, Kedem Royal Winery. *Turn around.* View of I.B.M. tower across river. (E.R.M. 67.50.)

102.20 *Turn right* on Main Street (end of Dock Road).

102.25 *Turn right* on Church Street.

102.30 Presbyterian Church on left: Creosote Shingle Gothic, bracketed, ca. 1890.

102.30 United Methodist Church on right: clapboard, ca. 1850, cemetery.

102.30 *Turn around*.

102.35 *Turn right* on Main Street.

102.50 Locust Grove Fruit Farm and vineyard, both sides.

102.50 Yellow Victorian barn on right.

102.90 Cross brook: picturesque orchards.

103.00 *Bear right* on North Road.

103.40 Sunnycrest on right: mid-nineteenth-century. Home of (Civil War) Gen. Peter Wanzer.

103.45 White colonial home on right.

103.50 *Turn right* on Route 9W off Main Street, North Road.

104.60 Pass Blue Point Road on right. Hudson Valley Wine Co. orchards and winery are at end of road. (E.R.M. 69.20.)

105.70 Junction Routes 44 and 55. Mid-Hudson Bridge to right. (E.R.M. 70.50.)

106.00 End of interchange.

106.10 Cross over Central New England Railroad (New Haven-Conrail).

106.20 Highland town line.

106.40 *Turn right* off Route 9W onto White Street.

106.70 *Turn right* on Vineyard Avenue.

106.80 *Bear Left* downhill, along Twaalfskill Creek.

106.90 Mid-Hudson Hotel on left: ca. 1850, brick with stepped gable ends.

106.92 Cross West Shore Railroad tracks. Former ferry slips to left.

107.10 Cross railroad tracks again. Here is a former Highland depot remodeled as a house as a small copy of Lake Mohonk Mountain House.

107.15 Elting's Landing Historical Marker on right. Bombarded by the British in 1777, the ferry was established by Noah Elting in 1793. A horse-powered flat boat was used

in 1819, and the Dutchess & Ulster Steam Power Ferry was established in 1830.

107.20 Continue along River on Oakes Road, under bridges.

107.90 *Turn around*. Oakes. (E.R.M. 70.40.)

108.90 Mid-Hudson Hotel on right. Continue uphill on Vineyard Avenue, the right fork.

109.40 *Turn right* on Bellevue Road.

110.60 *Bear right* at fork.

110.80 *Bear right at fork*.

111.30 View of Culinary Institute of America across river. (E.R.M. 73.80.)

111.80 Small Binnewater Pond on right.

112.40 Krum Elbow on right. See article E.R.M. 74.25.

112.90 Orchard area. Road now called Red Top Road.

113.20 *Turn right* on Route 9W— Divided highway.

113.80 New York State Police Station on right.

114.60 End of divided highway.

114.90 Mother Cabrini School on right: two-story stone with later Carpenter Gothic elements, 1820. St. Francis Xavier Cabrini (Mother Cabrini) (1850-1917) was born in Italy and came to the United States in 1889. She founded the order of Sisters of the Sacred Heart of Jesus and devoted herself to founding orphanages. She was canonized by Pope Pius XII in 1946—the first U.S. citizen to be canonized.

115.40 West Park town line.

115.50 Site of former St. Gabriels School on right.

115.60 Santa Maria Novitiate (Christian Brothers) on right: two-story brick Italianate Victorian, Mid-nineteenth-century.

116.00 View of Vanderbilt mansion across river. (E.R.M. 77.00.)

116.10 Cross over West Shore Railroad.

116.40 Greek Revival house on right: ca. 1835, clapboard with temple facade.

116.40 The Hedges Restaurant on left: French Provincial building.

116.50 Van Benschoten House on right: two-story stone and shingle.

116.52 Rustic gateway on right.

116.60 Riverby on right: home of John Burroughs, two-story stone, ca. 1873, designed and landscaped by Burroughs. See article E.R.M. 77.20.

116.80 Holy Cross Episcopal Monastery on right.

116.90 Church of the Ascension (Episcopal) on right: stone, 1842, with two ogee windows, Hudson River Gothic stone parsonage.

117.30 Wildwycke Village on left (entrance). A shopping center utilizing the stone stables designed by Julian Burroughs in Tudor style, the barn has a bell and clock. Formerly part of the Oliver Hazard Payne estate.

117.30 Marist Brothers Novitiate entrance on right. Former estate of Oliver Hazard Payne. See article E.R.M. 77.20.

117.50 Old mill ruins on left: mid-nineteenth-century.

117.52 Ascension Church Cemetery on left.

117.70 *Turn left* on Black Creek Road.

117.75 Cross Black Creek.

117.80 Wiltwyck School on right: stone buildings.

118.30 Cross Route 9W at grade. Be careful. It is here called Broadway.

118.30 You are now on Main Street, Esopus.

118.50 *Turn right* at Post Office, Motts Garage.

118.80 Rosemont Mansion on left. See article E.R.M. 79.50.

119.00 *Turn around.* Indian Rock, Private Seaman House. See article E.R.M. 79.75.

119.50 *Turn right* on Main Street.

119.70 Esopus Methodist Church on right: ca. 1845, clapboard, Greek Revival elements.

119.80 *Turn right* on Route 9W (Broadway).

120.10 Mount St. Alphonsus on right: Redemptorist Father's Major Seminary, a massive 4½-story Romanesque gray stone building, 1900.

120.30 Roadside picnic table on right.

120.60 Mother of Perpetual Help Monastery on right, Redemptorist Nuns.

120.70 Ulster Park town line.

121.40 Dutch Reformed Church on left: brick with Gothic Revival elements and bell tower, 1827.

121.60 *Turn right* on River Road, Ulster County Route 24.

121.60 Orchard area. Husseys Mountain to west.

121.80 Old Red Schoolhouse with belfry to left.

123.10 Riverfront. Esopus Meadows on right. Lighthouse. See article E.R.M. 82.30.

124.40 View upriver to Catskill Mountains and Kingston-Rhinecliff Bridge.

125.60 *Bend left.*

125.70 *Turn right* off River Road onto Route 9W.

125.70 Village of Port Ewen (E.R.M. 85.25.)

125.72 Cemetery on right.

125.30 View of Catskill Mountains ahead.

126.50 *Turn right* on North Broadway.

126.50 Sleightsburg. See article E.R.M. 86.00.

127.00 *Turn around:* southern terminus of former Skillipot cable ferry to Rondout, across Rondout

Creek. View of Ponckhockie Cliffs.

127.10 *Turn left* on First Avenue.

127.20 *Turn right* on Parsell Street.

127.30 View of Rondout Lighthouse on left. E.R.M. 86.25.

127.32 *Turn right* on Second Street.

127.40 *Turn left* on North Broadway.

127.70 *Turn right* on Route 9W.

127.71 *Turn left* on Old Route 9W.

128.00 Begin Suspension Bridge across Rondout Creek.

128.20 End bridge. You are on Wurts Street, Rondout. E.R.M. 86.30.

128.30 Trinity Methodist Episcopal Church on left: 1867, yellow brick, Hudson River Gothic, with slate spire.

128.30 Veterans' Memorial on right.

128.40 Corner of Spring Street. Abandoned church on left: brick Gothic. ca. 1860, fine spire.

128.45 St. Mark's A.M.E. Church on right: fieldstone Gothic Revival with Tudor influences, ca. 1870, slate roof, crennelated belfry.

128.45 St. Peter's R.C. Church on left: yellow brick Hudson River Gothic with Romanesque belfry, ca. 1860.

128.50 *Turn right* on Rogers Street.

128.50 Redeemer Lutheran Church on right: fieldstone Tudor with crennelated square belfry, ca. 1900.

128.60 *Turn right* on Broadway.

128.60 Ponckhockie Cliffs on left.

128.80 Hudson River Maritime Center Museum on right at 41 Broadway.

128.90 Strand Area. Daily Freeman Building on right.

128.90 *Turn left* on the Strand.

129.10 Site of old Rhinecliff ferry house on right.

129.30 Ruins of old limestone furnace on left.

129.60 *Bend left* on North Street, Ponckhockie.

130.00 *Turn Right* on Delaware Avenue.

130.10 Cross Ulster & Delaware railroad track.

130.40 Kingston Point. *Turn around.* (E.R.M. 86.30.)

130.60 *Turn right* into park. Good view upriver. Area of old Dayline Park and lagoon where replica of *Half Moon* was anchored.

130.80 *Turn right* on Delaware Avenue.

131.00 Continue up hill on Delaware Avenue.

131.20 Victorian School House on left.

131.20 *Turn right* on Lyndsley Avenue.

131.30 Cordt's House on right: 1873, twenty-two-room Victorian mansion.

131.30 *Turn Around.* Good view looking south.

131.40 *Turn right* on Delaware Avenue.

131.50 *Turn left* on Abruyn Street.

131.55 Union Congregational Church on right: cast concrete, Hudson River Gothic, late nineteenth-century, formerly known as "The Children's Church," Ponckhockie, 1780.

131.60 *Turn right* on Walnut Street. Ponckhockie Cliffs ahead.

131.70 *Turn right* on Gill Street.

131.75 *Turn left* on Yedman Street.

131.80 *Turn left* on East Union Street (Tompkins).

131.90 *Turn right* on East Strand.

132.40 *Turn right* on Broadway.

132.70 St. Marys Church on right: Brick Tudor, ca. 1910, with square belfry.

133.80 *Turn right* on Broadway, Route 9W. Continue uphill.

133.90 *Turn right* on East Chestnut Street.

134.00 *Turn left* on Livingston Street.

134.01 Emanual Evangelical Lutheran Church: Hudson River Gothic, green brick with spire, ca. 1860.

134.10 *Turn left* on Delaware Avenue.

134.20 *Turn right* on Broadway.

Optional Side Trip to Old Kingston
(4.1 miles round trip).

0.00 Corner of East Chester Street and Broadway. Continue straight on Broadway, Route 28.

0.10 Kingston Hospital on right.

0.20 Kingston Library on left: red brick, composite style, ca. 1900.

0.20 Kingston City Hall on right: nineteenth-century, by Arthur Crooks. Modeled after Palazzo Vecchio in Florence, ca. 1875, mansard roof.

0.25 Kingston High School on left: yellow brick, Ionic Neo-classic, ca. 1900.

0.30 Kingston Municipal Auditorium on left (corner of Hoffman).

0.40 Bus terminal on left.

0.50 Y.M.C.A. on left: three-story red brick, ca. 1900.

0.60 Go under West Shore Railroad and Greenkill Avenue.

0.80 Junction Routes 28-32-213.

0.90 Octagon House on left: corner of Elmendorf Avenue, two-story red brick.

1.10 *Turn left* on Park Avenue. View of Catskill Mountains ahead.

1.20 First Baptist Church on right: stone, Hudson River Gothic with spire, fieldstone, ca. 1890.

1.30 Governor Clinton Hotel on right: red brick Georgian with temple portico, ca. 1910, now apartments.

1.30 *Turn right* on Clinton Avenue. Entering Stockade area, original part of town.

1.50 Senate House on left (Colonel Wessel Ten Broeck House), 1676. This was the first meeting place of the New York State Senate in 1777.

1.50 *Turn left* on North Front Street.

1.80 *Turn left* on Green Street.

2.10 *Turn left* on Pearl Street.

2.20 *Turn left* on Wall Street.

2.25 Old Dutch Church on right: fieldstone with spire, 1852, by Minard Lefever. Governor George Clinton (1739-1812) is buried in the churchyard.

2.30 Old courthouse on left: 1818, on site of earlier one.

2.40 *Turn right* on North Front Street.

2.50 *Turn right* on Fair Street.

2.51 Senate House Museum on left.

2.70 *Turn left* on Pearl Street.

2.80 Continue straight on Park Avenue.

3.00 *Turn right* on Broadway (Routes 28 and 32).

3.20 Octagon House on right.

3.50 Pass under Greenkill Avenue and West Shore railroad.

4.10 *Turn left* on East Chester Street. End of sidetrip.

Old houses in the Stockade Area.

1) Converse Street and Frog Alley: Pieter Cornelise Louw-Bogardus site, ca. 1668, earliest documented house in city.

2) St. James Street #84: Van Keuren House.

3) Wall Street #97: Van Steenbergh House, 1700, the only house that escaped burning by General Vaughan in 1777.

#225: Cornelius Elmendorf House, before 1777.

4) Green Street #7: Tobias Van Bruen House.

#135: Col. Abraham Hasbrouck House.

#138: Gerrett Van Keuren House.

#145: Rachel DuMond House, Frame, late eighteenth century.

#147: Egbert DuMond House, Federal style.

#175: Jacobus Coenradt Elmendorf House.

5) Main Street

#63: John Sudam House (also known as Van Leuven) ca. 1820, Federal style.

#74: Tobias Swart House, Colonial style.

#77: Dr. Elmendorf House.

#78: Brick House, ca. 1840.

6) Crown Street

#10: Cornelius Tappen House, First Post Office.

#42: Petrus Franciscus Rogan House, ca. 1750, also known as Franz House, Swiss settlers.

#43: Matthew Jansen House.

#53: Abraham DeWitt Lowe House (ca. 1750), Coffee House. Corner of North Front Street: Jacobus S. Bruyn House ca. 1750.

7) John Street

#20: DeWitt House, ca. 1830

#74: Jan Hendrickse Persen House, 1700s.

Corner of Greene Street: Luke Kiersted House, 1700s, frame.

8) Pearl Street

#26: The Columns (Reverend Hoes House), Greek Revival, served as a Rectory.

#109: Cornelius Masten House (1725), stone.

Corner of Wall Street: Johannes Masten House, frame.

9) Maiden Lane

#88: Coonradt Elmendorf Tavern. The Committee of Safety met here.

#129: John McLean House, before 1730

10) Clinton Avenue

#308: Abraham Masten House.

11) North Front Street

#3: Tremper House, 1801

#61: Anthony Freer House.

Corner of Green Street: Martinus Hoffman House (1660), also known as Jan Gacherie House.

12) Road to Hurley: Tjerck Claessen DeWitt House (1669).

There are many other old and interesting buildings in the Stockade Area and a leisurely walking tour is greatly recommended.

134.30 *Turn right* on East Chester Street.

134.40 Cross Ulster & Delaware Railroad.

135.50 Kingston Home for Elderly on left. (E.R.M. 88.25.) White brick Victorian.

135.50 *Turn right* on Route 32.

135.52 Town of Ulster Line.

135.60 You are on Old Flatbush Road (E.R.M. 89.60.)

135.80 Quarries on both sides.

136.10 View of Kingston-Rhinecliff Bridge to right.

136.40 *Turn right* on Ulster Landing Road.

136.60 Town of Ulster Park, Riverside picnic ground and boat launching site, entrance.

137.80 Driveway to Patroon Hill on right: two-story clapboard with tower, 1835.

138.00 Pass under Kingston-Rhinecliff Bridge. (E.R.M. 90.00.)

138.90 *Turn right.*

139.40 Entrance to Wrongside on right: two-story brick and clapboard, ca. 1825. Name given to the estate by the Livingstons, who felt their relative who built it should have done so on the east bank of the river.

141.70 View of Catskill Mountains.

141.80 Ulster Landing (E.R.M. 91.50.)

142.20 St. George's camp on right.

142.70 Ulster County Park. St. George's bathing beach entrance on right.

143.30 Pass road to Turkey Point on right.

143.70 *Turn right* on Route 32. (E.R.M. 92.85.)

143.70 Flatbush Center.

143.71 One-room red brick school-house on right.

144.20 Flatbush Reformed Church on right: organized in 1807, present building 1808, field-stone with square belfry.

144.20 Good view of Catskill Mountains: left to right, Overlook Mountain, High Peak, Wall of Manitou.

144.40 Old stone house and well house on right.

145.20 Glasco town line.

145.80 Glasco Center.

145.80 *Turn right* on Glasco Turnpike also called Delaware Avenue.

146.40 *Turn around* at site of former glass warehouse at corner of Hudson Street. (E.R.M. 94.50.)

147.00 *Turn right* on Route 32.

147.00 Overlook Mountain and Kaaterskill High Peak seen ahead.

147.50 *Turn right* on Route 9W: Barclay Heights.

148.40 Saugerties town line.

148.40 St. Mary of the Snow Cemetery on left.

148.50 *Turn right* on Spaulding Lane.

148.60 Schoonmaker House on right: one-story stone, eighteenth century.

148.61 *Turn left* on Simmons Street.

148.90 *Turn left* on Barclay Heights.

149.10 *Turn right* on Burt Street.

149.30 *Bear right*.

149.35 *Turn right* on Ferry Street.

149.40 Esopus Creek and marinas on left. (E.R.M. 96.50.)

149.70 *Turn around* at Saugerties Power Boat Association.

150.05 *Bear left* uphill.

150.30 *Turn right* on Route 9W.

150.40 *Turn right again* on Route 9W.

150.40 Trinity Church and Catskill Mountains on left. Hudson River on right.

150.60 *Turn left* on Route 9W Kaaterskill High Peak seen ahead.

150.62 Old Red Brick School on right.

150.70 Cross Esopus Creek on Truss Bridge, above the dam.

150.80 *Turn right* on Riply Street.

150.85 *Turn left* at site of former Cantine Coated Paper mill.

150.90 *Turn right* on Route 9W, Partition Street.

151.00 *Turn right* on Dock Street.

151.00 Pull off to right. Overlook point. Gorge and falls of the Esopus.

151.00 *Turn around*.

151.10 *Turn right* on Route 9W, Partition Street.

151.30 *Turn right* on Route 9W, Main Street.

151.40 Reformed Church and Parsonage on left.

151.50 Kiersted House on left: one-story stone with small wing, pre-Revolutionary.

151.70 Schoonmaker Homestead on left: one-story stone with smaller wings, pre-Revolutionary.

151.80 *Turn right* on Mynderse Street.

152.00 Salt Box House on right: ca. 1820.

152.00 Mynderse House on left: one-story stone, early eighteenth century. This is the possible setting for "Clawbonny" in Cooper's *Afloat and Ashore:* The original house dates from 1690, with new wings dating from 1743.

152.30 *Bear left* on Lighthouse Drive.

152.40 Esopus Creek on right: old mills.

152.60 Capt. John Field House on left: two-story brick, Greek Revival mansion with fluted Doric columns, ca. 1840.

152.60 Marinas on right.

153.00 Coast Guard Station on right.

153.10 Rock Point. Private estate.

153.10 *Turn around*: view of lighthouse (E.R.M. 96.50.).

153.80 *Turn right* uphill on Mynderse Road (no street sign).

153.90 View to left of Saint Marys of the Snow R.C. Church: light gray, Hudson River gothic, with spire.

154.10 Continue straight onto Route 9W.

154.20 Entrance to Seamon Park on right: extensive floral displays, annual autumn Chrysanthemum Festival.

154.40 Sawyer's Mill and Falls on Sawyer Kill to right: old mill undergoing restoration.

154.40 Cross Sawyer Kill. View of Catskill Mountains to left.

154.80 *Bear right.*

155.30 Malden-on-Hudson. Methodist Church: brick bracketed, with tall spire, 1867.

155.60 Battleship Maine Memorial, 1898: an old cannon.

155.60 *Turn right* on unnamed street. Loop around, bearing right all the time to Malden Landing, an old Hudson River village.

155.90 *Bear right again* back onto the Main Road.

155.90 Victorian gingerbread cottage with large cast-iron floral urn ahead.

156.00 Pass Maine Memorial again on right.

156.00 *Bear left.*

156.30 *Turn right* on Route 9W.

156.80 Cross bridge over West Shore Railroad.

157.40 *Turn right* on Emerick Road.

157.50 *Bear right.*

157.70 Cross grade crossing of West Shore railroad.

157.70 *Bear left.*

157.90 Cross bridge over brook.

158.00 *Turn around,* bearing left: Eve's Point. (E.R.M. 99.60.)

158.70 *Bear left.*

158.75 *Turn right* on Route 9W.

158.90 Good view of Catskill Mountains to left: Overlook, High Peak, Cloves.

158.92 Enter village of West Camp. (E.R.M. 100.30.)

158.92 *Bear right* on Route 9W.

159.20 St. Paul's Lutheran Church and Old Stone House on right.

159.90 *Bend right* under West Shore Railroad.

160.00 *Turn sharp left* on Route 9W. Enter township of Catskill.

160.00 Village of Cementon.

160.50 St. Mary's R.C. Church and Alpha Portland Cement Plant to right. (E.R.M. 102.)

160.50 Enter Greene County (E.R.M. 102.90).

161.00 Entrance to Alpha Cement Plant on right.

161.20 Alsen.

161.20 Lehigh Portland Cement Co. to right.

161.21 *Sharp left and right* under West Shore Railroad.

161.22 Kalkberg on left.

161.70 Pass under cement conveyor.

162.70 *Turn right* on Embought Road.

162.80 Cross West Shore Railroad at grade.

162.80 Kalkberg, behind.

163.50 View of Inbocht Bay to right.

163.80 Cross Mineral Spring Brook.

163.90 *Bend left.*

164.60 *Bear left* at Corner of Greenpoint Road (E.R.M. 104.00).

165.10 *Bear left* at Anbach Lane.

165.40 Fine view of Catskill Mountains to left, beyond the Kalkberg.

165.70 Kykuit Hill (E.R.M. 106.35).

165.70 Clauland House on right: 1½-story stone with one-story attachment, 1740.

166.30 Village of Catskill town line.

166.30 Embought Road becomes Broome Street.

166.70 *Turn right* on Grand Avenue.

166.80 Victorian red brick mansion on left.

167.20 *Turn left* on West Main Street.

167.40 Driveway to Hudson View House to right.

167.60 Hop O'Nose on right.

167.80 Old Mill on right. Union Cotton Mills, ca. 1860, two-story brick with tower.

167.90 Catskill Creek on right. Marinas.

168.10 Uncle Sam House on left. Two-story stucco, early nineteenth century. Martin Van Buren, eighth president of United States, was married here in 1807. Also, Sam Wilson

("Uncle Sam") lived here between 1817 and 1824.

168.11 *Turn right on West Bridge Street.*

168.15 Cross Catskill Creek on "Uncle Sam" bascule bridge.

168.20 *Turn right on Water Street.*

168.20 Site of Catskill Evening Line dock on right.

168.30 *Turn left on Bronson Street.*

168.35 *Turn right on Hill Street.*

168.40 *Turn left on Greene Street.*

168.50 *Turn right on Main Street.*

168.50 Dr. Albuisson House on southwest corner: two-story brick with stepped gable, fine doorway, and later bracketed cornice, ca. 1825.

168.70 Site of shale brick company: office building: two-story clapboard, ca. 1840, on creek to right.

168.90 Rip Van Winkle Bridge seen on left.

169.00 Catskill Landing. Catskill Point (E.R.M. 107.25).

169.00 County Highway Department garage. Former site of terminus of Greenbush Ferry, Catskill Mountain narrow gauge railway, and wharf of Hudson River Day Line.

169.00 *Turn around.*

169.80 First Reformed Church on right: red brick, Hudson River Gothic.

169.85 First Baptist Church on left: red brick Hudson River Gothic, two spires.

169.85 Greene County Courthouse on right: Ionic style with dome and frieze pediment entablature.

170.20 *Bear left.*

170.30 *Turn right up Summit Avenue.*

170.35 *Bear right and left again.*

170.40 *Turn right on Grand Street.*

170.45 *Turn right on North Street.*

170.70 *Turn left on Thompson Street.*

171.00 *Turn right on Spring Street.*

171.20 *Turn right on William Street.*

171.25 Great view of Catskill Mountains.

171.25 St. Luke Episcopal Church on left: stone with slate roof and spire, bracketed style.

171.50 *Turn left on Main Street.*

171.60 Howard Slide on left.

171.65 *Turn left on Bridge Street.*

171.70 *Turn left on Franklin Street.*

171.72 Christ Presbyterian Church and Old Courthouse on right: mid-nineteenth century with Corinthian columns made in same pattern as those used on the former Catskill Mountain House. First Court House, two-story brick, Palladian window, ca. 1812, now a Masonic Temple.

171.72 Howard Slide on left.

171.80 *Turn right on William Street.*

171.90 *Turn right on Spring Street.*

171.98 *Turn right on Bridge Street (Route 385).*

172.05 *Turn left on Liberty Street.*

172.05 St. Patrick's Church: red brick Hudson River Gothic, with spire, 1885.

172.10 *Turn left on Harrison Street.*

172.20 *Turn right into grounds of St. Anthony's Friary.*

172.20 Site of former Prospect Park Hotel (E.R.M. 107.30). Circle around building. View of Rip Van Winkle Bridge.

172.50 *Exit friary grounds. Turn right on Harrison Street.*

172.51 *Turn left on Prospect Avenue.*

172.70 *Turn right on William Street.*

172.70 Ionic style Greek Revival house on left: ca. 1840.

172.80 *Turn left on Woodland Avenue.*

172.81 Picturesque roofed gateway on right.

173.10 *Turn left on High Street.*

173.20 *Turn right on Spring Street.*

173.30 Former home and studio of artist Thomas Cole on right.

173.40 *Turn right on Route 23. Rip Van Winkle Bridge ahead.* (E.R.M. 108.30.)

173.70 *Turn left on Hamburg Road.*

174.30 Hamburg Village (E.R.M. 108.75). View across river of Olana Castle and Mount Merino.

174.90 *Turn right* on Route 385.

175.00 Athens Village line.

175.80 Lighthouse on right. (E.R.M. 111.25.)

176.90 *Turn left* on Fifth Street.

176.91 *Bear right.*

176.91 Van Loan-Haight-Gantly House on left. 38 Franklin Street. Two-story yellow brick, Federal style, built in 1812 for Gen. Samuel Haight, it has an oval ballroom and was very elegant for its day.

176.92 *Turn right* on Franklin Street.

177.10 *Turn right* on Third Street.

177.20 *Turn left* on South Washington Street.

178.30 House with conservatory on left: Clark House, ca. 1865.

178.31 *Turn left* on Second Street.

178.31 House with stepped gables.

178.40 Brooks Building, 1893. Formerly the Opera House.

178.80 *Turn right* on Leeds Road (South Vernon Street).

178.90 *Turn right* on First Street.

179.10 *Turn right* on South Montgomery Street.

179.30 *Turn left* on Washington Street (Route 385).

179.90 Zion Lutheran Church.

180.10 Old yellow brick schoolhouse. Hudson River Gothic.

180.30 Athens Boat Launching site.

180.40 Cross Murderers' Creek (E.R.M. 113.00).

180.60 *Turn right* on Brick Row. Group of row houses for railroad workers. Three-story brick, mid-nineteenth century.

180.70 *Turn left* along Brick Row.

181.80 *Turn around.* Go back to Route 385.

182.10 *Turn right* on Route 385.

182.10 View of Catskill Mountains to left and Berkshire and Green Mountains of Vermont on right.

182.30 Large yellow farmhouse with Mansard roof on left. Orchard area.

183.20 Entrance to Sleepy Hollow Lake Development on left.

183.90 *Turn right* on Fourmile Point Road.

184.60 Klinkenburg House on left: two-story stone with brick ends, early eighteenth century.

184.90 Pond on right.

185.30 Fourmile Point (E.R.M. 115.45): lighthouse of stone with clapboard wings, early nineteenth century.

185.30 *Turn around.*

186.70 *Turn right* on route 385.

186.80 Old cemetery on right.

187.00 Groesback House on right: Two-story clapboard, early nineteenth century.

187.00 Extensive view of Catskill Mountains to left.

187.10 Mansion on knoll at right: Two-story brick Victorian, ca. 1870.

187.20 Elmcrest Farm on right. Lampman House, Two-story clapboard, ca. 1800. Later enlarged and renovated with mansard roof and brackets.

187.20 Lampman Hill (E.R.M. 118.00).

187.20 *Turn right* on Ely Street, Coxsackie.

188.00 House with stepped gable to right.

188.00 *Turn right* on New Street (one way).

188.01 *Turn right* on South River Street.

188.01 Old foundry on left.

188.60 *Turn around.* (E.R.M. 118.50.)

188.90 *Bear right.*

189.20 Old brick stores in area.

189.20 Boat launching site (E.R.M. 119.00).

189.20 *Turn around.*

189.30 *Turn right* on Reed Street.
189.40 *Turn right* on Ely Street (becomes Mansion Street).
189.40 Heermance Memorial Library.
189.70 Large red brick school house, corner of Elm Street.
189.80 *Turn right* on Washington Avenue.
189.80 St. Mary's Catholic Church on left.
190.20 *Turn left* on Lafayette Avenue.
190.50 Van Dyk House on right: built by Abraham Van Dyk in early nineteenth century, Two-story brick, Federal style.
190.60 *Turn right* on Mansion Street (Route 385).
190.70 *Turn right* on Lawrence Avenue (just before West Shore Railroad bridge).
190.80 Old brick farmhouse.
191.20 Cross Coxsackie Creek (E.R.M. 121.50).
191.30 One-room schoolhouse on left. Now private home.
194.30 *Turn right* down Mill Street, New Baltimore (E.R.M. 125.50).
194.60 *Turn left* on Main Street (Alton Civil Institute).
194.65 *Turn around* at Church Street.
194.70 *Turn right* at Parsons-Bronck House: 1½-story, eighteenth century.
194.90 Old clapboard church, now a private home.
195.00 Continue straight on Route 144.
195.70 Requea Cemetery on right.
195.90 Greene-Albany County Line.
196.10 Cross Hannacroix Creek (E.R.M. 126.50).
196.20 Coeymans. Bronck House to right: 1½-story stone, mid-eighteenth century.
196.25 Road to Barren Island on right (closed to public). (E.R.M. 126.60.)
196.40 Coeymans. You are on Main Street.
196.70 Large Doric Greek Revival house.

196.90 Continue straight on Main Street. (E.R.M. 127.50.)
197.00 *Bear right* across bridge over Coeymans Creek (E.R.M. 127.55).
197.05 *Turn right* downhill.
197.20 Ariantje Coeymans House on right: Two-story stone, ca. 1728.
197.30 Ravena Yacht Club—boat sheds, launching ramp, view of Castleton Bridges.
197.30 *Turn around*.
197.60 *Turn right* on Main Street, route 144.
197.70 Powell & Minnock Brick Works to right).
197.70 *Bear left*. View of Castleton bridges.
197.90 Coeymans town line.
198.50 Pass beneath conveyor.
199.20 New York Thruway visible to left.
200.20 Cross over New York Central Castleton cutoff line (Conrail) (E.R.M. 129.8.)
200.30 Pass beneath New York Thruway Berkshire branch (E.R.M. 129.90).
201.30 Junction Route 396. Continue on Route 144.
201.70 Baker Farm on right: Two-story clapboard, 1791.
201.80 Thruway entrance on left.
202.00 Cedar Hill town line.
202.90 Cross Vloman Kill (E.R.M. 132.35).
202.91 *turn right* on Lyons Road.
203.10 Old mill-site on right.
203.60 *Turn left* along picnic area.
204.00 Boat launching area.
204.20 *Turn sharp right*.
204.40 Winne House to right: brick Victorian, white with mansard roof, ca. 1860.
204.50 Parda Hook (E.R.M. 133.20): site of Barent-Winne Docks, active in the nineteenth century, especially in the Albany rice trade.
204.50 *turn around*

204.60 *turn right* on Winne Road.
204.80 Pryor House (B.P.O.E.) on right: Italianate Victorian, ca. 1900.
204.90 *Turn right* on route 144.
204.92 Town of Bethlehem line.
205.00 Old Schoolhouse on left: brick, 1859, enlarged in 1907.
205.90 Our Lady of Angels seminary on right.
206.30 Old racetrack on left.
206.30 Halfway House on right: One-story stone, late eighteenth century.
206.30 Frothingham Lake on right.
206.40 *Turn right* on Mosher Road.
206.60 Town House on right: Italianate Victorian, ca. 1870.
206.70 *Bear left.*
206.90 *Bear right.*
207.00 *Bear left.*
207.20 Site of former icehouse on right.
207.40 Van Wies Point (E.R.M. 135.00).
207.40 Van Wies House on right: clapboard with some early stone elements, 1679. Hendrick Gerritse Van Wie, Dutch Colonist in Fort Orange, in 1664, built a house here in 1679.
207.40 Road now becomes Wheeler Road, or Van Wies Point Road.
208.20 *Turn right* on Route 144.
208.25 Van Wies Point School on left: One-room brick, mid-nineteenth century, now shingled.
208.50 Exxon tank farm to left.
208.70 Texaco tank farm.
209.00 Niagara Mohawk Kenwood generating station to right: (E.R.M. 138.75).
209.40 Cross West Shore Railroad Albany Branch (Conrail).
209.90 Glenmont.
210.00 *Turn left* on Retreat House Road.
210.10 Corning Hill on left: Former estate of Erastus Corning, railroad magnate and mayor of Albany.
210.60 *Turn right* on Corning Hill Road.

210.60 Kenwood.
210.70 *Turn left* on route 144.
210.80 Cross Norman's Kill.
211.10 Pass beneath Delaware & Hudson Railroad.
211.30 Academy of the Sacred Heart to left: Victorian Eclectic with Gothic and Mansard elements; Victorian yellow rick gatekeeper's cottage.
211.40 Housing Development on right.
211.60 Pass beneath Interstate 787.
211.70 You are on South Pearl Street, Albany.
211.70 Cherry Hill on left: Two-story clapboard with gambrel roof, ca. 1763. Until 1963, Cherry Hill served as the home of Philip Van Rensselaer and his descendants. Today it features many of the original furnishings, documents, and china and silver collections.
211.90 Entrance to port of Albany on right. (E.R.M. 139.00.)
212.00 *Turn left* on 4th Avenue
212.10 *Turn right* on Elizabeth Street.
212.30 *Turn right* Catherine Street.
212.40 *Turn right* on Clinton Street.
212.40 Schuyler Mansion on right, also called The Pastures: Two-story brick Georgian, 1762, built by Philip Schuyler, a descendent of one of Albany's earliest settlers. With Schuyler's active role in the Revolutionary War and in the formation of the new nation, the mansion became a headquarters where such notables as the Compte de Rochambeau, General Washington, General Lafayette, Benjamin Franklin, and Aaron Burr were entertained. Several years after the war, Schuyler's daughter Elizabeth was wed to Alexander Hamilton in the mansion's drawing room. Open daily except holidays.
212.45 *Turn left* on Schuyler Street.

212.50 *Turn left* on South Pearl Street.

212.60 *Turn right* on Ferry Street.

212.70 *Turn left* on Green Street.

212.80 St. John's Catholic Church.

212.85 Restored row houses.

213.20 *Turn right* on Madison Avenue.

213.60 *Turn left* on Broadway.

213.90 Former Day Line Building on right (l'Auberge des Fougères): Dutch Revival, 1907.

214.00 Delaware & Hudson Building on Right: now State University of New York. Built for the Delaware & Hudson Railroad Co. in 1918 (Marcus T. Reynolds architect) it is in Flemish-Gothic style with sleep slate roofs, ornamented dormers. It is built of granite, four-story, with thirteen-story central tower with large bronze weather vane styled after Henry Hudson's *Half Moon*. A one-story vaulted arcade runs across the front. Major renovation was undertaken in 1975. (E.R.M. 139.50.)

214.00 *Bear right* around rotary to *turn left* up State Street.

214.00 Federal Office Building on right: stone, Victorian Eclectic, 1870.

214.20 St. Peters Church on right: stone, 1802, later Gothic elements.

214.30 *Turn right* on Eagle Street.

214.31 Albany City Hall on right: modified French Romanesque, 1882, by Henry Hobson Richardson, with sixty-bell carillon (largest bell weighs 11,200 lbs.). Statue of Philip Schuyler by J. Massey Rhind.

214.31 Site of former Fort Frederick to left.

214.32 New York State Capitol building to left: A gigantic French Chateau, built between 1867 and 1898 at a cost of $25,000,000. Its design is eclectic. Thomas W. Fuller, Leopold Eidlitz, Henry Hobson Richardson, and Isaac G. Perry all worked on the building.

214.35 *Turn left* on Washington Street.

214.40 New York State Museum-State Education Building on right: with thirty-six Corinthian columns across the facade, built in 1912, designed by Palmer, Hornbostel & Jones, at a cost of $4,000,000.

214.70 *Turn left* on Dove Street.

214.80 *Turn left* on State Street.

215.00 New State Office Buildings on right.

215.50 *Turn right* on Broadway.

215.55 *Circle left around rotary* to head north on Broadway.

215.70 *Turn right* (north) on Broadway.

215.90 Former Union Station on right: French Renaissance Style, 1899. (E.R.M. 139.80.)

216.40 Pass beneath New York Central mainline (Conrail).

216.80 A statue of "Nipper," the Victor "his master's voice" dog, an R.C.A. trademark is prominent on the roof of a building to right.

217.30 Pass beneath Interstate 90. (E.R.M. 141.50.)

217.70 Albany Belt Co. on right.

217.80 Albany-Menands city line (E.R.M. 143.00).

218.00 Old Erie Canal bed parallel to right. D. & H. railroad also parallel to right.

218.40 Junction Route I-787.

218.50 Montgomery Ward Building on left: 9-story concrete.

218.60 Cross over Delaware & Hudson Railroad.

218.60 Former Van Rensselaer estate to left.

219.00 Victorian old folks home on left.

219.30 Junction Route 378. Bridge to Troy on right. E.R.M. 144.25.

219.70 St. Agnes Cemetery and Albany Rural Cemetery on left.
219.80 Doric style mansion to left.
219.90 Watervliet-Menands city line.
220.00 Jermain House on left: Two-story clapboard, Doric temple front, ca. 1840.
220.20 *Take right fork.*
220.50 Continue straight on Third Street.
220.80 Entrance to Watervliet Arsenel on left.
220.90 *Turn left at light.*
221.00 Old Arsenel buildings on left.
221.50 Watervliet city hall on left (E.R.M. 146.25).
221.70 Continue straight on Broadway.
221.90 Pass beneath highway.
222.00 Junction I-787. Continue straight.
222.20 *Turn right* on Twenty-fifth street, traffic light.
222.25 Pass beneath I-787.
222.30 Cross ditch (which is the west channel of Hudson River).
222.31 Green Island, The street is now called Albany Avenue.
222.50 *Bear left* on Hudson Avenue.
222.50 Old railroad freight sheds on left.
222.50 Bridge to Troy on right (former D. & H. Railroad bridge) (E.R.M. 146.75).
222.70 St. Mark's Chapel.
223.10 Park with view of dam and lock on right (E.R.M. 147.75).
223.20 *Turn left* on Tibbits Avenue.
223.30 Cross D. & H. Railroad track.
223.50 *Turn right.*
224.30 City of Cohoes line.
224.40 *Turn right* at Proctor & Schwarz Mill.
224.40 One block before traffic light, you are riding in bed of old Erie Canal.
224.80 Remains of lock and bridge footing on left.
224.90 *Turn right* on Bridge Street.
225.00 Cross sprout or channel of Mohawk River (E.R.M. 149.00).

225.00 View of Simmons Island to left.
225.10 Van Schaick Island.
225.11 *Turn right on first Street.*
225.20 *Turn left* on Hudson Avenue.
225.40 Cross Park Avenue and enter park.
225.42 Golf course on right. Site of Revolutionary encampment on left.
225.45 *Bend left.*
225.50 *Turn right* on Old Military Road.
225.60 Cross D. & H. Railroad (former Rensselaer & Saratoga Railroad).
225.70 *Turn left.*
226.00 Van Schaick House on left: two-story white brick with gambrel roof, 1777.
226.10 View of Hudson River to right.
226.30 View of Route 470 bridge across Hudson to right.
226.40 *Turn left* on Ontario Street, Route 470.
226.50 *Turn right* on Park Avenue (at light).
226.60 *Turn left* on Heartt Avenue.
226.65 View of lower Cohoes Falls, railroad and highway bridges across Mohawk River, and Harmony Mill.
226.70 *Turn left* on River Street.
226.71 *Turn right* on Ontario Street, Route 470.
226.72 Cross bridge over sprout of Mohawk River.
226.72 Rapids visible to right.
226.80 Simmons Island.
226.90 Cross west channel of Hudson and rapids, sprout of Mohawk River.
227.00 Cohoes (E.R.M. 149.80).
227.20 Cross bed of old Erie Canal.
227.21 *Turn right* on Saratoga Street (light).
227.30 *Turn left* on Oneida Street. Mill area.
227.40 Cross main line of Delaware & Hudson Railroad.
227.45 *Turn right.*
227.47 *Turn left* on New Courtlandt Street.

227.50 View of Mohawk River to right.

227.60 Junction with Mohawk Street. Harmony Mills to left.

227.80 Site of finding of Cohoes Mastodon: found in 1866, now in New York State Museum.

228.00 *Turn right* on Front Street. East Harmony tenements.

228.10 *Turn left* on Cataract Street.

228.20 *Turn left.* View of falls to right.

228.22 *Turn left on School Street. Power pond on right.*

228.25 *Turn right on North Mohawk Street.*

228.30 *Bear right* at light.

228.50 Upper view of Mohawk Falls. Cohoes Falls to right.

228.70 *Turn left* on Cascade Street and make U-turn.

228.70 *Turn right* on North Mohawk Street.

229.20 *Bear left* at light.

229.30 Tenements on left.

229.80 *Turn right* on Mohawk Street.

229.90 *Turn left* on Oneida Street (light).

230.00 Cross Delaware & Hudson main line.

230.10 *Turn left* on Saratoga Street (Route 32).

230.20 Cross Mohawk River (E.R.M. 150.45).

230.20 D. & H. railroad viaduct and falls to left.

230.20 Van Schaick Island to right.

230.50 Mansfield House on right: two-story clapboard, full Greek facade, ca. 1840.

230.60 Town of Waterford.

230.60 Waterford Museum to right.

230.70 Cross New York State Barge Canal. View of locks to left and right. (E.R.M. 151.00)

230.80 *Bear right* on Broad Street, Route 32 (E.R.M. 151.40)

230.90 Cross water-filled section of old Erie Canal and Lock No. 2.

231.00 *Turn left* on 3rd Street, Route 32 and 4N (light).

231.60 Good view of Hudson River to right.

231.90 Halfmoon (E.R.M. 155.00).

233.50 Champlain Canal Lock No. 1 to right.

234.50 Brookwood to right: Greek Revival with full temple facade and Ionic columns, ca. 1840.

237.00 Lock No. 2 to right. Melville Hydro plant (E.R.M. 159.00).

237.50 Leeland House.

237.50 Ten Broeck House: Two-story clapboard, late eighteenth century.

238.00 *Bear right.*

238.60 Town of Mechanicville.

239.60 Cross Anthony Kill (E.R.M. 161.00).

239.80 Lock No. 3 and bridge across Hudson to right (E.R.M. 161.75).

240.40 Boston & Main Railroad bridge across Hudson (E.R.M. 162.50).

240.50 Stillwater town line.

242.00 Village of Stillwater. Octagon houses.

242.30 *Bear right.*

242.70 Lock No. 4 and bridge to canal park to right.

242.70 Historic sites:
Fort Ingoldsby, 1709.
Fort Winslow, 1756.
Montressor's Blockhouse.
Storehouse and barracks, 1758.
Schuyler supply depot, 1777.

244.20 Leave Stillwater.

244.90 Bemis Heights.

245.20 Junction Routes 32 and 4. Continue straight on Route 4 to right.

250.60 Enter Saratoga Battlefield Historical Park.

250.20 Historical Park drive on left. Keep straight on Route 4.

247.60 *Turn right* on River Road.

251.50 Town of Saratoga line (E.R.M. 171.70).

251.80 Continue straight on River Road.

252.60 *Turn right* on Route 4.

254.50 Greek Revival farmhouse on left.

256.70 Victory Mills, site of Fort Vrooman and Fort Clinton on left.

257.60 Site of surrender of Gen. Burgoyne to Gen. Gates.

257.90 Village of Schuylerville.

257.92 Philip Schuyler House on right, 1777.

257.92 Site of oldest cotton mill in New York State.

258.10 Cross Fish Creek. Enter village (E.R.M. 178.80).

258.15 Junction Route 32.

258.20 Burgoyne Street, leading to battlefield and monument on left.

258.30 Junction Route 29 and bridge across Hudson on right (E.R.M. 178.80).

258.60 Junction Route 29 to Saratoga Springs on left.

258.60 Site of camp of Gen. Burgoyne.

259.10 Lock No. 5 to right (E.R.M. 180.00).

259.30 Northumberland town line.

260.30 *Turn left* on Route 32. Stark's Knob to left. (E.R.M. 181.40.)

261.20 Bacon Hill (E.R.M. 182.00).

261.20 *Turn right* on Saratoga County Route 29.

263.90 Fort Miller across river to right. (E.R.M. 185.00).

264.40 *Bear right.*

265.60 Old cemetery on left.

266.00 *Bear right.*

266.70 John McCrea House on left.

268.90 Continue straight on West River Road.

270.10 Villa (ca. 1820) to left (E.R.M. 192.25.).

270.30 Cross Delaware & Hudson main line.

270.50 *Turn right.*

270.52 *Turn left* on Route 28— Fort Edward Road.

272.60 *Turn right* on Sisson Road.

272.90 Cross D. & H. Railroad, Fenimore Branch (E.R.M. 192.80).

273.20 *Turn right* on Bluebird Road.

274.00 Continue straight.

274.30 Fenimore. Large water tower to left. (E.R.M. 196.00.)

274.30 *Bear left.* Road becomes Ferry Boulevard.

274.60 *Bear left.*

276.00 South Glens Falls village line.

276.40 Cross South Glens Falls branch of D. & H. Railroad.

276.50 *Turn right* on Spring Street.

277.90 *Turn left* on First Street.

277.00 *Turn right* on Hudson Street.

277.05 *Turn left* on River Street.

277.10 *Turn right* on Main Street, Route 9W.

277.10 Federal style house on left, with palladian window, (ca. 1810).

277.20 Cross Hudson River above Glens Falls and Cooper's Cave.

277.30 Glens Falls (E.R.M. 199.10).

277.30 End.

Lower East Side Road Route

Southbound Express Route to Rockaway Point

0.00 Start at corner of 42nd Street and West Side Highway, 12th Avenue. Head South on 12th Avenue, West Side Highway. (E.R.M. 0.00)

-4.00 (-3.28 E.R.M.) Enter Brooklyn-Battery Tunnel.

Ole Singstad was the tunnel's designer and chief engineer. It is a facility of the Triborough Bridge and Tunnel Authority. Construction started October 28, 1940, and halted for three and a half years during World War

II. The tunnel was opened to traffic May 25, 1950. The length between portals is 9,117 feet. The tunnel has two separate tubes, each with 21'4" roadways with two traffic lanes in each tube. Fifty-three large exhaust fans supply 4,150,000 cubic feet of fresh air each minute, completely changing the air every one and a half minutes. There is a large ventilation tower at the eastern edge of Governor's Island (no vehicular outlet). The tubes have a diameter of thirty-one feet and are of cast iron and were shield-driven under the East River through rock and earth. The land sections were constructed by cut and cover. Tolls are collected at the southern portal.

-5.50 Exit Brooklyn-Battery Tunnel.
-6.50 *Bear right* on Gowanus Expressway—becomes Belt Parkway.
-9.25 Owl's Head Park on left. Begin Shore Parkway. (-8.25 E.R.M.)
-11.75 Fort Hamilton. You are now on Shore Parkway, also known as Belt Parkway. (-11.20 E.R.M.)
-19.00 Exit 11S Flatbush Avenue. *Turn right.*
-20.50 Marine Parkway bridge. (-15.00 E.R.M.)
-21.00 *Turn right* Breezy Point Exit.
-24.25 Corner Bay 227th Street and Rockaway Point Boulevard. (-16.00 E.R.M.)

**Northbound Scenic Route-
Rockaway Point to Forty-second Street Manhattan.**

0.00 Start Tour: corner Bay 227th Street and Rockaway Point Boulevard. (-16.00 E.R.M.) Rockaway Point. You are in Queens County on a barrier sand bar parallel to the southern shore of Long Island, and separated from it by Jamaica Bay Inlet. There is a lighthouse here. Coney Island lies to the North. The view is across Lower New York Bay to Sandy Hook and Atlantic Highlands, both in New Jersey. Normally many ships can be seen from here entering or leaving the Narrows.
0.10 Rockaway Point Boulevard and Bay 222nd Street.
1.00 Rockaway Point Village. Bay 204th Street.
1.20 Rockaway Point Gatehouse. Private residential development. View of Marine Parkway Bridge ahead to left.

Abandoned apartment house project on right. In 1979, these high-rise structures were demolished in thirty seconds by the use of explosives. This was the first use of this method in the New York City area. Remains were two twenty-foot high hills of rubbish.
1.90 Fort Tilden on right.
2.50 Roxbury Village. Residential development.
2.80 Coast Guard base on left.
2.90 Beach 169th Street.
3.00 *Bear left* onto Marine Parkway Bridge.
3.20 View of Rockaway Inlet and Riis Park bathing pavilion. Jacob Riis Park. This large recreation park and ocean bathing beach, with large public parking areas and bath houses, was named for the Danish-American journalist and philanthropist Jacob

361

August Riis (1849-1914). His book *How The Other Half Lives*, subtitled *Studies Among the Tenements of New York* (1890), brought attention to the wretched living conditions of the poor in New York and ultimately led to reforms. A reprint, with many historical photograpahic illustrations is available from Dover Publishing of New York City. Riis became a lifelong personal friend of Theodore Roosevelt.

3.30 Begin Marine Parkway Bridge. Be cautious of unusual pavement.

The Rockaway Peninsula is ten miles long and has a residential population of over 100,000, which is estimated to rise to 125,000 by 1980. The Marine Parkway Bridge is the main acces route for commuters.

Marine Parkway Bridge—A facility of the Triborough Bridge and Tunnel Authority, across Rockaway Inlet. Construction was started in June of 1936, and the span was opened to traffic on July 3, 1937. The bridge was designed by Wardell Hardesty. Emil Praeger was chief construction engineer. The total length of bridge, including viaducts, is 4,022 feet. The length of the lift-truss span is 540 feet, the length of each side truss span is 540 feet. Normal clearance at lift span above mean high water is 55 feet. Raised position under clearance is 150 feet. There are four traffic lanes. Tolls are collected at the northern end.

-15.00 E.R.M. View of Coney Island and Staten Island to left. Jamaica Bay to right.

4.10 North end of bridge. Enter Brooklyn.

4.30 Pay toll. Start of Flatbush Avenue, Brooklyn.

4.40 Floyd Bennett Field on right. Dunes on left. This airport is named for a pioneer American aviator who flew over the North Pole and participated in several arctic expeditions. He lived from 1890 until 1928.

4.60 Dead Horse Bay on left.

4.90 Boat basin on left. Deep Creek on left.

5.80 *Turn* onto Belt Parkway *westbound*. Also called Route 27-A.

6.80 Cross Gerritsen Inlet.

6.90 You are on Plum Island.

7.30 Plum Beach on left. Shell Bank Creek and Plum Beach channel on right. There are extensive tidal flats on left.

7.60 *Turn off* at Exit 14—Knapp Street.

7.60 Western end of Brooklyn Marine Park.

7.90 *Turn left* on Knapp Street. Cross over parkway.

8.00 *Turn right* on Emmons Avenue. (if heading southbound, enter Parkway East here.)

8.30 Sheepshead bay on left. Home port to many commercial fishing, party, and private pleasure boats. Excursion boats and small passenger ferries operate from here to Breezy Point and Rockaway Point Village.

8.60 Breezy Point ferry terminal on left.

8.70 F.W.I.L. Lundy Brothers' Seafood Restaurant on right founded by Frederick William Irving Lundy. This large, ornate building has long been a Brooklyn institution. It has excellent seafood and is well worth a stop. The waiters act in a very independent manner. This is traditional; don't take it personally.

8.80 Footbridge over Sheepshead Bay to left. (Ocean Avenue Footbridge.)

9.00 *Turn left* on Shore Boulevard. Head of Sheepshead Bay.

9.10 *Turn left again* on Shore Boulevard.

9.30 The footbridge you passed before is now on your left again.

10.00 *Dead End. Turn Around.* Kingsborough Community College. Manhattan Beach Air Force Base. You are now in the Manhattan Beach section of Brooklyn. This was once a great society summer resort in the nineteenth century with the great Manhattan Beach Hotel, which was a resort, open only in the summertime. John Philip Sousa, the "march king," dedicated a famous march to this popular pleasure mecca. Let us read how William H. Bishop described this resort in Scribner's Magazine in 1880:

We emerge from the train in a station forming part of the hotel itself. A Coney Island hotel of consequence has its railway station, and two or three special lines of land and water transportation, as another might have elevators or steam-heating. We pass through a wide corridor, wainscoted and ceiled up (as are all the interiors that meet the eye in the neighborhood) with cheerful, varnished pine, and out upon the enormous piazza. A multitude of people are dining at little tables on it, set with linen, glass and silver, and others are moving up and down in close procession.

Thalatta! Thalatta! what a charming glimpse of the sea! A wide esplanade between is green with turf and gay with flowers—geranium, heliotrope, lobelia, coleus, the queenly, tropical leaves of the Canna Indica—all growing finely out of the two feet of earth the careful gardeners have put down for their sustenance. They have a peculiar value from their situation; a lively fancy makes a species of jewels of them instead of flowers, in their setting of silvery white sand. In the center is a music stand shaped like a scallop shell. Benches are scattered profusely along;—the beach below is full of parasols and summer costumes bright against the water; pink-legged children with their skirts very much tucked up, are wading in it, reflected in the shallows. . . .
(Scribners Magazine, May 1880, New York/Article- "Manhattan Beach," by William H. Bishop.)

These hotels were of monstrous size and built of wood. They sported mansard roofs, spires, steeples, oriental style towers and much gingerbread wood carving. None are left.

Other famous hotels were the Hotel Brighton and Oriental Hotel—a name perpetuated in Oriental Boulevard.

10.10 *Turn left* on Norfolk Street.

10.20 *Turn right* on Oriental Boulevard.

10.30 Manhattan Beach Park on left.

11.00 *Bear right on Corbin Place.*

11.10 Chambers Square.

11.10 *Bear left* on Gerald Street.

11.15 *Bear right.* Road becomes Brighton Beach Avenue.

11.35 Brighton Beach Carousel on left (site of Hotel Brighton).

11.45 Pass Coney Island Avenue.

11.45 Elevated railway trestle overhead.

11.90 *Turn left* under concrete arches, onto Ocean Parkway.

12.00 Seaside Park on right.

12.10 *Turn right* on Surf Avenue.

12.10 Famous Coney Island Boardwalk on left.

12.40 New York City Acquarium on left.

12.60 Enter amusement area.

12.70 Cross Stillwell Avenue.

12.70 *The* original Nathans Hot Dogs on left.

12.80 Site of former Dreamland Park on left. This adult amusement park featured gigantic sculpture, gaudy recreations of scenes from Wagner's operas, such as "The Dragon's Gorge," and fun-house type attractions. It was very gaudy and greatly popularized by the well-known popular ballad, "Meet Me Tonight in Dreamland."

13.00 Site of once-famous Steeplechase Park.

Steeplechase Park. Known as "the funny place" was a twenty-five acre amusement park founded by George C. Tilyou in 1897. It burned to the ground in 1907, but was rebuilt in 1908 and operated until 1964 when the site was purchased for a housing project. Many of the amusements were located inside a six-story high great steel shed. The park was named for its most popular ride— a sort of roller-coaster arranged with multiple tracks. On each track was a wooden steeplechase horse, much like those on a carousel. At the start of the ride all the

horses were lined up at the top of the highest elevation. When the operator released the brakes the horses would start off over the long, winding course—zooming past one another in a great simulation of a genuine steeplechase. Other rides were the ferris wheel and great parachute jump ride. Riders were given a close simulation of an actual parachute free fall of over one hundred feet from atop a great steel tower.

13.00 Abe Stark Center on left.

13.00 Cross West 21st Street.

13.00 Site of former Luna Park on right.

Luna Park was the third of the great Coney Island adult amusement parks. It was modeled after the Great White Way of the Chicago World's Fair and was rather similar to the still-existing Tivoli Gardens in Copenhagen Denmark. Luna Park was opened by Thompson and Dundy in 1903. It burned down with considerable loss of life after World War II. Luna Park was beautiful and fantastic. Among the attractions were Mundy's menagerie and Wormwood's Monkey Theater and the "Chute the chutes." This was a ride where you coasted down a roller coaster track into a pool of water with a great splash. The writer remembers visiting Luna Park as a child and getting stuck in a dark underground tunnel in a little cart pulled by a donkey. The ride was called "The Coal Mine," and the little cart jumped the track on a curve, and we had to sit for about an hour until the custodian came searching for us with a kerosene lamp.

13.90 Gatehouse to Seagate—a private residential area.

-13.00 E.R.M. Atlantic Highlands visible to left.

13.90 *Turn around* head back.

13.95 *Turn left* on West 36th Street. Make sure car doors are locked. This is a rough neighborhood, and motorists are often mugged.

14.20 *Turn right* on Neptune Avenue.

15.10 *Turn left* on West 17th Street —becomes Cropsey Avenue.

15.20 Cross bridge over Coney Island Creek.

15.30 *Turn left* onto Belt Parkway Westbound at (Bay 50th Street).

15.50 Gravesend Bay on left.

15.55 Dreier Offerman Park on left.

16.20 Pass Exit 5 for Bay Parkway.

16.20 New Utrecht (-12.20 E.R.M.)

16.20 Bensonhurst Park on left.

16.50 Dyker Beach Park on right. Exit 4. (-11.25 E.R.M.)

16.70 View of Gravesend Bay, Lower New York Bay, and Verrazano Narrows Bridge to left.

17.60 Fort Hamilton. Veterans' Administration Hospital to right.

18.50 Pass beneath Verrazano Narrows Bridge. (-11.00 E.R.M.)

18.55 Fort Lafayette site on left. The Narrows. (-10.75 E.R.M.)

20.00 View of Statue of Liberty and World Trade Center.

20.70 Owl's Head Park on right. (-8.25 E.R.M.)

20.75 *Bear left on Interstate 278— Brooklyn-Queens Expressway.*

20.90 Cross above 69th Street.

21.00 Start of Gowanus Elevated Highway.

21.30 Cross above former Bay Ridge terminal tracks of New York Connecting Railroad.

21.50 Brooklyn Army Terminal on left. Bay Ridge section. (-8.10 E.R.M.)

21.70 Bush terminal on left. (-7.00 E.R.M.)

21.90 Williamsburg Savings Bank building visible ahead.

21.90 Get off expressway at 38th Street Exit.

22.10 *Turn left* on 4th Avenue.

22.30 *Turn right* on 33rd Street (Burger King on corner).

22.50 *Turn left* on 5th Avenue. (Southbound use 32nd Street between Fifth and Fourth Avenues.)

22.50 Greenwood Cemetery on right.

22.80 Entrance to Greenwood Cemetary (corner 5th Avenue and 24th Street).

Greenwood Cemetery. One of the nation's most famous cemeteries and among the most beautiful, it is one of the finest remaining examples of the Romantic landscape tradition. The statues are some of the best Victorian sculpture extant in America. The first burial was held here in 1840, and Greenwood soon rose to be the most fashionable cemetery in America. Among the famous buried here are Nathaniel Currier, James M. Ives, Rev. Henry Ward Beecher, DeWitt Clinton, Mayor William Jay Gaynor, Peter Cooper, Horace Greeley, William Marcy "Boss" Tweed, Samuel F.B. Morse, Duncan Phyfe, James Renwick Jr. (architect of St. Patrick's Cathedral), and Lola Montez (mistress of King Ludwig I of Bavaria.) (Sightseeing is permitted on weekdays only.)

Wealthy families who erected large tombs and mausoleums were the Whitneys, Lorillards, Aspinwalls, Schemerhorns, Howlands, Havemeyers, and Pierreponts. Two famous graves bear statues of their owners. That of seventeen-year old Charlotte Canda, who was killed in a carriage accident returning home from a ball and of a certain seacaptain named Correja attracted particular attention during the Victorian age. The tomb of the wealthy theatrical entrepreneur William Niblo (owner of the famous Niblo's Garden in Manhattan). is among the loveliest. It is in Gothic style and at the edge of beautiful little Crescent Water with its smooth reflections and gracefully swimming swans and ducks. The sections, roads, and paths bear such poetic names as Sylvan Water, Valley Water, Twilight Dell, Green Bough Avenue, Fern Avenue, Ocean Hill, Woodbine Path, Cedar Dell, etc. The largest tomb is that of the multi-millionaire Stephen Whitney on Ocean Hill. It is an eight-sided Gothic chapel surrounded by rhododendron, ivy, and ornamental trees.

There is an example of the rare Egyptian Revival architecture in the tomb of Dr. James Anderson on Cliff Path overlooking Sylvan Water. The main entrance gate at Fifth Avenue and 24th Street has been called "the culmination of Gothic Revival." It was built entirely of brown-stone and is a collection of pointed arches, medieval sculpture, and elaborately carved towers massed vertically to turn the visitor's thoughts heavenward. It was designed in 1861 by Richard Michell Upjohn, who also designed the Connecticut state capitol. He was the son of the leading proponent of Gothic Revival architecture in America.

Greenwood Cemetery comprises 478 acres including Gowan's Heights, Brooklyn's highest spot with an elevation of 216 feet. This was an important locality in the Battle of Long Island and is described in some detail by N. P. Willis in his *American Scenery.*

The area embraced by the cemetery was a glacial moraine with the usual erratic boulders scattered about. This prompted the minor poet Wendell Phillips Garrison (1840-1907), son of William Lloyd Garrison, to write the following peom, which is included in his *Post Meridian Sonnets* of 1898:

At Greenwood Cemetery

Here was the ancient strand, the utmost reach,
Of the great Northern ice-wave; hitherto
With its last pulse it mounted, then withdrew,
Leaving its fringe of wreck-age on the beach:
Boulder and pebble and sand-matrix—each
From crag or valley ravished; scanty clues
To its old site affording in its new,
Yet real, as the men of science teach,
Life hath not less its terminal moraine:
Look how on that discharged from melting snows
Another rears itself, the spoil of plain

*And Mountain also, marked
    by stones in rows,
With legend meet for such
    promiscuous pain:
"Here rests-Hier ruhet, or
    ici repose.*

*(An American Anthology,
edited by Edmund Clar-
ence Stedman, Boston;
Houghton Mifflin Co.,
1900 p.794.)*

Alternate Route 1—
Through Greenwood Cemetery

22.80 Enter cemetery at 5th Avenue
and 24th Street gateway.
Inside cemetery follow
signs to Fort Hamilton
entrance.

24.00 Leave cemetery at Fort Hamilton entrance.

24.00 *Turn left* on Fort Hamilton
Parkway.

24.10 *Turn right* on Caton Avenue at
intersection with McDonald
Avenue.

Alternate Route 2—
Around cemetery on streets

22.80 Corner 5th Avenue and 24th
Street. Continue straight on
5th Avenue.

23.00 *Turn right* on 19th Street.

23.75 *Turn right* on 10th Avenue.

23.80 *Turn left* on McDonald Avenue.

24.30 *Turn left* on Caton Avenue.

Continuation of Combined Route.

24.10 Corner of Caton Avenue and
McDonald Avenue.

24.20 *Bend right* on Caton Avenue.

24.60 *Bend left* on Caton Avenue.

24.70 *Turn left* on Coney Island
Avenue.

24.80 *Turn right* on Parkside Avenue.

25.10 Parade Grounds on right.

25.10 Prospect Park on left—covers
526 acres and was designed
by Vaux and Olmsted in 1857.

25.40 *Turn left* on Ocean Avenue.

25.90 *Bear right.*

26.00 *Turn left* on Flatbush Avenue.

26.10 Lefferts Homestead on left.
This house was built by Pieter
Lefferts (1753-1791) to replace one accidently burned
down on August 22, 1776
when the Americans were
burning adjacent grain fields
prior to the Battle of Long

Island so that the grain
would not fall into British
hands. It originally stood at
563 Flatbush Avenue, but was
later moved to its present
site in Prospect Park. It is
open as a museum and is
maintained by the Daughters
of the American Revolution.
Pieter Lefferts was a dele-
gate to the Constitutional
Convention, a lieutenant in
the American Army, and later
a senator.

26.30 Brooklyn Zoo on left.

26.40 Brooklyn Botanic Garden on
right.
This is among the world's
finest botanical gardens and
has an international reputation. It is extremely beautiful
and the rose display is excep-

tional. The gardens cover fifty acres and a large conservatory and museum. Special gardens include the Japanese Garden, Cranford Rose Garden, Fragrance Garden, Rock Garden, Iris Garden, Shakespeare Garden, Children's Garden, Ryoanji, Roji, and Tallman Gardens. The Botanic Garden is a cultural institution affiliated with the City of New York. It is a private institution. Twenty percent of the support of the garden comes as a subsidy from the city. The rest comes from gifts of private citizens. Every tree, shrub, and flower is purchased with private funds.

Generally speaking, the gardens are open daily except Mondays (unless the Monday is a holiday, in which case the garden will be open).

Do not plan your picnic lunch or rest break here. Go to Prospect Park instead. The Botanic Garden is only for study and contemplation.

26.70 Brooklyn Public Library on right.

26.80 Grand Army Plaza and Triumphal Arch. Designed by Olmstead, Vaux & Co. in 1866.

26.80 *Bear left around circle.*

27.00 *Turn right off circle onto Prospect Park West.*

27.10 *Turn right* on President Street.

27.20 *Turn right* on Eighth Avenue.

27.30 *Turn right* on St. John's Place.

27.40 *Turn right* on Plaza Street.

27.45 Montauk Club on right. Designed by Francis H. Kimball in 1891 in the Venetian Gothic style, built of yellow brick and terra cotta, it found its inspiration in the Ca d'Oro at Venice.

27.60 *Turn right* on Prospect Park West.

28.00 Litchfield Mansion on left. Located inside Prospect Park. It was designed in the modified Italianate style in 1855-56 by Alexander Jackson Davis. The classic collonade has unusual corncob capitals.

28.50 *Turn right* on 15th Street. Make sure car doors are locked and that you always have room to move ahead. Attacks on motorists are common in this area.

28.70 Park Slope area. Armory on right.

29.50 *Turn right* on Hamilton Avenue, under viaduct.

29.70 Cross Gowanus Canal (-6.52 E.R.M.)

30.10 *Stay on Hamilton Avenue. Do not enter tunnel.*

30.30 *Stay on Hamilton Avenue.* Do not enter tunnel.

30.80 Former site of India Wharf and Atlantic Basin on left.

-5.10 E.R.M. View of Manhattan and Governor's Island.

30.80 *Turn around.*

30.90 *Turn left* on Union Street.

31.20 *Turn left* on Hicks Street.

31.60 St. Peter's Church: red brick, Hudson River Gothic.

31.80 *Turn right* on Atlantic Avenue.

32.10 *Turn left* on Boerum Place.

32.40 *Turn left* on Fulton Street.

32.40 Borough Hall on right: Greek Revival, ca. 1846-1848, Ionic details, Gamaliel King, architect.

32.40 Municipal Building on right: modified Roman Eclectic, 1924. McKenzie, Voorhees, Gmelin and Walker, architects.

32.50 Cross Court Street, you are now on Joralemon Street.

32.60 Packer Collegiate Institute, 170 Joralemon Street: Ivy-covered Gothic Revival, 1854, Minard Lafever, architect.

32.61 *Turn right* on Clinton Street.

32.70 St. Anne's Episcopal Church on left: Victorian Gothic, 1867-69, Renwick and Sands, architects.

32.80 *Turn right* on Cadman Plaza West.

33.00 *Turn right* on Montague Street.

33.10 Franklin Trust Building on left: Romanesque Revival skyscraper. Tile Mansard roofs and dormer windows. George L. Morse, architect, 1888.

33.30 *Turn right* on Hicks Street.

33.50 *Turn left* on Clark Street.

33.60 *Turn right* on Brooklyn Heights Terrace.

33.60 Columbia Heights.

33.65 *Turn right* on Pineapple Street.

33.70 *Turn right* on Willow Street.

33.90 *Turn left* on Pierrepont Street.

34.10 Monroe Unitarian Church on left, formerly named Church of the Saviour: Gothic Revival, 1844, Minard Lafever, architect.

34.20 *Turn right* on Cadman Plaza West.

34.20 Main Post Office on left: French Renaissance with Romanesque Revival forms and German Renaissance details, 1885-91, Mifflin E. Bell, architect.

34.40 *Turn right* on Joralemon Street.

34.70 *Turn right* on Hicks Street.

34.70 Grace Episcopal Church on left: Gothic Revival, Richard Upjohn, architect, 1847-48.

34.80 *Turn left* on Montague Street.

34.90 *Turn left* on Montague Terrace.

35.00 *Turn right* on Remsen Street.

35.05 View of Lower Manhattan and Upper New York Bay. Flagpole. (-5.00 E.R.M.)

35.05 *Turn around.*

35.05 *Continue* back East on Remsen Street.

35.40 *Turn left* on Court Street.

35.60 Supreme Court Southern District of New York on right.

35.65 Post Office on right.

35.60 *Turn right* on Tillary Street. *Get into left lane immediately.*

35.70 *Turn left* on Adams Street. *Stay in center lane for* Brooklyn Bridge.

35.90 Begin Brooklyn Bridge.

36.20 Begin suspension span.

36.90 End suspension span (E.R.M.-4.5). Brooklyn Bridge. The oldest, and by many considered the most beautiful, remaining major suspension span in the United States, it was built between 1869 and 1883 by John A. Roebling (1806-1869) and his son Washington Augustus Roebling (1837-1926). The elder Roebling was born in Mulhouse, Germany, and studied engineering in Berlin. He came to America in 1831 and developed a strong type of steel cable, opening a plant in Trenton, New Jersey. Early suspension spans included the Allegheny Bridge at Pittsburgh, several aqueduct bridges for the D. & H. Canal, a bridge between Cincinnati and Covington across the Ohio River and the great Niagara Falls Suspension Bridge of 1855. The Brooklyn Bridge was his greatest achievement. Early in its construction, he suffered a serious injury on a ferry boat while supervising the work and died a few days later. His son supervised completion of the bridge: but he also was a victim of his work. He was stricken with caisson disease in 1872 as a result of continuous underground work. Although an invalid, he supervised from his bed in Brooklyn Heights, until the bridge was opened to traffic in 1883. In 1888, he took over supervision of the Roebling Plant in Trenton.

The Brooklyn Bridge has an overall length of 5,589 feet with a center span of 1,595 feet. The two major towers are built of dressed stone with twin pointed archways. Their style is Gothic Revival with crowning mouldings somewhat reminiscent of the Egyptian style. Box girder spans are supported by four main cables with much cross bracing, which creates an attractive gossamer effect.

It was opened for traffic on May 24, 1883. On May 30, a great panic took place when someone among the crowd of strollers screamed that the bridge was giving way. People fought to get off and became jammed together in the stairways. Forty people were injured, and twelve were crushed to death.

The bridge, as originally built, carried two dual-width vehicle road ways, two horse-car tracks and a wide boardwalk in the center. During later years it also carried electric streetcars and rapid transit railway trains. Various authorities give the initial cost as betwen $13,000,000 and $15,000,000. However, within the first twenty-six years in service, increasing loads-particularly electric trains-made it necessary to spend an additional $15,000,000 on partial reconstruction and strengthening. Twenty workmen lost their lives in the construction of the bridge. Today it carries only motor traffic and pedestrians.

36.90 Manhattan end suspension span.
Take exit to Park Row South.

37.30 New York City Hall seen straight ahead: Federal Style with French influence, 1803-1812, John McComb Jr. and Joseph Francois Mangin, architects.

37.30 New York Municipal Building to right.

37.40 *Turn left* on Broadway.

37.40 Woolworth Building straight ahead, 233 Broadway. This is a Gothic skyscraper built 1911-1913, its exterior clad with self-washing terra-cotta. The architect was Cass Gilbert. The interior has much exquisite detailing and artwork. With 60 stories and a height of 792 feet, it was world's tallest when built.

37.50 Western Electric corporate headquarters on left, 222 Broadway.

37.50 St. Paul's Chapel. A unit of Trinity Episcopal Parish, and the oldest church structure in Manhattan, Georgian style structure, built in 1764-66, Thomas McBean, architect. The steeple was built in 1793-94 by James C. Lawrence. George Washington worshiped here regularly during his residence in New York on right.

37.55 American Telephone and Telegraph Building, 195 Broadway, on right: Roman Eclectic, built in 1913, William Welles Bosworth, architect.

37.60 *Turn left* on John Street.

38.00 *Turn right* on South Street.

38.00 South Street Seaport Museum on left.

38.10 *Turn right* on Wall Street.

38.20 *Turn left* on Water Street.

38.30 *Turn right* on Hanover Square.

38.35 India House on left: Classic Revival, ca. 1837, architect unknown. It is assumed to have been erected by Richard F. Carman as an office block after a disasterous fire in 1835. It later housed the

New York Cotton Exchange and the Hanover Bank, and is presently a private club. It houses a superb maritime museum.

38.40 *Bear left* on Beaver Street.

38.40 Delmonico's Restaurant on left.

38.50 *Turn right* on Broad Street.

38.60 New York Stock Exchange on left: Beaux Arts Eclectic, 1901-04, George B. Post, architect. The pediment group of statury is by John Quincy Adams Ward, assisted by Paul W. Bartlett.

38.65 *Cross* Wall Street *Continue Straight* on Nassau Street.

38.65 Federal Hall on right (formerly U.S. Subtreasury). A national memorial, built in 1834-42 in Greek Revival Style by Town and Davis and S. Thomson and Frazee, it is now a museum. It stands on the site of the older Federal Hall, which was a Georgian style building, remodeled by Charles Pierre L'Enfant from New York's Second City Hall into a Federal Capitol. On April 30, 1789, George Washington was inaugurated as the first president of the United States on the front portico of this older building.

38.70 U.S. Federal Reserve Bank seen straight ahead: Italian Renaissance Eclectic, 1928, York and Sawyer, architects. Chase Manhattan Bank on right. Marine Midland Bank on left. World Trade Center seen down Cedar Street.

38.70 *Turn left* on Cedar Street.

38.80 *Turn left* on Broadway.

38.83 Monument on right: Revolutionary Prisoners' Monument.

38.90 Wall Street on left.

38.90 Trinity Church on right. This is the third Episcopal church on this site, built in 1840-46 by Richard Upjohn in Gothic Revival style. The bronze doors in Italian style, depicting Biblical scenes, were carved by Karl Bitter under the supervision of Richard Morris Hunt.

39.00 Bowling Green, site of early recreation ground.

39.10 United States Customs House on left: Beaux Arts Eclectic, 1901-07, Cass Gilbert, architect. Sculptured figures on north fascade are by Daniel C. French. The interiors are also very fine, but the building is not open to the general public.

39.10 *Cross* Battery Place: Broadway becomes State Street.

39.20 Castle Garden and Battery Park on right (-3.85 E.R.M.).

39.30 Shrine of St. Elizabeth Seton on left (Our Lady of the Rosary), 7 State Street: Federal style wtih Ionic trim. The east wing dates back to ca. 1793; there is a colonnaded west wing (1805). The architect is unknown. This was once the private home of Elizabeth Ann Seton (1774-1821) and her husband William Magee Seton, a wealthy merchant. Born Elizabeth Ann Bayley, she came from a prominent and well-to-do family and knew George Washington socially in her youth. She married William Seton in 1794, lived in this house and had five children. She was widowed in Pisa, Italy, in 1803 and introduced to the Catholic doctrine by the Filicchi family of that city. Although brought up in the Episcopal faith, she entered the Catholic Church at St. Peter's Church, Barclay

Street, upon her return home in 1805. She was disowned by her family because of her conversion and ran a school in this house to support her children. She later entered religious orders and moved to Emmitsburg, Maryland, in 1809. She subsequently founded the order of the Sisters of Charity, which now numbers 7,500 members. She was Canonized Saint Elizabeth Ann Seton at Rome on September 14, 1975—the first native-born American saint.

39.30 Staten Island Ferry Terminal on right. (-4.20 E.R.M.)

39.30 *Bend left* on State Street.

39.35 *Turn left* on Whitehall Street.

39.40 United States Army Building on right. Granite and red brick in Gothic Revival style.

39.50 *Turn left* on Pearl Street.

39.65 *Turn right* on State Street.

39.70 *Turn left* on Battery Place.

39.75 Whitehall Building on right.

39.80 Pier A on left. (E.R.M. -3.84.)

39.90 Site of landfill for Battery Park City on left.

39.90 Downtown Athletic Club on right.

40.10 Brady Building on right. Gothic styled skyscraper designed by Cass Gilbert as a trial of that style prior to designing the Woolworth Building. Former headquarters of the Delaware, Lackawanna & Western Railroad.

40.10 Pass foot of Cedar Street.

40.20 Pass foot of Liberty Street. Jersey Central Railroad ferries formerly landed to the left.

40.30 Foot of Cortlandt Street. (E.R.M. -3.71.) Fulton's first commercial voyage of the *North River Steamboat of Clermont* departed from here. This was also the site of the first steam ferry to Jersey City, and later terminal of Pennsylvania Railroad and West Shore Railroad ferries.

40.30 World Trade Center on right.

40.35 Pass foot of Vesey Street. Former site of Washington Market.

40.40 New York Telephone Co. Building, 140 West Street, on right. It is built in vertical modern style. Designed by McKenzie, Voorhees and Gmelin, Architects, it was completed between 1923 and 1927.

40.45 Foot of Barclay Street. Former Lackawanna Railroad ferry to Hoboken on left.

40.60 Foot of Chambers Street. Former Erie Railroad ferry to Jersey City on left.

41.00 Foot of Vestry Street.

41.10 Foot of Desbrosses Street. Former Pennsylvania Railroad, West Shore Railroad ferries and Hudson River Day Line, terminals on left.

41.20 Foot of Canal Street (E.R.M. -2.50.)

41.40 Former New York Central Railroad St. Johns Park Freight Terminal on right.

42.80 Chelsea (E.R.M. -1.20.) Foot of West 23rd Street.

43.20 Foot of 30th Street. (E.R.M. -1.00.) Heliport on left.

43.40 Foot of West 34th Street. (E.R.M. -.50.) New Convention Center to be built on right over old railroad yards.

43.60 Yellow brick Lincoln Tunnel Ventilator Tower on left.

43.80 Foot of West 42nd Street. (E.R.M. 0.00.) Base Line.

East Side Road Route

0.00 Start East Side Road Route, corner of West 42nd Street and 12th Avenue, New York City (Manhattan). Former West Shore Railroad ferry terminal for Weekhawken and West New York was situated at foot of the West 42nd Street. The Hudson River Day Line, pier 81 is slightly to the south, and the Circle Line, pier 83, is slightly to the north.

Head north on 12th Avenue (E.R.M. 0.00.)

0.20 *Go UP* on West Side elevated highway ("Miller highway"). This elevated highway, starting just north of the exit of the Brooklyn Battery Tunnel, has been largely demolished and removed to the south. The section north of West 42nd Street is also scheduled for ultimate demolition and the entire route is to be replaced by a new Westway. There is much political delay, and it is impossible to tell when this will come about. The original elevated structure began to literally fall apart from corrosion several years ago owing to delayed and improper maintenance and damage from salt used to melt ice and snow.

0.30 New passenger liner terminal on left. West 49th Street. (E.R.M. 0.30.)

0.50 DeWitt Clinton Park on right between West 52nd and West 54th Streets.

0.75 Pass West 57th Street on right.

1.20 Former New York Central car-float slips on left and freight yards on right.

1.50 *Turn right* on West 72nd Street Exit. Note elegant older apartment houses and town-houses.

1.60 *Turn left* on Riverside Drive. Townhouses and apartments on right. Riverside Park on left. This was the most fashionable residential street in the city in 1910.

1.90 Cross West 79th Street. Yacht Basin to left. (E.R.M. 1.85.)

2.30 Cross West 86th Street on right.

2.40 Soldiers' and Sailors Monument on left. (2.45 E.R.M.)

3.60 Cross West 110th Street, Cathedral Parkway.

Note: Two blocks to the East (.20 mile), at the corner of 110th Street and Amsterdam Avenue is the:

Cathedral Church of Saint John the Divine (Episcopal). Although still uncompleted, this is the largest church structure in the United States. It is the largest Gothic Cathedral in the world and will hold 40,000 standees. Construction was started in 1892. The choir, apse, and original crossing were designed by Heins & LaFarge (won in competition) in Romanesque Eclectic style, and completed in 1907. After 1911, a contract was awarded to Ralph Adams Cram of Cram & Ferguson for completion of the nave, final crossing and transept, in French Gothic Eclectic. The cathedral is in use but still unfinished and there are various differing plans for the ultimate completed design.

The high area between 110th Street and 125th Street to the south and north, and Morningside Avenue on the east and the Hudson River on the west is known as Morningside Heights. In the early twentieth century, after the relocation of Columbia University here, it was known as the "Acropolis of America."

Columbia University is located between Broadway and Amsterdam Avenue and 116th and 120 Streets. It was founded in 1754 as King's College by grant of King George II and located downtown. In 1784, it was reorganized as Columbia College, and in 1912 the name was changed to Columbia University, although this name was used unofficially from 1896. Around the turn of the century, the university moved to its present site. The medical school was founded in 1767.

4.10 Cross West 120th Street.

4.10 Riverside Church and Interchurch Center on right. (E.R.M. 4.30.)

4.20 Grant's Tomb on left. (E.R.M. 4.40.)

4.30 Site of former Claremont Inn on left. In later years this was an elegant restaurant located immediately north of Grant's Tomb. It had formal gardens and delicate small arbors and pavilions. Its history is told by Benson Lossing in his *The Hudson* of 1866:

"Upon a high promontory overlooking the Hudson, on the south side of Manhattanville, is Jones's Claremont Hotel, a fashionable place of resort for the pleasure-seekers who frequent the Bloomingdale and Kingsbridge roads on pleasant afternoons. At such times it is often thronged with visitors,

and presents a lively appearance. The main, or older portion of the building, was erected, I believe, by the elder Dr. Post, early in the present century, as a summer residence, and named by him Claremont. [Editor's note: Actually it was built in 1797.] *It still* [1866] *belongs to the Post family. It was an elegant country mansion, upon a most desirable spot, overlooking many leagues of the Hudson. There, more than fifty years ago, lived Viscount Courtenay, afterwards Earl of Devon. He left England, it was reported, because of political troubles. When the War of 1812 broke out, he returned thither, leaving his furniture and plate, which were sold at auction. The latter is preserved with care by the family of the purchaser. Courtenay was a great lion in New York, for he was a handsome bachelor, with title, fortune, and a reputation—a combination of excellences calculated to captivate the heart-desires of the opposite sex.*

Claremont was the residence, for a while, of Joseph Buonaparte, ex-king of Spain, when he first took refuge in the United States, after the Battle of Waterloo and the downfall of the Napoleon dynasty. Here, too, Francis James Jackson, the successor of Mr. Erskine, the British minister at Washington at the opening of the War of 1812, resided a short time. He was familiarly known as "Copenhagen Jackson," because of his then recent participation in measures for the seizure of the Danish fleet by the British at Copenhagen. He was politically and socially unpopular, and presented a strong contrast to the polished Courtenay."

The restaurant remained a resort of society on into the mid-twentieth century, much as described by Lossing, and the writer remembers being taken there for refreshments on Sunday afternoon. It was burned and demolished by the city in 1951.

On the grounds is a small grave marked with the simple inscription, "Here lies an amiable child." It was sometimes surmised that this was a "natural" child of Viscount Courtenay, although there is no evidence to support this opinion.

4.45 South end of Harlem Valley Viaduct. (E.R.M. 4.75.)

4.60 Cross above West 125th Street on right.

4.80 North end of Harlem Valley Viaduct (E.R.M. 5.00.), Manhattanville.

4.80 Cross West 135th Street on right.

4.80 New sewage treatment plant on riverfront to left. (E.R.M. 5.00.)

6.00 Trinity Parish Cemetery on right, between West 153rd and West 155th Streets.

6.60 Cross West 165th Street. Carmansville. (See E.R.M. 7.00.)

6.60 Columbia Presbyterian Medical Center on right. (See E.R.M. 7.10.)

6.80 Pass beneath George Washington Bridge (See E.R.M. 7.30.)

6.80 Jeffrey's Hook and lighthouse to left under ridge (E.R.M. 7.30.).

7.50 Pavilion Overlook on left. Fort Washington Park on hill on

right. (See article in River section under E.R.M. 7.30.)

7.60 Fort Tryon Park on right. (See E.R.M. 8.20.)

7.90 *Turn right* on Fort Tryon and Cloisters Exit.
(Note: This short sidetrip is possible headed northbound only.)

8.10 The cloisters (see E.R.M. 8.30.).
Circle around and go back to Riverside Drive Northbound.

8.37 Cross over Dyckman Street on low viaduct. Former ferry to Englewood on left. (E.R.M. 8.70.)

8.38 Tubby Hook on left. (E.R.M. 8.70.)

8.40 Inwood Park on right. (E.R.M. 8.75.)

8.40 Road now becomes Route 9A.

9.00 Stop: pay toll.

9.10 South end of Henry Hudson Bridge over Spuyten Duyvil Creek. Henry Hudson Monument seen ahead.

9.50 North end of Henry Hudson Bridge. Riverdale.

9.55 *Turn right Exit* 18, Kappock Street.

9.62 *Turn right* on Palisade Avenue.

9.90 Pass under Henry Hudson Bridge (E.R.M. 9.90.).

10.20 *Northbound*—Continue straight on Palisade Avenue.
Southbound—Turn left on Kappock Street to enter Henry Hudson Bridge.

11.00 Riverdale Park on left.

11.30 *Turn right* on West 248th Street.

11.40 *Turn left* on Independence Avenue.

11.55 Villa Pauline on left. The home of conductor Arturo Toscanini from 1940 to 1957, it has five acres of grounds and half-timbered Tudor house with porte-cochere. The house commands a fine view of the Hudson River and Palisades, of which Toscanini was very fond.

Toscanini was very fond of the writings of Washington Irving, and he was a frequent visitor to the Sunnyside restoration. The tie that bound the American author and the famous conductor was their mutual love for the Hudson River.

Tapes and recordings of every performance the Maestro ever conducted that was broadcast or recorded are carefully stored at the Villa Pauline.

11.70 *Turn left* on West 252nd Street.

11.75 *Turn right* on Sycamore Avenue.

11.77 *Turn left* on 254th Street (Riverdale Railroad Station at end of street).

11.80 *Turn right* on Palisade Avenue.

12.20 Passionist Fathers' Retreat House on left. Visitation Monastery on right.

12.50 *Turn right* on 261st Street. (Mount St. Vincent Railroad Station, end of street.) Mount St. Vincent College on left. Former Font Hill home of Edwin Forrest on left. (12.20 E.R.M.)

12.65 *Turn left* on Riverdale Avenue.

12.80 Entrance to Mount St. Vincent College on left.

12.90 Pass 263rd Street—New York City/Yonkers city line.

13.00 *Turn left* on Valentine Place (P.S. 27 on left). (12.30 E.R.M.)

13.20 *Turn right* on Hawthorne Avenue.

13.45 Hawthorne High School on right.

13.70 Pass Ludlow Street. (Ludlow Railroad station end of street) (13.00 E.R.M.)

14.10 *Turn right* on Vark Street.

14.20 *Turn left* on Riverdale Avenue.

14.60 Cross Main Street (Municipal Pier at end of street (14.10 E.R.M.)

14.65 Cross Dock Street (Yonkers Railroad station at end of street). Cross over Nepperhan River—now in underground sewer.

14.65 Philips Manor restoration on left.

14.65 Street name changes to Warburton Avenue. Continue straight.

15.70 Trevor Park on left: Twenty-three-acre former private estate of John B. Trevor. Glenview, the Trevor mansion is in Victorian Gothic style and now serves as the home of the Hudson River Museum. There is also a modern planetarium. Open daily except Mondays. (14.60 E.R.M.)

16.83 Greystone section (16.10 E.R.M.). (Greystone Railroad station at end of Odel Avenue to left.)

17.90 Cross Brook. Yonkers city line. Enter village of Hastings-on-Hudson.

18.70 Cross Washington Street.

18.78 Cross over viaduct.

18.82 Cross Main Street (Hastings-on-Hudson Railroad station at end of street).

19.10 *Turn left* on Broadway (Route 9). (Southbound turn right on Warburton Avenue.)

19.15 Pass Edgar's Lane on right: site of Revolutionary battle.

19.40 Dobbs Ferry/Hastings-on-Hudson town line. (18.65 E.R.M.)

19.60 St. Christopher's School on left: Gothic Revival mansion by Alexander Jackson Davis, built for E.B. Strange, a New York silk merchant.

19.80 Sacred Heart School on left. Note: Here Broadway goes uphill to the right. Livingston Avenue drops downhill straight ahead. *Bear right* on Broadway.

20.20 Former Summerfield Methodist Church on left, 303 Broadway. This orange brick building with dark stone trim was built in 1894. It has been used subsequently as a Greek Orthodox Church, an art gallery, and an apartment house.

20.25 Estherwood (now the Masters School) on right up Clinton Avenue: a large mansion built in 1890 by James Jennings McComb.

20.50 *Turn left* on Broadway, Route 9.

20.50 Sacred Heart Church on left: ca. 1890, fieldstone.

20.70 Dobbs Ferry School on left: Three stories, red brick Tudor style, ca. 1900.

20.90 Mount Mercy College on left.

21.00 Dobbs Ferry/Irvington town line.

21.10 Nuits, the Cottenet mansion on left: 1892.

21.20 *Turn left* on Ardsley Avenue. *Bear left* on Hudson Road. Note railroad station ca. 1890 on right.
    Bear left on Hudson Road East. This is Ardsley-on-Hudson (E.R.M. 20.10.)

22.30 *Turn left* on Broadway.

22.50 Pass Ardsley Avenue again. This time *go straight*.

22.50 Cyrus W. Field gatehouse on right, southeast corner of Ardsley Road and Broadway.

22.50 Nevis on left (1835), former home of James Alexander Hamilton, third son of Alexander Hamilton, now a laboratory and arboretum belonging to Columbia University.

23.00 O'Dell Tavern on left: ca. 1690.

23.20 Pass Station Road on left. Irvington railroad station at end of street (E.R.M. 20.80.).

23.40 Pass Main Street, Irvington on left.

23.50 St. Barnabas Episcopal Church on left: stone gothic, 1853.

23.60 Irvington Presbyterian Church on left: 1869, James Renwick architect, Romanesque style, windows designed by Louis Comfort Tiffany.

23.80 Abbotsford section.

23.90 Penny Bridge over Sunnyside Brook, Sunnyside Monument.

23.90 Washington Irving Monument on left. Consists of bronze and marble panels over a bridge with bas reliefs in bronze of Rip Van Winkle and Boabdil, the last king of Granada, two characters immortalized by Irving, facing a central marble shaft topped by a bust of Irving. Sculpture by Daniel Chester French (1850-1931), best known for his statues of the Minuteman at Concord, Massachusetts, and Lincoln, in the Lincoln Memorial at Washington.

23.90 *Turn left* on Sunnyside Lane.

24.60 Cross Old Croton Aqueduct (now a footpath).

25.00 Sunnyside Restoration parking lot. See article (E.R.M. 21.45.).

25.00 *Turn around* and return to Broadway, Route 9.

25.80 *Turn left* on Broadway.

25.85 Irvington/Tarrytown town line.

25.85 Shadow Brook estate on left.

26.00 David Maun cottage on right: 1826 clapboard saltbox.

26.00 Belvedere Estate on left.

26.10 Lyndhurst on left. See article E.R.M. 22.25.

26.70 Hilton Inn on left. Carroll Castle on hill to right.

26.80 Cross over New York State Thruway, Tappan Zee Bridge to left. (E.R.M. 23.20.)

27.10 St. Vincent De Paul Academy on left.

27.30 Hopkins gatehouse on right: brick, Victorian, mansard roof, mid-nineteenth century.

27.50 Washington Irving School on left: Two stories.

27.60 First Baptist Church on Right.

27.61 Christ Church on left: 1837, brick Gothic with crenellated tower. Washington Irving was a vestryman here.

27.80 Cross Main Street, Tarrytown. Railroad station at end of street. Half-timbered commercial block on northwest corner.

27.90 Second Reformed Church on right: 1837 Greek Revival, Ionic portico.

27.95 Lovett House on right: clapboard, gabled roof, ca. 1890.

28.00 Warner Library on left. See description under Tarrytown article. (E.R.M. 24.00.)

28.10 Patriots' Park and monument to captors of Major André on left. This is the spot where Major André was captured.

28.10 Cross André Brook.

28.10 Tarrytown/North Tarrytown line.

28.20 Church of the Immaculate Conception on left. Formerly St. Mark's Church, it is a gray stone Gothic mid-nineteenth-century structure.

28.30 First Reformed Church (ca. 1870): red brick Gothic.

28.40 *Bear left* downhill on Route 9: North Broadway.

28.60 *Turn left* here for .10 mile to Philipsburg Manor Restoration. (E.R.M. 24.50.) See Pocantico River article for full description.

28.70 Cross Pocantico River on Washington Irving Memorial Bridge. This is Sleepy Hollow. The old Headless Horseman Bridge, where Icabod Crane met the Headless Horseman, was slightly to the west.

28.70 Kingsland Point Park to the left.

28.75 Sleepy Hollow. This is the area immortalized by Washington Irving in his Legend of Sleepy Hollow.

28.75 Old Dutch Reformed church of Sleepy Hollow on right. Parking for church and grave of Washington Irving, behind church. According to Irving, the Dutch called this area "die Slapering Haven." This church was greatly beloved by Irving. The weather vane is marked "V.F. (Verdyk Flypse) 1700." The bell was cast in Holland in 1685 and is marked: "Si Deus pro Nobis, Quis Contra Nos-1685." The Church was built by Frederick Philipse I in 1697 or 1699 (the records are not clear). Its walls are thirty inches thick. A popular Currier and Ives print of 1867 made this quaint church familiar to millions. The adjoining churchyard contains the graves of such locally notable families as the Van Tassels, Eckers Van Werts. Swartwouts, Beekmans, and Buckhouts.

29.25 Sleepy Hollow Cemetery main gate on right. This is a large and beautifully landscaped cemetery containing the graves of such notables as Washington Irving, Carl Schurz, Robert G. Ingersoll, Andrew Carnegie, and Whitelaw Reid.

29.25 Philipse Manor section of North Tarrytown on left.

29.55 North end of Sleepy Hollow Cemetery on right.

29.75 Sleepy Hollow Manor on left.

31.00 Phelps Memorial Hospital on left.

31.10 Junction with Route 117.

31.60 Archville. Cross Old Croton Aqueduct.

32.10 I.B.M. entrance on left.

32.20 Sleepy Hollow Country Club entrance on right. (E.R.M. 26.50.) Brick and limestone mansion in Renaissance style built in 1895 by McKim, Mead & White for Elliott Shepard.

32.25 St. Mary's Episcopal Church on right: Scarborough. Built in 1851, it was copied from the fourteenth-century Gothic church of St. Mary in Scarborough in Yorkshire. Stained glass windows by John Bolton of Pelham, who popularized the craft in America in the mid-nineteenth century. Washington Irving planted the ivy on the church.

32.50 Sleepy Hollow Country club exit on right.

32.60 Scarborough School on left.

32.90 Rosemond on right. Home of John L. Worden, commander of the *Monitor*. It is a two-story brick Greek Revival building, ca. 1840. (E.R.M. 27.00.)

32.90 Corner of Scarborough Road on right.

32.90 Scarborough Presbyterian Church on right. Freestone and smooth sandstone are combined in this Neo-Baroque structure, built in 1893. The high tower is surmounted by a belfry and cupola.

33.25 Beechwood on left: Two-story frame, 1835.

33.30 Sparta Burying Ground on left: pre-Revolutionary time to present.

33.60 Ossining town line (E.R.M. 28.65.).

34.80 Highland Avenue Methodist Church on right: ca. 1860, fieldstone Gothic with elaborate companile.

34.90 The Mud House on left: Two-story cement block Victorian

house with mansard roof, ca. 1870.

34.95 First Presbyterian Church on left: Hudson River Gothic, red brick with large clock, ca. 1880.

35.10 Site of Union Hotel.

35.10 First Baptist Church on left: red brick Hudson River Gothic, bracketted with wooden belfry.

35.12 Westchester County Savings Bank on left.(E.R.M. 28.75.)

35.12 Trinity Episcopal Church on right: Gothic, ca. 1880.

35.15 Junction Route 133. *Bear left* downhill on Route 9.

35.61 St. Augustine's R.C. Church on left: gray brick Hudson River Gothic, 1856. Demolished 1980.

35.80 Peter Pan Inn on right.

36.20 Mariandale Dominican Sisters Nursing Home on left.

36.20 Crawbuckie Point on left. (E.R.M. 29.50.)

36.30 Sheraton Inn on left.

36.60 Junction Route 9A. Continue on Route 9.

36.90 Crotonville.

37.00 Cross Croton River. (E.R.M. 30.25.)

37.40 *Turn right* at Exit.

37.50 *Turn right* on Croton Point Avenue.

37.60 *Turn right* on South Riverside Avenue.

37.80 Van Cortlandt Manor Restoration. (E.R.M. 30.25.) This manor house was the center of the great 86,000-acre Van Cortlandt Manor Estate which was erected in 1697. It ran twelve miles along the Hudson from the Croton River to Anthony's Nose. The history of the Van Cortlandt dynasty is as follows:

Oloff Stevenson Van Cortlandt, father of the first proprietor of the estate, was a lineal descendant of the Dukes of Courland in Poland. His ancestors emigrated to Holland when deprived of the Duchy of Courland. The family name was Stevense or Stevensen, van (or from) Courland. They adopted the latter as a surname, the true orthography of which in Dutch is Korte (short), and Landt (land), a term expressing the form of the ancient Duchy of Courland. He emigrated to New Amsterdam in 1637 and soon became rich and poweful. He was colonel of the burghery, president of the "nine men," Schepen of the city, and eventually became burgomaster form 1655 till the end of the Dutch regime in 1664.

His son Stephanus Van Cortlandt (1643-1700) first Lord of the Manor, assembled a large estate along the Hudson by 1687. His eldest son, Johannes Van Cortlandt, had built a rough stone house, or trading post and hunting lodge on the site of the present manor house in 1683. This was the nucleus of the present structure. This was used by Gov. Thomas Dongan as a hunting lodge in the duck hunting seasons. Stephanus Van Cortlandt was granted manorial rights in 1697, which included the rights of Courts Baron and Court Leet, and the right to send his own representative to the provincial assembly. He paid an annual rent to the Crown of forty shillings on the Feast of the Annunciation of the Blessed Virgin Mary. At the age of 34, he became the first American-born Mayor of

the City of New York. He also served as Chief Justice of the Province and was a member of the Governor's Council. He married Gertrude Schuyler and had eleven children.

His son, Philip Van Cortlandt (1683-1746), second Lord of the Manor, married Catherine DePeyster. They used the manor house only as a summer home residing principally in New York city.

Phillip's son, Pierre Van-Cortlandt (1721-1814). third Lord of the Manor, established his permanent home here in 1749 and greatly enlarged and improved the old stone structure. Pierre served as Lieutenant Governor of New York from 1775 to 1795.

The Van Cortlandt family were pro-American during the Revolution, and this provoked the ire of the British, who partially burned the manor in 1777. It was restored in 1780. Benjamin Franklin, John Jay, General Layafatette, Baron von Steuben, Rochambeau, and George Washington were all guests at Van Cortlandt manor. The great preacher George Whitefield preached from the front verandah, and it is claimed that he could be heard across the Hudson.

The house has rubblestone walls three feet thick and with loop-holes. Notable features are the double stairs that climb to the verandah and the broad paneled Dutch door.

The manor house was lived in by Van Cortlandts for 260 years—seven generations. Anne Stevenson Van Cortlandt, who died in 1940, was the last direct descendant to live here. After her death, the house deteriorated for thirteen years and was in danger of being demolished when it was purchased by John D. Rockefeller, Jr. The present restoration, by Sleepy Hollow Restorations, includes the ferry house, ferry house kitchen, a smokehouse, the necessary, a red-brick long walk between the manor and ferry houses, and colonial gardens of herbs, flowers, and fruit trees.

37.80 *Turn around.*

38.00 *Turn left* on Croton Point Avenue.

38.00 View of Croton Bay on left.

38.20 Pass under Route 9.

38.30 Cross trestle over New York Central/Conrail Railroad tracks.

38.30 Croton-Harmon station to left. Armtrak and M.T.A. service.

38.35 Harmon car shops on right: ca. 1860.

38.70 Pass sand pits.

39.10 Croton Point Park (E.R.M. 30.50.). *Turn around* at traffic circle.

39.90 Cross railroad trestle.

40.00 Pass under Route 9.

40.10 *Turn right* onto Route 9 North.

40.40 Prickly Pear Hill appears ahead.

40.40 Croton-On-Hudson on right.

40.70 Junction Route 129 (Municipal Place) (E.R.M. 32.00.).

41.15 Croton North station on left (E.R.M. 32.40.).

42.70 Old Oscawana on left (E.R.M. 33.25.).

43.30 *Get off expressway* at Montrose Exit, Route 9A. (Southbound—Enter Route 9.)

43.40 *Turn left* on Route 9A (New York and Albany Post Road).

44.20 *Turn left* on Cruger's Station Road.

44.80 Cruger's Station—original site of Boscobel—on right. (35.00 E.R.M.)

44.80 *Turn left* on Cruger's Avenue. (Battery Place on right.)

45.00 Name of road changes to Cortlandt Street.

45.30 Cross Furnace Brook, Oscawana Park.

45.40 Oscawana Island on right. (E.R.M. 34.65).

45.70 *Turn left* on Furnace Dock Road (E.R.M. 33.50).

46.40 *Turn left* on Albany Post Road.

46.40 Chimney Corners.

46.50 Cross Furnace Brook.

46.52 *Turn left* on Route 9A (New York & Albany Post Road).

46.60 Pass under Route 9.

47.41 Cross over New York Central Railroad (Conrail).

47.80 Franklin D. Roosevelt V.A. Hospital on left (E.R.M. 35.25).

47.90 *Turn left* on Dutch Road, Montrose.

48.60 *Turn right* on Sunset Road (Bony Hollow Road).

49.00 Episcopal Church of the Divine Love on right. Brick, 1869.

49.00 Cross Montrose Point Road (E.R.M. 35.75).

49.00 Entrance to George's Island Park and Montrose Point on left.

49.40 *Turn left* on King's Ferry Road.

49.60 Town of Cortlandt line.

49.60 Post Hannock House. The owner operated the King's Ferry in 1664. It served as Col. Livingston's Headquarters in 1781, and, in 1782, Washington presented medals here to the captors of Major André.

49.70 Green Cove on left. Henry Hudson anchored here. Many Indians came down to the ship and one of them was killed in an affray. (E.R.M. 36.25.)

49.70 Lake Meahagh on right. Also called Knickerbocker Pond.

49.80 *Turn left* on Riverview Avenue.

50.10 Cross Broadway. *Bend right.* Street becomes Hardie Street.

50.20 Verplanck Point: launching ramp, view of Stony Point.

50.50 Old King's Ferry Wharf. View of Stony Point, Buckberg Mountain, and Tomkins Cove. *Turn around.* (E.R.M. 36.75.)

50.90 *Turn left* on Broadway.

51.80 St. Mary's R.C. Cemetery on right (St. Patrick's).

51.80 Georgia-Pacific Co. Gypsum Division Buchanan Plant on left.

52.00 Village of Buchanan line.

52.20 Pass under power line.

52.20 South gate Indian Point atomic power plant on left.

52.30 Main gate Indian Point atomic power plant on left. This is the visitors' entrance. (E.R.M. 38.25.)

52.60 Pass Bleakley Avenue (Indian Point Road) on right.

52.70 Lent's Cove Park on left. Charles Point visible across cove.

52.70 *Turn around.* (E.R.M. 39.00.)

52.80 *Turn left* on Bleakley Avenue (Indian Point Road).

53.20 *Turn left* on Route 9A, Albany Post Road.

53.20 Sanitas wallpaper plant on right.

53.30 Cross Dickey Brook (E.R.M. 39.00).

53.40 Pass under New York Central railroad (Conrail).

53.45 *Turn left* onto Route 9, after passing beneath it.

53.90 Charles Point on left. (E.R.M. 39.25).

54.20 Travis Point on left. (E.R.M. 39.45).

54.30 Mount St. Francis Church on left.

54.60 Pass South Street Peekskill Exit (to railroad station).

54.70 Cross viaduct over Central Avenue.

54.80 Main Street Peekskill Exit, pass.

54.80 Peekskill Bay, Jones Point, and Dunderberg Mountain to left. (E.R.M. 39.50).

55.00 Fort Hill on right. (St. Mary's School) (E.R.M. 39.60).

55.10 Manitou Mountain ahead.

55.20 Scenic parking area (available southbound only).

55.40 *Turn left* on Routes 202 and 6, across bridge.

55.50 Cross Annsville Creek (E.R.M. 39.75).

55.60 Begin around traffic circle.

55.80 *Turn right* on Route 9 North.

Optional Sidetrip.

55.80 *Turn right* on Route 9 North.

56.20 Confluence of Peekskill Hollow Brook and Annsville Creek with Canopus Creek (Here called Sprout Brook) on right.

56.40 Annsville Union Church on right.

57.50 Cross Annsville Creek.

57.50 Wallace Pond on left.

58.40 Westchester/Putnam county line.

59.30 Cross Appalachain Trail. Continental village over hill to right.

59.40 Graymoor: Mount of Atonement Monastery. Founded in 1898 by Father Lewis Wattson and Mother Lurana White, an Anglican priest and nun. On October 30th, 1909, the entire religious community was received at once into the Roman Catholic Church, Father Wattson taking the new name of Father Paul James Francis. Father Paul in later years became known as the "prophet of reunion" because of his work for Anglican-Roman unity. He died in 1940. The Christopher Inn is a halfway house for the rehabilitation of unfortunate men.

59.40 *Turn right uphill.*

59.50 Convent on left.
59.70 Christopher Inn on left.
59.80 Main buildings atop hill.
60.40 Take loop road around top of hill.
60.50 Christopher Inn on right.
60.70 Convent on right.
60.80 *Turn left* on Route 9 South.
60.90 Cross Appalachian Trail.
64.40 Traffic Circle. Bear right. End of sidetrip.

Return to Main Route.

55.80 Continue around traffic circle on Routes U.S. 6 and U.S. 202 West.
55.95 End of circle. Take Routes U.S. 6 and 202 West.
56.20 Entrance to Camp Smith on right. (E.R.M. 40.30.)
56.20 Peekskill Bay and Dunderberg Mountain on left.
56.40 Roa Hook on left (E.R.M. 40.30.).
57.40 Fish Island on left. (E.R.M. 40.75.).
57.60 Manitou Mountain on right.
57.80 Round Island on left (E.R.M. 41.00.).
58.10 Iona Island on left (E.R.M. 41.50.).
58.40 Cross Broccy Creek (E.R.M. 41.60.).
58.75 Scenic lookout parking on left. Bear Mountain across river.
59.30 Anthony's Nose on right (E.R.M. 42.40.).
59.45 Entrance to Bear Mountain Bridge. Bear right on Route 9D (E.R.M. 42.50.).
59.65 Westchester/Putnam county line. North end of Camp Smith Reservation.
60.25 Appalachian trail on right.
60.70 Pass Manitou on left. It is .50 mile to the Manitou railroad station. There is a marker here stating the first chain

across the river was forced by the British on October 17, 1777.

60.75 Cross Copper Mine Brook (E.R.M. 44.40.).
61.00 South Mountain Pass on right.
61.15 Manitou Chapel on left.
62.37 Canada Hill on right (E.R.M. 44.40.).
62.65 Garrison Inn Restaurant on left.
63.00 Manitou School on left: One-room Gothic, ca. 1860.
63.10 St. James Chapel on left: painted red, ca. 1770.
63.20 Manitoga Nature Conservancy on right. This is an 80-acre forest preserve with four miles of walking trails, sponsored by the Nature Conservancy, a national non-profit land conservation organization.
63.90 St. Francis Retreat House on left.
64.10 Sugarloaf Mountain on right (E.R.M. 45.50.).
64.40 Site of Beverly Robinson House on right (E.R.M. 45.70).
64.50 Entrance drive to Wing and Wing on right (1857).
64.60 Castle Rock on right (1881) (E.R.M. 46.40).
64.60 Glenclyffe (E.R.M. 45.65).
64.70 Capuchin Franciscan friary and Sisters of the Cross convent

on left (ca. 1890 and 1932).
(E.R.M. 46.40.)

64.80 Castle Rock on top of hill to right. Built in 1881 for William H. Osborn. (E.R.M. 46.40.)

64.90 Highlands Country Club on left.

65.10 Garrison town line.

65.20 *Turn left* off Route 9D.

65.20 Jacob Mandeville House (1737) on right.

65.30 *Turn sharp blind right.*

65.40 *Bend to right.*

65.60 Arden point on left across railroad tracks (E.R.M. 46.75).

65.80 *Turn left* on bridge across railroad tracks.

65.81 *Turn left.*

65.80 Golden Eagle Hotel (1840) ahead.

65.85 Garrison Village (E.R.M. 47.35).

65.90 New Railroad Depot (ca. 1880) on left.

65.90 *Turn around.* Excellent view across river to West Point South Dock. There is a foot-passenger ferry here. the new railroad depot is now also used as a theater. A park with bandstand gazebo is near the river bank. Old auto ferry slips are visible.

65.95 Old yellow clapboard depot (ca. 1853) on left, now a store.

66.00 *Turn right* over bridge across railroad. Continue straight up hill.

66.20 Glover House (ca.1850) on left.

66.30 St. Josephs R.C. Church on left: white frame Hudson River Gothic.

66.40 *Turn left* on Route 9D.

66.50 St. Philip's Church in the Highlands on left: Episcopal, 1863, by Richard Upjohn, who is buried in adjoining graveyard. The architect was a vestryman of this church. The parish was founded in 1770. Multicolored slate roof. Buttressed tower.

66.80 Cross Philips Brook (E.R.M.

47.70). Site of Connecticut camps on right.

66.90 Garrison town line.

67.30 Moore House (1847), now Malcolm Gordon School, on left: stone Gothic by Richard Upjohn.

67.50 Entrance to St. Basil's Academy on left: former Jacob Ruppert mansion, Tudor style, ca.1920. (E.R.M. 48.25.)

67.90 Entrance to Dick's Castle on right. (E.R.M. 48.35).

67.90 Start across Indian Brook Viaduct (E.R.M. 48.40).

68.00 End Indian Brook Viaduct.

68.50 Entrance to Boscobel on left. (E.R.M. 48.65).

68.90 Rossiter House on left.

69.00 Cross viaduct over Foundry Brook.

69.10 *Turn left* on Old Road.

69.20 Foundry Brook on left (E.R.M. 49.00).

69.35 *Putnam County Historical Society* on left.

69.40 *West Point Foundry Museum* on left.

69.45 *Continue Straight* on Route 9D (Chestnut Street).

69.60 St. Mary's Church in the Highlands on left: Episcopal, 1868, by George E. Harney—bluestone walls, simple gable roof, stone spire, modeled upon an English parish church.

69.70 *Turn left* on Main Street. Cold Spring: Manitou Hotel on right.

70.00 *Turn left* on Lunn Terrace.

70.10 *Turn right* across railroad bridge.

70.15 *Turn right* immediately after crossing bridge.

70.20 *Turn left* on Main Street.

70.30 *Circle around bandstand* on riverfront. Turn around at Front Street. Cold Spring. (E.R.M. 49.50.)
Three-story brick house with stepped gables to the south.

Historic Hudson View Inn (1837) is to the north. The view across the river extends to West Point, Washington Valley, Crow'Nest Mountain.

Continue back on Main Street and retrace route over railroad bridge to corner of Lunn Terrace and Main Street.

70.60 *Turn right* on Main Street.

70.70 *Turn left* on Fair Street.

71.30 *Run back into* Route 9D. Continue straight.

(Southbound: continue straight-right onto Fair Street. Do not go uphill on Route 9D.)

71.30 Little Stony Point and Mother Cronk's Cove on left. (E.R.M. 50.50 and 51.00.)

71.40 Old stone crusher area.

71.70 Mount Taurus (Bull Hill) on right. (E.R.M. 50.55.)

72.50 Site of former Storm King railroad station on left. (E.R.M. 51.25.)

72.50 Enter tunnel under Breakneck Ridge (E.R.M. 51.50.)

72.70 Exit tunnel.

72.70 Putnam/Dutchess county line.

72.80 Catskill Aqueduct pumping station on left. (E.R.M. 51.55.)

73.60 Pollepel Island (Bannermans Island) on left. (E.R.M. 52.80.)

74.00 Dutchess Manor Restaurant (ca. 1870) on left.

74.00 Sugarloaf Mountain on right.

74.80 Dutchess Junction on left. (E.R.M. 54.90.)

75.70 City of Beacon line.

76.10 Craig House (Tioranda) on left. Built in 1859 by Richard Morris Hunt for shipping magnate George Joseph Howland, it is Gothic-Victorian with contrasting black and white glazed bricks. It now serves as a sanitarium.

76.10 Route 9D here called Howland Avenue.

76.40 Mount Beacon inclined railway base depot on right. (E.R.M. 56.00.)

76.40 *Turn left* on Route 9D: Wolcott Avenue.

76.70 St. Luke's Episcopal Church on right: 1868 by Frederick C. Withers, stone English Gothic. The church yard has the grave of Chancellor James Kent. (E.R.M. 55.00.)

76.80 Cross Fishkill Creek.

76.90 Cross New Haven Railroad (now Conrail).

77.50 Continue straight west towards the river. Do not turn right on Route 9D. (Southbound continue straight onto Route 9D.)

77.70 Nabisco, Inc. printing and carton plant on left.

78.00 View of Newburgh Bay and Northern Highlands. You are on Wolcott Ave.

Note: Do not cross bridge over railroad to Beacon station (Conrail, M.T.A., and Amtrak): .30 mile to Fishkill Landing—former ferry terminal for Newburgh. (E.R.M. 56.30.)

78.35 *Bear right* uphill on Ferry Street.

78.40 *Turn left* on Route 9D. North Avenue.

78.80 Southern Dutchess Country Club on left.

79.00 Beacon town line.

79.20 Cross Interstate 84. Newburgh-Beacon Bridge to left. (E.R.M. 57.20.)

79.50 Site of former Verplanck House on right.

79.60 Entrance Matteawan State Hospital on right. (E.R.M. 57.30.)

80.00 Purdy Ridge on right. (E.R.M. 58.50.)

80.80 Entrance to Castle Point U.S. Veterans' Hospital on left.

80.90 *Turn left* on Castle Point Road.
81.00 Cross Hospital, private road.
82.00 *Bend sharp right* on River Road South.
82.40 Castle Hill Veterans' Hospital on right. (E.R.M. 59.50.)
82.90 *Turn right* on Spring Street.
83.50 *Turn left* on Market Street. Chelsea. (E.R.M. 60.25.)
83.70 Continue straight along railroad on North River Road.
84.40 City of New York Delaware Aqueduct tunnel and intake station on left. (E.R.M. 60.30.)
84.40 View of Danskammer Point and Soap Hill across river, to left.
84.80 Continue on North River Road. Derick Brinkerhoff House to left: 1½—story clapboard, ca. 1820.
85.20 *Turn left.*
85.80 Mother of Good Counsel Novitiate on left.
86.20 *Turn right.*
86.30 *Turn left* on Wheeler Hill Road.
87.10 *Turn sharp left* on New Hamburg Road, Route 28.
87.50 Cross Wappinger's Creek. (E.R.M. 63.00.)
87.70 New Hamburg depot on left.
87.80 *Turn left* on Bridge Street.
87.85 Cross Main Street.
87.95 *Bear left* on Bridge Street.
88.00 Cross railroad bridge.
88.05 *Turn left* on Main Street.
88.10 *Turn right* on Railroad Avenue.
88.15 *Turn right* on River Street (E.R.M. 63.30).
88.35 *Turn right* on Point Street.
88.70 *Turn right* on Reed Road. Cross railroad bridge.
89.00 *Turn left* on Channingville Road.
89.30 *Turn left* on Sheafe Road.
91.00 Entrance George Clinton estate on left.
91.20 Children's Aid Society Camps on left.
91.40 Lone Star Industries on left.
91.70 Cobalt Lake on left (Lake Pontusco) (E.R.M. 64.90).

92.70 Oak Grove. Road becomes Old Post Road. (Sheafe Road southbound.)
92.11 *Turn left* on route 9D.
93.00 I.B.M. Country Club on right.
93.40 I.B.M. plant on left. (E.R.M. 67.60.)
94.80 Locust Grove on left. (E.R.M. 68.80.)
95.00 Southwood on left. (E.R.M. 69.10.)
95.60 Poughkeepsie Rural Cemetery on left. (E.R.M. 69.50.)
95.90 *Turn right* on Market Street (southbound turn right on Route 9).
95.90 Central Hudson Power Company headquarters on left.
96.10 Entrance to Springside on right: summer home of Matthew Vassar, with grounds landscaped by Andrew Jackson Downing.
96.50 Eastman Park on left.
96.60 Soldiers' Memorial Fountain on left.
96.70 Adriance Memorial Library on right.
96.80 Brick Armory on right.
96.80 *Turn left* on Church Street.
97.10 *Turn right* on Route 9. (Southbound—Exit right on Laurel Street and circle under Route 9, then turn right on Church Street.)
97.10 Mid-Hudson Bridge to left. (E.R.M. 70.50.)
97.40 Church of the Holy Comforter on right: Stone Gothic, 1860, Richard Upjohn.
97.50 Cross Fall Kill (E.R.M. 70.52).
97.60 St. Peter's Church on right: Italianate Victorian, 1853.
97.70 Pass beneath railroad viaduct (E.R.M. 70.52).
98.20 *Turn left* on North Road, Albany Post Road.
98.30 *Cross railroad grade crossing.*
98.50 *Continue straight* (Southbound bear right on Route 9).
98.50 Poughkeepsie city line.

98.50 Marist College on left. (E.R.M. 71.50.)

98.70 Western Instrument Co. on right.

99.00 Hudson River State Hospital on right. (E.R.M. 72.75.)

100.00 South entrance Culinary Institute of America on left. (E.R.M. 73.80.)

100.10 North entrance Culinary Institute of America on left.

101.10 Hyde Park town line.

101.10 Cross Maritje Kill (E.R.M. 74.00).

101.90 Franklin D. Roosevelt National Historical Site on left. (E.R.M. 74.75.)

102.80 Stoutenburgh-Bergh House on right: Pre-revolutionary, one-story stone.

102.80 *Turn left* on Eymard Seminary Road.

103.50 Crumwald (1889), Eymard Seminary (E.R.M. 76.40).

103.50 *Turn around.*

104.20 *Turn left* on Route 9 off Eymard Seminary Road.

104.80 *Turn left* on Main Street.

104.90 Vanderbilt Stables on right.

105.00 *Turn left* on Curry Lane.

105.40 *Turn sharp right* on River Road.

105.60 Pass River Road Arena.

105.70 Hyde Park depot and landing on left. (E.R.M. 76.40.) Street becomes Main Street.

106.10 *Bear left* on West Market Street.

106.30 *Turn left* on Route 9.

106.30 Federal style mansion on left.

106.50 Entrance to Vanderbilt Mansion National Historical Site to left.

106.50 *Turn left* into driveway. (E.R.M. 77.00.)

106.70 Cross pond to parking area.

107.50 Exit north gate.

107.50 *Turn left* on Route 9.

107.50 St. James Episcopal Church on right: stone Gothic, 1844, by Augustus Thomas Cowman,

architect. The parish was founded 1811 by Dr. Samuel Bard and Gen. Morgan Lewis. The first minister was Rev. John McVickar (1787-1868). Franklin D. Roosevelt was senior warden. In 1939, King George VI and Queen Elizabeth worshipped here.

107.55 Vanderbilt Barns on right: ca. 1900, Stanford White, architect.

107.60 Cross Bard Rock Creek (E.R.M. 77.75).

110.00 *Turn left* into Norrie State Park.

110.10 Enter Margaret Lewis Norrie State Park.

110.30 Cross Indian Kill.

110.50 Pass under railroad.

110.70 Cross Indian Kill (picnic area).

110.90 Norrie Point Yacht Club. (E.R.M. 79.75.)

111.00 *Circle around.*

112.00 Exit Norrie State Park.

112.00 *Turn left* on Post Road, towards Staatsburg.

112.05 Cross Indian Kill.

112.60 Staatsburg village center (E.R.M. 81.20).

112.70 St. Margaret's Episcopal Church on right.

113.10 *Turn left* into Ogden Mills State Park.

113.20 Cross over railroad tracks.

113.90 Mansion. Circle around. (E.R.M. 81.60.)

113.90 *Turn left* on Post Road.

114.90 Dinsmore golf course on right. This is possibly the second oldest in United States.

115.70 *Turn left* on Route 9.

116.00 *Turn left* on Fishing Flats Road.

116.60 Cross Landsman Kill. (E.R.M. 82.90.)

117.00 Ruins of Rhinecliff on left. (E.R.M. 83.20.) (Sisters of St. Ursula.)

117.20 Esopus Meadows on left. (E.R.M. 82.30.)

117.50 Wildercliff on left. (E.R.M. 83.30.)

117.80 *Turn sharp left* on Route 85. (Southbound sharp right on South Mill Road.)

117.80 Old Schoolhouse on right. 1-story Carpenter Gothic, now a residence.

118.00 Wilderstein on left. (E.R.M. 83.50.)

118.80 Pius XII School on right: formerly Cardinal Farley Military Academy, and earlier Ellerslie, home of Levi P. Morton. (E.R.M. 84.50.)

119.60 Rhinecliff town line. Road becomes Kelly Street.

119.80 *Turn left* on Butler Street.

119.90 *Turn left* on James Street.

120.00 *Turn right* on Grinell Street.

120.30 *Turn right* on Shatzell Street.

120.35 *Turn left* on Charles Street.

120.40 *Turn left* on Corning Street.

120.45 *Turn right* on Dutchess Terrace.

120.50 Rhinecliff Depot, Amtrak. (E.R.M. 86.25.)

120.50 *Turn right* on Hutton Street.

120.70 *Turn left* on Long Dock Landing Road.

120.70 Leave Rhinecliff.

121.50 *Turn left* on River Road.

122.50 Entrance to Ferncliff Carmelite Sisters Nursing Home. (E.R.M. 88.25.)

123.00 Astor estate gatehouse on left: stone Victorian mansard ca. 1860.

123.80 Mary Astor chateau (Teen Challenge School) on left.

123.80 Mount Rutsen on right. (E.R.M. 88.75.)

125.10 Entrance to Leacote Farm on left: stone Gothic Revival based on design of Lyndhurst, ca. 1880.

125.10 Cross Route 199. Kingston-Rhinecliff Bridge to left. (E.R.M. 90.00.)

125.20 Eighteenth-century stone house on left.

125.50 Gatehouse to Steen Valetje on left.

126.00 Rokeby on left: Two-story stuccoed stone, Federal style, ca. 1815, later mansard roof, tower, and other renovations.

126.00 Road becomes Annandale Road.

127.10 *Turn left* on Station Hill Road.

127.90 Cross railroad.

128.00 Barrytown depot and landing. *Turn around.* (E.R.M. 91.75.)

128.10 Cross railroad.

128.40 Sacred Heart Church on left: carpenter Gothic, 1874.

128.80 *Turn left* on Annandale Road.

129.00 St. John's Church on right: Episcopal, Carpenter Gothic, mid-nineteenth century.

129.20 Moore House on left: pre-revolutionary stone and brick with gable ends.

129.40 Drive to Montgomery Place on left. (E.R.M. 92.75.)

129.70 Cross Saw Kill.

129.70 Annandale-on-Hudson (E.R.M. 92.60).

130.10 Blithewood gatehouse on left.

130.30 Bard College on right.

130.30 *Turn right* into college grounds.

130.40 *Bard Hall:* two-story stone Gothic, ca. 1860.

130.50 Bard College library, two-story brick with Ionic columns, copy of a classic Greek temple, 1893.

130.50 *Turn around at circle.*

130.70 *Turn right* on Annandale Road.

130.70 Chapel of the Holy Innocents: stone Gothic, ca. 1860.

131.10 Ward Manor gatehouse straight ahead: two-story stone castellated structure with tower, 1915.

131.10 *Turn right* on Route 103 (Cruger Road to the left). (E.R.M. 93.75.)

131.30 *Turn left* on Robbins Road.

131.40 *Turn left* on Manor Road.

131.50 Ward Mansion: two-story stuccoed Tudor-style, ca. 1918.

131.50 *Turn around at circle.*

131.70 *Turn left* on Route 103.
131.80 *Turn left* on Route 9G.
132.50 Beckwith Hill on right.
133.30 *Turn left* on Kidd Lane.
134.10 *Turn right* over bridge across Stony Creek.
134.30 Mansion on left: ca. 1850. You are now on Washburn Avenue.
134.90 *Turn left* on Broadway, Route 402.
134.90 Tivoli.
135.80 Tivoli Depot. View of Saugerties across river. (E.R.M. 95.80.)
135.80 *Turn around*.
136.30 *Turn left* on Woods Road, Route 35.
136.50 St. Paul's Church on left. Brick with bell tower. ca. 1850.
136.90 Trivoli Town line.
137.60 Enter Clermont State Park.
137.80 *Turn left* on Park Road.
138.10 Clermont: Livingston Mansion (E.R.M. 97.90).
138.10 *Turn around* (parking available here).
138.40 Continue straight on Route 35 after leaving park.
138.50 *Turn left* on Route 35.
139.10 Ridgely: Carmelite Sisters' convent on left, the former Thomas Hunt mansion, late nineteenth century.
139.30 Chiddingstone on left: Two-story brick mansion, bracketed, ca. 1890.
139.50 Southwood on left: Two-story, brick and stone mansion, mansard roof and brackets, late nineteenth century.
139.50 Clermont Farm on right.
139.60 Midwood on left: Two-story clapboard home with bracketed cornice, mid-nineteenth century (Washburn).
140.10 Oaklawn on left: childhood home of Eleanor Roosevelt, mid-nineteenth century, much altered.

140.20 Holcroft on left: two-story brick mansion, ca. 1890.
140.50 Northwood on left: two-story brick house with mansard roof, mid-nineteenth century.
141.40 Cheviot Cemetery on right.
141.40 *Turn left* on Cheviot Road.
141.60 Cheviot depot (E.R.M. 100.50).
141.60 *Turn around*.
141.80 *Turn left* on Cheviot Road Extension.
142.10 *Turn left* on Route 35.
142.60 Mansion on right: two-story brick, ca. 1850.
142.80 *Go straight*. Junction of Routes 35 and 9G. Southbound *bear right*.
142.80 Views of Catskill Mountains and Kaaterskill Clove to left.
142.90 *Turn left at light*. To Germantown.
143.00 Site of Diell Rockerfeller Grist and Saw Mill, 1751.
143.30 Germantown Depot (E.R.M. 101.50).
143.30 *Turn around*.
143.70 *Turn left* on Route 9G.
144.50 Germantown town line.
144.60 Shapp's Landing Road on right. (1684).
144.90 *Turn left* on Anchorage Road.
145.20 North Germantown line (E.R.M. 103.00).
145.90 Extensive view to left: includes cement works at Alsen, Duck Cove, DeWitt Point, Inbocht Bay, and Kalkberg—also distant Catskills.
145.90 You are on Northern Boulevard.
146.40 North Germantown.
146.40 Peary House on left: board and batten Carpenter Gothic, mid-nineteenth century (Crawford).
146.50 Cross narrow bridge.
146.70 North Germantown town line.
146.90 *Turn left* on Route 9G.
147.70 Germantown/Livingston township line.
147.70 Cross Roeliff Jansen's Kill (E.R.M. 105.25).

147.90 *Turn right* on "Ye Waggon Road from Manor House."

148.50 Linlithgo (E.R.M. 105.25).

148.50 Livingston Memorial Chapel: parts from 1722, rebuilt 1870, Dutch Reformed.

148.50 *Turn around.*

149.10 *Turn right* on Route 9G.

149.90 Cross Fox Creek culvert.

151.50 *Turn right* into drive of Olana Castle.

151.80 Lake on right.

152.50 Olana Castle (E.R.M. 108.00). Parking area.

152.50 *Turn around.*

153.50 *Turn right* on Route 9G.

154.20 Church Hill on right.

154.40 Rip Van Winkle Bridge on left. (E.R.M. 108.60.)

154.40 Junction Routes 9G and 23. Continue around circle. Do not cross bridge.

154.50 *Turn* onto Mount Merino Road.

154.50 Extensive views to left: panorama of entire Great Wall of Manitou: From south to north: Overlook Mountain, Indian Head Mountain, Twin Mountain, Kaaterskill High Peak, Round Top, South Mountain, North Mountain, Acra Point, Mount Thomas Cole, Windham Mountain.

156.40 Pass beneath power lines.

156.40 Mount Merino on right. (E.R.M. 110.00.)

156.50 Mansion on right: 2½-story brick, ca. 1840.

157.00 *Turn left* off Mount Merino Road, onto Routes 9G and 23B.

157.10 Hudson city line.

157.30 Cross brook. Road becomes South 3rd Street.

157.50 *Turn left* on Warren Street.

157.80 *Turn right* on Front Street.

157.80 Washington Hose Company No. 3.

157.80 The Parade on left. (E.R.M. 112.00.) Panoramic views.

158.00 *Turn right* on State Street.

158.50 Hudson Library. Old Brick School on right.

158.60 Brick armory on left.

158.70 Row houses.

159.00 Junction Routes 9G and 23B.

159.00 *Turn left* on Green State. Route 9G. (Southbound *turn right* on State Street.)

159.40 Junction Routes 23B and 9G. *Turn left* on Route 9G, Fairview Avenue. (Southbound *turn right* on Green Street.)

159.70 Hudson city line. Cross railroad track.

160.00 Fireman's home on left.

162.10 Stottsville town line. Greenport/Stockport town line.

162.10 *Bend left* on route 9. (Southbound bend right on Route 9G, Fairview Avenue.) (E.R.M. 114.25.)

162.40 Green water tower on right.

162.40 Views of Taconics on right and Catskills on left.

163.40 Columbiaville Falls (E.R.M. 115.80). Columbiaville was incorporated in 1812. There were a cotton factory and saw, paper, and grist mills.

163.50 Cross Stockport Creek.

163.50 *Turn left* on Southers Road.

163.70 Greek Revival house on right.

163.90 *Turn left* to Stockport.

164.60 Stockport Station (E.R.M. 115.80).

164.60 *Turn around.*

164.65 Maj. Abram Staats House on left: One-story stone, ca. 1664, much altered.

165.30 *Turn left* on Southers Road.

166.40 *Turn sharp left.*

166.50 Stockport Landing, Judson Point (E.R.M. 116.75).

166.70 *Bear left.*

167.20 Hay-rick on left.

167.80 *Turn left* on Route 9J.

168.10 View of Catskills to left.

169.40 Stockport-Stuyvesant line. Patent granted to Arent Van Dendbergh in 1666. Sold to Hans Hendricksen in 1667.

169.60 Greek Revival house on right.
170.20 Newton Hook station.
170.20 *Turn left* across railroad tracks.
170.50 Nutten Hook (E.R.M. 118.80).
170.50 *Turn around.*
170.80 *Turn left* on Route 9J.
172.70 Town line.
172.90 Powell Patent marker on left. (southwest corner). Patent granted in 1664.
173.20 Stuyvesant Landing (E.R.M. 121.45).
173.40 Junction with Route 398 on right.
173.40 Wendover Mansion on left: Two-story brick, early nineteenth century, with possible earlier portions.
173.50 Van Schaack houses: built in 1790 and 1820, in brick Federal and Italian villa styles, now Stuyvesant Home.
173.70 Stuyvesant town line.
173.90 Henry Hudson landed here September 19, 1609.
174.00 Northwest corner of Powell Patent of 1664.
174.20 Bracketed villa on right.
174.40 View of Catskills to left.
175.00 Go under New York Central Railroad loop track to Alfred H. Smith Memorial Bridge.
175.30 Cross brook.
175.70 Cross brook.
175.90 Go under railroad loop track to bridge.
178.80 Columbia/Rensselaer county line. Cross Brook. (E.R.M. 126.60).
180.00 Schodack Landing. (E.R.M. 127.55).
180.10 Ten Eyck House on right: 1½-story brick, gambrel roof, mid-nineteenth century.
180.80 Schodack Island to left. (E.R.M. 129.00).
181.50 Pass beneath Alfred H. Smith Memorial Bridge. This single-track railroad bridge was named in honor of former president of the New York

Central Railroad. (E.R.M. 129.80.)
181.60 Pass beneath New York Thruway Berkshire Branch Bridge (E.R.M. 129.90).
182.70 Cross Muitze's Kill.
183.00 Cross Vlockie Kill (E.R.M. 131.25).
183.50 Junction Route 150 to right.
183.50 Castleton-on-Hudson (E.R.M. 131.50).
183.60 House with stepped gable on right.
183.80 Ressurection Rest Home on right.
184.20 Castleton town line.
184.40 Cross Moordener Kill (E.R.M. 132.50).
185.00 Becker House on right: Two-story clapboard, rebuilt after fire ca. 1860.
185.20 Cross Vierda Kill (E.R.M. 133.75).
186.20 Staats Island Road on left.
186.60 Town of Schodack-East Greenbush Line.
187.00 East Greenbush, Hayes Road on right. (E.R.M. 135.50.)
187.00 Genet Schoolhouse on right: Carpenter Gothic, ca. 1850.
189.60 Port of Albany and Sunoco tank farm on left.
189.60 Niagara Mohawk Kenwood generating station to left. (E.R.M. 138.75.)
190.70 *Go straight.* (Southbound bear right on Route 9J.)
190.70 Junction Routes U.S. 9 and 20.
190.80 Cross bridge over New York Central Railroad (Conrail).
191.10 *Turn left* on Akin Avenue.
191.20 *Turn left* on Nelson Avenue.
191.30 *Turn right* on Belmore Place.
191.40 *Turn left* on Riverside Avenue.
191.80 *Turn around* at foot of Riverside Avenue.
191.80 G.A.F. plant on east. Port of Albany on south.
192.20 Fort Crailo on right: Two-story brick, ca. 1700, renovated. One of the early buildings of

Rensselaerwyck, it is now a museum.

192.40 Cross over Routes 9 and 20. Go North on Broadway.

192.60 Pass entrance of bridge to Albany. (E.R.M. 139.65.)

192.70 Cross Quackendary Kill.

192.75 *Turn right* on Herrick Street.

192.85 Cross bridge over railroad.

192.85 St. John's Byzantine style church seen ahead on right.

192.95 *Turn left* on East Street.

193.10 Amtrak Albany-Rensselaer passenger station on left.

193.30 Go straight.

193.40 *Turn left* on Harrison Street.

193.50 *Turn right* on Broadway.

194.20 *Turn right* on Washington Avenue.

194.30 *Bear left uphill*.

194.40 Continue straight ahead.

194.80 Cross over Interstate 90.

194.90 St. Anthony-on-Hudson on left.

195.00 Franciscan mission house on left.

195.90 North Greenbush-Rensselaer town line. Road becomes Washington Avenue Extension.

196.40 *Turn left* on Route 4.

196.40 Defreestville (E.R.M. 140.75).

198.10 Junction Route 405 on right.

199.20 Troy-North Greenbush town line.

199.50 Hudson Valley Community College on right.

199.50 Immaculate Conception Monastery on left.

199.60 Cross Wynants Kill (E.R.M. 144.50).

200.30 Junction Route 378 on left.

200.30 *Turn right* on Route 4, Norden Avenue. (Southbound bend left on Route 4.)

200.60 *Turn right* on 4th Street, Troy. (E.R.M. 144.80.)

201.40 Cross Poesten Kill (E.R.M. 145.60).

202.00 Junction Route 7.

202.05 First Baptist Church on right.

202.10 St. Paul's Episcopal Church on right.

202.30 *Bend right* along river on Route 4, River Street.

202.50 *Bend left* along river on Route 4, River Street.

202.60 Junction Route 787. Lift bridge to Green Island on left. (E.R.M. 146.75.)

202.70 Cluet-Peabody plant on left.

204.30 Green Island on left, across river.

204.30 Continue north on Route 4, Second Avenue.

205.10 Junction Route 470. Van Schaick Island on left, across river. (E.R.M. 149.90.)

205.50 Old Lansing Inn on right. Lansingburgh.

205.80 Standard Manufacturing Company mill on right.

206.20 Junction Route 142. Go straight.

206.30 Bridge to Waterford on left. (E.R.M. 151.40.)

206.30 Old streetcar barn on left.

206.30 Route 4 crosses the Hudson here. *Continue straight* on Marion Avenue.

207.20 Troy city line.

207.40 Road becomes River Road.

207.70 Continue straight.

208.10 Pleasantdale town line.

208.70 Cross B. & M. Railroad track (abandoned).

209.30 Cross B. & M. Railroad track (abandoned).

210.20 Campbell Island to left. (E.R.M. 153.75.)

215.00 Lock No. 2 on left (River Road). (E.R.M. 159.00.)

215.50 Quack Island on left. (Linden Street.) (E.R.M. 159.35.)

216.50 *Turn left* on Locust Avenue.

216.60 *Turn right* on Main Street, Hemstreet Park.

216.90 *Turn left* on River Road.

218.10 Cross Boston & Maine Railroad. (main line, active.) (E.R.M. 162.50.)

219.80 *Bend sharp right*. Hoosic River on left. (E.R.M. 163.50.)

222.55 Site of Fort Schaghticoke on left. (Southbound stay to right.) Early eighteenth century fortification.

224.95 Cross bridge over Boston & Maine Railroad.

225.60 *Turn left* on Route 40.

226.20 Cross Hoosic River.

226.30 *Bear left.*

227.00 Village of Schaghticoke.

227.10 *Turn left* on Route 67.

227.40 Rensselaer County Fairgrounds on left.

227.40 Elmwood Cemetery on right.

231.40 *Turn right* on River Road, Route 113. (E.R.M. 164.30.)

232.30 Rensselaer-Washington county line.

238.30 Sarles ferry site on left. (E.R.M. 172.45.)

243.70 Saratoga Battle Monument visible on hill across river to left.

243.70 Cross Route 29.

243.70 Bridge to Schuylerville on left. (E.R.M. 178.80.)

245.10 Cross Batten Kill. (E.R.M. 180.00.)

245.20 *Turn left.*

245.50 Site of Hessian Camp of 1777 on left.

245.70 *Turn right.*

245.70 Site of British camp and river crossing of 1777 on left.

245.90 *Turn left.*

246.80 Thomson (E.R.M. 181.30).

247.00 *Turn left* off Route 113. *Then immediate right* on Route 4.

248.60 *Turn left at fork.*

248.80 *Turn left over bridge* at Lock No. 6. (E.R.M. 184.25.)

248.90 Fort Miller. (E.R.M. 185.00.)

249.40 *Turn right.*

249.80 *Turn right.*

249.90 Cross bridge over Champlain Canal.

250.00 *Turn left* on Route 4.

251.50 Lock floodgate on canal to left.

252.20 Cross Moses Kill (E.R.M. 187.25).

253.10 South Argyle (E.R.M. 188.50).

254.60 Fort Edward Center: original burial place of Jenny M'Crea (E.R.M. 190.25).

256.60 Cross Champlain Canal, Lock No. 7 (E.R.M. 192.20).

256.70 *Turn right.*

256.75 Enter town of Fort Edward.

256.80 Old Fort House Museum.

256.90 Junction Route 197. Continue on Route 4.

257.30 Old Fort Edward area on left. (E.R.M. 192.50.)

257.50 Pass beneath Delaware & Hudson Railroad main line. Amtrak Depot. (E.R.M. 192.80.)

257.60 Junction Route 197 on left. Continue straight. (E.R.M. 192.90.)

257.80 United Methodist Church on left.

257.85 Cross railroad grade crossing, D. & H.

257.90 Cross bridge over railroad, D. & H.

258.00 *Bear left* on Route 4.

258.50 Union Cemetery on right.

258.50 Fort Edward village line.

259.00 Union Cemetery on right.

259.50 Mullen Mansion on right, ca. 1800.

259.90 Washington County Courthouse on right. brick Victorian, 1878.

260.10 Junction Routes 4 and 254.

260.10 *Turn left* on route 254.

260.10 Hudson Falls town square (E.R.M. 196.00).

260.70 Washington-Warren county line. Warren County has area of 883 square miles. Taken from Washington County in 1813 it was named for Gen. Joseph Warren, killed at Battle of Bunker Hill. Lake George is the county seat.

261.40 Junction Route 254 and 32.

261.40 *Go straight on route* 32.

261.60 (Southbound take far right fork at traffic light.)

261.90 Glens Falls city line.

262.00 Pass beneath Delaware & Hudson Glens Falls branch.

262.20 (Southbound bear left on Route 32.)

262.20 Route 32 becomes Warren Street.

262.20 Flintcote Plant on left.

262.60 *Turn left* on Prospect Street.

262.70 *Turn right* on Oakland Avenue.

262.80 Pulp log dump on left.

263.10 Finch-Pruyn Paper Mill on left.

263.10 Junction Route 9 and 32-A with Oakland Avenue. (E.R.M. 199.10.)

263.10 Cooper's Cave and Glens Fall on Hudson River to left.

263.10 End.

East Side Railroad Route

Service on this line is provided from Grand Central Terminal in Manhattan as far north as Poughkeepsie by the Metropolitan Transit Authority, making all local stops. Through trains to Albany and beyond are operated by the National Railroad Passenger Corporation, Amtrak.

The route is over the former tracks of the New York & Harlem, Hudson River Railroad, and New York Central Railroad. In later years, these lines have been operated by the: New York Central & Hudson River Railroad; the New York Central Railroad; Penn Central Railroad; and Conrail—who still own much of the track.

Our trip commences at Grand Central Terminal on Forty-second Street in Manhattan, at Park Avenue—which here actually passes through an upper level of the terminal. The original station was built in 1871 and expanded in 1884 and 1900. The present terminal was built between 1903 and 1913. It is in the Beaux Arts Eclectic Style and was designed by Warren and Wetmore and Reed and Stem. Col. William J. Wilgus was the principal engineer. Grand Central has two levels of tracks. Forty-one tracks carry through traffic on the upper level, and suburban trains use tracks on the lower level. On the upper level, there is a run-around loop track. In consequence of an accident in the Park Avenue tunnel in 1902, the legislature passed an act requiring trains to be operated through the tunnel by electric traction. Beneath both levels is the giant power plant that moves the trains and lights and heats the buildings. Tracks and switches in underground caverns carved out of solid rock stretch out for seventy-nine acres.

Mile

0 Grand Central Terminal. The train remains in a tunnel beneath Park Avenue for three and one half miles, and then comes out on an elevated trestle above Park Avenue in the Harlem section of Manhattan.

4 125th Street Station—an elevated station. After leaving 125th Street, the line crosses the Harlem River on a large vertical lift bridge.

5 The Bronx (138th Street). Beyond here the Hudson division splits to the west from the Harlem division, which continues straight to White Plains, Brewster, and a connection with the Boston & Albany at Chatham. Local trains also use this line to Woodlawn Junction to reach the former New York, New Haven & Hartford line to Boston.

7 Sedgwick Avenue.

8 High Bridge, West 169th Street, Bronx. Pass beneath the High Bridge of the Old Croton Aqueduct. Parallel Harlem River and Spuyten Duyvil Creek to Spuyten Duyvil Station.

9	Morris Heights, West 177th Street, Bronx.	**49**	Garrison.
10	University Heights, West 207th Street, Bronx. Former Putnam Division splits off at Kingsbridge.	**52**	Cold Spring.
		54	Storm King.
		56	Dutchess.
		58	Becon.
10	Marble Hill, West 225 Street.	**62**	Chelsea.
11	Spuyten Duyvil. Junction with West Side Manhattan freight line, former southern end of Hudson River Railroad.	**64**	New Hamburg. (Cross Wappinger's Creek south of depot.)
		67	Camelot.
		73	Poughkeepsie.
13	Riverdale.	**78**	Hyde Park.
13	Mount St. Vincent.	**83**	Staatsburg.
14	Ludlow.	**88**	Rhinecliff.
15	Yonkers.	**94**	Barrytown.
16	Glenwood.	**98**	Tivoli.
18	Greystone.	**104**	Germantown.
19	Hastings-on-Hudson.	**105**	North Germantown.
20	Dobbs Ferry.	**109**	Greendale.
21	Ardsley-on-Hudson.	**114**	Hudson.
22	Irvington.	**118**	Stockport. (Cross Stockport Creek south of depot.)
23	Sunnyside restoration.		
25	Tarrytown.	**121**	Newton Hook.
26	Philipse Manor.	**124**	Stuyvesant.
29	Scarborough.	**130**	Schodack Landing.
31	Ossining. (Here tracks pass through tunnel beneath Sing Sing prison.)	**134**	Castleton-on-Hudson.
		142	Rensselaer. (Now Albany-Rensselaer—the present Amtrak station for the Albany area.)
33	Croton-Harmon. End of electrification for through trains. Cross Croton River south of station.		
			The main line crosses the Hudson River here, as do Montreal-bound trains operating further north via the Delaware & Hudson Railroad.
34	Croton-on-Hudson.		
36	Oscawana.		
37	Crugers. (Tracks cut inland to Peekskill.)	**143**	Albany (Union Station is now out of service). Trains use the upper railroad bridge formerly used for freight only. The lower bridge to Union Station is deactivated.)
39	Montrose.		
41	Peekskill. (Tracks cross Annsville Creek north of station.)		
45	Manitou.		

Albany & Troy Branch of Conrail

(freight service only)

0	Albany.	**6½**	Adams Street, Troy.
1	Rensselaer.	**7**	Troy, Union Station (formerly connections with D & H and B & M).
5	Iron Works,		
6	Madison Street, Troy.		

Delaware & Hudson Railroad Main Line
(Passenger service by Amtrak)

0 Albany-Rensselaer
Cross Hudson River on freight bridge. Switch to former D & H tracks near old Albany Union Station. Head north along west shore of Hudson River.
3 Menands.
4 Cemetery (Albany Rural Cemetery and St. Agnes Cemetery).
5 Colonie. (Large yards of D & H located here.)
6 Watervliet.
9 Cohoes. (Cross Mohawk River on 960-feet long bridge built in 1927. View of falls to west.)
11 West Waterford.
19 Mechanicville. (Junction with Boston & Maine.) Line cuts inland here to Fort Edward.
25 Round Lake.
32 Ballston Spa. (Junction with D & H line from Schenectady.)
38 Saratoga Springs.
54 Cross Hudson River.
55 Fort Edward. (Branch to Glens Falls, formerly to Lake George, cuts off to west.)
63 Smith's Basin. (Line parallels Champlain Canal to Whitehall.)
67 Fort Ann.
71 Comstock.
77 Whitehall (formerly Skenesborough.) Rutland branch cuts

off to east. Southern end of Lake Champlain. Railroad follows western shoreline to Plattsburg.
100 Ticonderoga (Lake Champlain to right).
109 Crown Point.
117 Port Henry.
128 Westport.
137 Essex.
142 Willsboro.
150 Douglas.
154 Port Kent (ferry to Burlington, Vermont).
167 Plattsburg.
177 West Chazy.
183 Chazy.
190 Rouses Point.
Connects with Napierville Junction Railway to:
Lacolle.
Napierville.
St. Edouard.
St. Mathieu.
Delson.
Cross St. Lawrence River.
Enter Canadian Pacific trackage.
238 Montreal West.
241 Westmount.
243 Montreal, Windsor Station.

Delaware and Hudson Glens Falls Branch
(freight only)

0 Fort Edward.
2 Hudson Falls.
6 Glens Falls.
15 Lake George. (Track abandoned between Glens Falls and Lake George.) Formerly connection

with Lake George Steamboat Co. to Bolton Landing, Sabbath Day Point, Huelet's Landing, Hague, Silver Bay, and Baldwin (Ticonderoga).

West Side Railroad Route

Over lines of the New Jersey Junction Railroad and the West Shore Railroad, now Conrail.

Presently freight service only. Any excursions would probably operate from Erie-Lackawanna Terminal at Hoboken. The Weehawken Terminal is entirely gone.

Mile

-4 Hoboken Terminal. Switch onto tracks of New Jersey Junction Railroad and run along foot of Palisades to Weehawken. Pick up West Shore tracks.

0 Weehawken. Formerly ferries to West Forty-second Street and Cortlandt Street. One-mile-long tunnel beneath Palisades to the Hackensack Meadows.

2 North Bergen.

5 Cross Overpeck Creek.

6 Little Ferry. (Tracks of New York, Susquehanna & Western Railway are parallel on the left. Hackensack River to Left.)

7 Ridgefield Park.

8 West View. The dome of the Bergen County Courthouse, across the river in Hackensack is visible. Neo-classic style by J. R. Gordon, 1912.

9 Bogota.

10 Teaneck.

11 West Englewood.

12 Bergenfield. formerly, along with Dumont, part of town of Schraalenberg. Railroad shortened name to Bergen Fields. Old South Dutch Reformed Church visible to left.

13 Dumont. Northern part of Old Schraalenburgh. Old North Dutch Reformed Church visible to right.

Former end of much local commuter service. Extensive coach yards were north of station. World War I Camp Merritt was to the east of here.

15 Haworth. Exclusive residential area.

16 Harrington Park. Former summer resort. Town layed out by Vaux & Olmsted. Exclusive residential town. The Oradell Reservoir on the Hackensack River is to West.

18 West Norwood, New Jersey.

20 Tappan, New York Treason Hill, where Major André was hung, is just west of tracks. He was tried here.

21 Orangeburg. Large Rockland State Hospital (mental) west of here. This was the site of the large World War II Camp Shanks, used for embarkation and mustering out.

22 Blauvelt.

25 West Nyack.

26 Cross bridge over New York Thruway.

27 Lake De Forest on Hackensack River to west.

27 Valley Cottage. In 1753 a large tract here was sold to John Ryder by Peter Geslar.

29 Congers-Rockland Lake. Named for Abraham B. Conger, who settled here in 1840. Home of wireless inventor A. Frederick Collins.

30 Tunnel beneath Palisades to Hudson Valley.

31 Views of Haverstraw Bay to right.

33 Haverstraw.

34 West Haverstraw. This is the former end of suburban service. It was formerly a junc-

tion with the New Jersey &
New York Railroad.

35 Stony Point.

37 Tomkins Cove.

40 Jones Point. Dunderberg Mountain, Snake Creek.

41 Iona Island. Doodletown Bight.

42 Bear Mountain. Steamboat docks. Anthony's Nose across river. Cross Popolopen Creek. Bear Mountain Bridge above.

43 Tunnel.

43 Fort Montgomery.

46 Buttermilk Falls to left.

47 Highland Falls.

48 West Point (South Dock).

48 Tunnel beneath Parade Grounds and Trophy Point.

49 Cro'Nest Mountain to left.

51 Mother Cronk's Cove.

52 Storm King Mountain to left.

53 Cornwall. Formerly New York, Ontario & Western Railway cut off here to the west, toward Oswego.

54 Cross Moodna Creek.

57 Newburgh.

61 Roseton.

64 Cedarcliff.

65 Marlborough.

69 Milton.

73 Highland. Mid-Hudson and Poughkeepsie Railroad bridges above.

78 Railroad leaves the river and cuts inland to Glenmont.

79 West Park.

81 Esopus.

83 Ulster Park.

86 Port Ewen. Explosive storage yards south of depot.

87 High Wilbur trestle over Rondout Creek.

88 Short tunnel.

89 Kingston Union Station. Former junction with Ulster & Dela-

ware and New York, Ontario & Western, Ellenville & Kingston Branch.

91 Lake Katerine. I.B.M. plant to west, south of depot. Views of Catskill Mountains to west.

96 Mount Marion The mountain is to the west. The railroad now parallels the New York Thruway.

97 Cross Esopus Creek above Glenerie Falls to right.

100 Saugerties.

102 Malden-on-Hudson.

105 Alsen (Cementon). Kalkberg to west. Inbocht Bay to east.

108 Kykuit Flats and Hill to east.

111 Catskill.

112 High trestle above Catskill Creek.

115 West Athens.

121 Coxsackie.

125 New Baltimore.

128 Ravena (station for Coeymans). Main line of West Shore cuts off to northwest. Train enters the Albany Branch.

133 Selkirk. Cross the Boston & Albany, Castleton Bridge Line.

136 Wemple.

138 Glenmont.

139 Kenwood. Enter trackage of Delaware & Hudson line from Binghamton. Former Albany & Susquehanna Railroad.

139 Cross Norman's Kill. Vale of Tawasentha to west.

140 Port of Albany to right.

142 Albany. Former Union Sation. Connections north to Delaware & Hudson main line and west to former New York Central main line to Buffalo and Chicago, Conrail.

INDEX

NOTE: In addition to the regular page references, certain entries in this index include the Equivalent River Mileage (ERM) number. This will enable the index to also serve as a ready reference guide for determining approximate situation of various localities.

Index